C# 2008 Programmer's Reference

C# 2008
Programmer's Reference

C# 2008
Programmer's Reference

Wei-Meng Lee

WILEY

Wiley Publishing, Inc.

C# 2008 Programmer's Reference

Published by
Wiley Publishing, Inc.
10475 Crosspoint Boulevard
Indianapolis, IN 46256
www.wiley.com

Copyright © 2009 by Wiley Publishing, Inc., Indianapolis, Indiana

Published simultaneously in Canada

ISBN: 978-0-470-28581-7

Manufactured in the United States of America

10 9 8 7 6 5 4 3 2 1

Library of Congress Cataloging-in-Publication Data

Lee, Wei-Meng.
   C# 2008 programmer's reference / Wei-Meng Lee.
     p. cm.
   Includes index.
   ISBN 978-0-470-28581-7 (paper/website)
    1. C# (Computer program language)   I. Title.
  QA76.73.C154L33   2009
  005.13'3—dc22

2009036345

To my family and wife, Shihua, for their support and love.

About the Author

Wei-Meng Lee, Microsoft MVP, is a technologist and founder of Developer Learning Solutions (www.learn2develop.net), a technology company specializing in hands-on training in the latest Microsoft and Apple technologies.

Wei-Meng writes extensively for online publications such as DevX.com and the O'Reilly Network and magazines such as *CoDe Magazine* and *asp.netPRO* magazine on topics ranging from .NET to Mac OS X. He is also the author of *Professional Windows Vista Gadgets Programming* (Wrox) and *Practical .NET 2.0 Networking Projects* (Apress).

You can contact Wei-Meng at weimenglee@learn2develop.net.

About the Technical Editor

Andrew Moore is a graduate of Purdue University–Calumet in Hammond, Indiana, and has been developing software since 1998 for radar systems, air traffic management, discrete-event simulation, and business communications applications using C, C++, C#, and Java on the Windows, UNIX, and Linux platforms. Andrew is the author of Wrox Blox articles titled "Create Amazing Custom User Interfaces with WPF, C#, and XAML in .NET 3.0,", ".NET 3.5 CD Audio Player," and "Power Programming with ReSharper." He is currently a senior software engineer at Interactive Intelligence, Inc. in Indianapolis developing Microsoft-based applications for business communications. Andrew lives in Indiana with his wife, Barbara, and children, Sophia and Andrew.

Credits

Acquisitions Editor
Katie Mohr

Development Editor
Maryann Steinhart

Technical Editor
Andrew Moore

Production Editor
Christine O'Connor

Copy Editor
Foxxe Editorial Services

Editorial Manager
Mary Beth Wakefield

Production Manager
Tim Tate

Vice President and Executive Group Publisher
Richard Swadley

Vice President and Executive Publisher
Joseph B. Wikert

Project Coordinator, Cover
Lynsey Stanford

Proofreader
C.M. Jones

Indexer
Robert Swanson

Acknowledgments

Writing a book is like running a long race — you need stamina, training, and perseverance. But these are not the most important factors that ensure you reach the finishing line. The most important factor is the motivation that keeps you going, on and on, even though you may be physically exhausted and don't think you can move any farther. While this is not the first book I have written, I am always very excited when embarking on a new book project. After the excitement comes a lot of hard work — coping with missed deadlines, changing work schedules, writer's block, and so forth.

For this book, I am extremely lucky to work with two very important people — my acquisitions editor, Katie Mohr, and development editor, Maryann Steinhart. Both Katie and Maryann have been very patient with me when the going gets tough. Katie has always egged me on, and offered many suggestions to scope the book to what it is today. Maryann has been the studious timekeeper, with a gentle but firm voice telling me to press forward when I missed the deadline. Maryann has also painstakingly read and reread every sentence I wrote, and I am always surprised with her attention to detail which has definitely made this book a better one. With heart-felt sincerity, I want to say a big thank you to both of them!

I would also like to thank the technical editor, Andrew Moore, for giving me many suggestions for improving the book. Writing this book has made me learn a lot of things I never knew. Thanks, Andrew!

Last but not least, I want to take this opportunity to thank my parents and my wife, Shihua, for their understanding and support when I have had to take time away to work on this book. Thanks!

Contents

Contents

Contents

Contents

Contents

Contents

Contents

Introduction

Since the release of the Microsoft .NET Framework in July 2000, the C# programming language has gone through a few iterations to its latest version, 3.0. Over the years, the C# language has gained a lot of followers, partly due to its syntax, which is familiar to Java and C programmers. The clear syntax of the language made it easy to learn, and it's a popular choice for beginning programmers. In addition, the C# language is gaining a lot of traction in the Visual Basic camp, especially among VB6 programmers, who needed to move to .NET and did not want to learn a totally new variant of the Visual Basic language — Visual Basic .NET.

The latest version of C# 3.0 comes with .NET Framework 3.5. It contains many new features that makes the language more intuitive and powerful. Coupled with Visual Studio 2008, Microsoft's flagship development environment, developing applications using C# is now available to a wide audience.

In writing this book, I used the approach I believe is the easiest way to learn a new language — by examples. Often, books and articles get into too much of the theory without showing the readers what the concept looks like in code. For each topic, I try to provide numerous examples to illustrate the concept, and I would encourage you to make changes to the program to explore further. If you are an experienced programmer, you can jump directly to a particular chapter, as each chapter comes with independent examples.

Who This Book Is For

This book is for programmers of all levels. Beginning programmers should find the C# language easy to learn through the many code examples provided in each chapter. Experienced programmers can jump directly to individual chapters covering the topics of interest to them.

A conscious effort is made to illustrate each topic with independent code examples so that readers who want clarification on a topic do not need to wade through the entire chapter.

This book is ideal for the working programmer as well as students taking a semester course in C# programming. The sample projects covered in chapters16 to 20 provide numerous project ideas as well as motivation for readers to get started working on bigger projects.

What This Book Covers

This book is divided into three parts. Part I covers the C# language fundamentals; Part II covers application development using C#, and Part III provides three appendices that cover the list of C# keywords, the .NET class libraries, and document generation using the Sandcastle utility.

Part I: C# Fundamentals

❑ Chapter 1 introduces the .NET Framework. It examines the key components in the .NET Framework as well as the role played by each of the components. In addition, it discusses the relationships between the various versions of the framework, from version 1.0 to the latest 3.5.

❑ Chapter 2 covers the use of Microsoft Visual Studio 2008 as the tool for C# development. Visual Studio 2008 is an extremely versatile and powerful environment for developing .NET applications. This chapter explores some of the common features that you will likely use in the process of your development work.

❑ Chapter 3 introduces the syntax of the C# language and covers all the important topics: C# keywords, variables, constants, comments, XML documentation, data types, flow control, loops, operators, and preprocessor directives.

❑ Chapter 4 tackles one of the most important topics in C# programming — classes and objects. Classes are essentially templates in from which you create objects. In C# .NET programming, everything you deal with involves classes and objects. This chapter provides a firm foundation in the use and creation of classes for code reuse.

❑ Chapter 5 explains how interfaces can be used to define the contract for a class. It also discusses difference between an interface and an abstract class.

❑ Chapter 6 looks at how inheritance facilitates code reuse, enabling you to extend the functionality of code that you have already written. This book explains the different types of inheritance and how to define overloaded methods and operators.

❑ Chapter 7 introduces the concept of delegates and events used in object oriented programming, and discusses what a delegate is and how delegates are used to implement events.

❑ Chapter 8 examines strings handling in C# and the various ways to manipulate them. For more complex strings pattern matching, you can use regular expressions. This chapter also covers the various ways to format your strings data.

❑ Chapter 9 looks into the basics of generics and how you can use them to enhance efficiency and type safety in your applications. Generics enable developers to define type-safe data structures without binding to specific fixed data types at design time.

❑ Chapter 10 explains how to write multithreaded applications using the Thread class in the .NET Framework. It also shows you how to create and synchronize threads as well as how to write thread-safe Windows applications.

❑ Chapter 11 delves into the concepts of files and streams in .NET. With streams, you can perform a wide range of tasks, including compressing and decompressing data, serializing and deserializing data, and encrypting and decrypting data. This chapter covers the various ways to manipulate files and the various stream objects in .NET.

❑ Chapter 12 deals with exception handling. An exception is a situation that occurs when your program encounters an error that it is not expecting during runtime. Understanding how to handle exceptions makes your program more robust and resilient.

❑ Chapter 13 examines arrays and collections. It discusses the many collection classes that you can use to represent groups of data in .NET.

- ❑ Chapter 14 introduces a new feature in .NET 3.5: Language Integrated Query (LINQ). It covers all the important implementations of LINQ — LINQ to Objects, LINQ to XML, LINQ to Dataset, and LINQ to SQL.

- ❑ Chapter 15 explores the concept of assemblies. In .NET, the basic unit deployable is called an assembly. Assemblies play an important part of the development process where understanding how they work is useful in helping you develop scalable and efficient .NET applications.

Part II: Application Development Using C#

- ❑ Chapter 16 demonstrates how you can build a Windows application using the C# language. The sample application illustrates how to perform FTP using the classes available in the .NET Framework. You will also see how to perform printing in a.NET application and how to deploy Windows applications using the ClickOnce technology.

- ❑ Chapter 17 takes you through building an ASP.NET web application in C#. You perform data binding using the new `LinqDataSource` control and see how to AJAX-enable your web pages.

- ❑ Chapter 18 illustrates Windows Mobile development using the .NET Compact Framework, a subset of the .NET Framework. It examines the basics of the Windows Mobile development and builds a sample RSS reader application. Finally, it shows you how to create a professional setup package for your application so that it can be distributed to your readers for installation.

- ❑ Chapter 19 helps you get started with Silverlight and provides an opportunity for you to get a feel for Silverlight development works. It covers Silverlight 1.0 and 2, and contains several examples showing the capabilities of Silverlight, including animation, media, and .NET integration.

- ❑ Chapter 20 provides a quick introduction to the new Windows Communication Foundation (WCF) technology and shows how it addresses some of the limitations of today's web services technology. While most books and conferences focus heavily on the theory behind WCF, this chapter shows you how to build WCF services and then explains the theory behind them. It ends with an example that creates a ticketing application, allowing multiple clients to obtain updated seat information in real time.

Part III: Appendixes

- ❑ Appendix A lists the various keywords in C# that are predefined and have special meanings to the compiler.

- ❑ Appendix B summarizes the features of the various versions of the .NET Framework and explains how to use the Object Browser feature in Visual Studio 2008 to browse the available namespaces and classes in the .NET Framework.

- ❑ Appendix C shows you how to generate MSDN-style documentation for your project using Visual Studio 2008 and a third-party documentation generation tool — Sandcastle.

What You Need to Use This Book

For all the examples demonstrated in this book, I used Microsoft Visual Studio Team System 2008. However, Microsoft has released a plethora of editions of Visual Studio designed for the different types of C# developers:

❑ Visual Web Developer 2008 Express Edition

❑ Visual C# 2008 Express Edition

❑ Visual Studio 2008 Standard Edition

❑ Visual Studio 2008 Professional Edition

❑ Visual Studio 2008 Team System 2008 Architecture Edition

❑ Visual Studio 2008 Team System 2008 Database Edition

❑ Visual Studio 2008 Team System 2008 Development Edition

❑ Visual Studio 2008 Team System 2008 Test Edition

❑ Visual Studio 2008 Team System 2008 Team Suite

> *For a detailed discussion of the features available in each edition, check out the following URL:* http://msdn.microsoft.com/en-us/vs2008/products/cc149003.aspx.

Express editions are designed for hobbyists and are available for download at no charge. This is a great way to get started with Visual Studio 2008 and is ideal for students and beginning programmers. However, if you are a professional developer, you should purchase either the Standard or Professional Edition. If you are developing Windows Mobile applications, you need the Professional Edition (or higher). If you are working in a large development environment and need to develop collaboratively with other developers on large projects, check out the Team System editions.

> *If you are not ready to purchase Visual Studio 2008, you can always download a 90-day trial edition of Visual Studio 2008 Professional from* http://msdn.microsoft.com/en-us/vs2008/products/cc268305.aspx.

Depending on the edition of Visual Studio you are using, some of the steps illustrated in this book may not appear exactly the same on your screen. However, the differences are minor, and you should not have any problem in following the steps outlines in each chapter.

In addition, readers using Windows Vista should launch Visual Studio 2008 (as well as the Command Prompt window) in Administrator mode. To do so:

❑ Click on Vista Start button.

❑ Locate the program you want to launch (Visual Studio 2008, or Command Prompt).

❑ Right-click on the program and select Run as Administrator.

Conventions

A number of conventions are used throughout the book to help you get the most from the text and keep track of what's happening.

> **Boxes like this one hold important, not-to-be forgotten information that is directly relevant to the surrounding text.**

Tips, hints, tricks, and asides to the current discussion are offset and placed in italics like this.

As for styles in the text:

❑ New terms and important words are *highlighted* introduced.

❑ Keyboard strokes look like this: Ctrl+A.

❑ Filenames, URLs, and code within the text looks like this: `persistence.properties`.

❑ Code is presented in two different ways:

```
Code examples nearly always look like this.
```

```
Gray highlighting is used to show where new code is added to existing code,
or to point out a specific section of code that's being explained in the text.
```

Source Code

As you work through the examples in this book, you may choose either to type in all the code manually or to use the source code files that accompany the book. All of the source code used in this book is available for download at `www.wrox.com`. Once at the site, simply locate the book's title (either by using the Search box or by using one of the title lists), and click the Download Code link on the book's detail page to obtain all the source code for the book.

Because many books have similar titles, you may find it easiest to search by ISBN; this book's ISBN is 978-0-470-28581-7.

Once you download the code, just decompress it with your favorite compression tool. Alternatively, you can go to the main Wrox code download page at `www.wrox.com/dynamic/books/download.aspx` to see the code available for this book and all other Wrox books.

Errata

Every effort is made to ensure that there are no errors in the text or in the code. However, no one is perfect, and mistakes do occur. If you find an error such as a spelling mistake or faulty piece of code in one of our books, we would be grateful for your feedback. By sending in errata, you may save another reader hours of frustration, and at the same time you will be helping us provide even higher-quality information.

To find the errata page for this book, go to www.wrox.com and locate the title using the Search box or one of the title lists. Then, on the book details page, click the Book Errata link. On this page, you can view all errata that has been submitted for this book and posted by Wrox editors. A complete book list including links to each book's errata is also available at www.wrox.com/misc-pages/booklist.shtml.

If you don't spot "your" error on the Book Errata page, go to www.wrox.com/contact/techsupport .shtml, and complete the form there to send us the error you have found. We'll check the information and, if appropriate, post a message to the book's errata page and fix the problem in subsequent editions of the book.

p2p.wrox.com

For author and peer discussion, join the P2P forums at p2p.wrox.com. The forums are a web-based system for you to post messages relating to Wrox books and related technologies and interact with other readers and technology users. The forums offer a subscription feature to email you topics of interest of your choosing when new posts are made to the forums. Wrox authors, editors, other industry experts, and your fellow readers are present on these forums.

At http://p2p.wrox.com, you will find a number of different forums that will help you not only as you read this book but also as you develop your own applications. To join the forums, just follow these steps:

1. Go to p2p.wrox.com, and click the Register link.

2. Read the terms of use, and click Agree.

3. Complete the required information to join as well as any optional information you wish to provide, and click Submit.

4. You will receive an email with information describing how to verify your account and complete the joining process.

You can read messages in the forums without joining P2P but to post your own messages, you must join.

Once you join, you can post new messages and respond to messages other users post. You can read messages at any time on the web. If you would like to have new messages from a particular forum emailed to you, click the Subscribe to this Forum icon by the forum name in the forum listing.

For more information about how to use the Wrox P2P, be sure to read the P2P FAQs for answers to questions about how the forum software works as well as many common questions specific to P2P and Wrox books. To read the FAQs, click the FAQ link on any P2P page.

Part I
C# Fundamentals

The .NET Framework

The .NET Framework is a development framework created by Microsoft to enable developers to build applications that run on Microsoft (and other) platforms. Understanding the basics of the .NET Framework is essential because a large part of C# development revolves around using the classes in that framework.

This chapter explains the key components in the .NET Framework as well as the role played by each of the components. In addition, it examines the relationships among the various versions of the Framework, from version 1.0 to the latest 3.5.

What's the .NET Framework?

The .NET Framework has two components:

❑   Common Language Runtime

❑   .NET Framework class library

The Common Language Runtime (CLR) is the agent that manages your .NET applications at execution time. It provides core services such as memory, thread, and resource management. Applications that run on top of the CLR are known as *managed code*; all others are known as unmanaged code.

The .NET Framework class library is a comprehensive set of reusable classes that provides all the functionalities your application needs. This library enables you to develop applications ranging from desktop Windows applications to ASP.NET web applications, and Windows Mobile applications that run on Pocket PCs.

Common Language Runtime

The Common Language Runtime (CLR) is the virtual machine in the .NET Framework. It sits on top of the Windows operating system (Windows XP, Windows Vista, Windows Server 2008, and so on). A .NET application is compiled into a bytecode format known as MSIL

(Microsoft Intermediate Language). During execution, the CLR JIT (just-in-time) compiles the bytecode into the processor's native code and executes the application. Alternatively, MSIL code can be precompiled into native code so that JIT compiling is no longer needed; that speeds up the execution time of your application.

The CLR also provides the following services:

- Memory management/garbage collection
- Thread management
- Exception handling
- Security

.NET developers write applications using a .NET language such as C#, VB.NET, or C++. The MSIL bytecode allows .NET applications to be portable (at least theoretically) to other platforms because the application is compiled to native code only during runtime.

> At the time of writing, Microsoft's implementation of the .NET Framework runs only on Windows operating systems. However, there is an open-source implementation of the .NET Framework, called "Mono," that runs on Mac and Linux.

Figure 1-1 shows the relationships between the CLR, unmanaged and managed code.

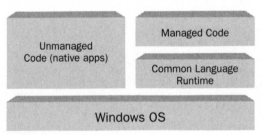

Figure 1-1

.NET Framework Class Library

The .NET Framework class library contains classes that allow you to develop the following types of applications:

- Console applications
- Windows applications
- Windows services

- ❏ ASP.NET Web applications
- ❏ Web Services
- ❏ Windows Communication Foundation (WCF) applications
- ❏ Windows Presentation Foundation (WPF) applications
- ❏ Windows Workflow Foundation (WF) applications

The library's classes are organized using a hierarchy of namespaces. For example, all the classes for performing I/O operations are located in the `System.IO` namespace, and classes that manipulate regular expressions are located in the `System.Text.RegularExpressions` namespace.

The .NET Framework class library is divided into two parts:

- ❏ * Framework Class Library (FCL)
- ❏ * Base Class Library (BCL)

The BCL is a subset of the entire class library and contains the set of classes that provide core functionalities for your applications. Some of the classes in the BCL are contained in the `mscorlib.dll`, `System.dll`, and `System.core.dll` assemblies. The BCL is available to all the languages using the .NET Framework. It encapsulates all the common functions such as file handling, database access, graphics manipulation, and XML document manipulation.

The FCL is the entire class library and it provides the classes for you to develop all the different types of applications listed previously.

Figure 1-2 shows the key components that make up the .NET Framework.

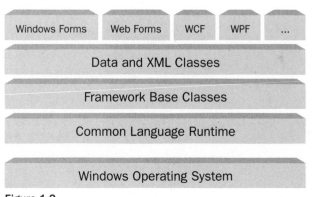

Figure 1-2

Assemblies and the Microsoft Intermediate Language (MSIL)

In .NET, an application compiled into MSIL bytecode is stored in an assembly. The assembly is contained in one or more PE (portable executable) files and may end with an EXE or DLL extension.

Some of the information contained in an assembly includes:

❑ **Manifest** — Information about the assembly, such as identification, name, version, and so on.

❑ **Versioning** — The version number of an assembly.

❑ **Metadata** — Information that describes the types and methods of the assembly.

Assemblies are discussed in more detail in Chapter 15.

To get a better idea of a MSIL file and its content, take a look at the following example, which has two console applications — one written in C# and the other written in VB.NET.

The following C# code displays the "Hello, World" string in the console window:

```
using System;
using System.Collections.Generic;
using System.Linq;
using System.Text;

namespace HelloWorldCS
{
    class Program
    {
        static void Main(string[] args)
        {
            Console.WriteLine("Hello, World!");
            Console.ReadLine();
        }
    }
}
```

Likewise, the following VB.NET code displays the "Hello, World" string in the console window:

```
Module Module1

    Sub Main()
        Console.WriteLine("Hello, World!")
        Console.ReadLine()
    End Sub

End Module
```

When both programs are compiled, the assembly for each program has an .exe extension. To view the content of each assembly, you can use the ildasm (MSIL Disassembler) tool.

Launch the ildasm tool from the Visual Studio 2008 Command Prompt window (Start ⇨ Programs ⇨ Microsoft Visual Studio 2008 ⇨ Visual Studio Tools ⇨ Visual Studio 2008 Command Prompt).

The following command uses the ildasm tool to view the assemblies for the C# and VB.NET programs:

```
C:\MSIL>ildasm HelloWorldCS.exe
C:\MSIL>ildasm HelloWorldVB.exe
```

Figure 1-3 shows the content of the C# and VB.NET assemblies, respectively.

Figure 1-3

The Main method of the C# MSIL looks like this:

```
.method private hidebysig static void  Main(string[] args) cil managed
{
  .entrypoint
  // Code size       19 (0x13)
  .maxstack  8
  IL_0000:  nop
  IL_0001:  ldstr      "Hello, World!"
  IL_0006:  call       void [mscorlib]System.Console::WriteLine(string)
  IL_000b:  nop
  IL_000c:  call       string [mscorlib]System.Console::ReadLine()
  IL_0011:  pop
  IL_0012:  ret
} // end of method Program::Main
```

The Main method of the VB.NET MSIL looks very similar to that of the C# program:

```
.method public static void  Main() cil managed
{
  .entrypoint
  .custom instance void [mscorlib]System.STAThreadAttribute::.ctor() = ( 01 00 00 00 )
  // Code size       20 (0x14)
  .maxstack  8
  IL_0000:  nop
  IL_0001:  ldstr      "Hello, World!"
  IL_0006:  call       void [mscorlib]System.Console::WriteLine(string)
  IL_000b:  nop
  IL_000c:  call       string [mscorlib]System.Console::ReadLine()
  IL_0011:  pop
  IL_0012:  nop
  IL_0013:  ret
} // end of method Module1::Main
```

The important thing to note here is that regardless of the language you use to develop your .NET applications, all .NET applications are compiled to the MSIL bytecode as this example shows. This means that you can mix and match languages in a .NET project — you can write a component in C# and use VB.NET to derive from it.

Versions of the .NET Framework and Visual Studio

Microsoft officially released the .NET Framework in January 2002. Since then, the .NET Framework has gone through a few iterations, and at the time of writing it stands at version 3.5. While technically you can write .NET applications using a text editor and a compiler, it is always easier to write .NET applications using Visual Studio, the integrated development environment from Microsoft. With Visual Studio, you can use its built-in debugger and support for IntelliSense to effectively and efficiently build .NET applications. The latest version of Visual Studio is Visual Studio 2008.

The following table shows the various versions of the .NET Framework, their release dates, and the versions of Visual Studio that contain them.

Version	Version Number	Release Date	Versions of Visual Studio shipped
1.0	1.0.3705.0	2002-01-05	Visual Studio .NET 2002
1.1	1.1.4322.573	2003-04-01	Visual Studio .NET 2003
2.0	2.0.50727.42	2005-11-07	Visual Studio 2005
3.0	3.0.4506.30	2006-11-06	Shipped with Windows Vista
3.5	3.5.21022.8	2007-11-19	Visual Studio 2008

Starting with Visual Studio 2005, Microsoft dropped the .Net name from the Visual Studio.

The .NET Framework 3.5 builds upon version 2.0 and 3.0 of the .NET Framework, so it essentially contains the following components:

❑ .NET Framework 2.0 and .NET Framework 2.0 Service Pack 1

❑ .NET Framework 3.0 and .NET Framework 3.0 Service Pack 1

❑ New features in .NET 3.5

> **.NET Framework version 3.5 is dependent on .NET 2.0 and 3.0. If you have a computer with .NET 1.0, 1.1, and 2.0 installed, these three versions are completely separate from each other. When you install .NET 3.5 on a computer without the .NET Framework installed, it will first install .NET 2.0, followed by .NET 3.0, and then finally the new assemblies new in .NET 3.5.**

Figure 1-4 summarizes the relationships between .NET 2.0, 3.0, and 3.5.

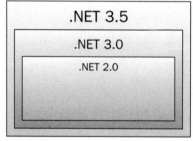

Figure 1-4

Summary

This chapter provided a quick overview of the .NET Framework and the various versions that make up the latest .NET Framework (3.5). Regardless of the language you use, all .NET applications will compile to a bytecode format known as MSIL. The MSIL is then JIT-compiled during runtime by the CLR to generate the native code to be executed by the processor.

In the next chapter, you start your journey to C# programming by learning use the development environment of Visual Studio 2008.

2

Getting Started with Visual Studio 2008

Microsoft Visual Studio 2008 is an extremely versatile and powerful environment for developing .NET applications. This chapter explores some of the commonly used features that you will likely use in the process of your development work. Because there are literally hundreds and thousands of ways in which you can customize Visual Studio 2008, this chapter can only explore, for the most part, the default settings in Visual Studio. While some of the topics covered are discussed in more detail in subsequent chapters, you'll want to breeze through this chapter to get an overall look at this version of Visual Studio.

This chapter examines:

❏ Components of the IDE (Menu bar, Toolbar, Toolbox, and so on)

❏ Code and Text Editor and the features it contains, including IntelliSense and Refactoring support

❏ Using the debugger in Visual Studio 2008

❏ Unit testing in Visual Studio 2008

Visual Studio 2008 Overview

In early 2008, Microsoft released the latest version of Visual Studio — Visual Studio 2008. With it comes a plethora of editions designed for the different types of developers in mind:

❏ Visual Web Developer 2008 Express Edition

❏ Visual Basic 2008 Express Edition

❏ Visual C# 2008 Express Edition

❏ Visual C++ 2008 Express Edition

❏ Visual Studio 2008 Standard Edition

- ❑ Visual Studio 2008 Professional Edition
- ❑ Visual Studio 2008 Team System 2008 Architecture Edition
- ❑ Visual Studio 2008 Team System 2008 Database Edition
- ❑ Visual Studio 2008 Team System 2008 Development Edition
- ❑ Visual Studio 2008 Team System 2008 Test Edition
- ❑ Visual Studio 2008 Team System 2008 Team Suite

For a detailed discussion of the features available in each edition, check out the following URL: `http://msdn.microsoft.com/en-us/vs2008/products/cc149003.aspx`.

The Express editions are designed for hobbyists and are available for download at no charge. This is a great way to get started with Visual Studio 2008 and is ideal for students and beginning programmers. However, if you are a professional developer, you should purchase either the Standard or Professional Edition. Note that if you are developing Windows Mobile applications, you need the Professional Edition (or higher). If you are working in a large development environment and need to develop collaboratively with other developers on large projects, check out the Team System editions.

If you are not ready to purchase Visual Studio 2008, you can always download a 90-day trial edition of Visual Studio 2008 Professional from `http://msdn.microsoft.com/en-us/vs2008/products/cc268305.aspx`.

Choosing the Development Settings

The first time you launch Visual Studio 2008, you choose the default environment settings. If you are going to use the C# language most of the time, choose the Visual C# Development Settings (see Figure 2-1). Choosing this option does not mean that you cannot use other languages (such as Visual Basic); it just means that C# will be listed as the default project type when you create a new project.

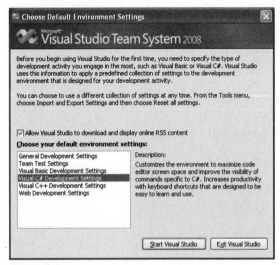

Figure 2-1

If the Visual C# Development Settings is chosen, Visual C# appears at the top of the Project Types list (see the left screenshot in Figure 2-2). In contrast, choosing the General Development Settings puts the Visual Basic language at the top (see the right screenshot in Figure 2-2).

Figure 2-2

Resetting the Development Settings

If for some reason you want to change the development settings after you have set them, you can always select Tools ⇨ Import and Export Settings to reset the settings. In the Import and Export Settings Wizard dialog that appears (see Figure 2-3), you can:

Figure 2-3

- ❑ Export the settings to a file so that they can be exported to another machine
- ❑ Import a saved setting
- ❑ Reset all the settings

To reset to another setting, check the Reset All Settings option and click Next. In the next step, you can choose either to save your current settings or to just reset the settings without saving. Once you have selected the option, click Next, and you can select another setting (see Figure 2-4).

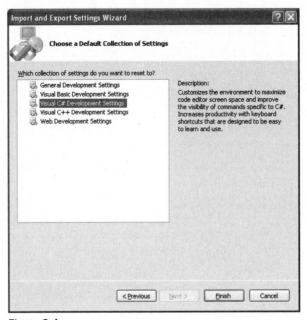

Figure 2-4

Creating a New Project

After you select a default setting, Visual Studio 2008 takes a couple of minutes to initialize. Once that's done, you will see something as shown in Figure 2-5.

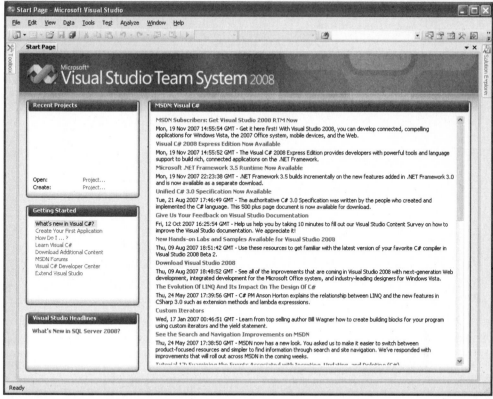

Figure 2-5

To create a new project, select File ⇨ New ⇨ Project (see Figure 2-6).

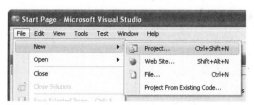

Figure 2-6

In the Visual C# development setting, you see the New Project dialog shown in Figure 2-7.

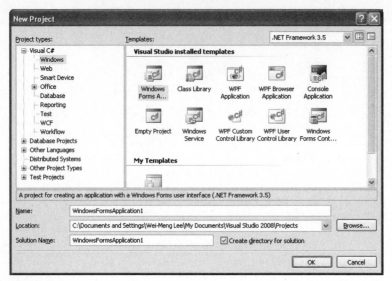

Figure 2-7

The default project name (WindowsFormApplication1 in this example) is provided, along with the following:

❑ The default location for saving the project.

❑ The solution name. The solution name by default is the same as your project name and is changed automatically to be the same as the project name. However, you can modify the solution name if you want it to have a different name than the project name.

❑ A separate directory to store the solution; if you uncheck the Create Directory For Solution checkbox, a solution is not be created for your project.

You can target a different version of the .NET Framework by selecting it from the dropdown list at the top right corner of the New Project dialog (see Figure 2-8).

Remember: A solution contains one or more projects.

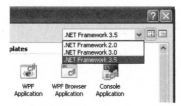

Figure 2-8

Components of the IDE

Figure 2-9 shows the various parts of the Visual Studio 2008 development environment.

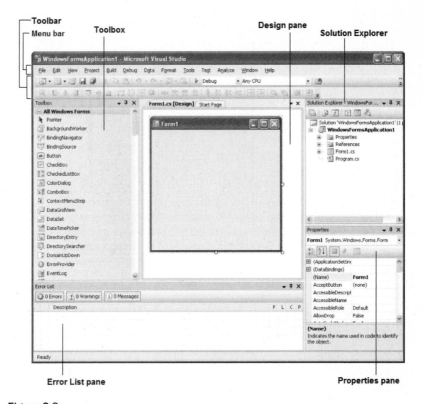

Figure 2-9

These parts are described in the following sections.

Menu Bar

The Menu bar contains standard Visual Studio commands. For example, Figure 2-10 shows that the File menu (see Figure 2-10) contains commands that enable you to create new projects, open existing projects, save the current form, and so on.

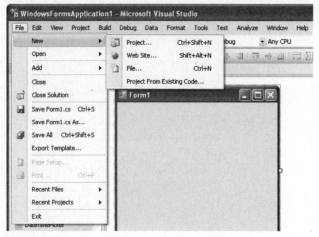

Figure 2-10

To customize the items displayed in the Menu bar, select Tools ⇨ Customize to display the Customize dialog (see Figure 2-11). Click on the Commands tab; the list of main menu items (Action, Addins, Analyze, and so forth) is on the left. Selecting a main menu item displays the list of available submenu items on the right. You can rearrange the submenu items by dragging them and dropping them onto the desired main menu item.

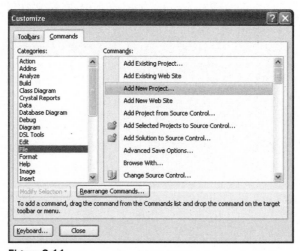

Figure 2-11

To add a new submenu item to a main menu item, click the Rearrange Commands button. In the Rearrange Commands dialog (see Figure 2-12), select the menu you want to customize, and click the Add button. You can then select the various submenu items from the different categories to add to the menu.

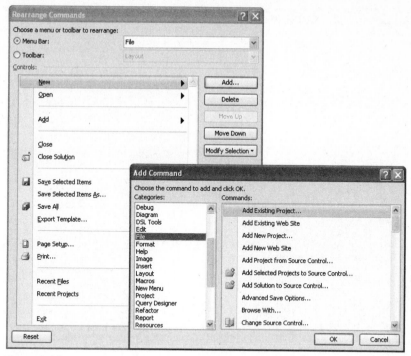

Figure 2-12

Toolbar

The Toolbar (see Figure 2-13) contains shortcuts to many of the often used commands contained in the Menu bar.

Figure 2-13

As with the Menu bar, the Toolbar is also customizable. To add additional toolbars, simply right-click on any existing toolbar and check the toolbar(s) you want to add to Visual Studio from the list of toolbars available (see Figure 2-14).

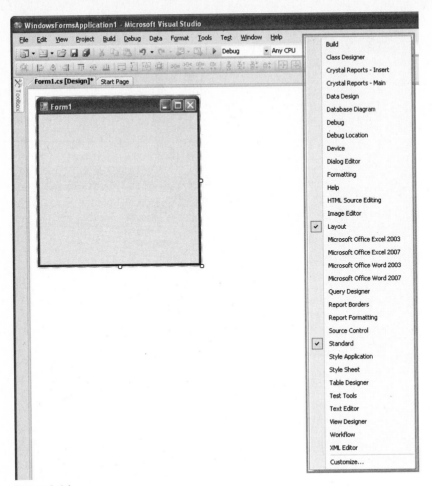

Figure 2-14

To customize the Toolbar, select Tools ⇨ Customize. On the Toolbars tab of the Customize dialog (see Figure 2-15), check the toolbar(s) you want to add to Visual Studio. You can create your own custom toolbar by clicking the New button.

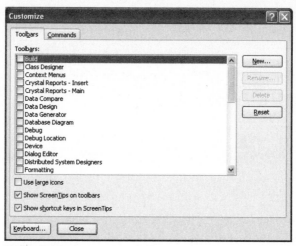

Figure 2-15

As with the Menu bar, you can also rearrange the items displayed in each toolbar. To customize the items displayed in the Toolbar, select Toolsv ⇨Customize to open the Customize dialog and then click the Rearrange Commands button. The Rearrange Commands dialog allows you to add/delete items from each toolbar (see Figure 2-16).

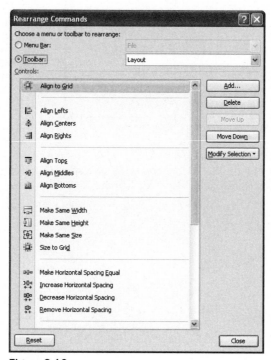

Figure 2-16

Each toolbar in the Toolbar can also be physically rearranged in Visual Studio by dragging the four-dot line on the left edge of the toolbar (see Figure 2-17) and relocating it to the new desired position.

Figure 2-17

Toolbox

The Toolbox (see Figure 2-18) contains all the controls that you can use in your applications. You can drag controls from the Toolbox and drop them onto the design surface of your application.

Figure 2-18

Each tab in the Toolbox contains controls that are related to a specific purpose. You can create your own tab to house your own controls. To do so, right-click on the Toolbox and select Add Tab. Name the newly created tab (see Figure 2-19).

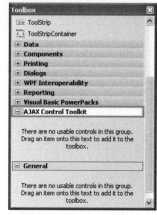

Figure 2-19

To add controls to the Toolbox, right-click on the tab to which you want the controls added and select Choose Items. The Choose Toolbox Items dialog (see Figure 2-20) opens.

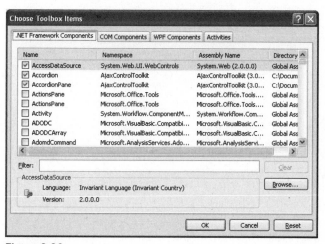

Figure 2-20

You can add the following types of controls to the Toolbox:

❑ .NET Framework components

❑ COM components

❑ WPF components

❑ Workflow activities

You can also click the Browse button to locate the .dll file that contains your own custom controls.

Another way to add controls to the Toolbox is to simply drag the DLL containing the controls and drop it directly onto the Toolbox.

You can relocate the Toolbox by dragging it and repositioning it on the various anchor points on the screen. Figure 2-21 shows the anchor points displayed by Visual Studio 2008 when you drag the Toolbox.

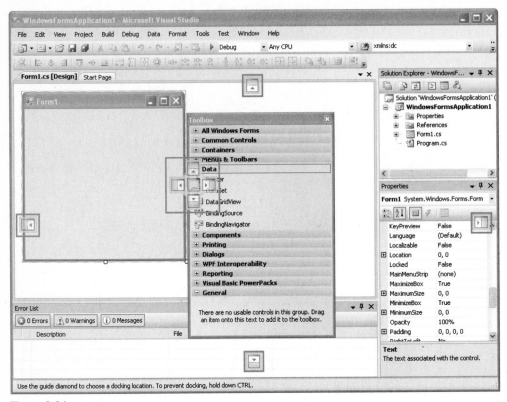

Figure 2-21

If you have limited screen real estate, you might want to auto-hide the Toolbox by clicking the Auto Hide button (see Figure 2-22).

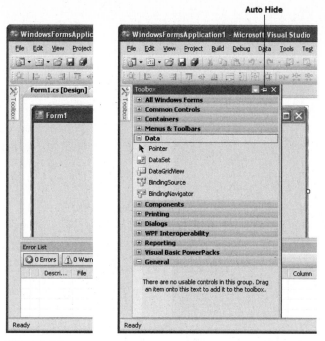

Figure 2-22

Missing Controls in Toolbox

Sometimes, for some unknown reasons, the controls in the Toolbox may suddenly go missing. The usual remedy is to right-click the Toolbox and select Reset Toolbox. This works most of the time. However, if that fails to work, you may need to do the following:

Navigate to `C:\Documents and Settings\<user_name>\Local Settings\Application Data\Microsoft\VisualStudio\9.0`.

Within this folder are some hidden files. Simply delete the following files: `toolbox.tbd`, `toolboxIndex.tbd`, `toolbox_reset.tbd`, and `toolboxIndex_reset.tbd`.

Then restart Visual Studio 2008. Your controls should now come back up!

Solution Explorer

The Solution Explorer window contains all the files and resources used in your project. A solution contains one or more projects. Figure 2-23 shows the various buttons available in the Solution Explorer.

> The buttons in the Solution Explorer window are context sensitive, which means that some buttons will not be visible when certain items are selected. For instance, if you select the project name, the View Code and View Designer buttons will not be shown.

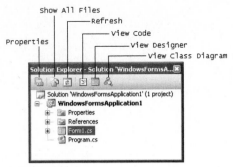

Figure 2-23

To add additional items such as a Windows Form or a Class to your current project, right-click the project name in Solution Explorer, select Add (see Figure 2-24), and then choose the item you want to add from the list.

Figure 2-24

You can also add new (or existing) projects to the current solution. To do so, right-click on the solution name in Solution Explorer, select Add (see Figure 2-25), and then select what you want to add.

Figure 2-25

When you have multiple projects in a solution, one of the projects will be set as the startup project (the project name that is displayed in bold in Solution Explorer is the startup project). That is, when you press F5 to debug the application, the project set as the startup project will be debugged. To change the startup project, right-click the project that you want to set as the startup and select Set as Startup Project (see Figure 2-26).

Figure 2-26

To debug multiple projects at the same time when you press the F5 key, set multiple projects as the startup projects. To do so, right-click on the solution name in Solution Explorer and select Properties.

Select the Multiple Startup Projects option (see Figure 2-27), and set the appropriate action for each project (None, Start, or Start Without Debugging).

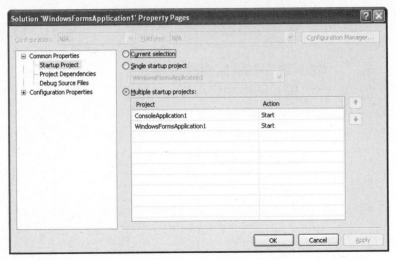

Figure 2-27

Then when you press F5, the projects configured to start launch at the same time.

Properties

The Properties window shows the list of properties associated with the various items in your projects (Windows Forms, controls, projects, solutions, etc).

Figure 2-28 shows the Properties window displaying the list of properties of a Windows Form (Form1, in this example). By default, the properties are displayed in Categorized view, but you can change it to Alphabetical view, which lists all the properties in alphabetical order.

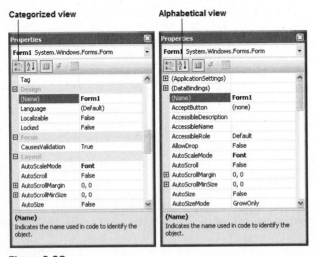

Figure 2-28

All default property values are displayed in normal font, while nondefault values are displayed in bold. This feature is very useful for debugging because it enables you to quickly trace the property values that you have changed.

Besides displaying properties of items, the Properties window also displays events. When the Properties window is displaying an item (such as a Windows Form or a control) that supports events, you can click the Events icon (see left side of Figure 2-29) to view the list of events supported by that item. To create an event handler stub for an event, simply double-click the event name and Visual Studio 2008 automatically creates an event handler for you (see right side of Figure 2-29).

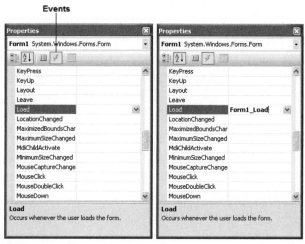

Figure 2-29

Error List

The Error List window (see Figure 2-30) is used to display:

❑ Errors, warnings, and messages produced as you edit and compile code.

❑ Syntax errors noted by IntelliSense.

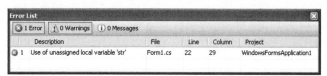

Figure 2-30

To display the Error List window, select View ⇨ Error List.

You can double-click on an error message to open the source file and locate the position of the error. Once the error is located, press F1 for help.

Output Window

The Output window (View ⇨ Output) displays status messages for your application when you are debugging in Visual Studio 2008. The Output window is useful for displaying debugging messages in your application. For example, you can use the `Console.WriteLine()` statement to display a message to the Output window:

```
Console.WriteLine(DateTime.Now.ToString());
```

Figure 2-31 shows the message displayed in the Output window.

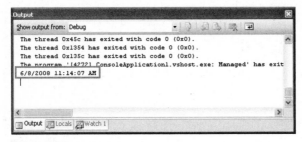

Figure 2-31

Designer Window

The Designer window enables you to visually design the UI of your application. Depending on the type of projects you are creating, the Designer displays a different design surface where you can drag and drop controls onto it. Figure 2-32 shows the Designer for creating different types of projects — Windows Forms (left), Windows Mobile (right), and Web (bottom left).

To switch to the code-behind of the application, you can either double-click on the surface of the designer, or right-click the item in Solution Explorer and select View Code. For example, if you are developing a Windows Forms application, you can right-click on a form, say `Form1.cs`, in Solution Explorer and select View Code. The code-behind for `Form1` then displays (see Figure 2-33).

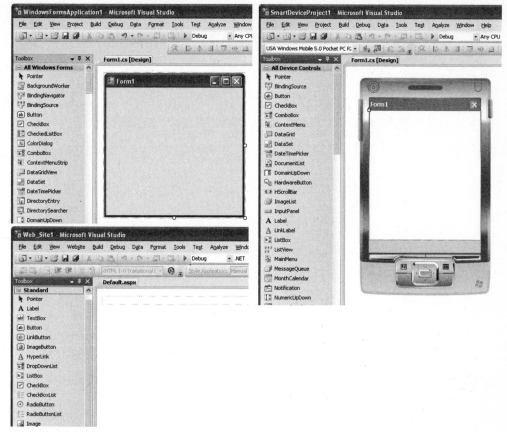

Figure 2-32

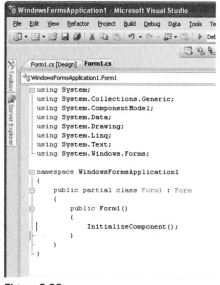

Figure 2-33

Code View

Code view is where you write the code for your application. You can switch between design view and code view by clicking on the relevant tabs (see Figure 2-34).

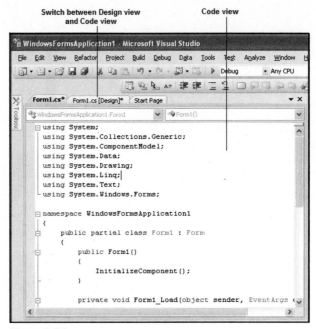

Figure 2-34

In Visual Studio, you can right-click on the tabs (see Figure 2-35) to arrange the code view either horizontally or vertically, to maximize the use of your monitor(s).

Figure 2-35

Figure 2-36 shows the code view and design view displaying horizontally.

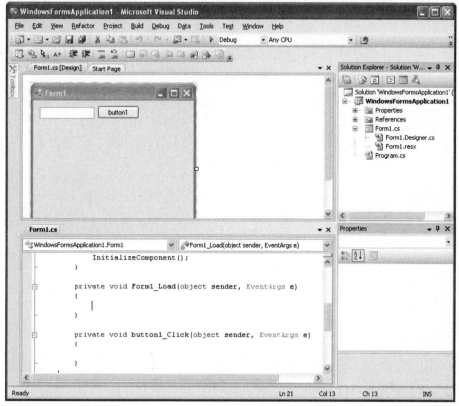

Figure 2-36

Figure 2-37 shows the code view and design view displaying vertically.

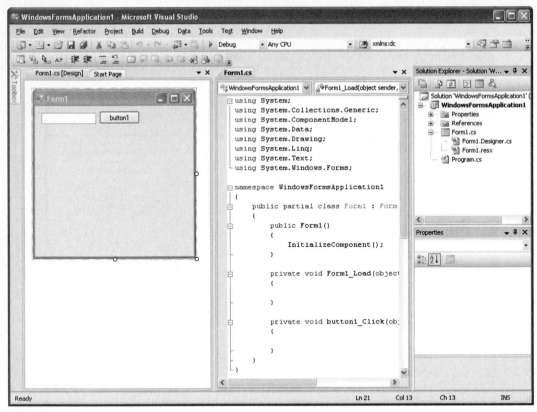

Figure 2-37

Having multiple views at the same time is useful if you have a big monitor (or multiple monitors).

Code and Text Editor

Within the code view of Visual Studio 2008 is the Code and Text Editor, which provides several rich features that make editing your code easy and efficient, including:

- ❑ Code Snippets
- ❑ IntelliSense statement completion
- ❑ IntelliSense support for object properties, methods and events
- ❑ Refactoring support

Code Snippets

The Code Snippet feature in Visual Studio 2008 enables you to insert commonly used code blocks into your project, thereby improving the efficiency of your development process. To insert a code snippet, right-click on the location where you want to insert the code snippet in the Code Editor, and select Insert Snippet (see Figure 2-38).

Figure 2-38

Select the snippet category by clicking on the category name (see the top of Figure 2-39) and then selecting the code snippet you want to insert (see bottom of Figure 2-39).

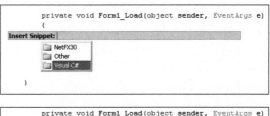

Figure 2-39

For example, suppose that you select the `try` code snippet. The following block of code will be inserted automatically:

```
private void Form1_Load(object sender, EventArgs e)
{
    try
    {

    }
    catch (Exception)
    {

        throw;
    }
}
```

You can also use the Surround With code snippets feature. Suppose that you have the following statements:

```
private void Form1_Load(object sender, EventArgs e)
{
    int num1 = 5;
    int num2 = 0;
    int result = num1 / num2;
}
```

The third statement is dangerous because it could result in a division-by-zero runtime error, so it would be good to wrap the code in a `try-catch` block. To do so, you can highlight the block of code you want to put within a `try-catch` block and right-click it. Select Surround With (see Figure 2-40), and then select the `try` code snippet.

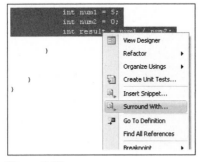

Figure 2-40

Your code now looks like this:

```
private void Form1_Load(object sender, EventArgs e)
{
    try
    {
        int num1=5;
        int num2 = 0;
        int result = num1 / num2;
    }
    catch (Exception)
    {

        throw;
    }
}
```

IntelliSense

IntelliSense is one of the most useful tools in Visual Studio 2008. IntelliSense automatically detects the properties, methods, events, and so forth of an object as you type in the code editor. You do not need to remember the exact member names of an object because IntelliSense helps you by dynamically providing you with a list of relevant members as you enter your code.

For example, when you type the word Console in the code editor followed by the ., IntelliSense displays a list of relevant members pertaining to the Console class (see Figure 2-41).

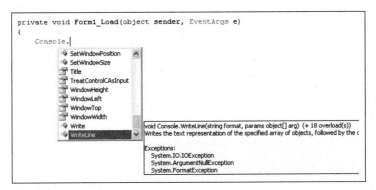

Figure 2-41

When you have selected the member you want to use, press the Tab key and IntelliSense will insert the member into your code.

IntelliSense in Visual Studio 2008 has some great enhancements. For example, the IntelliSense dropdown list often obscures the code that is behind when it pops up. You can now make the dropdown list disappear momentarily by pressing the Control key. Figure 2-42 shows the IntelliSense dropdown list blocking the code behind it (top) and having it be translucent by pressing the Control key (bottom).

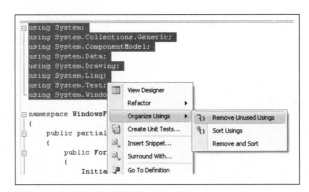

Figure 2-42

You can also use IntelliSense to tidy up the namespaces at the top of your code. For example, you often import a lot of namespaces at the beginning of your code and some of them might not ever be used by your application. In Visual Studio 2008, you can select the namespaces, right-click, and select Organize Usings (see Figure 2-43).

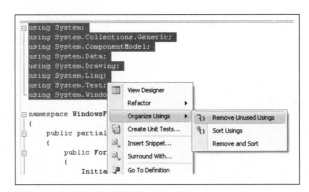

Figure 2-43

Then you can choose to:

❑ Remove all unused using statements

❑ Sort the using statements alphabetically

❑ Remove all unused using statements and sort the remaining namespace alphabetically

Refactoring Support

Another useful feature available in Visual Studio 2008 is code refactoring. Even though the term may sound unfamiliar, many of you have actually used it. In a nutshell, code refactoring means restructuring your code so that the original intention of the code is preserved. For example, you may rename a variable so that it better reflects its usage. In that case, the entire application that uses the variable needs to be updated with the new name. Another example of code refactoring is extracting a block of code and placing it into a function for more efficient code reuse. In either case, you would need to put in significant amount of effort to ensure that you do not inadvertently inject errors into the modified code. In Visual Studio 2008, you can perform code refactoring easily. The following sections explain how to use this feature.

Rename

Renaming variables is a common programming task. However, if you are not careful, you may inadvertently rename the wrong variable (most people use the find-and-replace feature available in the IDE, which is susceptible to wrongly renaming variables). In C# refactoring, you can rename a variable by selecting it, right-clicking, and choosing Refactoring ➪ Rename (see Figure 2-44).

Figure 2-44

You are prompted for a new name (see Figure 2-45). Enter a new name, and click OK.

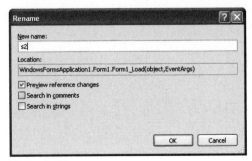

Figure 2-45

You can preview the change (see Figure 2-46) before it is applied to your code.

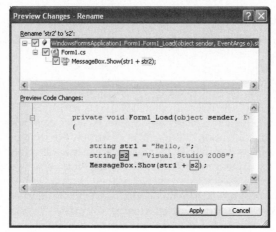

Figure 2-46

Click the Apply button to change the variable name.

Extract Method

Very often, you write repetitive code within your application. Consider the following example:

```
private void Form1_Load(object sender, EventArgs e)
{
    int num = 10, sum = 0;
    for (int i = 1; i <= num; i++)
    {
        sum += i;
    }
}
```

Here, you are summing up all the numbers from 1 to num, a common operation. It would be better for you to package this block of code into a function. So, highlight the code (see Figure 2-47), right-click it, and select Refactor ⇨ Extract Method.

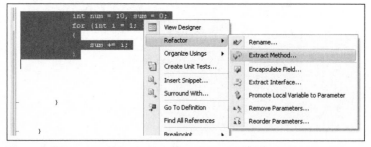

Figure 2-47

Supply a new name for your method (see Figure 2-48). You can also preview the default method signature that the refactoring engine has created for you. Click OK.

Figure 2-48

The block of statements is now encapsulated within a function and the original block of code is replaced by a call to that function:

```
private void Form1_Load(object sender, EventArgs e)
{
    Summation();
}

private static void Summation()
{
    int num = 10, sum = 0;
    for (int i = 1; i <= num; i++)
    {
        sum += i;
    }
}
```

However, you still need to do some tweaking because the variable sum should be returned from the function. The code you highlight will affect how the refactoring engine works. For example, if you include the variables declaration in the highlighting, a void function is created.

While the method extraction feature is useful, you must pay close attention to the new method signature and the return type. Often, some minor changes are needed to get what you want. Here's another example:

```
Single radius = 3.5f;
Single height = 5;
double volume = Math.PI * Math.Pow(radius, 2) * height;
```

If you exclude the variables declaration in the refactoring (instead of selecting all the three lines; see Figure 2-49) and name the new method `VolumeofCylinder`, a method with two parameters is created:

```csharp
private void Form1_Load(object sender, EventArgs e)
{
    Single radius = 3.5f;
    Single height = 5;
    double volume = VolumeofCylinder(radius, height);
}

private static double VolumeofCylinder(Single radius, Single height)
{
    return Math.PI * Math.Pow(radius, 2) * height;
}
```

Figure 2-49

Here are some observations:

- Variables that are defined outside of the highlighted block for refactoring are used as an input parameter in the new method.

- If variables are declared within the block selected for refactoring, the new method will have no signature.

- Values that are changed within the block of highlighted code will be passed into the new method by reference.

Reorder and Remove Parameters

You can use code refactoring to reorder the parameters in a function. Consider the following function from the previous example:

```csharp
private static double VolumeofCylinder(Single radius, Single height)
{
    return Math.PI * Math.Pow(radius, 2) * height;
}
```

Highlight the function signature, right-click it, and select Refactor ⇨ Reorder Parameters (see Figure 2-50).

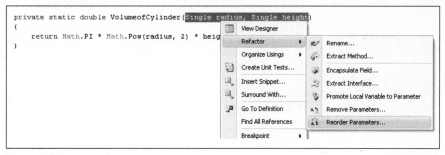

Figure 2-50

You can then rearrange the order of the parameter list (see Figure 2-51).

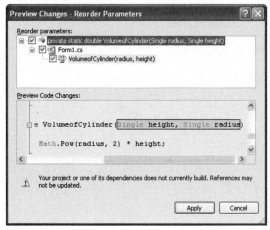

Figure 2-51

Click OK. You can preview the changes before they are made (see Figure 2-52).

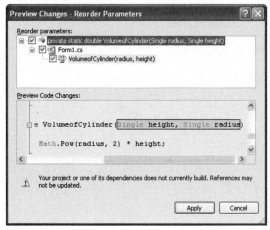

Figure 2-52

Once you click the Apply button, your code is changed automatically:

```
private void Form1_Load(object sender, EventArgs e)
{
    Single radius = 3.5f;
    Single height = 5;
    double volume = VolumeofCylinder(height, radius);
}

private static double VolumeofCylinder(Single height, Single radius)
{
    return Math.PI * Math.Pow(radius, 2) * height;
}
```

All statements that call the modified function will have their arguments order changed automatically.

You can also remove parameters from a function by highlighting the function signature, right-clicking, and selecting Refactor ⇨ Remove Parameters. Then remove the parameter(s) you want to delete (see Figure 2-53). All statements that call the modified function will have their calls changed automatically.

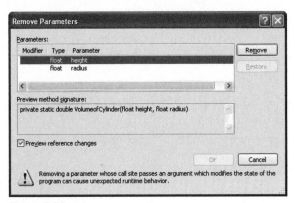

Figure 2-53

Encapsulate Field

Consider the following string declaration:

```
namespace WindowsFormsApplication1
{
    public partial class Form1 : Form
    {
        public string caption;

        private void Form1_Load(object sender, EventArgs e)
        {
            //...
        }
    }
}
```

Instead of exposing the `caption` variable as public, it is a better idea to encapsulate it as a property and use the `set` and `get` accessors to access it. To do that, right-click on the `caption` variable and select Refactor ⇨ Encapsulate Field (see Figure 2-54).

Figure 2-54

Assign a name to your property (see Figure 2-55). You have the option to update all external references or all references (including the one within the class), and you can choose to preview your reference changes. When you're ready, click OK.

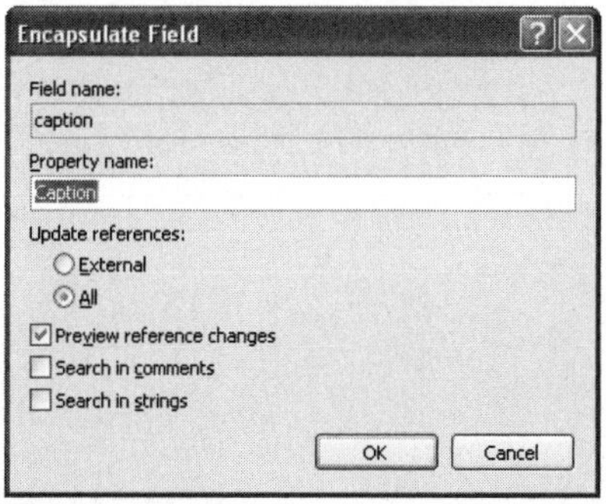

Figure 2-55

After you've previewed the changes (see Figure 2-56), click Apply to effect the change.

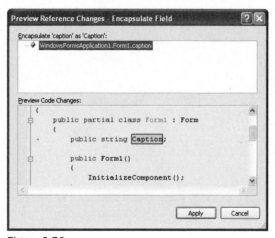

Figure 2-56

Here is the result after applying the change:

```
namespace WindowsFormsApplication1
{
    public partial class Form1 : Form
    {
        private string caption;

        public string Caption
        {
            get { return caption; }
            set { caption = value; }
        }

        private void Form1_Load(object sender, EventArgs e)
        {
            //...
        }
    }
}
```

Extract Interface

You can use the refactoring engine to extract an interface from a class definition. Consider the following `Contact` class:

```
namespace WindowsFormsApplication1
{
    class Contact
    {
        public string FirstName
        {
            get;
            set;
        }
        public string LastName
        {
            get;
            set;
        }
        public string Email
        {
            get;
            set;
        }
        public DateTime DOB
        {
            get;
            set;
        }
    }
}
```

Right-click the `Contact` class name and select Refactor ⇨ Extract Interface (see Figure 2-57).

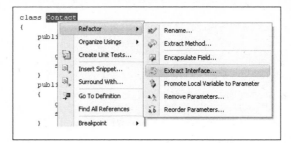

Figure 2-57

The Extract Interface dialog opens, and you can select the individual public members to form the interface (see Figure 2-58).

Figure 2-58

The new interface is saved in a new `.cs` file. In this example, the filename is `IContact.cs`:

```
using System;
namespace WindowsFormsApplication1
{
    interface IContact
    {
        DateTime DOB { get; set; }
        string Email { get; set; }
        string FirstName { get; set; }
        string LastName { get; set; }
    }
}
```

The original `Contact` class definition has now been changed to implements the newly created interface:

```
class Contact : WindowsFormsApplication1.IContact
{
    public string FirstName
    ...
```

Promote Local Variable to Parameter

You can promote a local variable into a parameter. Here's an example:

```
private void Form1_Load(object sender, EventArgs e)
{
    LogError("File not found.");
}

private void LogError(string message)
{
    string SourceFile = "Form1.cs";
    Console.WriteLine(SourceFile + ": " + message);
}
```

You want to promote the variable `SourceFile` into a parameter so that callers of this function can pass in its value through an argument. To do so, select the variable `SourceFile`, right-click, and then select Refactor ⇨ Promote Local Variable to Parameter (see Figure 2-59).

Figure 2-59

Note that the local variable to be promoted must be initialized or an error will occur. The promoted variable is now in the parameter list and the call to it is updated accordingly:

```
private void Form1_Load(object sender, EventArgs e)
{
    LogError("File not found.", "Form1.cs");
}
```

```
private void LogError(string message, string SourceFile)
{
    Console.WriteLine(SourceFile + ": " + message);
}
```

Debugging

Debugging is an important part of the development cycle. Naturally, Visual Studio 2008 contains debugging tools that enable you to observe the runtime behavior of your program. This section takes a look at those tools.

Suppose that you have the following program:

```
using System;
using System.Windows.Forms;

namespace WindowsFormsApplication1
{
    public partial class Form1 : Form
    {
        public Form1()
        {
            InitializeComponent();
        }

        private void Form1_Load(object sender, EventArgs e)
        {
            Console.WriteLine("Start");
            printAllOddNumbers(9);
            Console.WriteLine("End");
        }

        private void printAllOddNumbers(int num)
        {
            for (int i = 1; i <= num; i++)
            {
                if (i % 2 == 1)
                {
                    Console.WriteLine(i);
                }
            }
        }
    }
}
```

The following sections show how you can insert breakpoints into the application so that you can debug the application during runtime.

Setting Breakpoints

To set a breakpoint in your application, in the Visual Studio 2008 Code Editor, click in the left column beside the statement at which you want to set the breakpoint (see Figure 2-60).

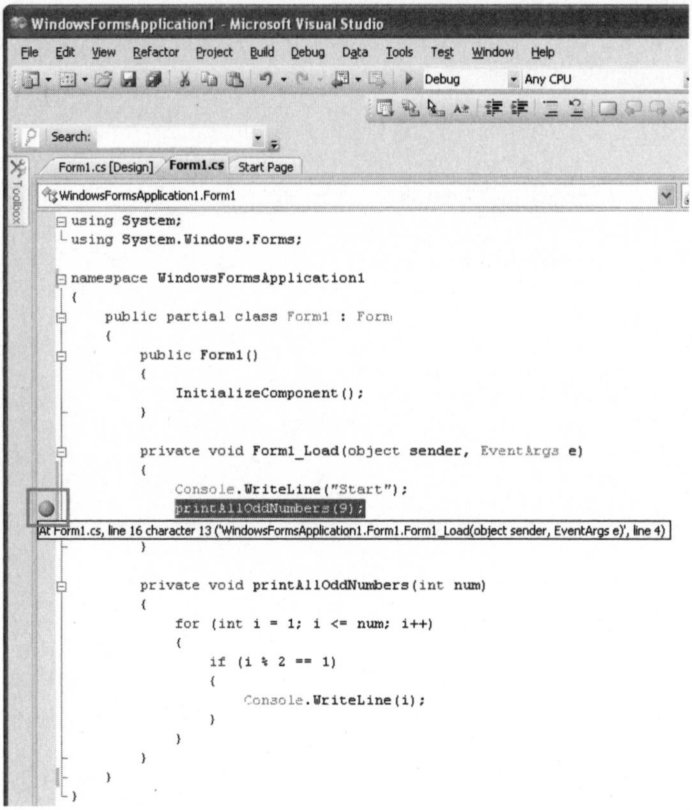

Figure 2-60

Press F5 to debug the application. When the execution reaches the statement with the breakpoint set, Visual Studio 2008 pauses the application and shows the breakpoint (see Figure 2-61).

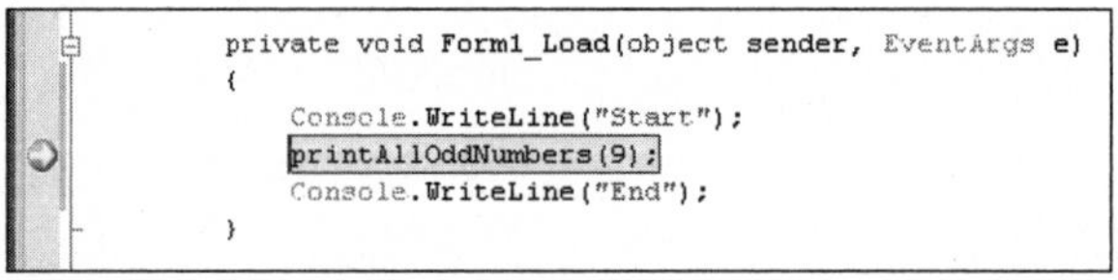

Figure 2-61

Stepping through the Code

With the application stopped at the breakpoint, you have a choice of what to do:

❑ **Step Into** — Press F11 (see Figure 2-62). Stepping into the code means that if the breakpoint statement is a function call, execution is transferred to the first statement in the function and you can step through the function one statement at a time.

❑ **Step Over** — Press F10. Stepping over the code means that if the breakpoint statement is a function call, the entire function is executed and control is transferred to the next statement after the function.

❑ **Step Out** — Press Shift+F11 to step out of the code (Step Out). If the statement at the breakpoint is part of a function, execution is resumed until the function exits. The control is transferred to the returning point in the calling function.

Step Into and Step Over are basically the same, except when it comes to executing functions.

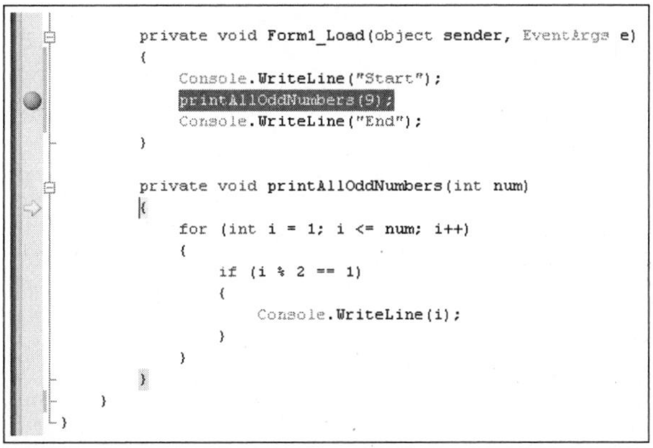

```
        private void Form1_Load(object sender, EventArgs e)
        {
            Console.WriteLine("Start");
            printAllOddNumbers(9);
            Console.WriteLine("End");
        }

        private void printAllOddNumbers(int num)
        {
            for (int i = 1; i <= num; i++)
            {
                if (i % 2 == 1)
                {
                    Console.WriteLine(i);
                }
            }
        }
    }
}
```

Figure 2-62

While you are at a breakpoint stepping through the code (using either F10 or F11), you can also examine the values of variables by hovering the mouse over the object you want to examine. Figure 2-63 shows value of i when the mouse is over i.

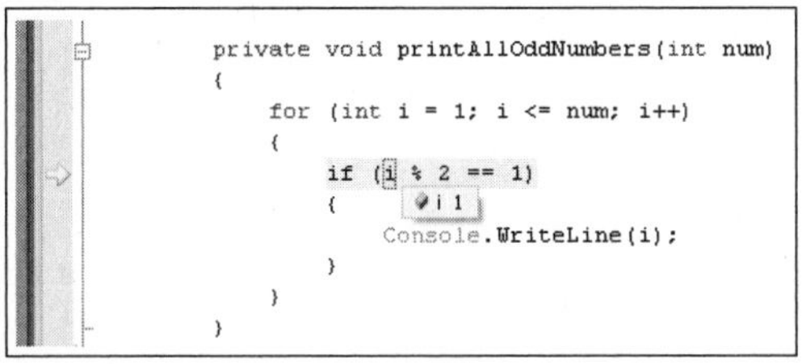

```
        private void printAllOddNumbers(int num)
        {
            for (int i = 1; i <= num; i++)
            {
                if (i % 2 == 1)
                {          ⬦ i  1
                    Console.WriteLine(i);
                }
            }
        }
```

Figure 2-63

Watching

You can also right-click on the object you want to monitor and select Add Watch or QuickWatch (see Figure 2-64).

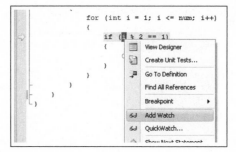

Figure 2-64

When you use the Add Watch feature, the variable you are watching will be displayed in the Watch window (see Figure 2-65). As you step through your code, changes in the variable are reflected in the Watch window. In addition, you have the option to change the value of the variable directly in the Watch window.

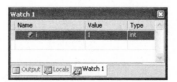

Figure 2-65

The QuickWatch feature also enables you to monitor the value of variables, except that the execution cannot continue until you have closed the QuickWatch window (see Figure 2-66). You can also enter an expression to evaluate and at the same time add a variable into the Add Watch window.

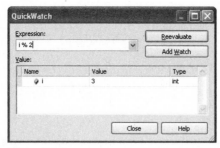

Figure 2-66

Autos and Immediate Windows

To automatically view all the relevant variables in scope, you can launch the Autos window (see Figure 2-67) during a breakpoint by selecting Debug ⇨ Windows ⇨ Autos.

Figure 2-67

You can use the Immediate Window (see Figure 2-68) at runtime to evaluate expressions, execute statements, print variable values, and so on. You can launch the Immediate window during a breakpoint by selecting Debug ⇨ Windows ⇨ Immediate.

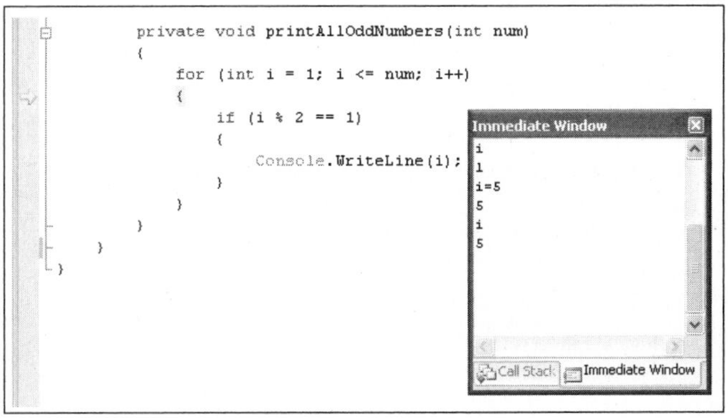

```
private void printAllOddNumbers(int num)
{
    for (int i = 1; i <= num; i++)
    {
        if (i % 2 == 1)
        {
            Console.WriteLine(i);
        }
    }
}
```

Immediate Window
```
i
1
i=5
5
i
5
```

Figure 2-68

Unit Testing

Application testing is one of the tasks that every programmer worth his salt needs to do. For example, after writing a class, you often need to write additional code to instantiate the class and test the various methods and properties defined within it. Visual Studio 2008 Professional (and higher) provides a Unit Testing feature to auto-generate the code needed to test your application.

This section demonstrates how unit testing is performed in Visual Studio 2008. Use the following `Point` class definition located within a Class Library project:

```csharp
using System;
using System.Collections.Generic;
using System.Linq;
using System.Text;

namespace UnitTesting
{
    class Point
    {
        public Point() { }
        public Point(int x, int y)
        {
            this.x = x;
            this.y = y;
        }

        public int x { get; set; }
        public int y { get; set; }

        //---calculates the length between 2 points
        public double length(Point pointOne)
        {
            return Math.Sqrt(
                Math.Pow(this.x - pointOne.x, 2) +
                Math.Pow(this.y - pointOne.y, 2));
        }
    }
}
```

Creating the Test

For this example, create a unit test to test the `length()` method. To do so, right-click on the `length()` method and select Create Unit Tests (see Figure 2-69).

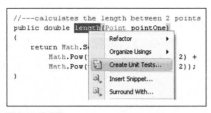

Figure 2-69

In the Create Unit Tests dialog, select any other additional members you want to test and click OK (see Figure 2-70).

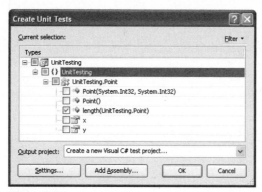

Figure 2-70

You are prompted to name the test project. Use the default `TestProject1` and click Create. You may also be prompted with the dialog shown in Figure 2-71. Click Yes.

Figure 2-71

The `TestProject1` is be added to Solution Explorer (see Figure 2-72).

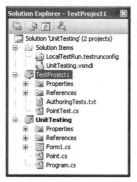

Figure 2-72

The content of the `PointTest.cs` class is now displayed in Visual Studio 2008. This class contains the various methods that you can use to test the `Point` class. In particular, note the `lengthTest()` method:

```
/// <summary>
///A test for length
///</summary>
[TestMethod()]
public void lengthTest()
{
    Point target = new Point(); // TODO: Initialize to an appropriate value
    Point pointOne = null; // TODO: Initialize to an appropriate value
    double expected = 0F; // TODO: Initialize to an appropriate value
    double actual;
    actual = target.length(pointOne);
    Assert.AreEqual(expected, actual);
    Assert.Inconclusive("Verify the correctness of this test method.");
}
```

The `lengthTest()` method has the `[TestMethod]` attribute prefixing it. Methods with that attribute are known as *test methods*.

Now modify the implementation of the `lengthTest()` method to basically create and initialize two `Point` objects and then call the `length()` method of the `Point` class to calculate the distance between the two points:

```
/// <summary>
///A test for length
///</summary>
[TestMethod()]
public void lengthTest()
{
    int x = 3;
    int y = 4;

    Point target = new Point(x, y);
    Point pointOne = new Point(0,0);
    double expected = 5F;
    double actual;
    actual = target.length(pointOne);
    Assert.AreEqual(expected, actual,
        "UnitTesting.Point.length did not return the expected value.");
}
```

Once the result is returned from the `length()` method, you use the `AreEqual()` method from the `Assert` class to check the returned value against the expected value. If the expected value does not match the returned result, the error message set in the `AreEqual()` method is displayed.

Running the Test

Before you run the unit test, take a look at the Test Tools toolbar (see Figure 2-73) automatically shown in Visual Studio 2008.

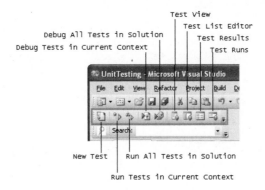

Figure 2-73

To run the unit test, click the Run All Tests in Solution button in the toolbar. In this case, the lengthTest() method passed the test. The length between two points (3,4) and (0,0) is indeed 5 (see Figure 2-74).

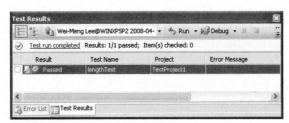

Figure 2-74

You can make modifications to the lengthTest() method to test other parameters. In the Test Results window, you have the option to view the previous test results (see Figure 2-75).

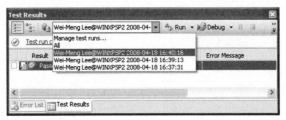

Figure 2-75

Testing with Floating Point Numbers

You need to take special note when your test involves comparing floating point numbers. Consider the following example:

```
[TestMethod()]
public void lengthTest()
{
    int x = 4;
    int y = 5;

    Point target = new Point(x, y);
    Point pointOne = new Point(1,2);
    double expected = 4.24264F;
    double actual;
    actual = target.length(pointOne);
    Assert.AreEqual(expected, actual,
        "UnitTesting.Point.length did not return the expected value.");
}
```

When you run the test, the test will fail (see Figure 2-76).

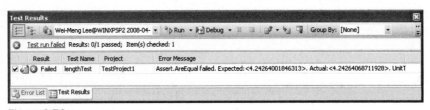

Figure 2-76

Why is this so? The reason is that floating point numbers (such as `Single` and `Double`) are not stored exactly as what they have been assigned. For example, in this case, the value of 4.24264 is stored internally as 4.2426400184631348, and the result returned by the `length()` method is actually 4.2426406871192848. The `AreEqual()` method actually fails if you compare them directly.

To address this issue, the `AreEqual()` method supports a third parameter — `delta` — that specifies the maximum difference allowed for the two numbers that you are comparing. In this case, the difference between the two numbers is 0.0000066865615. And so the following code will pass the test:

```
Assert.AreEqual(expected, actual, 0.0000066865616,
    "UnitTesting.Point.length did not return the expected value.");
```

But this code will fail:

```
Assert.AreEqual(expected, actual, 0.0000066865615,
    "UnitTesting.Point.length did not return the expected value.");

Assert.AreEqual(expected, actual, 0.0000066865614,
    "UnitTesting.Point.length did not return the expected value.");
```

Although the documentation says that the delta specifies the maximum difference allowed for the two numbers, in actual testing the difference should be *less* than the delta for the `Assert.AreEqual()` method to pass. This explains why that first statement fails.

Adding Additional Test Methods

You can insert additional test methods by adding new subroutines to the `PointTest.cs` file and prefixing them with the `[TestMethod]` attribute. For example, the following test method uses the `AreSame()` method of the `Assert` class to check whether two objects are pointing to the same reference:

```
[TestMethod()]
public void objectTest()
{
    Point point1 = new Point(4, 5);
    Point point2 = new Point() { x = 4, y = 5 };
    Point point3 = point2;

    //---Failed---
    Assert.AreSame(point1, point2, "point1 is not the same as point2");

    //---Passed---
    Assert.AreSame(point2, point3, "point2 is not the same as point3");
}
```

Figure 2-77 shows the test results.

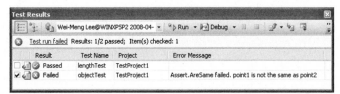

Figure 2-77

Summary

This chapter provided a quick overview of the common features and tools available in Visual Studio 2008. Visual Studio 2008 is highly configurable, so you'll want to take some time to familiarize yourself with the environment. If you're totally new to C#, some Visual Studio features like code refactoring and unit testing may not seem all that important to you now, but once you've gotten some C# under your belt, you'll want to take another look at those features.

When you're ready, the next chapter gets you started in writing code in C#.

C# Language Foundations

The best way to get started in a new programming language is to create a simple program and then examine the various parts that compose it. With this principle in mind, you'll create a simple C# program — first using Visual Studio 2008 and then using a plain text editor.

In this chapter you build and run the HelloWorld application, using Visual Studio 2008 as well as using the command line. After that, you tackle the syntax of the C# language and all the important topics, such as:

- ❑ C# keywords
- ❑ Variables
- ❑ Constants
- ❑ Comments
- ❑ XML documentation
- ❑ Data types
- ❑ Flow control
- ❑ Loops
- ❑ Operators
- ❑ Preprocessor directives

Using Visual Studio 2008

The easiest way to create your first C# program is to use Visual Studio 2008.

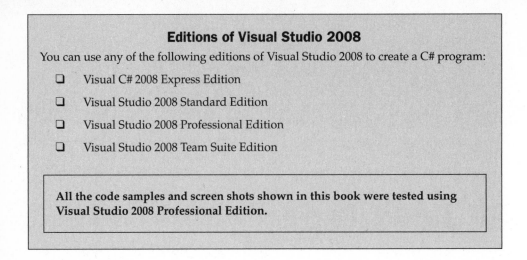

Editions of Visual Studio 2008

You can use any of the following editions of Visual Studio 2008 to create a C# program:

❑ Visual C# 2008 Express Edition

❑ Visual Studio 2008 Standard Edition

❑ Visual Studio 2008 Professional Edition

❑ Visual Studio 2008 Team Suite Edition

All the code samples and screen shots shown in this book were tested using Visual Studio 2008 Professional Edition.

1. Launch Visual Studio 2008.

2. Create a new Console Application project by selecting File ⇨ New ⇨ Project.

3. Expand the Visual C# item on the left of the dialog, and select Windows. Then, select the Console Application template on the right (see Figure 3-1). Name the project HelloWorld.

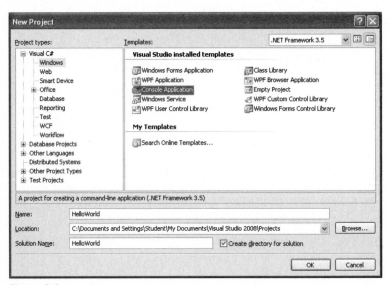

Figure 3-1

4. Click OK. Figure 3-2 shows the skeleton of the console application.

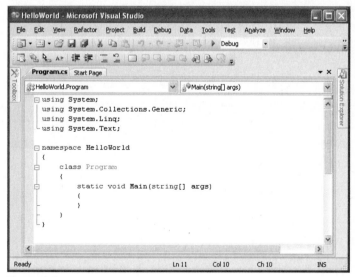

Figure 3-2

5. Type the following highlighted code into the `Main()` method as shown:

```
using System;
using System.Collections.Generic;
using System.Linq;
using System.Text;

namespace HelloWorld
{
    class Program
    {
        static void Main(string[] args)
        {
            Console.WriteLine("Hello, world! This is my first C# program!");
            Console.ReadLine();
            return;
        }
    }
}
```

6. To debug the application and see how it looks like when executed, press F5 in Visual Studio 2008. Figure 3-3 shows the output in the Console window.

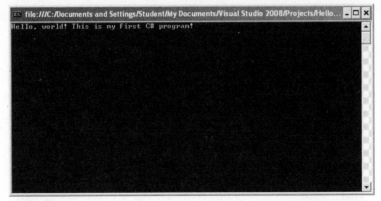

Figure 3-3

To return to Visual Studio 2008, press the Enter key and the console window will disappear.

Using the C# Compiler (csc.exe)

Besides using Visual Studio 2008 to compile and run the application, you can build the application using Visual Studio 2008 and use the C# compiler (csc.exe) to manually compile and then run the application. This option is useful for large projects where you have a group of programmers working on different sections of the application.

Alternatively, if you prefer to code a C# program using a text editor, you can use the Notepad (Programs ➪ Accessories ➪ Notepad) application included in every Windows computer. (Be aware, however, that using Notepad does not give you access to the IntelliSense feature, which is available only in Visual Studio 2008.)

1. Using Notepad, create a text file, name it HelloWorld.cs, and save it into a folder on your hard disk, say in C:\C#.

2. Populate HelloWorld.cs with the following:

```csharp
using System;
using System.Collections.Generic;
using System.Linq;
using System.Text;

namespace HelloWorld
{
    class Program
    {
        static void Main(string[] args)
        {
            Console.WriteLine("Hello, world! This is my first C# program!");
            Console.ReadLine();
            return;
        }
    }
}
```

3. Use the command-line C# compiler (`csc.exe`) that ships with Visual Studio 2008 to compile the program. The easiest way to invoke `csc.exe` is to use the Visual Studio 2008 command prompt, which has all the path references added for you.

4. To launch the Visual Studio 2008 command prompt, select Start ⇨ Programs ⇨ Microsoft Visual Studio 2008 ⇨ Visual Studio Tools ⇨ Visual Studio 2008 Command Prompt.

5. In the command prompt, change to the directory containing the C# program (C:\C# for this example), and type the following command (see Figure 3-4):

```
C:\C#>csc HelloWorld.cs
```

Figure 3-4

6. Once the program is compiled, you will find the `HelloWorld.exe` executable in the same directory (C:\C#). Type the following to execute the application (see Figure 3-5):

```
C:\C#>HelloWorld
```

Figure 3-5

7. To return to the command prompt, press Enter.

Dissecting the Program

Now that you have written your first C# program, let's take some time to dissect it and understand some of the important parts.

The first few lines specify the various namespaces:

```
using System;
using System.Collections.Generic;
using System.Linq;
using System.Text;
```

As mentioned in Chapter 1, all the class libraries in the .NET Framework are grouped using namespaces. In C#, you use the `using` keyword to indicate that you will be using library classes from the specified namespace. In this example, you use the `Console` class's `WriteLine()` method to write a message to the console. The `Console` class belongs to the `System` namespace, and if you do not have the `using System` statement at the top of the program, you need to specify the fully qualified name for `Console`, which is:

```
System.Console.WriteLine("Hello, world! This is my first C# program!");
```

The next keyword of interest is `namespace`. It allows you to assign a namespace to your class, which is `HelloWorld` in this example:

```
namespace HelloWorld
{
    class Program
    {
        static void Main(string[] args)
        {
            Console.WriteLine("Hello, world! This is my first C# program!");
            Console.ReadLine();
            return;
        }
    }
}
```

Next, you define the class name as `Program`:

```
class Program
{
    static void Main(string[] args)
    {
        Console.WriteLine("Hello, world! This is my first C# program!");
        Console.ReadLine();
        return;
    }
}
```

All C# code must be contained within a class. Because this class is within the `HelloWorld` namespace, its fully qualified name is `HelloWorld.Program`.

Classes and objects are discussed in detail in Chapter 4.

Within the `Program` class, you have the `Main()` method:

```
class Program
{
    static void Main(string[] args)
    {
        Console.WriteLine("Hello, world! This is my first C# program!");
        Console.ReadLine();
        return;
    }
}
```

Every C# program must have an entry point, which in this case is `Main()`. An entry point is the method that is first executed when an application starts up. The `static` keyword indicates that this method can be called without creating an instance of the class.

Chapters 4 and 5 provide more information about object-oriented programming.

Unlike languages such as VB.NET in which a method can be either a function or a subroutine (a function returns a value; a subroutine does not), C# only supports functions. If a function does not return a result, you simply prefix the function name with the `void` keyword; otherwise, you indicate the return type by specifying its type.

You will find more about functions in Chapter 4.

Finally, you write the statements within the `Main()` method:

```
static void Main(string[] args)
{
    Console.WriteLine("Hello, world! This is my first C# program!");
    Console.ReadLine();
    return;
}
```

The `WriteLine()` method from the `Console` class writes a string to the command prompt. Notice that in C# you end each statement with a semicolon (`;`), which indicates to the compiler the end of each statement. Hence, you can rewrite the `WriteLine()` statement like this:

```
Console.WriteLine(
    "Hello, world! This is my first C# program!");
```

This is useful when you have a long statement and need to format it to fit into multiple lines for ease of reading.

The use of the `ReadLine()` statement is to accept inputs from the user. The statement is used here mainly to keep the command window visible. If you run this program in Visual Studio 2008 without using the `ReadLine()` method, the program will print the hello world statement and then close the window immediately.

Passing Arguments to Main()

If you run a program in the command prompt as described earlier in the chapter, you can pass in arguments to the application. For example, you might want the program to display your name. To do so, pass in the name like this:

```
C:\C#>HelloWorld Wei-Meng Lee
```

The argument passed into the program can be accessed by the `args` parameter (a string array) defined in the `Main()` method. Hence, you need to modify the program by displaying the values contained in the `args` string array, like this:

```csharp
using System;
using System.Collections.Generic;
using System.Linq;
using System.Text;

namespace HelloWorld
{
    class Program
    {
        static void Main(string[] args)
        {
            Console.Write("Hello, ");
            for (int i = 0; i < args.Length; i++)
                Console.Write("{0} ",args[i]);
            Console.Write("! This is my first C# program!");

            Console.ReadLine();
            return;
        }
    }
}
```

Chapter 8 covers string arrays in depth.

Language Syntax

C# is a case-sensitive language that is highly expressive yet simple to learn and use. The following sections describe the various syntax of the language.

Keywords

In any programming language, there is always a list of identifiers that have special meanings to the compiler. These identifiers are known as keywords, and you should not use them as identifiers in your program.

Here's the list of keywords in C# 2008:

abstract	event	new	struct
as	explicit	null	switch
base	extern	object	this
bool	false	operator	throw
break	finally	out	true
byte	fixed	override	try
case	float	params	typeof
catch	for	private	uint
char	foreach	protected	ulong
checked	goto	public	unchecked
class	if	readonly	unsafe
const	implicit	ref	ushort
continue	in	return	using
decimal	int	sbyte	virtual
default	interface	sealed	volatile
delegate	internal	short	void
do	is	sizeof	while
double	lock	stackalloc	
else	long	static	
enum	namespace	string	

Variables

In C#, you declare variables using the following format:

```
datatype identifier;
```

The following example declares and uses four variables:

```
class Program
    {
        static void Main(string[] args)
        {
            //---declare the variables---
            int num1;
            int num2 = 5;
            float num3, num4;

            //---assign values to the variables---
            num1 = 4;
            num3 = num4 = 6.2f;

            //---print out the values of the variables---
            Console.WriteLine("{0} {1} {2} {3}", num1, num2, num3, num4);
            Console.ReadLine();
            return;
        }
    }
```

Note the following:

- ❑ num1 is declared as an `int` (integer).

- ❑ num2 is declared as an `int` and assigned a value at the same time.

- ❑ num3 and num4 are declared as `float` (floating point number)

- ❑ You need to declare a variable before you can use it. If not, C3 compiler will flag that as an error.

- ❑ You can assign multiple variables in the same statement, as is shown in the assignment of num3 and num4.

This example will print out the following output:

```
4 5 6.2 6.2
```

The following declaration is also allowed:

```
//---declares both num5 and num6 to be float
// and assigns 3.4 to num5---
float num5 = 3.4f, num6;
```

But this one is not allowed:

```
//---cannot mix different types in a declaration statement---
int num7, float num8;
```

The name of the variable cannot be one of the C# keywords. If you absolutely must use one of the keywords as a variable name, you need to prefix it with the @ character, as the following example shows:

```
int @new = 4;
Console.WriteLine(@new);
```

Scope of Variables

The scope of a variable (that is, its visibility and accessibility) that you declare in C# is affected by the location in which the variable is declared. Consider the following example where a variable num is declared within the Program class:

```
using System;
using System.Collections.Generic;
using System.Linq;
using System.Text;

namespace HelloWorld
{
    class Program
    {
        static int num = 7;

        static void Main(string[] args)
        {
            Console.WriteLine("num in Main() is {0}", num); //---7---
            HelloWorld.Program.Method1();

            Console.ReadLine();
            return;
        }

        static private void Method1()
        {
            Console.WriteLine("num in Method1() is {0}", num); //---7---
        }
    }
}
```

Because the num variable is declared in the class, it is visible (that is, global) to all the methods declared within the class, and you see the following output:

```
num in Main() is 7
num in Method1() is 7
```

However, if you declare another variable with the same name (num) within Main() and Method1(), like this:

```
using System;
using System.Collections.Generic;
using System.Linq;
using System.Text;

namespace HelloWorld
{
    class Program
    {
        static int num = 7;

        static void Main(string[] args)
        {
            int num = 5;
            Console.WriteLine("num in Main() is {0}", num); //---5---
            HelloWorld.Program.Method1();

            Console.ReadLine();
            return;
        }

        static private void Method1()
        {
            int num = 10;
            Console.WriteLine("num in Method1() is {0}", num); //---10---
        }
    }
}
```

You get a very different output:

```
num in Main() is 5
num in Method1() is 10
```

That's because the num variables in Main() and Method1() have effectively hidden the num variable in the Program class. In this case, the num in the Program class is known as the global variable while the num variables in Main and Method1 are known as local variables. The num variable in Main() is only visible within Main(). Likewise, this also applies to the num variable in Method1().

What if you need to access the num declared in the Program class? In that case, you just need to specify its full name:

```
Console.WriteLine("num in Program is {0}", HelloWorld.Program.num); //---7---
```

While a local variable can hide the scope of a global variable, you cannot have two variables with the same scope and identical names. The following makes it clear:

```csharp
static void Main(string[] args)
{
    int num = 5;
    Console.WriteLine("num in Main() is {0}", num); //---5---

    int num = 6; //---error: num is already declared---

    return;
}
```

However, two identically named variables in different scope would be legal, as the following shows:

```csharp
static void Main(string[] args)
{
    for (int i = 0; i < 5; i++)
    { //---i is visible within this loop only---
        Console.WriteLine(i);
    } //---i goes out of scope here---

    for (int i = 0; i < 3; i++)
    { //---i is visible within this loop only---
        Console.WriteLine(i);
    } //---i goes out of scope here---

    Console.ReadLine();
    return;
}
```

Here, the variable i appears in two `for` loops (looping is covered later in this chapter). The scope for each i is restricted to within the loop, so there is no conflict in the scope and this is allowed.

Declaring another variable named i outside the loop or inside it will cause a compilation error as the following example shows:

```csharp
static void Main(string[] args)
{
    int i = 4; //---error---

    for (int i = 0; i < 5; i++)
    {
        int i = 6; //---error---
        Console.WriteLine(i);
    }

    for (int i = 0; i < 3; i++)
    {
        Console.WriteLine(i);
    }

    Console.ReadLine();
    return;
}
```

This code results in an error: "A local variable named 'i' cannot be declared in this scope because it would give a different meaning to 'i', which is already used in a 'parent or current' scope to denote something else."

Constants

To declare a constant in C#, you use the `const` keyword, like this:

```
//---declared the PI constant---
const float PI=3.14f;
```

You cannot change the value of a constant (during runtime) once it has been declared and assigned a value.

As a good programming practice, you should always use constants whenever you use values that do not change during runtime.

Comments

In C#, you can insert comments into your program using either `//` or a mirrored pair of `/*` and `*/`. The following example shows how to insert comments into your program using `//`:

```
//---declare the variables---
int num1;              //---num1 variable---
int num2 = 5;          //---num2 variable---
float num3, num4;      //---num3 and num4 variables---
```

And here's an example of how to insert a multi-line block of comments into your program:

```
/*
Declares the following variables:
  num1, num2, num3, num4
*/

int num1;
int num2 = 5;
float num3, num4;
```

In general, use the `//` for short, single-line comments and `/* */` for multi-line comments.

XML Documentation

One of the very cool features available in Visual Studio 2008 is the support for XML documentation. This feature enables you to insert comments into your code using XML elements and then generate a separate XML file containing all the documentation. You can then convert the XML file into professional-looking documentation for your code.

To insert an XML comment into your code, position the cursor before a class or method name and type three / characters (left window in Figure 3-6). The XML template is automatically inserted for you (see the right window in Figure 3-6).

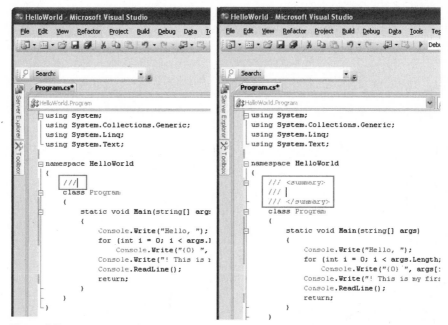

Figure 3-6

The following code shows the XML documentation template created for the Program class, the Main() method, and the AddNumbers() method (you need to fill in the description for each element):

```csharp
using System;
using System.Collections.Generic;
using System.Linq;
using System.Text;

namespace HelloWorld
{
    /// <summary>
    /// This is my first C# program.
    /// </summary>
    class Program
    {
        /// <summary>
        /// The entry point for the program
        /// </summary>
        /// <param name="args">Argument(s) from the command line</param>
```

(continued)

(continued)

```csharp
        static void Main(string[] args)
        {
            Console.Write("Hello, ");
            for (int i = 0; i < args.Length; i++)
                Console.Write("{0} ", args[i]);
            Console.Write("! This is my first C# program!");
            Console.ReadLine();
            return;
        }

        /// <summary>
        /// Adds two numbers and returns the result
        /// </summary>
        /// <param name="num1">Number 1</param>
        /// <param name="num2">Number 2</param>
        /// <returns>Sum of Number 1 and 2</returns>
        private int AddNumbers(int num1, int num2)
        {
            //---implementations here---
        }
    }
}
```

To enable generation of the XML document containing the XML comments, right-click the project name in Solution Explorer and select Properties.

> You can also generate the XML documentation file using the `csc.exe` compiler at the command prompt using the `/doc` option:
>
> ```
> csc Program.cs /doc:HelloWorld.xml
> ```

In the Build tab, tick the XML Documentation File checkbox and use the default path suggested: `bin\Debug\HelloWorld.XML` (see Figure 3-7).

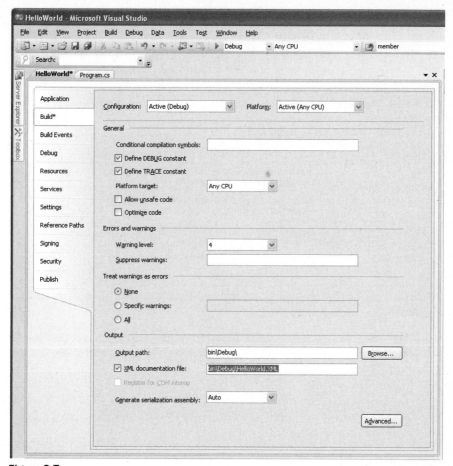

Figure 3-7

Build the project by right-clicking the project name in Solution Explorer and selecting Build.

You will now find the HelloWorld.xml file (see Figure 3-8) located in the bin\Debug\ folder of the project.

Figure 3-8

You can now convert this XML file into a MSDN-style documentation file. Appendix C shows you how to use the SandCastle tool to do this.

Data Types

C# is a strongly typed language and as such all variables and objects must have a declared data type. The data type can be one of the following:

❑ Value

❑ Reference

❑ User-defined

❑ Anonymous

You'll find more information about user-defined types in Chapter 4 and about anonymous types in Chapter 14.

Value Types

A value type variable contains the data that it is assigned. For example, when you declare an int (integer) variable and assign a value to it, the variable directly contains that value. And when you assign a value type variable to another, you make a copy of it. The following example makes this clear:

```
class Program
{
    static void Main(string[] args)
    {
        int num1, num2;
        num1 = 5;
        num2 = num1;
        Console.WriteLine("num1 is {0}. num2 is {1}", num1, num2);

        num2 = 3;
        Console.WriteLine("num1 is {0}. num2 is {1}", num1, num2);
        Console.ReadLine();
        return;
    }
}
```

The output of this program is:

```
num1 is 5. num2 is 5
num1 is 5. num2 is 3
```

As you can observe, num2 is initially assigned a value of num1 (which is 5). When num2 is later modified to become 3, the value of num1 remains unchanged (it is still 5). This proves that the num1 and num2 each contains a copy of its own value.

Following is another example of value type. Point is a structure that represents an ordered pair of integer x and y coordinates that defines a point in a two-dimensional plane (structure is another example of value types). The Point class is found in the System.Drawing namespace and hence to test the following statements you need to import the System.Drawing namespace.

Chapter 4 discusses structures in more detail.

```
Point pointA, pointB;
pointA = new Point(3, 4);
pointB = pointA;
Console.WriteLine("point A is {0}. pointB is {1}",
    pointA.ToString(), pointB.ToString());

pointB.X = 5;
pointB.Y = 6;
Console.WriteLine("point A is {0}. pointB is {1}",
    pointA.ToString(), pointB.ToString());
```

These statements yield the following output:

```
point A is {X=3,Y=4}. pointB is {X=3,Y=4}
point A is {X=3,Y=4}. pointB is {X=5,Y=6}
```

As in the earlier example, changing the value of the pointB does not change the value of pointA.

Predefined Value Types

The .NET Framework ships with a set of predefined C# and .NET value types. These are described in the following table.

C# Type	.NET Framework Type	Bits	Range
bool	System.Boolean		True or false
byte	System.Byte	8	Unsigned 8-bit integer values from 0 to 255
sbyte	System.SByte	8	Signed 8-bit integer values from −128 to 127
char	System.Char	16	16-bit Unicode character from U+0000 to U+ffff
decimal	System.Decimal	128	Signed 128-bit number from $\pm 1.0 \times 10-28$ to $\pm 7.9 \times 1028$
double	System.Double	64	Signed 64-bit floating point number; approximately from $\pm 5.0 \times 10-324$ to $\pm 1.7 \times 10308$
float	System.Single	32	Signed 32-bit floating point number; approximately from $\pm 1.5 \times 10-45$ to $\pm 3.4 \times 1038$
int	System.Int32	32	Signed 32-bit integer number from −2,147,483,648 to 2,147,483,647
uint	System.UInt32	32	Unsigned 32-bit integer number from 0 to 4,294,967,295
long	System.Int64	64	Signed 64-bit integer number from −9,223,372,036,854,775,808 to 9,223,372,036,854,775,807
ulong	System.UInt64	64	Unsigned 64-bit integer number from 0 to 18,446,744,073,709,551,615
short	System.Int1616		Signed 16-bit integer number from −32,768 to 32,767
ushort	System.UInt16	16	Unsigned 16-bit integer number from 0 to 65,535

To declare a variable of a predefined type, you can either use the C# type or the .NET Framework type. For example, to declare an integer variable, you can either use the int or System.Int32 type, as shown here:

```
int num1 = 5;
//---or---
System.Int32 num2 = 5;
```

To get the type of a variable, use the GetType() method:

```
Console.WriteLine(num1.GetType()); //---System.Int32---
```

To get the .NET equivalent of a C# type, use the typeof() method. For example, to learn the .NET type equivalent of C#'s float type, you can use the following statements:

```
Type t = typeof(float);
Console.WriteLine(t.ToString()); //---System.Single---
```

To get the size of a type, use the sizeof() method:

```
Console.WriteLine("{0} bytes", sizeof(int)); //---4 bytes---
```

In C#, all noninteger numbers are always treated as a double. And so if you want to assign a noninteger number like 3.99 to a float variable, you need to append it with the F (or f) suffix, like this:

```
float price = 3.99F;
```

If you don't do this, the compiler will issue an error message: "Literal of type double cannot be implicitly converted to type 'float'; use an 'F' suffix to create a literal of this type."

Likewise, to assign a noninteger number to a decimal variable, you need to use the M suffix:

```
decimal d = 4.56M; //---suffix M to convert to decimal---
float f = 1.23F;   //---suffix F to convert to float---
```

You can also assign integer values using hexadecimal representation. Simply prefix the hexadecimal number with 0x, like this:

```
int num1 = 0xA;
Console.WriteLine(num1); //---10---
```

Nullable Type

All value types in C# have a default value when they are declared. For example, the following declaration declares a Boolean and an int variable:

```
Boolean married; //---default value is false---
int age; //--- default value is 0---
```

> **To learn the default value of a value type, use the** `default` **keyword, like this:**
>
> ```
> object x;
> x = default(int);
> Console.WriteLine(x);   //---0---
> x = default(bool);
> Console.WriteLine(x);   //---false---
> ```

However, C# forbids you from using a variable if you do not explicitly initialize it. The following statements, for instance, cause the compiler to complain:

```
Boolean married;
//---error: Use of unassigned local variable 'married'---
Console.WriteLine(married);
```

To use the variable, you first need to initialize it with a value:

```
Boolean married = false;
Console.WriteLine(married); //---now OK---
```

Now `married` has a default value of `false`. There are times, though, when you do not know the marital status of a person, and the variable should be neither `true` nor `false`. In C#, you can declare value types to be *nullable*, meaning that they do not yet have a value.

To make the `married` variable nullable, the above declaration can be rewritten in two different ways (all are equivalent):

```
Boolean? married = null;
//---or---
Nullable<Boolean> married = null;
```

The syntax `T?` (example, `Boolean?`) is shorthand for `Nullable<T>` (example, `Nullable<Boolean>`), where T is a type.

You read this statement as "Nullable of Boolean." The <> represents a generic type and will be discussed in more detail in Chapter 9.

In this case, married can take one of the three values: `true`, `false`, or `null`.

The following code snippet prints out "Not Married":

```
Boolean? married = null;
if (married == true)
    Console.WriteLine("Married");
else
    Console.WriteLine("Not Married"); //---this will be printed---
```

That's because the if statement evaluates to false (married is currently null), so the else block executes. A much better way to check would be to use the following snippet:

```
if (married == true)
    Console.WriteLine("Married");
else if (married==false)
    Console.WriteLine("Not Married");
else
    Console.WriteLine("Not Sure"); //---this will be printed---
```

Once a nullable type variable is set to a value, you can set it back to nothing by using null, as the following example shows:

```
married = true;    //---set it to True---
married = null; //---reset it back to nothing---
```

To check the value of a nullable variable, use the HasValue property, like this:

```
if (married.HasValue)
{
    //---this line will be executed only
    // if married is either true or false---
    Console.WriteLine(married.Value);
}
```

You can also use the == operator to test against null, like the following:

```
if (married == null)
{
    //---causes a runtime error---
    Console.WriteLine(married.Value);
}
```

But this results in an error because attempting to print out the value of a null variable using the Value property causes an exception to be thrown. Hence, always use the HasValue property to check a nullable variable before attempting to print its value.

When dealing with nullable types, you may want to assign a nullable variable to another variable, like this:

```
int? num1 = null;
int num2 = num1;
```

In this case, the compiler will complain because num1 is a nullable type while num2 is not (by default, num2 cannot take on a null value unless it is declared nullable). To resolve this, you can use the null *coalescing operator* (??). Consider the following example:

```
int? num1 = null;
int num2 = num1 ?? 0;
Console.WriteLine(num2); //---0---
```

In this statement, if num1 is null, 0 will be assigned to num2. If num1 is not null, the value of num1 will be assigned to num2, as evident in the following few statements:

```
num1 = 5;
num2 = num1 ?? 0;
Console.WriteLine(num2); //---5---
```

Reference Types

For reference types, the variable stores a reference to the data rather than the actual data. Consider the following:

```
Button btn1, btn2;
btn1 = new Button();
btn1.Text = "OK";

btn2 = btn1;
Console.WriteLine("{0} {1}", btn1.Text, btn2.Text);

btn2.Text = "Cancel";
Console.WriteLine("{0} {1}", btn1.Text, btn2.Text);
```

Here, you first declare two Button controls — btn1 and btn2. btn1's Text property is set to "OK" and then btn2 is assigned btn1. The first output will be:

```
OK OK
```

When you change btn2's Text property to "Cancel", you invariably change btn1's Text property, as the second output shows:

```
Cancel Cancel
```

That's because btn1 and btn2 are both pointing to the same Button object. They both contain a reference to that object instead of storing the value of the object. The declaration statement (Button btn1, btn2;) simply creates two variables that contain references to Button objects (in the example these two variables point to the same object).

To remove the reference to an object in a reference type, simply use the null keyword:

```
btn2 = null;
```

When a reference type is set to null, attempting to access its members results in a runtime error.

Value Types versus Reference Types

For any discussion about value types and reference types, it is important to understand how the .NET Framework manages the data in memory.

Basically, the memory is divided into two parts — the stack and the heap. The stack is a data structure used to store value-type variables. When you create an int variable, the value is stored on the stack. In addition, any call you make to a function (method) is added to the top of the stack and removed when the function returns.

In contrast, the heap is used to store reference-type variables. When you create an instance of a class, the object is allocated on the heap and its address is returned and stored in a variable located on the stack.

Memory allocation and deallocation on the stack is much faster than on the heap, so if the size of the data to be stored is small, it's better to use a value-type variable than reference-type variable. Conversely, if the size of data is large, it is better to use a reference-type variable.

C# supports two predefined reference types — object and string — which are described in the following table.

C# Type	.NET Framework Type	Descriptions
object	System.Object	Root type from which all types in the CTS (Common Type System) derive
string	System.String	Unicode character string

Chapter 4 explores the System.Object type, and Chapter 8 covers strings in more detail.

Enumerations

You can create your own set of named constants by using enumerations. In C#, you define an enumeration by using the enum keyword. For example, say that you need a variable to store the day of a week (Monday, Tuesday, Wednesday, and so on):

```
static void Main(string[] args)
{
    int day = 1; //---1 to represent Monday---
    //...
    Console.ReadLine();
    return;
}
```

In this case, rather than use a number to represent the day of a week, it would be better if the user could choose from a list of possible named values representing the days in a week. The following code example declares an enumeration called Days that comprises seven names (Sun, Mon, Tue, and so forth). Each name has a value assigned (Sun is 0, Mon is 1, and so on):

```
namespace HelloWorld
{
    public enum Days
    {
        Sun = 0,
        Mon = 1,
        Tue = 2,
        Wed = 3,
        Thur = 4,
        Fri = 5,
        Sat = 6
    }

    class Program
    {
        static void Main(string[] args)
        {
            Days day = Days.Mon;
            Console.WriteLine(day);          //---Mon---
            Console.WriteLine((int) day);    //---1---

            Console.ReadLine();
            return;
        }
    }
}
```

Instead of representing the day of a week using an int variable, you can create a variable of type Days. Visual Studio 2008's IntelliSense automatically displays the list of allowed values in the Days enumeration (see Figure 3-9).

Figure 3-9

By default, the first value in an enumerated type is zero. However, you can specify a different initial value, such as:

```
public enum Ranking
{
    First = 100,
    Second = 50,
    Third = 25
}
```

To print out the value of an enumerated type, you can use the `ToString()` method to print out its name, or typecast the enumerated type to `int` to obtain its value:

```
Console.WriteLine(day);            //---Mon---
Console.WriteLine(day.ToString()); //---Mon---
Console.WriteLine((int)day);       //---1---
```

For assigning a value to an enumerated type, you can either use the name directly or typecast the value to the enumerated type:

```
Days day;
day = (Days)3;   //---Wed---
day = Days.Wed; //---Wed---
```

Arrays

An array is a data structure containing several variables of the same type. For example, you might have an array of integer values, like this:

```
int[] nums;
```

In this case, `nums` is an array that has yet to contain any elements (of type `int`). To make `nums` an array containing 10 elements, you can instantiate it with the `new` keyword followed by the type name and then the size of the array:

```
nums = new int[10];
```

The index for each element in the array starts from 0 and ends at n-1 (where n is the size of the array). To assign a value to each element of the array, you can specify its index as follows:

```
nums[0] = 0;
nums[1] = 1;
//...
nums[9] = 9;
```

Arrays are reference types, but array elements can be of any type.

Instead of assigning values to each element in an array individually, you can combine them into one statement, like this:

```
int[] nums = { 0, 1, 2, 3, 4, 5, 6, 7, 8, 9 };
```

Arrays can be single-dimensional (which is what you have seen so far), multi-dimensional, or jagged. You'll find more about arrays in Chapter 13, in the discussion of collections.

Implicit Typing

In the previous versions of C#, all variables must be explicitly typed-declared. For example, if you want to declare a string variable, you have to do the following:

```
string str = "Hello World";
```

In C# 3.0, this is not mandatory — you can use the new `var` keyword to implicitly declare a variable. Here's an example:

```
var str = "Hello world!";
```

Here, `str` is implicitly declared as a string variable. The type of the variable declared is based on the value that it is initialized with. This method of variable declaration is known as *implicit typing*. Implicitly typed variables must be initialized when they are declared. The following statement will not compile:

```
var str;   //---missing initializer---
```

Also notice that IntelliSense will automatically know the type of the variable declared, as evident in Figure 3-10.

Figure 3-10

You can also use implicit typing on arrays. For example, the following statement declares `points` to be an array containing two `Point` objects:

```
var points = new[] { new Point(1, 2), new Point(3, 4) };
```

When using implicit typing on arrays, all the members in the array must be of the same type. The following won't compile since its members are of different types — string and Boolean:

```
//---No best type found for implicitly-typed array---
var arr = new[] { "hello", true, "world" };
```

Implicit typing is useful in cases where you do not know the exact type of data you are manipulating and want the compiler to determine it for you. Do not confuse the `Object` type with implicit typing.

Variables declared as Object types need to be cast during runtime, and IntelliSense does not know their type at development time. On the other hand, implicitly typed variables are statically typed during design time, and IntelliSense is capable of providing detailed information about the type. In terms of performance, an implicitly typed variable is no different from a normal typed variable.

Implicit-typing is very useful when using LINQ queries. Chapter 14 discusses LINQ in more detail.

Type Conversion

C# is a strongly typed language, so when you are assigning values of variables from one type to another, you must take extra care to ensure that the assignment is compatible. Consider the following statements where you have two variables — one of type int and another of type short:

```
int num;
short sNum = 20;
```

The following statement assigns the value of sNum to num:

```
num = sNum; //---OK---
```

This statement works because you're are assigning the value of a type (short) whose range is smaller than that of the target type (int). In such instances, C# allows the assignment to occur, and that's known as *implicit conversion*.

Converting a value from a smaller range to a bigger range is known as widening.

The following table shows the implicit conversion between the different built-in types supported by C#.

Convert from (type)	To (type)
sbyte	short, int, long, float, double, or decimal
byte	short, ushort, int, uint, long, ulong, float, double, or decimal
short	int, long, float, double, or decimal
ushort	int, uint, long, ulong, float, double, or decimal
int	long, float, double, or decimal
uint	long, ulong, float, double, or decimal
long	float, double, or decimal
char	ushort, int, uint, long, ulong, float, double, or decimal
float	double
ulong	float, double, or decimal

If you try to assign the value of a type whose range is bigger than the target type, C# will raise an error. Consider the following example:

```
num = 5;
sNum = num; //---not allowed---
```

In this case, num is of type int and it may contain a big number (such as 40,000). When assigning it to a variable of type short, that could cause a loss of data. To allow the assignment to proceed, C# requires you to explicitly *type-cast* (convert) the value to the target type. This process is known as *explicit conversion*.

> **Converting a value from a bigger range to a smaller range is known as narrowing. Narrowing can result in a loss of data, so be careful when performing a narrowing operation.**

The preceding statement could be made valid when you perform a type casting operation by prefixing the variable that you want to assign with the target type in parentheses:

```
num = 5;
sNum = (short) num;   //---sNum is now 5---
```

When performing type casting, you are solely responsible for ensuring that the target variable can contain the value assigned and that no loss of data will happen. In the following example, the assignment will cause an overflow, changing the value of num to −25536, which is not the expected value:

> **By default, Visual Studio 2008 checks statements involving constant assignments for overflow during compile time. However, this checking is not enforced for statements whose values cannot be determined at runtime.**
>
> ```
> int num = 40000;
> short sNum;
> sNum =(short) num;   //--- -25536; no exception is raised ---
> ```

To ensure that an exception is thrown during runtime when an overflow occurs, you can use the checked keyword, which is used to explicitly enable overflow-checking for integral-type arithmetic operations and conversions:

```
try
{
    sNum = checked((short)num);   //---overflow exception---
}
catch (OverflowException ex)
{
    Console.WriteLine(ex.Message);
}
```

If you try to initialize a variable with a value exceeding its range, Visual Studio 2008 raises an error at compile time, as the following shows:

```
int num = 400000 * 400000;
//---overflows at compile time in checked mode
```

To turn off the automatic check mode, use the unchecked keyword, like this:

```
unchecked
{
    int num = 400000 * 400000;
}
```

The compiler will now ignore the error and proceed with the compilation.

Another way to perform conversion is to use the System.Convert class to perform the conversion for you. The System.Convert class converts the value of a variable from one type into another type. It can convert a value to one of the following types:

Boolean	Int16	UInt32	Decimal
Char	Int32	UInt64	DateTime
SByte	Int64	Single	String
Byte	UInt16	Double	

Using an earlier example, you can convert a value to Int16 using the following statement:

```
sNum = Convert.ToInt16(num);
```

If a number is too big (or too small) to be converted to a particular type, an overflow exception is thrown, and you need to catch the exception:

```
int num = 40000;
short sNum;
try
{
    sNum = Convert.ToInt16(num); //---overflow exception---
}
catch (OverflowException ex)
{
    Console.WriteLine(ex.Message);
}
```

When converting floating point numbers to integer values, you need to be aware of one subtle difference between type casting and using the Convert class. When you perform a type casting on a floating point number, it truncates the fractional part, but the Convert class performs numerical rounding for you, as the following example shows:

```
int num;
float price = 5.99F;
num = (int)price;              //---num is 5---
num = Convert.ToInt16(price); //---num is 6---
```

When converting a string value type to a numerical type, you can use the Parse() method that is available to all built in numeric types (such as int, float, double, and so on). Here's how you can convert the value stored in the str variable into an integer:

```
string str = "5";
int num = int.Parse(str);
```

Beware that using the Parse() method may trigger an exception, as demonstrated here:

```
string str = "5a";
int num = int.Parse(str); //---format exception---
```

This statement causes a format exception to be raised during runtime because the Parse() method cannot perform the conversion. A safer way would be to use the TryParse() method, which will try to perform the conversion. It returns a false if the conversion fails, or else it returns the converted value in the out parameter:

```
int num;
string str = "5a";
if (int.TryParse(str, out num))
    Console.WriteLine(num);
else
    Console.WriteLine("Cannot convert");
```

Flow Control

In C#, there are two ways to determine the selection of statements for execution:

❑   if-else statement
❑   switch statement

if-else Statement

The most common flow-control statement is the if-else statement. It evaluates a Boolean expression and uses the result to determine the block of code to execute. Here's an example:

```
int num = 9;
if (num % 2 == 0)
    Console.WriteLine("{0} is even", num);
else
    Console.WriteLine("{0} is odd", num);
```

In this example, if num modulus 2 equals to 0, the statement "9 is even" is printed; otherwise (else), "9 is odd" is printed.

> Remember to wrap the Boolean expression in a pair of parentheses when using the if statement.

If you have multiple statements to execute after an if-else expression, enclose them in { }, like this:

```
int num = 9;
if (num % 2 == 0)
{
        Console.WriteLine("{0} is even", num);
        Console.WriteLine("Print something here...");
}
else
{
        Console.WriteLine("{0} is odd", num);
        Console.WriteLine("Print something here...");
}
```

Here's another example of an if-else statement:

```
int num = 9;
string str = string.Empty;

if (num % 2 == 0)
    str = "even";
else
    str = "odd";
```

You can rewrite these statements using the conditional operator (?:), like this:

```
str = (num % 2 == 0) ? "even" : "odd";
Console.WriteLine(str); //---odd---
```

?: *is also known as the ternary operator.*

The conditional operator has the following format:

```
condition ? first_expression : second_expression;
```

If condition is true, the first expression is evaluated and becomes the result; if false, the second expression is evaluated and becomes the result.

switch Statement

You can evaluate multiple expressions and conditionally execute blocks of code by using `if-else` statements. Consider the following example:

```
string symbol = "YHOO";
if (symbol == "MSFT")
{
    Console.WriteLine(27.96);
}
else if (symbol == "GOOG")
{
    Console.WriteLine(437.55);
}
else if (symbol == "YHOO")
{
    Console.WriteLine(27.15);
}
else
    Console.WriteLine("Stock symbol not recognized");
```

One problem with this is that multiple `if` and `else-if` conditions make the code unwieldy — and this gets worse when you have lots of conditions to check. A better way would be to use the `switch` keyword:

```
switch (symbol)
{
    case "MSFT": Console.WriteLine(27.96);
        break;
    case "GOOG": Console.WriteLine(437.55);
        break;
    case "YHOO": Console.WriteLine(27.15);
        break;
    default: Console.WriteLine("Stock symbol not recognized");
        break;
}
```

The `switch` keyword handles multiple selections and uses the `case` keyword to match the condition. Each `case` statement must contain a unique value and the statement, or statements, that follow it is the block to execute. Each `case` statement must end with a `break` keyword to jump out of the `switch` block. The `default` keyword defines the block that will be executed if none of the preceding conditions is met.

The following example shows multiple statements in a `case` statement:

```
string symbol = "MSFT";
switch (symbol)
{
    case "MSFT":
        Console.Write("Stock price for MSFT: ");
        Console.WriteLine(27.96);
        break;
    case "GOOG":
```

```
                Console.Write("Stock price for GOOG: ");
                Console.WriteLine(437.55);
            break;
        case "YHOO":
                Console.Write("Stock price for YHOO: ");
                Console.WriteLine(27.15);
            break;
        default: Console.WriteLine("Stock symbol not recognized");
            break;
    }
```

In C#, fall-throughs are not allowed; that is, each case block of code must include the break keyword so that execution can be transferred out of the switch block (and not "fall through" the rest of the case statements). However, there is one exception to this rule — when a case block is empty. Here's an example:

```
string symbol = "INTC";
switch (symbol)
{
    case "MSFT": Console.WriteLine(27.96);
        break;
    case "GOOG": Console.WriteLine(437.55);
        break;
    case "INTC":
    case "YHOO": Console.WriteLine(27.15);
        break;
    default: Console.WriteLine("Stock symbol not recognized");
        break;
}
```

The case for "INTC" has no execution block/statement and hence the execution will fall through into the case for "YHOO", which will incorrectly print the output "27.15". In this case, you need to insert a break statement after the "INTC" case to prevent the fall-through:

```
switch (symbol)
{
    case "MSFT": Console.WriteLine(27.96);
        break;
    case "GOOG": Console.WriteLine(437.55);
        break;
    case "INTC":
        break;
    case "YHOO": Console.WriteLine(27.15);
        break;
    default: Console.WriteLine("Stock symbol not recognized");
        break;
}
```

Looping

A loop is a statement, or set of statements, repeated for a specified number of times or until some condition is met. C# supports the following looping constructs:

❑ for

❑ foreach

❑ while and do-while

for Loop

The for loop executes a statement (or a block of statements) until a specified expression evaluates to false. The for loop has the following format:

```
for (statement; expression; statement(s))
{
    //---statement(s)
}
```

The expression inside the for loop is evaluated first, before the execution of the loop.

Consider the following example:

```
int[] nums = { 1, 2, 3, 4, 5, 6, 7, 8, 9 };
for (int i =0; i<9; i++)
{
    Console.WriteLine(nums[i].ToString());
}
```

Here, nums is an integer array with nine members. The initial value of i is 0 and after each iteration it increments by 1. The loop will continue as long as i is less than 9. The loop prints out the numbers from the array:

```
1
2
3
4
5
6
7
8
9
```

Here's another example:

```
string[] words = { "C#","3.0","Programming","is","fun"};
for (int j = 2; j <= 4; ++j) {
    Console.WriteLine(words[j]);
}
```

This code prints the strings in the words array, from index 2 through 4. The output is:

```
Programming
is
fun
```

You can also omit statements and expressions inside the for loop, as the following example illustrates:

```
for (; ; )
{
    Console.Write("*");
}
```

In this case, the for loop prints out a series of *s continuously (infinite loop).

Nested for Loop

It is common to nest two or more for loops within one another. The following example prints out the times table from 1 to 10:

```
for (int i = 1; i <= 10; i++)
{
    Console.WriteLine("Times table for {0}", i);
    Console.WriteLine("==================");
    for (int j = 1; j <= 10; j++)
    {
        Console.WriteLine ("{0} x {1} = {2}", i, j, i*j );
    }
}
```

Figure 3-11 shows the output.

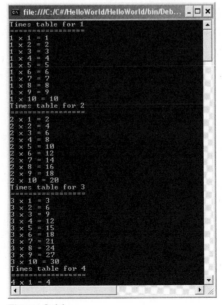

Figure 3-11

Here, one `for` loop is nested within another `for` loop. The first pass of the outer loop (represented by i in this example) triggers the inner loop (represented by j). The inner loop will execute to completion and then the outer loop will move to the second pass, which triggers the inner loop again. This repeats until the outer loop has finished executing.

foreach

One common use for the `for` loop is to iterate through a series of objects in a collection. In C# there is another looping construct that is very useful for just this purpose — the `foreach` statement, which iterates over each element in a collection. Take a look at an example:

```
int[] nums = { 1, 2, 3, 4, 5, 6, 7, 8, 9 };
foreach (int i in nums)
{
    Console.WriteLine(i);
}
```

This code block prints out all the numbers in the nums array (from 1 to 9). The value of i takes on the value of each individual member of the array during each iteration. However, you cannot change the value of i within the loop, as the following example demonstrates:

```
int[] nums = { 1, 2, 3, 4, 5, 6, 7, 8, 9 };
foreach (int i in nums)
{
    i += 4; //---error: cannot change the value of i---
    Console.WriteLine(i);
}
```

Here is another example of the use of the `foreach` loop:

```
string[] words = { "C#", "3.0", "Programming", "is", "fun" };
foreach (string w in words)
{
    Console.WriteLine(w);
}
```

This code block prints out:

```
C#
3.0
Programming
is
fun
```

while and do-while Loops

In addition to `for` and `foreach` statements, you can use a `while` statement to execute a block of code repeatedly. The `while` statement executes a code block until the specified condition is false. Here's an example:

```
int[] nums = { 1, 2, 3, 4, 5, 6, 7, 8, 9 };
int i = 0;
while (i < 9)
{
    Console.WriteLine(nums[i++]);
}
```

This code iterates through all the elements (from index 0 to 8) in the `nums` array and prints out each number to the console window.

The `while` statement checks the condition before executing the block of code. To execute the code at least once before evaluating the condition, use the `do-while` statement. It executes its code and then evaluates the condition specified by the `while` keyword, as the following example shows:

```
string reply;
do
{
    Console.WriteLine("Are you sure you want to quit? [y/n]");
    reply = Console.ReadLine();
} while (reply != "y");
```

In this code, you first print the message on the console and then wait for the user to enter a string. If the string entered is not `y`, the loop continues. It will exit when the user enters `y`.

Exiting from a Loop

To break out of a loop prematurely (before the exit condition is met), you can use one of the following keywords:

- ❑ `break`
- ❑ `return`
- ❑ `throw`
- ❑ `goto`

break

The `break` keyword allows you to break out of a loop prematurely:

```
int counter = 0;
do
{
    Console.WriteLine(counter++);
    //---exits the loop when counter is more than 100
    if (counter > 100) break;
} while (true);
```

In this example, you increment the value of counter in an infinite do-while loop. To break out of the loop, you use a if statement to check the value of counter. If the value exceeds 100, you use the break keyword to exit the do-while loop.

You can also use the break keyword in while, for, and foreach loops.

return

The return keyword allows you to terminate the execution of a method and return control to the calling method. When you use it within a loop, it will also exit from the loop. In the following example, the FindWord() function searches for a specified word ("car") inside a given array. As soon as a match is found, it exits from the loop and returns control to the calling method:

```
class Program
{
    static string FindWord(string[] arr, string word)
    {
        foreach (string w in arr)
        {
            //---if word is found, exit the loop and return back to the
            // calling function---
            if (w.StartsWith(word))
                return w;
        }
        return string.Empty;
    }

    static void Main(string[] args)
    {

        string[] words = {
                "-online", "4u", "adipex", "advicer", "baccarrat", "blackjack",
                "bllogspot", "booker", "byob", "car-rental-e-site",
                "car-rentals-e-site", "carisoprodol", "casino", "casinos",
                "chatroom", "cialis", "coolcoolhu", "coolhu", "credit-card-debt",
                "credit-report-4u"
        };

        Console.WriteLine(FindWord(words, "car")); //---car-rental-e-site---
    }
}
```

throw

The throw keyword is usually used with the try-catch-finally statements to throw an exception. However, you can also use it to exit a loop prematurely. Consider the following block of code that contains the Sums() function to perform some addition and division on an array:

```
class Program
{
    static double Sums(int[] nums, int num)
    {
        double sum = 0;
        foreach (double n in nums)
```

```
        {
            if (n == 0)
                throw new Exception("Nums contains zero!");
            sum += num / n;
        }
        return sum;
    }

    static void Main(string[] args)
    {
        int[] nums = { 1, 2, 3, 4, 0, 6, 7, 8, 9 };
        try
        {
            Console.WriteLine(Sums(nums, 2));
        }
        catch (Exception e)
        {
            Console.WriteLine(e.Message);
        }
    }
}
```

When the `foreach` loop reaches the fifth element of the array (0), it throws an exception and exits the loop. The exception is then caught by the `try-catch` loop in the `Main()` method.

goto

The `goto` keyword transfers program control directly to a labeled statement. Using `goto` is not considered a best practice because it makes your program hard to read. Still, you want to be aware of what it does, so the following example shows its use:

```
string[] words = {
    "-online", "4u", "adipex", "advicer", "baccarrat", "blackjack",
    "bllogspot", "booker", "byob", "car-rental-e-site",
    "car-rentals-e-site", "carisoprodol", "casino", "casinos",
    "chatroom", "cialis", "coolcoolhu", "coolhu", "credit-card-debt",
    "credit-report-4u"
};

foreach (string word in words)
{
    if (word == "casino")
        goto Found;
}
goto Resume;

Found:
    Console.WriteLine("Word found!");

Resume:
    //---other statements here---
```

In this example, if the word casino is found in the words array, control is transferred to the label named Found: and execution is continued from there. If the word is not found, control is transferred to the label named Resume:.

Skipping an Iteration

To skip to the next iteration in the loop, you can use the continue keyword. Consider the following block of code:

```
for (int i = 0; i < 9; i++)
{
    if (i % 2 == 0)
    {
        //---print i if it is even---
        Console.WriteLine(i);
        continue;
    }
    //---print this when i is odd---
    Console.WriteLine("******");
}
```

When i is an even number, this code block prints out the number and skips to the next number. Here's the result:

```
0
******
2
******
4
******
6
******
8
```

Operators

C# comes with a large set of operators that allows you to specify the operation to perform in an expression. These operators can be broadly classified into the following categories:

❑   Assignment

❑   Relational

❑   Logical (also known as conditional)

❑   Mathematical

Assignment Operators

You've already seen the use of the assignment operator (=). It assigns the result of the expression on its left to the variable on its right:

```
string str = "Hello, world!";   //---str is now "Hello, world!"---
int num1 = 5;
int result = num1 * 6;          //---result is now 30---
```

You can also assign a value to a variable during declaration time. However, if you are declaring multiple variables on the same line, only the variable that has the equal operator is assigned a value, as shown in the following example:

```
int num1, num2, num3 = 5; //---num1 and num2 are unassigned; num3 is 5---
int i, j = 5, k; //---i and k are unassigned; j is 5---
```

You can also use multiple assignment operators on the same line by assigning the value of one variable to two or more variables:

```
num1 = num2 = num3;
Console.WriteLine(num1); //---5---
Console.WriteLine(num2); //---5---
Console.WriteLine(num3); //---5---
```

If each variable has a unique value, it has to have its own line:

```
int num1 = 4
int num2 = 3
int num3 = 5
```

Self-Assignment Operators

A common task in programming is to change the value of a variable and then reassign it to itself again. For example, you could use the following code to increase the salary of an employee:

```
double salary = 5000;
salary = salary + 1000; //---salary is now 6000---
```

Similarly, to decrease the salary, you can use the following:

```
double salary = 5000;
salary = salary - 1000; //---salary is now 4000---
```

To halve the salary, you can use the following:

```
double salary = 5000;
salary = salary / 2; //---salary is now 2500---
```

To double his pay, you can use the following:

```
double salary = 5000;
salary = salary * 2; //---salary is now 10000---
```

All these statements can be rewritten as follows using self-assignment operators:

```
salary += 1000;    //---same as salary = salary + 1000---
salary -= 1000;    //---same as salary = salary - 1000---
salary /= 2;       //---same as salary = salary / 2---
salary *= 2;       //---same as salary = salary * 2---
```

A self-assignment operator alters its own value before assigning the altered value back to itself. In this example, +=, -=, /=, and *= are all self-assignment operators.

You can also use the modulus self-assignment operator like this:

```
int num = 5;
num %= 2; //---num is now 1---
```

Prefix and Postfix Operators

The previous section described the use of the self-assignment operators. For example, to increase the value of a variable by 1, you would write the statement as follows:

```
int num = 5;
num += 1;   //---num is now 6---
```

In C#, you can use the prefix or postfix operator to increment/decrement the value of a variable by 1. The preceding statement could be rewritten using the prefix operator like this:

```
++num;
```

Alternatively, it could also be rewritten using the postfix operator like this:

```
num++;
```

To decrement a variable, you can use either the prefix or postfix operator, like this:

```
--num;
//---or---
num--;
```

So what is the difference between the prefix and postfix operators? The following example makes it clear:

```
int num1 = 5;
int num2 = 5;
int result;

result = num1++;
Console.WriteLine(num1); //---6---
Console.WriteLine(result); //---5---

result = ++num2;
Console.WriteLine(num2); //---6---
Console.WriteLine(result); //---6---
```

As you can see, if you use the postfix operator (num1++), the value of num1 is assigned to result before the value of num1 is incremented by1. In contrast, the prefix operator (++num2) first increments the value of num2 by 1 and then assigns the new value of num2 (which is now 6) to result.

Here's another example:

```
int num1 = 5;
int num2 = 5;
int result;

result = num1++ + ++num2;
Console.WriteLine(num1); //---6---
Console.WriteLine(num2); //---6---
Console.WriteLine(result); //---11---
```

In this case, both num1 and num2 are initially 5. Because a postfix operator is used on num1, its initial value of 5 is used for adding. And because num2 uses the prefix operator, its value is incremented before adding, hence the value 6 is used for adding. This adds up to 11 (5 + 6). After the first statement, both num1 and num2 would have a value of 6.

Relational Operators

You use relational operators to compare two values and the result of the comparison is a Boolean value — true or false. The following table lists all of the relational operators available in C#.

Operator	Description
==	Equal
!=	Not equal
>	Greater than
>=	Greater than or equal to
<	Lesser than
<=	Lesser than or equal to

The following statements compare the value of num with the numeric 5 using the various relational operators:

```
int num = 5;
Console.WriteLine(num == 5); //---True---
Console.WriteLine(num != 5); //---False---
Console.WriteLine(num > 5);  //---False---
Console.WriteLine(num >= 5); //---True---
Console.WriteLine(num < 5);  //---False---
Console.WriteLine(num <= 5); //---True---
```

A common mistake with the equal relational operator is omitting the second = sign. For example, the following statement prints out the numeric 5 instead of True:

```
Console.WriteLine(num = 5);
```

A single = is the assignment operator.

C programmers often make the following mistake of using a single = for testing equality of two numbers:

```
if (num = 5)   //---use == for testing equality---
{
    Console.WriteLine("num is 5");
}
```

Fortunately, the C# compiler will check for this mistake and issue a "Cannot implicitly convert type 'int' to 'bool'" error.

Logical Operators

C# supports the use of logical operators so that you can evaluate multiple expressions. The following table lists the logical operators supported in C#.

Operator	Description
&&	And
||	Or
!	Not

For example, consider the following code example:

```
if (age < 12 || height < 120)
{
    Console.WriteLine("Student price applies");
}
```

In this case, student price applies if either the age is less than 12, or the height is less than 120cm. As long as at least one of the conditions evaluates to true, the statement is true. Following is the truth table for the Or (||) operator.

Operand A	Operand B	Result
false	false	false
false	true	true
true	false	true
true	true	true

However, if the condition is changed such that student price applies only if a person is less than 12 years old *and* with height less than 120cm, the statement would be rewritten as:

```
if (age < 12 && height < 120)
{
    Console.WriteLine("Student price applies");
}
```

The truth table for the And (&&) operator follows.

Operand A	Operand B	Result
false	false	false
false	true	false
true	false	false
true	true	true

The Not operator (!) negates the result of an expression. For example, if student price does not apply to those more than 12 years old, you could write the expression like this:

```
if (!(age <= 12))
    Console.WriteLine("Student price does not apply");
```

Following is the truth table for the Not operator.

Operand A	Result
false	true
true	false

Short-Circuit Evaluation

C# uses short-circuiting when evaluating logical operators. In short-circuiting, the second argument in a condition is evaluated only when the first argument is not sufficient to determine the value of the entire condition. Consider the following example:

```
int div = 0;
int num = 5;
if ((div == 0) || (num / div == 1))
{
    Console.WriteLine(num); //---5---
}
```

Here the first expression evaluates to true, so there is no need to evaluate the second expression (because an Or expression evaluates to true as long as at least one expression evaluates to true). The second expression, if evaluated, will result in a division-by-zero error. In this case, it won't, and the number 5 is printed.

If you reverse the placement of the expressions, as in the following example, a division-by-zero error occurs:

```
if ((num / div == 1) || (div == 0))
{
    Console.WriteLine(num);
}
```

Short-circuiting also applies to the `&&` operator — if the first expression evaluates to false, the second expression will not be evaluated because the final evaluation is already known.

Mathematical Operators

C# supports five mathematical operators, shown in the following table.

Operator	Description
+	Addition
−	Subtraction
/	Division
*	Multiplication
%	Modulus

One interesting thing about the division operator (`/`) is that when you divide two integers, the fractional part is discarded:

```
int num1 = 6;
int num2 = 4;
double result = num1 / num2;
Console.WriteLine(result); //---1---
```

Here both `num1` and `num2` are integers and hence after the division result only contains the integer portion of the division. To divide correctly, one of the operands must be a noninteger, as the following shows:

```
int num1 = 6;
double num2 = 4;
double result = num1 / num2;
Console.WriteLine(result); //---1.5---
```

Alternatively, you can use type casting to force one of the operands to be of type double so that you can divide correctly:

```
int num1 = 6;
int num2 = 4;
double result = (double) num1 / num2;
Console.WriteLine(result); //---1.5---
```

The modulus operator (%) returns the reminder of a division:

```
int num1 = 6;
int num2 = 4;
int remainder = num1 % num2;
Console.WriteLine(remainder); //---2---
```

The % operator is commonly used for testing whether a number is odd or even, like this:

```
if (num1 % 2 == 0)
    Console.WriteLine("Even");
else
    Console.WriteLine("Odd");
```

Operator Precedence

When you use multiple operators in the same statement, you need be aware of the precedence of each operator (that is, which operator will evaluate first). The following table shows the various C# operators grouped in the order of precedence. Operators within the same group have equal precedence (operatorsinclude some keywords).

Category	Operators
Primary	x.y f(x) a[x] x++ x--newtypeofcheckedunchecked
Unary	+ — ! ~ ++x --x (T)x
Multiplicative	* / %
Additive	+ —
Shift	<< >>
Relational and type testing	< > <= >= is as
Equality	== !=
Logical AND	&
Logical XOR	^
Logical OR		
Conditional AND	&&
Conditional OR	||
Conditional	?:
Assignment	= *= /= %= += -= <<= >>= &= ^= |=

When you are in doubt of the precedence of two operators, always use parentheses to force the compiler to evaluate the expression first. For example, the formula to convert a temperature from Fahrenheit to Celsius is:

```
Tc = (5/9)*(Tf-32);
```

When implemented in C#, the formula looks like this:

```
double fahrenheit = 100;
double celcius = 5.0 / 9.0 * fahrenheit - 32;
Console.WriteLine("{0:##.##} degrees C",celcius);   //---23.56 degrees C---
```

But this produces a wrong answer because `5.0 / 9.0` and `fahrenheit - 32` must be evaluated separately before their results are multiplied to get the final answer. What's happened is that, according to the precedence table, `5.0 / 9.0 * fahrenheit` is evaluated first and then 32 is subtracted from the result. This gives the incorrect answer of 23.56 degrees C.

To correct this, you use parentheses to group all the expressions that need to be evaluated first, like this:

```
double fahrenheit = 100;
double celcius = (5.0 / 9.0) * (fahrenheit - 32);
Console.WriteLine("{0:##.##} degrees C",celcius);   //---37.78 degrees C---
```

This code gives the correct answer of 37.78 degrees C.

Preprocessor Directives

So far the programs you have seen in this chapter are pretty straightforward; you compile the entire program and run it from beginning until end. However, there are times when you want to inject debugging statements into your program — generally using methods such as `Console.WriteLine()` or `MessageBox.Show()` — and then remove them when the program is ready for deployment. But one common mistake is that programmers often forget to remove all those statements after debugging. The end result is that production code often contains many redundant code statements.

A better way is to instruct the C# compile to conditionally omit some of the code during compilation. For example, you can delineate some parts of your code as debugging statements that should not be present in the production code. To do so, you can use preprocessor directives, which are special instructions to a special program (known as the processor) that will prepare your code before sending it to the compiler. C# supports the following preprocessor directives, most of which are discussed in the following sections:

#define	#elif	#line	#pragma warning
#undef	#endif	#region	#pragma checksum
#if	#warning	#endregion	
#else	#error	#pragma	

#define and #undef

The #define preprocessor directive allows you to define a symbol so that you can use the #if preprocessor directive to evaluate and then make conditional compilation. To see how the #define preprocessor directive works, assume that you have a console application named TestDefine (saved in C:\) created using Visual Studio 2008 (see Figure 3-12).

Figure 3-12

The Main() method is located in the Program.cs file. The program basically asks the user to enter a number and then sums up all the odd number from 1 to that number:

```csharp
using System;
using System.Collections.Generic;
using System.Linq;
using System.Text;

namespace TestDefine
{
    class Program
    {
        static void Main(string[] args)
        {
            Console.Write("Please enter a number: ");
            int num = int.Parse(Console.ReadLine());
            int sum = 0;
            for (int i = 1; i <= num; i++)
            {
                //---sum up all odd numbers---
                if (i % 2 == 1)
                    sum += i;
            }
            Console.WriteLine(
                "Sum of all odd numbers from 1 to {0} is {1}",
                num, sum);

            Console.ReadLine();
        }
    }
}
```

Suppose that you want to add some debugging statements to the program so that you can print out the intermediate results. The additional lines of code are highlighted:

```csharp
using System;
using System.Collections.Generic;
using System.Linq;
using System.Text;

namespace TestDefine
{
    class Program
    {
        static void Main(string[] args)
        {
            Console.Write("Please enter a number: ");
            int num = int.Parse(Console.ReadLine());
            int sum = 0;
            for (int i = 1; i <= num; i++)
            {
                //---sum up all odd numbers---
                if (i % 2 == 1)
                {
                    sum += i;
                    Console.WriteLine("i={0}, sum={1}", i, sum);
                }
            }
            Console.WriteLine(
                "Sum of all odd numbers from 1 to {0} is {1}",
                num, sum);

            Console.ReadLine();
        }
    }
}
```

You do not want the debugging statements to be included in the production code so you first define a symbol (such as DEBUG) using the #define preprocessor directive and wrap the debugging statements with the #if and #endif preprocessor directives:

```csharp
#define DEBUG
using System;
using System.Collections.Generic;
using System.Linq;
using System.Text;

namespace TestDefine
{
    class Program
    {
        static void Main(string[] args)
        {
```

```
Console.Write("Please enter a number: ");
int num = int.Parse(Console.ReadLine());
int sum = 0;
for (int i = 1; i <= num; i++)
{
    //---sum up all odd numbers---
    if (i % 2 == 1)
    {
        sum += i;
#if DEBUG
        Console.WriteLine("i={0}, sum={1}", i, sum);
#endif
    }
}
Console.WriteLine(
    "Sum of all odd numbers from 1 to {0} is {1}",
    num, sum);

Console.ReadLine();
        }
    }
}
```

DEBUG *is a common symbol that developers use to indicate debugging statements, which is why most books use it in examples. However, you can define any symbol you want using the* #define *preprocessor directive.*

Before compilation, the preprocessor will evaluate the #if preprocessor directive to see if the DEBUG symbol has been defined. If it has, the statement(s) wrapped within the #if and #endif preprocessor directives will be included for compilation. If the DEBUG symbol has not been defined, the statement — the statement(s) wrapped within the #if and #endif preprocessor — will be omitted from the compilation.

To test out the TestDefine program, follow these steps:

1. Launch the Visual Studio 2008 command prompt (Start ⇨ Programs ⇨ Microsoft Visual Studio 2008 ⇨ Visual Studio Tools ⇨ Visual Studio 2008 Command Prompt).

2. Change to the path containing the program (C:\TestDefine).

3. Compile the application by issuing the command:

```
csc Program.cs.
```

4. Run the program by issuing the command:

```
Program.exe.
```

Figure 3-13 shows the output of the application. As you can see, the debugging statement prints out the intermediate results.

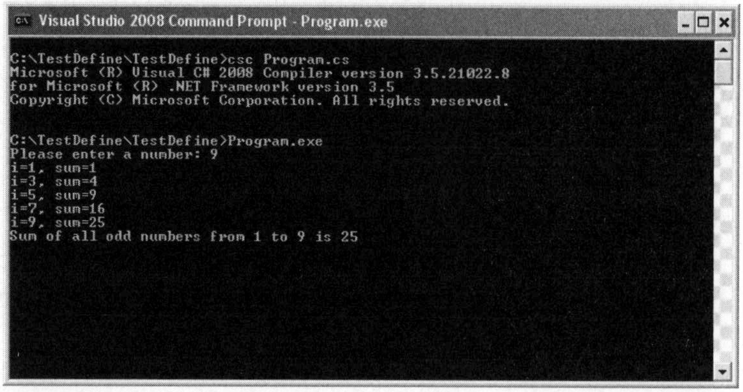

Figure 3-13

To undefine a symbol, you can use the #undef preprocessor directive, like this:

```
#undef DEBUG
using System;
using System.Collections.Generic;
using System.Linq;
using System.Text;
...
```

If you recompile the program now, the debugging statement will be omitted.

Another popular way of using the #define preprocessor directive is to omit the definition of the symbol and inject it during compilation time. For example, if you remove the #define preprocessor directive from the program, you can define it using the /define compiler option:

1.   In Visual Studio 2008 command prompt, compile the program using:

    csc Program.cs /define:DEBUG.

2.   Run the program by issuing the command:

    Program.exe.

The output is identical to what you saw in Figure 3-13 — the debugging statement prints out the intermediate results.

If you now recompile the program by defining another symbol (other than DEBUG), you will realize that the debugging output does not appear (see Figure 3-14).

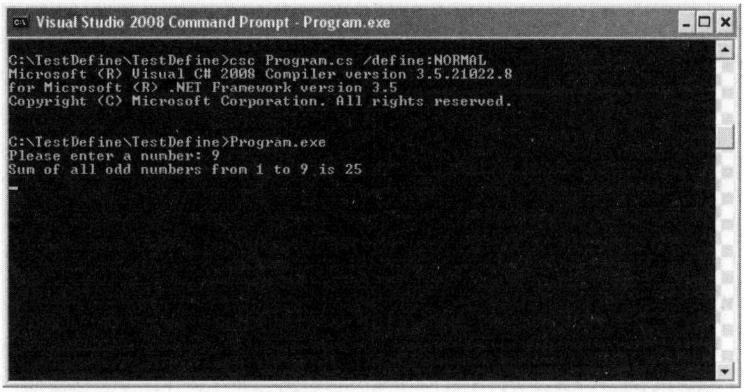

Figure 3-14

#if, #else, #elif, and #endif

As you saw in the preceding section, the #if and #endif preprocessor directives defines a block of code to include for compilation if a specified symbol is defined. You can also use the #else and #elif preprocessor directives to create compound conditional directives.

Using the previous example, you can add the #else and #elif preprocessor directives as follows:

```csharp
using System;
using System.Collections.Generic;
using System.Linq;
using System.Text;

namespace TestDefine
{
    class Program
    {
        static void Main(string[] args)
        {
            Console.Write("Please enter a number: ");
            int num = int.Parse(Console.ReadLine());
            int sum = 0;
            for (int i = 1; i <= num; i++)
            {
                //---sum up all odd numbers---
                if (i % 2 == 1)
                {
                    sum += i;
#if DEBUG
                    Console.WriteLine("i={0}, sum={1}", i, sum);
#elif NORMAL
                    Console.WriteLine("sum={0}", sum);
#else
                    Console.WriteLine(".");
#endif
```

(continued)

(continued)

```
                }
            }
            Console.WriteLine(
                "Sum of all odd numbers from 1 to {0} is {1}",
                num, sum);

            Console.ReadLine();
        }
    }
}
```

Figure 3-15 shows the different output when different symbols are defined. The top screen shows the output when the DEBUG symbol is defined. The middle screen shows the output when the NORMAL symbol is defined. The bottom screen shows the output when no symbol is defined.

Figure 3-15

The #if preprocessor directive can also test for multiple conditions using the logical operators. Here are some examples:

```
#if (DEBUG || NORMAL)   //---either DEBUG or NORMAL is defined---
#if (DEBUG && NORMAL)   //---both DEBUG and NORMAL are defined---
#if (!DEBUG && NORMAL) //---DEBUG is not defined AND NORMAL is defined---
```

#warning and #error

The #warning preprocessor directive lets you generate a warning from a specific location of your code. The following example shows how you can use it to display warning messages during compilation time.

```
            for (int i = 1; i <= num; i++)
            {
                //---sum up all odd numbers---
                if (i % 2 == 1)
                {
                    sum += i;
#if DEBUG
#warning Debugging mode is on
                    Console.WriteLine("i={0}, sum={1}", i, sum);
#elif NORMAL
#warning Normal mode is on
                    Console.WriteLine("sum={0}", sum);
#else
#warning Default mode is on
                    Console.WriteLine(".");
#endif
                }
            }
```

Figure 3-16 shows the output when the DEBUG symbol is defined using the /define compiler option.

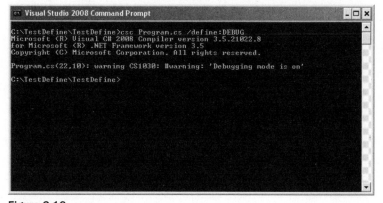

Figure 3-16

The `#error` preprocessor directive lets you generate an error. Consider the following example:

```
                for (int i = 1; i <= num; i++)
                {
                    //---sum up all odd numbers---
                    if (i % 2 == 1)
                    {
                        sum += i;
#if DEBUG
#warning Debugging mode is on
                        Console.WriteLine("i={0}, sum={1}", i, sum);
#elif NORMAL
#error This mode is obsolete.
                        Console.WriteLine("sum={0}", sum);
#else
#warning Default mode is on
                        Console.WriteLine(".");
#endif
                    }
                }
```

Here, if the NORMAL symbol is defined, an error message is shown and the statement defined within the conditional directive is ignored. Figure 3-17 shows that when you define the NORMAL symbol, the error message is displayed and the compilation is aborted.

Figure 3-17

#line

The `#line` preprocessor directive lets you modify the compiler's line number and (optionally) the file name output for errors and warnings.

The `#line` preprocessor directive is injected in the following example. The highlighted code indicates statements that will cause the debugger to issue warning messages:

```
1. using System;
2. using System.Collections.Generic;
3. using System.Linq;
4. using System.Text;
5.
6. namespace TestDefine
7. {
8.     class Program
9.     {
10.         static void Main(string[] args)
```

```
11.          {
12. #line 25
13.              int i;                           //---treated as line 25---
14.              char c;                          //---treated as line 26---
15.              Console.WriteLine("Line 1");     //---treated as line 27---
16. #line hidden                                 //---treated as line 28---
17.              Console.WriteLine("Line 2");     //---treated as line 29---
18.              Console.WriteLine("Line 3");     //---treated as line 30---
19. #line default
20.              double d;                        //---treated as line 20---
21.              Console.WriteLine("Line 4");     //---treated as line 21---
22. #line 45 "Program1.cs"                       //---treated as line 22---
23.              Single s;                        //---treated as line 45---
24.              Console.WriteLine("Line 5");     //---treated as line 46---
25.              Console.ReadLine();              //---treated as line 47---
26.          }
27.      }
28. }
```

The line numbers are for illustration purposes and are not part of the program.

The four highlighted lines are numbered 13, 14, 20, and 23. When you build the program in Visual Studio 2008, the lines reported are 25, 26, 20, and 45 (see Figure 3-18).

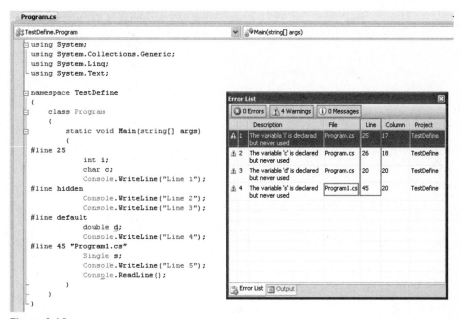

Figure 3-18

Let's take a look at the #line directives in the example program:

❑ #line 25 means that you want to modify the line number to use the specified line number (25 in this case) instead of the actual line number of the statement in error. This is useful if you need to assign a fixed line number to a particular part of the code so that you can trace it easily. Interestingly, the next line will continue from 25, that is, the next line is now line 26. This is evident from the warning message for the char c; line.

❑ #line default means that the compiler will report the actual line number.

❑ #line 45 "Program1.cs" means that you want to fix the line number at 45 and specify the name of the file in error (Program1.cs in this case). An example usage of it would be that the statement in error might be a call to an external DLL and by specifying the filename of the DLL here, it is clearer that the mistake might be from that DLL.

What about the #line hidden statement? That preprocessor directive indicates to the debugger to skip the block of code beginning with the #line hidden preprocessor directive. The debugger will skip the line(s) until the next #line preprocessor directive is found. This is useful for skipping over method calls that you are not interested in (such as those not written by you).

Interestingly, you can replace the #line hidden preprocessor directive with #line 16707566 (0xFeeFee) and it will still work correctly.

#region and #endregion

The #region and #region preprocessor directives are used in conjunction with Visual Studio's Code Editor. Let's work with the following example:

```
using System;
using System.Collections.Generic;
using System.Linq;
using System.Text;

namespace TestDefine
{
    class Program
    {
        static void Main(string[] args)
        {
            //---implementions here---
        }

        private void Method1()
        {
            //---implementions here---
        }

        private void Method2()
        {
            //---implementions here---
        }
```

```
        private void Method3()
        {
            //---implementions here---
        }

    }
}
```

Often, you have many functions that perform specific tasks. In such cases, it is often good to organize them into regions so that they can be collapsed and expanded as and when needed. Using this example, you can group all the methods — Method1(), Method2(), and Method3() — into a region using the #region and #region preprocessor directives:

```
using System;
using System.Collections.Generic;
using System.Linq;
using System.Text;

namespace TestDefine
{
    class Program
    {
        static void Main(string[] args)
        {

        }

        #region "Helper functions"

        private void Method1()
        {
            //---implementions here---
        }

        private void Method2()
        {
            //---implementions here---
        }

        private void Method3()
        {
            //---implementions here---
        }

        #endregion
    }
}
```

In Visual Studio 2008, you can now collapse all the methods into a group called "Helper functions". Figure 3-19 shows the Code Editor before and after the region is collapsed.

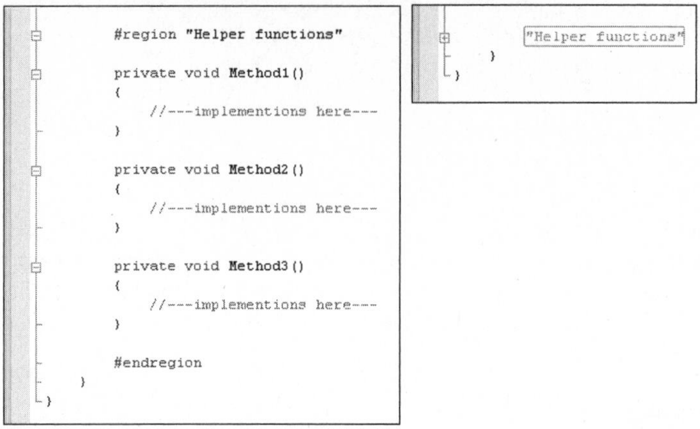

Figure 3-19

The #region and #region preprocessor directives do not affect the logic of your code. They are used purely in Visual Studio 2008 to better organize your code.

#pragma warning

The #pragma warning directive enables or disables compiler warning messages. For example, consider the following program:

```csharp
using System;
using System.Collections.Generic;
using System.Linq;
using System.Text;

namespace TestDefine
{
    class Program
    {
        int num = 5;
        static void Main(string[] args)
        {
        }
    }
}
```

In this program, the variable num is defined but never used. When you compile the application, the C# compiler will show a warning message (see Figure 3-20).

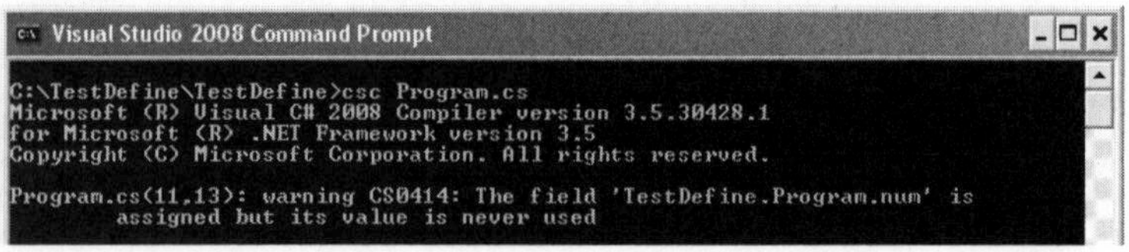

Figure 3-20

To suppress the warning message, you can use the #pragma warning directive together with the warning number of the message that you want to suppress:

```
using System;
using System.Collections.Generic;
using System.Linq;
using System.Text;

#pragma warning disable 414
namespace TestDefine
{
    class Program
    {
        int num = 5;
        static void Main(string[] args)
        {
        }
    }
}
```

This example suppresses warning message number 414 ("The private field 'field' is assigned but its value is never used"). With the #pragma warning directive, the compiler will now suppress the warning message (see Figure 3-21).

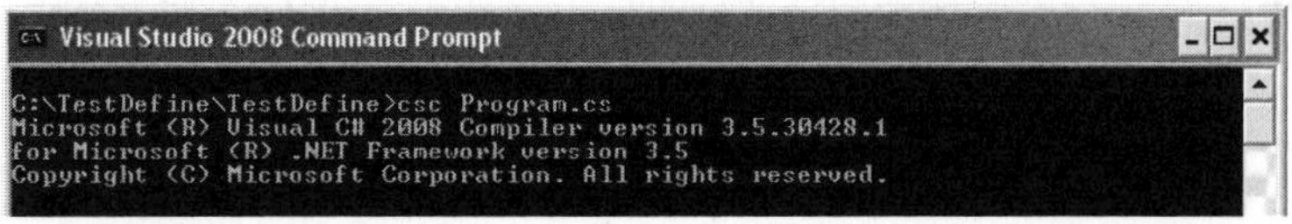

Figure 3-21

You can suppress multiple warning messages by separating the message numbers with a comma (,) like this:

```
#pragma warning disable 414, 3021, 1959
```

Summary

In this chapter, you explored the basic syntax of the C# language and saw how to use Visual Studio 2008 to compile and run a working C# application. You examined the different data types available in the .NET Framework and how you can perform type conversion from one type to another. You have also seen the various ways to perform looping, and the various processor directives with which you can change the way your program is compiled.

4

Classes and Objects

One of the most important topics in C# programming — in fact, the cornerstone of .NET development — is classes and objects.

Classes are essentially templates from which you create objects. In C# .NET programming, everything you deal with involves classes and objects. This chapter assumes that you already have a basic grasp of object-oriented programming. It tackles:

- ❏ How to define a class
- ❏ How to create an object from a class
- ❏ The different types of members in a class
- ❏ The root of all objects — `System.Object`

Classes

Everything you encounter in .NET in based on classes. For example, you have a Windows Forms application containing a default form called `Form1`. `Form1` itself is a class that inherits from the base class `System.Windows.Forms.Form`, which defines the basic behaviors that a Windows Form should exhibit:

```
using System.Data;
using System.Drawing;
using System.Linq;
using System.Text;
using System.Windows.Forms;

namespace Project1
{
    public partial class Form1 : Form
    {
        public Form1()
        {
            InitializeComponent();
        }
    }
}
```

Within the `Form1` class, you code in your methods. For example, to display a "`Hello World`" message when the form is loaded, add the following statement in the `Form1_Load()` method:

```
public partial class Form1 : Form
{
    public Form1()
    {
        InitializeComponent();
    }

    protected override void OnLoad(EventArgs e)
    {
        MessageBox.Show("Hello World!");
    }
}
```

The following sections walk you through the basics of defining your own class and the various members you can have in the class.

Defining a Class

You use the `class` keyword to define a class. The following example is the definition of a class called `Contact`:

```
public class Contact
{
    public int ID;
    public string FirstName;
    public string LastName;
    public string Email;
}
```

This `Contact` class has four public members — `ID`, `FirstName`, `LastName`, and `Email`. The syntax of a class definition is:

```
<access_modifiers> class Class_Name
{
    //---Fields, properties, methods, and events---
}
```

Using Partial Classes

Instead of defining an entire class by using the `class` keyword, you can split the definition into multiple classes by using the `partial` keyword. For example, the `Contact` class defined in the previous section can be split into two partial classes like this:

```
public partial class Contact
{
    public int ID;
    public string Email;
```

```
    }

public partial class Contact
{
    public string FirstName;
    public string LastName;
}
```

When the application is compiled, the C# compiler will group all the partial classes together and treat them as a single class.

Uses for Partial Classes

There are a couple of very good reasons to use partial classes. First, using partial classes enables the programmers on your team to work on different parts of a class without needing to share the same physical file. While this is useful for projects that involve big class files, be wary: a huge class file may signal a design fault, and refactoring may be required.

Second, and most compelling, you can use partial classes to separate your application business logic from the designer-generated code. For example, the code generated by Visual Studio 2008 for a Windows Form is kept separate from your business logic. This prevents developers from messing with the code that is used for the user interface. At the same time, it prevents you from losing your changes to the designer-generated code when you change the user interface.

Creating an Instance of a Class (Object Instantiation)

A class works like a template. To do anything useful, you need to use the template to create an actual object so that you can work with it. The process of creating an object from a class is known as *instantiation*.

To instantiate the Contact class defined earlier, you first create a variable of type Contact:

```
Contact contact1;
```

At this stage, contact1 is of type Contact, but it does not actually contain the object data yet. For it to contain the object data, you need to use the new keyword to create a new instance of the Contact class, a process is known as *object instantiation*:

```
contact1 = new Contact();
```

Alternatively, you can combine those two steps into one, like this:

```
Contact contact1 = new Contact();
```

Once an object is instantiated, you can set the various members of the object. Here's an example:

```
contact1.ID = 12;
contact1.FirstName = "Wei-Meng";
contact1.LastName = "Lee";
contact1.Email = "weimenglee@learn2develop.net";
```

You can also assign an object to an object, like the following:

```
Contact contact1 = new Contact();
Contact contact2 = contact1;
```

In these statements, contact2 and contact1 are now both pointing to the same object. Any changes made to one object will be reflected in the other object, as the following example shows:

```
Contact contact1 = new Contact();
Contact contact2 = contact1;

contact1.FirstName = "Wei-Meng";
contact2.FirstName = "Jackson";

//---prints out "Jackson"---
Console.WriteLine(contact1.FirstName);
```

It prints out "Jackson" because both contact1 and contact2 are pointing to the same object, and when you assign "Jackson" to the FirstName property of contact2, contact1's FirstName property also sees "Jackson".

Anonymous Types (C# 3.0)

C# 3.0 introduces a new feature known as *anonymous types*. Anonymous types enable you to define data types without having to formally define a class. Consider the following example:

```
var book1 = new
{
    ISBN = "978-0-470-17661-0",
    Title="Professional Windows Vista Gadgets Programming",
    Author = "Wei-Meng Lee",
    Publisher="Wrox"
};
```

Chapter 3 discusses the new C# 3.0 keyword var.

Here, book1 is an object with 4 properties: ISBN, Title, Author, and Publisher (see Figure 4-1).

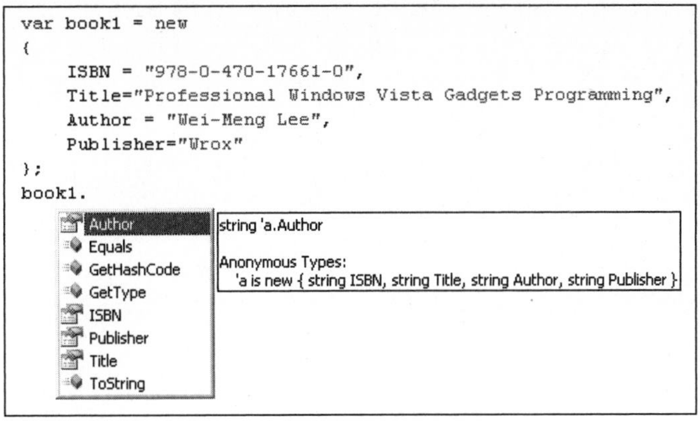

```
var book1 = new
{
    ISBN = "978-0-470-17661-0",
    Title="Professional Windows Vista Gadgets Programming",
    Author = "Wei-Meng Lee",
    Publisher="Wrox"
};
book1.
```

| Author |
| Equals |
| GetHashCode |
| GetType |
| ISBN |
| Publisher |
| Title |
| ToString |

string 'a.Author

Anonymous Types:
'a is new { string ISBN, string Title, string Author, string Publisher }

Figure 4-1

In this example, there's no need for you to define a class containing the four properties. Instead, the object is created and its properties initialized with their respective values.

> C# anonymous types are immutable, which means all the properties are read-only — their values cannot be changed once they are initialized.

You can use variable names when assigning values to properties in an anonymous type; for example:

```
var Title = "Professional Windows Vista Gadgets Programming";
var Author = "Wei-Meng Lee";
var Publisher = "Wrox";

var book1 = new
{
    ISBN = "978-0-470-17661-0",
    Title,
    Author,
    Publisher
};
```

In this case, the names of the properties will assume the names of the variables, as shown in Figure 4-2.

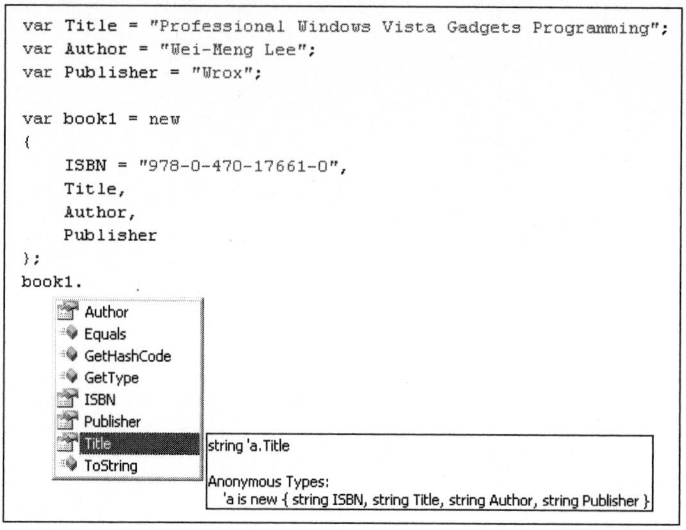

```
var Title = "Professional Windows Vista Gadgets Programming";
var Author = "Wei-Meng Lee";
var Publisher = "Wrox";

var book1 = new
{
    ISBN = "978-0-470-17661-0",
    Title,
    Author,
    Publisher
};
book1.
```

Figure 4-2

However, you cannot create anonymous types with literals, as the following example demonstrates:

```
//---error---
var book1 = new
{
    "978-0-470-17661-0",
    "Professional Windows Vista Gadgets Programming",
    "Wei-Meng Lee",
    "Wrox"
};
```

When assigning a literal value to a property in an anonymous type, you must use an identifier, like this:

```
var book1 = new
{
    ISBN = "978-0-470-17661-0",
    Title="Professional Windows Vista Gadgets Programming",
    Author = "Wei-Meng Lee",
    Publisher="Wrox"
};
```

So, how are anonymous types useful for your application? Well, they enable you to shape your data from one type to another. You will look into more about this in Chapter 14, which tackles LINQ.

Class Members

Variables and functions defined in a class are known as a class's members. The `Contact` class definition, for instance, has four members that you can access once an object is instantiated:

```
public class Contact
{
    public int ID;
    public string FirstName;
    public string LastName;
    public string Email;
}
```

Members of a class are classified into two types:

Type	Description
Data	Members that store the data needed by your object so that they can be used by functions to perform their work. For example, you can store a person's name using the `FirstName` and `LastName` members.
Function	Code blocks within a class. Function members allow the class to perform its work. For example, a function contained within a class (such as the `Contact` class) can validate the email of a person (stored in the Email member) to see if it is a valid email address.

Data members can be further grouped into *instance members* and *static members*.

Instance Members

By default, all data members are *instance members* unless they are constants or prefixed with the `static` keyword (more on this in the next section). The variables defined in the `Contact` class are instance members:

```
public int ID;
public string FirstName;
public string LastName;
public string Email;
```

Instance members can be accessed only through an instance of a class and each instance of the class (object) has its own copy of the data. Consider the following example:

```
Contact contact1 = new Contact();
contact1.ID = 12;
contact1.FirstName = "Wei-Meng";
contact1.LastName = "Lee";
contact1.Email = "weimenglee@learn2develop.net";

Contact contact2 = new Contact();
contact2.ID = 35;
contact2.FirstName = "Jason";
contact2.LastName = "Will";
contact2.Email = "JasonWill@company.net";
```

The objects `contact1` and `contact2` each contain information for a different user. Each object maintains its own copy of the ID, `FirstName`, `LastName`, and `Email` data members.

Static Members

Static data members belong to the class rather than to each instance of the class. You use the `static` keyword to define them. For example, here the `Contact` class has a static member named `count`:

```
public class Contact
{
    public static int count;
    public int ID;
    public string FirstName;
    public string LastName;
    public string Email;
}
```

The `count` static member can be used to keep track of the total number of `Contact` instances, and thus it should not belong to any instances of the `Contact` class but to the class itself.

To use the `count` static variable, access it through the `Contact` class:

```
Contact.count = 4;
Console.WriteLine(Contact.count);
```

You cannot access it via an instance of the class, such as `contact1`:

```
//---error---
contact1.count = 4;
```

Constants defined within a class are implicitly static, as the following example shows:

```
public class Contact
{
    public const ushort MAX_EMAIL = 5;
    public static int count;
    public int ID;
    public string FirstName;
    public string LastName;
    public string Email;
}
```

In this case, you can only access the constant through the class name but not set a value to it:

```
Console.WriteLine(Contact.MAX_EMAIL);
Contact.MAX_EMAIL = 4; //---error---
```

Access Modifiers

Access modifiers are keywords that you can add to members of a class to restrict their access. Consider the following definition of the `Contact` class:

```
public class Contact
{
    public const ushort MAX_EMAIL = 5;
    public static int count;
    public int ID;
    public string FirstName;
    public string LastName;
    private string _Email;
}
```

Unlike the rest of the data members, the `_Email` data member has been defined with the `private` keyword. The `public` keyword indicates that the data member is visible outside the class, while the `private` keyword indicates that the data member is only visible within the class.

> *By convention, you can denote a private variable by beginning its name with the underscore (_) character. This is recommended, but not mandatory.*

For example, you can access the `FirstName` data member through an instance of the `Contact` class:

```
//---this is OK---
contact1.FirstName = "Wei-Meng";
```

But you cannot access the `_Email` data member outside the class, as the following statement demonstrates:

```
//---error: _Email is inaccessible---
contact1._Email = "weimenglee@learn2develop.net";
```

> *C# has four access modifiers — `private`, `public`, `protected`, and `internal`. The last two are discussed with inheritance in the next chapter.*

If a data member is declared without the `public` keyword, its scope (or access) is `private` by default. So, `_Email` can also be declared like this:

```
public class Contact
{
    public const ushort MAX_EMAIL = 5;
    public static int count;
    public int ID;
    public string FirstName;
    public string LastName;
    string _Email;
}
```

Function Members

A function member contains executable code that performs work for the class. The following are examples of function members in C#:

❑ Methods

❑ Properties

❑ Events

❑ Indexers

❑ User-defined operators

❑ Constructors

❑ Destructors

Events and indexers are covered in detail in Chapters 7 and 13.

Methods

In C#, every function must be associated with a class. A function defined with a class is known as a *method*. In C#, a method is defined using the following syntax:

```
[access_modifiers] return_type method_name(parameters)
{
    //---Method body---
}
```

Here's an example — the `ValidateEmail()` method defined in the `Contact` class:

```
public class Contact
{
    public static ushort MAX_EMAIL;
    public int ID;
    public string FirstName;
    public string LastName;
    public string Email;

    public Boolean ValidateEmail() {
        //---implementation here---
        Boolean valid=true;
        return valid;
    }
}
```

If the method does not return a value, you need to specify the return type as void, as the following PrintName() method shows:

```
public class Contact
{
    public static ushort MAX_EMAIL;
    public int ID;
    public string FirstName;
    public string LastName;
    public string Email;

    public Boolean ValidateEmail() {
        //---implementation here---
        //...
        Boolean valid=true;
        return valid;
    }

    public void PrintName()
    {
        Console.WriteLine("{0} {1}", this.FirstName, this.LastName);
    }
}
```

Passing Arguments into Methods

You can pass values into a method using *arguments*. The words parameter and argument are often used interchangeably, but they mean different things. A parameter is what you use to define a method. An argument is what you actually use to call a method.

In the following example, x and y are examples of parameters:

```
public int AddNumbers(int x, int y) {}
```

When you call the method, you pass in values/variables. In the following example, num1 and num2 are examples of arguments:

```
Console.WriteLine(AddNumbers(num1, num2));
```

Consider the method named AddNumbers() with two parameters, x and y:

```
public int AddNumbers(int x, int y)
{
    x++;
    y++;
    return x + y;
}
```

When you call this method, you also need to pass two integer arguments (num1 and num2), as the following example shows:

```
int num1 = 4, num2 = 5;
//---prints out 11---
Console.WriteLine(AddNumbers(num1, num2));
Console.WriteLine(num1); //---4---
Console.WriteLine(num2); //---5---
```

In C#, all arguments are *passed by value* by default. In other words, the called method gets a copy of the value of the arguments passed into it. In the preceding example, for instance, even though the value of x and y are both incremented within the method, this does not affect the values of num1 and num2.

If you want to pass in arguments to methods *by reference*, you need to prefix the parameters with the ref keyword. Values of variables passed in by reference will be modified if there are changes made to them in the method. Consider the following rewrite of the AddNumbers() function:

Because C# functions can only return single values, passing arguments by reference is useful when you need a method to return multiple values.

```
public int AddNumbers(ref int x, ref int y)
{
    x++;
    y++;
    return x + y;
}
```

In this case, the values of variables passed into this function will be modified, as the following example illustrates:

```
int num1 = 4, num2 = 5;
//---prints out 11---
Console.WriteLine(AddNumbers(ref num1, ref num2));
Console.WriteLine(num1); //---5---
Console.WriteLine(num2); //---6---
```

After calling the AddNumbers() function, num1 becomes 5 and num2 becomes 6. Observe that you need to prefix the arguments with the ref keyword when calling the function. In addition, you cannot pass literal values as arguments into a method that requires parameters to be passed in by reference:

```
//---invalid arguments---
Console.WriteLine(AddNumbers(4, 5));
```

Also note that the ref keyword requires that all the variables be initialized first. Here's an example:

```
public void GetDate(ref int day, ref int month, ref int year)
{
    day = DateTime.Now.Day;
    month = DateTime.Now.Month;
    year = DateTime.Now.Year;
}
```

The `GetDate()` method takes in three reference parameters and uses them to return the day, month, and year.

If you pass in the day, month and year reference variables without initializing them, an error will occur:

```
//---Error: day, month, and year not initialized---
int day, month, year;
GetDate(ref day, ref month, ref year);
```

If your intention is to use the variables solely to obtain some return values from the method, you can use the `out` keyword, which is identical to the `ref` keyword except that it does not require the variables passed in to be initialized first:

```
public void GetDate(out int day, out int month, out int year)
{
    day = DateTime.Now.Day;
    month = DateTime.Now.Month;
    year = DateTime.Now.Year;
}
```

Also, the `out` parameter in a function must be assigned a value before the function returns. If it isn't, a compiler error results.

Like the `ref` keyword, you need to prefix the arguments with the `out` keyword when calling the function:

```
int day, month, year;
GetDate(out day, out month, out year);
```

The this Keyword

The `this` keyword refers to the current instance of an object (in a nonstatic class; discussed later in the section Static Classes). In the earlier section on methods, you saw the use of `this` :

```
Console.WriteLine("{0} {1}", this.FirstName, this.LastName);
```

While the `FirstName` and `LastName` variable could be referenced without using the `this` keyword, prefixing them with it makes your code more readable, indicating that you are referring to an instance member.

However, if instance members have the same names as your parameters, using `this` allows you to resolve the ambiguity:

```
public void SetName(string FirstName, string LastName)
{
    this.FirstName = FirstName;
    this.LastName = LastName;
}
```

Another use of the `this` keyword is to pass the current object as a parameter to another method. For example:

```
public class AddressBook
{
    public void AddContact(Contact c)
    {
        Console.WriteLine(c.ID);
        Console.WriteLine(c.FirstName);
        Console.WriteLine(c.LastName);
        Console.WriteLine(c.Email);
        //---other implementations here---
        //...
    }
}
```

The `AddContact()` method takes in a `Contact` object and prints out the details of the contact. Suppose that the `Contact` class has a `AddToAddressBook()` method that takes in an `AddressBook` object. This method adds the `Contact` object into the `AddressBook` object:

```
public class Contact
{
    public int ID;
    public string FirstName;
    public string LastName;
    public string Email;

    public void AddToAddressBook(AddressBook addBook)
    {
        addBook.AddContact(this);
    }
}
```

In this case, you use the `this` keyword to pass in the current instance of the `Contact` object into the `AddressBook` object. To test out that code, use the following statements:

```
Contact contact1 = new Contact();
contact1.ID = 12;
contact1.FirstName = "Wei-Meng";
contact1.LastName = "Lee";
contact1.Email = "weimenglee@learn2develop.net";

AddressBook addBook1 = new AddressBook();
contact1.AddToAddressBook(addBook1);
```

Properties

Properties are function members that provide an easy way to read or write the values of private data members. Recall the `Contact` class defined earlier:

```
public class Contact
{
    public int ID;
    public string FirstName;
    public string LastName;
    public string Email;
}
```

You've seen that you can create a `Contact` object and set its public data members (`ID`, `FirstName`, `LastName`, and `Email`) directly, like this:

```
Contact c = new Contact();
c.ID = 1234;
c.FirstName = "Wei-Meng";
c.LastName = "Lee";
c.Email = "weimenglee@learn2develop.net";
```

However, if the `ID` of a person has a valid range of values — such as from 1 to 9999 — the following value of 12345 would still be assigned to the ID data member:

```
c.ID = 12345;
```

Technically, the assignment is valid, but logically it should not be allowed — the number assigned is beyond the range of values permitted for `ID`. Of course you can perform some checks before assigning a value to the ID member, but doing so violates the spirit of encapsulation in object-oriented programming — the checks should be done within the class.

A solution to this is to use properties.

The `Contact` class can be rewritten as follows with its data members converted to properties:

```
public class Contact
{
    int _ID;
    string _FirstName, _LastName, _Email;
    public int ID
    {
        get
        {
            return _ID;
        }
        set
        {
            _ID = value;
        }
    }
}
```

(continued)

(continued)

```csharp
    public string FirstName
    {
        get
        {
            return _FirstName;
        }
        set
        {
            _FirstName = value;
        }
    }
    public string LastName
    {
        get
        {
            return _LastName;
        }
        set
        {
            _LastName = value;
        }
    }
    public string Email
    {
        get
        {
            return _Email;
        }
        set
        {
            _Email = value;
        }
    }
}
```

Note that the public members (ID, FirstName, LastName, and Email) have been replaced by properties with the set and get accessors.

The set accessor sets the value of a property. Using this example, you can instantiate a Contact class and then set the value of the ID property, like this:

```csharp
Contact c = new Contact();
c.ID = 1234;
```

In this case, the set accessor is invoked:

```csharp
public int ID
{
    get
    {
        return _ID;
    }
```

```
        set
        {
            _ID = value;
        }
    }
```

The `value` keyword contains the value that is being assigned by the `set` accessor. You normally assign the value of a property to a private member so that it is not visible to code outside the class, which in this case is _ID.

When you retrieve the value of a property, the `get` accessor is invoked:

```
public int ID
{
    get
    {
        return _ID;
    }
    set
    {
        _ID = value;
    }
}
```

The following statement shows an example of retrieving the value of a property:

```
Console.WriteLine(c.ID);  //---prints out 1234---
```

The really useful part of properties is the capability for you to perform checking on the value assigned. For example, before the ID property is set, you want to make sure that the value is between 1 and 9999, so you perform the check at the `set` accessor, like this:

```
public int ID
{
    get
    {
        return _ID;
    }
    set
    {
        if (value > 0 && value <= 9999)
        {
            _ID = value;
        }
        else
        {
            _ID = 0;
        };
    }
}
```

Using properties, you can now prevent users from setting invalid values.

Read-Only and Write-Only Properties

When a property definition contains the get and set accessors, that property can be read as well as written. To make a property read-only, you simply leave out the set accessor, like this:

```
public int ID
{
    get
    {
        return _ID;
    }
}
```

You can now read but not write values into the ID property:

```
Console.WriteLine(c1.ID); //---OK---
c1.ID = 1234;             //---Error---
```

Likewise, to make a property write-only, simply leave out the get accessor:

```
public int ID
{
    set
    {
        _ID = value;
    }
}
```

You can now write but not read from the ID property:

```
Console.WriteLine(c1.ID); //---Error---
c1.ID = 1234;             //---OK---
```

You can also restrict the visibility of the get and set accessors. For example, the set accessor of a public property could be set to private to allow only members of the class to call the set accessor, but any class could call the get accessor. The following example demonstrates this:

```
public int ID
{
    get
    {
        return _ID;
    }
    private set
    {
        _ID = value;
    }
}
```

In this code, the set accessor of the ID property is prefixed with the private keyword to restrict its visibility. That means that you now cannot assign a value to the ID property but you can access it:

```
c.ID = 1234;                //---error---
Console.WriteLine(c.ID);    //---OK---
```

You can, however, access the ID property anywhere within the Contact class itself, such as in the Email property:

```
public string Email
{
    get
    {
        //...
        this.ID = 1234;
        //...
    }
    //...
}
```

Partial Methods (C# 3.0)

Earlier on, you saw that a class definition can be split into one or more class definitions. In C# 3.0, this concept is extended to methods — you can now have partial methods. To see how partial methods works, consider the Contact partial class:

```
public partial class Contact
{
    //...
    private string _Email;
    public string Email
    {
        get
        {
            return _Email;
        }
        set
        {
            _Email = value;
        }
    }
}
```

Suppose you that want to allow users of this partial class to optionally log the email address of each contact when its Email property is set. In that case, you can define a partial method — LogEmail() in this example — like this:

```
public partial class Contact
{
    //...
}

public partial class Contact
{
    //...
```

(continued)

(continued)

```
        private string _Email;
        public string Email
        {
            get
            {
                return _Email;
            }
            set
            {
                _Email = value;
                LogEmail();
            }
        }

        //---partial methods are private---
        partial void LogEmail();
}
```

The partial method `LogEmail()` is called when a contact's email is set via the `Email` property. Note that this method has no implementation. Where is the implementation? It can optionally be implemented in another partial class. For example, if another developer decides to use the `Contact` partial class, he or she can define another partial class containing the implementation for the `LogEmail()` method:

```
public partial class Contact
{
    partial void LogEmail()
    {
        //---code to send email to contact---
        Console.WriteLine("Email set: {0}", _Email);
    }
}
```

So when you now instantiate an instance of the `Contact` class, you can set its `Email` property as follows and a line will be printed in the output window:

```
Contact contact1 = new Contact();
contact1.Email = "weimenglee@learn2develop.net";
```

What if there is no implementation of the `LogEmail()` method? Well, in that case the compiler simply removes the call to this method, and there is no change to your code.

Partial methods are useful when you are dealing with generated code. For example, suppose that the `Contact` class is generated by a code generator. The signature of the partial method is defined in the class, but it is totally up to you to decide if you need to implement it.

> **A partial method must be declared within a partial class or partial struct.**

Partial methods must adhere to the following rules:

- ❑ Must begin with the `partial` keyword and the method must return void

- ❑ Can have `ref` but not `out` parameters

- ❑ They are implicitly private, and therefore they cannot be virtual (virtual methods are discussed in the next chapter)

- ❑ Parameter and type parameter names do not have to be the same in the implementing and defining declarations

Automatic Properties (C# 3.0)

In the `Contact` class defined in the previous section, apart from the `ID` property, the properties are actually not doing much except assigning their values to private members:

```
public string FirstName
{
    get
    {
        return _FirstName;
    }
    set
    {
        _FirstName = value;
    }
}
public string LastName
{
    get
    {
        return _LastName;
    }
    set
    {
        _LastName = value;
    }
}
public string Email
{
    get
    {
        return _Email;
    }
    set
    {
        _Email = value;
    }
}
```

In other words, you are not actually doing any checking before the values are assigned. In C# 3.0, you can shorten those properties that have no filtering (checking) rules by using a feature known as *automatic properties*. The Contact class can be rewritten as:

```
public class Contact
{
    int _ID;
    public int ID
    {
        get
        {
            return _ID;
        }
        set
        {
            if (value > 0 && value <= 9999)
            {
                _ID = value;
            }
            else
            {
                _ID = 0;
            };
        }
    }
    public string FirstName {get; set;}
    public string LastName {get; set;}
    public string Email {get; set;}
}
```

Now there's no need for you to define private members to store the values of the properties. Instead, you just need to use the get and set keywords, and the compiler will automatically create the private members in which to store the properties values. If you decide to add filtering rules to the properties later, you can simply implement the set and get accessor of each property.

To restrict the visibility of the get and set accessor when using the automatic properties feature, you simply prefix the get or set accessor with the private keyword, like this:

```
public string FirstName {get; private set;}
```

This statement sets the FirstName property as read-only.

You might be tempted to directly convert these properties (FirstName, LastName, and Email) into public data members. But if you did that and then later decided to convert these public members into properties, you would need to recompile all of the assemblies that were compiled against the old class.

Constructors

Instead of initializing the individual properties of an object after it has been instantiated, it is sometimes useful to initialize them at the time of instantiation. *Constructors* are class methods that are executed when an object is instantiated.

Using the `Contact` class as the example, the following constructor initializes the `ID` property to 9999 every time an object is instantiated:

```
public class Contact
{
    int _ID;
    public int ID
    {
        get
        {
            return _ID;
        }
        set
        {
            if (value > 0 && value <= 9999)
            {
                _ID = value;
            }
            else
            {
                _ID = 0;
            };
        }
    }
    public string FirstName { get; set; }
    public string LastName { get; set; }
    public string Email { get; set; }

    public Contact()
    {
        this.ID = 9999;
    }
}
```

The following statement proves that the constructor is called:

```
Contact c = new Contact();
//---prints out 9999---
Console.WriteLine(c.ID);
```

Constructors have the same name as the class and they do not return any values. In this example, the constructor is defined without any parameters. A constructor that takes in no parameters is called a *default constructor*. It is invoked when you instantiate an object without any arguments, like this:

```
Contact c = new Contact();
```

If you do not define a default constructor in your class, an implicit default constructor is automatically created by the compiler.

You can have as many constructors as you need to, as long as each constructor's *signature* (parameters) is different. Let's now add two more constructors to the `Contact` class:

```
public class Contact
{
    //...
    public Contact()
    {
        this.ID = 9999;
    }

    public Contact(int ID)
    {
        this.ID = ID;
    }

    public Contact(int ID, string FirstName, string LastName,
                   string Email)
    {
        this.ID = ID;
        this.FirstName = FirstName;
        this.LastName = LastName;
        this.Email = Email;
    }
}
```

When you have multiple methods (constructors in this case) with the same name but different signatures, the methods are known as *overloaded*. IntelliSense will show the different signatures available when you try to instantiate a `Contact` object (see Figure 4-3).

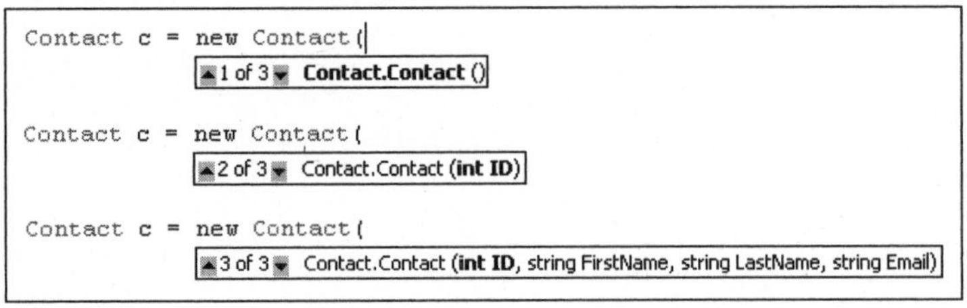

```
Contact c = new Contact(|
            ▲1 of 3▼  Contact.Contact ()

Contact c = new Contact(
            ▲2 of 3▼  Contact.Contact (int ID)

Contact c = new Contact(
            ▲3 of 3▼  Contact.Contact (int ID, string FirstName, string LastName, string Email)
```

Figure 4-3

You can create instances of the `Contact` class using the different constructors:

```
//---first constructor is called---
Contact c1 = new Contact();

//---second constructor is called---
Contact c2 = new Contact(1234);

//---third constructor is called---
Contact c3 = new Contact(1234, "Wei-Meng", "Lee", "weimenglee@learn2develop.net");
```

Constructor Chaining

Suppose that the Contact class has the following four constructors:

```
public class Contact
{
    //...

    public Contact()
    {
        this.ID = 9999;
    }

    public Contact(int ID)
    {
        this.ID = ID;
    }

    public Contact(int ID, string FirstName, string LastName)
    {
        this.ID = ID;
        this.FirstName = FirstName;
        this.LastName = LastName;
    }

    public Contact(int ID, string FirstName, string LastName, string Email)
    {
        this.ID = ID;
        this.FirstName = FirstName;
        this.LastName = LastName;
        this.Email = Email;
    }
}
```

Instead of setting the properties individually in each constructor, each constructor itself sets some of the properties for other constructors. A more efficient way would be for some constructors to call the other constructors to set some of the properties. That would prevent a duplication of code that does the same thing. The Contact class could be rewritten like this:

```
public class Contact
{
    //...

    //---first constructor---
    public Contact()
    {
        this.ID = 9999;
    }

    //---second constructor---
    public Contact(int ID)
    {
```

(continued)

(continued)

```
        this.ID = ID;
    }

    //---third constructor---
    public Contact(int ID, string FirstName, string LastName)
        : this(ID)
    {
        this.FirstName = FirstName;
        this.LastName = LastName;
    }

    //---fourth constructor---
    public Contact(int ID, string FirstName, string LastName, string Email)
        : this(ID,FirstName, LastName)
    {
        this.Email = Email;
    }
}
```

In this case, the fourth constructor is calling the third constructor using the `this` keyword. In addition, it is also passing in the arguments required by the third constructor. The third constructor in turn calls the second constructor. This process of one constructor calling another is call *constructor chaining*.

To prove that constructor chaining works, use the following statements:

```
Contact c1 = new Contact(1234, "Wei-Meng", "Lee", "weimenglee@learn2develop.net");
Console.WriteLine(c1.ID);          //---1234---
Console.WriteLine(c1.FirstName);   //----Wei-Meng---
Console.WriteLine(c1.LastName);    //---Lee---
Console.WriteLine(c1.Email);       //--- weimenglee@learn2develop.net---
```

To understand the sequence of the constructors that are called, insert the following highlighted statements:

```
class Contact
{
    //...

    //---first constructor---
    public Contact()
    {
        this.ID = 9999;
        Console.WriteLine("First constructor");
    }

    //---second constructor---
    public Contact(int ID)
    {
        this.ID = ID;
```

```
        Console.WriteLine("Second constructor");
    }

    //---third constructor---
    public Contact(int ID, string FirstName, string LastName)
        : this(ID)
    {
        this.FirstName = FirstName;
        this.LastName = LastName;
        Console.WriteLine("Third constructor");
    }

    //---fourth constructor---
    public Contact(int ID, string FirstName, string LastName, string Email)
        : this(ID, FirstName, LastName)
    {
        this.Email = Email;
        Console.WriteLine("Fourth constructor");
    }
}
```

The statement:

```
Contact c1 = new Contact(1234, "Wei-Meng", "Lee", "weimenglee@learn2develop.net");
```

prints the following output:

```
Second constructor
Third constructor
Fourth constructor
```

Static Constructors

If your class has static members, it is only sometimes necessary to initialize them before an object is created and used. In that case, you can add *static constructors* to the class. For example, suppose that the Contact class has a public static member count to record the number of the Contact object created. You can add a static constructor to initialize the static member, like this:

```
public class Contact
{
    //...
    public static int count;

    static Contact()
    {
        count = 0;
        Console.WriteLine("Static constructor");
    }

    //---first constructor---
```

(continued)

(continued)

```
    public Contact()
    {
        count++;
        Console.WriteLine("First constructor");
    }

    //...
}
```

When you now create instances of the Contact class, like this:

```
Contact c1 = new Contact();
Contact c2 = new Contact();
Console.WriteLine(Contact.count);
```

the static constructor is only called once, evident in the following output:

```
Static constructor
First constructor
First constructor
2
```

Note the behavior of static constructors:

- ❑ A static constructor does not take access modifiers or have parameters.
- ❑ A static constructor is called automatically to initialize the class before the first instance is created or any static members are referenced.
- ❑ A static constructor cannot be called directly.
- ❑ he user has no control on when the static constructor is executed in the program.

Copy Constructor

The C# language does not provide a copy constructor that allows you to copy the value of an existing object into a new object when it is created. Instead, you have to write your own.

The following copy constructor in the Contact class copies the values of the properties of an existing object (through the otherContact parameter) into the new object:

```
class Contact
{
    //...
    //---a copy constructor---
    public Contact(Contact otherContact)
    {
        this.ID = otherContact.ID;
        this.FirstName = otherContact.FirstName;
```

```
        this.LastName = otherContact.LastName;
        this.Email = otherContact.Email;
    }
    //...
}
```

To use the copy constructor, first create a `Contact` object:

```
Contact c1 = new Contact(1234, "Wei-Meng", "Lee",
                         "weimenglee@learn2develop.net");
```

Then, instantiate another `Contact` object and pass in the first object as the argument:

```
Contact c2 = new Contact(c1);
Console.WriteLine(c2.ID);        //---1234---
Console.WriteLine(c2.FirstName); //----Wei-Meng---
Console.WriteLine(c2.LastName);  //---Lee---
Console.WriteLine(c2.Email);     //--- weimenglee@learn2develop.net---
```

Object Initializers (C# 3.0)

Generally, there are two ways in which you can initialize an object — through its constructor(s) during instantiation or by setting its properties individually after instantiation. Using the `Contact` class defined in the previous section, here is one example of how to initialize a `Contact` object using its constructor:

```
Contact c1 = new Contact(1234, "Wei-Meng", "Lee", "weimenglee@learn2develop.net");
```

You can also set an object's properties explicitly:

```
Contact c1 = new Contact();
c1.ID = 1234;
c1.FirstName = "Wei-Meng";
c1.LastName = "Lee";
c1.Email = "weimenglee@learn2develop.net";
```

In C# 3.0, you have a third way of initializing objects — when they are instantiated. This feature is known as the *object initializers*. The following statement shows an example:

```
Contact c1 = new Contact()
    {
        ID = 1234,
        FirstName = "Wei-Meng",
        LastName = "Lee",
        Email = "weimenglee@learn2develop.net"
    };
```

Here, when instantiating a `Contact` class, you are also setting its properties directly using the `{ }` block. To use the object initializers, you instantiate an object using the `new` keyword and then enclose the properties that you want to initialize within the `{ }` block. You separate the properties using commas.

Do not confuse the object initializer with a class's constructor(s). You should continue to use the constructor (if it has one) to initialize an object. The following example shows that you use the `Contact`'s constructor to initialize the `ID` property and then the object initializers to initialize the rest of the properties:

```
Contact c2 = new Contact(1234)
    {
        FirstName = "Wei-Meng",
        LastName = "Lee",
        Email = "weimenglee@learn2develop.net"
    };
```

Destructors

In C#, a constructor is called automatically when an object is instantiated. When you are done with the object, the Common Language Runtime (CLR) will destroy them automatically, so you do not have to worry about cleaning them up. If you are using unmanaged resources, however, you need to free them up manually.

When objects are destroyed and cleaned up by the CLR, the object's *destructor* is called. A C# destructor is declared by using a tilde (~) followed by the class name:

```
class Contact : Object
{
    //---constructor---
    public Contact()
    {
        //...
    }

    //---destructor---
    ~Contact()
    {
        //---release unmanaged resources here---
    }
    //...
}
```

The destructor is a good place for you to place code that frees up unmanaged resources, such as COM objects or database handles. One important point is that you cannot call the destructor explicitly — it will be called automatically by the garbage collector.

To manually dispose of your unmanaged resources without waiting for the garbage collector, you can implement the `IDisposable` interface and the `Dispose()` method.

Chapter 5 discusses the concept of interfaces in more detail.

The following shows the `Contact` class implementing the `IDisposable` class and implementing the `Dispose()` method:

```
class Contact : IDisposable
{
    //...
    ~Contact()
    {
        //---call the Dispose() method---
        Dispose();
    }

    public void Dispose()
    {
        //---release unmanaged resources here---
    }
}
```

You can now manually dispose of unmanaged resources by calling the `Dispose()` method directly:

```
Contact c1 = new Contact();
//...
//---done with c1 and want to dispose it---
c1.Dispose();
```

There is now a call to the `Dispose()` method within the destructor, so you must make sure that the code in that method is safe to be called multiple times — manually by the user and also automatically by the garbage collector.

The Using Statement

C# provides a convenient syntax for automatically calling the `Dispose()` method, using the `using` keyword. In the following example, the `conn` object is only valid within the *using* block and will be disposed automatically after the execution of the block.

```
using System.Data.SqlClient;

...

using (SqlConnection conn = new SqlConnection())
{
    conn.ConnectionString = "...";
    //...
}
```

Using the `using` keyword is a good way for you to ensure that resources (especially COM objects and unmanaged code, which will not be unloaded automatically by the garbage collector in the CLR) are properly disposed of once they are no longer needed.

Static Classes

You can also apply the `static` keyword to class definitions. Consider the following `FilesUtil` class definition:

```
public class FilesUtil
{
    public static string ReadFile(string Filename)
    {
        //---implementation---
        return "file content...";
    }

    public static void WriteFile(string Filename, string content)
    {
        //---implementation---
    }
}
```

Within this class are two static methods — `ReadFile()` and `WriteFile()`. Because this class contains only static methods, creating an instance of this class is not very useful, as Figure 4-4 shows.

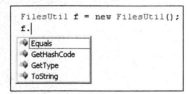

Figure 4-4

As shown in Figure 4-4, an instance of the `FilesUtil` class does not expose any of the static methods defined within it. Hence, if a class contains nothing except static methods and properties, you can simply declare the class as static, like this:

```
public static class FilesUtil
{
    public static string ReadFile(string Filename)
    {
        //---implementation---
        return "file content...";
    }

    public static void WriteFile(string Filename, string content)
    {
        //---implementation---
    }
}
```

The following statements show how to use the static class:

```
//---this is not allowed for static classes---
FilesUtil f = new FilesUtil();

//---these are OK---
Console.WriteLine(FilesUtil.ReadFile(@"C:\TextFile.txt"));
FilesUtil.WriteFile(@"C:\TextFile.txt", "Some text content to be written");
```

Use static classes when the methods in a class are not associated with a particular object. You need not create an instance of the static class before you can use it.

System.Object Class

In C#, all classes inherit from the `System.Object` base class (inheritance is discussed in the next chapter). This means that all classes contain the methods defined in the `System.Object` class.

All class definitions that do not inherit from other classes by default inherit directly from the `System.Object` class. The earlier `Contact` class definition:

```
public class Contact
```

for example, is equivalent to:

```
public class Contact: Object
```

You can create an instance of the `System.Object` class if you want, but it is by itself not terribly useful:

```
Object o = new object();
```

The `System.Object` class exposes four instance methods (see Figure 4-5):

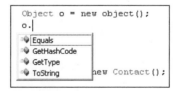

Figure 4-5

❑ `Equals()` — Checks whether the value of the current object is equal to that of another object. By default, the `Equals()` method checks for *reference equality* (that is, if two objects are pointing to the same object). You should override this method for your class.

❑ `GetHashCode()` — Returns a hash code for the class. The `GetHashCode()` method is suitable for use in hashing algorithms and data structures, such as a hash table. There will be more about hashing in Chapter 11

❑ `GetType()` — Returns the type of the current object

❑ `ToString()` — Returns the string representation of an object

In addition, the `System.Object` class also has two static methods (see Figure 4-6):

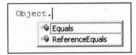

Figure 4-6

❑   `Equals()` — Returns true if the two objects are equal (see next section for more details)

❑   `ReferenceEquals()` — Returns true if two objects are from the same instance

All classes that inherit from `System.Object` also inherit all the four instance methods, a couple of which you will learn in more details in the following sections.

Testing for Equality

Consider the following three instances of the `Contact` class, which implicitly inherits from the `System`
`.Object` class:

```
Contact c1 = new Contact()
{
    ID = 1234,
    FirstName = "Wei-Meng",
    LastName = "Lee",
    Email = "weimenglee@learn2develop.net"
};

Contact c2 = new Contact()
{
    ID = 1234,
    FirstName = "Wei-Meng",
    LastName = "Lee",
    Email = "weimenglee@learn2develop.net"
};

Contact c3 = new Contact()
{
    ID = 4321,
    FirstName = "Lee",
    LastName = "Wei-Meng",
    Email = "weimenglee@gmail.com"
};
```

As you can see, c1 and c2 are identical in data member values, while c3 is different. Now, let's use the following statements to see how the Equals() and ReferenceEquals() methods work:

```
Console.WriteLine(c1.Equals(c2)); //---False---
Console.WriteLine(c1.Equals(c3)); //---False---
c3 = c1;
Console.WriteLine(c1.Equals(c3)); //---True---

Console.WriteLine(Object.ReferenceEquals(c1, c2)); //---False---
Console.WriteLine(Object.ReferenceEquals(c1, c3)); //---True---
```

The first statement might be a little surprising to you; did I not just mention that you can use the Equals() method to test for value equality?

```
Console.WriteLine(c1.Equals(c2)); //---False---
```

In this case, c1 and c2 have the exact same values for the members, so why does the Equals() method return False in this case? It turns out that the Equals() method must be overridden in the Contact class definition. This is because by itself, the System.Object class does not know how to test for the equality of your custom class; the Equals() method is a virtual method and needs to be overridden in derived classes. By default, the Equals() method tests for reference equality.

The second statement is straightforward, as c1 and c3 are two different objects:

```
Console.WriteLine(c1.Equals(c3)); //---False---
```

The third and fourth statements assign c1 to c3, which means that c1 and c3 are now two different variables pointing to the same object. Hence, Equals() returns True:

```
c3 = c1;
Console.WriteLine(c1.Equals(c3)); //---True---
```

The fifth and sixth statements test the reference equality of c1 against c2 and then c1 against c3:

```
Console.WriteLine(Object.ReferenceEquals(c1, c2)); //---False---
Console.WriteLine(Object.ReferenceEquals(c1, c3)); //---True---
```

> **If two objects have reference equality, they also have value equality, but the reverse is not necessarily true.**

Implementing Equals

By default the Equals() method tests for reference equality. To ensure that it tests for value equality rather than reference equality, you need to override the Equals() virtual method.

Using the same `Contact` class used in the previous section, add the methods highlighted in the following code:

```csharp
public class Contact
{
    public int ID;
    public string FirstName;
    public string LastName;
    public string Email;

    public override bool Equals(object obj)
    {
        //---check for null obj---
        if (obj == null) return false;

        //---see if obj can be cast to Contact---
        Contact c = obj as Contact;
        if ((System.Object)c == null) return false;

        //---check individual fields---
        return (ID == c.ID) && (FirstName == c.FirstName) &&
            (LastName == c.LastName) && (Email == c.Email);
    }

    public bool Equals(Contact c)
    {
        //---check for null obj---
        if (c == null) return false;

        //---check individual fields---
        return (ID == c.ID) && (FirstName == c.FirstName) &&
            (LastName == c.LastName) && (Email == c.Email);
    }

    public override int GetHashCode()
    {
        return ID;
    }
}
```

Essentially, you're adding the following:

- ❑ The `Equals(object obj)` method to override the `Equals()` virtual method in the `System.Object` class. This method takes in a generic object (`System.Object`) as argument.

- ❑ The `Equals(Contact c)` method to test for value equality. This method is similar to the first method, but it takes in a `Contact` object as argument.

- ❑ The `GetHashCode()` method to override the `GetHashCode()` virtual method in the `System.Object` class.

The as Keyword

In the `Equals(object obj)` method you saw the use of the as keyword:

```
Contact c = obj as Contact;
```

The as operator performs conversions between compatible types. In this case, it tries to cast the `obj` object into a `Contact` object. The as keyword is discussed in detail in Chapter 5.

Notice that the `Equals()` methods essentially performs the following to determine if two objects are equal in value:

- ❏ It checks whether the object passed is in `null`. If it is, it returns `false`.

- ❏ It checks whether the object passed is a `Contact` object (the second `Equals()` method need not check for this). If it isn't, it returns `false`.

- ❏ Last, it checks to see whether the individual members of the passed-in `Contact` object are of the same value as the members of the current object. Only when all the members have the same values (which members to test are determined by you) does the `Equals()` method return `true`. In this case, all the four members' values must be equal to the passed-in `Contact` object.

The following statement will now print out `True`:

```
Console.WriteLine(c1.Equals(c2)); //---True---
```

ToString() Method

All objects in C# inherits the `ToString()` method, which returns a string representation of the object. For example, the `DateTime` class's `ToString()` method returns a string containing the date and time, as the following shows:

```
DateTime dt = new DateTime(2008, 2, 29);
//---returns 2/29/2008 12:00:00 AM---
Console.WriteLine(dt.ToString());
```

For custom classes, you need to override the `ToString()` method to return the appropriate string. Using the example of the `Contact` class, an instance of the `Contact` class's `ToString()` method simply returns the string `"Contact"`:

```
Contact c1 = new Contact()
{
    ID = 1234,
    FirstName = "Wei-Meng",
    LastName = "Lee",
    Email = "weimenglee@learn2develop.net"
};

//---returns "Contact"---
Console.WriteLine(c1.ToString());
```

This is because the `ToString()` method from the `Contact` class inherits from the `System.Object` class, which simply returns the name of the class.

To ensure that the `ToString()` method returns something appropriate, you need to override it:

```
class Contact
{
    public int ID;
    public string FirstName;
    public string LastName;
    public string Email;

    public override string ToString()
    {
        return ID + "," + FirstName + "," +
            LastName + "," + Email;
    }
    //...
}
```

In this implementation of the `ToString()` method, you return the concatenation of the various data members, as evident in the output of the following code:

```
Contact c1 = new Contact()
{
    ID = 1234,
    FirstName = "Wei-Meng",
    LastName = "Lee",
    Email = "weimenglee@learn2develop.net"
};

//---returns "1234,Wei-Meng,Lee,weimenglee@learn2develop.net"---
Console.WriteLine(c1.ToString());
```

Attributes

Attributes are descriptive tags that can be used to provide additional information about types (classes), members, and properties. Attributes can be used by .NET to decide how to handle objects while an application is running.

There are two types of attributes:

❑ Attributes that are defined in the CLR.

❑ Custom attributes that you can define in your code.

CLR Attributes

Consider the following `Contact` class definition:

```csharp
class Contact
{
    public string FirstName;
    public string LastName;

    public void PrintName()
    {
        Console.WriteLine("{0} {1}", this.FirstName, this.LastName);
    }

    [Obsolete("This method is obsolete. Please use PrintName()")]
    public void PrintName(string FirstName, string LastName)
    {
        Console.WriteLine("{0} {1}", FirstName, LastName);
    }
}
```

Here, the `PrintName()` method is overloaded — once with no parameter and again with two input parameters. Notice that the second `PrintName()` method is prefixed with the `Obsolete` attribute:

```csharp
[Obsolete("This method is obsolete. Please use PrintName()")]
```

That basically marks the method as one that is not recommended for use. The class will still compile, but when you try to use this method, a warning will appear (see Figure 4-7).

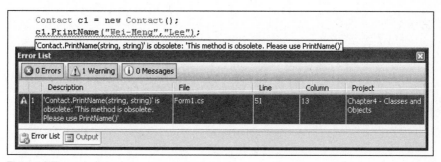

Figure 4-7

The `Obsolete` attribute is overloaded — if you pass in `true` for the second parameter, the message set in the first parameter will be displayed as an error (by default the message is displayed as a warning):

```csharp
[Obsolete("This method is obsolete. Please use PrintName()", true)]
```

Figure 4-8 shows the error message displayed when you use the `PrintName()` method marked with the `Obsolete` attribute with the second parameter set to `true`.

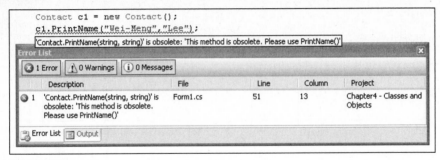

Figure 4-8

Attributes can also be applied to a class. In the following example, the Obsolete attribute is applied to the Contact class:

```
[Obsolete("This class is obsolete. Please use NewContact")]
class Contact
{
    //...
}
```

Custom Attributes

You can also define your own custom attributes. To do so, you just need to define a class that inherits directly from System.Attribute. The following Programmer class is one example of a custom attribute:

```
public class Programmer : System.Attribute
{
    private string _Name;
    public double Version;
    public string Dept { get; set; }
    public Programmer(string Name)
    {
        this._Name = Name;
    }
}
```

In this attribute, there are:

❑   One private member (_Name)

❑   One public member (Version)

❑   One constructor, which takes in one string argument

Here's how to apply the `Programmer` attribute to a class:

```
[Programmer("Wei-Meng Lee", Dept="IT", Version=1.5)]
class Contact
{
    //...
}
```

You can also apply the `Programmer` attribute to methods (as the following code shows), properties, structure, and so on:

```
[Programmer("Wei-Meng Lee", Dept="IT", Version=1.5)]
class Contact
{
    [Programmer("Jason", Dept = "CS", Version = 1.6)]
    public void PrintName()
    {
        Console.WriteLine("{0} {1}", this.FirstName, this.LastName);
    }
    //...
}
```

Use the `AttributeUsage` attribute to restrict the use of any attribute to certain types:

```
[System.AttributeUsage(System.AttributeTargets.Class |
                       System.AttributeTargets.Method |
                       System.AttributeTargets.Property)]
public class Programmer : System.Attribute
{
    private string _Name;
    public double Version;
    public string Dept { get; set; }
    public Programmer(string Name)
    {
        this._Name = Name;
    }
}
```

In this example, the `Programmer` attribute can only be used on class definitions, methods, and properties.

Structures

An alternative to using classes is to use a *struct* (for structure). A struct is a lightweight user-defined type that is very similar to a class, but with some exceptions:

- ❑ Structs do not support inheritance or destructors.

- ❑ A struct is a value type (class is a reference type).

- ❑ A struct cannot declare a default constructor.

Structs implicitly derive from `object` and unlike classes, a struct is a value type. This means that when an object is created from a struct and assigned to another variable, the variable will contain a copy of the struct object.

Like classes, structs support constructor, properties, and methods. The following code shows the definition for the `Coordinate` struct:

```
using System;
using System.Collections.Generic;
using System.ComponentModel;
using System.Data;
using System.Drawing;
using System.Linq;
using System.Text;
using System.Windows.Forms;

namespace WindowsFormsApplication1
{
    public partial class Form1 : Form
    {
        public Form1()
        {
            InitializeComponent();
        }
    }
}

public struct Coordinate
{
    public double latitude { get; set; }
    public double longitude { get; set; }
}
```

The `Coordinate` struct contains two properties (defined using the automatic properties feature). You can add a constructor to the struct if you want:

```
public struct Coordinate
{
    public double latitude { get; set; }
    public double longitude { get; set; }

    public Coordinate(double lat, double lng)
    {
        latitude = lat;
        longitude = lng;
    }
}
```

Remember, a struct cannot have a default constructor.

166

Note that the compiler will complain with the message "Backing field for automatically implemented property 'Coordinate.latitude' must be fully assigned before control is returned to the caller" when you try to compile this application. This restriction applies only to structs (classes won't have this problem). To resolve this, you need to call the default constructor of the struct, like this:

```
public struct Coordinate
{
    public double latitude { get; set; }
    public double longitude { get; set; }

    public Coordinate(double lat, double lng)
        : this()
    {
        latitude = lat;
        longitude = lng;
    }
}
```

You can also add methods to a struct. The following shows the ToString() method defined in the Coordinate struct:

```
public struct Coordinate
{
    public double latitude { get; set; }
    public double longitude { get; set; }

    public Coordinate(double lat, double lng)
        : this()
    {
        latitude = lat;
        longitude = lng;
    }

    public override string ToString()
    {
        return latitude + "," + longitude;
    }
}
```

To use the Coordinate struct, create a new instance using the new keyword and then initialize its individual properties:

```
public partial class Form1 : Form
{
    public Form1()
    {
        InitializeComponent();
    }

    private void Form1_Load(object sender, EventArgs e)
```

(continued)

(continued)

```
        {
            Coordinate pt1 = new Coordinate();
            pt1.latitude = 1.33463167;
            pt1.longitude = 103.74697;
        }
    }
```

Or you can use the object initializer feature:

```
    private void Form1_Load(object sender, EventArgs e)
    {
        //...
        Coordinate pt2 = new Coordinate()
        {
            latitude = 1.33463167,
            longitude = 103.74697
        };
    }
```

Because structs are value types, assigning one struct to another makes a copy of its value, as the following code sample shows:

```
    private void Form1_Load(object sender, EventArgs e)
    {
        //...
        Coordinate pt2 = new Coordinate()
        {
            latitude = 1.33463167,
            longitude = 103.74697
        };

        Coordinate pt3;
        pt3 = pt2;
        Console.WriteLine("After assigning pt2 to pt3");
        Console.WriteLine("pt2: {0}", pt2.ToString());
        Console.WriteLine("pt3: {0}", pt3.ToString());

        pt3.latitude = 1.45631234;
        pt3.longitude = 101.32355;

        Console.WriteLine("After changing pt3");
        Console.WriteLine("pt2: {0}", pt2.ToString());
        Console.WriteLine("pt3: {0}", pt3.ToString());
    }
```

Here's the program's output:

```
After assigning pt2 to pt3
pt2: 1.33463167,103.74697
pt3: 1.33463167,103.74697
After changing pt3
pt2: 1.33463167,103.74697
pt3: 1.45631234,101.32355
```

Notice that after changing the properties of pt3, the `latitude` and `longitude` properties of pt2 and pt3 are different.

Memory Allocation

When you use the `new` keyword to create an instance of a class, the object will be allocated on the heap. When using structs, the struct object is created on the stack instead. Because of this, using structs yields better performance gains. Also, when passing a struct to a method, note that it is passed by value instead of passed by reference.

In general, use classes when dealing with large collections of data. When you have smaller sets of data to deal with, using structs is more efficient.

Summary

This chapter explained how to define a class and the various components that make up a class — properties, methods, constructors, and destructors. In addition, it explored the new features in C# 3.0 — object initializers, anonymous types, and automatic properties. While you need to use the `new` keyword to instantiate a new object, you can also create static classes that can be used without instantiation. Finally, you saw how to use structs, the lightweight alternative to classes, that behave much like classes but are value types.

5

Interfaces

When defining a class, you have to provide the implementation for all its methods and properties. However, there are times when you do not want to provide the actual implementation of how a class might work. Rather, you want to describe the functionalities of the class. This set of descriptions is like a contract, dictating what the class will do, the types of parameters needed, and the type of return results. In object-oriented programming, this contract is known as an *interface*.

An interface defines a class and its members without providing any implementation. When using interfaces in programming, generally three parties are involved:

- ❑ **Interface definition** — The interface defines the composition of a class, such as methods, properties, and so on. However, the interface does not provide any implementation for any of these members.

- ❑ **Implementing class** — The class that implements a particular interface provides the implementation for all the members defined in that interface.

- ❑ **Clients** — Objects that instantiate from the implementing classes are known as the *client*. The client invokes the methods defined in the interface, whose implementation is provided by the implementing class.

Differences between an Interface and an Abstract Base Class

Conceptually, an abstract class is similar to an interface; however, they do have some subtle differences:

- ❑ An abstract class can contain a mixture of concrete methods (implemented) and abstract methods (an abstract class needs at least one abstract method); an interface does not contain any method implementations.

- ❑ An abstract class can contain constructors and destructors; an interface does not.

- ❑ A class can implement multiple interfaces, but it can inherit from only one abstract class.

This chapter explains how to define an interface and how to implement the interface using a class.

Defining an Interface

Defining an interface is similar to defining a class — you use the `interface` keyword followed by an identifier (the name of the interface) and then specify the interface body. For example:

```
interface IPerson
{
    string Name { get; set; }
    DateTime DateofBirth { get; set; }
    ushort Age();
}
```

Here you define the `IPerson` interface containing three members — two properties and one function. You do not use any access modifiers on interface members — they are implicitly `public`. That's because the real use of an interface is to define the publicly accessible members (such as methods and properties) of a class so that all implementing classes have the same public members. The implementation of each individual member is left to the implementing class.

The declaration for the `Name` property consists simply of `get` and `set` accessors without implementation:

```
string Name { get; set; }
```

And the `Age()` method simply contains its return type (and input parameters, if any) but without its implementation:

```
ushort Age();
```

It's important to note that you cannot create an instance of the interface directly; you can only instantiate a class that implements that interface:

```
//---error---
IPerson person = new IPerson();
```

Interface Naming Convention

By convention, begin the name of an interface with a capital I (such as `IPerson`, `IManager`, `IEmployee`, and so on) so that it is clear that you are dealing with an interface.

Implementing an Interface

Once an interface is defined, you can create a new class to implement it. The class that implements that particular interface must provide all the implementation for the members defined in that interface.

For example, here's an `Employee` class that implements the `IPerson` interface:

```
public class Employee : IPerson
{
    public string Name { get; set; }
    public DateTime DateofBirth { get; set; }
    public ushort Age()
    {
        return (ushort)(DateTime.Now.Year - this.DateofBirth.Year);
    }
}
```

To implement an interface, you define your class and add a colon (:) followed by the interface name:

```
public class Employee : IPerson
```

You then provide the implementation for the various members:

```
{
    public string Name { get; set; }
    public DateTime DateofBirth { get; set; }
    public ushort Age()
    {
        return (ushort)(DateTime.Now.Year - this.DateofBirth.Year);
    }
}
```

Notice that I'm using the new automatic properties feature (discussed in Chapter 4) in C# 3.0 to implement the Name *and* DateofBirth *properties. That's why the implementation looks the same as the declaration in the interface.*

As explained, all implemented members must have the `public` access modifiers.

You can now use the class as you would a normal class:

```
Employee e1 = new Employee();
e1.DateofBirth = new DateTime(1980, 7, 28);
e1.Name = "Janet";
Console.WriteLine(e1.Age());  //---prints out 28---
```

This could be rewritten using the new object initializer feature (also discussed in Chapter 4) in C# 3.0:

```
Employee e1 = new Employee() {
    DateofBirth = new DateTime(1980, 7, 28), Name = "Janet"
};
Console.WriteLine(e1.Age());  //---prints out 28---
```

Implementing Multiple Interfaces

A class can implement any number of interfaces. This makes sense because different interfaces can define different sets of behaviors (that is, members) and a class may exhibit all these different behaviors at the same time.

For example, the IPerson interface defines the basic information about a user, such as name and date of birth, while another interface such as IAddress can define a person's address information, such as street name and ZIP code:

```
interface IAddress
{
    string Street { get; set; }
    uint Zip { get; set; }
    string State();
}
```

An employee working in a company has personal information as well as personal address information, and you can define an Employee class that implements both interfaces, like this:

```
public class Employee : IPerson, IAddress
{
    //---implementation here---
}
```

The full implementation of the Employee class looks like this:

```
public class Employee : IPerson, IAddress
{
    //---IPerson---
    public string Name { get; set; }
    public DateTime DateofBirth { get; set; }
    public ushort Age()
    {
        return (ushort)(DateTime.Now.Year - this.DateofBirth.Year);
    }

    //---IAddress---
    public string Street { get; set; }
    public uint Zip { get; set; }
    public string State()
    {
        //---some implementation here---
        return "CA";
    }
}
```

You can now use the `Employee` class like this:

```
Employee e1 = new Employee()
{
    DateofBirth = new DateTime(1980, 7, 28),
    Name = "Janet",
    Zip = 123456,
    Street = "Kingston Street"
};
Console.WriteLine(e1.Age());
Console.WriteLine(e1.State());
```

Extending Interfaces

You can extend interfaces if you need to add new members to an existing interface. For example, you might want to define another interface named `IManager` to store information about managers. Basically, a manager uses the same members defined in the `IPerson` interface, with perhaps just one more additional property — `Dept`. In this case, you can define the `IManager` interface by extending the `IPerson` interface, like this:

```
interface IPerson
{
    string Name { get; set; }
    DateTime DateofBirth { get; set; }
    ushort Age();
}

interface IManager : IPerson
{
    string Dept { get; set; }
}
```

To use the `IManager` interface, you define a `Manager` class that implements the `IManager` interface, like this:

```
public class Manager : IManager
{
    //---IPerson---
    public string Name { get; set; }
    public DateTime DateofBirth { get; set; }
    public ushort Age()
    {
        return (ushort)(DateTime.Now.Year - this.DateofBirth.Year);
    }

    //---IManager---
    public string Dept { get; set; }
}
```

The `Manager` class now implements all the members defined in the `IPerson` interface, as well as the additional member defined in the `IManager` interface. You can use the `Manager` class like this:

```
Manager m1 = new Manager()
{
    Name = "John",
    DateofBirth = new DateTime(1970, 7, 28),
    Dept = "IT"
};
Console.WriteLine(m1.Age());
```

You can also extend multiple interfaces at the same time. The following example shows the `IManager` interface extending both the `IPerson` and the `IAddress` interfaces:

```
interface IManager : IPerson, IAddress
{
    string Dept { get; set; }
}
```

The `Manager` class now needs to implement the additional members defined in the `IAddress` interface:

```
public class Manager : IManager
{
    //---IPerson---
    public string Name { get; set; }
    public DateTime DateofBirth { get; set; }
    public ushort Age()
    {
        return (ushort)(DateTime.Now.Year - this.DateofBirth.Year);
    }

    //---IManager---
    public string Dept { get; set; }

    //---IAddress---
    public string Street { get; set; }
    public uint Zip { get; set; }
    public string State()
    {
        //---some implementation here---
        return "CA";
    }
}
```

You can now access the `Manager` class like this:

```
Manager m1 = new Manager()
{
    Name = "John",
    DateofBirth = new DateTime(1970, 7, 28),
    Dept = "IT",
```

```
            Street = "Kingston Street",
            Zip = 12345
    };
    Console.WriteLine(m1.Age());
    Console.WriteLine(m1.State());
```

Interface Casting

In the preceding example, the IManager interface extends both the IPerson and IAddress interfaces. So an instance of the Manager class (which implements the IManager interface) will contain members defined in both the IPerson and IAddress interfaces:

```
Manager m1 = new Manager()
{
    Name = "John",                         //---from IPerson---
    DateofBirth = new DateTime(1970, 7, 28), //---from IPerson---
    Dept = "IT",                           //---from IManager---
    Street = "Kingston Street",            //---from IAddress---
    Zip = 12345                            //---from IAddress---
};
Console.WriteLine(m1.Age());               //---from IPerson---
Console.WriteLine(m1.State());             //---from IAddress---
```

In addition to accessing the members of the Manager class through its instance (in this case m1), you can access the members through the interface that it implements. For example, since m1 is a Manager object that implements both the IPerson and IAddress interfaces, you can cast m1 to the IPerson interface and then assign it to a variable of type IPerson, like this:

```
//---cast to IPerson---
IPerson p = (IPerson) m1;
```

This is known as interface casting. Interface casting allows you to cast an object to one of its implemented interfaces and then access its members through that interface.

You can now access members (the Age() method and Name and DateofBirth properties) through p:

```
Console.WriteLine(p.Age());
Console.WriteLine(p.Name);
Console.WriteLine(p.DateofBirth);
```

Likewise, you can cast the m1 to the IAddress interface and then assign it to avariable to of type IAddress:

```
//---cast to IAddress---
IAddress a = (IAddress) m1;
Console.WriteLine(a.Street);
Console.WriteLine(a.Zip);
Console.WriteLine(a.State());
```

Note that instead of creating an instance of a class and then type casting it to an interface, like this:

```
Manager m2 = new Manager();
IPerson p = (IPerson) m2;
```

You can combine them into one statement:

```
IPerson p = (IPerson) new Manager();
```

The is and as Operators

Performing a direct cast is safe only if you are absolutely sure that the object you are casting implements the particular interface you are trying to assign to. Consider the following case where you have an instance of the Employee class:

```
Employee e1 = new Employee();
```

The Employee class implements the IPerson and IAddress interfaces. And so if you try to cast it to an instance of the IManager interface, you will get a runtime error:

```
//---Error: Invalid cast exception---
IManager m = (IManager) e1;
```

To ensure that the casting is done safely, use the is operator. The is operator checks whether an object is compatitble with a given type. It enables you to rewrite the casting as:

```
if (m1 is IPerson)
{
    IPerson p = (IPerson) m1;
    Console.WriteLine(p.Age());
    Console.WriteLine(p.Name);
    Console.WriteLine(p.DateofBirth);
}
```

```
if (m1 is IAddress)
{
    IAddress a = (IAddress) m1;
    Console.WriteLine(a.Street);
    Console.WriteLine(a.Zip);
    Console.WriteLine(a.State());
}
```

```
if (e1 is IManager)
{
    IManager m = (IManager) e1;
}
```

Using the is operator means that the compiler checks the type twice — once in the is statement and again when performing the actual casting. So this is actually not very efficient. A better way would be to use the as operator.

The as operator performs conversions between compatible types. Here's the preceding casting rewritten using the as operator:

```
IPerson p = m1 as IPerson;
if (p != null)
{
    Console.WriteLine(p.Age());
    Console.WriteLine(p.Name);
    Console.WriteLine(p.DateofBirth);
}

IAddress a = m1 as IAddress;
if (a != null)
{
    Console.WriteLine(a.Street);
    Console.WriteLine(a.Zip);
    Console.WriteLine(a.State());
}

Employee e1 = new Employee();
//---m is null after this statement---
IManager m = e1 as IManager;
if (m != null)
{
    //...
}
```

If the conversion fails, the as operator returns null, so you need to check for null before you actually use the instance of the interface.

Overriding Interface Implementations

When implementing an interface, you can mark any of the methods from the interface as virtual. For example, you can make the Age() method of the Employee class virtual so that any other classes that inherit from the Employee class can override its implementation:

```
public interface IPerson
{
    string Name { get; set; }
    DateTime DateofBirth { get; set; }
    ushort Age();
}

public class Employee : IPerson
{
    public string Name { get; set; }
    public DateTime DateofBirth { get; set; }
    public virtual ushort Age()
    {
        return (ushort)(DateTime.Now.Year - this.DateofBirth.Year);
    }
}
```

Suppose there is a new class called `Director` that inherits from the `Employee` class. The `Director` class can override the `Age()` method, like this:

```
public class Director : Employee
{
    public override ushort Age()
    {
        return base.Age() + 1;
    }
}
```

Notice that the `Age()` method increments the age returned by the base class by 1. To use the `Director` class, create an instance of it and set its date of birth as follows:

```
Director d = new Director();
d.DateofBirth = new DateTime(1970, 7, 28);
```

When you print out the age using the `Age()` method, you get 39 (2008 – 1970 = 38; increment it by 1 and the result is 39):

```
Console.WriteLine(d.Age()); //---39---
```

This proves that the overriden method in the `Age()` method is invoked. If you typecast d to the `IPerson` interface, assign it to an instance of the `IPerson` interface, and invoke the `Age()` method, it will still print out 39:

```
IPerson p = d as IPerson;
Console.WriteLine(p.Age());    //---39---
```

An interesting thing happens if, instead of overriding the `Age()` method in the `Director` class, you create a new `Age()` class using the `new` keyword:

```
public class Director : Employee
{
    public new ushort Age()
    {
        return (ushort)(base.Age() + 1);
    }
}
```

Create an instance of the `Director` class and invoke its `Age()` method; it returns 39, as the following statements show:

```
Director d = new Director();
d.DateofBirth = new DateTime(1970, 7, 28);
Console.WriteLine(d.Age()); //---39---
```

However, if you typecast d to an instance of the IPerson interface and then use that interface to invoke the Age() method, you get 38 instead:

```
IPerson p = d as IPerson;
Console.WriteLine(p.Age()); //---38---
```

What's happened is that the instance of the IPerson interface (p) uses the Age() method defined in the Employee class.

Summary

An interface defines the contract for a class — the various members that a class must have, the result returned for each method, and so on. However, an interface does not provide the implementation for a class; the actual implementation is left to the implementing classes. This chapter presented different ways in which you can work with interfaces — implementing multiple interfaces, extending interfaces, casting to an interface, and so forth.

6

Inheritance

Inheritance is one of the fundamental concepts in object-oriented programming. Inheritance facilitates code reuse and allows you to extend the functionality of code that you have already written. This chapter looks at:

❑   How inheritance works

❑   Implementing inheritance in C#

❑   Defining abstract methods and classes

❑   Sealing classes and methods

❑   Defining overloaded methods

❑   The different types of access modifiers you can use in inheritance

❑   Using inheritance in interfaces

Understanding Inheritance in C#

The following Employee class contains information about employees in a company:

```
public class Employee
{
    public string Name { get; set; }
    public DateTime DateofBirth { get; set; }
    public ushort Age()
    {
        return (ushort)(DateTime.Now.Year - this.DateofBirth.Year);
    }
}
```

`Manager` is a class containing information about managers:

```
public class Manager
{
    public string Name { get; set; }
    public DateTime DateofBirth { get; set; }
    public ushort Age()
    {
        return (ushort)(DateTime.Now.Year - this.DateofBirth.Year);
    }
    public Employee[] subordinates { get; set; }
}
```

The key difference between the `Manager` class and the `Employee` class is that `Manager` has an additional property, `subordinates`, that contains an array of employees under the supervision of a manager. In fact, a manager is actually an employee, except that he has some additional roles. In this example, the `Manager` class could *inherit* from the `Employee` class and then add the additional `subordinates` property that it requires, like this:

```
public class Manager: Employee
{
    public Employee[] subordinates { get; set; }
}
```

By inheriting from the `Employee` class, the Manager class has all the members defined in the `Employee` class made available to it. The relationships between the `Employee` and `Manager` classes can be represented using a class diagram as shown in Figure 6-1.

Figure 6-1

`Employee` is known as the *base class* and Manager is a *derived class*. In object-oriented programming, inheritance is classified into two types: implementation and interface. This chapter explores both.

Implementation Inheritance

Implementation inheritance is when a class derives from another base class, inheriting all the base class's members. To add new members to a class, you can define another class that derives from the existing base class. Using implementation inheritance, the new derived class inherits all of the implementation provided in the base class.

To understand how inheritance works in C#, define a simple class as follows:

```
public class Shape
{
    //---properties---
    public double length { get; set; }
    public double width { get; set; }
    //---method---
    public double Perimeter()
    {
        return 2 * (this.length + this.width);
    }
}
```

Here, the Shape class contains two properties and a single method. By itself, this class does not specify a particular shape, but it does assume that a basic shape contains length and width. It also assumes that the perimeter of a shape is simply double the sum of its length and width.

Using this base class, you can define other shapes such as square, rectangle, and circle. Let's start with the rectangle shape. Using Shape as the base class, you can define a Rectangle class (a derived class because it derives from the Shape class) by inheriting from the Shape class, like this:

```
public class Rectangle : Shape
{
}
```

In C#, you use the colon (:) operator to indicate that a class inherits from another class (known as the base class). This example reads: "The Rectangle class inherits from the Shape class." This means that whatever members the Shape class has are inherited by the Rectangle class. (In this example, the Rectangle class has no implementation; that will be added in the next few sections.)

C# supports only single-class inheritance, which means that a class can inherit directly from only one base class. If you do not specify the base class, the C# compiler assumes that it is inheriting from the System .Object class. Because the Shape class did not specify who it is inheriting from, it is equivalent to:

```
public class Shape : Object
{
    //---properties---
    public double length { get; set; }
    public double width { get; set; }

    //---method---
    public double Perimeter()
    {
        return 2 * (this.length + this.width);
    }
}
```

To use the Rectangle class, you instantiate it as you would other classes:

```
Rectangle r = new Rectangle();
```

Because the `Rectangle` class inherits all the members of the `Shape` class, you can access its members as if they are defined within the `Rectangle` class itself:

```
r.length = 4;
r.width = 5;
Console.WriteLine(r.Perimeter()); //---18---
```

Abstract Class

The `Shape` class does not specify a particular shape, and thus it really does not make sense for you to instantiate it directly, like this:

```
Shape someShape = new Shape();
```

Instead, all other shapes should inherit from this base class. To ensure that you cannot instantiate the `Shape` class directly, you can make it an *abstract* class by using the `abstract` keyword:

```
public abstract class Shape
{
    //---properties---
    public double length { get; set; }
    public double width { get; set; }

    //---method---
    public double Perimeter()
    {
        return 2 * (this.length + this.width);
    }
}
```

Once a class is defined as abstract, you can no longer instantiate it directly; the following is now not permitted:

```
//---cannot instantiate directly---
Shape someShape = new Shape();
```

The `abstract` keyword indicates that the class is defined solely for the purpose of inheritance; other classes need to inherit from it in order to have objects of this base type.

Abstract Methods

Besides making a class abstract by using the `abstract` keyword, you can also create *abstract methods*. An abstract method has no implementation, and its implementation is left to the classes that inherit from the class that defines it. Using the `Shape` class as an example, you can now define an abstract method called `Area()` that calculates the area of a shape:

```
public abstract class Shape
{
    //---properties---
    public double length { get; set; }
```

```
    public double width { get; set; }

    //---method---
    public double Perimeter()
    {
        return 2 * (this.length + this.width);
    }

    //---abstract method---
    public abstract double Area();
}
```

It is logical to make the `Area()` method an abstract one because at this point you don't really know what shape you are working on (circle, square, or triangle, for example), and thus you don't know how to calculate its area.

An abstract method is defined just like a normal method without the normal method block (`{}`). Classes that inherit from a class containing abstract methods must provide the implementation for those methods.

The `Rectangle` class defined earlier must now implement the `Area()` abstract method, using the `override` keyword:

```
public class Rectangle : Shape
{
    //---provide the implementation for the abstract method---
    public override double Area()
    {
        return this.length * this.width;
    }
}
```

Instead of using the `this` keyword to access the `length` and `width` properties, you can also use the `base` keyword:

```
public class Rectangle : Shape
{
    public override double  Area()
    {
        return base.length * base.width;
    }
}
```

The `base` keyword is used to access members (such as properties and variables) of the base class from within a derived class. You can also use the `base` keyword to access methods from the base class; here's an example:

```
public class Rectangle : Shape
{
    public override sealed double Area()
    {
        return this.length * this.width;
```

(continued)

(continued)

```
            //return base.length * base.width;
        }

        public override double Perimeter()
        {
            //---invokes the Perimeter() method in the Shape class---
            return base.Perimeter();
        }
    }
```

You can now use the `Rectangle` class like this:

```
Rectangle r = new Rectangle();
r.length = 4;
r.width = 5;
Console.WriteLine(r.Perimeter()); //---18---
Console.WriteLine(r.Area()); //---20---
```

An abstract method can only be defined in an abstract class.

The `base` keyword refers to the *parent class* of a derived class, *not* the root class. Consider the following example where you have three classes — `Class3` inherits from `Class2`, which in turn inherits from `Class1`:

```
public class Class1
{
    public virtual void PrintString()
    {
        Console.WriteLine("Class1");
    }
}

public class Class2: Class1
{
    public override void PrintString()
    {
        Console.WriteLine("Class2");
    }
}

public class Class3 : Class2
{
    public override void PrintString()
    {
        base.PrintString();
    }
}
```

In `Class3`, the `base.PrintString()` statement invokes the `PrintString()` method defined in its parent, `Class2`. The following statements verify this:

```
Class3 c3 = new Class3();
//---prints out "Class2"---
c3.PrintString();
```

Virtual Methods

Using the `Rectangle` class, you can find the perimeter and area of a rectangle with the `Perimeter()` and `Area()` methods, respectively. But what if you want to define a `Circle` class? Obviously, the perimeter (circumference) of a circle is not the length multiply by its width. For simplicity, though, let's assume that the diameter of a circle can be represented by the `Length` property.

The definition of `Circle` will look like this:

```
public class Circle : Shape
{
}
```

However, the `Perimeter()` method should be reimplemented as the circumference of a circle is defined to be 2*π*radius (or π*diameter). But the `Perimeter()` method has already been defined in the base class `Shape`. In this case, you need to indicate to the compiler that the `Perimeter()` method in the `Shape` class can be reimplemented by its derived class. To do so, you need to prefix the `Perimeter()` method with the `virtual` keyword to indicate that all derived classes have the option to change its implementation:

```
public abstract class Shape
{
    //---properties---
    public double length { get; set; }
    public double width { get; set; }

    //---make this method as virtual---
    public virtual double Perimeter()
    {
        return 2 * (this.length + this.width);
    }

    //---abstract method---
    public abstract double Area();
}
```

The `Circle` class now has to provide implementation for both the `Perimeter()` and `Area()` methods (note the use of the `override` keyword):

```
public class Circle : Shape
{
    //---provide the implementation for the abstract method---
    public override double Perimeter()
```

(continued)

(continued)

```
    {
        return Math.PI * (this.length);
    }

    //---provide the implementation for the virtual method---
    public override double Area()
    {
        return Math.PI * Math.Pow(this.length /2 ,2);
    }
}
```

Bear in mind that when overriding a method in the base class, the new method must have the same signature (parameter) as the overridden method. For example, the following is not allowed because the new `Perimeter()` method has a single input parameter, but this signature does not match that of the `Perimeter()` method defined in the base class (`Shape`):

```
public class Circle : Shape
{
    //---signature does not match Perimeter() in base class---
    public override double Perimeter(int Diameter)
    {
        //...
    }
}
```

If you need to implement another new method also called `Perimeter()` in the `Circle` class but with a different signature, use the `new` keyword, like this:

```
public class Circle : Shape
{
    //---a new Perimeter() method---
    public new double Perimeter(int diameter)
    {
        //...
    }
}
```

When a class has multiple methods each with the same name but a different signature (parameter), the methods are known as *overloaded*. The `Perimeter()` method of the `Circle` class is now overloaded (see Figure 6-2). Note that IntelliSense shows that the first method is from the `Shape` base class, while the second one is from the `Circle` class.

```
Circle c = new Circle();
c.Perimeter (|
▲1 of 2▼  double Shape.Perimeter ()

Circle c = new Circle();
c.Perimeter (
▲2 of 2▼  double Circle.Perimeter (int diameter)
```

Figure 6-2

See the "Overloading Methods" section later in this chapter.

Sealed Classes and Methods

So far you've seen the class definition for `Shape`, `Rectangle`, and `Circle`. Now let's define a class for the shape `Square`. As you know, a square is just a special version of rectangle; it just happens to have the same length and width. In this case, the `Square` class can simply inherit from the `Rectangle` class:

```
public class Square : Rectangle
{
}
```

You can instantiate the `Square` class as per normal and all the members available in the `Rectangle` would then be available to it:

```
Square s = new Square();
s.length = 5;
s.width = 5;
Console.WriteLine(s.Perimeter());   //---20---
Console.WriteLine(s.Area());        //---25---
```

To ensure that no other classes can derive from the `Square` class, you can *seal* it using the `sealed` keyword. A class prefixed with the `sealed` keyword prevents other classes inheriting from it. For example, if you seal the `Square` class, like this:

```
public sealed class Square : Rectangle
{
}
```

The following will result in an error:

```
//---Error: Square is sealed---
public class Rhombus : Square
{
}
```

A sealed class cannot contain virtual methods. In the following example, the `Square` class is sealed, so it cannot contain the virtual method called `Diagonal()`:

```
public sealed class Square : Rectangle
{
    //---Error: sealed class cannot contain virtual methods---
    public virtual Single Diagonal()
    {
        //---implementation here---
    }
}
```

This is logical because a sealed class does not provide an opportunity for a derived class to implement its virtual method. By the same argument, a sealed class also cannot contain abstract methods:

```
public sealed class Square : Rectangle
{
    //---Error: sealed class cannot contain abstract method---
    public abstract Single Diagonal();
}
```

You can also seal methods so that other derived classes cannot override the implementation that you have provided in the current class. For example, recall that the `Rectangle` class provides the implementation for the abstract `Area()` method defined in the `Shape` class:

```
public class Rectangle : Shape
{
    public override double Area()
    {
        return this.length * this.width;
    }
}
```

To prevent the derived classes of `Rectangle` (such as `Square`) from modifying the `Area()` implementation, prefix the method with the `sealed` keyword:

```
public class Rectangle : Shape
{
    public override sealed double Area()
    {
        return this.length * this.width;
    }
}
```

Now if you try to override the `Area()` method in the `Square` class, you get an error:

```
public  sealed class Square : Rectangle
{
    //---Error: Area() is sealed in Rectangle class---
    public override double Area()
    {
        //---implementation here---
    }
}
```

Overloading Methods

When you have multiple methods in a class having the same name but different signatures (parameters), they are known as *overloaded methods*. Consider the following class definition:

```
public class BaseClass
{
    public void Method(int num)
    {
        Console.WriteLine("Number in BaseClass is " + num);
    }

    public void Method(string st)
    {
        Console.WriteLine("String in BaseClass is " + st);
    }
}
```

Here, `BaseClass` has two methods called `Method()` with two different signatures — one `integer` and another one `string`.

When you create an instance of `BaseClass`, you can call `Method()` with either an integer or string argument and the compiler will automatically invoke the appropriate method:

```
BaseClass b = new BaseClass();

//---prints out: Number in BaseClass is 5---
b.Method(5);

//---prints out: String in BaseClass is This is a string---
b.Method("This is a string");
```

Suppose that you have another class inheriting from `BaseClass` with a `Method()` method that has a different signature, like this:

```
public class DerivedClass : BaseClass
{
    //---overloads the method---
    public void Method(char ch)
    {
        Console.WriteLine("Character in DerivedClass is " + ch);
    }
}
```

Then, `DerivedClass` now has three overloaded `Method()` methods, as illustrated in Figure 6-3.

```
DerivedClass d = new DerivedClass();
d.Method(
 ▲1 of 3▼  void DerivedClass.Method (char ch)


DerivedClass d = new DerivedClass();
d.Method(
 ▲2 of 3▼  void BaseClass.Method (int num)


DerivedClass d = new DerivedClass();
d.Method(
 ▲3 of 3▼  void BaseClass.Method (string st)
```

Figure 6-3

You can now pass three different types of arguments into `Method()` — character, integer, and string:

```
DerivedClass d = new DerivedClass();

//---prints out: Character in DerivedClass is C---
d.Method('C');

//---prints out: Number in BaseClass is 5---
d.Method(5);

//---prints out: String in BaseClass is This is a string---
d.Method("This is a string");
```

What happens if you have a `Method()` having the same signature as another one in the base class, such as the following?

```
public class DerivedClass : BaseClass
{
    //---overloads the method with the same parameter list---
    public void Method(int num)
    {
        Console.WriteLine("Number in DerivedClass is " + num);
    }

    //---overloads the method
    public void Method(char ch)
    {
        Console.WriteLine("Character in DerivedClass is " + ch);
    }
}
```

In this case, `Method(int num)` in `DerivedClass` will hide the same method in `BaseClass`, as the following printout proves:

```
DerivedClass d = new DerivedClass();

//---prints out: Number in DerivedClass is 5---
d.Method(5);

//---prints out: String in BaseClass is This is a string---
d.Method("This is a string");

//---prints out: Character in DerivedClass is C---
d.Method('C');
```

If hiding `Method(int num)` in `BaseClass` is your true intention, use the new keyword to denote that as follows (or else the compiler will issue a warning):

```
//---overloads the method with the same parameter list
public new void Method(int num)
{
    Console.WriteLine("Number in DerivedClass is " + num);
}
```

> In C#, you use the new keyword to hide methods in the base class by *signature*. C# does not support hiding methods by name as is possible in VB.NET by using the Shadows keyword.

The following table summarizes the different keywords used for inheritance.

Modifier	Description
new	Hides an inherited method with the same signature.
static	A member that belongs to the type itself and not to a specific object.
virtual	A method that can be overridden by a derived class.
abstract	Provides the signature of a method/class but does not contain any implementation.
override	Overrides an inherited virtual or abstract method.
sealed	A method that cannot be overridden by derived classes; a class that cannot be inherited by other classes.
extern	An "extern" method is one in which the implementation is provided elsewhere and is most commonly used to provide definitions for methods invoked using .NET interop.

Overloading Operators

Besides overloading methods, C# also supports the overloading of operators (such as +, -, /, and *). Operator overloading allows you to provide your own operator implementation for your specific type. To see how operator overloading works, consider the following program containing the Point class representing a point in a coordinate system:

```
using System;
using System.Collections.Generic;
using System.Linq;
using System.Text;

namespace OperatorOverloading
{
    class Program
    {
        static void Main(string[] args)
        {
        }
    }

    class Point
    {
        public Single X { get; set; }
        public Single Y { get; set; }

        public Point(Single X, Single Y)
        {
            this.X = X;
            this.Y = Y;
        }
```

(continued)

(continued)

```
        public double DistanceFromOrigin()
        {
            return (Math.Sqrt(Math.Pow(this.X, 2) + Math.Pow(this.Y, 2)));
        }
    }
}
```

The `Point` class contains two public properties (`X` and `Y`), a constructor, and a method — `DistanceFromOrigin()`.

If you constantly perform calculations where you need to add the distances of two points (from the origin), your code may look like this:

```
static void Main(string[] args)
{
    Point ptA = new Point(4, 5);
    Point ptB = new Point(2, 7);

    double distanceA, distanceB;

    distanceA = ptA.DistanceFromOrigin(); //---6.40312423743285---
    distanceB = ptB.DistanceFromOrigin(); //---7.28010988928052---

    Console.WriteLine(distanceA + distanceB);   //---13.6832341267134---

    Console.ReadLine();
}
```

A much better implementation is to overload the + operator for use with the `Point` class. To overload the + operator, define a public static operator within the `Point` class as follows:

```
class Point
{
    public Single X { get; set; }
    public Single Y { get; set; }

    public Point(Single X, Single Y)
    {
        this.X = X;
        this.Y = Y;
    }
    public double DistanceFromOrigin()
    {
        return (Math.Sqrt(Math.Pow(this.X, 2) + Math.Pow(this.Y, 2)));
    }

    public static double operator +(Point A, Point B)
    {
        return (A.DistanceFromOrigin() + B.DistanceFromOrigin());
    }
}
```

The `operator` keyword overloads a built-in operator. In this example, the overloaded + operator allows it to "add" two `Point` objects by adding the result of their `DistanceFromOrigin()` methods:

```
static void Main(string[] args)
{
    Point ptA = new Point(4, 5);
    Point ptB = new Point(2, 7);

    Console.WriteLine(ptA + ptB);   //---13.6832341267134---
    Console.ReadLine();
}
```

You can also use the `operator` keyword to define a conversion operator, as the following example shows:

```
class Point
{
    public Single X { get; set; }
    public Single Y { get; set; }

    public Point(Single X, Single Y)
    {
        this.X = X;
        this.Y = Y;
    }
    public double DistanceFromOrigin()
    {
        return (Math.Sqrt(Math.Pow(this.X, 2) + Math.Pow(this.Y, 2)));
    }

    public static double operator +(Point A, Point B)
    {
        return (A.DistanceFromOrigin() + B.DistanceFromOrigin());
    }

    public static implicit operator double(Point pt)
    {
        return (pt.X / pt.Y);
    }
}
```

Here, the `implicit` keyword indicates that you want to implicitly perform a conversion of the `Point` class to a `double` value (this value is defined to be the ratio of the X and Y coordinates).

Now when you assign a `Point` object to a double variable, the ratio of the X and Y coordinates is assigned automatically, as the following statements prove:

```
static void Main(string[] args)
{
    Point ptA = new Point(4, 5);
    Point ptB = new Point(2, 7);

    double ratio = ptA;   //---implicitly convert to a double type---
```

(continued)

(continued)

```
          ptB = ptA;              //---assign to another Point object---
          Console.WriteLine(ratio);      //---0.8---
          Console.WriteLine((double)ptB); //---0.8---

      Console.ReadLine();
   }
```

Extension Methods (C# 3.0)

Whenever you add additional methods to a class in previous versions of C#, you need to subclass it and then add the required method. For example, consider the following predefined (meaning you cannot modify it) classes:

```
public abstract class Shape
{
    //---properties---
    public double length { get; set; }
    public double width { get; set; }

    //---make this method as virtual---
    public virtual double Perimeter()
    {
        return 2 * (this.length + this.width);
    }

    //---abstract method---
    public abstract double Area();
}

public class Rectangle : Shape
{
    public override sealed double Area()
    {
        return this.length * this.width;
    }
}
```

The only way to add a new method `Diagonal()` to the `Rectangle` class is to create a new class that derives from it, like this:

```
public class NewRectangle : Rectangle
{
    public double Diagonal()
    {
        return Math.Sqrt(Math.Pow(this.length, 2) + Math.Pow(this.width, 2));
    }
}
```

In C# 3.0, you just use the new *extension method* feature to add a new method to an existing type. To add the `Diagonal()` method to the existing `Rectangle` class, define a new static class and define the extension method (a static method) within it, like this:

```
public static class MethodsExtensions
{
    public static double Diagonal(this Rectangle rect)
    {
        return Math.Sqrt(Math.Pow(rect.length, 2) + Math.Pow(rect.width, 2));
    }
}
```

In this example, `Diagonal()` is the extension method that is added to the `Rectangle` class. You can use the `Diagonal()` method just like a method from the `Rectangle` class:

```
Rectangle r = new Rectangle();
r.length = 4;
r.width = 5;
//---prints out: 6.40312423743285---
Console.WriteLine(r.Diagonal());
```

The first parameter of an extension method is prefixed by the `this` keyword, followed by the type it is extending (`Rectangle` in this example, indicating to the compiler that this extension method must be added to the `Rectangle` class). The rest of the parameter list (if any) is then the signature of the extension method. For example, to pass additional parameters into the `Diagonal()` extension method, you can declare it as:

```
public static double Diagonal(this Rectangle rect, int x, int y)
{
    //---additional implementation here---
    return Math.Sqrt(Math.Pow(rect.length, 2) + Math.Pow(rect.width, 2));
}
```

To call this modified extension method, simply pass in two arguments, like this:

```
Console.WriteLine(r.Diagonal(3,4));
```

Figure 6-4 shows IntelliSense providing a hint on the parameter list.

```
Rectangle r = new Rectangle();
r.length = 4;
r.breadth = 5;
Console.WriteLine(r.Area());
Console.WriteLine(r.Diagonal(
                  (extension) double Rectangle.Diagonal (int x, int y)
```

Figure 6-4

Although an extension method is a useful new feature in the C# language, use it sparingly. If an extension method has the same signature as another method in the class it is trying to extend, the method in the class will take precedence and the extension method will be ignored.

Access Modifiers

Chapter 4 discussed two primary access modifiers — `public` and `private`, and introduced two others: `protected` and `internal`. Let's take a look at how the latter are used. Consider the following class definition:

```
public class A
{
    private int v;
    public int w;
    protected int x;
    internal int y;
    protected internal int z;
}
```

The A class has four data members, each with a different access modifiers. The fifth data member, z, has a combination of two access modifiers — `protected` and `internal`. To see the difference between all these different modifiers, create an instance of A and observe the members displayed by IntelliSense.

Figure 6-5 shows that only the variables w, y, and z are accessible.

Figure 6-5

At this moment, you can conclude that:

❑   The `private` keyword indicates that the member is not visible outside the type (class).

❑   The `public` keyword indicates that the member is visible outside the type (class).

❑   The `protected` keyword indicates that the member is not visible outside the type (class).

❑   The `internal` keyword indicates that the member is visible outside the type (class).

❑   The `protected internal` keyword combination indicates that the member is visible outside the type (class).

Now define a second class, B, that inherits from class A:

```
public class B : A
{
    public void Method()
    {

    }
}
```

Try to access the class A variables from within Method(). In Figure 6-6, IntelliSense shows the variables that are accessible.

```
public class A
{
    private int v;
    public int w;
    protected int x;
    internal int y;
    protected internal int z;
}

public class B : A
{
    public void Method()
    {
        base.|
    }                Equals
}                    GetHashCode
                     GetType
                     MemberwiseClone
                     ToString
                     w
                     x
                     y
                     z
```

Figure 6-6

As you can see, member x is now visible (in addition to w, y, and z), so you can conclude that:

❑ The private keyword indicates that the member is not visible outside the type (class) or to any derived classes.

❑ The public keyword indicates that the member is visible outside the type (class) and to all derived classes.

❑ The protected keyword indicates that the member is not visible outside the type (class) but is visible to any derived classes.

❑ The internal keyword indicates that the member is visible outside the type (class) as well as to all derived classes.

❑ The protected internal keyword combination indicates that the item is visible outside the type (class) as well as to all derived classes.

From these conclusions, the difference among private, public, and protected is obvious. However, there is no conclusive difference between internal and protected internal. The internal access modifier indicates that the member is only visible within its containing assembly. The protected internal keyword combination indicates that the member is visible to any code within its containing assembly as well as derived types.

Besides applying the access modifiers to data members, you can also use them on type definitions. However, you can only use the private and public access modifiers on class definitions.

Inheritance and Constructors

Consider the following `BaseClass` definition consisting of one default constructor:

```
public class BaseClass
{
    //---default constructor---
    public BaseClass()
    {
        Console.WriteLine("Constructor in BaseClass");
    }
}
```

Anther class, `DerivedClass` inheriting from the `BaseClass`, also has a default constructor:

```
public class DerivedClass : BaseClass
{
    //---default constructor---
    public DerivedClass()
    {
        Console.WriteLine("Constructor in DerivedClass");
    }
}
```

So when an object of `DerivedClass` is instantiated, which constructor will be invoked first? The following statement shows that the constructor in the base class will be invoked before the constructor in the current class will be invoked:

```
DerivedClass dc = new DerivedClass();
```

The outputs are:

```
Constructor in BaseClass
Constructor in DerivedClass
```

What happens if there is no default constructor in the base class, but perhaps a parameterized constructor like the following?

```
public class BaseClass
{
    //---constructor---
    public BaseClass(int x)
    {
        Console.WriteLine("Constructor in BaseClass");
    }
}
```

In that case, the compiler will complain that `BaseClass` does not contain a default constructor.

> **Remember that if a base class contains constructors, one of them must be a default constructor.**

Calling Base Class Constructors

Suppose `BaseClass` contains two constructors — one default and one parameterized:

```
public class BaseClass
{
    //---default constructor---
    public BaseClass()
    {
        Console.WriteLine("Default constructor in BaseClass");
    }

    //---parameterized constructor---
    public BaseClass(int x)
    {
        Console.WriteLine("Parameterized Constructor in BaseClass");
    }
}
```

And `DerivedClass` contains one default constructor:

```
public class DerivedClass : BaseClass
{
    //---default constructor---
    public DerivedClass()
    {
        Console.WriteLine("Constructor in DerivedClass");
    }
}
```

When an instance of the `DerivedClass` is created like this:

```
DerivedClass dc = new DerivedClass();
```

The default constructor in `BaseClass` is first invoked followed by the `DerivedClass`. However, you can choose which constructor you want to invoke in `BaseClass` by using the `base` keyword in the default constructor in `DerivedClass`, like this:

```
public class DerivedClass : BaseClass
{
    //---default constructor---
    public DerivedClass(): base(4)
    {
        Console.WriteLine("Constructor in DerivedClass");
    }
}
```

In this example, when an instance of the `DerivedClass` is created, the parameterized constructor in `BaseClass` is invoked first (with the argument 4 passed in), followed by the default constructor in `DerivedClass`. This is shown in the output:

```
DerivedClass dc = new DerivedClass();
//---prints out:---
 //Parameterized Constructor in BaseClass
//Constructor in DerivedClass
```

203

Figure 6-7 shows that IntelliSense lists the overloaded constructors in BaseClass.

```
public class DerivedClass : BaseClass
{
    //---default constructor---
    public DerivedClass(): base(
    {                         [ 1 of 2   BaseClass.BaseClass () ]
        Console.WriteLine("Constructor in DerivedClass");
    }
}
```

```
public class DerivedClass : BaseClass
{
    //---default constructor---
    public DerivedClass(): base(
    {                         [ 2 of 2   BaseClass.BaseClass (int x) ]
        Console.WriteLine("Constructor in DerivedClass");
    }
}
```

Figure 6-7

Interface Inheritance

When an interface inherits from a base interface, it inherits all the base interface's functions' signatures (but no implementation).

Let's explore the concept of interface inheritance by using the hierarchy of various classes defined earlier in the chapter, starting from the root class Shape, with the Circle and Rectangle classes inheriting from it (the Square class in turn inherits from the Rectangle class), as Figure 6-8 shows.

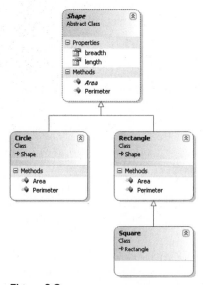

Figure 6-8

One problem with this class hierarchy is that for the Circle class, using the inherited length property to represent the diameter is a bit awkward. Likewise, for the Square class the width property should not be visible because the length and width of a square are the same. Hence, these classes could be better rearranged.

As you recall from Chapter 5, you can use an interface to define the signature of a class's members. Likewise, you can use interfaces to define the hierarchy of a set of classes. If you do so, developers who implement this set of classes will have to follow the rules as defined in the interfaces.

You can use interfaces to redefine the existing classes, as shown in Figure 6-9.

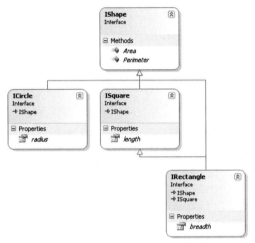

Figure 6-9

Here, the IShape interface contains two methods — Area() and Perimeter():

```
public interface IShape
{
    //---methods---
    double Perimeter();
    double Area();
}
```

Remember, an interface simply defines the members in a class; it does not contain any implementation. Also, there is no modifier (like virtual or abstract) prefixing the function members here, so you need not worry about the implementation of the Perimeter() and Area() methods — they could be implemented by other derived classes.

The ICircle interface inherits from the IShape interface and defines an additional radius property:

```
public interface ICircle : IShape
{
    //---property---
    double radius { get; set; }
}
```

The ISquare interface inherits from the IShape interface and defines an additional length property:

```
public interface ISquare : IShape
{
    //---property---
    double length { get; set; }
}
```

The IRectangle interface inherits from both the IShape and ISquare interfaces. In addition, it also defines a width property:

```
public interface IRectangle : IShape, ISquare
{
    //---property---
    double width { get; set; }
}
```

So what does the implementation of these interfaces look like? First, implement the ISquare interface, like this:

```
public class Square : ISquare
{
    //---property---
    public double length { get; set; }

    //---methods---
    public double Perimeter()
    {
        return 4 * (this.length);
    }

    public double Area()
    {
        return (Math.Pow(this.length, 2));
    }
}
```

Here, you provide the implementation for the length property as well as the two methods — Perimeter() and Area().

You not need to implement the IShape class because you can't provide any meaningful implementation of the Area() and Perimeter() methods here.

Because the IRectangle interface inherits from both the ISquare and IShape interfaces and the ISquare interface has already been implemented (by the Square class), you can simply inherit from the Square class and implement the IRectangle interface, like this:

```
public class Rectangle : Square, IRectangle
{
    //---property---
    public double width { get; set; }
}
```

> If you implement the `IRectangle` interface directly (without inheriting from the `Square` class, you need to provide the implementation of the `length` property as well as the methods `Perimeter()` and `Area()`.

You need only provide the implementation for the `width` property here. The implementation for the `Area()` and `Perimeter()` methods is inherited from the `Square` class.

The last implementation is the `ICircle` interface, for which you will implement the `radius` property as well as the `Perimeter()` and `Area()` methods:

```
public class Circle : ICircle
{
    public double radius { get; set; }
    public double Perimeter()
    {
        return (2 * Math.PI * (this.radius));
    }

    //---provide the implementation for the virtual method---
    public double Area()
    {
        return (Math.PI * Math.Pow(this.radius, 2));
    }
}
```

Figure 6-10 shows the classes that you have implemented for these three interfaces.

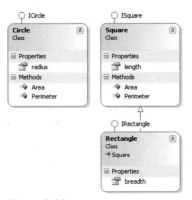

Figure 6-10

Explicit Interface Members Implementation

A class can implement one or more interfaces. To implement a member in an interface, you simply need to match the member name and its signature with the one defined in the interface. However, there are times when two interfaces may have the same member name and signature. Here's an example:

```
public interface IFileLogging
{
    void LogError(string str);
}

public interface IConsoleLogging
{
    void LogError(string str);
}
```

In this example, both IFileLogging and IConsoleLogging have the same LogError() method. Suppose that you have a class named Calculation that implements both interfaces:

```
public class Calculation : IFileLogging, IConsoleLogging
{

}
```

The implementation of the LogError() method may look like this:

```
public class Calculation : IFileLogging, IConsoleLogging
{
    //---common to both interfaces---
    public void LogError(string str)
    {
        Console.WriteLine(str);
    }
}
```

In this case, the LogError() method implementation will be common to both interfaces and you can invoke it via an instance of the Calculation class:

```
Calculation c = new Calculation();
//---prints out: Some error message here---
c.LogError("Some error message here");
```

In some cases, you need to differentiate between the two methods in the two interfaces. For example, the LogError() method in the IFileLogging interface may write the error message into a text file, while the LogError() method in the IConsoleLogging interface may write the error message into the console window. In that case, you must explicitly implement the LogError() method in each of the two interfaces. Here's how:

```
public class Calculation : IFileLogging, IConsoleLogging
{
    //---common to both interfaces---
    public void LogError(string str)
```

```
    {
        Console.WriteLine(str);
    }

    //---only available to the IFileLogging interface---
    void IFileLogging.LogError(string str)
    {
        Console.WriteLine("In IFileLogging: " + str);
    }

    //---only available to the IConsoleLogging interface---
    void IConsoleLogging.LogError(string str)
    {
        Console.WriteLine("In IConsoleLogging: " + str);
    }
}
```

This example has three implementations of the `LogError()` method:

❑ One common to both interfaces that can be accessed via an instance of the `Calculation` class.

❑ One specific to the `IFileLogging` interface that can be accessed only via an instance of the `IFileLogging` interface.

❑ One specific to the `IConsoleLogging` interface that can be accessed only via an instance of the `IConsoleLogging` interface.

> **You cannot use the `public` access modifier on the explicit interface methods' implementation.**

To invoke these implementations of the `LogError()` method, use the following statements:

```
//---create an instance of Calculation---
Calculation c = new Calculation();

//---prints out: Some error message here---
c.LogError("Some error message here");

//---create an instance of IFileLogging---
IFileLogging f = c;
//---prints out: In IFileLogging: Some error message here---
f.LogError("Some error message here");

//---create an instance of IConsoleLogging---
IConsoleLogging l = c;
//---prints out: In IConsoleLogging: Some error message here---
l.LogError("Some error message here");
```

Another use of explicit interface member implementation occurs when two interfaces have the same method name but different signatures. For example:

```
public interface IFileLogging
{
    void LogError(string str);
}

public interface IConsoleLogging
{
    void LogError();
}
```

Here, the LogError() method in the IFileLogging interface has a string input parameter, while there is no parameter in the IConsoleLogging interface. When you now implement the two interfaces, you can provide two overloaded LogError() methods, together with an implementation specific to each interface as illustrated here:

```
public class Calculation : IFileLogging, IConsoleLogging
{
    //---common to both interfaces---
    public void LogError(string str)
    {
        Console.WriteLine("In LogError(str): " + str);
    }
    public void LogError()
    {
        Console.WriteLine("In LogError()");
    }

    //---only available to the IFileLogging interface---
    void IFileLogging.LogError(string str)
    {
        Console.WriteLine("In IFileLogging: " + str);
    }

    //---only available to the IConsoleLogging interface---
    void IConsoleLogging.LogError()
    {
        Console.WriteLine("In IConsoleLogging");
    }
}
```

As you can see , the first two LogError() methods are overloaded and are common to both interfaces. This means that you can access them via an instance of the Calculation class. The next two implementations are specific to the IFileLogging and IConsoleLogging interfaces and can be accessed only via an instance of each interface:

```
//---create an instance of Calculation---
Calculation c = new Calculation();

//---prints out: In LogError()---
```

```
c.LogError();

//---prints out: In LogError(str)---
c.LogError("Some error message here");

//---create an instance of IFileLogging---
IFileLogging f = c;
//---prints out: In IFileLogging: Some error message here---
f.LogError("Some error message here");

//---create an instance of IConsoleLogging---
IConsoleLogging l = c;
//---prints out: In IConsoleLogging---
l.LogError();
```

Abstract Classes versus Interfaces

An abstract class defines the members and optionally provides the implementations of each member. Members that are not implemented in the abstract class must be implemented by classes that inherit from it.

An interface, on the other hand, defines the signatures of members but does not provide any implementation. All the implementations must be provided by classes that implement it.

So which one should you use? There are no hard-and-fast rules, but here are a couple of points to note:

❑ You can add additional members to classes as and when needed. In contrast, once an interface is defined (and implemented by classes), adding additional members will break existing code.

❑ Classes support only single-inheritance but can implement multiple interfaces. So if you need to define multiple contracts (rules) for a type, it is always better to use an interface.

Summary

This chapter explained how inheritance works in C# and the types of inheritances available — implementation and interface. One important topic covered in this chapter is that of abstract class versus interface, both of which have their uses in C#.

The chapter also described how you can provide overloaded methods and operators, as well as add capabilities to a class without deriving from it by using the extension method feature new in C# 3.0.

7

Delegates and Events

Two of the most important aspects of object-oriented programming are delegates and events. A delegate basically enables you to reference a function without directly invoking the function. Delegates are often used to implement techniques called callbacks, which means that after a function has finished execution, a call is made to a specific function to inform it that the execution has completed. In addition, delegates are also used in event handling. Despite the usefulness of delegates, it is a topic that not all .NET programmers are familiar with. An event, on the other hand, is used by classes to notify clients when something of interest has happened. For example, a `Button` control has the `Click` even, which allows your program to be notified when someone clicks the button.

This chapter explores the following:

- ❑   What is a delegate?
- ❑   Using delegates
- ❑   Implementing callbacks using a delegate
- ❑   What are events?
- ❑   How to handle and implement events in your program

Delegates

In C#, a delegate is a reference type that contains a reference to a method. Think of a delegate as a pointer to a function. Instead of calling a function directly, you use a delegate to point to it and then invoke the method by calling the delegate. The following sections explain how to use a delegate and how it can help improve the responsiveness of your application.

Creating a Delegate

To understand the use of delegates, begin by looking at the conventional way of invoking a function. Consider the following program:

```
using System;
using System.Collections.Generic;
using System.Linq;
using System.Text;

namespace Delegates
{
    class Program
    {
        static void Main(string[] args)
        {
            int num1 = 5;
            int num2 = 3;
            Console.WriteLine(Add(num1, num2).ToString());
            Console.WriteLine(Subtract(num1, num2).ToString());
            Console.ReadLine();
        }

        static int Add(int num1, int num2)
        {
            return (num1 + num2);
        }

        static int Subtract(int num1, int num2)
        {
            return (num1 - num2);
        }
    }
}
```

The program contains three methods: `Main()`, `Add()`, and `Subtract()`. Notice that the `Add()` and `Subtract()` methods have the same signature. In the `Main()` method, you invoke the `Add()` and `Subtract()` methods by calling them directly, like this:

```
Console.WriteLine(Add(num1, num2).ToString());
Console.WriteLine(Subtract(num1, num2).ToString());
```

Now create a delegate type with the same signature as the `Add()` method:

```
namespace Delegates
{
    class Program
    {
        delegate int MethodDelegate(int num1, int num2);

        static void Main(string[] args)
        {
            ...
```

You define a delegate type by using the `delegate` keyword, and its declaration is similar to that of a function, except that a delegate has no function body.

To make a delegate object point to a function, you create an object of that delegate type (`MethodDelegate`, in this case) and instantiate it with the method you want to point to, like this:

```
static void Main(string[] args)
{
    int num1 = 5;
    int num2 = 3;
    MethodDelegate method = new MethodDelegate(Add);
```

Alternatively, you can also assign the function name to it directly, like this:

```
MethodDelegate method = Add;
```

This statement declares `method` to be a delegate that points to the `Add()` method. Hence instead of calling the `Add()` method directly, you can now call it using the `method` delegate:

```
//---Console.WriteLine(Add(num1, num2).ToString());---
Console.WriteLine(method(num1, num2).ToString());
```

The beauty of delegates is that you can make the delegate call whatever function it refers to, without knowing exactly which function it is calling until runtime. Any function can be pointed by the delegate, as long as the function's signature matches the delegate's.

For example, the following statements check the value of the `Operation` variable before deciding which method the `method` delegate to point to:

```
char Operation = 'A';
MethodDelegate method = null;
switch (Operation)
{
    case 'A': method = new MethodDelegate(Add);
        break;
    case 'S': method = new MethodDelegate(Subtract);
        break;
}
if (method != null)
    Console.WriteLine(method(num1, num2).ToString());
```

You can also pass a delegate to a method as a parameter, as the following example shows:

```
using System;
using System.Collections.Generic;
using System.Linq;
using System.Text;

namespace Delegates
{
    class Program
    {
        delegate int MethodDelegate(int num1, int num2);

        static void PerformMathOps(MethodDelegate method, int num1, int num2)
        {
            Console.WriteLine(method(num1, num2).ToString());
        }

        static void Main(string[] args)
        {
            int num1 = 5;
            int num2 = 3;
            char Operation = 'A';

            MethodDelegate method = null;
            switch (Operation)
            {
                case 'A': method = new MethodDelegate(Add);
                    break;
                case 'S': method = new MethodDelegate(Subtract);
                    break;
            }
            if (method != null)
                PerformMathOps(method, num1, num2);

            Console.ReadLine();
        }

        static int Add(int num1, int num2)
        {
            return (num1 + num2);
        }

        static int Subtract(int num1, int num2)
        {
            return (num1 - num2);
        }
    }
}
```

In this example, the PerformMathOps() function takes in three arguments — a delegate of type MethodDelegate and two integer values. Which method to invoke is determined by the Operation variable. Once the delegate is assigned to point to a method (Add() or Subtract()), it is passed to the PerformMathOps() method.

Delegates Chaining (Multicast Delegates)

In the previous section, a delegate pointed to a single function. In fact, you can make a delegate point to multiple functions. This is known as *delegates chaining*. Delegates that point to multiple functions are known as *multicast delegates*.

Consider the following example:

```
using System;
using System.Collections.Generic;
using System.Linq;
using System.Text;

namespace Delegates
{
    class Program
    {
        delegate void MethodsDelegate();

        static void Main(string[] args)
        {
            MethodsDelegate methods = Method1;
            methods += Method2;
            methods += Method3;

            //---call the delegated method(s)---
            methods();
            Console.ReadLine();
        }

        static private void Method1()
        {
            Console.WriteLine("Method 1");
        }

        static private void Method2()
        {
            Console.WriteLine("Method 2");
        }

        static private void Method3()
        {
            Console.WriteLine("Method 3");
        }
    }
}
```

This program three methods: `Method1()`, `Method2()`, and `Method3()`. The `methods` delegate is first assigned to point to `Method1()`. The next two statements add `Method2()` and `Method3()` to the delegate by using the += operator:

```
MethodsDelegate methods = Method1;
methods += Method2;
methods += Method3;
```

When the `methods` delegate variable is called, the following output results:

```
Method 1
Method 2
Method 3
```

The output shows that the three methods are called in succession, in the order they were added.

What happens when your methods each return a value and you call them using a multicast delegate? Here's an example in which the three methods each return an integer value:

```
class Program
{
    delegate int MethodsDelegate(ref int num1, ref int num2);

    static void Main(string[] args)
    {
        int num1 = 0, num2 = 0;
        MethodsDelegate methods = Method1;
        methods += Method2;
        methods += Method3;

        //---call the delegated method(s)---
        Console.WriteLine(methods(ref num1, ref num2));
        Console.WriteLine("num1: {0} num2: {1}", num1, num2);
        Console.ReadLine();
    }

    static private int Method1(ref int num1, ref int num2)
    {
        Console.WriteLine("Method 1");
        num1 = 1;
        num2 = 1;
        return 1;
    }

    static private int Method2(ref int num1, ref int num2)
    {
        Console.WriteLine("Method 2");
        num1 = 2;
        num2 = 2;
        return 2;
    }

    static private int Method3(ref int num1, ref int num2)
```

```
        {
            Console.WriteLine("Method 3");
            num1 = 3;
            num2 = 3;
            return 3;
        }
    }
```

When the `methods` delegate is called, `Method1()`, `Method2()`, and `Method3()` are called in succession. However, only the last method (`Method3()`) returns a value back to the `Main()` function, as the output shows:

```
Method 1
Method 2
Method 3
3
num1: 3 num2: 3
```

If one of the methods pointed to by a delegate causes an exception, no results are returned. The following modifications to the preceding program shows that `Method2()` throws an exception and is caught by the `Try-Catch` block:

```
class Program
{
    delegate int MethodsDelegate(ref int num1, ref int num2);
    static void Main(string[] args)
    {
        int num1 = 0, num2 = 0;
        MethodsDelegate methods = Method1;
        methods += Method2;
        methods += Method3;

        try
        {
            //---call the delegated method(s)---
            Console.WriteLine(methods(ref num1, ref num2));
            Console.WriteLine("num1: {0} num2: {1}", num1, num2);
        }
        catch (Exception ex)
        {
            Console.WriteLine(ex.Message);
        }

        Console.WriteLine("num1: {0} num2: {1}", num1, num2);
        Console.ReadLine();
    }

    static private int Method1(ref int num1, ref int num2)
    {
        Console.WriteLine("Method 1");
        num1 = 1;
        num2 = 1;
```

(continued)

219

(continued)

```
            return 1;
        }

        static private int Method2(ref int num1, ref int num2)
        {
            throw new Exception();
            Console.WriteLine("Method 2");
            num1 = 2;
            num2 = 2;
            return 2;
        }

        static private int Method3(ref int num1, ref int num2)
        {
            Console.WriteLine("Method 3");
            num1 = 3;
            num2 = 3;
            return 3;
        }
    }
```

The following output shows that num1 and num2 retain the values set by the last method that was successfully invoked by the delegate:

```
Method 1
Exception of type 'System.Exception' was thrown.
num1: 1 num2: 1
```

Just as you use the += operator to add a method to a delegate, you use the −= operator to remove a method from a delegate:

```
        static void Main(string[] args)
        {
            int num1 = 0, num2 = 0;
            MethodsDelegate methods = Method1;
            methods += Method2;
            methods += Method3;
            //...
            //...
            //---removes Method3---
            methods -= Method3;
```

Implementing Callbacks Using Delegates

One of the useful things you can do with delegates is to implement callbacks. Callbacks are methods that you pass into a function that will be called when the function finishes execution. For example, you have a function that performs a series of mathematical operations. When you call the function, you also pass it a callback method so that when the function is done with its calculation, the callback method is called to notify you of the calculation result.

Following is an example of how to implement callbacks using delegates:

```
class Program
{
    delegate void callbackDelegate(string Message);

    static void Main(string[] args)
    {
        callbackDelegate result = ResultCallback;
        AddTwoNumbers(5, 3, result);

        Console.ReadLine();
    }

    static private void AddTwoNumbers(
        int num1, int num2, callbackDelegate callback)
    {
        int result = num1 + num2;
        callback("The result is: " + result.ToString());
    }

    static private void ResultCallback(string Message)
    {
        Console.WriteLine(Message);
    }
}
```

First, you declare two methods:

❑   AddTwoNumbers() — Takes in two integer arguments and a delegate of type callbackDelegate

❑   ResultCallback() — Takes in a string argument and displays the string in the console window

Then you declare a delegate type:

```
delegate void callbackDelegate(string Message);
```

Before you call the AddTwoNumbers() function, you create a delegate of type callbackDelegate and assign it to point to the ResultCallback() method. The AddTwoNumbers() function is then called with two integer arguments and the result callback delegate:

```
callbackDelegate result = ResultCallback;
AddTwoNumbers(5, 3, result);
```

In the AddTwoNumbers() function, when the calculation is done, you invoke the callback delegate and pass to it a string:

```
static private void AddTwoNumbers(
    int num1, int num2, callbackDelegate callback)
{
    int result = num1 + num2;
    callback("The result is: " + result.ToString());
}
```

The `callback` delegate calls the `ResultCallback()` function, which prints the result to the console. The output is:

```
The result is: 8
```

Asynchronous Callbacks

Callbacks are most useful if they are asynchronous. The callback illustrated in the previous example is *synchronous*, that is, the functions are called sequentially. If the `AddTwoNumbers()` function takes a long time to execute, all the statements after it will block. Figure 7-1 shows the flow of execution when the callback is synchronous.

Figure 7-1

A better way to organize the program is to call the `AddTwoNumbers()` method asynchronously, as shown in Figure 7-2. Calling a function asynchronously allows the main program to continue executing without waiting for the function to return.

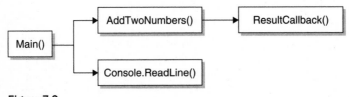

Figure 7-2

In this asynchronous model, when the `AddTwoNumbers()` function is called, the statement(s) after it can continue to execute. When the function finishes execution, it calls the `ResultCallback()` function.

Here's the rewrite of the previous program, using an asynchronous callback:

```
using System;
using System.Collections.Generic;
using System.Linq;
using System.Text;
using System.Runtime.Remoting.Messaging;

namespace Delegates
{
    class Program
    {
        //---delegate to the AddTwoNumbers() method---
        delegate int MethodDelegate(int num1, int num2);

        static void Main(string[] args)
```

```
        {
                //---assign the delegate to point to AddTwoNumbers()---
                MethodDelegate del = AddTwoNumbers;

                //---creates a AsyncCallback delegate---
                AsyncCallback callback = new AsyncCallback(ResultCallback);

                //---invoke the method asychronously---
                Console.WriteLine("Invoking the method asychronously...");
                IAsyncResult result = del.BeginInvoke(5, 3, callback, null);
                Console.WriteLine("Continuing with the execution...");

                Console.ReadLine();
        }

        //---method to add two numbers---
        static private int AddTwoNumbers(int num1, int num2)
        {
                //---simulate long execution---
                System.Threading.Thread.Sleep(5000);

                return num1 + num2;
        }

        static private void ResultCallback(IAsyncResult ar)
        {
                MethodDelegate del =
                    (MethodDelegate)((AsyncResult)ar).AsyncDelegate;
                //---get the result---
                int result = del.EndInvoke(ar);
                Console.WriteLine("Result of addition is: " + result);
        }
    }
}
```

First, you define a delegate type so that you can point to the `AddTwoNumbers()` method:

```
delegate int MethodDelegate(int num1, int num2);
```

Then create a delegate, and assign it to point to the `AddTwoNumbers()` method:

```
//---assign the delegate to point to AddTwoNumbers()---
MethodDelegate del = AddTwoNumbers;
```

Next, define a delegate of type `AsyncCallback`:

```
//---creates a AsyncCallback delegate---
AsyncCallback callback = new AsyncCallback(ResultCallback);
```

The `AsyncCallback` is a delegate that references a method to be called when an asynchronous operation completes. Here, you set it to point to `ResultCallback` (which you will define later).

To call the AddTwoNumbers() methods asynchronously, you use the BeginInvoke() method of the del delegate, passing it two integer values (needed by the AddTwoNumbers() method), as well as a delegate to call back when the method finishes executing:

```
//---invoke the method asychronously---
Console.WriteLine("Invoking the method asynchronously...");
IAsyncResult result = del.BeginInvoke(5, 3, callback, null);
Console.WriteLine("Continuing with the execution...");
```

The BeginInvoke() method calls the delegate asynchronously, and the next statement continues execution after the async delegate is called. This method returns a variable of type IAsyncResult to represent the status of an asynchronous operation.

To obtain the result of the calculation, you define the ResultCallback() method, which takes in an argument of type IAsyncResult:

```
static private void ResultCallback(IAsyncResult ar)
{
    MethodDelegate del =
        (MethodDelegate)((AsyncResult)ar).AsyncDelegate;
    //---get the result---
    int result = del.EndInvoke(ar);
    Console.WriteLine("Result of addition is: " + result);
}
```

Within the ResultCallback() method, you first obtain the delegate to the AddTwoNumbers() method by using the AsyncDelegate property, which returns the delegate on which the asynchronous call was invoked. You then obtain the result of the asynchronous call by using the EndInvoke() method, passing it the IAsyncResult variable (ar).

Finally, to demonstrate the asynchronous calling of the AddTwoNumbers() method, you can insert a Sleep() statement to delay the execution (simulating long execution):

```
static private int AddTwoNumbers(int num1, int num2)
{
    //---simulate long execution---
    System.Threading.Thread.Sleep(5000);
    return num1 + num2;
}
```

Figure 7-3 shows the output of this program.

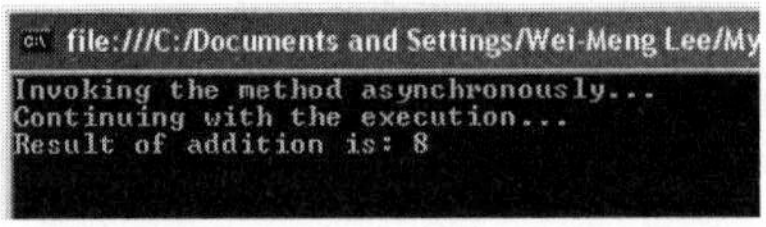

Figure 7-3

When using asynchronous callbacks, you can make your program much more responsive by executing different parts of the program in different threads.

Chapter 10 discusses more about threading.

Anonymous Methods and Lambda Expressions

Beginning with C# 2.0, you can use a feature known as *anonymous methods* to define a delegate. An anonymous method is an "inline" statement or expression that can be used as a delegate parameter. To see how it works, take a look at the following example:

```
class Program
{
    delegate void MethodsDelegate(string Message);

    static void Main(string[] args)
    {
        MethodsDelegate method = Method1;

        //---call the delegated method---
        method("Using delegate.");
        Console.ReadLine();
    }

    static private void Method1(string Message)
    {
        Console.WriteLine(Message);
    }
}
```

Instead of defining a separate method and then using a delegate variable to point to it, you can shorten the code using an anonymous method:

```
class Program
{
    delegate void MethodsDelegate(string Message);

    static void Main(string[] args)
    {
        MethodsDelegate method = delegate(string Message)
        {
            Console.WriteLine(Message);
        };

        //---call the delegated method---
        method("Using anonymous method.");

        Console.ReadLine();
    }
}
```

In this expression, the `method` delegate is an anonymous method:

```
MethodsDelegate method = delegate(string Message)
{
    Console.WriteLine(Message);
};
```

Anonymous methods eliminate the need to define a separate method when using delegates. This is useful if your delegated method contains a few simple statements and is not used by other code because you reduce the coding overhead in instantiating delegates by not having to create a separate method.

In C# 3.0, anonymous methods can be further shortened using a new feature known as *lambda expressions*. Lambda expressions are a new feature in .NET 3.5 that provides a more concise, functional syntax for writing anonymous methods.

The preceding code using anonymous methods can be rewritten using a lambda expression:

```
class Program
{
    delegate void MethodsDelegate(string Message);

    static void Main(string[] args)
    {
        MethodsDelegate method = (Message) => { Console.WriteLine(Message); };

        //---call the delegated method---
        method("Using Lambda Expression.");

        Console.ReadLine();
    }
}
```

Lambda expressions are discussed in more detail in Chapter 14.

Events

One of the most important techniques in computer science that made today's graphical user interface operating systems (such as Windows, Mac OS X, Linux, and so on) possible is event-driven programming. Event-driven programming lets the OS react appropriately to the different clicks made by the user. A typical Windows application has various widgets such as buttons, radio buttons, and checkboxes that can raise events when, say, a user clicks them. The programmer simply needs to write the code to handle that particular event. The nice thing about events is that you do not need to know when these events will be raised — you simply need to provide the implementation for the event handlers that will handle the events and the OS will take care of invoking the necessary event handlers appropriately.

In .NET, events are implemented using delegates. An object that has events is known as a *publisher*. Objects that subscribe to events (in other words, handle events) are known as *subscribers*. When an object exposes events, it defines a delegate so that whichever object wants to handle this event will have to provide a function for this delegate. This delegate is known as an *event*, and the function that handles this delegate is known as an *event handler*. Events are part and parcel of every Windows application. For example, using Visual Studio 2008 you can create a Windows application containing a `Button` control (see Figure 7-4).

Figure 7-4

When you double-click the `Button` control, an event handler is automatically added for you:

```csharp
public partial class Form1 : Form
{
    public Form1()
    {
        InitializeComponent();
    }

    private void button1_Click(object sender, EventArgs e)
    {

    }
}
```

But how does your application know which event handler is for which event? Turns out that Visual Studio 2008 automatically wires up the event handlers in the code-behind of the form (`FormName .Designer.cs`; see Figure 7-5) located in a function called `InitializeComponent()`:

```csharp
this.button1.Location = new System.Drawing.Point(12, 12);
this.button1.Name = "button1";
this.button1.Size = new System.Drawing.Size(75, 23);
this.button1.TabIndex = 0;
this.button1.Text = "button1";
this.button1.UseVisualStyleBackColor = true;
this.button1.Click += new System.EventHandler(this.button1_Click);
```

Figure 7-5

Notice that the way you wire up an event handler to handle the `Click` event is similar to how you assign a method name to a delegate.

Alternatively, you can manually create the event handler for the `Click` event of the `Button` control. In the `Form()` constructor, type `+ =` after the `Click` event and press the Tab key. Visual Studio 2008 automatically completes the statement (see Figure 7-6).

```
public Form1()
{
    InitializeComponent();
    this.button1.Click+=
                        new EventHandler(button1_Click);   (Press TAB to insert)
}
```

Figure 7-6

Press the Tab key one more time, and Visual Studio 2008 inserts the stub of the event handler for you (see Figure 7-7).

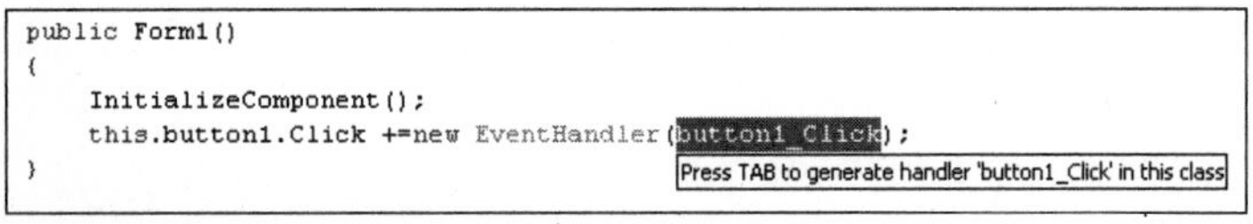

```
public Form1()
{
    InitializeComponent();
    this.button1.Click +=new EventHandler (button1_Click);
                                           Press TAB to generate handler 'button1_Click' in this class
}
```

Figure 7-7

The completed code looks like this:

```
public Form1()
{
    InitializeComponent();
    this.button1.Click += new EventHandler(button1_Click);
}

void button1_Click(object sender, EventArgs e)
{

}
```

Notice that `Click` is the event and the event handler must match the signature required by the event (in this case, the event handler for the `Click` event must have two parameter — `object` and `EventArgs`). By convention, event handlers in the .NET Framework return void and have two parameters. The first is the source of the event (that is, the object that raises this event), and the second is an object derived from `EventArgs`. The `EventArgs` parameter allows data to be passed from an event to the event handler. The `EventArgs` class is discussed further later in this chapter.

Using the new lambda expressions in C# 3.0, the preceding event handler can also be written like this:

```
public Form1()
{
    InitializeComponent();
    this.button1.Click += (object sender, EventArgs e) =>
    {
        MessageBox.Show("Button clicked!");
    };
}
```

Handling Events

Let's take a look at how to handle events using a couple of simple examples. The Timer class (located in the System.Timers namespace) is a class that generates a series of recurring events at regular intervals. You usually use the Timer class to perform some background tasks, such as updating a ProgressBar control when downloading some files from a server, or displaying the current time.

The Timer class has one important event that you need to handle — Elapsed. The Elapsed event is fired every time a set time interval has elapsed.

The following program shows how you can use the Timer class to display the current time in the console window:

```
using System;
using System.Collections.Generic;
using System.Linq;
using System.Text;
using System.Runtime.Remoting.Messaging;
using System.Timers;
namespace Events
{
    class Program
    {
        static void Main(string[] args)
        {
            Timer t = new Timer(1000);
            t.Elapsed += new ElapsedEventHandler(t_Elapsed);
            t.Start();
            Console.ReadLine();
        }

        static void t_Elapsed(object sender, ElapsedEventArgs e)
        {
            Console.SetCursorPosition(0, 0);
            Console.WriteLine(DateTime.Now);
        }
    }
}
```

First, you instantiate a `Timer` class by passing it a value. The value is the time interval (in milliseconds) between the `Timer` class's firing (raising) of its `Elapsed` event. You next wire the `Elapsed` event with the event handler `t_Elapsed`, which displays the current time in the console window. The `Start()` method of the `Timer` class activates the `Timer` object so that it can start to fire the `Elapsed` event. Because the event is fired every second, the console is essentially updating the time every second (see Figure 7-8).

Figure 7-8

Another useful class that is available in the .NET Framework class library is the `FileSystemWatcher` class (located in the `System.IO` namespace). It watches the file system for changes and enables you to monitor these changes by raising events. For example, you can use the `FileSystemWatcher` class to monitor your hard drive for changes such as when a file/directory is deleted, is created, or has its contents changed.

To see how the `FileSystemWatcher` class works, consider the following program:

```
using System;
using System.Collections.Generic;
using System.Linq;
using System.Text;
using System.Runtime.Remoting.Messaging;
using System.IO;

namespace Events
{
    class Program
    {
        static void Main(string[] args)
        {
            FileSystemWatcher fileWatcher = new FileSystemWatcher()
            {
                Path = @"c:\",
                Filter = "*.txt"
            };

            //---wire up the event handlers---
            fileWatcher.Deleted += new FileSystemEventHandler(fileWatcher_Deleted);
            fileWatcher.Renamed += new RenamedEventHandler(fileWatcher_Renamed);
            fileWatcher.Changed += new FileSystemEventHandler(fileWatcher_Changed);
            fileWatcher.Created += new FileSystemEventHandler(fileWatcher_Created);

            //---begin watching---
            fileWatcher.EnableRaisingEvents = true;
            Console.ReadLine();
        }

        static void fileWatcher_Created(object sender, FileSystemEventArgs e)
```

```
    {
        Console.WriteLine("File created: " + e.FullPath);
    }

    static void fileWatcher_Changed(object sender, FileSystemEventArgs e)
    {
        Console.WriteLine("File changed: " + e.FullPath);
    }

    static void fileWatcher_Renamed(object sender, RenamedEventArgs e)
    {
        Console.WriteLine("File renamed: " + e.FullPath);
    }

    static void fileWatcher_Deleted(object sender, FileSystemEventArgs e)
    {
        Console.WriteLine("File deleted: " + e.FullPath);
    }
    }
}
```

You first create an instance of the `FileSystemWatcher` class by initializing its `Path` and `Filter` properties:

```
FileSystemWatcher fileWatcher = new FileSystemWatcher()
{
    Path = @"c:\",
    Filter = "*.txt"
};
```

Here, you are monitoring the C:\ drive and all its files ending with the `.txt` extension.

You then wire all the events with their respective event handlers:

```
//---wire up the event handlers---
fileWatcher.Deleted += new FileSystemEventHandler(fileWatcher_Deleted);
fileWatcher.Renamed += new RenamedEventHandler(fileWatcher_Renamed);
fileWatcher.Changed += new FileSystemEventHandler(fileWatcher_Changed);
fileWatcher.Created += new FileSystemEventHandler(fileWatcher_Created);
```

These statements handle four events:

❑　`Deleted` — Fires when a file is deleted

❑　`Renamed` — Fires when a file is renamed

❑　`Changed` — Fires when a file's content is changed

❑　`Created` — Fires when a file is created

Finally, you define the event handlers for the four events:

```csharp
static void fileWatcher_Created(object sender, FileSystemEventArgs e)
{
    Console.WriteLine("File created: " + e.FullPath);
}

static void fileWatcher_Changed(object sender, FileSystemEventArgs e)
{
    Console.WriteLine("File changed: " + e.FullPath);
}

static void fileWatcher_Renamed(object sender, RenamedEventArgs e)
{
    Console.WriteLine("File renamed: " + e.FullPath);
}

static void fileWatcher_Deleted(object sender, FileSystemEventArgs e)
{
    Console.WriteLine("File deleted: " + e.FullPath);
}
```

To test the program, you can create a new text file in C:\ drive, make some changes to its content, rename it, and then delete it. The output window will look like Figure 7-9.

Figure 7-9

Implementing Events

So far you have been subscribing to events by writing event handlers. Now you will implement events in your own class. For this example, you create a class called `AlarmClock`. `AlarmClock` allows you to set a particular date and time so that you can be notified (through an event) when the time is up. For this purpose, you use the `Timer` class.

First, define the `AlarmClock` class as follows:

```csharp
using System;
using System.Collections.Generic;
using System.Linq;
using System.Text;
using System.Timers;

class AlarmClock
{

}
```

Declare a `Timer` variable and define the `AlarmTime` property to allow users of this class to set a date and time:

```
class AlarmClock
{
    Timer t;
    public DateTime AlarmTime { get; set; }
}
```

Next, define the `Start()` method so that users can start the monitoring by turning on the `Timer` object:

```
class AlarmClock
{
    //...
    public void Start()
    {
        t.Start();
    }
}
```

Next, define a public event member in the `AlarmClock` class:

```
public event EventHandler TimesUp;
```

The `EventHandler` is a predefined delegate, and this statement defines `TimesUp` as an event for your class.

Define a protected virtual method in the `AlarmClock` class that will be used internally by your class to raise the `TimesUp` event:

```
protected virtual void onTimesUp(EventArgs e)
{
    if (TimesUp != null)
        TimesUp(this, e);
}
```

The `EventArgs` class is the base class for classes that contain event data. This class does not pass any data back to an event handler.

The next section explains how you can create another class that derives from this `EventArgs` base class to pass back information to an event handler.

Define the constructor for the `AlarmClock` class so that the `Timer` object (t) will fire its `Elapsed` event every 100 milliseconds. In addition, wire the `Elapsed` event with an event handler. The event handler will check the current time against the time set by the user of the class. If the time equals or exceeds the user's set time, the event handler calls the onTimesUp() method that you defined in the previous step:

```
public AlarmClock()
{
    t = new Timer(100);
    t.Elapsed += new ElapsedEventHandler(t_Elapsed);
}

void t_Elapsed(object sender, ElapsedEventArgs e)
{
    if (DateTime.Now >= this.AlarmTime)
    {
        onTimesUp(new EventArgs());
        t.Stop();
    }
}
```

That's it! The entire AlarmClock class is:

```
using System;
using System.Collections.Generic;
using System.Linq;
using System.Text;

using System.Timers;

class AlarmClock
{
    Timer t;
    public DateTime AlarmTime { get; set; }

    public void Start()
    {
        t.Start();
    }

    public AlarmClock()
    {
        t = new Timer(100);
        t.Elapsed += new ElapsedEventHandler(t_Elapsed);
    }

    void t_Elapsed(object sender, ElapsedEventArgs e)
    {
        if (DateTime.Now >= this.AlarmTime)
        {
            onTimesUp(new EventArgs());
```

```
                t.Stop();
            }
        }

    public event EventHandler TimesUp;
    protected virtual void onTimesUp(EventArgs e)
    {
        if (TimesUp != null)
            TimesUp(this, e);
    }
}
```

To use the `AlarmClock` class, you first create an instance of the `AlarmClock` class and then set the time for the alarm by using the `AlarmTime` property. You then wire the `TimesUp` event with an event handler so that you can print a message when the set time is up:

```
class Program
{
    static void Main(string[] args)
    {
        AlarmClock c = new AlarmClock()
        {
            //---alarm to sound off at 16 May 08, 9.50am---
            AlarmTime = new DateTime(2008, 5, 16, 09, 50, 0, 0),
        };
        c.Start();
        c.TimesUp += new EventHandler(c_TimesUp);

        Console.ReadLine();
    }

    static void c_TimesUp(object sender, EventArgs e)
    {
        Console.WriteLine("Times up!");
    }
}
```

Difference between Events and Delegates

Events are implemented using delegates, so what is the difference between an event and a delegate? The difference is that for an event you cannot directly assign a delegate to it using the = operator; you must use the += operator.

To understand the difference, consider the following class definitions — `Class1` and `Class2`:

```
namespace DelegatesVsEvents
{
    class Program
    {
        static void Main(string[] args)
        {
        }
    }

    class Class1
    {
        public delegate void Class1Delegate();
        public Class1Delegate del;
    }

    class Class2
    {
        public delegate void Class2Delegate();
        public event Class2Delegate evt;     }
}
```

In this code, `Class1` exposes a public delegate `del`, of type `Class1Delegate`. `Class2` is similar to `Class1`, except that it exposes an event `evt`, of type `Class2Delegate`. `del` and `evt` each expect a delegate, with the exception that `evt` is prefixed with the `event` keyword.

To use `Class1`, you create an instance of `Class1` and then assign a delegate to the `del` delegate using the "=" operator:

```
static void Main(string[] args)
{
    //---create a delegate---
    Class1.Class1Delegate d1 =
        new Class1.Class1Delegate(DoSomething);

    Class1 c1 = new Class1();

    //---assign a delegate to del of c1---
    c1.del = new Class1.Class1Delegate(d1);
}

static private void DoSomething()
{
    //...
}
```

To use `Class2`, you create an instance of `Class2` and then assign a delegate to the `evt` event using the += operator:

```
static void Main(string[] args)
{
    //...

    //---create a delegate---
    Class2.Class2Delegate e2 =
        new Class2.Class2Delegate(DoSomething);

    Class2 c2 = new Class2();

    //---assign a delegate to evt of c2---
    c2.evt += new Class2.Class2Delegate(d1);
}
```

If you try to use the = operator to assign a delegate to the `evt` event, you will get a compilation error:

```
c2.evt = new Class2.Class2Delegate(d1); //---error---
```

This important restriction of event is important because defining a delegate as an event will ensure that if multiple clients are subscribed to an event, another client will not be able to set the delegate to null (or simply set it to another delegate). If the client succeeds in doing so, all the other delegates set by other client will be lost. Hence, a delegate defined as an event can only be set with the += operator.

Passing State Information to an Event Handler

In the preceding program, you simply raise an event in the `AlarmClock` class; there is no passing of information from the class back to the event handler. To pass information from an event back to an event handler, you need to implement your own class that derives from the `EventArgs` base class.

In this section, you modify the previous program so that when the set time is up, the event passes a message back to the event handler. The message is set when you instantiate the `AlarmClock` class.

First, define the `AlarmClockEventArgs` class that will allow the event to pass back a string to the event handler. This class must derive from the `EventArgs` base class:

```
public class AlarmClockEventArgs : EventArgs
{
    public AlarmClockEventArgs(string Message)
    {
        this.Message = Message;
    }
    public string Message { get; set; }
}
```

Next, define a delegate called `AlarmClockEventHandler` with the following signature:

```
public delegate void AlarmClockEventHandler(object sender, AlarmClockEventArgs e);
```

Replace the original `TimesUp` event statement with the following statement, which uses the `AlarmClockEventHandler` class:

```
//---public event EventHandler TimesUp;---
public event AlarmClockEventHandler TimesUp;
```

Add a `Message` property to the class so that users of this class can set a message that will be returned by the event when the time is up:

```
public string Message { get; set; }
```

Modify the `onTimesUp` virtual method by changing its parameter type to the new `AlarmClockEventArgs` class:

```
protected virtual void onTimesUp(AlarmClockEventArgs e)
{
    if (TimesUp != null)
        TimesUp(this, e);
}
```

Finally, modify the `t_Elapsed` event handler so that when you now call the `onTimesUp()` method, you pass in an instance of the `AlarmClockEventArgs` class containing the message you want to pass back to the event handler:

```
void t_Elapsed(object sender, ElapsedEventArgs e)
{
    if (DateTime.Now >= this.AlarmTime)
    {
        onTimesUp(new AlarmClockEventArgs(this.Message));
        t.Stop();
    }
}
```

Here's the complete program:

```
using System;
using System.Collections.Generic;
using System.Linq;
using System.Text;
using System.Timers;

public class AlarmClockEventArgs : EventArgs
{
```

```
        public AlarmClockEventArgs(string Message)
        {
            this.Message = Message;
        }
        public string Message { get; set; }
}

public delegate void AlarmClockEventHandler(object sender, AlarmClockEventArgs e);

class AlarmClock
{
    Timer t;

    public event AlarmClockEventHandler TimesUp;

    protected virtual void onTimesUp(AlarmClockEventArgs e)
    {
        if (TimesUp != null)
            TimesUp(this, e);
    }

    public DateTime AlarmTime { get; set; }
    public string Message { get; set; }

    public AlarmClock()
    {
        t = new Timer(100);
        t.Elapsed += new ElapsedEventHandler(t_Elapsed);
    }

    public void Start()
    {
        t.Start();
    }

    void t_Elapsed(object sender, ElapsedEventArgs e)
    {
        if (DateTime.Now >= this.AlarmTime)
        {
            onTimesUp(new AlarmClockEventArgs(this.Message));
            t.Stop();
        }
    }
}
```

With the modified `AlarmClock` class, your program will now look like this:

```
namespace Events
{
    class Program
    {
        static void c_TimesUp(object sender, AlarmClockEventArgs e)
        {
            Console.WriteLine(DateTime.Now.ToShortTimeString() + ": " + e.Message);
        }

        static void Main(string[] args)
        {
            AlarmClock c = new AlarmClock()
            {
                //---alarm to sound off at 16 May 08, 9.50am---
                AlarmTime = new DateTime(2008, 5, 16, 09, 50, 0, 0),
                Message = "Meeting with customer."
            };
            c.TimesUp += new AlarmClockEventHandler(c_TimesUp);
            c.Start();
            Console.ReadLine();
        }
    }
}
```

Figure 7-10 shows the output when the `AlarmClock` fires the `TimesUp` event.

Figure 7-10

Summary

This chapter discussed what delegates are and how you can use them to invoke other functions, as well as how you can use delegates to implement callbacks so that your application is more efficient and responsive. One direct application of delegates is events, which make GUI operating systems such as Windows possible. One important difference between delegates and events is that you cannot assign a delegate to an event by using the = operator.

Strings and Regular Expressions

One of the most common data types used in programming is the string. In C#, a string is a group of one or more characters declared using the `string` keyword. Strings play an important part in programming and are an integral part of our lives — our names, addresses, company names, email addresses, web site URLs, flight numbers, and so forth are all made up of strings. To help manipulate those strings and pattern matching, you use *regular expressions*, sequences of characters that define the patterns of a string. In this chapter, then, you will:

❑   Explore the `System.String` class

❑   Learn how to represent special characters in string variables

❑   Manipulate strings with various methods

❑   Format strings

❑   Use the `StringBuilder` class to create and manipulate strings

❑   Use Regular Expressions to match string patterns

The System.String Class

The .NET Framework contains the `System.String` class for string manipulation. To create an instance of the `String` class and assign it a string, you can use the following statements:

```
String str1;
str1 = "This is a string";
```

C# also provides an alias to the `String` class: `string` (lowercase "s"). The preceding statements can be rewritten as:

```
string str1; //---equivalent to String str1;---
str1 = "This is a string";
```

You can declare a string and assign it a value in one statement, like this:

```
string str2 = "This is another string";
```

In .NET, a string is a reference type but behaves very much like a value type. Consider the following example of a typical reference type:

```
Button btn1 = new Button() { Text = "Button 1" };
Button btn2 = btn1;

btn1.Text += " and 2"; //---btn1.text is now "Button 1 and 2"---
Console.WriteLine(btn1.Text); //---Button 1 and 2---
Console.WriteLine(btn2.Text); //---Button 1 and 2---
```

Here, you create an instance of a Button object (btn1) and then assign it to another variable (btn2). Both btn1 and btn2 are now pointing to the same object, and hence when you modify the Text property of btn1, the changes can be seen in btn2 (as is evident in the output of the WriteLine() statements).

Because strings are reference types, you would expect to see the same behavior as exhibited in the preceding block of code. For example:

```
string str1 = "String 1";
string str2 = str1;
```

str1 and str2 should now be pointing to the same instance. Make some changes to str1 by appending some text to it:

```
str1 += " and some other stuff";
```

And then print out the value of these two strings:

```
Console.WriteLine(str1); //---String 1 and some other stuff---
Console.WriteLine(str2); //---String 1---
```

Are you surprised to see that the values of the two strings are different? What actually happens when you do the string assignment (string str2 = str1) is that str1 is copied to str2 (str2 holds a copy of str1; it does not points to it). Hence, changes made to str1 are not reflected in str2.

> **A string cannot be a value type because of its unfixed size. All values types (int, double, and so on) have fixed size.**

A string is essentially a collection of Unicode characters. The following statements show how you enumerate a string as a collection of char and print out the individual characters to the console:

```
string str1 = "This is a string";
foreach (char c in str1)
{
    Console.WriteLine(c);
}
```

Here's this code's output:

```
T
h
i
s

i
s

a

s
t
r
i
n
g
```

Escape Characters

Certain characters have special meaning in strings. For example, strings are always enclosed in double quotation marks, and if you want to use the actual double-quote character in the string, you need to tell the C# compiler by "escaping" the character's special meaning. For instance, say you need to represent the following in a string:

```
"I don't necessarily agree with everything I say." Marshall McLuhan
```

Because the sentence contains the double-quote characters, simply using a pair of double-quotes to contain it will cause an error:

```
//---error---
string quotation;
quotation = ""I don't necessarily agree with everything I say." Marshall McLuhan";
```

To represent the double-quote character in a string, you use the backslash (\) character to turn off its special meanings, like this:

```
string quotation =
    "\"I don't necessarily agree with everything I say.\" Marshall McLuhan";
Console.WriteLine(quotation);
```

The output is shown in Figure 8-1.

Figure 8-1

A backslash, then, is another special character. To represent the C:\Windows path, for example, you need to turn off the special meaning of \ by using another \, like this:

```
string path = "C:\\Windows";
```

What if you really need two backslash characters in your string, as in the following?

```
"\\servername\path"
```

In that case, you use the backslash character twice, once for each of the backslash characters you want to turn off, like this:

```
string UNC = "\\\\servername\\path";
```

In addition to using the \ character to turn off the special meaning of characters like the double-quote (") and backslash (\), there are other escape characters that you can use in strings.

One common escape character is the \n. Here's an example:

```
string lines = "Line 1\nLine 2\nLine 3\nLine 4\nLine 5";
Console.WriteLine (lines);
```

The \n escape character creates a newline, as Figure 8-2 shows.

Figure 8-2

You can also use \t to insert tabs into your string, as the following example shows (see also Figure 8-3):

```
string columns1 = "Column 1\tColumn 2\tColumn 3\tColumn 4";
string columns2 = "1\t5\t25\t125";
Console.WriteLine(columns1);
Console.WriteLine(columns2);
```

Figure 8-3

You learn more about formatting options in the section "String Formatting" later in this chapter.

Besides the \n and \t escape characters, C# also supports the \r escape character. \r is the carriage return character. Consider the following example:

```
string str1 = "        One";
string str2 = "Two";
Console.Write(str1);
Console.Write(str2);
```

The output is shown in Figure 8-4.

Figure 8-4

However, if you prefix a \r escape character to the beginning of str2, the effect will be different:

```
string str1 = "        One";
string str2 = "\rTwo";
Console.Write(str1);
Console.Write(str2);
```

The output is shown in Figure 8-5.

Figure 8-5

The \r escape character simply brings the cursor to the beginning of the line, and hence in the above statements the word "Two" is printed at the beginning of the line. The \r escape character is often used together with \n to form a new line (see Figure 8-6):

```
string str1 = "Line 1\n\r";
string str2 = "Line 2\n\r";
Console.Write(str1);
Console.Write(str2);
```

By default, when you use the \n to insert a new line, the cursor is automatically returned to the beginning of the line. However, some legacy applications still require you to insert newline and carriage return characters in strings.

Figure 8-6

The following table summarizes the different escape sequences you have seen in this section:

Sequence	Purpose
\n	New line
\r	Carriage return
\r\n	Carriage return; New line
\"	Quotation marks
\\	Backslash character
\t	Tab

In C#, strings can also be @-quoted. Earlier, you saw that to include special characters (such as double-quote, backslash, and so on) in a string you need to use the backslash character to turn off its special meaning:

```
string path="C:\\Windows";
```

You can actually use the @ character, and prefix the string with it, like this:

```
string path=@"C:\Windows";
```

Using the @ character makes your string easier to read. Basically, the compiler treats strings that are prefixed with the @ character verbatim — that is, it just accepts all the characters in the string (inside the quotes). To better appreciate this, consider the following example where a string containing an XML snippet is split across multiple lines (with each line ending with a carriage return):

```
string XML = @"
    <Books>
        <title>C# 3.0 Programmers' Reference</title>
    </Book>";
Console.WriteLine(XML);
```

Figure 8-7 shows the output. The `WriteLine()` method prints out the line verbatim.

Figure 8-7

To illustrate the use of the @ character on a double-quoted string, the following:

```
string quotation =
    "\"I don't necessarily agree with everything I say.\" Marshall McLuhan";
Console.WriteLine(quotation);
```

can be rewritten as:

```
string quotation =
    @"""I don't necessarily agree with everything I say."" Marshall McLuhan";
Console.WriteLine(quotation);
```

Escape Code for Unicode

C# supports the use of escape code to represent Unicode characters. The four-digit escape code format is: `\udddd`. For example, the following statement prints out the £ symbol:

```
string symbol = "\u00A3";
Console.WriteLine(symbol);
```

For more information on Unicode, check out `http://unicode.org/Public/UNIDATA/NamesList.txt`.

String Manipulations

Often, once your values are stored in string variables, you need to perform a wide variety of operations on them, such as comparing the values of two strings, inserting and deleting strings from an existing string, concatenating multiple strings, and so on. The `String` class in the .NET Framework provides a host of methods for manipulating strings, some of the important ones of which are explained in the following sections.

You can find out about all of the `String` class methods at www.msdn.com.

Testing for Equality

Even though `string` is a reference type, you will use the `==` and `!=` operators to compare the value of two strings (not their references).

Consider the following three string variables:

```
string str1 = "This is a string";
string str2 = "This is a ";
str2 += "string";
string str3 = str2;
```

The following statements test the equality of the values contained in each variable:

```
Console.WriteLine(str1 == str2); //--True---
Console.WriteLine(str1 == str3); //--True---
Console.WriteLine(str2 != str3); //---False---
```

As you can see from the output of these statements, the values of each three variables are identical. However, to compare their reference equality, you need to cast each variable to object and then check their equality using the `==` operator, as the following shows:

```
Console.WriteLine((object)str1 == (object)str2); //--False---
Console.WriteLine((object)str2 == (object)str3); //--True---
```

However, if after the assignment the original value of the string is changed, the two strings' references will no longer be considered equal, as the following shows:

```
string str3 = str2;
Console.WriteLine((object)str2 == (object)str3); //--True---

str2 = "This string has changed";
Console.WriteLine((object)str2 == (object)str3); //--False---
```

Besides using the `==` operator to test for value equality, you can also use the `Equals()` method, which is available as an instance method as well as a static method:

```
Console.WriteLine(str1 == str2); //--True---
Console.WriteLine(str1.Equals(str2)); //--True---
Console.WriteLine(string.Equals(str1,str2)); //--True---
```

Comparing Strings

String comparison is a common operation often performed on strings. Consider the following two string variables:

```
string str1 = "Microsoft";
string str2 = "microsoft";
```

You can use the `String.Compare()` static method to compare two strings:

```
Console.WriteLine(string.Compare(str1, str2));       // 1;str1 is greater than str2
Console.WriteLine(string.Compare(str2, str1));       // -1;str2 is less than str1
Console.WriteLine(string.Compare(str1, str2, true)); // 0;str1 equals str2
```

The lowercase character "m" comes before the capital "M," and hence `str1` is considered greater than `str2`. The third statement compares the two strings without considering the casing (that is, case-insensitive; it's the third argument that indicates that the comparison should ignore the casing of the strings involved).

The `String.Compare()` static method is overloaded, and besides the two overloaded methods (first two statements and the third statement) just shown, there are additional overloaded methods as described in the following table.

Method	Description
`Compare(String, String)`	Compares two specified `String` objects.
`Compare(String, String, Boolean)`	Compares two specified `String` objects, ignoring or respecting their case.
`Compare(String, String, StringComparison)`	Compares two specified `String` objects. Also specifies whether the comparison uses the current or invariant culture, honors or respects case, and uses word or ordinal sort rules.
`Compare(String, String, Boolean, CultureInfo)`	Compares two specified `String` objects, ignoring or respecting their case, and using culture-specific information for the comparison.
`Compare(String, Int32, String, Int32, Int32)`	Compares substrings of two specified `String` objects.
`Compare(String, Int32, String, Int32, Int32, Boolean)`	Compares substrings of two specified `String` objects, ignoring or respecting their case.
`Compare(String, Int32, String, Int32, Int32, StringComparison)`	Compares substrings of two specified `String` objects.
`Compare(String, Int32, String, Int32, Int32, Boolean, CultureInfo)`	Compares substrings of two specified `String` objects, ignoring or respecting their case, and using culture-specific information for the comparison.

Alternatively, you can use the `CompareTo()` instance method, like this:

```
Console.WriteLine(str1.CompareTo(str2)); // 1; str1 is greater than str2
Console.WriteLine(str2.CompareTo(str1)); // -1; str2 is less than str1
```

Note that comparisons made by the `CompareTo()` instance method are always case sensitive.

Creating and Concatenating Strings

The `String` class in the .NET Framework provides a number of methods that enable you to create or concatenate strings.

The most direct way of concatenating two strings is to use the "+" operator, like this:

```
string str1 = "Hello ";
string str2 = "world!";
string str3 = str1 + str2;
Console.WriteLine(str3); //---Hello world!---
```

The `String.Format()` static method takes the input of multiple objects and creates a new string. Consider the following example:

```
string Name = "Wei-Meng Lee";
int age = 18;
string str1 = string.Format("My name is {0} and I am {1} years old",
              Name, age);

//---str1 is now "My name is Wei-Meng Lee and I am 18 years old"---
Console.WriteLine(str1);
```

Notice that you supplied two variables of `string` and `int` type and the `Format()` method automatically combines them to return a new string.

The preceding example can be rewritten using the `String.Concat()` static method, like this:

```
string str1 = string.Concat("My name is ", Name, " and I am ", age ,
                            " years old");
//---str1 is now "My name is Wei-Meng Lee and I am 18 years old"---
Console.WriteLine(str1);
```

Strings Are Immutable

In .NET, all string objects are *immutable*. This means that once a string variable is initialized, its value cannot be changed. And when you modify the value of a string, a new copy of the string is created and the old copy is discarded. Hence, all methods that process strings return a copy of the modified string — the original string remains intact.

For example, the `Insert()` instance method inserts a string into the current string and returns the modified string:

```
str1 = str1.Insert(10, "modified ");
```

In this statement, you have to assign the returned result to the original string to ensure that the new string is modified.

The `String.Join()` static method is useful when you need to join a series of strings stored in a string array. The following example shows the strings in a string array joined using the `Join()` method:

```
string[] pts = { "1,2", "3,4", "5,6" };
string str1 = string.Join("|", pts);
Console.WriteLine(str1); //---1,2|3,4|5,6---
```

To insert a string into an existing string, use the instance method `Insert()`, as demonstrated in the following example:

```
string str1 = "This is a string";
str1 = str1.Insert(10, "modified ");
Console.WriteLine(str1); //---This is a modified string---
```

The `Copy()` instance method enables you to copy part of a string into a char array. Consider the following example:

```
string str1 = "This is a string";
char[] ch = { '*', '*', '*', '*', '*', '*','*', '*' };
str1.CopyTo(0, ch, 2, 4);
Console.WriteLine(ch); //---**This**---
```

The first parameter of the `CopyTo()` method specifies the index of the string to start copying from. The second parameter specifies the char array. The third parameter specifies the index of the array to copy into, while the last parameter specifies the number of characters to copy.

If you need to pad a string with characters to achieve a certain length, use the `PadLeft()` and `PadRight()` instance methods, as the following statements show:

```
string str1 = "This is a string";
string str2;

str2 = str1.PadLeft(20, '*');
Console.WriteLine(str2); //---"****This is a string"---

str2 = str1.PadRight(20, '*');
Console.WriteLine(str2); //---"This is a string****"---
```

Trimming Strings

To trim whitespace from the beginning of a string, the end of a string, or both, you can use the `TrimStart()`, `TrimEnd()`, or `Trim()` instance methods, respectively. The following statements demonstrate the use of these methods:

```
string str1 = "   Computer   ";
string str2;
Console.WriteLine(str1); //---"   Computer   "---
str2 = str1.Trim();
Console.WriteLine(str2); //---"Computer"---

str2 = str1.TrimStart();
Console.WriteLine(str2); //---"Computer   "---

str2 = str1.TrimEnd();
Console.WriteLine(str2); //---"   Computer"---
```

Splitting Strings

One common operation with string manipulation is splitting a string into smaller strings. Consider the following example where a string contains a serialized series of points:

```
string str1 = "1,2|3,4|5,6|7,8|9,10";
```

Each point ("1, 2", "3, 4", and so on) is separated with the | character. You can use the `Split()` instance method to split the given string into an array of strings:

```
string[] strArray = str1.Split('|');
```

Once the string is split, the result is stored in the string array `strArray` and you can print out each of the smaller strings using a `foreach` statement:

```
foreach (string s in strArray)
    Console.WriteLine(s);
```

The output of the example statement would be:

```
1,2
3,4
5,6
7,8
9,10
```

You can further split the points into individual coordinates and then create a new `Point` object, like this:

```
string str1 = "1,2|3,4|5,6|7,8|9,10";
string[] strArray = str1.Split('|');

foreach (string s in strArray)
{
    string[] xy= s.Split(',');
    Point p = new Point(Convert.ToInt16(xy[0]), Convert.ToInt16(xy[1]));
    Console.WriteL   ine(p.ToString());
}
```

The output of the above statements would be:

```
{X=1,Y=2}
{X=3,Y=4}
{X=5,Y=6}
{X=7,Y=8}
{X=9,Y=10}
```

Searching and Replacing Strings

Occasionally, you need to search for a specific occurrence of a string within a string. For this purpose, you have several methods that you can use.

To look for the occurrence of a word and get its position, use the `IndexOf()` and `LastIndexOf()` instance methods. `IndexOf()` returns the position of the first occurrence of a specific word from a string, while `LastIndexOf()` returns the last occurrence of the word. Here's an example:

```
string str1 = "This is a long long long string...";
Console.WriteLine(str1.IndexOf("long"));     //---10---
Console.WriteLine(str1.LastIndexOf("long")); //---20---
```

To find all the occurrences of a word, you can write a simple loop using the `IndexOf()` method, like this:

```
int position = -1;
string str1 = "This is a long long long string...";
do
{
    position = str1.IndexOf("long", ++position);
    if (position > 0)
        Console.WriteLine(position);
} while (position > 0);
```

This prints out the following:

```
10
15
20
```

To search for the occurrence of particular character, use the `IndexOfAny()` instance method. The following statements search the `str1` string for the any of the characters a, b, c, d, or e, specified in the `char` array:

```
char[] anyof = "abcde".ToCharArray();
Console.WriteLine(str1.IndexOfAny(anyof)); //---8---
```

To obtain a substring from within a string, use the `Substring()` instance method, as the following example shows:

```
string str1 = "This is a long string...";
string str2;
Console.WriteLine(str1.Substring(10)); //---long string...---
Console.WriteLine(str1.Substring(10, 4)); //---long---
```

To find out if a string begins with a specific string, use the `StartsWith()` instance method. Likewise, to find out if a string ends with a specific string, use the `EndsWith()` instance method. The following statements illustrate this:

```
Console.WriteLine(str1.StartsWith("This")); //---True---
Console.WriteLine(str1.EndsWith("...")); //---True---
```

To remove a substring from a string beginning from a particular index, use the `Remove()` instance method:

```
str2 = str1.Remove(10);
Console.WriteLine(str2); //---"This is a"---
```

This statement removes the string starting from index position 10. To remove a particular number of characters, you need to specify the number of characters to remove in the second parameter:

```
str2 = str1.Remove(10,5);   //---remove 5 characters from index 10---
Console.WriteLine(str2); //---"This is a string..."---
```

To replace a substring with another, use the `Replace()` instance method:

```
str2 = str1.Replace("long", "short");
Console.WriteLine(str2); //---"This is a short string..."---
```

To remove a substring from a string without specifying its exact length, use the `Replace()` method, like this:

```
str2 = str1.Replace("long ", string.Empty);
Console.WriteLine(str2); //---"This is a string..."---
```

Changing Case

To change the casing of a string, use the `ToUpper()` or `ToLower()` instance methods. The following statements demonstrate their use:

```
string str1 = "This is a string";
string str2;

str2 = str1.ToUpper();
Console.WriteLine(str2); //---"THIS IS A STRING"---

str2 = str1.ToLower();
Console.WriteLine(str2); //---"this is a string"---
```

String Formatting

You've seen the use of the `Console.WriteLine()` method to print the output to the console. For example, the following statement prints the value of num1 to the console:

```
int num1 = 5;
Console.WriteLine(num1); //---5---
```

You can also print the values of multiple variables like this:

```
int num1 = 5;
int num2 = 12345;
Console.WriteLine(num1 + " and " + num2); //---5 and 12345---
```

If you have too many variables to print (say more than five), though, the code can get messy very quickly. A better way would be to use a *format specifier*, like this:

```
Console.WriteLine("{0} and {1}", num1, num2); //---5 and 12345---
```

A format specifier ({0}, {1}, and so forth) automatically converts all data types to string. Format specifiers are labeled sequentially ({0}, {1}, {2}, and so on). Each format specifier is then replaced with the value of the variable to be printed. The compiler looks at the number in the format specifier, takes the argument with the same index in the argument list, and makes the substitution. In the preceding example, num1 and num2 are the arguments for the format specifiers.

What happens if you want to print out the value of a number enclosed with the {} characters? For example, say that you want to print the string {5} when the value of num1 is 5. You can do something like this:

```
num1 = 5;
Console.WriteLine("{{{0}}}", num1); //---{5}---
```

Why are there two additional sets of {} characters for the format specifier? Well, if you only have one additional set of {} characters, the compiler interprets this to mean that you want to print the string literal {0}, as the following shows:

```
num1 = 5;
Console.WriteLine("{{0}}", num1); //---{0}---
```

The two additional sets of {} characters indicate to the compiler that you want to specify a format specifier and at the same time surround the value with a pair of {} characters.

And as demonstrated earlier, the String class contains the Format() static method, which enables you to create a new string (as well as perform formatting on string data). The preceding statement could be rewritten using the following statements:

```
string formattedString = string.Format("{{{0}}}", num1);
Console.WriteLine(formattedString); //---{5}---
```

To format numbers, you can use the format specifiers as shown here:

```
num1=5;
Console.WriteLine("{0:N}", num1);        //---5.00---

Console.WriteLine("{0:00000}", num1);    //---00005---
//---OR---
Console.WriteLine("{0:d5}", num1);       //---00005---

Console.WriteLine("{0:d4}", num1);       //---0005---

Console.WriteLine("{0,5:G}", num1);      //---    5 (4 spaces on left)---
```

For a detailed list of format specifiers you can use for formatting strings, please refer to the MSDN documentation under the topics "Standard Numeric Format Strings" and "Custom Numeric Format Strings."

You can also print out specific strings based on the value of a number. Consider the following example:

```
num1 = 0;
Console.WriteLine("{0:yes;;no}", num1); //---no---
num1 = 1;
Console.WriteLine("{0:yes;;no}", num1); //---yes---
num1 = 5;
Console.WriteLine("{0:yes;;no}", num1); //---yes---
```

In this case, the format specifier contains two strings: yes and no. If the value of the variable (num) is nonzero, the first string will be returned (yes). If the value is 0, then it returns the second string (no). Here is another example:

```
num1 = 0;
Console.WriteLine("{0:OK;;Cancel}", num1); //---Cancel---
num1 = 1;
Console.WriteLine("{0:OK;;Cancel}", num1); //---OK---
num1 = 5;
Console.WriteLine("{0:OK;;Cancel}", num1); //---OK---
```

For decimal number formatting, use the following format specifiers:

```
double val1 = 3.5;
Console.WriteLine("{0:##.00}", val1);    //---3.50---
Console.WriteLine("{0:##.000}", val1);   //---3.500---
Console.WriteLine("{0:0##.000}", val1);  //---003.500---
```

There are times when numbers are represented in strings. For example, the value 9876 may be represented in a string with a comma denoting the thousandth position. In this case, you cannot simply use the Parse() method from the int class, like this:

```
string str2 = "9,876";
int num3 = int.Parse(str2); //---error---
```

To correctly parse the string, use the following statement:

```
int num3 = int.Parse(
    str2,
    System.Globalization.NumberStyles.AllowThousands);
Console.WriteLine(num3);   //---9876---
```

Here is another example:

```
string str3 = "1,239,876";
num3 = int.Parse(
    str3,
    System.Globalization.NumberStyles.AllowThousands);
Console.WriteLine(num3);   //---1239876---
```

What about the reverse — formatting a number with the comma separator? Here is the solution:

```
num3 = 9876;
Console.WriteLine("{0:#,0}", num3); //---9,876---

num3 = 1239876;
Console.WriteLine("{0:#,0}", num3); //---1,239,876---
```

Last, to format a special number (such as a phone number), use the following format specifier:

```
long phoneNumber = 1234567890;
Console.WriteLine("{0:###-###-####}", phoneNumber); //---123-456-7890---
```

The StringBuilder Class

Earlier in this chapter you saw how to easily concatenate two strings by using the + operator. That's fine if you are concatenating a small number of strings, but it is not recommended for large numbers of strings. The reason is that `String` objects in .NET are *immutable*, which means that once a string variable is initialized, its value cannot be changed. When you concatenate another string to an existing one, you actually discard its old value and create a new string object containing the result of the concatenation. When you repeat this process several times, you incur a performance penalty as new temporary objects are created and old objects discarded.

> One important application of the `StringBuilder` class is its use in .NET interop with native C/C++ APIs that take string arguments and modify strings. One example of this is the Windows API function `GetWindowText()`. This function has a second argument that takes a `TCHAR*` parameter. To use this function from .NET code, you would need to pass a `StringBuilder` object as this argument.

Consider the following example, where you concatenate all the numbers from 0 to 9999:

```
int counter = 9999;
string s = string.Empty;
for (int i = 0; i <= counter; i++) {
    s += i.ToString();
}
Console.WriteLine(s);
```

At first glance, the code looks innocent enough. But let's use the `Stopwatch` object to time the operation. Modify the code as shown here:

```
int counter = 9999;
System.Diagnostics.Stopwatch sw = new System.Diagnostics.Stopwatch();
sw.Start();

string s = string.Empty;
for (int i = 0; i <= counter; i++) {
    s += i.ToString();
}

sw.Stop();
Console.WriteLine("Took {0} ms", sw.ElapsedMilliseconds);

Console.WriteLine(s);
```

On average, it took about 374 ms on my computer to run this operation. Let's now use the `StringBuilder` class in .NET to perform the string concatenation, using its `Append()` method:

```
System.Diagnostics.Stopwatch sw = new System.Diagnostics.Stopwatch();
sw.Start();

StringBuilder sb = new StringBuilder();
for (int i = 0; i <= 9999; i++) {
    sb.Append (i.ToString());
}

sw.Stop();

Console.WriteLine("Took {0} ms", sw.ElapsedMilliseconds);
Console.WriteLine(sb.ToString());
```

On average, it took about 6 ms on my computer to perform this operation. As you can deduce, the improvement is drastic — 98% ((374–6)/374). If you increase the value of the loop variant (counter), you will find that the improvement is even more dramatic.

The `StringBuilder` class represents a mutable string of characters. Its behavior is like the `String` object except that its value can be modified once it has been created.

The `StringBuilder` class contains some other important methods, which are described in the following table.

Method	Description
Append	Appends the string representation of a specified object to the end of this instance.
AppendFormat	Appends a formatted string, which contains zero or more format specifiers, to this instance. Each format specification is replaced by the string representation of a corresponding object argument.
AppendLine	Appends the default line terminator, or a copy of a specified string and the default line terminator, to the end of this instance.
CopyTo	Copies the characters from a specified segment of this instance to a specified segment of a destination Char array.
Insert	Inserts the string representation of a specified object into this instance at a specified character position.
Remove	Removes the specified range of characters from this instance.
Replace	Replaces all occurrences of a specified character or string in this instance with another specified character or string.
ToString	Converts the value of a StringBuilder to a String.

Regular Expressions

When dealing with strings, you often need to perform checks on them to see if they match certain patterns. For example, if your application requires the user to enter an email address so that you can send them a confirmation email later on, it is important to at least verify that the user has entered a correctly formatted email address. To perform the checking, you can use the techniques that you have learnt earlier in this chapter by manually looking for specific patterns in the email address. However, this is a tedious and mundane task.

A better approach would be to use regular expressions — a language for describing and manipulating text. Using regular expressions, you can define the patterns of a text and match it against a string. In the .NET Framework, the System.Text.RegularExpressions namespace contains the RegEx class for manipulating regular expressions.

Searching for a Match

To use the RegEx class, first you need to import the System.Text.RegularExpressions namespace:

```
using System.Text.RegularExpressions;
```

The following statements shows how you can create an instance of the RegEx class, specify the pattern to search for, and match it against a string:

```
string s = "This is a string";
Regex r = new Regex("string");
if (r.IsMatch(s))
{
    Console.WriteLine("Matches.");
}
```

In this example, the Regex class takes in a string constructor, which is the pattern you are searching for. In this case, you are searching for the word "string" and it is matched against the s string variable. The IsMatch() method returns True if there is a match (that is, the string s contains the word "string").

To find the exact position of the text "string" in the variable, you can use the Match() method of the RegEx class. It returns a Match object that you can use to get the position of the text that matches the search pattern using the Index property:

```
string s = "This is a string";
Regex r = new Regex("string");
if (r.IsMatch(s))
{
    Console.WriteLine("Matches.");
}

Match m = r.Match(s);
if (m.Success)
{
    Console.WriteLine("Match found at " + m.Index);
    //---Match found at 10---
}
```

What if you have multiple matches in a string? In this case, you can use the Matches() method of the RegEx class. This method returns a MatchCollection object, and you can iteratively loop through it to obtain the index positions of each individual match:

```
string s = "This is a string and a long string indeed";
Regex r = new Regex("string");

MatchCollection mc = r.Matches(s);
foreach (Match m1 in mc)
{
    Console.WriteLine("Match found at " + m1.Index);
    //---Match found at 10---
    //---Match found at 28---
}
```

More Complex Pattern Matching

You can specify more complex searches using *regular expressions operators*. For example, to know if a string contains either the word "Mr" or "Mrs", you can use the operator |, like this:

```
string gender = "Mr Wei-Meng Lee";
Regex r = new Regex("Mr|Mrs");
if (r.IsMatch(gender))
{
    Console.WriteLine("Matches.");
}
```

The following table describes regular expression operators commonly used in search patterns.

Operator	Description
.	Match any one character
[ ]	Match any one character listed between the brackets
[^]	Match any one character not listed between the brackets
?	Match any character one time, if it exists
*	Match declared element multiple times, if it exists
+	Match declared element one or more times
{n}	Match declared element exactly n times
{n,}	Match declared element at least n times
{n,N}	Match declared element at least n times, but not more than N times
^	Match at the beginning of a line
$	Match at the end of a line
\<	Match at the beginning of a word
\>	Match at the end of a word
\b	Match at the beginning or end of a word
\B	Match in the middle of a word
\d	Shorthand for digits (0–9)
\w	Shorthand for word characters (letters and digits)
\s	Shorthand for whitespace

Another common search pattern is verifying a string containing a date. For example, if a string contains a date in the format "yyyy/mm/dd", you would specify the search pattern as follows: "(19|20)\d\d[- /.](0[1-9]|1[012])[- /.](0[1-9]|[12][0-9]|3[01])". This pattern will match dates ranging from 1900-01-01 to 2099-12-31.

```
string date = "2007/03/10";
Regex r = new Regex(@"(19|20)\d\d[- /.](0[1-9]|1[012])[- /.]
(0[1-9]|[12][0-9]|3[01])");
if (r.IsMatch(date))
{
    Console.WriteLine("Matches.");
}
```

You can use the following date separators with the pattern specified above:

```
string date = "2007/03/10";
string date = "2007-03-10";
string date = "2007 03 10";
string date = "2007.03.10";
```

Some commonly used search patterns are described in the following table.

Pattern	Description
[0-9]	Digits
[A-Fa-f0-9]	Hexadecimal digits
[A-Za-z0-9]	Alphanumeric characters
[A-Za-z]	Alphabetic characters
[a-z]	Lowercase letters
[A-Z]	Uppercase letters
[\t]	Space and tab
[\x00-\x1F\x7F]	Control characters
[\x21-\x7E]	Visible characters
[\x20-\x7E]	Visible characters and spaces
[!"#$%&'()*+,-./:;<=>?@[\\\]_`{|}~]	Punctuation characters
[\t\r\n\v\f]	Whitespace characters
\w+([-+.']\w+)*@\w+([-.]\w+)*\.\w+([-.]\w+)*	Email address
http(s)?://([\w-]+\.)+[\w-]+(/[\w- ./?%&=]*)?	Internet URL
((\(\d{3}\) ?)|(\d{3}-))?\d{3}-\d{4}	U.S. phone number
\d{3}-\d{2}-\d{4}	U.S. Social Security number
\d{5}(-\d{4})?	U.S. ZIP code

To verify that an email address is correctly formatted, you can use the following statements with the specified regular expression:

```
string email = "weimenglee@learn2develop.net";
Regex r = new Regex(@"^[\w-\.]+@([\w-]+\.)+[\w-]{2,4}$");
if (r.IsMatch(email))
    Console.WriteLine("Email address is correct.");
else
    Console.WriteLine("Email address is incorrect.");
```

There are many different regular expressions that you can use to validate an email address. However, there is no perfect regular expression to validate all email addresses. For more information on validating email addresses using regular expressions, check out the following web sites: http://regular-expressions.info/email.html *and* http://fightingforalostcause.net/misc/2006/compare-email-regex.php.

Summary

String manipulations are common operations, so it's important that you have a good understanding of how they work and the various methods and classes that deal with them. This chapter provided a lot of information about how strings are represented in C# and about using regular expressions to perform matching on strings.

9

Generics

One of the new features in the .NET Framework (beginning with version 2.0) is the support of generics in Microsoft Intermediate Language (MSIL). Generics use type parameters, which allow you to design classes and methods that defer the specification of one or more types until the class or method is declared and instantiated by client code. Generics enable developers to define type-safe data structures, without binding to specific fixed data types at design time.

Generics are a feature of the IL and not specific to C# alone, so languages such as C# and VB.NET can take advantage of them.

This chapter discusses the basics of generics and how you can use them to enhance efficiency and type safety in your applications. Specifically, you will learn:

❏ Advantages of using generics

❏ How to specify constraints in a generic type

❏ Generic interfaces, structs, methods, operators, and delegates

❏ The various classes in the .NET Framework class library that support generics

Understanding Generics

Let's look at an example to see how generics work. Suppose that you need to implement your own custom stack class. A stack is a last-in, first-out (LIFO) data structure that enables you to push items into and pop items out of the stack. One possible implementation is:

```
public class MyStack
{
    private int[] _elements;
    private int _pointer;

    public MyStack(int size)
    {
        _elements = new int[size];
```

(continued)

(continued)

```
            _pointer = 0;
        }

        public void Push(int item)
        {
            if (_pointer > _elements.Length - 1)
            {
                throw new Exception("Stack is full.");
            }
            _elements[_pointer] = item;
            _pointer++;
        }

        public int Pop()
        {
            _pointer--;
            if (_pointer < 0)
            {
                throw new Exception("Stack is empty.");
            }
            return _elements[_pointer];
        }
    }
```

In this case, the MyStack class allows data of int type to be pushed into and popped out of the stack. The following statements show how to use the MyStack class:

```
        MyStack stack = new MyStack(3);
        stack.Push(1);
        stack.Push(2);
        stack.Push(3);

        Console.WriteLine(stack.Pop()); //---3---
        Console.WriteLine(stack.Pop()); //---2---
        Console.WriteLine(stack.Pop()); //---1---
```

As you can see, this stack implementation accepts stack items of the int data type. To use this implementation for another data type, say String, you need to create another class that uses the string type. Obviously, this is not a very efficient way of writing your class definitions because you now have several versions of essentially the same class to maintain.

A common way of solving this problem is to use the Object data type so that the compiler will use late-binding during runtime:

```
public class MyStack
{
    private object[] _elements;
    private int _pointer;

    public MyStack(int size)
```

```
    {
        _elements = new object[size];
        _pointer = 0;
    }

    public void Push(object item)
    {
        if (_pointer > _elements.Length - 1)
        {
            throw new Exception("Stack is full.");
        }
        _elements[_pointer] = item;
        _pointer++;
    }

    public object Pop()
    {
        _pointer--;
        if (_pointer < 0)
        {
            throw new Exception("Stack is empty.");
        }
        return _elements[_pointer];
    }
}
```

One problem with this approach is that when you use the stack class, you may inadvertently pop out the wrong data type, as shown in the following highlighted code:

```
MyStack stack = new MyStack(3);
stack.Push(1);
stack.Push(2);
stack.Push("A");

//---invalid cast---
int num = (int) stack.Pop();
```

Because the Pop() method returns a variable of Object type, IntelliSense cannot detect during design time if this code is correct. It is only during runtime that when you try to pop out a string type and try to typecast it into an int type that an error occurs. Besides, type casting (boxing and unboxing) during runtime incurs a performance penalty.

To resolve this inflexibility, you can make use of generics.

Generic Classes

Using generics, you do not need to fix the data type of the items used by your stack class. Instead, you use a generic type parameter (`<T>`) that identifies the data type parameter on a class, structure, interface, delegate, or procedure. Here's a rewrite of the `MyStack` class that shows the use of generics:

```
public class MyStack<T>
{
    private T[] _elements;
    private int _pointer;

    public MyStack(int size)
    {
        _elements = new T[size];
        _pointer = 0;
    }

    public void Push(T item)
    {
        if (_pointer > _elements.Length - 1)
        {
            throw new Exception("Stack is full.");
        }
        _elements[_pointer] = item;
        _pointer++;
    }

    public T Pop()
    {
        _pointer--;
        if (_pointer < 0)
        {
            throw new Exception("Stack is empty.");
        }
        return _elements[_pointer];
    }
}
```

As highlighted, you use the type `T` as a placeholder for the eventual data type that you want to use for the class. In other words, during the design stage of this class, you do not specify the actual data type that the `MyStack` class will deal with. The `MyStack` class is now known as a *generic type*.

When declaring the private member array `_element`, you use the generic parameter `T` instead of a specific type such as `int` or `string`:

```
private T[] _elements;
```

In short, you replace all specific data types with the generic parameter `T`.

You can use any variable name you want to represent the generic parameter. `T` is chosen as the generic parameter for illustration purposes.

If you want the `MyStack` class to manipulate items of type `int`, specify that during the instantiation stage (`int` is called the type argument):

```
MyStack<int> stack = new MyStack<int>(3);
```

The stack object is now known as a *constructed* type, and you can use the `MyStack` class normally:

```
stack.Push(1);
stack.Push(2);
stack.Push(3);
```

A constructed type is a generic type with at least one type argument.

In Figure 9-1 IntelliSense shows that the `Push()` method now accepts arguments of type `int`.

```
MyStack<int> stack = new MyStack<int>(3);
stack.Push(|
void MyStack<int>.Push (int item)
```

Figure 9-1

Trying to push a `string` value into the stack like this:

```
stack.Push("A");   //---Error---
```

generates a compile-time error. That's because the compiler checks the data type used by the `MyStack` class during compile time. This is one of the key advantages of using generics in C#.

To use the `MyStack` class for `String` data types, you simply do this:

```
MyStack<string> stack = new MyStack<string>(3);
stack.Push("A");
stack.Push("B");
stack.Push("C");
```

Figure 9-2 summarizes the terms used in a generic type.

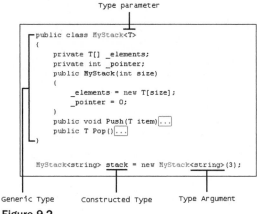

Figure 9-2

Using the default Keyword in Generics

In the preceding implementation of the generic `MyStack` class, the `Pop()` method throws an exception whenever you call it when the stack is empty:

```
public T Pop()
{
    _pointer--;
    if (_pointer < 0)
    {
        throw new Exception("Stack is empty.");
    }
    return _elements[_pointer];
}
```

Rather than throwing an exception, you might want to return the default value of the type used in the class. If the stack is dealing with `int` values, it should return 0; if the stack is dealing with `string`, it should return an empty string. In this case, you can use the `default` keyword to return the default value of a type:

```
public T Pop()
{
    _pointer--;
    if (_pointer < 0)
    {
        return default(T);
    }
    return _elements[_pointer];
}
```

For instance, if the stack deals with `int` values, calling the `Pop()` method on an empty stack will return 0:

```
MyStack<int> stack = new MyStack<int>(3);
stack.Push(1);
stack.Push(2);
stack.Push(3);

Console.WriteLine(stack.Pop()); //---3---
Console.WriteLine(stack.Pop()); //---2---
Console.WriteLine(stack.Pop()); //---1---
Console.WriteLine(stack.Pop()); //---0---
```

Likewise, if the stack deals with the `string` type, calling `Pop()` on an empty stack will return an empty string:

```
MyStack<string> stack = new MyStack<string>(3);
stack.Push("A");
stack.Push("B");
stack.Push("C");

Console.WriteLine(stack.Pop()); //---"C"---
Console.WriteLine(stack.Pop()); //---"B"---
Console.WriteLine(stack.Pop()); //---"A"---
Console.WriteLine(stack.Pop()); //---""---
```

The default keyword returns null for reference types (that is, if T is a reference type) and 0 for numeric types. If the type is a struct, it will return each member of the struct initialized to 0 (for numeric types) or null (for reference types).

Advantages of Generics

It's not difficult to see the advantages of using generics:

❏ **Type safety** — Generic types enforce type compliance at compile time, not at runtime (as in the case of using Object). This reduces the chances of data-type conflict during runtime.

❏ **Performance** — The data types to be used in a generic class are determined at compile time, so there's no need to perform type casting during runtime, which is a computationally costly process.

❏ **Code reuse** — Because you need to write the class only once and then customize it for use with the various data types, there is a substantial amount of code reuse.

Using Constraints in a Generic Type

Using the MyStack class, suppose that you want to add a method called Find() that allows users to check if the stack contains a specific item. You implement the Find() method like this:

```
public class MyStack<T>
{
    private T[] _elements;
    private int _pointer;

    public MyStack(int size)
    {
        _elements = new T[size];
        _pointer = 0;
    }

    public void Push(T item)
    {
        if (_pointer > _elements.Length - 1)
        {
            throw new Exception("Stack is full.");
        }
        _elements[_pointer] = item;
        _pointer++;
    }

    public T Pop()
    {
        _pointer--;
        if (_pointer < 0)
        {
            return default(T);
            //throw new Exception("Stack is empty.");
        }
```

(continued)

(continued)

```
            return _elements[_pointer];
    }

    public bool Find(T keyword)
    {
        bool found = false;
        for (int i=0; i<_pointer; i++)
        {
            if (_elements[i] == keyword)
            {
                found = true;
                break;
            }
        }
        return found;
    }
}
```

But the code will not compile. This is because of the statement:

```
    if (_elements[i] == keyword)
```

That's because the compiler has no way of knowing if the actual type of item and keyword (type T) support this operator (see Figure 9-3). For example, you cannot by default compare two struct objects.

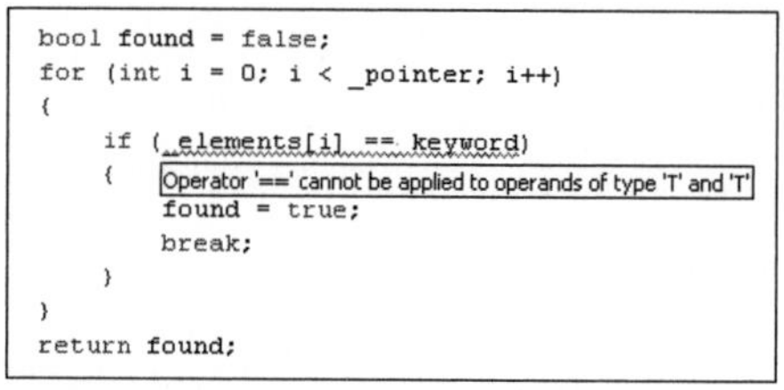

```
bool found = false;
for (int i = 0; i < _pointer; i++)
{
    if (_elements[i] == keyword)
    {   Operator '==' cannot be applied to operands of type 'T' and 'T'
        found = true;
        break;
    }
}
return found;
```

Figure 9-3

A better way to resolve this problem is to apply constraint to the generic class so that only certain data types can be used. In this case, because you want to perform comparison in the Find() method, the data type used by the generic class must implement the IComparable<T> interface. This is enforced by using the where keyword:

```
public class MyStack<T> where T : IComparable<T>
{
    private T[] _elements;
    private int _pointer;

    public MyStack(int size)
    {
        _elements = new T[size];
        _pointer = 0;
    }

    public void Push(T item)
```

```
    {
        if (_pointer > _elements.Length - 1)
        {
            throw new Exception("Stack is full.");
        }
        _elements[_pointer] = item;
        _pointer++;
    }

    public T Pop()
    {
        _pointer--;
        if (_pointer < 0)
        {
            return default(T);
        }
        return _elements[_pointer];
    }

    public bool Find(T keyword)
    {
        bool found = false;
        for (int i=0; i<_pointer; i++)
        {
            if (_elements[i].CompareTo(keyword) == 0)
            {
                found = true;
                break;
            }
        }
        return found;
    }
}
```

For the comparison, you use the CompareTo() method to compare two items of type T (which must implement the IComparable interface). The CompareTo() method returns 0 if the two objects are equal. You can now search for an item by using the Find() method:

```
MyStack<string> stack = new MyStack<string>(3);
stack.Push("A");
stack.Push("B");
stack.Push("C");

if (stack.Find("B"))
    Console.WriteLine("Contains B");
```

In this case, the code works because the string type implements the IComparable interface. Suppose that you have the following Employee class definition:

```
public class Employee
{
    public string ID { get; set; }
    public string Name { get; set; }
}
```

When you try to use the `MyStack` class with the `Employee` class, you get an error:

```
MyStack<Employee> stack = new MyStack<Employee>(3);   //---Error---
```

That's because the `Employee` class does not implement the `IComparable<T>` interface. To resolve this, simply implement the `IComparable<Employee>` interface in the `Employee` class and implement the `CompareTo()` method:

```
public class Employee : IComparable<Employee>
{
    public string ID { get; set; }
    public string Name { get; set; }

    public int CompareTo(Employee obj)
    {
        return this.ID.CompareTo(obj.ID);
    }
}
```

You can now use the `Employee` class with the generic `MyStack` class:

```
MyStack<Employee> stack = new MyStack<Employee>(2);
stack.Push(new Employee() { ID = "123", Name = "John" });
stack.Push(new Employee() { ID = "456", Name = "Margaret" });

Employee e1 = new Employee() { ID = "123", Name = "John" };

if (stack.Find(e1))
    Console.WriteLine("Employee found.");
```

Specifying Multiple Constraints

You can specify multiple constraints in a generic type. For example, if you want the `MyStack` class to manipulate objects of type `Employee` and also implement the `Icomparable` interface, you can declare the generic type as:

```
public class MyStack<T> where T : Employee,  IComparable<T>
{
    //...
}
```

Here, you are constraining that the `MyStack` class must use types derived from `Employee` and they must also implement the `IComparable` interface.

> The base class constraint must always be specified first, before specifying the interface.

Assuming that you have the following Manager class deriving from the Employee class:

```
public class Manager : Employee, IComparable<Manager>
{
    public int CompareTo(Manager obj)
    {
        return base.CompareTo(obj);
    }
}
```

The following statement is now valid:

```
MyStack<Manager> stackM = new MyStack<Manager>(3);
```

Multiple Type Parameter

So far you have seen only one type parameter used in a generic type, but you can have multiple type parameters. For example, the following MyDictionary class uses two generic type parameters — K and V:

```
public class MyDictionary<K, V>
{
    //...
}
```

To apply constraints on multiple type parameters, use the where keyword multiple times:

```
public class MyDictionary<K, V>
    where K : IComparable<K>
    where V : ICloneable
{
    //...
}
```

Generic Interfaces

Generics can also be applied on interfaces. The following example defines the IMyStack interface:

```
interface IMyStack<T> where T : IComparable<T>
{
    void Push(T item);
    T Pop();
    bool Find(T keyword);
}
```

A class implementing a generic interface must supply the same type parameter as well as satisfy the constraints imposed by the interface.

The following shows the generic MyStack class implementing the generic IMyStack interface:

```
public class MyStack<T> : IMyStack<T> where T : IComparable<T>
{
    //...
}
```

Figure 9-4 shows the error reported by Visual Studio 2008 if the generic `MyStack` class does not provide the constraint imposed by the generic interface.

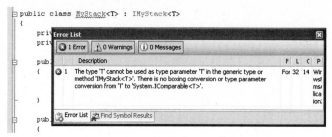

Figure 9-4

Generic Structs

Generics can also be applied to structs. For example, suppose that you have a `Coordinate` struct defined as follows:

```
public struct Coordinate
{
    public int x, y, z;
}
```

The coordinates for the `Coordinate` struct takes in `int` values.

You can use generics on the `Coordinate` struct, like this:

```
public struct Coordinate<T>
{
    public T x, y, z;
}
```

To use `int` values for the `Coordinate` struct, you can do so via the following statements:

```
Coordinate<int> pt1;
pt1.x = 5;
pt1.y = 6;
pt1.z = 7;
```

To use `float` values for the `Coordinate` struct, utilize the following statements:

```
Coordinate<float> pt2;
pt2.x = 2.0F;
pt2.y = 6.3F;
pt2.z = 2.9F;
```

Generic Methods

In addition to generic classes and interfaces, you can also define generic methods. Consider the following class definition and the method contained within it:

```
public class SomeClass
{
    public void DoSomething<T>(T t)
    {
    }
}
```

Here, `DoSomething()` is a generic method. To use a generic method, you need to provide the type when calling it:

```
SomeClass sc = new SomeClass();
sc.DoSomething<int>(3);
```

The C# compiler, however, is smart enough to deduce the type based on the argument passed into the method, so the following statement automatically infers T to be of type String:

```
sc.DoSomething("This is a string"); //---T is String---
```

This feature is known as *generic type inference*.

You can also define a constraint for the generic type in a method, like this:

```
public class SomeClass
{
    public void DoSomething<T>(T t) where T : IComparable<T>
    {
    }
}
```

If you need the generic type to be applicable to the entire class, define the type T at the class level:

```
public class SomeClass<T> where T : IComparable<T>
{
    public void DoSomething(T t)
    {
    }
}
```

In this case, you specify the type during the instantiation of SomeClass:

```
SomeClass<int> sc = new SomeClass<int>();
sc.DoSomething(3);
```

You can also use generics on static methods, in addition to instance methods as just described. For example, the earlier `DoSomething()` method can be modified to become a static method:

```
public class SomeClass
{
    public static void DoSomething<T>(T t) where T : IComparable<T>
    {
    }
}
```

To call this static generic method, you can either explicitly specify the type or use generic type inference:

```
SomeClass.DoSomething(3);
//---or---
SomeClass.DoSomething<int>(3);
```

Generic Operators

Generics can also be applied to operators. Consider the generic MyStack class discussed earlier in this chapter. Suppose that you want to be able to join two MyStack objects together, like this:

```
MyStack<string> stack1 = new MyStack<string>(4);
stack1.Push("A");
stack1.Push("B");

MyStack<string> stack2 = new MyStack<string>(2);
stack2.Push("C");
stack2.Push("D");

stack1 += stack2;
```

In this case, you can overload the + operator, as highlighted in the following code:

```
public class MyStack<T> where T : IComparable<T>
{
    private T[] _elements;
    private int _pointer;

    public MyStack(int size)
    {
        _elements = new T[size];
        _pointer = 0;
    }

    public void Push(T item)
    {
        if (_pointer > _elements.Length - 1)
        {
            throw new Exception("Stack is full.");
        }
        _elements[_pointer] = item;
        _pointer++;
    }

    public T Pop()
    {
        _pointer--;
        if (_pointer < 0)
        {
            return default(T);
        }
        return _elements[_pointer];
    }
```

```
public bool Find(T keyword)
{
    bool found = false;
    for (int i = 0; i < _pointer; i++)
    {
        if (_elements[i].CompareTo(keyword) == 0)
        {
            found = true;
            break;
        }
    }
    return found;
}

public bool Empty
{
    get{
        return (_pointer <= 0);
    }
}

public static MyStack<T> operator +
    (MyStack<T> stackA, MyStack<T> stackB)
{
    while (!stackB.Empty)
    {
        T item = stackB.Pop();
        stackA.Push(item);
    }
    return stackA;
}
}
```

The + operator takes in two operands — the generic MyStack objects. Internally, you pop out each element from the second stack and push it into the first stack. The Empty property allows you to know if a stack is empty.

To print out the elements of stack1 after the joining, use the following statements:

```
stack1 += stack2;
while (!stack1.Empty)
    Console.WriteLine(stack1.Pop());
```

Here's the output:

```
C
D
B
A
```

Generic Delegates

You can also use generics on delegates. The following class definition contains a generic delegate, MethodDelegate:

```
public class SomeClass<T>
{
    public delegate void MethodDelegate(T t);
    public void DoSomething(T t)
    {
    }
}
```

When you specify the type for the class, you also need to specify it for the delegate:

```
SomeClass<int> sc = new SomeClass<int>();
SomeClass<int>.MethodDelegate del;
del = new SomeClass<int>.MethodDelegate(sc.DoSomething);
```

You can make direct assignment to the delegate using a feature known as delegate inferencing, as the following code shows:

```
del = sc.DoSomething;
```

Generics and the .NET Framework Class Library

The .NET Framework class library contains a number of generic classes that enable users to create strongly typed collections. These classes are grouped under the System.Collections.Generic namespace (the nongeneric versions of the classes are contained within the System.Collections namespace). The following tables show the various classes, structures, and interfaces contained within this namespace.

The following table provides a look at the classes contained within the System.Collections.Generic namespace.

Class	Description
Comparer<(Of <(T)>)>	Provides a base class for implementations of the IComparer<(Of <(T)>)> generic interface.
Dictionary<(Of <(TKey, TValue)>)>	Represents a collection of keys and values.
Dictionary<(Of <(TKey, TValue)>)>..::.KeyCollection	Represents the collection of keys in a Dictionary<(Of <(TKey, TValue)>)>. This class cannot be inherited.
Dictionary<(Of <(TKey, TValue)>)>..::.ValueCollection	Represents the collection of values in a Dictionary<(Of <(TKey, TValue)>)>. This class cannot be inherited.

Class	Description
EqualityComparer<(Of <(T)>)>	Provides a base class for implementations of the IEqualityComparer<(Of <(T)>)> generic interface.
HashSet<(Of <(T)>)>	Represents a set of values.
KeyedByTypeCollection<(Of <(TItem)>)>	Provides a collection whose items are types that serve as keys.
KeyNotFoundException	The exception that is thrown when the key specified for accessing an element in a collection does not match any key in the collection.
LinkedList<(Of <(T)>)>	Represents a doubly linked list.
LinkedListNode<(Of <(T)>)>	Represents a node in a LinkedList<(Of <(T)>)>. This class cannot be inherited.
List<(Of <(T)>)>	Represents a strongly typed list of objects that can be accessed by index. Provides methods to search, sort, and manipulate lists.
Queue<(Of <(T)>)>	Represents a first-in, first-out collection of objects.
SortedDictionary<(Of <(TKey, TValue)>)>	Represents a collection of key/value pairs that are sorted on the key.
SortedDictionary<(Of <(TKey, TValue)>)>..::.KeyCollection	Represents the collection of keys in a SortedDictionary<(Of <(TKey, TValue)>)>. This class cannot be inherited.
SortedDictionary<(Of <(TKey, TValue)>)>..::.ValueCollection	Represents the collection of values in a SortedDictionary<(Of <(TKey, TValue)>)>. This class cannot be inherited.
SortedList<(Of <(TKey, TValue)>)>	Represents a collection of key/value pairs that are sorted by key based on the associated IComparer<(Of <(T)>)> implementation.
Stack<(Of <(T)>)>	Represents a variable size last-in, first-out (LIFO) collection of instances of the same arbitrary type.
SynchronizedCollection<(Of <(T)>)>	Provides a thread-safe collection that contains objects of a type specified by the generic parameter as elements.
SynchronizedKeyedCollection<(Of <(K, T)>)>	Provides a thread-safe collection that contains objects of a type specified by a generic parameter and that are grouped by keys.
SynchronizedReadOnlyCollection<(Of <(T)>)>	Provides a thread-safe, read-only collection that contains objects of a type specified by the generic parameter as elements.

The structures contained within the `System.Collections.Generic` namespace are described in the following table.

Structure	Description
`Dictionary<(Of <(TKey, TValue>)>)..::.Enumerator`	Enumerates the elements of a `Dictionary<(Of <(TKey, TValue>)>)`
`Dictionary<(Of <(TKey, TValue>)>)..::.KeyCollection..::.Enumerator`	Enumerates the elements of a `Dictionary<(Of <(TKey, TValue>)>)..::.KeyCollection`
`Dictionary<(Of <(TKey, TValue>)>)..::.ValueCollection..::.Enumerator`	Enumerates the elements of a `Dictionary<(Of <(TKey, TValue>)>)..::.ValueCollection`
`HashSet<(Of <(T>)>)..::.Enumerator`	Enumerates the elements of a `HashSet<(Of <(T>)>)` object
`KeyValuePair<(Of <(TKey, TValue>)>)`	Defines a key/value pair that can be set or retrieved
`LinkedList<(Of <(T>)>)..::.Enumerator`	Enumerates the elements of a `LinkedList<(Of <(T>)>)`
`List<(Of <(T>)>)..::.Enumerator`	Enumerates the elements of a `List<(Of <(T>)>)`
`Queue<(Of <(T>)>)..::.Enumerator`	Enumerates the elements of a `Queue<(Of <(T>)>)`
`SortedDictionary<(Of <(TKey, TValue>)>)..::.Enumerator`	Enumerates the elements of a `SortedDictionary<(Of <(TKey, TValue>)>)`
`SortedDictionary<(Of <(TKey, TValue>)>)..::.KeyCollection..::.Enumerator`	Enumerates the elements of a `SortedDictionary<(Of <(TKey, TValue>)>)..::.KeyCollection`
`SortedDictionary<(Of <(TKey, TValue>)>)..::.ValueCollection..::.Enumerator`	Enumerates the elements of a `SortedDictionary<(Of <(TKey, TValue>)>)..::.ValueCollection`
`Stack<(Of <(T>)>)..::.Enumerator`	Enumerates the elements of a `Stack<(Of <(T>)>)`

Following are descriptions of the interfaces contained within the System.Collections.Generic namespace.

Interface	Description
ICollection<(Of <(T>)>)	Defines methods to manipulate generic collections
IComparer<(Of <(T>)>)	Defines a method that a type implements to compare two objects
IDictionary<(Of <(TKey, TValue>)>)	Represents a generic collection of key/value pairs
IEnumerable<(Of <(T>)>)	Exposes the enumerator, which supports a simple iteration over a collection of a specified type
IEnumerator<(Of <(T>)>)	Supports a simple iteration over a generic collection
IEqualityComparer<(Of <(T>)>)	Defines methods to support the comparison of objects for equality
Ilist<(Of <(T>)>)	Represents a collection of objects that can be individually accessed by index

Prior to .NET 2.0, all the data structures contained in the System.Collection namespace are object-based. With .NET 2.0, Microsoft has released generic equivalents of some of these classes. The following table shows the mapping of these classes in the two namespaces.

System.Collection	System.Collection.Generic
Comparer	Comparer<T>
HashTable	Dictionary<K,T>
–	LinkedList<T>
ArrayList	List<T>
Queue	Queue<T>
SortedList	SortedDictionary<K,T>
Stack	Stack<T>
ICollection	ICollection<T>
System.IComparable	IComparable<T>
IDictionary	IDictionary<K,T>
IEnumerable	IEnumerable<T>
IEnumerator	IEnumerator<T>
IList	IList<T>

The Stack<T>, Queue<T>, *and* Dictionary<K,T> *generic classes are discussed in more detail in Chapter 13, "Collections."*

Using the LinkedList<T> Generic Class

One of the new classes in the System.Collection.Generic namespace is the LinkedList<T> generic class. A *linked list* is a data structure containing a series of interconnected nodes. Linked lists have wide usage in computer science and are often used to store related data.

There are several types of linked lists:

❑　Singly linked list

❑　Doubly linked list

❑　Circularly linked list

Figure 9-5 shows a singly linked list. Every node has a field that "points" to the next node. To move from one node to another (known as *list traversal*), you start from the first node and follow the links leading to the next node.

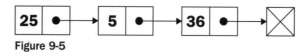

Figure 9-5

Figure 9-6 shows a doubly linked list. Doubly linked list nodes contains an additional field to point to the previous node. You can traverse a doubly linked list in either direction. The LinkedList<T> class implements a doubly linked list.

Figure 9-6

Figure 9-7 shows a circularly linked list. A circularly linked list has its first and last node linked together. A circularly linked list can either be a singly linked list (as shown in Figure 9-5) or a doubly linked list.

Figure 9-7

The next example shows how to use the `LinkedList<T>` class available in the .NET Framework to store a list of random numbers. As each random number is generated, it is inserted into the linked list in numeric sorted order (from small to big). The end result is a list of sorted random numbers. Specifically, the example uses the `LinkedList<T>` class members shown in the following table.

Member	Description
AddAfter()	Adds a new node after an existing node
AddBefore()	Adds a new node before an existing node
First	Gets the first node
Last	Gets the last node

Each node in the `LinkedList<T>` class is an object of type `LinkedListNode<T>`. The following table shows the properties in the `LinkedListNode<T>` that are used in this example.

Property	Description
Next	Gets the next node
Previous	Gets the previous node
Value	Gets the value contained in the node

Now for the example, first create an instance of the `LinkedList<T>` class using the `int` type:

```
LinkedList<int> Numbers = new LinkedList<int>();
```

Define the `InsertNumber()` function, which accepts an `int` parameter:

```
private void InsertNumber(int number)
{
    //---start from first node---
    LinkedListNode<int> currNode = Numbers.First;
    LinkedListNode<int> newNode = new LinkedListNode<int>(number);

    if (currNode == null)
    {
        Numbers.AddFirst(newNode);
        return;
    }
    while (currNode != null)
    {
        if (currNode.Value > number)
        {
            if (currNode.Previous != null)
                //---Case 1 - add the node to the previous node---
                Numbers.AddAfter(currNode.Previous, newNode);
```

(continued)

(continued)

```
                else
                    //--- Case 2 - the current node is the first node---
                    Numbers.AddBefore(currNode, newNode);
                break;
            }
            else if (currNode.Next == null)
            {
                //--- Case 3 - if last node has been reached---
                Numbers.AddAfter(currNode, newNode);
                break;
            }
            //---traverse to the next node---
            currNode = currNode.Next;
        }
    }
```

The `InsertNumber()` function initially creates a new node to contain the random number generated. It then traverses the linked list to find the correct position to insert the number. Take a look at the different possible cases when inserting a number into the linked list.

Figure 9-8 shows the case when the node to be inserted (11) is between two nodes (9 and 15, the current node). In this case, it must be added after node 9.

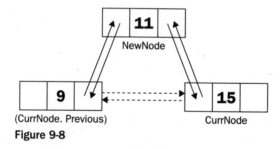

Figure 9-8

Figure 9-9 shows the case when the node to be inserted (11) is smaller than the first node (current node) in the linked list. In this case, it must be added before the current node.

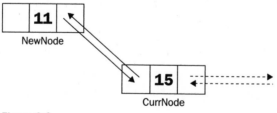

Figure 9-9

Figure 9-10 shows the case when the node to be inserted is larger than the last node (current node) in the linked list. In this case, it must be added after the current node.

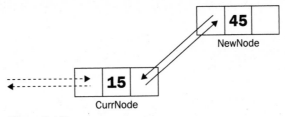

Figure 9-10

To insert a list of random numbers into the linked list, you can use the following statements:

```
Random rnd = new Random();
for (int i = 0; i < 20; i++)
    InsertNumber(rnd.Next(100)); //---random number from 0 to 100---
```

To print out all the numbers contained within the linked list, traverse the link starting from the first node:

```
//---traverse forward---
LinkedListNode<int> node = Numbers.First;
while (node != null)
{
    Console.WriteLine(node.Value);
    node = node.Next;
}
```

The result is a list of 20 random numbers in sorted order.

Alternatively, you can traverse the list backward from the last node:

```
//---traverse backward---
LinkedListNode<int> node = Numbers.Last;
while (node != null)
{
    Console.WriteLine(node.Value);
    node = node.Previous;
}
```

The result would be a list of random numbers in reverse-sort order.

System.Collections.ObjectModel

The `System.Collections.ObjectModel` namespace in the .NET class library contains several generic classes that deal with collections. These classes are described in the following table.

Generic Class	Description
Collection<T>	Provides the base class for a generic collection.
KeyedCollection<TKey,TItem>	Provides the abstract base class for a collection whose keys are embedded in the values.
ObservableCollection<T>	Represents a dynamic data collection that provides notifications when items get added, removed, or when the whole list is refreshed.
ReadOnlyCollection<T>	Provides the base class for a generic read-only collection.
ReadOnlyObservableCollection<T>	Represents a read-only ObservableCollection<T>.

Let's take a look at `Collection<T>`, one of the classes available. It is similar to the generic `List<T>` class. Both `Collection<T>` and `List<T>` implement the `IList<T>` and `ICollection<T>` interfaces. The main difference between the two is that `Collection<T>` contains virtual methods that can be overridden, whereas `List<T>` does not have any.

The List<T> generic class is discussed in details in Chapter 13.

The following code example shows how to use the generic `Collection<T>` class:

```
using System;
using System.Collections.Generic;
using System.Linq;
using System.Text;
using System.Collections.ObjectModel;

namespace CollectionEg1
{
    class Program
    {
        static void Main(string[] args)
        {
            Collection<string> names = new Collection<string>();
            names.Add("Johnny");
            names.Add("Michael");
            names.Add("Wellington");
            foreach (string name in names)
            {
                Console.WriteLine(name);
            }
            Console.ReadLine();
        }
    }
}
```

Here's the example's output:

```
Johnny
Michael
Wellington
```

To understand the usefulness of the generic `Collection<T>` class, consider the following example where you need to write a class to contain the names of all the branches a company has:

```
using System;
using System.Collections.Generic;
using System.Linq;
using System.Text;

using System.Collections.ObjectModel;

namespace CollectionEg2
{
    class Program
    {
        static void Main(string[] args)
        {
        }
    }

    public class Branch
    {
        private List<string> _branchNames = new List<string>();
        public List<string> BranchNames
        {
            get
            {
                return _branchNames;
            }
        }
    }
}
```

In this example, the `Branch` class exposes a public read-only property called `BranchNames` of type `List<T>`. To add branch names to a `Branch` object, you first create an instance of the `Branch` class and then add individual branch names to the `BranchNames` property by using the `Add()` method of the `List<T>` class:

```
static void Main(string[] args)
{
    Branch b = new Branch();
    b.BranchNames.Add("ABC");
    b.BranchNames.Add("XYZ");
}
```

Suppose now that your customers request an event for the `Branch` class so that every time a branch name is deleted, the event fires so that the client of `Branch` class can be notified. The problem with the generic `List<T>` class is that there is no way you can be informed when an item is removed.

A better way to resolve this issue is to expose BranchName as a property of type Collection<T> instead of List<T>. That's because the generic Collection<T> type provides four overridable methods — ClearItems(), InsertItem(), RemoveItem(), and SetItem() — which allow a derived class to be notified when a collection has been modified.

Here's how rewriting the Branch class, using the generic Collection<T> type, looks:

```csharp
public class Branch
{
    public Branch()
    {
        _branchNames = new BranchNamesCollection(this);
    }

    private BranchNamesCollection _branchNames;
    public Collection<string> BranchNames
    {
        get
        {
            return _branchNames;
        }
    }

    //---event raised when an item is removed---
    public event EventHandler ItemRemoved;

    //---called from within the BranchNamesCollection class---
    protected virtual void RaiseItemRemovedEvent(EventArgs e)
    {
        if (ItemRemoved != null)
        {
            ItemRemoved(this, e);
        }
    }

    private class BranchNamesCollection : Collection<string>
    {
        private Branch _b;
        public BranchNamesCollection(Branch b)
        {
            _b = b;
        }

        //---fired when an item is removed---
        protected override void RemoveItem(int index)
        {
            base.RemoveItem(index);
            _b.RaiseItemRemovedEvent(EventArgs.Empty);
        }
    }
}
```

There is now a class named `BranchNamesCollection` within the `Branch` class. The `BranchNamesCollection` class is of type `Collection<string>`. It overrides the `RemoveItem()` method present in the `Collection<T>` class. When an item is deleted from the collection, it proceeds to remove the item by calling the `base RemoveItem()` method and then invoking a function defined in the `Branch` class: `RaiseItemRemovedEvent()`. The `RaiseItemRemovedEvent()` function then raises the `ItemRemoved` event to notify the client that an item has been removed.

To service the `ItemRemoved` event in the `Branch` class, modify the code as follows:

```
static void Main(string[] args)
{
    Branch b = new Branch();
    b.ItemRemoved += new EventHandler(b_ItemRemoved);

    b.BranchNames.Add("ABC");
    b.BranchNames.Add("XYZ");
    b.BranchNames.Remove("XYZ");

    foreach (string branchName in b.BranchNames)
    {
        Console.WriteLine(branchName);
    }
    Console.ReadLine();
}

static void b_ItemRemoved(object sender, EventArgs e)
{
    Console.WriteLine("Item removed!");
}
```

And here's the code's output:

```
Item removed!
```

> As a rule of thumb, use the generic `Collection<T>` class (because it is more extensible) as a return type from a public method, and use the generic `List<T>` class for internal implementation.

Summary

Generics allow you define type-safe data structures without binding to specific fixed data types at design time. The end result is that your code becomes safer without sacrificing performance. In addition to showing you how to define your own generic class, this chapter also examined some of the generic classes provided in the .NET Framework class library, such as the generic `LinkedList<T>` and `Collection<T>` classes.

10

Threading

Today's computer runs at more than 2GHz, a blazing speed improvement over just a few years ago. Almost all operating systems today are multitasking, meaning you can run more than one application at the same time. However, if your application is still executing code sequentially, you are not really utilizing the speed advancements of your latest processor. How many times have you seen an unresponsive application come back to life after it has completed a background task such as performing some mathematical calculations or network transfer? To fully utilize the extensive processing power of your computer and write responsive applications, understanding and using threads is important.

> **A thread is a sequential flow of execution within a program. A program can consist of multiple threads of execution, each capable of independent execution.**

This chapter explains how to write multithreaded applications using the Thread class in the .NET Framework. It shows you how to:

❑ Create a new thread of execution and stop it

❑ Synchronize different threads using the various thread classes available

❑ Write thread-safe Windows applications

❑ Use the BackgroundWorker component in Windows Forms to program background tasks.

The Need for Multithreading

Multithreading is one of the most powerful concepts in programming. Using multithreading, you can break a complex task in a single application into multiple threads that execute independently of one another. One particularly good use of multithreading is in tasks that are synchronous in nature, such as Web Services calls. By default, Web Services calls are blocking calls — that is, the caller code does not continue until the Web Service returns the result. Because Web Services calls are often slow, this can result in sluggish client-side performance unless you take special steps to make the call an asynchronous one.

To see how multithreading works, first take a look at the following example:

```
class Program
{
    static void Main(string[] args)
    {
        DoSomething();
        Console.WriteLine("Continuing with the execution...");
        Console.ReadLine();
    }

    static void DoSomething()
    {
        while (true)
        {
            Console.WriteLine("Doing something...");
        }
    }
}
```

This is a simple application that calls the DoSomething() function to print out a series of strings (in fact, it is an infinite loop, which will never stop; see Figure 10-1). Right after calling the DoSomething() function, you try to print a string ("Continuing with the execution...") to the console window. However, because the DoSomething() function is busy printing its own output, the "Console .WriteLine("Continuing with the execution...");" statement never gets a chance to execute.

Figure 10-1

This example illustrates the sequential nature of application — statements are executed sequentially. The DoSomething() function is analogous to consuming a Web Service, and as long as the Web Service does not return a value to you (due to network latency or busy web server, for instance), the rest of your application is blocked (that is, not able to continue).

Starting a Thread

You can use threads to break up statements in your application into smaller chunks so that they can be executed in parallel. You could, for instance, use a separate thread to call the DoSomething() function in the preceding example and let the remaining of the code continue to execute.

Every application contains one main thread of execution. A multithreaded application contains two or more threads of execution.

In C#, you can create a new thread of execution by using the Thread class found in the System .Threading namespace. The Thread class creates and controls a thread. The constructor of the Thread class takes in a ThreadStart delegate, which wraps the function that you want to run as a separate thread. The following code shows to use the Thread class to run the DoSomething() function as a separate thread:

> **Import the** System.Threading **namespace when using the** Thread **class.**

```
class Program
{
    static void Main(string[] args)
    {
        Thread t = new Thread(new ThreadStart(DoSomething));
        t.Start();

        Console.WriteLine("Continuing with the execution...");
        Console.ReadLine();
    }

    static void DoSomething()
    {
        while (true)
        {
            Console.WriteLine("Doing something...");
        }
    }
}
```

Note that the thread is not started until you explicitly call the Start() method. When the Start() method is called, the DoSomething() function is called and control is immediately returned to the Main() function. Figure 10-2 shows the output of the example application.

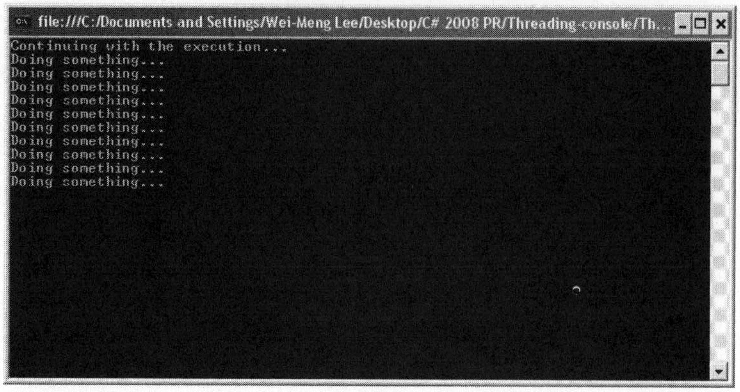

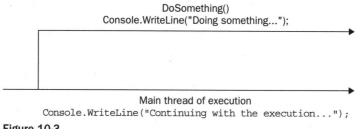

Figure 10-2

Figure 10-3 shows graphically the two different threads of execution.

DoSomething()
Console.WriteLine("Doing something...");

Main thread of execution
Console.WriteLine("Continuing with the execution...");

Figure 10-3

As shown in Figure 10-2, it just so happens that before the `DoSomething()` method gets the chance to execute, the main thread has proceeded to execute its next statements. Hence, the output shows the main thread executing before the `DoSomething()` method. In reality, both threads have an equal chance of executing, and one of the many possible outputs could be:

```
Doing something...
Doing something...
Continuing with the execution...
Doing something...
Doing something...
...
```

A thread executes until:

❑ It reaches the end of its life (method exits), or

❑ You prematurely kill (abort) it.

Aborting a Thread

You can use the Abort() method of the Thread class to abort a thread after it has started executing. Here's an example:

```
class Program
{
    static void Main(string[] args)
    {
        Thread t = new Thread(new ThreadStart(DoSomething));
        t.Start();
        Console.WriteLine("Continuing with the execution...");

        while (!t.IsAlive) ;

        Thread.Sleep(1);
        t.Abort();

        Console.ReadLine();
    }

    static void DoSomething()
    {
        try
        {
            while (true)
            {
                Console.WriteLine("Doing something...");
            }
        }
        catch (ThreadAbortException ex)
        {
            Console.WriteLine(ex.Message);
        }
    }
}
```

When the thread is started, you continue with the next statement and print out the message "Continuing with the execution... ". You then use the IsAlive property of the Thread class to find out the execution status of the thread and block the execution of the Main() function (with the while statement) until the thread has a chance to start. The Sleep() method of the Thread class blocks the current thread (Main()) for a specified number of milliseconds. Using this statement, you are essentially giving the DoSomething() function a chance to execute. Finally, you kill the thread by using the Abort() method of the Thread class.

The `ThreadAbortException` exception is fired on any thread that you kill. Ideally, you should clean up the resources in this exception handler (via the `finally` statement):

```
static void DoSomething()
{
    try
    {
        while (true)
        {
            Console.WriteLine("Doing something...");
        }
    }
    catch (ThreadAbortException ex)
    {
        Console.WriteLine(ex.Message);
    }
    finally {
        //---clean up your resources here---
    }
}
```

The output of the preceding program may look like this:

```
Continuing with the execution...
Doing something...
Doing something...
Doing something...
Doing something...
Doing something...
Doing something...
Doing something...
Thread was being aborted.
```

Notice that I say the program *may* look like this. When you have multiple threads running in your application, you don't have control over which threads are executed first. The OS determines the actual execution sequence and that is dependent on several factors such as CPU utilization, memory usage, and so on. It is possible, then, that the output may look like this:

```
Doing something...
Continuing with the execution...
Doing something...
Doing something...
Doing something...
Doing something...
Doing something...
Doing something...
Thread was being aborted.
```

While you can use the `Abort()` method to kill a thread, it is always better to exit it gracefully whenever possible.

Here's a rewrite of the previous program:

```
class Program
{
    private static volatile bool _stopThread = false;

    static void Main(string[] args)
    {
        Thread t = new Thread(new ThreadStart(DoSomething));
        t.Start();

        Console.WriteLine("Continuing with the execution...");

        while (!t.IsAlive) ;

        Thread.Sleep(1);
        _stopThread = true;
        Console.WriteLine("Thread ended.");
        Console.ReadLine();
    }

    static void DoSomething()
    {
        try
        {
            while (!_stopThread)
            {
                Console.WriteLine("Doing something...");
            }
        }
        catch (ThreadAbortException ex)
        {
            Console.WriteLine(ex.Message);
        }
        finally {
            //---clean up your resources here---
        }
    }
}
```

First, you declare a static Boolean variable call _stopThread:

```
private static volatile bool _stopThread = false;
```

Notice that you prefix the declaration with the volatile keyword, which is used as a hint to the compiler that this variable will be accessed by multiple threads. The variable will then not be subjected to compiler optimization and will always have the most up-to-date value.

To use the _stopThread variable to stop the thread, you modify the DoSomething() function, like this:

```
while (!_stopThread)
{
    Console.WriteLine("Doing something...");
}
```

Finally, to stop the thread in the `Main()` function, you just need to set the `_stopThread` variable to `true`:

```
_stopThread = true;
Console.WriteLine("Thread ended.");
```

The output of this program *may* look like this:

```
Continuing with the execution.
Doing something...
Doing something...
Doing something...
Doing something...
Doing something...
Doing something...
Thread ended.
Doing something...
```

The `DoSomething()` function may print another message after the `"Thread ended."` message. That's because the thread might not end immediately. To ensure that the `"Thread ended."` message is printed only after the `DoSomething()` function ends, you can use the `Join()` method of the `Thread` class to join the two threads:

```
static void Main(string[] args)
{
    Thread t = new Thread(new ThreadStart(DoSomething));
    t.Start();

    Console.WriteLine("Continuing with the execution...");

    while (!t.IsAlive) ;

    Thread.Sleep(1);
    _stopThread = true;

    //---joins the current thread (Main()) to t---
    t.Join();
    Console.WriteLine("Thread ended.");
    Console.ReadLine();
}
```

The `Join()` method essentially blocks the calling thread until the thread terminates. In this case, the `Thread ended` message will be blocked until the thread (t) terminates.

The output of the program now looks like this:

```
Continuing with the execution.
Doing something...
Doing something...
Doing something...
Doing something...
Doing something...
Doing something...
Thread ended.
```

Figure 10-4 shows graphically the two different threads of execution.

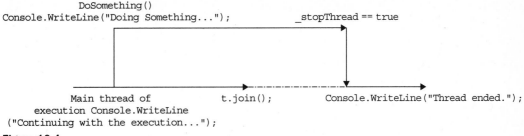

Figure 10-4

Passing Parameters to Threads

In the past few examples, you've seen how to create a thread using the `ThreadStart` delegate to point to a method. So far, though, the method that you have been pointing to does not have any parameters:

```
static void DoSomething()
{
    ...
    ...
}
```

What if the function you want to invoke as a thread has a parameter? In that case, you have two choices:

❑   Wrap the function inside a class, and pass in the parameter via a property.

❑   Use the `ParameterizedThreadStart` delegate instead of the `ThreadStart` delegate.

Using the same example, the first choice is to wrap the `DoSomething()` method as a class and then expose a property to take in the parameter value:

```
class Program
{
    static void Main(string[] args)
    {
        SomeClass sc = new SomeClass();
        sc.msg = "useful";
        Thread t = new Thread(new ThreadStart(sc.DoSomething));
        t.Start();
    }

}

class SomeClass
```

(continued)

(continued)

```
        {
    public string msg { get; set; }
    public void DoSomething()
    {
        try
        {
            while (true)
            {
                Console.WriteLine("Doing something...{0}", msg);
            }
        }
        catch (ThreadAbortException ex)
        {
            Console.WriteLine(ex.Message);
        }
        finally
        {
            //---clean up your resources here---
        }
    }
        }
```

In this example, you create a thread for the DoSomething() method by creating a new instance of the SomeClass class and then passing in the value through the msg property.

For the second choice, you use the ParameterizedThreadStart delegate instead of the ThreadStart delegate. The ParameterizedThreadStart delegate takes a parameter of type object, so if the function that you want to invoke as a thread has a parameter, that parameter must be of type object.

To see how to use the ParameterizedThreadStart delegate, modify the DoSomething() function by adding a parameter:

```
    static void DoSomething(object msg)
    {
        try
        {
            while (true)
            {
                Console.WriteLine("Doing something...{0}", msg);
            }
        }
        catch (ThreadAbortException ex)
        {
            Console.WriteLine(ex.Message);
        }
        finally {
            //---clean up your resources here---
        }
    }
```

To invoke DoSomething() as a thread and pass it a parameter, you use the ParameterizedThreadStart delegate as follows:

```
static void Main(string[] args)
{
    Thread t = new Thread(new ParameterizedThreadStart(DoSomething));
    t.Start("useful");
    Console.WriteLine("Continuing with the execution...");
    ...
```

The argument to pass to the function is passed in the Start() method.

Thread Synchronization

Multithreading enables you to have several threads of execution running at the same time. However, when a number of different threads run at the same time, they all compete for the same set of resources, so there must be a mechanism to ensure synchronization and communication among threads.

One key problem with multithreading is thread safety. Consider the following subroutine:

```
static void IncrementVar()
{
    _value += 1;
}
```

If two threads execute the same routine at the same time, it is possible that _value variable will not be incremented correctly. One thread may read the value for _value and increment the value by 1. Before the incremented value can be updated, another thread may read the old value and increment it. In the end, _value is incremented only once. For instances like this, it is important that when _value is incremented, no other threads can access the region of the code that is doing the incrementing. You accomplish that by locking all other threads during an incrementation.

In C#, you can use the following ways to synchronize your threads:

❏   The Interlocked class

❏   The C# lock keyword

❏   The Monitor class

The following sections discuss each of these.

Using Interlocked Class

Because incrementing and decrementing are such common operations in programming, the .NET Framework class library provides the `Interlocked` class for performing atomic operations for variables that are shared by multiple threads. You can rewrite the preceding example using the `Increment()` method from the static `Interlocked` class:

```
static void IncrementVar()
{
    Interlocked.Increment(ref _value);
}
```

You need to pass in the variable to be incremented by reference to the `Increment()` method. When a thread encounters the `Increment()` statement, all other threads executing the same statement must wait until the incrementing is done.

The `Interlocked` class also includes the `Decrement()` class that, as its name implies, decrements the specified variable by one.

Using C# Lock

The `Interlocked` class is useful when you are performing atomic increment or decrement operations. What happens if you have multiple statements that you need to perform atomically? Take a look at the following program:

```
class Program
{
    //---initial balance amount---
    static int balance = 500;

    static void Main(string[] args)
    {
        Thread t1 = new Thread(new ThreadStart(Debit));
        t1.Start();

        Thread t2 = new Thread(new ThreadStart(Credit));
        t2.Start();

        Console.ReadLine();
    }

    static void Credit()
    {
        //---credit 1500---
        for (int i = 0; i < 15; i++)
        {
            balance += 100;
            Console.WriteLine("After crediting, balance is {0}", balance);
        }
    }

    static void Debit()
```

```
    {
        //---debit 1000---
        for (int i = 0; i < 10; i++)
        {
            balance -= 100;
            Console.WriteLine("After debiting, balance is {0}", balance);
        }
    }
}
```

Here two separate threads are trying to modify the value of `balance`. The `Credit()` function increments `balance` by 1500 in 15 steps of 100 each, and the `Debit()` function decrements `balance` by 1000 in 10 steps of 100 each. After each crediting or debiting you also print out the value of `balance`. With the two threads executing in parallel, it is highly probably that different threads may execute different parts of the functions at the same time, resulting in the inconsistent value of the `balance` variable.

Figure 10-5 shows one possible outcome of the execution. Notice that some of the lines showing the balance amount are inconsistent — the first two lines show that after crediting twice, the balance is still 500, and further down the balance jumps from 1800 to 400 and then back to 1700. In a correctly working scenario, the balance amount always reflects the amount credited or debited. For example, if the balance is 500, and 100 is credited, the balance should be 600. To ensure that crediting and debiting work correctly, you need to obtain a *mutually exclusive* lock on the block of code performing the crediting or debiting. A mutually exclusive lock means that once a thread is executing a block of code that is locked, other threads that also want to execute that code block will have to wait.

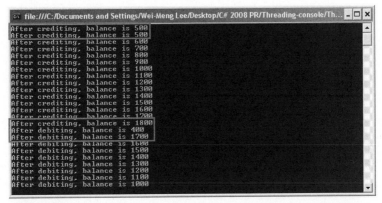

Figure 10-5

To enable you to create a mutually exclusive lock on a block of code (the code that is locked is called a *critical section*), C# provides the `lock` keyword. Using it, you can ensure that a block of code runs to completion without any interruption by other threads.

To lock a block of code, give the `lock` statement an object as argument. The preceding code could be written as follows:

```csharp
class Program
{
    //---used for locking---
    static object obj = new object();

    //---initial balance amount---
    static int balance = 500;

    static void Main(string[] args)
    {
        Thread t1 = new Thread(new ThreadStart(Debit));
        t1.Start();

        Thread t2 = new Thread(new ThreadStart(Credit));
        t2.Start();

        Console.ReadLine();
    }

    static void Credit()
    {
        //---credit 1500---
        for (int i = 0; i < 15; i++)
        {
            lock (obj)
            {
                balance += 100;
                Console.WriteLine("After crediting, balance is {0}", balance);
            }
        }
    }

    static void Debit()
    {
        //---debit 1000---
        for (int i = 0; i < 10; i++)
        {
            lock (obj)
            {
                balance -= 100;
                Console.WriteLine("After debiting, balance is {0}", balance);
            }
        }
    }
}
```

Notice that you first create an instance of an object that will be used for locking purposes:

```csharp
//---used for locking---
static object obj = new object();
```

In general, it is best to avoid using a public object for locking purposes. This prevents situations in which threads are all waiting for a public object, which may itself be locked by some other code.

To delineate a block of code to lock, enclose the statements with the `lock` statement:

```
lock (obj)
{
    //---place code here---
}
```

As long as one thread is executing the statements within the block, all other threads will have to wait for the statements to be completed before they can execute the statements.

Figure 10-6 shows one possible outcome of the execution.

```
After debiting, balance is 300
After debiting, balance is 200
After debiting, balance is 100
After debiting, balance is 0
After debiting, balance is -100
After debiting, balance is -200
After debiting, balance is -300
After debiting, balance is -400
After debiting, balance is -500
After crediting, balance is -400
After crediting, balance is -300
After crediting, balance is -200
After crediting, balance is -100
After crediting, balance is 0
After crediting, balance is 100
After crediting, balance is 200
After crediting, balance is 300
After crediting, balance is 400
After crediting, balance is 500
After crediting, balance is 600
After crediting, balance is 700
After crediting, balance is 800
After crediting, balance is 900
After crediting, balance is 1000
```

Figure 10-6

Notice that the value of `balance` is now consistent after each credit/debit operation.

Monitor Class

The limitation of the `lock` statement is that you do not have the capability to release the lock halfway through the critical section. This is important because there are situations in which one thread needs to release the lock so that other threads have a chance to proceed before the first thread can resume its execution.

For instance, you saw in Figure 10-6 that on the fifth line the balance goes into a negative value. In real life this might not be acceptable. The bank might not allow your account to go into a negative balance, and thus you need to ensure that you have a positive balance before any more debiting can proceed. Hence, you need to check the value of `balance`. If it is 0, then you should release the lock and let the crediting thread have a chance to increment the balance before you do any more debiting.

For this purpose, you can use the Monitor class provided by the .NET Framework class library. Monitor is a static class that controls access to objects by providing a lock. Here's a rewrite of the previous program using the Monitor class:

```
class Program
{
    //---used for locking---
    static object obj = new object();

    //---initial balance amount---
    static int balance = 500;

    static void Main(string[] args)
    {
        Thread t1 = new Thread(new ThreadStart(Debit));
        t1.Start();

        Thread t2 = new Thread(new ThreadStart(Credit));
        t2.Start();

        Console.ReadLine();
    }

    static void Credit()
    {
        //---credit 1500---
        for (int i = 0; i < 15; i++)
        {
            Monitor.Enter(obj);
            balance += 100;
            Console.WriteLine("After crediting, balance is {0}", balance);
            Monitor.Exit(obj);
        }
    }

    static void Debit()
    {
        //---debit 1000---
        for (int i = 0; i < 10; i++)
        {
            Monitor.Enter(obj);
            balance -= 100;
            Console.WriteLine("After debiting, balance is {0}", balance);
            Monitor.Exit(obj);
        }
    }
}
```

The Enter() method of the Monitor class acquires a lock on the specified object, and the Exit() method releases the lock. The code enclosed by the Enter() and Exit() methods is the critical section. The C# lock statement looks similar to the Monitor class; in fact, it is implemented with the Monitor class. The following lock statement, for instance:

```
lock (obj)
{
    balance -= 100;
    Console.WriteLine("After debiting, balance is {0}", balance);
}
```

Is equivalent to this Monitor class usage:

```
Monitor.Enter(obj);
try
{
    balance -= 100;
    Console.WriteLine("After debiting, balance is {0}", balance);
}
finally
{
    Monitor.Exit(obj);
}
```

Now the code looks promising, but the debiting could still result in a negative balance. To resolve this, you need to so some checking to ensure that the debiting does not proceed until there is a positive balance. Here's how:

```
static void Debit()
{
    //---debit 1000---
    for (int i = 0; i < 10; i++)
    {
        Monitor.Enter(obj);

        if (balance == 0)
            Monitor.Wait(obj);

        balance -= 100;
        Console.WriteLine("After debiting, balance is {0}", balance);
        Monitor.Exit(obj);
    }
}
```

When you use the Wait() method of the Monitor class, you release the lock on the object and enter the object's waiting queue. The next thread that is waiting for the object acquires the lock. If the balance is 0, the debit thread would give up control and let the credit thread have the lock.

However, this code modification may result in the scenario shown in Figure 10-7, in which after debiting the balance five times, balance becomes 0. On the sixth time, the lock held by the debit thread is released to the credit thread. The credit thread credits the balance 15 times. At that point, the program freezes. Turns out that the credit thread has finished execution, but the debit thread is still waiting for the lock to be explicitly returned to it.

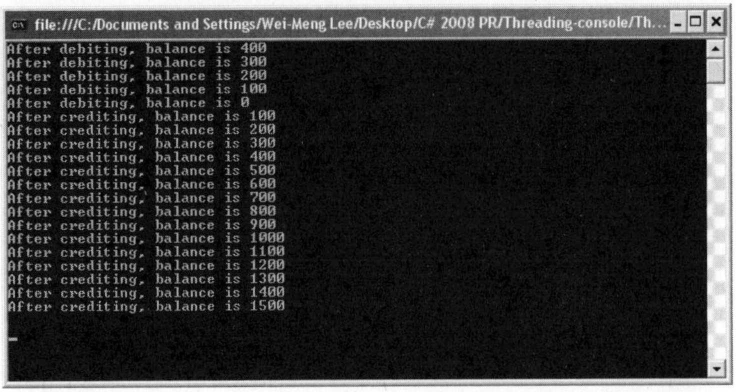

Figure 10-7

To resolve this, you call the `Pulse()` method of the `Monitor` class in the credit thread so that it can send a signal to the waiting thread that the lock is now released and is now going to pass back to it. The modified code for the `Credit()` function now looks like this:

```
static void Credit()
{
    //---credit 1500---
    for (int i = 0; i < 15; i++)
    {
        Monitor.Enter(obj);
        balance += 100;

        if (balance > 0)
            Monitor.Pulse(obj);

        Console.WriteLine("After crediting, balance is {0}", balance);
        Monitor.Exit(obj);
    }
}
```

Figure 10-8 shows that the sequence now is correct.

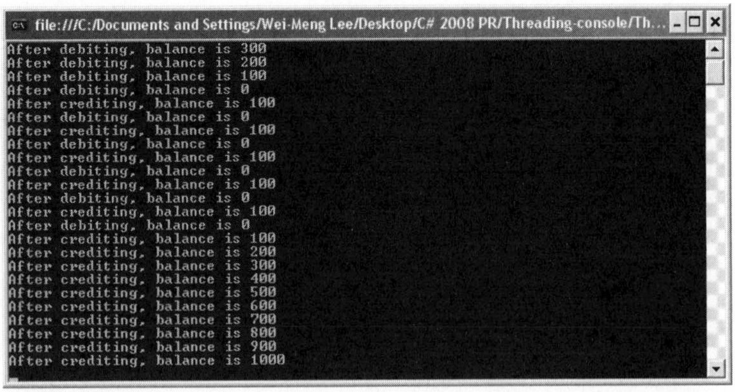

Figure 10-8

The complete program is as follows:

```
class Program
{
    //---used for locking---
    static object obj = new object();

    //---initial balance amount---
    static int balance = 500;

    static void Main(string[] args)
    {
        Thread t1 = new Thread(new ThreadStart(Debit));
        t1.Start();

        Thread t2 = new Thread(new ThreadStart(Credit));
        t2.Start();

        Console.ReadLine();
    }

    static void Credit()
    {
        //---credit 1500---
        for (int i = 0; i < 15; i++)
        {
            Monitor.Enter(obj);
            balance += 100;

            if (balance > 0)
                Monitor.Pulse(obj);

            Console.WriteLine("After crediting, balance is {0}", balance);
            Monitor.Exit(obj);
        }
    }

    static void Debit()
    {
        //---debit 1000---
        for (int i = 0; i < 10; i++)
        {
            Monitor.Enter(obj);

            if (balance == 0)
                Monitor.Wait(obj);

            balance -= 100;
            Console.WriteLine("After debiting, balance is {0}", balance);
            Monitor.Exit(obj);
        }
    }
}
```

Thread Safety in Windows Forms

One of the common problems faced by Windows programmers is the issue of updating the UI in multithreaded situations. To improve the efficiency of their applications, Windows developers often use threads to perform different tasks in parallel. One thread may be consuming a Web Service, another performing file I/O, another doing some mathematical calculations, and so on. As each thread completes, the developers may want to display the result on the Windows form itself.

However, it is important to know that controls in Windows Forms are bound to a specific thread and are thus not thread safe; this means that if you are updating a control from another thread, you should not call the control's member directly. Figure 10-9 shows the conceptual illustration.

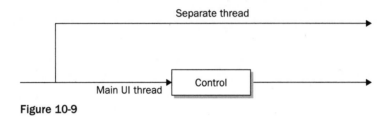

Figure 10-9

To update a Windows Forms control from another thread, use a combination of the following members of that particular control:

❑ InvokeRequired **property** — Returns a Boolean value indicating if the caller must use the Invoke() method when making call to the control if the caller is on a different thread than the control. The InvokeRequired property returns true if the calling thread is not the thread that created the control or if the window handle has not yet been created for that control.

❑ Invoke() **method** — Executes a delegate on the thread that owns the control's underlying windows handle.

❑ BeginInvoke() **method** — Calls the Invoke() method asynchronously.

❑ EndInvoke() **method** — Retrieves the return value of the asynchronous operation started by the BeginInvoke() method.

To see how to use these members, create a Windows application project in Visual Studio 2008. In the default Form1, drag and drop a Label control onto the form and use its default name of Label1. Figure 10-10 shows the control on the form.

Figure 10-10

Double-click the form to switch to its code-behind. The `Form1_Load` event handler is automatically created for you.

Add the following highlighted code:

```csharp
private void Form1_Load(object sender, EventArgs e)
{
    if (label1.InvokeRequired)
    {
        MessageBox.Show("Need to use Invoke()");
    }
    else
    {
        MessageBox.Show("No need to use Invoke()");
    }
}
```

This code checks the `InvokeRequired` property to determine whether you need to call `Invoke()` if you want to call the `Label` control's members. Because the code is in the same thread as the `Label` control, the value for the `InvokeRequired` property would be `false` and the message box will print the message `No need to use Invoke()`.

Now to write some code to display the current time on the `Label` control and to update the time every second, making it look like a clock. Define the `PrintTime()` function as follows:

```csharp
private void PrintTime()
{
    try
    {
        while (true)
        {
            if (label1.InvokeRequired)
            {
                label1.Invoke(myDelegate, new object[]
                {
                    label1, DateTime.Now.ToString()
                });
                Thread.Sleep(1000);
            }
            else
                label1.Text = DateTime.Now.ToString();
        }
    }
    catch (Exception ex)
    {
        Console.WriteLine(ex.Message);
    }
}
```

Because the `PrintTime()` function is going to be executed on a separate thread (you will see this later), you need to use the `Invoke()` method to call a delegate (`myDelegate`, which you will define shortly) so that the time can be displayed in the Label control. You also insert a delay of one second so that the time is refreshed every second.

Define the `updateLabel` function so that you can set the `Label`'s control `Text` property to a specific string:

```
private void updateLabel(Control ctrl, string str)
{
    ctrl.Text = str;
}
```

This function takes in two parameters — the control to update, and the string to display in the control. Because this function resides in the UI thread, it cannot be called directly from the `PrintTime()` function; instead, you need to use a delegate to point to it. So the next step is to define a delegate type for this function and then create the delegate:

```
public partial class Form1 : Form
{
    //---delegate type for the updateLabel() function---
    private delegate void delUpdateControl(Control ctrl, string str);

    //---a delegate---
    private delUpdateControl myDelegate;
```

Finally, create a thread for the `PrintTime()` method in the `Form1_Load` event handler and start it:

```
private void Form1_Load(object sender, EventArgs e)
{
    //...
    //...
    myDelegate = new delUpdateControl(updateLabel);
    Thread t = new Thread(PrintTime);
    t.Start();
}
```

That's it! When you run the application, the time is displayed and updated every second on the `Label` control (see Figure 10-11). At the same time, you can move the form, resize it, and so forth, and it is still responsive.

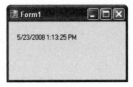

Figure 10-11

Using the BackgroundWorker Control

Because threading is such a common programming task in Windows programming, Microsoft has provided a convenient solution to implementing threading: the BackgroundWorker control for Windows applications. The BackgroundWorker control enables you to run a long background task such as network access, file access, and so forth and receive continual feedback on the progress of the task. It runs on a separate thread.

This section creates a simple Windows application that will show you how the BackgroundWorker component can help make your applications more responsive.

First, start Visual Studio 2008 and create a new Windows application. Populate the default Windows form with the following controls (see Figure 10-12).

Control	Name	Text
Label		Number
Label	lblResult	label2
Label		Progress
TextBox	txtNum	
Button	btnStart	Start
Button	btnCancel	Cancel
ProgressBar	ProgressBar1	

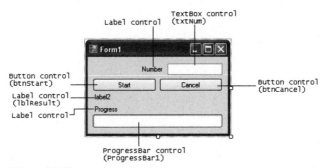

Figure 10-12

Drag and drop the BackgroundWorker component from the Toolbox onto the form. The BackgroundWorker is a nonvisual control, so it appears below the form in the component section (see Figure 10-13).

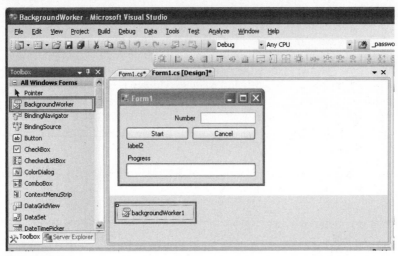

Figure 10-13

Right-click on the `BackgroundWorker` component, and select Properties. Set the `WorkerReportsProgress` and `WorkerSupportsCancellation` properties to `True` so that the component can report on the progress of the thread as well as be aborted halfway through the thread (see Figure 10-14).

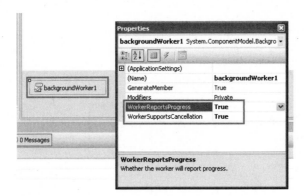

Figure 10-14

Here is how the application works. The user enters a number in the `TextBox` control (`txtNum`) and clicks the Start button. The application then sums all of the numbers from 0 to that number. The progress bar at the bottom of the page displays the progress of the summation. The speed in which the progress bar updates is dependent upon the number entered. For small numbers, the progress bar fills up very quickly. To really see the effect of how summation works in a background thread, try a large number and watch the progress bar update itself. Notice that the window is still responsive while the summation is underway. To abort the summation process, click the Cancel button. Once the summation is done, the result is printed on the `Label` control (`lblResult`).

Switch to the code behind of the Windows form to do the coding. When the Start button is clicked, you first initialize some of the controls on the form. You then get the BackgroundWorker component to spin off a separate thread by using the RunWorkAsync() method. You pass the number entered by the user as the parameter for this method:

```
private void btnStart_Click(object sender, EventArgs e)
{
    lblResult.Text = string.Empty;
    btnCancel.Enabled = true;
    btnStart.Enabled = false;
    progressBar1.Value = 0;

    backgroundWorker1.RunWorkerAsync(txtNum.Text);
}
```

Now, double-click the BackgroundWorker control in design view to create the event handler for its DoWork event.

```
private void backgroundWorker1_DoWork(object sender, DoWorkEventArgs e)
{
    BackgroundWorker worker = (BackgroundWorker)sender;
    e.Result = SumNumbers(double.Parse(e.Argument.ToString()), worker, e);
}
```

The DoWork event of the BackgroundWorker component invokes the SumNumbers() function (which you will define next) in a separate thread. This event is fired when you call the RunWorkerAsync() method (as was done in the previous step).

> The DoWork event handler runs on a separate thread from the UI. Be sure not to manipulate any Windows Forms controls created on the UI thread from this method.

The SumNumbers() function basically sums up all the numbers from 0 to the number specified:

```
private double SumNumbers(
    double number, BackgroundWorker worker, DoWorkEventArgs e)
{
    int lastPercent = 0;
    double sum = 0;
    for (double i = 0; i <= number; i++)
    {
        //---check if user cancelled the process---
        if (worker.CancellationPending)
        {
            e.Cancel = true;
        }
        else
        {
            sum += i;
            if (i % 10 == 0)
```

(continued)

(continued)

```
            {
                int percentDone = (int)((i / number) * 100);
                //---update the progress bar if there is a change---
                if (percentDone > lastPercent)
                {
                    worker.ReportProgress(percentDone);
                    lastPercent = percentDone;
                }
            }
        }
    }
    return sum;
}
```

It takes in three arguments — the number to sum up to, the `BackgroundWorker` component, and the `DoWorkEventArgs`. Within the `For` loop, you check to see if the user has clicked the Cancel button (this event is defined a little later in this chapter) by checking the value of the `CancellationPending` property. If the user has canceled the process, set `e.Cancel` to `True`. After every 10 iterations, you calculate the progress completed so far. If there is progress (when the current progress percentage is greater than the last one recorded), you update the progress bar by calling the `ReportProgress()` method of the `BackgroundWorker` component. Do not call the `ReportProgress()` method unnecessarily because frequent calls to update the progress bar will freeze the UI of your application.

It is important to note that in this method (which was invoked by the `DoWork` event), you cannot directly access Windows controls because they are not thread-safe. Trying to do so will trigger a runtime error, a useful feature in Visual Studio 2008.

The `ProgressChanged` event is invoked whenever the `ReportProgress()` method is called. In this case, you use it to update the progress bar. To generate the event handler for the `ProgressChanged` event, switch to design view and look at the properties of the `BackgroundWorker` component. In the Properties window, select the Events icon and double-click the `ProgressChanged` event (see Figure 10-15).

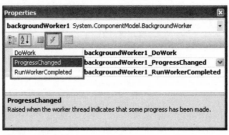

Figure 10-15

Code the event handler for the `ProgressChanged` event as follows:

```
private void backgroundWorker1_ProgressChanged(
    object sender, ProgressChangedEventArgs e)
{
    //---updates the progress bar and label control---
    progressBar1.Value = e.ProgressPercentage;
    lblResult.Text = e.ProgressPercentage.ToString() + "%";
}
```

Now double-click the `RunWorkerCompleted` event to generate its event handler:

```
private void backgroundWorker1_RunWorkerCompleted(
    object sender, RunWorkerCompletedEventArgs e)
{
    if (e.Error != null)
        MessageBox.Show(e.Error.Message);
    else if (e.Cancelled)
        MessageBox.Show("Cancelled");
    else
    {
        lblResult.Text = "Sum of 1 to " +
        txtNum.Text + " is " + e.Result;
    }
    btnStart.Enabled = true;
    btnCancel.Enabled = false;
}
```

The `RunWorkerCompleted` event is fired when the thread (`SumNumbers()`, in this case) has completed running. Here you print the result accordingly.

Finally, when the user clicks the Cancel button, you cancel the process by calling the `CancelAsync()` method:

```
private void btnCancel_Click(object sender, EventArgs e)
{
    //---Cancel the asynchronous operation---
    backgroundWorker1.CancelAsync();
    btnCancel.Enabled = false;
}
```

Testing the Application

To test the application, press F5, enter a large number (say, 9999999), and click the Start button. The progress bar updating should begin updating. When the process is complete, the result is printed in the Label control (see Figure 10-16).

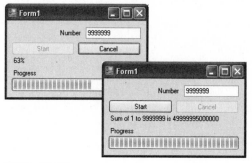

Figure 10-16

Summary

This chapter explans the rationale for threading and how it can improve the responsiveness of your applications. Threading is a complex topic and you need to plan carefully before using threads in your application. For instance, you must identify the critical regions so that you can ensure that the different threads accessing the critical region are synchronized. Finally, you saw that Windows Forms controls are not thread-safe and that you need to use delegates when updating UI controls from another thread.

Files and Streams

At some stage in your development cycle, you need to store data on some persistent media so that when the computer is restarted the data is still be available. In most cases, you either store the data in a database or in files. A file is basically a sequence of characters stored on storage media such as your hard disks, thumb drives, and so on. When you talk about files, you need to understand another associated term — streams. A stream is a channel in which data is passed from one point to another. In .NET, streams are divided into various types: file streams for files held on permanent storage, network streams for data transferred across the network, memory streams for data stored in internal storage, and so forth.

With streams, you can perform a wide range of tasks, including compressing and decompressing data, serializing and deserializing data, and encrypting and decrypting data. This chapter examines:

- ❑ Manipulating files and directories
- ❑ How to quickly read and write data to files
- ❑ The concepts of streams
- ❑ Using the `BufferedStream` class to improve the performance of applications reading from a stream
- ❑ Using the `FileStream` class to read and write to files
- ❑ Using the `MemoryStream` class to use the internal memory store as a buffer
- ❑ Using the `NetworkStream` class for network programming
- ❑ The various types of cryptographic classes available in .NET
- ❑ Performing compressions and decompression on streams
- ❑ Serializing and deserializing objects into binary and XML data

Working with Files and Directories

The `System.IO` namespace in the .NET Framework contains a wealth of classes that allow synchronous and asynchronous reading and writing of data on streams and files. In the following sections, you will explore the various classes for dealing with files and directories.

> **Remember to import the** `System.IO` **namespace when using the various classes in the** `System.IO` **namespace.**

Working with Directories

The .NET Framework class library provides two classes for manipulating directories:

❑ `DirectoryInfo` class

❑ `Directory` class

The `DirectoryInfo` class exposes instance methods for dealing with directories while the `Directory` class exposes static methods.

DirectoryInfo Class

The `DirectoryInfo` class provides various instance methods and properties for creating, deleting, and manipulating directories. The following table describes some of the common methods you can use to programmatically manipulate directories.

Method	Description
`Create`	Creates a directory.
`CreateSubdirectory`	Creates a subdirectory.
`Delete`	Deletes a directory.
`GetDirectories`	Gets the subdirectories of the current directory.
`GetFiles`	Gets the file list from a directory.

And here are some of the common properties:

Properties	Description
`Exists`	Indicates if a directory exists.
`Parent`	Gets the parent of the current directory.
`FullName`	Gets the full path name of the directory.
`CreationTime`	Gets or sets the creation time of current directory.

Refer to the MSDN documentation for a full list of methods and properties.

To see how to use the `DirectoryInfo` class, consider the following example:

```
static void Main(string[] args)
{
    string path = @"C:\My Folder";
    DirectoryInfo di = new DirectoryInfo(path);

    try
    {
        //---if directory does not exists---
        if (!di.Exists)
        {
            //---create the directory---
            di.Create();  //---c:\My Folder---

            //---creates subdirectories---
            di.CreateSubdirectory("Subdir1"); //---c:\My Folder\Subdir1---
            di.CreateSubdirectory("Subdir2"); //---c:\My Folder\Subdir2---
        }

        //---print out some info about the directory---
        Console.WriteLine(di.FullName);
        Console.WriteLine(di.CreationTime);

        //---get and print all the subdirectories---
        DirectoryInfo[] subDirs = di.GetDirectories();
        foreach (DirectoryInfo subDir in subDirs)
            Console.WriteLine(subDir.FullName);

        //---get the parent of C:\My folder---
        DirectoryInfo parent = di.Parent;
        if (parent.Exists)
        {
            //---prints out C:\---
            Console.WriteLine(parent.FullName);
        }

        //---creates C:\My Folder\Subdir3---
        DirectoryInfo newlyCreatedFolder =
            di.CreateSubdirectory("Subdir3");

        //---deletes C:\My Folder\Subdir3---
        newlyCreatedFolder.Delete();
    }
    catch (IOException ex)
    {
        Console.WriteLine(ex.Message);
    }
    catch (Exception ex)
    {
        Console.WriteLine(ex.Message);
    }

    Console.ReadLine();
}
```

In this example, you first create an instance of the `DirectoryInfo` class by instantiating it with a path (C:\My Folder). You check if the path exists by using the `Exist` property. If it does not exist, you create the folder (C:\My Folder) and then create two subdirectories underneath it (Subdir1 and Subdir2).

Next, you print out the full pathname (using the `FullName` property) of the folder and its creation date (using the `CreationTime` property). You then get all the subdirectories under C:\My Folder and display their full pathnames. You can get the parent of the C:\My Folder using the `Parent` property.

Finally, you create a subdirectory named Subdir3 under C:\My Folder and pass a reference to the newly created subdirectory to the `newlyCreatedFolder` object. You then delete the folder, using the `Delete()` method.

Directory Class

The `Directory` class is similar to `DirectoryInfo` class. The key difference between is that `Directory` exposes static members instead of instance members. The `Directory` class also exposes only methods — no properties. Some of the commonly used methods are described in the following table.

Method	Description
CreateDirectory	Creates a subdirectory.
Delete	Deletes a specified directory.
Exists	Indicates if a specified path exists.
GetCurrentDirectory	Gets the current working directory.
GetDirectories	Gets the subdirectories of the specified path.
GetFiles	Gets the file list from a specified directory.
SetCurrentDirectory	Sets the current working directory.

Refer to the MSDN documentation for a full list of methods and properties.

Here's the previous program using the `DirectoryInfo` class rewritten to use the `Directory` class:

```
static void Main(string[] args)
{
    string path = @"C:\My Folder";
    try
    {
        //---if directory does not exists---
        if (!Directory.Exists(path))
        {
            //---create the directory---
            Directory.CreateDirectory(path);

            //---set the current directory to C:\My Folder---
            Directory.SetCurrentDirectory(path);
```

```
                    //---creates subdirectories---
                    //---c:\My Folder\Subdir1---
                    Directory.CreateDirectory("Subdir1");
                    //---c:\My Folder\Subdir2---
                    Directory.CreateDirectory("Subdir2");
                }

                //---set the current directory to C:\My Folder---
                Directory.SetCurrentDirectory(path);

                //---print out some info about the directory---
                Console.WriteLine(Directory.GetCurrentDirectory());
                Console.WriteLine(Directory.GetCreationTime(path));

                //---get and print all the subdirectories---
                string[] subDirs = Directory.GetDirectories(path);
                foreach (string subDir in subDirs)
                    Console.WriteLine(subDir);

                //---get the parent of C:\My folder---
                DirectoryInfo parent = Directory.GetParent(path);
                if (parent.Exists)
                {
                    //---prints out C:\---
                    Console.WriteLine(parent.FullName);
                }

                //---creates C:\My Folder\Subdir3---
                Directory.CreateDirectory("Subdir3");

                //---deletes C:\My Folder\Subdir3---
                Directory.Delete("Subdir3");
            }
            catch (IOException ex)
            {
                Console.WriteLine(ex.Message);
            }
            catch (Exception ex)
            {
                Console.WriteLine(ex.Message);
            }
            Console.ReadLine();
        }
```

As you can see, most of the methods in the Directory class require you to specify the directory you are working with. If you like to specify the directory path by using relative path names, you need to set the current working directory using the SetCurrentDirectory() method; if not, the default current directory is always the location of your program. Also, notice that some methods (such as GetParent()) still return DirectoryInfo objects.

In general, if you are performing a lot of operations with directories, use the DirectoryInfo class. Once it is instantiated, the object has detailed information about the directory you are currently working on. In contrast, the Directory class is much simpler and is suitable if you are occasionally dealing with directories.

Working with Files Using the File and FileInfo Classes

The .NET Framework class library contains two similar classes for dealing with files — FileInfo and File.

The File class provides static methods for creating, deleting, and manipulating files, whereas the FileInfo class exposes instance members for files manipulation.

Like the Directory class, the File class only exposes static methods and does not contain any properties.

Consider the following program, which creates, deletes, copies, renames, and sets attributes in files, using the File class:

```csharp
static void Main(string[] args)
{
    string filePath = @"C:\temp\textfile.txt";
    string fileCopyPath = @"C:\temp\textfile_copy.txt";
    string newFileName = @"C:\temp\textfile_newcopy.txt";

    try
    {
        //---if file already existed---
        if (File.Exists(filePath))
        {
            //---delete the file---
            File.Delete(filePath);
        }

        //---create the file again---
        FileStream fs = File.Create(filePath);
        fs.Close();

        //---make a copy of the file---
        File.Copy(filePath, fileCopyPath);

        //--rename the file---
        File.Move(fileCopyPath, newFileName);

        //---display the creation time---
        Console.WriteLine(File.GetCreationTime(newFileName));

        //---make the file read-only and hidden---
        File.SetAttributes(newFileName, FileAttributes.ReadOnly);
        File.SetAttributes(newFileName, FileAttributes.Hidden);
    }
    catch (IOException ex)
    {
        Console.WriteLine(ex.Message);
    }
    catch (Exception ex)
    {
        Console.WriteLine(ex.Message);
    }
    Console.ReadLine();
}
```

This program first checks to see if a file exists by using the `Exists()` method. If the file exists, the program deletes it using the `Delete()` method. It then proceeds to create the file by using the `Create()` method, which returns a `FileStream` object (more on this in subsequent sections). To make a copy of the file, you use the `Copy()` method. The `Move()` method moves a file from one location to another. Essentially, you can use the `Move()` method to rename a file. Finally, the program sets the `ReadOnly` and `Hidden` attribute to the newly copied file.

In addition to the `File` class, you have the `FileInfo` class that provides instance members for dealing with files. Once you have created an instance of the `FileInfo` class, you can use its members to obtain more information about a particular file. Figure 11-1 shows the different methods and properties exposed by an instance of the `FileInfo` class, such as the `Attributes` property, which retrieves the attributes of a file, the `Delete()` method that allows you to delete a file, and so on.

Figure 11-1

Reading and Writing to Files

The `File` class contains four methods to write content to a file:

❑ `WriteAllText()` — Creates a file, writes a string to it, and closes the file

❑ `AppendAllText()` — Appends a string to an existing file

❑ `WriteAllLines()` — Creates a file, writes an array of string to it, and closes the file

❑ `WriteAllBytes()` — Creates a file, writes an array of byte to it, and closes the file

The following statements show how to use the various methods to write some content to a file:

```
string filePath = @"C:\temp\textfile.txt";
string strTextToWrite = "This is a string";
string[] strLinesToWrite = new string[] { "Line1", "Line2" };
byte[] bytesToWrite =
    ASCIIEncoding.ASCII.GetBytes("This is a string");

File.WriteAllText(filePath, strTextToWrite);
File.AppendAllText(filePath, strTextToWrite);
File.WriteAllLines(filePath, strLinesToWrite);
File.WriteAllBytes(filePath,bytesToWrite);
```

The `File` class also contains three methods to read contents from a file:

❑   `ReadAllText()` — Opens a file, reads all text in it into a string, and closes the file

❑   `ReadAllLines()` — Opens a file, reads all the text in it into a string array, and closes the file

❑   `ReadAllBytes()` — Opens a file, reads all the content in it into a byte array, and closes the file

The following statements show how to use the various methods to read contents from a file:

```
string filePath = @"C:\temp\textfile.txt";
string strTextToRead = (File.ReadAllText(filePath));
string[] strLinestoRead = File.ReadAllLines(filePath);
byte[] bytesToRead = File.ReadAllBytes(filePath);
```

The beauty of these methods is that you need not worry about opening and closing the file after reading or writing to it; they close the file automatically after they are done.

StreamReader and StreamWriter Classes

When dealing with text files, you may also want to use the `StreamReader` and `StreamWriter` classes. `StreamReader` is derived from the TextReader class, an abstract class that represents a reader that can read a sequential series of characters.

You'll see more about streams in the "The Stream Class" section later in this chapter.

The following code snippet uses the `StreamReader` class to read lines from a text file:

```
try
{
    using (StreamReader sr = new StreamReader(filePath))
    {
        string line;
        while ((line = sr.ReadLine()) != null)
        {
            Console.WriteLine(line);
        }
    }
}
catch (Exception ex)
{
    Console.WriteLine(ex.ToString());
}
```

In addition to the `ReadLine()` method, the `StreamReader` class supports the following methods:

❑   `Read()` — Reads the next character from the input stream

❑   `ReadBlock()` — Reads a maximum of specified characters

❑   `ReadToEnd()` — Reads from the current position to the end of the stream

The `StreamWriter` class is derived from the abstract `TextWriter` class and is used for writing characters to a stream. The following code snippet uses the `StreamWriter` class to write lines to a text file:

```
try
{
    using (StreamWriter sw = new  StreamWriter(filePath))
    {
        sw.Write("Hello, ");
        sw.WriteLine("World!");
    }
}
catch (Exception ex)
{
    Console.WriteLine(ex.ToString());
}
```

BinaryReader and BinaryWriter Classes

If you are dealing with binary files, you can use the `BinaryReader` and `BinaryWriter` classes. The following example reads binary data from one file and writes it into another, essentially making a copy of the file:

```
string filePath = @"C:\temp\VS2008Pro.png";
string filePathCopy = @"C:\temp\VS2008Pro_copy.png";

//---open files for reading and writing---
FileStream fs1 = File.OpenRead(filePath);
FileStream fs2 = File.OpenWrite(filePathCopy);

BinaryReader br = new BinaryReader(fs1);
BinaryWriter bw = new BinaryWriter(fs2);

//---read and write individual bytes---
for (int i = 0; i <= br.BaseStream.Length - 1; i++)
    bw.Write(br.ReadByte());

//---close the reader and writer---
br.Close();
bw.Close();
```

This program first uses the `File` class to open two files — one for reading and one for writing. The `BinaryReader` class is then used to read the binary data from the `FileStream`, and the `BinaryWriter` is used to write the binary data to the file.

The `BinaryReader` class contains many different read methods for reading different types of data — `Read()`, `Read7BitEncodedInt()`, `ReadBoolean()`, `ReadByte()`, `ReadBytes()`, `ReadChar()`, `ReadChars()`, `ReadDecimal()`, `ReadDouble()`, `ReadInt16()`, `ReadInt32()`, `ReadInt64()`, `ReadSByte()`, `ReadSingle()`, `ReadString()`, `ReadUInt16()`, `ReadUInt32()`, and `ReadUInt64()`.

Creating a FileExplorer

Now that you have seen how to use the various classes to manipulate files and directories, let's put them to good use by building a simple file explorer that displays all the subdirectories and files within a specified directory.

The following program contains the PrintFoldersinCurrentDirectory() function, which recursively traverses a directory's subdirectories and prints out its contents:

```
class Program
{
    static string path = @"C:\Program Files\Microsoft Visual Studio 9.0\VC#";
    static void Main(string[] args)
    {
        DirectoryInfo di = new DirectoryInfo(path);
        Console.WriteLine(di.FullName);
        PrintFoldersinCurrentDirectory(di, -1);
        Console.ReadLine();
    }

    private static void PrintFoldersinCurrentDirectory(
        DirectoryInfo directory, int level)
    {
        level++;

        //---print all the subdirectories in the current directory---
        foreach (DirectoryInfo subDir in directory.GetDirectories())
        {
            for (int i = 0; i <= level * 3; i++)
                Console.Write(" ");
            Console.Write("|__");

            //---display subdirectory name---
            Console.WriteLine(subDir.Name);

            //---display all the files in the subdirectory---
            FileInfo[] files = subDir.GetFiles();
            foreach (FileInfo file in files)
            {
                //---display the spaces---
                for (int i = 0; i <= (level+1) * 3; i++)
                    Console.Write(" ");

                //---display filename---
                Console.WriteLine("* " + file.Name);
            }

            //---explore its subdirectories recursively---
            PrintFoldersinCurrentDirectory(subDir, level);
        }
    }
}
```

Figure 11-2 shows the output of the program.

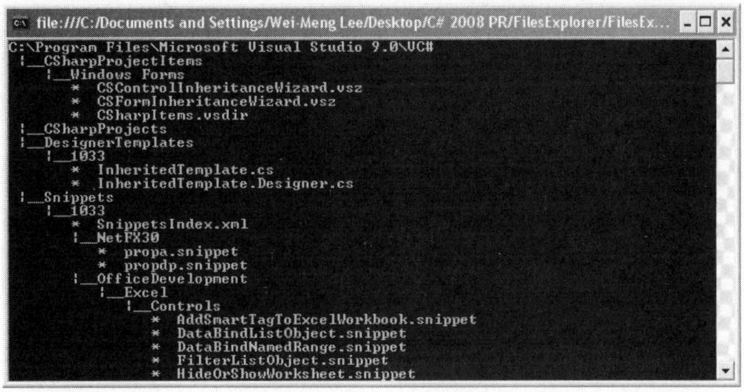

Figure 11-2

The Stream Class

A stream is an abstraction of a sequence of bytes. The bytes may come from a file, a TCP/IP socket, or memory. In .NET, a stream is represented, aptly, by the `Stream` class. The `Stream` class provides a generic view of a sequence of bytes.

The `Stream` class forms the base class of all other streams, and it is also implemented by the following classes:

❑ `BufferedStream` — Provides a buffering layer on another stream to improve performance

❑ `FileStream` — Provides a way to read and write files

❑ `MemoryStream` — Provides a stream using memory as the backing store

❑ `NetworkStream` — Provides a way to access data on the network

❑ `CryptoStream` — Provides a way to supply data for cryptographic transformation

❑ Streams fundamentally involve the following operations:

    ❑ Reading

    ❑ Writing

    ❑ Seeking

> The `Stream` class is defined in the `System.IO` namespace. Remember to import that namespace when using the class.

The following code copies the content of one binary file and writes it into another using the `Stream` class:

```
try
{
    const int BUFFER_SIZE = 8192;
    byte[] buffer = new byte[BUFFER_SIZE];
    int bytesRead;

    string filePath = @"C:\temp\VS2008Pro.png";
    string filePath_backup = @"C:\temp\VS2008Pro_bak.png";

    Stream s_in = File.OpenRead(filePath);
    Stream s_out = File.OpenWrite(filePath_backup);

    while ((bytesRead = s_in.Read(buffer, 0, BUFFER_SIZE)) > 0)
    {
        s_out.Write(buffer, 0, bytesRead);
    }
    s_in.Close();
    s_out.Close();
}
catch (Exception ex)
{
    Console.WriteLine(ex.ToString());
}
```

This first opens a file for reading using the static `OpenRead()` method from the `File` class. In addition, it opens a file for writing using the static `OpenWrite()` method. Both methods return a `FileStream` object.

While the `OpenRead()` and `OpenWrite()` methods return a `FileStream` object, you can actually assign the returning type to a `Stream` object because the `FileStream` object inherits from the `Stream` object.

To copy the content of one file into another, you use the `Read()` method from the `Stream` class and read the content from the file into an byte array. `Read()` returns the number of bytes read from the stream (in this case the file) and returns 0 if there are no more bytes to read. The `Write()` method of the `Stream` class writes the data stored in the byte array into the stream (which in this case is another file). Finally, you close both the `Stream` objects.

In addition to the `Read()` and `Write()` methods, the `Stream` object supports the following methods:

- ❑ `ReadByte()` — Reads a byte from the stream and advances the position within the stream by one byte, or returns -1 if at the end of the stream

- ❑ `WriteByte()` — Writes a byte to the current position in the stream and advances the position within the stream by 1 byte

- ❑ `Seek()` — Sets the position within the current stream

The following example writes some text to a text file, closes the file, reopens the file, seeks to the fourth position in the file, and reads the next six bytes:

```
try
{
    const int BUFFER_SIZE = 8192;
    string text = "The Stream class is defined in the System.IO namespace.";
    byte[] data = ASCIIEncoding.ASCII.GetBytes(text);
    byte[] buffer = new byte[BUFFER_SIZE];
    string filePath = @"C:\temp\textfile.txt";

    //---writes some text to file---
    Stream s_out = File.OpenWrite(filePath);
    s_out.Write(data, 0, data.Length);
    s_out.Close();

    //---opens the file for reading---
    Stream s_in = File.OpenRead(filePath);

    //---seek to the fourth position---
    s_in.Seek(4, SeekOrigin.Begin);

    //---read the next 6 bytes---
    int bytesRead = s_in.Read(buffer, 0, 6);
    Console.WriteLine(ASCIIEncoding.ASCII.GetString(buffer, 0, bytesRead));

    s_in.Close();
    s_out.Close();
}
catch (Exception ex)
{
    Console.WriteLine(ex.ToString());
}
```

BufferedStream

To improve its performance, the BufferedStream class works with another Stream object. For instance, the previous example used a buffer size of 8192 bytes when reading from a text file. However, that size might not be the ideal size to yield the optimum performance from your computer. You can use the BufferedStream class to let the operating system determine the optimum buffer size for you. While you can still specify the buffer size to fill up your buffer when reading data, your buffer will now be filled by the BufferedStream class instead of directly from the stream (which in the example is from a file). The BufferedStream class fills up its internal memory store in the size that it determines is the most efficient.

The `BufferedStream` class is ideal when you are manipulating large streams. The following shows how the previous example can be speeded up using the `BufferedStream` class:

```
try
{
    const int BUFFER_SIZE = 8192;
    byte[] buffer = new byte[BUFFER_SIZE];
    int bytesRead;

    string filePath = @"C:\temp\VS2008Pro.png";
    string filePath_backup = @"C:\temp\VS2008Pro_bak.png";

    Stream s_in = File.OpenRead(filePath);
    Stream s_out = File.OpenWrite(filePath_backup);

    BufferedStream bs_in = new BufferedStream(s_in);
    BufferedStream bs_out = new BufferedStream(s_out);

    while ((bytesRead = bs_in.Read(buffer, 0, BUFFER_SIZE)) > 0)
    {
        bs_out.Write(buffer, 0, bytesRead);
    }
    bs_out.Flush();
    bs_in.Close();
    bs_out.Close();

}
catch (Exception ex)
{
    Console.WriteLine(ex.ToString());
}
```

You use a `BufferedStream` object over a `Stream` object, and all the reading and writing is then done via the `BufferedStream` objects.

The FileStream Class

The `FileStream` class is designed to work with files, and it supports both synchronous and asynchronous read and write operations. Earlier, you saw the use of the `Stream` object to read and write to file. Here is the same example using the `FileStream` class:

```
try
{
    const int BUFFER_SIZE = 8192;
    byte[] buffer = new byte[BUFFER_SIZE];
    int bytesRead;

    string filePath = @"C:\temp\VS2008Pro.png";
    string filePath_backup = @"C:\temp\VS2008Pro_bak.png";

    FileStream fs_in = File.OpenRead(filePath);
    FileStream fs_out = File.OpenWrite(filePath_backup);
```

```
                    while ((bytesRead = fs_in.Read(buffer, 0, BUFFER_SIZE)) > 0)
                    {
                        fs_out.Write(buffer, 0, bytesRead);
                    }

                    fs_in.Dispose();
                    fs_out.Dispose();
                    fs_in.Close();
                    fs_out.Close();
                }
                catch (Exception ex)
                {
                    Console.WriteLine(ex.ToString());
                }
```

If the size of the file is large, this program will take a long time because it uses the blocking `Read()` method. A better approach would be to use the asynchronous read methods `BeginRead()` and `EndRead()`.

`BeginRead()` starts an asynchronous read from a `FileStream` object. Every `BeginRead()` method called must be paired with the `EndRead()` method, which waits for the pending asynchronous read operation to complete. To read from the stream synchronously, you call the `BeginRead()` method as usual by providing it with the buffer to read, the offset to begin reading, size of buffer, and a call back delegate to invoke when the read operation is completed. You can also provide a custom object to distinguish different asynchronous operations (for simplicity you just pass in `null` here):

```
            IAsyncResult result =
                fs_in.BeginRead(buffer, 0, BUFFER_SIZE,
                new AsyncCallback(readCompleted), null);
```

The following program shows how you can copy the content of a file into another asynchronously:

```
    class Program
    {
        static FileStream fs_in;
        static FileStream fs_out;
        const int BUFFER_SIZE = 8192;
        static byte[] buffer = new byte[BUFFER_SIZE];

        static void Main(string[] args)
        {
            try
            {
                string filePath = @"C:\temp\VS2008Pro.png";
                string filePath_backup = @"C:\temp\VS2008Pro_bak.png";

                //---open the files for reading and writing---
                fs_in = File.OpenRead(filePath);
                fs_out = File.OpenWrite(filePath_backup);

                Console.WriteLine("Copying file...");
```

(continued)

(continued)

```csharp
            //---begin to read asynchronously---
            IAsyncResult result =
                fs_in.BeginRead(buffer, 0, BUFFER_SIZE,
                new AsyncCallback(readCompleted), null);

            //---continue with the execution---
            for (int i = 0; i < 100; i++)
            {
                Console.WriteLine("Continuing with the execution...{0}", i);
                System.Threading.Thread.Sleep(250);
            }
        }
        catch (Exception ex)
        {
            Console.WriteLine(ex.ToString());
        }
        Console.ReadLine();
    }
```

```csharp
    //---when a block of data is read---
    static void readCompleted(IAsyncResult result)
    {
        //---simulate slow reading---
        System.Threading.Thread.Sleep(500);

        //---reads the data---
        int bytesRead = fs_in.EndRead(result);

        //---writes to another file---
        fs_out.Write(buffer, 0, bytesRead);

        if (bytesRead > 0)
        {
            //---continue reading---
            result =
                fs_in.BeginRead(buffer, 0, BUFFER_SIZE,
                new AsyncCallback(readCompleted), null);
        }
        else
        {
            //---reading is done!---
            fs_in.Dispose();
            fs_out.Dispose();
            fs_in.Close();
            fs_out.Close();
            Console.WriteLine("File copy done!");
        }
    }
}
```

Because the reading may happen so fast for a small file, you can insert `Sleep()` statements to simulate reading a large file. Figure 11-3 shows the output.

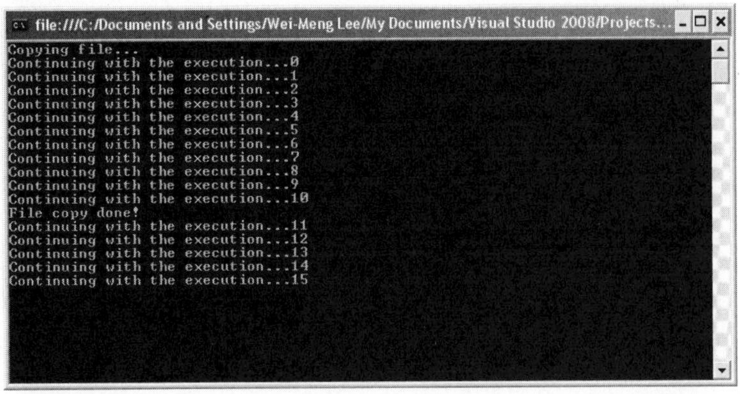

Figure 11-3

MemoryStream

Sometimes you need to manipulate data in memory without resorting to saving it in a file. A good example is the `PictureBox` control in a Windows Form. For instance, you have a picture displayed in the `PictureBox` control and want to send the picture to a remote server, say a Web Service. The `PictureBox` control has a `Save()` method that enables you to save the image to a `Stream` object.

Instead of saving the image to a `FileStream` object and then reloading the data from the file into a byte array, a much better way would be to use a `MemoryStream` object, which uses the memory as a backing store (which is more efficient compared to performing file I/O; file I/O is relatively slower).

The following code shows how the image in the `PictureBox` control is saved into a `MemoryStream` object:

```
//---create a MemoryStream object---
MemoryStream ms1 = new MemoryStream();

//---save the image into a MemoryStream object---
pictureBox1.Image.Save(ms1, System.Drawing.Imaging.ImageFormat.Jpeg);
```

To extract the image stored in the `MemoryStream` object and save it to a byte array, use the `Read()` method of the `MemoryStream` object:

```
//---read the data in ms1 and write to buffer---
ms1.Position = 0;
byte[] buffer = new byte[ms1.Length];
int bytesRead = ms1.Read(buffer, 0, (int)ms1.Length);
```

With the data in the byte array, you can now proceed to send the data to the Web Service. To verify that the data stored in the byte array is really the image in the `PictureBox` control, you can load it back to another `MemoryStream` object and then display it in another `PictureBox` control, like this:

```
//---read the data in buffer and write to ms2---
MemoryStream ms2 = new MemoryStream();
ms2.Write(buffer,0,bytesRead);

//---load it in another PictureBox control---
pictureBox2.Image = new Bitmap(ms2);
```

NetworkStream Class

The `NetworkStream` class provides methods for sending and receiving data over `Stream` sockets in blocking mode. Using the `NetworkStream` class is more restrictive than using most other Stream implementations. For example, the `CanSeek()` properties of the `NetworkStream` class are not supported and always return false. Similarly, the `Length()` and `Position()` properties throw `NotSupportedException`. It is not possible to perform a `Seek()` operation, and the `SetLength()` method also throws `NotSupportedException`.

Despite these limitations, the `NetworkStream` class has made network programming very easy and encapsulates much of the complexity of socket programming. Developers who are familiar with streams programming can use the `NetworkStream` class with ease.

This section leads you through creating a pair of socket applications to illustrate how the `NetworkStream` class works. The server will listen for incoming TCP clients and send back to the client whatever it receives.

Building a Client-Server Application

The following code is for the server application:

```csharp
using System;
using System.Collections.Generic;
using System.Linq;
using System.Text;
using System.Net;
using System.Net.Sockets;

namespace Server
{
    class Program
    {
        const int PORT_NO = 5000;
        const string SERVER_IP = "127.0.0.1";

        static void Main(string[] args)
        {
            //---listen at the specified IP and port no.---
            IPAddress localAdd = IPAddress.Parse(SERVER_IP);
            TcpListener listener = new TcpListener(localAdd, PORT_NO);
            Console.WriteLine("Listening...");
```

```
                    listener.Start();

                    //---incoming client connected---
                    TcpClient client = listener.AcceptTcpClient();

                    //---get the incoming data through a network stream---
                    NetworkStream nwStream = client.GetStream();
                    byte[] buffer = new byte[client.ReceiveBufferSize];

                    //---read incoming stream---
                    int bytesRead = nwStream.Read(buffer, 0, client.ReceiveBufferSize);

                    //---convert the data received into a string---
                    string dataReceived = Encoding.ASCII.GetString(buffer, 0, bytesRead);
                    Console.WriteLine("Received : " + dataReceived);

                    //---write back the text to the client---
                    Console.WriteLine("Sending back : " + dataReceived);
                    nwStream.Write(buffer, 0, bytesRead);

                    client.Close();
                    listener.Stop();
                    Console.ReadLine();
                }
            }
        }
```

Basically, you use the `TcpListener` class to listen for an incoming TCP connection. Once a connection is made, you use a `NetworkStream` object to read data from the client, using the `Read()` method as well as write data to the client by using the `Write()` method.

For the client, you use the `TcpClient` class to connect to the server using TCP and, as with the server, you use the `NetworkStream` object to write and read data to and from the client:

```
using System;
using System.Collections.Generic;
using System.Linq;
using System.Text;
using System.Net;
using System.Net.Sockets;

namespace Client
{
    class Program
    {
        const int PORT_NO = 5000;
        const string SERVER_IP = "127.0.0.1";

        static void Main(string[] args)
        {
            //---data to send to the server---
            string textToSend = DateTime.Now.ToString();

            //---create a TCPClient object at the IP and port no.---
```

(continued)

(continued)

```
            TcpClient client = new TcpClient(SERVER_IP, PORT_NO);

            NetworkStream nwStream = client.GetStream();
            byte[] bytesToSend = ASCIIEncoding.ASCII.GetBytes(textToSend);

            //---send the text---
            Console.WriteLine("Sending : " + textToSend);
            nwStream.Write(bytesToSend, 0, bytesToSend.Length);

            //---read back the text---
            byte[] bytesToRead = new byte[client.ReceiveBufferSize];
            int bytesRead = nwStream.Read(bytesToRead, 0,
                client.ReceiveBufferSize);

            Console.WriteLine("Received : " +
                Encoding.ASCII.GetString(bytesToRead, 0, bytesRead));
            Console.ReadLine();

            client.Close();
        }
    }
}
```

Figure 11-4 shows how the server and client look like when you run both applications.

Figure 11-4

Building a Multi-User Server Application

The client-server applications built in the previous section can accept only a single client. A client connects and sends some data to the server; the server receives it, sends the data back to the client, and then exits. While this is a simple demonstration of a client-server application, it isn't a very practical application because typically a server should be able to handle multiple clients simultaneously and runs indefinitely. So let's look at how you can extend the previous server so that it can handle multiple clients simultaneously.

To do so, you can create a class named `Client` and code it as follows:

```
using System;
using System.Collections.Generic;
using System.Linq;
using System.Text;
using System.Net.Sockets;

namespace Server
{
    class Client
    {
        //---create a TCPClient object---
        TcpClient _client = null;

        //---for sending/receiving data---
        byte[] buffer;

        //---called when a client has connected---
        public Client(TcpClient client)
        {
            _client = client;
            //---start reading data asynchronously from the client---
            buffer = new byte[_client.ReceiveBufferSize];
            _client.GetStream().BeginRead(
                buffer, 0, _client.ReceiveBufferSize,
                receiveMessage, null);
        }

        public void receiveMessage(IAsyncResult ar)
        {
            int bytesRead;
            try
            {
                lock (_client.GetStream())
                {
                    //---read from client---
                    bytesRead = _client.GetStream().EndRead(ar);
                }

                //---if client has disconnected---
                if (bytesRead < 1)
                    return;
                else
                {
                    //---get the message sent---
                    string messageReceived =
                        ASCIIEncoding.ASCII.GetString(buffer, 0, bytesRead);
                    Console.WriteLine("Received : " + messageReceived);
```

(continued)

341

(continued)

```
                    //---write back the text to the client---
                    Console.WriteLine("Sending back : " + messageReceived);
                    byte[] dataToSend =
                        ASCIIEncoding.ASCII.GetBytes(messageReceived);
                    _client.GetStream().Write(dataToSend, 0, dataToSend.Length);
                }

                //---continue reading from client---
                lock (_client.GetStream())
                {
                    _client.GetStream().BeginRead(
                        buffer, 0, _client.ReceiveBufferSize,
                        receiveMessage, null);
                }
            }
            catch (Exception ex)
            {
                Console.WriteLine(ex.ToString());
            }
        }
    }
}
```

Here, the constructor of the Client class takes in a TcpClient object and starts to read from it asynchronously using the receiveMessage() method (via the BeginRead() method of the NetworkStream object). Once the incoming data is read, the constructor continues to wait for more data.

To ensure that the server supports multiple users, you use a TcpListener class to listen for incoming client connections and then use an infinite loop to accept new connections. Once a client is connected, you create a new instance of the Client object and continue waiting for the next client. So the Main() function of your application now looks like this:

```
using System;
using System.Collections.Generic;
using System.Linq;
using System.Text;
using System.Net;
using System.Net.Sockets;

namespace Server
{
    class Program
    {
        const int PORT_NO = 5000;
        const string SERVER_IP = "127.0.0.1";

        static void Main(string[] args)
        {
            //---listen at the specified IP and port no.---
            IPAddress localAddress = IPAddress.Parse(SERVER_IP);
            TcpListener listener = new TcpListener(localAddress, PORT_NO);
            Console.WriteLine("Listening...");
            listener.Start();
```

```
        while (true)
        {
            //---incoming client connected---
            Client user = new Client(listener.AcceptTcpClient());
        }
    }
}
}
```

Figure 11-5 shows the server with two clients connected to it.

Figure 11-5

Cryptography

The .NET framework contains a number of cryptography services that enable you to incorporate security services into your .NET applications. These libraries are located under the System.Security .Cryptography namespace and provide various functions such as encryption and decryption of data, as well as other operations such as hashing and random-number generation. One of the core classes that support the cryptographic services is the CryptoStream class, which links data streams to cryptographic transformations.

This section explores how to use some of the common security APIs to make your .NET applications more secure.

Hashing

The most common security function that you will perform is hashing. Consider the situation where you need to build a function to authenticate users before they can use your application. You would require the user to supply a set of login credentials, generally containing a user name and a password. This login information needs to be persisted to a database. Quite commonly, developers store the passwords of users verbatim on a database. That's a big security risk because hackers who get a chance to glance at the users' database would be able to obtain the passwords of your users. A better approach is to store the *hash values* of the users' passwords instead of the passwords themselves. A hashing algorithm has the following properties:

- ❑ It maps a string of arbitrary length to small binary values of a fixed length, known as a *hash value*.

- ❑ The hash value of a string is unique, and small changes in the original string will produce a different hash value.

- ❑ It is improbable that you'd find two different strings that produce the same hash value.

- ❑ It is impossible to use the hash value to find the original string.

Then, when the user logs in to your application, the hash value of the password provided is compared with the hash value stored in the database. In this way, even if hackers actually steal the users' database, the actual password is not exposed. One downside to storing the hash values of users' passwords is that in the event that a user loses her password, there is no way to retrieve it. You'd need to generate a new password for the user and request that she change it immediately. But this inconvenience is a small price to pay for the security of your application.

There are many hashing algorithms available in .NET, but the most commonly used are the SHA1 and MD5 implementations. Let's take a look at how they work in .NET.

Using Visual Studio 2008, create a new Console application project. Import the following namespaces:

```
using System.IO;
using System.Security.Cryptography;
```

Define the following function:

```
static void Hashing_SHA1()
{
    //---ask the user to enter a password---
    Console.Write("Please enter a password: ");
    string password = Console.ReadLine();

    //---hash the password---
    byte[] data = ASCIIEncoding.ASCII.GetBytes(password);
    byte[] passwordHash;
    SHA1CryptoServiceProvider sha = new SHA1CryptoServiceProvider();
    passwordHash = sha.ComputeHash(data);

    //---ask the user to enter the same password again---
    Console.Write("Please enter password again: ");
    password = Console.ReadLine();
```

```
//---hash the second password and compare it with the first---
data = System.Text.Encoding.ASCII.GetBytes(password);

if (ASCIIEncoding.ASCII.GetString(passwordHash) ==
    ASCIIEncoding.ASCII.GetString(sha.ComputeHash(data)))
      Console.WriteLine("Same password");
else
      Console.WriteLine("Incorrect password");
}
```

You first ask the user to enter a password, after which you will hash it using the SHA1 implementation. You then ask the user to enter the same password again. To verify that the second password matches the first, you hash the second password and then compare the two hash values. For the SHA1 implementation, the hash value generated is 160 bits in length (the byte array `passwordHash` has 20 members: 8 bits × 20 = 160 bits). In this example, you convert the hash values into strings and perform a comparison. You could also convert them to Base64 encoding and then perform a comparison. Alternatively, you can also evaluate the two hash values by using their byte arrays, comparing them byte by byte. As soon as one byte is different, you can conclude that the two hash values are not the same.

To test the function, simply call the `Hashing_SHA1()` function in `Main()`:

```
static void Main(string[] args)
{
    Hashing_SHA1();
    Console.Read();
}
```

Figure 11-6 shows the program in action.

Figure 11-6

You can also use the MD5 implementation to perform hashing, as the following function shows:

```
static void Hashing_SHA1()
{
    //---ask the user to enter a password---
    Console.Write("Please enter a password: ");
    string password = Console.ReadLine();

    //---hash the password---
    byte[] data = ASCIIEncoding.ASCII.GetBytes(password);
    byte[] passwordHash;
```

(continued)

(continued)

```
            MD5CryptoServiceProvider md5 = new MD5CryptoServiceProvider();
            passwordHash = md5.ComputeHash(data);

            //---ask the user to enter the same password again---
            Console.Write("Please enter password again: ");
            password = Console.ReadLine();

            //---hash the second password and compare it with the first---
            data = System.Text.Encoding.ASCII.GetBytes(password);

            if (ASCIIEncoding.ASCII.GetString(passwordHash) ==
                ASCIIEncoding.ASCII.GetString(md5.ComputeHash(data)))
                Console.WriteLine("Same password");
            else
                Console.WriteLine("Incorrect password");
    }
```

The main difference is that the hash value for MD5 is 128 bits in length.

Salted Hash

With hashing, you simply store the hash value of a user's password in the database. However, if two users use identical passwords, the hash values for these two passwords will be also identical. Imagine a hacker seeing that the two hash values are identical; it would not be hard for him to guess that the two passwords must be the same. For example, users often like to use their own names or birth dates or common words found in the dictionary as passwords. So, hackers often like to use dictionary attacks to correctly guess users' passwords. To reduce the chance of dictionary attacks, you can add a "salt" to the hashing process so that no two identical passwords can generate the same hash values. For instance, instead of hashing a user's password, you hash his password together with his other information, such as email address, birth date, last name, first name, and so on. The idea is to ensure that each user will have a unique password hash value. While the idea of using the user's information as a salt for the hashing process sounds good, it is quite easy for hackers to guess. A better approach is to randomly generate a number to be used as the salt and then hash it together with the user's password.

The following function, `Salted_Hashing_SHA1()`, generates a random number using the `RNGCryptoServiceProvider` class, which returns a list of randomly generated bytes (the salt). It then combines the salt with the original password and performs a hash on it.

```
        static void Salted_Hashing_SHA1()
        {
            //---Random Number Generator---
            byte[] salt = new byte[8];

            RNGCryptoServiceProvider rng = new RNGCryptoServiceProvider();
            rng.GetBytes(salt);

            //---ask the user to enter a password---
            Console.Write("Please enter a password: ");
            string password = Console.ReadLine();
```

```
//---add the salt to the password---
password += ASCIIEncoding.ASCII.GetString(salt);

//---hash the password---
byte[] data = ASCIIEncoding.ASCII.GetBytes(password);
SHA1CryptoServiceProvider sha = new SHA1CryptoServiceProvider();
byte[] passwordHash;
passwordHash = sha.ComputeHash(data);

//---ask the user to enter the same password again---
Console.Write("Please enter password again: ");
password = Console.ReadLine();
Console.WriteLine(ASCIIEncoding.ASCII.GetString(salt));

//---adding the salt to the second password---
password += ASCIIEncoding.ASCII.GetString(salt);

//---hash the second password and compare it with the first---
data = ASCIIEncoding.ASCII.GetBytes(password);
if (ASCIIEncoding.ASCII.GetString(passwordHash) ==
    ASCIIEncoding.ASCII.GetString(sha.ComputeHash(data)))
    Console.WriteLine("Same password");
else
    Console.WriteLine("Incorrect password");
}
```

If you use salted hash for storing passwords, the salt used for each password should be stored separately from the main hash database so that hackers do not have a chance to obtain it easily.

Encryption and Decryption

Hashing is a one-way process, which means that once a value is hashed, you can't obtain its original value by reversing the process. This characteristic is particularly well suited for authentications as well as digitally signing a document.

In reality, there are many situations that require information to be performed in a two-way process. For example, to send a secret message to a recipient, you need to "scramble" it so that only the recipient can see it. This process of scrambling is known as *encryption*. Undoing the scrambling process to obtain the original message is known as *decryption*. There are two main types of encryption: symmetric and asymmetric.

Symmetric Encryption

Symmetric encryption is also sometimes known as *private key encryption*. You encrypt a secret message using a key that only you know. To decrypt the message, you need to use the same key. Private key encryption is effective only if the key can be kept a secret. If too many people know the key, its effectiveness is reduced, and if the key's secrecy is compromised somehow, then the message is no longer secure.

Despite the potential weakness of private key encryption, it is very easy to implement and, computationally, it does not take up too many resources.

For private key encryption (symmetric), the .NET Framework supports the DES, RC2, Rijndael, and TripleDES algorithms.

To see how symmetric encryption works, you will use the `RijndaelManaged` class in the following `SymmetricEncryption()` function. Three parameters are required — the string to be encrypted, the private key, and the initialization vector (IV). The IV is a random number used in the encryption process to ensure that no two strings will give the same cipher text (the encrypted text) after the encryption process. You will need the same IV later on when decrypting the cipher text.

To perform the actual encryption, you initialize an instance of the `CryptoStream` class with a `MemoryStream` object, the cryptographic transformation to perform on the stream, and the mode of the stream (`Write` for encryption and `Read` for decryption):

```
static string SymmetricEncryption(string str, byte[] key, byte[] IV)
{
    MemoryStream ms = new MemoryStream();
    try
    {
        //---creates a new instance of the RijndaelManaged class---
        RijndaelManaged RMCrypto = new RijndaelManaged();

        //---creates a new instance of the CryptoStream class---
        CryptoStream cryptStream =
            new CryptoStream(
            ms, RMCrypto.CreateEncryptor(key, IV),
            CryptoStreamMode.Write);

        StreamWriter sWriter = new StreamWriter(cryptStream);

        //---encrypting the string---
        sWriter.Write(str);
        sWriter.Close();
        cryptStream.Close();

        //---return the encrypted data as a string---
        return System.Convert.ToBase64String(ms.ToArray());
    }
    catch (Exception ex)
    {
        Console.WriteLine(ex.ToString());
        return (String.Empty);
    }
}
```

The encrypted string is returned as a Base64-encoded string. You can check the allowable key sizes for the `RijndaelManaged` class by using the following code:

```
KeySizes[] ks;
RijndaelManaged RMCrypto = new RijndaelManaged();
ks = RMCrypto.LegalKeySizes;

//---print out the various key sizes---
Console.WriteLine(ks[0].MaxSize);    // 256
Console.WriteLine(ks[0].MinSize);    // 128
Console.WriteLine(ks[0].SkipSize);   //  64
```

The valid key sizes are: 16 bytes (128 bit), 24 bytes (128 bits + 64 bits), and 32 bytes (256 bits).

You can get the system to generate a random key and IV (which you need to supply in the current example) automatically:

```
//---generate key---
RMCrypto.GenerateKey();
byte[] key = RMCrypto.Key;
Console.WriteLine("Key : " + System.Convert.ToBase64String(key));

//---generate IV---
RMCrypto.GenerateIV();
byte[] IV = RMCrypto.IV;
Console.WriteLine("IV : " + System.Convert.ToBase64String(IV));
```

If the IV is null when it is used, the GenerateIV() method is called automatically. Valid size for the IV is 16 bytes.

To decrypt a string encrypted using the RijndaelManaged class, you can use the following SymmetricDecryption() function:

```
static string SymmetricDecryption(string str, byte[] key, byte[] IV)
{
    try
    {
        //---converts the encrypted string into a byte array---
        byte[] b = System.Convert.FromBase64String(str);

        //---converts the byte array into a memory stream for decryption---
        MemoryStream ms = new MemoryStream(b);

        //---creates a new instance of the RijndaelManaged class---
        RijndaelManaged RMCrypto = new RijndaelManaged();

        //---creates a new instance of the CryptoStream class---
        CryptoStream cryptStream =
            new CryptoStream(
                ms, RMCrypto.CreateDecryptor(key, IV),
                CryptoStreamMode.Read);

        //---decrypting the stream---
        StreamReader sReader = new StreamReader(cryptStream);

        //---converts the decrypted stream into a string---
        String s = sReader.ReadToEnd();
        sReader.Close();

        return s;
    }
    catch (Exception ex)
    {
        Console.WriteLine(ex.ToString());
        return String.Empty;
    }
}
```

The following code snippet shows how to use the `SymmetricEncryption()` and `SymmetricDecryption()` functions to encrypt and decrypt a string:

```
RijndaelManaged RMCrypto = new RijndaelManaged();

//---generate key---
RMCrypto.GenerateKey();
byte[] key = RMCrypto.Key;
Console.WriteLine("Key : " + System.Convert.ToBase64String(key));

//---generate IV---
RMCrypto.GenerateIV();
byte[] IV = RMCrypto.IV;
Console.WriteLine("IV : " + System.Convert.ToBase64String(IV));

//---encrypt the string---
string cipherText =
    SymmetricEncryption("This is a test string.", key, IV);
Console.WriteLine("Ciphertext: " + cipherText);

//---decrypt the string---
Console.WriteLine("Original string: " +
    SymmetricDecryption(cipherText, key, IV));
```

Figure 11-7 shows the output.

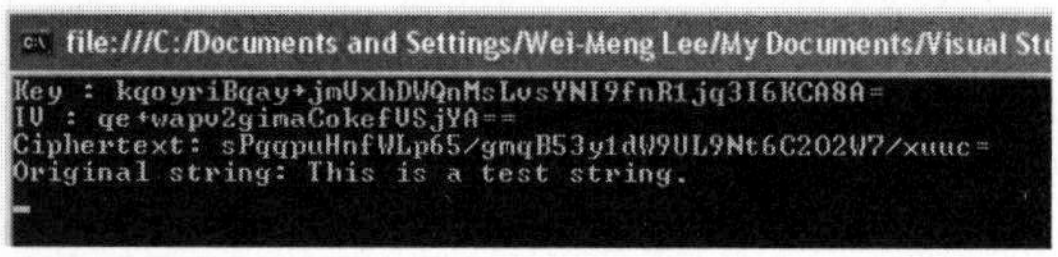

Figure 11-7

Asymmetric Encryption

Private key encryption requires the key used in the encryption process to be kept a secret. A more effective way to transport secret messages to your intended recipient is to use asymmetric encryption (also known as *public key encryption*), which involves a pair of keys involved. This pair, consisting of a private key and a public key, is related mathematically such that messages encrypted with the public key can only be decrypted with the corresponding private key. The reverse is also true; messages encrypted with the private key can only be decrypted with the public key. Let's see an example for each scenario.

Before you send a message to your friend Susan, Susan needs to generate the key pair containing the private key and the public key. Susan then freely distributes the public key to you (and all her other friends) but keeps the private key to herself. When you want to send a message to Susan, you use her public key to encrypt the message. Upon receiving the encrypted message, Susan proceeds to decrypt it with her private key. Susan is the only one who can decrypt the message because the key pair works in such a way that only messages encrypted with the public key can be decrypted with the private key. And there is no need to exchange keys, thus eliminating the risk of compromising the secrecy of the key.

Now suppose that Susan sends a message encrypted with her private key to you. To decrypt the message, you need the public key. The scenario may seem odd because the public key is not a secret; everyone knows it. But using this method guarantees that the message has not been tampered with and confirms that it indeed comes from Susan. If the message had been modified, you would not be able to decrypt it. The fact that you can decrypt the message using the public key proves that the message has not been modified.

In computing, public key cryptography is a secure way to encrypt information, but it's computationally expensive because it is time-consuming to generate the key pairs and to perform encryption and decryption. Therefore, it's generally used only for encrypting a small amount of sensitive information.

For public key (asymmetric) encryptions, the .NET Framework supports the DSA and RSA algorithms. The RSA algorithm is used in the following AsymmetricEncryption() function. This function takes in two parameters: the string to be encrypted and the public key:

```
static string AsymmetricEncryption(string str, string publicKey)
{
    try
    {
        //---Creates a new instance of RSACryptoServiceProvider---
        RSACryptoServiceProvider RSA = new RSACryptoServiceProvider();

        //---Loads the public key---
        RSA.FromXmlString(publicKey);

        //---Encrypts the string---
        byte[] encryptedStr =
            RSA.Encrypt(ASCIIEncoding.ASCII.GetBytes(str), false);

        //---Converts the encrypted byte array to string---
        return System.Convert.ToBase64String(encryptedStr);
    }
    catch (Exception ex)
    {
        Console.WriteLine(ex.ToString());
        return String.Empty;
    }
}
```

The encrypted string is returned as a Base64-encoded string. To decrypt a string encrypted with the public key, define the following AsymmetricDecryption() function. It takes in two parameters (the encrypted string and the private key) and returns the decrypted string.

```
static string AsymmetricDecryption(string str, string privateKey)
{
    try
    {
        //---Creates a new instance of RSACryptoServiceProvider---
        RSACryptoServiceProvider RSA = new RSACryptoServiceProvider();

        //---Loads the private key---
        RSA.FromXmlString(privateKey);
```

(continued)

351

(continued)

```
            //---Decrypts the string---
            byte[] DecryptedStr =
                RSA.Decrypt(System.Convert.FromBase64String(str), false);

            //---Converts the decrypted byte array to string---
            return ASCIIEncoding.ASCII.GetString(DecryptedStr);
        }
        catch (Exception ex)
        {
            Console.WriteLine(ex.ToString());
            return String.Empty;
        }
    }
```

The following code snippet shows how to use the `AsymmetricEncryption()` and `AsymmetricDecryption()` functions to encrypt and decrypt a string:

```
        string publicKey, privateKey;
        RSACryptoServiceProvider RSA =
            new RSACryptoServiceProvider();

        //---get public key---
        publicKey = RSA.ToXmlString(false);
        Console.WriteLine("Public key: " + publicKey);
        Console.WriteLine();

        //---get private and public key---
        privateKey = RSA.ToXmlString(true);
        Console.WriteLine("Private key: " + privateKey);
        Console.WriteLine();

        //---encrypt the string---
        string cipherText =
            AsymmetricEncryption("C# 2008 Programmer's Reference", publicKey);
        Console.WriteLine("Ciphertext: " + cipherText);
        Console.WriteLine();

        //---decrypt the string---
        Console.WriteLine("Original string: " +
            AsymmetricDecryption(cipherText, privateKey));
        Console.WriteLine();
```

You can obtain the public and private keys generated by the RSA algorithm by using the `ToXmlString()` method from the `RSACryptoServiceProvider` class. This method takes in a `Bool` variable, and returns a public key if the value `false` is supplied. If the value `true` is supplied, it returns both the private and public keys.

Figure 11-8 shows the output.

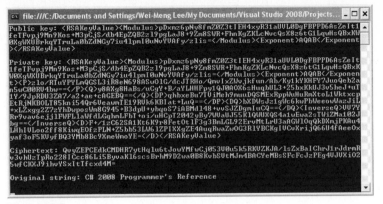

Figure 11-8

Compressions for Stream Objects

The `System.IO.Compression` namespace contains classes that provide basic compression and decompression services for streams. This namespace contains two classes for data compression: `DeflateStream` and `GZipStream`. Both support lossless compression and decompression and are designed for dealing with streams.

Compression is useful for reducing the size of data. If you have huge amount of data to store in your SQL database, for instance, you can save on disk space if you compress the data before saving it into a table. Moreover, because you are now saving smaller blocks of data into your database, the time spent in performing disk I/O is significantly reduced. The downside of compression is that it takes additional processing power from your machine (and requires additional processing time), and you need to factor in this additional time before deciding you want to use compression in your application.

Compression is extremely useful in cases where you need to transmit data over networks, especially slow and costly networks such as General Packet Radio Service (GPRS).connections. In such cases, using compression can drastically cut down the data size and reduce the overall cost of communication. Web Services are another area where using compression can provide a great advantage because XML data can be highly compressed.

But once you've decided the performance cost is worth it, you'll need help deciphering the utilization of these two compression classes, which is what this section is about.

Compression

The compression classes read data (to be compressed) from a byte array, compress it, and store the results in a `Stream` object. For decompression, the compressed data stored in a `Stream` object is decompressed and then stored in another `Stream` object.

Let's see how you can perform compression. First, define the `Compress()` function, which takes in two parameters: `algo` and `data`. The first parameter specifies which algorithm to use (GZip or Deflate), and the second parameter is a byte array that contains the data to compress. A MemoryStream object will be used to store the compressed data. The compressed data stored in the MemoryStream is then copied into another byte array and returned to the calling function. The Compress() function is defined as follows:

```csharp
static byte[] Compress(string algo, byte[] data)
{
    try
    {
        //---the ms is used for storing the compressed data---
        MemoryStream ms = new MemoryStream();
        Stream zipStream = null;
        switch (algo)
        {
            case "Gzip": zipStream =
                new GZipStream(ms, CompressionMode.Compress, true);
                break;
            case "Deflat": zipStream =
                new DeflateStream(ms, CompressionMode.Compress, true);
                break;
            default: return null;
        }

        //---compress the data stored in the data byte array---
        zipStream.Write(data, 0, data.Length);
        zipStream.Close();

        //---store the compressed data into a byte array---
        ms.Position = 0;
        byte[] c_data = new byte[ms.Length];

        //---read the content of the memory stream into the byte array---
        ms.Read(c_data, 0, (int)ms.Length);
        return c_data;
    }
    catch (Exception ex)
    {
        Console.WriteLine(ex.ToString());
        return null;
    }
}
```

Decompression

The following Decompress() function decompresses the data compressed by the Compress() function. The first parameter specifies the algorithm to use, while the byte array containing the compressed data is passed in as the second parameter, which is then copied into a MemoryStream object.

```csharp
static byte[] Decompress(string algo, byte[] data)
{
    try
    {
        //---copy the data (compressed) into ms---
        MemoryStream ms = new MemoryStream(data);
```

```
        Stream zipStream = null;
        //---decompressing using data stored in ms---

        switch (algo)
        {
            case "Gzip": zipStream =
                new GZipStream(ms, CompressionMode.Decompress, true);
                break;
            case "Deflat": zipStream =
                new DeflateStream(ms, CompressionMode.Decompress, true);
                break;
            default: return null;
        }

        //---used to store the de-compressed data---
        byte[] dc_data;

        //---the de-compressed data is stored in zipStream;
        // extract them out into a byte array---
        dc_data = RetrieveBytesFromStream(zipStream, data.Length);

        return dc_data;
    }
    catch (Exception ex)
    {
        Console.WriteLine(ex.ToString());
        return null;
    }
}
```

The compression classes then decompress the data stored in the memory stream and store the decompressed data into another Stream object. To obtain the decompressed data, you need to read the data from the Stream object. This is accomplished by the RetrieveBytesFromStream() function, which is defined next:

```
static byte[] RetrieveBytesFromStream(Stream stream, int bytesblock)
{
    //---retrieve the bytes from a stream object---
    byte[] data = null;
    int totalCount = 0;
    try
    {
        while (true)
        {
            //---progressively increase the size of the data byte array---
            Array.Resize(ref data, totalCount + bytesblock);
            int bytesRead = stream.Read(data, totalCount, bytesblock);
            if (bytesRead == 0)
            {
                break;
            }
            totalCount += bytesRead;
        }
```

(continued)

(continued)

```
                //---make sure the byte array contains exactly the number
                // of bytes extracted---
                Array.Resize(ref data, totalCount);
                return data;
            }
            catch (Exception ex)
            {
                Console.WriteLine(ex.ToString());
                return null;
            }
        }
```

The RetrieveBytesFromStream() function takes in two parameters — a Stream object and an integer — and returns a byte array containing the decompressed data. The integer parameter is used to determine how many bytes to read from the stream object into the byte array at a time. This is necessary because you do not know the exact size of the decompressed data in the stream object. And hence it is necessary to dynamically expand the byte array in blocks to hold the decompressed data during runtime. Reserving too large a block wastes memory, and reserving too small a block loses valuable time while you continually expand the byte array. It is therefore up to the calling routine to determine the optimal block size to read.

The block size is the size of the compressed data (data.Length):

```
                //---the de-compressed data is stored in zipStream;
                // extract them out into a byte array---
                dc_data = RetrieveBytesFromStream(zipStream, data.Length);
```

In most cases, the uncompressed data is a few times larger than the compressed data, so you would at most expand the byte array dynamically during runtime a couple of times. For instance, suppose that the compression ratio is 20% and the size of the compressed data is 2MB. In that case, the uncompressed data would be 10MB, and the byte array would be expanded dynamically five times. Ideally, the byte array should not be expanded too frequently during runtime because it severely slows down the application. Using the size of the compressed data as a block size is a good compromise.

Use the following statements to test the Compress() and Decompress() functions:

```
        static void Main(string[] args)
        {
            byte[] compressedData = Compress("Gzip",
                System.Text.Encoding.ASCII.GetBytes(
                "This is a uncompressed string"));
            Console.WriteLine("Compressed: {0}",
                ASCIIEncoding.ASCII.GetString(compressedData));
            Console.WriteLine("Uncompressed: {0}",
                ASCIIEncoding.ASCII.GetString(Decompress("Gzip", compressedData)));
            Console.ReadLine();
        }
```

The output is as shown in Figure 11-9.

Figure 11-9

The compressed data contains some unprintable characters, so you may hear some beeps when it prints. To display the compressed data using printable characters, you can define two helper functions — byteArrayToString() and stringToByteArray():

```
//---converts a byte array to a string---
static string byteArrayToString(byte[] data)
{
    //---copy the compressed data into a string for presentation---
    System.Text.StringBuilder s = new System.Text.StringBuilder();
    for (int i = 0; i <= data.Length - 1; i++)
    {
        if (i != data.Length - 1)
            s.Append(data[i] + " ");
        else
            s.Append(data[i]);
    }
    return s.ToString();
}

//---converts a string into a byte array---
static byte[] stringToByteArray(string str)
{
    //---format the compressed string into a byte array---
    string[] eachByte = str.Split(' ');
    byte[] data = new byte[eachByte.Length];
    for (int i = 0; i <= eachByte.Length - 1; i++)
        data[i] = Convert.ToByte(eachByte[i]);
    return data;
}
```

To use the two helper functions, make the following changes to the statements:

```
static void Main(string[] args)
{
    byte[] compressedData = Compress("Gzip",
        System.Text.Encoding.ASCII.GetBytes(
        "This is a uncompressed string"));

    string compressedDataStr = byteArrayToString(compressedData);
    Console.WriteLine("Compressed: {0}", compressedDataStr);

    byte[] data = stringToByteArray(compressedDataStr);
    Console.WriteLine("Uncompressed: {0}",
        ASCIIEncoding.ASCII.GetString(Decompress("Gzip", data)));

    Console.ReadLine();
}
```

Figure 11-10 shows the output when using the two helper functions.

Figure 11-10

Alternatively, you can also convert the compressed data to a Base64-encoded string, like this:

```
byte[] compressedData = Compress("Gzip",
    System.Text.Encoding.ASCII.GetBytes(
    "This is a uncompressed string"));

string compressedDataStr = Convert.ToBase64String(compressedData);
Console.WriteLine("Compressed: {0}", compressedDataStr);

byte[] data = Convert.FromBase64String((compressedDataStr));
Console.WriteLine("Uncompressed: {0}",
    ASCIIEncoding.ASCII.GetString(Decompress("Gzip", data)));
```

Figure 11-11 shows the output using the base64 encoding.

Figure 11-11

Serialization

Many a time you may need to persist the value of an object to secondary storage. For example, you may want to save the values of a couple of `Point` objects representing the positioning of an item on-screen to secondary storage. The act of "flattening" an object into a serial form is known as *serialization*. The .NET Framework supports binary and XML serialization.

Binary Serialization

Consider the following class, `BookMark`, which is used to stored information about web addresses and their descriptions:

```csharp
using System;
using System.Collections.Generic;
using System.Linq;
using System.Text;
using System.IO;
using System.Runtime.Serialization.Formatters.Binary;

namespace Serialization
{
    class Program
    {
        static void Main(string[] args)
        {
        }
    }

    class BookMark
    {
        private DateTime _dateCreated;
        public BookMark()
        {
            _dateCreated = DateTime.Now;
        }
        public DateTime GetDateCreated()
        {
            return _dateCreated;
        }
        public string URL { get; set; }
        public string Description { get; set; }
        public BookMark NextURL { get; set; }
    }
}
```

The `BookMark` class contains properties as well as private variables. The `NextURL` property links multiple `BookMark` objects, much like a linked list. Let's now create two `BookMark` objects and link them:

```
static void Main(string[] args)
{
    BookMark bm1, bm2;

    bm1 = new BookMark
    {
        URL = "http://www.amazon.com",
        Description = "Amazon.com Web site"
    };

    bm2 = new BookMark()
    {
        URL = "http://www.wrox.com",
        Description = "Wrox.com Web site",
        NextURL = null
    };

    //---link the first BookMark to the next---
    bm1.NextURL = bm2;
}
```

You can serialize the objects into a binary stream by writing the `Serialize()` function:

```
static void Main(string[] args)
{
    //...
}
```

```
static MemoryStream Serialize(BookMark bookMark)
{
    MemoryStream ms = new MemoryStream();
    FileStream fs = new FileStream(
        @"C:\Bookmarks.dat",
        FileMode.Create,
        FileAccess.Write);

    BinaryFormatter formatter = new BinaryFormatter();
    //---serialize to memory stream---
    formatter.Serialize(ms, bookMark);
    ms.Position = 0;

    //---serialize to file stream---
    formatter.Serialize(fs, bookMark);
    return ms;
}
```

> For binary serialization, you need to import the `System.Runtime.Serialization` `.Formatters.Binary` **namespace.**

The `Serialize()` function takes in a single parameter (the `BookMark` object to serialize) and returns a `MemoryStream` object representing the serialized `BookMark` object. You use the `BinaryFormatter` class from the `System.Runtime.Serialization.Formatters.Binary` namespace to serialize an object. One side effect of this function is that it also serializes the `BookMark` object to file, using the `FileStream` class.

Before you serialize an object, you need to prefix the class that you want to serialize name with the `[Serializable]` attribute:

```
[Serializable]
class BookMark
{
    private DateTime _dateCreated;
    public BookMark()
    {
        _dateCreated = DateTime.Now;
    }
    public DateTime GetDateCreated()
    {
        return _dateCreated;
    }
    public string URL { get; set; }
    public string Description { get; set; }
    public BookMark NextURL { get; set; }
}
```

The following statement serializes the bm1 `BookMark` object, using the `Serialize()` function:

```
static void Main(string[] args)
{
    BookMark bm1, bm2;

    bm1 = new BookMark
    {
        URL = "http://www.amazon.com",
        Description = "Amazon.com Web site"
    };

    bm2 = new BookMark()
    {
        URL = "http://www.wrox.com",
        Description = "Wrox.com Web site",
        NextURL = null
    };

    //---link the first BookMark to the next---
    bm1.NextURL = bm2;

    //========Binary Serialization=========
    //---serializing an object graph into a memory stream---
    MemoryStream ms = Serialize(bm1);
}
```

To prove that the object is serialized correctly, you deserialize the memory stream (that is, "unflatten" the data) and assign it back to a `BookMark` object:

```csharp
static void Main(string[] args)
{
    BookMark bm1, bm2;

    bm1 = new BookMark
    {
        URL = "http://www.amazon.com",
        Description = "Amazon.com Web site"
    };

    bm2 = new BookMark()
    {
        URL = "http://www.wrox.com",
        Description = "Wrox.com Web site",
        NextURL = null
    };

    //---link the first BookMark to the next---
    bm1.NextURL = bm2;


    //========Binary Serialization=========
    //---serializing an object graph into a memory stream---
    MemoryStream ms = Serialize(bm1);

    //---deserializing a memory stream into an object graph---
    BookMark bm3 = Deserialize(ms);
}
```

Here is the definition for the `DeSerialize()` function:

```csharp
static void Main(string[] args)
{
    //...
}

static MemoryStream Serialize(BookMark bookMark)
{
    //...
}

static BookMark Deserialize(MemoryStream ms)
{
    BinaryFormatter formatter = new BinaryFormatter();
    return (BookMark)formatter.Deserialize(ms);
}
```

To display the values of the deserialized `BookMark` object, you can print out them out like this:

```
static void Main(string[] args)
{
    BookMark bm1, bm2;

    bm1 = new BookMark
    {
        URL = "http://www.amazon.com",
        Description = "Amazon.com Web site"
    };

    bm2 = new BookMark()
    {
        URL = "http://www.wrox.com",
        Description = "Wrox.com Web site",
        NextURL = null
    };

    //---link the first BookMark to the next---
    bm1.NextURL = bm2;


    //========Binary Serialization=========
    //---serializing an object graph into a memory stream---
    MemoryStream ms = Serialize(bm1);


    //---deserializing a memory stream into an object graph---
    BookMark bm3 = Deserialize(ms);

    //---print out all the bookmarks---
    BookMark tempBookMark = bm3;
    do
    {
        Console.WriteLine(tempBookMark.URL);
        Console.WriteLine(tempBookMark.Description);
        Console.WriteLine(tempBookMark.GetDateCreated());
        Console.WriteLine("---");
        tempBookMark = tempBookMark.NextURL;
    } while (tempBookMark != null);

    Console.ReadLine();
}
```

If the objects are serialized and deserialized correctly, the output is as shown in Figure 11-12.

Figure 11-12

But what does the binary stream look like? To answer that question, take a look at the `c:\BookMarks` `.dat` file that you have created in the process. To view the binary file, simply drag and drop the `BookMarks.dat` file into Visual Studio 2008. You should see something similar to Figure 11-13.

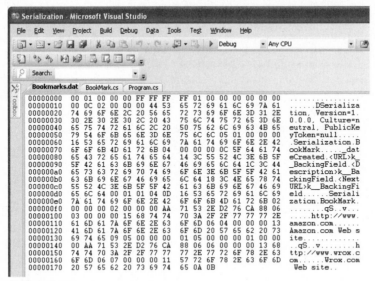

Figure 11-13

A few observations are worth noting at this point:

❑ Private variables and properties are all serialized. In binary serialization, both the private variables and properties are serialized. This is known as *deep serialization*, as opposed to *shallow serialization* in XML serialization (which only serializes the public variables and properties). The next section discusses XML serialization.

❑ Object graphs are serialized and preserved. In this example, two `BookMark` objects are linked, and the serialization process takes care of the relationships between the two objects.

There are times when you do not want to serialize all of the data in your object. If you don't want to persist the date and time that the `BookMark` objects are created, for instance, you can prefix the variable name (that you do not want to serialize) with the `[NonSerialized]` attribute:

```
[Serializable]
class BookMark
{
    [NonSerialized]
    private DateTime _dateCreated;
    public BookMark()
    {
        _dateCreated = DateTime.Now;
    }
    public DateTime GetDateCreated()
```

```
        {
            return _dateCreated;
        }
        public string URL { get; set; }
        public string Description { get; set; }
        public BookMark NextURL { get; set; }
    }
```

The `dateCreated` variable will not be serialized. Figure 11-14 shows that when the `dateCreated` variable is not serialized, its value is set to the default date when the object is deserialized.

Figure 11-14

XML Serialization

You can also serialize an object into an XML document. There are many advantages to XML serialization. For instance, XML documents are platform-agnostic because they are in plain text format and that makes cross-platform communication quite easy. XML documents are also easy to read and modify, which makes XML a very flexible format for data representation.

The following example illustrates XML serialization and shows you some of its uses.

Defining a Sample Class

Let's define a class so that you can see how XML serialization works. For this example, you define three classes that allow you to store information about a person, such as name, address, and date of birth. Here are the class definitions:

```
using System;
using System.Collections.Generic;
using System.Linq;
using System.Text;
using Microsoft.VisualBasic;
using System.IO;
using System.Xml.Serialization;
using System.Xml;

namespace Serialization
{
    class Program
    {
        static void Main(string[] args)
```

(continued)

(continued)

```
        {
        }
    }

    public class Member
    {
        private int age;
        public MemberName Name;
        public MemberAddress[] Addresses;
        public DateTime DOB;
        public int currentAge
        {
            get
            {
                //---add a reference to Microsoft.VisualBasic.dll---
                age = (int)DateAndTime.DateDiff(
                    DateInterval.Year, DOB,
                    DateTime.Now,
                    FirstDayOfWeek.System,
                    FirstWeekOfYear.System);
                return age;
            }
        }
    }

    public class MemberName
    {
        public string FirstName { get; set; }
        public string LastName { get; set; }
    }

    public class MemberAddress
    {
        public string Line1;
        public string Line2;
        public string City;
        public string Country;
        public string Postal;
    }
}
```

The various classes are deliberately designed to illustrate the various aspects of XML serialization. They may not adhere to the best practices for defining classes.

Here are the specifics for the classes:

- ❏ The Member class contains both private and public members. It also contains a read-only property.
- ❏ The Member class contains a public array containing the address of a Member.
- ❏ The Member class contains a variable of Date data type.
- ❏ The MemberName class contains two properties.
- ❏ The MemberAddress class contains only public members.

Serializing the Class

To serialize a Member object into a XML document, you can use the XMLSerializer class from the System.Xml.Serialization namespace:

```
static void Main(string[] args)
{
}
```

```
//========XML Serialization=========
static void XMLSerialize(Member mem)
{
    StreamWriter sw = new StreamWriter(@"c:\Members.xml");
    try
    {
        XmlSerializer s = new XmlSerializer(typeof(Member));
        s.Serialize(sw, mem);
    }
    catch (Exception ex)
    {
        Console.WriteLine(ex.ToString());
    }
    finally
    {
        sw.Close();
    }
}
```

For XML serialization, you need to import the System.Xml.Serialization namespace.

In the XMLSerialize() function, you first create a new StreamWriter object so that you can save the serialized XML string to a file. The Serialize() method from the XMLSerializer class serializes the Member object into an XML string, which is then written to file by using the StreamWriter class.

To test the XMLSerialize() function, assume that you have the following object declarations:

```csharp
static void Main(string[] args)
{
    MemberAddress address1 = new MemberAddress()
    {
        Line1 = "One Way Street",
        Line2 = "Infinite Loop",
        Country = "SINGAPORE",
        Postal = "456123"
    };

    MemberAddress address2 = new MemberAddress()
    {
        Line1 = "Two Way Street",
        Country = "SINGAPORE",
        Postal = "456123"
    };

    Member m1 = new Member()
    {
        Name = new MemberName()
        {
            FirstName = "Wei-Meng",
            LastName = "Lee"
        },
        DOB = Convert.ToDateTime(@"5/1/1972"),
        Addresses = new MemberAddress[] { address1, address2 }
    };
}
```

To serialize the Member object, invoke the XMLSerialize() method like this:

```csharp
static void Main(string[] args)
{
    MemberAddress address1 = new MemberAddress()
    {
        Line1 = "One Way Street",
        Line2 = "Infinite Loop",
        Country = "SINGAPORE",
        Postal = "456123"
    };

    MemberAddress address2 = new MemberAddress()
    {
        Line1 = "Two Way Street",
        Country = "SINGAPORE",
        Postal = "456123"
    };

    Member m1 = new Member()
    {
        Name = new MemberName()
        {
```

```
                    FirstName = "Wei-Meng",
                    LastName = "Lee"
            },
            DOB = Convert.ToDateTime(@"5/1/1972"),
            Addresses = new MemberAddress[] { address1, address2 }
        };

        XMLSerialize(m1);
    }
```

Figure 11-15 shows the XML document generated by the XMLSerialize() function.

Figure 11-15

As you can see, the object is serialized into an XML document with a format corresponding to the structure of the object. Here are some important points to note:

❑   The City information is not persisted in the XML document (nor as the Line2 in the second Address element) because it was not assigned in the objects. You will see later how to persist empty elements, even though a value is not assigned.

❑   All read/write properties in the object are persisted in the XML document, except the read-only currentAge property in the Member class.

❑   Only public variables are persisted; private variables are not persisted in XML serialization.

❑   The default name for each element in the XML document is drawn from the variable (or class) name. In most cases this is desirable, but sometimes the element names might not be obvious.

Deserializing the Class

To deserialize the XML document, simply use the `Deserialize()` method from the `XMLSerializer` class. Define the `XMLDeserialize()` function as follows:

```
static void Main(string[] args)
{
    //...
}
```

```
//========XML Serialization=========
static Member XMLDeserialize(string xmlFile)
{
    Member obj;
    XmlReader xr = XmlReader.Create(xmlFile);
    try
    {
        XmlSerializer s = new XmlSerializer(typeof(Member));
        obj = (Member)s.Deserialize(xr);
    }
    catch (Exception ex)
    {
        Console.WriteLine(ex.ToString());
        obj = null;
    }
    finally
    {
        xr.Close();
    }

    return obj;
}
```

Here, you can use the `XmlReader` class's `Create()` method to open an XML file for reading. The `XmlReader` class is used to read the data from the XML file. The deserialized object is then returned to the calling function.

> Remember to import the `System.Xml` namespace for the `XmlReader` class.

To test the `XMLDeserialize()` function, call it directly after an object has been serialized, like this:

```
static void Main(string[] args)
{
    MemberAddress address1 = new MemberAddress()
    {
        Line1 = "One Way Street",
        Line2 = "Infinite Loop",
        Country = "SINGAPORE",
        Postal = "456123"
```

```
    };

    MemberAddress address2 = new MemberAddress()
    {
        Line1 = "Two Way Street",
        Country = "SINGAPORE",
        Postal = "456123"
    };

    Member m1 = new Member()
    {
        Name = new MemberName()
        {
            FirstName = "Wei-Meng",
            LastName = "Lee"
        },
        DOB = Convert.ToDateTime(@"5/1/1972"),
        Addresses = new MemberAddress[] { address1, address2 }
    };

    XMLSerialize(m1);

    Member m2 = XMLDeserialize(@"c:\Members.xml");

    Console.WriteLine("{0}, {1}", m2.Name.FirstName, m2.Name.LastName);
    Console.WriteLine("{0}", m2.currentAge);
    foreach (MemberAddress a in m2.Addresses)
    {
        Console.WriteLine("{0}", a.Line1);
        Console.WriteLine("{0}", a.Line2);
        Console.WriteLine("{0}", a.Country);
        Console.WriteLine("{0}", a.Postal);
        Console.WriteLine();
    }
    Console.ReadLine();
}
```

The output of these statements is shown in Figure 11-16.

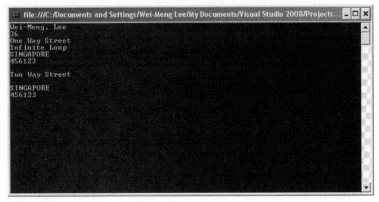

Figure 11-16

Customizing the Serialization Process

Despite the fairly automated task performed by the XMLSerializer object, you can customize the way the XML document is generated. Here's an example of how you can modify classes with a few attributes:

```
[XmlRoot("MemberInformation",
    Namespace = "http://www.learn2develop.net",
    IsNullable = true)]
public class Member
{
    private int age;

    //---specify the element name to be MemberName---
    [XmlElement("MemberName")]
    public MemberName Name;

    //---specify the sub-element(s) of Addresses to be Address---
    [XmlArrayItem("Address")]
    public MemberAddress[] Addresses;
    public DateTime DOB;
    public int currentAge
    {
        get
        {
            //---add a reference to Microsoft.VisualBasic.dll---
            age = (int)DateAndTime.DateDiff(
                DateInterval.Year, DOB,
                DateTime.Now,
                FirstDayOfWeek.System,
                FirstWeekOfYear.System);
            return age;
        }
    }
}

public class MemberName
{
    public string FirstName { get; set; }
    public string LastName { get; set; }
}

public class MemberAddress
{
    public string Line1;
    public string Line2;

    //---empty element if city is not specified---
    [XmlElement(IsNullable = true)]
    public string City;

    //---specify country and postal as attribute---
    [XmlAttributeAttribute()]
    public string Country;
```

```
        [XmlAttributeAttribute()]
     public string Postal;
}
```

When the class is serialized again, the XML document will look like Figure 11-17.

Figure 11-17

Notice that the root element of the XML document is now <MemberInformation>. Also, <MemberAddress> has now been changed to <Address>, and the <Country> and <Postal> elements are now represented as attributes. Finally, the <City> element is always persisted regardless of whether or not it has been assigned a value.

Here are the uses of each attribute:

❑

```
   [XmlRoot("MemberInformation",
      Namespace = "http://www.learn2develop.net",
      IsNullable = true)]
public class Member
{
...
```

Sets the root element name of the XML document to MemberInformation (default element name is Member, which follows the class name), with a specific namespace. The IsNullable attribute indicates if empty elements must be displayed.

❏

```
//---specify the element name to be MemberName---
[XmlElement("MemberName")]
public MemberName Name;
...
```

Specifies that the element name MemberName be used in place of the current variable name (as defined in the class as Name).

❏

```
//---specify the sub-element(s) of Addresses to be Address---
[XmlArrayItem("Address")]
public MemberAddress[] Addresses;
...
```

Specifies that the following variable is repeating (an array) and that each repeating element be named as Address.

❏

```
//---empty element if city is not specified---
[XmlElement(IsNullable = true)]
public string City;
...
```

Indicates that the document must include the City element even if it is empty.

❏

```
//---specify country and postal as attribute---
[XmlAttributeAttribute()]
public string Country;

[XmlAttributeAttribute()]
public string Postal;
...
```

Indicates that the Country and Postal property be represented as an attribute.

XML Serialization Needs a Default Constructor

There is one more thing that you need to note when doing XML serialization. If your class has a constructor (as in the following example), you also need a default constructor:

```
[XmlRoot("MemberInformation",
    Namespace = "http://www.learn2develop.net",
    IsNullable = true)]
public class Member
{
    private int age;
```

```
        public Member(MemberName Name)
        {
            this.Name = Name;
        }
```

```
        //---specify the element name to be MemberName---
        [XmlElement("MemberName")]
        public MemberName Name;
        ...
```

This example results in an error when you try to perform XML serialization on it. To solve the problem, simply add a default constructor to your class definition:

```
        [XmlRoot("MemberInformation",
            Namespace = "http://www.learn2develop.net",
            IsNullable = true)]
        public class Member
        {
            private int age;

            public Member() { }

            public Member(MemberName Name)
            {
                this.Name = Name;
            }
            ...
```

Uses of XML Serialization

XML serialization can help you to preserve the state of your object (just like the binary serialization that you saw in previous section) and makes transportation easy. More significantly, you can use XML serialization to manage configuration files. You can define a class to store configuration information and use XML serialization to persist it on file. By doing so, you have the flexibility to modify the configuration information easily because the information is now represented in XML; at the same time, you can programmatically manipulate the configuration information by accessing the object's properties and methods.

Summary

In this chapter, you explored the basics of files and streams and how to use the Stream object to perform a wide variety of tasks, including network communication, cryptography, and compression. In addition, you saw how to preserve the state of objects using XML and binary serialization. In the .NET Framework, the Stream object is extremely versatile and its large number of derived classes is designed to deal with specific tasks such as file I/O, memory I/O, network I/O, and so on.

12

Exception Handling

An exception is a situation that occurs when your program encounters an error that it is not expecting during runtime. Examples of exceptions include trying to divide a number by zero, trying to write to a file that is read-only, trying to delete a nonexistent file, and trying to access more members of an array than it actually holds. Exceptions are part and parcel of an application, and as a programmer you need to look out for them by handling the various exceptions that may occur. That means your program must be capable of responding to the exceptions by offering some ways to remedy the problem instead of exiting midway through your program (that is, crashing).

Handling Exceptions

To understand the importance of handling exceptions, consider the following case, a classic example of dividing two numbers:

```
using System;
using System.Collections.Generic;
using System.Linq;
using System.Text;

namespace ConsoleApp
{
    class Program
    {
        static void Main(string[] args)
        {
            int num1, num2, result;

            Console.Write("Please enter the first number:");
            num1 = int.Parse(Console.ReadLine());

            Console.Write("Please enter the second number:");
            num2 = int.Parse(Console.ReadLine());

            result = num1 / num2;
```

(continued)

(continued)

```
                Console.WriteLine("The result of {0}/{1} is {2}", num1, num2, result);

                Console.ReadLine();
            }
        }
    }
```

In this example, there are several opportunities for exceptions to occur:

❑   If the user enters a noninteger value for num1 or num2.

❑   If the user enters a non-numeric value for num1 and num2.

❑   If num2 is zero, resulting in a division by zero error.

Figure 12-1 shows the program halting abruptly when the user enters 3.5 for num1.

Figure 12-1

Hence, you need to anticipate all the possible scenarios and handle the exceptions gracefully.

Handling Exceptions Using the try-catch Statement

In C#, you can use the try-catch statement to enclose a block of code statements that may potentially cause exceptions to be raised. You enclose these statements within the catch block and that block to catch the different types of exceptions that may occur.

Using the previous example, you can enclose the statements that ask the user to input num1 and num2 and then performs the division within a catch block. You then use the catch block to catch possible exceptions, like this:

```
        static void Main(string[] args)
        {
            int num1, num2, result;
            try
            {
```

```
        Console.Write("Please enter the first number:");
        num1 = int.Parse(Console.ReadLine());

        Console.Write("Please enter the second number:");
        num2 = int.Parse(Console.ReadLine());

        result = num1 / num2;
        Console.WriteLine("The result of {0}/{1} is {2}",
            num1, num2, result);
    }
    catch (Exception ex)
    {
        Console.WriteLine(ex.Message);
    }

    Console.ReadLine();
}
```

The Exception class is the base class for all exceptions; that is, it catches all the various types of exceptions. The class contains the details of the exception that occurred, and includes a number of properties that help identify the code location, the type, the help file, and the reason for the exception. The following table describes these properties.

Property	Description
Data	Gets a collection of key/value pairs that provide additional user-defined information about the exception.
HelpLink	Gets or sets a link to the help file associated with this exception.
HResult	Gets or sets HRESULT, a coded numerical value that is assigned to a specific exception.
InnerException	Gets the Exception instance that caused the current exception.
Message	Gets a message that describes the current exception.
Source	Gets or sets the name of the application or the object that causes the error.
StackTrace	Gets a string representation of the frames on the call stack at the time the current exception was thrown.
TargetSite	Gets the method that throws the current exception.

In the preceding program, if you type in a numeric value for num1 and then an alphabetical character for num2, the exception is caught and displayed like this:

```
Please enter the first number:6
Please enter the second number:a
Input string was not in a correct format.
```

If, though, you enter 0 for the second number, you get a different description for the error:

```
Please enter the first number:7
Please enter the second number:0
Attempted to divide by zero.
```

Notice that two different types of exceptions are caught using the same Exception class. The description of the exception is contained within the Message property of the Exception class.

You can use the ToString() *method of the* Exception *class to retrieve more details about the exception, such as the description of the exception as well as the stack trace.*

However, there are cases where you would like to print your own custom error messages for the different types of exceptions. Using the preceding code, you would not be able to do that — you would need a much finer way to catch the different types of possible exceptions.

To know the different types of exceptions that your program can cause (such as entering "a" for num1 or division by zero), you can set a breakpoint at a line within the catch block and try entering different values. When an exception is raised during runtime, IntelliSense tells you the error and the type of the exception raised. Figure 12-2 shows that the FormatException exception is raised when you enter a for num1.

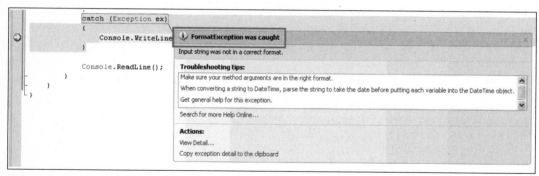

Figure 12-2

If you are not sure what type of exception your program is going to raise during runtime, it is always safe to use the base Exception class. If not — if the exception that is raised does not match the exception you are trying to catch — a runtime error will occur. Here's an example:

```csharp
static void Main(string[] args)
{
    int num1, num2, result;
    try
    {
        Console.Write("Please enter the first number:");
        num1 = int.Parse(Console.ReadLine());

        Console.Write("Please enter the second number:");
```

```
        num2 = int.Parse(Console.ReadLine());

        result = num1 / num2;
        Console.WriteLine("The result of {0}/{1} is {2}",
            num1, num2, result);
    }
    catch (DivideByZeroException ex)
    {
        Console.WriteLine(ex.Message);
    }
    Console.ReadLine();
}
```

If a division-by-zero exception occurs (entering 0 for num2), the exception is caught. However, if you enter an alphabetic character for num1 or num2, a FormatException exception is raised. And because you are only catching the DivideByZeroException exception, this exception goes unhandled and a runtime error results.

Handling Multiple Exceptions

To handle different types of exceptions, you can have one or more catch blocks in the try-catch statement. The following example shows how you can catch three different exceptions:

❑ DivideByZeroException — Thrown when there is an attempt to divide an integral or decimal value by zero.

❑ FormatException — Thrown when the format of an argument does not meet the parameter specifications of the invoked method.

❑ Exception — Represents errors that occur during application execution.

This example handles the three different exceptions and then prints out a custom error message:

```
static void Main(string[] args)
{
    int num1, num2, result;
    try
    {
        Console.Write("Please enter the first number:");
        num1 = int.Parse(Console.ReadLine());

        Console.Write("Please enter the second number:");
        num2 = int.Parse(Console.ReadLine());

        result = num1 / num2;
        Console.WriteLine("The result of {0}/{1} is {2}",
            num1, num2, result);
    }
    catch (DivideByZeroException ex)
    {
        Console.WriteLine("Division by zero error.");
    }
```

(continued)

(continued)

```
            catch (FormatException ex)
            {
                Console.WriteLine("Input error.");
            }
            catch (Exception ex)
            {
                Console.WriteLine(ex.Message);
            }
            Console.ReadLine();
    }
```

In this program, typing in a numeric value for num1 and an alphabetic character for num2 produces the FormatException exception, which is caught and displayed like this?

```
Please enter the first number:6
Please enter the second number:a
Input error.
```

Entering 0 for the second number throws the DivideByZeroException exception, which is caught and displays a different error message:

```
Please enter the first number:7
Please enter the second number:0
Division by zero error.
```

So far, all the statements are located in the Main() function. What happens if you have a function called PerformDivision() that divides the two numbers and returns the result, like this?

```
class Program
{
    static void Main(string[] args)
    {
        int num1, num2;
        try
        {
            Console.Write("Please enter the first number:");
            num1 = int.Parse(Console.ReadLine());

            Console.Write("Please enter the second number:");
            num2 = int.Parse(Console.ReadLine());

            Program myApp = new Program();

            Console.WriteLine("The result of {0}/{1} is {2}",
                num1, num2,
                myApp.PerformDivision(num1, num2));
        }
        catch (DivideByZeroException ex)
        {
            Console.WriteLine("Division by zero error.");
        }
        catch (FormatException ex)
        {
```

```
        Console.WriteLine("Input error.");
    }
    catch (Exception ex)
    {
        Console.WriteLine(ex.Message);
    }
    Console.ReadLine();
}

private int PerformDivision(int num1, int num2)
{
    return num1 / num2;
}
```

If num2 is zero, an exception is raised within the PerformDivision() function. You can either catch
the exception in the PerformDivision() function or catch the exception in the calling function — Main()
in this case. When an exception is raised within the PerformDivision() function, the system searches
the function to see if there is any catch block for the exception. If none is found, the exception is passed
up the call stack and handled by the calling function. If there is no try-catch block in the calling function,
the exception continues to be passed up the call stack again until it is handled. If no more frames exist
in the call stack, the default exception handler handles the exception and your program has a runtime error.

Throwing Exceptions Using the throw Statement

Instead of waiting for the system to encounter an error and raise an exception, you can programmatically
raise an exception by *throwing* one. Consider the following example:

```
private int PerformDivision(int num1, int num2)
{
    if (num1 == 0) throw new ArithmeticException();
    if (num2 == 0) throw new DivideByZeroException();
    return num1 / num2;
}
```

In this program, the PerformDivision() function throws an ArithmeticException exception when
num1 is zero and it throws a DivideByZeroException exception when num2 is zero. Because there is no
catch block in PerformDivision(), the exception is handled by the calling Main() function. In
Main(), you can catch the ArithmeticException exception like this:

```
class Program
{
    static void Main(string[] args)
    {
        int num1, num2, result;
        try
        {
            Console.Write("Please enter the first number:");
            num1 = int.Parse(Console.ReadLine());

            Console.Write("Please enter the second number:");
```

(continued)

383

(continued)

```
            num2 = int.Parse(Console.ReadLine());

            Program myApp = new Program();

            Console.WriteLine("The result of {0}/{1} is {2}",
                num1, num2,
                myApp.PerformDivision(num1, num2));
        }
        catch (ArithmeticException ex)
        {
            Console.WriteLine("Numerator cannot be zero.");
        }
        catch (DivideByZeroException ex)
        {
            Console.WriteLine("Division by zero error.");
        }
        catch (FormatException ex)
        {
            Console.WriteLine("Input error");
        }
        catch (Exception ex)
        {
            Console.WriteLine(ex.Message);
        }
        Console.ReadLine();
    }

    private int PerformDivision(int num1, int num2)
    {
        if (num1 == 0) throw new  ArithmeticException();
        if (num2 == 0) throw new DivideByZeroException();
        return num1 / num2;
    }
}
```

One interesting thing about the placement of the multiple catch blocks is that you place all specific exceptions that you want to catch first before placing generic ones. Because the Exception class is the base of all exception classes, it should always be placed last in a catch block so that any exception that is not caught in the previous catch blocks is always caught. In this example, when the ArithmeticException exception is placed before the DivideByZeroException exception, IntelliSense displays an error (see Figure 12-3).

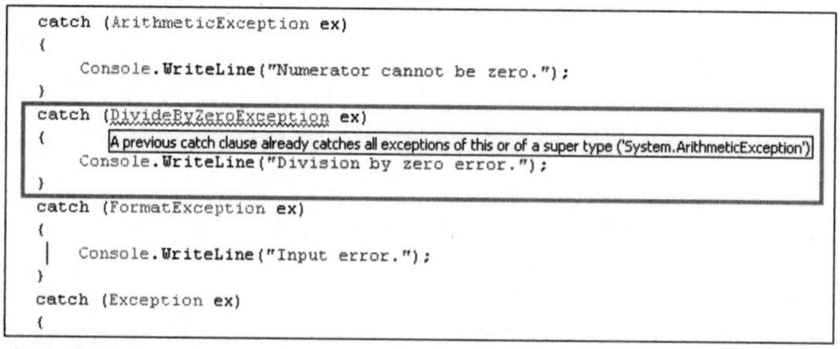

Figure 12-3

That's because the `DivideByZeroException` is derived from the `ArithmeticException` class, so if there is a division-by-zero exception, the exception is always handled by the `ArithmeticException` exception and the `DivideByZeroException` exception is never caught. To solve this problem, you must catch the `DivideByZeroException` exception first before catching the `ArithmeticException` exception:

```csharp
static void Main(string[] args)
{
    int num1, num2, result;
    try
    {
        Console.Write("Please enter the first number:");
        num1 = int.Parse(Console.ReadLine());

        Console.Write("Please enter the second number:");
        num2 = int.Parse(Console.ReadLine());

        Program myApp = new Program();

        Console.WriteLine("The result of {0}/{1} is {2}",
            num1, num2,
            myApp.PerformDivision(num1, num2));
    }
    catch (DivideByZeroException ex)
    {
        Console.WriteLine("Division by zero error.");
    }
    catch (ArithmeticException ex)
    {
        Console.WriteLine("Numerator cannot be zero.");
    }
    catch (FormatException ex)
    {
        Console.WriteLine("Input error.");
    }
    catch (Exception ex)
    {
        Console.WriteLine(ex.Message);
    }
    Console.ReadLine();
}
```

The following shows the output when different values are entered for num1 and num2:

```
Please enter the first number:5
Please enter the second number:0
Division by zero error.

Please enter the first number:0
Please enter the second number:5
Numerator cannot be zero.

Please enter the first number:a
Input error.
```

Rethrowing Exceptions

There are times when after catching an exception, you want to throw the same (or a new type) exception back to the calling function after taking some corrective actions. Take a look at this example:

```csharp
class Program
{
    static void Main(string[] args)
    {
        int num1, num2, result;
        try
        {
            Console.Write("Please enter the first number:");
            num1 = int.Parse(Console.ReadLine());

            Console.Write("Please enter the second number:");
            num2 = int.Parse(Console.ReadLine());

            Program myApp = new Program();

            Console.WriteLine("The result of {0}/{1} is {2}",
                num1, num2,
                myApp.PerformDivision(num1, num2));
        }
        catch (Exception ex)
        {
            Console.WriteLine(ex.Message);
            if (ex.InnerException != null)
                Console.WriteLine(ex.InnerException.ToString());
        }
        Console.ReadLine();
    }

    private int PerformDivision(int num1, int num2)
    {
        try
        {
            return num1 / num2;
        }
        catch (DivideByZeroException ex)
        {
            throw new Exception("Division by zero error.", ex);
        }
    }
}
```

Here, the `PerformDivision()` function tries to catch the `DivideByZeroException` exception and once it succeeds, it rethrows a new generic `Exception` exception, using the following statements with two arguments:

```csharp
        throw new Exception("Division by zero error.", ex);
```

The first argument indicates the description for the exception to be thrown, while the second argument is for the *inner exception*. The inner exception indicates the exception that causes the current exception. When this exception is rethrown, it is handled by the catch block in the Main() function:

```
catch (Exception ex)
{
    Console.WriteLine(ex.Message);
    if (ex.InnerException != null)
        Console.WriteLine(ex.InnerException.ToString());
}
```

To retrieve the source of the exception, you can check the InnerException property and print out its details using the ToString() method. Here's the output when num2 is zero:

```
Please enter the first number:5
Please enter the second number:0
Division by zero error.
System.DivideByZeroException: Attempted to divide by zero.
    at ConsoleApp.Program.PerformDivision(Int32 num1, Int32 num2) in C:\Documents
and Settings\Wei-Meng Lee\My Documents\Visual Studio 2008\Projects\ConsoleApp\
ConsoleApp\Program.cs:line 43
```

As you can see, the message of the exception is "Division by zero error" (set by yourself) and the InnerException property shows the real cause of the error — "Attempted to divide by zero."

Exception Chaining

The InnerException property is of type Exception, and it can be used to store a list of previous exceptions. This is known as *exception chaining*.

To see how exception chaining works, consider the following program:

```
class Program
{
    static void Main(string[] args)
    {
        Program myApp = new Program();

        try
        {
            myApp.Method1();
        }
        catch (Exception ex)
        {
            Console.WriteLine(ex.Message);
            if (ex.InnerException != null)
                Console.WriteLine(ex.InnerException.ToString());
        }
        Console.ReadLine();
    }

    private void Method1()
```

(continued)

(continued)

```
        {
            try
            {
                Method2();
            }
            catch (Exception ex)
            {
                throw new Exception(
                    "Exception caused by calling Method2() in Method1().", ex);
            }
        }

        private void Method2()
        {
            try
            {
                Method3();
            }
            catch (Exception ex)
            {
                throw new Exception(
                    "Exception caused by calling Method3() in Method2().", ex);
            }
        }

        private void Method3()
        {
            try
            {
                int num1 = 5, num2 = 0;
                int result = num1 / num2;
            }
            catch (DivideByZeroException ex)
            {
                throw new Exception("Division by zero error in Method3().", ex);
            }
        }
    }
```

In this program, the `Main()` function calls `Method1()`, which in turns calls `Method2()`. `Method2()` then calls `Method3()`. In `Method3()`, a division-by-zero exception occurs and you rethrow a new `Exception` exception by passing in the current exception (`DividebyZeroException`). This exception is caught by `Method2()`, which rethrows a new `Exception` exception by passing in the current exception. `Method1()` in turn catches the exception and rethrows a new `Exception` exception. Finally, the `Main()` function catches the exception and prints out the result as shown in Figure 12-4.

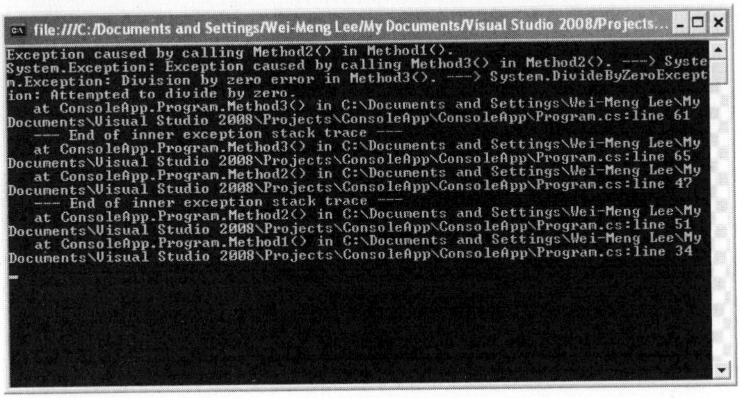

Figure 12-4

If you set a breakpoint in the catch block within the `Main()` function, you will see that the `InnerException` property contains details of each exception and that all the exceptions are chained via the `InnerException` property (see Figure 12-5).

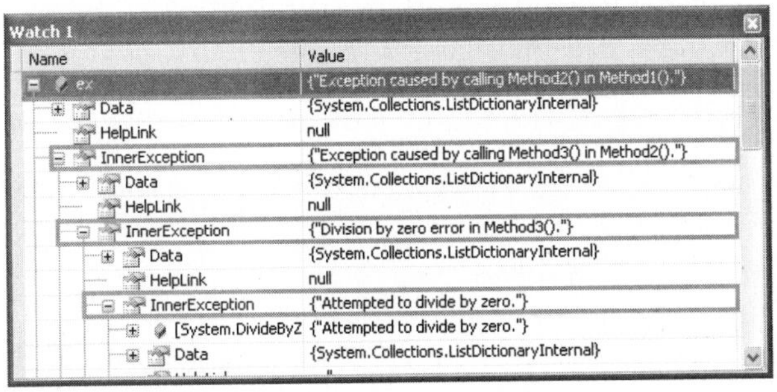

Figure 12-5

Using Exception Objects

Instead of -using the default description for each exception class you are throwing, you can customize the description of the exception by creating an instance of the exception and then setting the `Message` property. You can also specify the `HelpLink` property to point to a URL where developers can find more information about the exception. For example, you can create a new instance of the `ArithmeticException` class using the following code:

```
if (num1 == 0)
{
    ArithmeticException ex =
        new ArithmeticException("Value of num1 cannot be 0.")
    {
        HelpLink = "http://www.learn2develop.net"
    };
    throw ex;
}
```

Here's how you can modify the previous program by customizing the various existing exception classes:

```csharp
class Program
{
    static void Main(string[] args)
    {
        int num1, num2;
        try
        {
            Console.Write("Please enter the first number:");
            num1 = int.Parse(Console.ReadLine());

            Console.Write("Please enter the second number:");
            num2 = int.Parse(Console.ReadLine());

            Program myApp = new Program();

            Console.WriteLine("The result of {0}/{1} is {2}",
                num1, num2,
                myApp.PerformDivision(num1, num2));
        }
        catch (DivideByZeroException ex)
        {
            Console.WriteLine(ex.Message);
        }
        catch (ArithmeticException ex)
        {
            Console.WriteLine(ex.Message);
        }
        catch (FormatException ex)
        {
            Console.WriteLine(ex.Message);
        }
        catch (Exception ex)
        {
            Console.WriteLine(ex.Message);
        }
        Console.ReadLine();
    }

    private int PerformDivision(int num1, int num2)
    {
        if (num1 == 0)
        {
            ArithmeticException ex =
                new ArithmeticException("Value of num1 cannot be 0.")
            {
                HelpLink = "http://www.learn2develop.net"
            };
            throw ex;
        }
```

```
            if (num2 == 0)
            {
                DivideByZeroException ex =
                    new DivideByZeroException("Value of num2 cannot be 0.")
                {
                    HelpLink = "http://www.learn2develop.net"
                };
                throw ex;
            }

        return num1 / num2;
    }
}
```

Here's the output when different values are entered for num1 and num2:

```
Please enter the first number:0
Please enter the second number:5
Value of num1 cannot be 0.

Please enter the first number:5
Please enter the second number:0
Value of num2 cannot be 0.
```

The finally Statement

By now you know that you can use the try-catch block to enclose potentially dangerous code. This is especially useful for operations such as file manipulation, user input, and so on. Consider the following example:

```
FileStream fs = null;
try
{
    //---opens a file for reading---
    fs = File.Open(@"C:\textfile.txt",
        FileMode.Open, FileAccess.Read);

    //---tries to write some text into the file---
    byte[] data = ASCIIEncoding.ASCII.GetBytes("some text");
    fs.Write(data, 0, data.Length);

    //---close the file---
    fs.Close();
}
catch (Exception ex)
{
    Console.WriteLine(ex.ToString());
}

//---an error will occur here---
fs = File.Open(@"C:\textfile.txt", FileMode.Open, FileAccess.Read);
```

Suppose that you have a text file named `textfile.txt` located in C:\. In this example program, you first try to open the file for reading. After that, you try to write some text into the file, which causes an exception because the file was opened only for reading. After the exception is caught, you proceed to open the file again. However, this fails because the file is still open (the `fs.Close()` statement within the `try` block is never executed because the line before it has caused an exception). In this case, you need to ensure that the file is always closed — with or without an exception. For this, you can use the `finally` statement.

The statement(s) enclosed within a `finally` block is always executed, regardless of whether an exception occurs. The following program shows how you can use the `finally` statement to ensure that the file is always closed properly:

```
FileStream fs = null;
try
{
    //---opens a file for reading---
    fs = File.Open(@"C:\textfile.txt",
        FileMode.Open, FileAccess.Read);

    //---tries to write some text into the file---
    byte[] data = ASCIIEncoding.ASCII.GetBytes("1234567890");
    fs.Write(data, 0, data.Length);
}
catch (Exception ex)
{
    Console.WriteLine(ex.ToString());
}
finally
{
    //---close the file stream object---
    if (fs != null) fs.Close();
}

//---this will now be OK---
fs = File.Open(@"C:\textfile.txt", FileMode.Open, FileAccess.Read);
```

One important thing about exception handling is that the system uses a lot of resources to raise an exception; thus, you should always try to prevent the system from raising exceptions. Using the preceding example, instead of opening the file and then writing some text into it, it would be a good idea to first check whether the file is writable before proceeding to write into it. If the file is read-only, you simply inform the user that the file is read-only. That prevents an exception from being raised when you try to write into it.

The following shows how to prevent an exception from being raised:

```
FileStream fs = null;
try
{
    //---opens a file for reading---
    fs = File.Open(@"C:\textfile.txt",
        FileMode.Open, FileAccess.Read);

    //---checks to see if it is writeable---
    if (fs.CanWrite)
```

```
            {
                //---tries to write some text into the file---
                byte[] data = ASCIIEncoding.ASCII.GetBytes("1234567890");
                fs.Write(data, 0, data.Length);
            } else
                Console.WriteLine("File is read-only");
    }
    catch (Exception ex)
    {
        Console.WriteLine(ex.ToString());
    }
    finally
    {
        //---close the file stream object---
        if (fs != null) fs.Close();
    }
```

Creating Custom Exceptions

The .NET class libraries provide a list of exceptions that should be sufficient for most of your uses, but there may be times when you need to create your own custom exception class. You can do so by deriving from the Exception class. The following is an example of a custom class named AllNumbersZeroException:

```csharp
using System;
using System.Collections.Generic;
using System.Linq;
using System.Text;

public class AllNumbersZeroException : Exception
{
    public AllNumbersZeroException()
    {
    }
    public AllNumbersZeroException(string message)
        : base(message)
    {
    }
    public AllNumbersZeroException(string message, Exception inner)
        : base(message, inner)
    {
    }
}
```

To create your own custom exception class, you need to inherit from the Exception base class and implement the three overloaded constructors for it.

The `AllNumbersZeroException` class contains three overloaded constructors that initialize the constructor in the base class. To see how you can use this custom exception class, let's take another look at the program you have been using all along:

```csharp
static void Main(string[] args)
{
    int num1, num2, result;
    try
    {
        Console.Write("Please enter the first number:");
        num1 = int.Parse(Console.ReadLine());

        Console.Write("Please enter the second number:");
        num2 = int.Parse(Console.ReadLine());

        Program myApp = new Program();

        Console.WriteLine("The result of {0}/{1} is {2}",
            num1, num2,
            myApp.PerformDivision(num1, num2));
    }
    catch (AllNumbersZeroException ex)
    {
        Console.WriteLine(ex.Message);
    }
    catch (DivideByZeroException ex)
    {
        Console.WriteLine(ex.Message);
    }
    catch (ArithmeticException ex)
    {
        Console.WriteLine(ex.Message);
    }
    catch (FormatException ex)
    {
        Console.WriteLine(ex.Message);
    }
    catch (Exception ex)
    {
        Console.WriteLine(ex.Message);
    }
    Console.ReadLine();
}

private int PerformDivision(int num1, int num2)
{
    if (num1 == 0 && num2 == 0)
    {
        AllNumbersZeroException ex =
            new AllNumbersZeroException("Both numbers cannot be 0.")
```

```
                    {
                        HelpLink = "http://www.learn2develop.net"
                    };
                throw ex;
            }
            if (num1 == 0)
            {
                ArithmeticException ex =
                    new ArithmeticException("Value of num1 cannot be 0.")
                {
                    HelpLink = "http://www.learn2develop.net"
                };
                throw ex;
            }
            if (num2 == 0)
            {
                DivideByZeroException ex =
                    new DivideByZeroException("Value of num2 cannot be 0.")
                {
                    HelpLink = "http://www.learn2develop.net"
                };
                throw ex;
            }
            return num1 / num2;
        }
```

This program shows that if both num1 and num2 are zero, the AllNumbersException exception is raised with the custom message set.

Here's the output when 0 is entered for both num1 and num2:

```
Please enter the first number:0
Please enter the second number:0
Both numbers cannot be 0.
```

Summary

Handling exceptions is part and parcel of the process of building a robust application, and you should spend considerable effort in identifying code that is likely to cause an exception. Besides catching all the exceptions defined in the .NET Framework, you can also define your own custom exception containing your own specific error message.

13

Arrays and Collections

In programming, you often need to work with collections of related data. For example, you may have a list of customers and you need a way to store their email addresses. In that case, you can use an array to store the list of strings.

In .NET, there are many collection classes that you can use to represent groups of data. In addition, there are various interfaces that you can implement so that you can manipulate your own custom collection of data.

This chapter examines:

- ❑   Declaring and initializing arrays
- ❑   Declaring and using multidimensional arrays
- ❑   Declaring a parameter array to allow a variable number of parameters in a function
- ❑   Using the various `System.Collections` namespace interfaces
- ❑   Using the different collection classes (such as Dictionary, Stacks, and Queue) in .NET

Arrays

An *array* is an indexed collection of items of the same type. To declare an array, specify the type with a pair of brackets followed by the variable name. The following statements declare three array variables of type `int`, `string`, and `decimal`, respectively:

```
int[] num;
string[] sentences;
decimal[] values;
```

Array variables are actually objects. In this example, num, sentences, *and* values *are objects of type* System.Array.

These statements simply declare the three variables as arrays; the variables are not initialized yet, and at this stage you do not know how many elements are contained within each array.

To initialize an array, use the new keyword. The following statements declare and initialize three arrays:

```
int[] num = new int[5];
string[] sentences = new string[3];
decimal[] values = new decimal[4];
```

The num array now has five members, while the sentences array has three members, and the values array has four. The *rank specifier* of each array (the number you indicate within the []) indicates the number of elements contained in each array.

You can declare an array and initialize it separately, as the following statements show:

```
//---declare the arrays---
int[] num;
string[] sentences;
decimal[] values;

//---initialize the arrays with default values---
num = new int[5];
sentences = new string[3];
values = new decimal[4];
```

When you declare an array using the new keyword, each member of the array is initialized with the default value of the type. For example, the preceding num array contains elements of value 0. Likewise, for the sentences string array, each of its members has the default value of null.

To learn the default value of a value type, use the default keyword, like this:

```
object x;
x = default(int); //---0---
x = default(char); //---0 '\0'---
x = default(bool); //---false---
```

To initialize the array to some value other than the default, you use an initialization list. The number of elements it includes must match the array's rank specifier. Here's an example:

```
int[] num = new int[5] { 1, 2, 3, 4, 5 };
string[] sentences = new string[3] {
    "C#", "Programmers", "Reference"
};
decimal[] values = new decimal[4] {1.5M, 2.3M, 0.3M,5.9M};
```

Because the initialization list already contains the exact number of elements in the array, the rank specifier can be omitted, like this:

```
int[] num = new int[] { 1, 2, 3, 4, 5 };
string[] sentences = new string[] {
    "C#", "Programmers", "Reference"
};
decimal[] values = new decimal[] {1.5M, 2.3M, 0.3M,5.9M};
```

Use the new `var` keyword in C# to declare an implicitly typed array:

```
var num = new [] { 1, 2, 3, 4, 5 };
var sentences = new [] {
    "C#", "Programmers", "Reference"
};
var values = new [] {1.5M, 2.3M, 0.3M, 5.9M};
```

For more information on the `var` keyword, see Chapter 3.

In C#, arrays all derive from the abstract base class `Array` (in the System namespace) and have access to all the properties and methods contained in that. In Figure 13-1 IntelliSense shows some of the properties and methods exposed by the `num` array.

Figure 13-1

That means you can use the `Rank` property to learn the dimension of an array. To find out how many elements are contained within an array, you can use the `Length` property. The following statements produce the output shown in Figure 13-2.

```
Console.WriteLine("Dimension of num is {0}", num.Rank);
Console.WriteLine("Number of elements in num is {0}", num.Length);
```

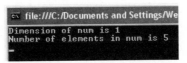

Figure 13-2

To sort an array, you can use the static `Sort()` method in the `Array` class:

```
int[] num = new int[] { 5, 3, 1, 2, 4 };
Array.Sort(num);
foreach (int i in num)
    Console.WriteLine(i);
```

These statements print out the array in sorted order:

```
1
2
3
4
5
```

Accessing Array Elements

To access an element in an array, you specify its index, as shown in the following statements:

```
int[] num = new int[5] { 1, 2, 3, 4, 5 };
Console.WriteLine(num[0]); //---1---
Console.WriteLine(num[1]); //---2---
Console.WriteLine(num[2]); //---3---
Console.WriteLine(num[3]); //---4---
Console.WriteLine(num[4]); //---5---
```

The index of an array starts from 0 to $n-1$. For example, num has size of 5 so the index runs from 0 to 4.

You usually use a loop construct to run through the elements in an array. For example, you can use the for statement to iterate through the elements of an array:

```
for (int i = 0; i < num.Length; i++)
    Console.WriteLine(num[i]);
```

You can also use the foreach statement, which is a clean way to iterate through the elements of an array quickly:

```
foreach (int n in num)
    Console.WriteLine(n);
```

Multidimensional Arrays

So far the arrays you have seen are all one-dimensional ones. Arrays may also be multidimensional. To declare a multidimensional array, you can the comma (,) separator. The following declares xy to be a 2-dimensional array:

```
int[,] xy;
```

To initialize the two-dimensional array, you use the new keyword together with the size of the array:

```
xy = new int[3,2];
```

With this statement, xy can now contain six elements (three rows and two columns). To initialize xy with some values, you can use the following statement:

```
xy = new int[3, 2] { { 1, 2 }, { 3, 4 }, { 5, 6 } }; ;
```

The following statement declares a three-dimensional array:

```
int[, ,] xyz;
```

To initialize it, you again use the new keyword together with the size of the array:

```
xyz = new int[2, 2, 2];
```

To initialize the array with some values, you can use the following:

```
int[, ,] xyz;
xyz = new int[,,] {
    { { 1, 2 }, { 3, 4 } },
    { { 5, 6 }, { 7, 8 } }
};
```

To access all the elements in the three-dimensional array, you can use the following code snippet:

```
for (int x = xyz.GetLowerBound(0); x <= xyz.GetUpperBound(0); x++)
    for (int y = xyz.GetLowerBound(1); y <= xyz.GetUpperBound(1); y++)
        for (int z = xyz.GetLowerBound(2); z <= xyz.GetUpperBound(2); z++)
            Console.WriteLine(xyz[x, y, z]);
```

The Array abstract base class contains the GetLowerBound() and GetUpperBound() methods to let you know the size of an array. Both methods take in a single parameter, which indicates the dimension of the array about which you are inquiring. For example, GetUpperBound(0) returns the size of the first dimension, GetUpperBound(1) returns the size of the second dimension, and so on.

You can also use the foreach statement to access all the elements in a multidimensional array:

```
foreach (int n in xyz)
    Console.WriteLine(n);
```

These statements print out the following:

```
1
2
3
4
5
6
7
8
```

Arrays of Arrays: Jagged Arrays

An array's elements can also contain arrays. An array of arrays is known as a *jagged array*. Consider the following statements:

```
Point[][] lines = new Point[5][];
lines[0] = new Point[4];
lines[1] = new Point[15];
lines[2] = new Point[7];
lines[3] = ...
lines[4] = ...
```

Here, lines is a jagged array. It has five elements and each element is a Point array. The first element is an array containing four elements, the second contains 15 elements, and so on.

> The Point *class represents an ordered pair of integer x- and y-coordinates that defines a point in a two-dimensional plane.*

You can use the array initializer to initialize the individual array within the lines array, like this:

```
Point[][] lines = new Point[3][];
lines[0] = new Point[] {
    new Point(2, 3), new Point(4, 5)
}; //---2 points in lines[0]---

lines[1] = new Point[] {
    new Point(2, 3), new Point(4, 5) , new Point(6, 9)
}; //---3 points in lines[1]---

lines[2] = new Point[] {
    new Point(2, 3)
}; //---1 point in lines[2]---
```

To access the individual Point objects in the lines array, you first specify which Point array you want to access, followed by the index for the elements in the Point array, like this:

```
//---get the first point in lines[0]---
Point ptA = lines[0][0]; //---(2,3)

//---get the third point in lines[1]---
Point ptB = lines[1][2]; //---(6,9)---
```

A jagged array can also contain multidimensional arrays. For example, the following declaration declares nums to be a jagged array with each element pointing to a two-dimensional array:

```
int[][,] nums = new int[][,]
{
    new int[,] {{ 1, 2 }, { 3, 4 }},
    new int[,] {{ 5, 6 }, { 7, 8 }}
};
```

To access an individual element within the jagged array, you can use the following statements:

```
Console.WriteLine(nums[0][0, 0]); //---1---
Console.WriteLine(nums[0][0, 1]); //---2---
Console.WriteLine(nums[0][1, 0]); //---3---
Console.WriteLine(nums[0][1, 1]); //---4---
Console.WriteLine(nums[1][0, 0]); //---5---
Console.WriteLine(nums[1][0, 1]); //---6---
Console.WriteLine(nums[1][1, 0]); //---7---
Console.WriteLine(nums[1][1, 1]); //---8---
```

Used on a jagged array, the `Length` property of the `Array` abstract base class returns the number of arrays contained in the jagged array:

```
Console.WriteLine(nums.Length); //---2---
```

Parameter Arrays

In C#, you can pass variable numbers of parameters into a function/method using a feature known as *parameter arrays*. Consider the following statements:

```
string firstName = "Wei-Meng";
string lastName = "Lee";
Console.WriteLine("Hello, {0}", firstName);
Console.WriteLine("Hello, {0} {1}", firstName, lastName);
```

Observe that the last two statements contain different numbers of parameters. In fact, the `WriteLine()` method is overloaded, and one of the overloaded methods has a parameter of type `params` (see Figure 13-3). The `params` keyword lets you specify a method parameter that takes an argument where the number of arguments is variable.

```
Console.WriteLine (|
▲ 15 of 19 ▼  void Console.WriteLine (string format, params object[] arg)
format: A composite format string.
```

Figure 13-3

A result of declaring the parameter type to be of `params` is that callers to the method do not need to explicitly create an array to pass into the method. Instead, they can simply pass in a variable number of parameters.

To use the `params` type in your own function, you define a parameter with the `params` keyword:

```
private void PrintMessage(string prefix, params string[] msg)
{
}
```

To extract the parameter array passed in by the caller, treat the `params` parameter like a normal array, like this:

```
private void PrintMessage(string prefix, params string[] msg)
{
    foreach (string s in msg)
        Console.WriteLine("{0}>{1}", prefix, s);
}
```

When calling the `PrintMessage()` function, you can pass in a variable number of parameters:

```
PrintMessage("C# Part 1", "Arrays", "Index", "Collections");
PrintMessage("C# Part 2", "Objects", "Classes");
```

These statements generate the following output:

```
C# Part 1>Arrays
C# Part 1>Index
C# Part 1>Collections
C# Part 2>Objects
C# Part 2>Classes
```

> A `params` **parameter must always be the last parameter defined in a method declaration.**

Copying Arrays

To copy from one array to another, use the `Copy()` method from the `Array` abstract base class:

```
int[] num = new int[5] { 1, 2, 3, 4, 5 };
int[] num1 = new int[5];
num.CopyTo(num1, 0);
```

These statements copy all the elements from the `num` array into the `num1` array. The second parameter in the `CopyTo()` method specifies the index in the array at which the copying begins.

Collections Interfaces

The `System.Collections` namespace contains several interfaces that define basic collection functionalities:

The interfaces described in the following list are the generic versions of the respective interfaces. Beginning with C# 2.0, you should always try to use the generic versions of the interfaces for type safety. Chapter 9 discusses the use of generics in the C# language.

Interface	Description
IEnumerable<T> and IEnumerator<T>	Enable you to loop through the elements in a collection.
ICollection<T>	Contains items in a collection and provides the functionality to copy elements to an array. Inherits from IEnumerable<T>.
IComparer<T> and IComparable<T>	Enable you to compare objects in a collection.
IList<T>	Inherits from ICollection and provides functionality to allow members to be accessed by index.
IDictionary<K,V>	Similar to IList<T>, but members are accessed by key value rather than index.

The ICollection<T> interface is the base interface for classes in the System.Collections namespace.

Dynamic Arrays Using the ArrayList Class

Arrays in C# have a fixed size once they are initialized. For example, the following defines a fixed-size array of five integer elements:

```
int[] num = new int[5];
```

If you need to dynamically increase the size of an array during runtime, use the ArrayList class instead. You use it like an array, but its size can be increased dynamically as required.

The ArrayList class is located within the System.Collections namespace, so you need to import that System.Collections namespace before you use it. The ArrayList class implements the IList interface.

To use the ArrayList class, you first create an instance of it:

```
ArrayList arrayList = new ArrayList();
```

Use the Add() method to add elements to an ArrayList object:

```
arrayList.Add("Hello");
arrayList.Add(25);
arrayList.Add(new Point(3,4));
arrayList.Add(3.14F);
```

Notice that you can add elements of different types to an ArrayList object.

To access an element contained within an `ArrayList` object, specify the element's index like this:

```
Console.WriteLine(arrayList[0]); //---Hello---
Console.WriteLine(arrayList[1]); //---25---
Console.WriteLine(arrayList[2]); //---{X=3, Y=4}
Console.WriteLine(arrayList[3]); //---3.14---
```

The `ArrayList` object can contain elements of different types, so when retrieving items from an `ArrayList` object make sure that the elements are assigned to variables of the correct type. Elements retrieved from an `ArrayList` object belong to `Object` type.

You can insert elements to an `ArrayList` object using the `Insert()` method:

```
arrayList.Insert(1, " World!");
```

After the insertion, the `ArrayList` object now has five elements:

```
Console.WriteLine(arrayList[0]); //---Hello---
Console.WriteLine(arrayList[1]); //---World!---
Console.WriteLine(arrayList[2]); //---25---
Console.WriteLine(arrayList[3]); //---{X=3,Y=4}---
Console.WriteLine(arrayList[4]); //---3.14---
```

To remove elements from an `ArrayList` object, use the `Remove()` or `RemoveAt()` methods:

```
arrayList.Remove("Hello");
arrayList.Remove("Hi");              //---cannot find item---
arrayList.Remove(new Point(3, 4));
arrayList.RemoveAt(1);
```

After these statements run, the `ArrayList` object has only two elements:

```
Console.WriteLine(arrayList[0]); //---World!---
Console.WriteLine(arrayList[1]); //---3.14---
```

If you try to remove an element that is nonexistent, no exception is raised (which is not very useful). It would be good to use the `Contains()` method to check whether the element exists before attempting to remove it:

```
if (arrayList.Contains("Hi"))
    arrayList.Remove("Hi");
else
    Console.WriteLine("Element not found.");
```

You can also assign the elements in an `ArrayList` object to an array using the `ToArray()` method:

```
object[] objArray;
objArray = arrayList.ToArray();

foreach (object o in objArray)
    Console.WriteLine(o.ToString());
```

Because the elements in the `ArrayList` can be of different types you must be careful handling them or you run the risk of runtime exceptions. To work with data of the same type, it is more efficient to use the generic equivalent of the `ArrayList` class — the `List<T>` class, which is type safe. To use the `List<T>` class, you simply instantiate it with the type you want to use and then use the different methods available just like in the `ArrayList` class:

```
List<int> nums = new List<int>();
nums.Add(4);
nums.Add(1);
nums.Add(3);
nums.Add(5);
nums.Add(7);
nums.Add(2);
nums.Add(8);

//---sorts the list---
nums.Sort();

//---prints out all the elements in the list---
foreach (int n in nums)
    Console.WriteLine(n);
```

> If you try to sort an ArrayList object containing elements of different types, you are likely to run into an exception because the compiler may not be able to compare the values of two different types.

Indexers and Iterators

Sometimes you may have classes that encapsulate an internal collection or array. Consider the following `SpamPhraseList` class:

```
public class SpamPhraseList
{
    protected string[] Phrases =
        new string[]{
            "pain relief","paxil","pharmacy","phendimetrazine",
            "phentamine","phentermine","pheramones","pherimones",
            "photos of singles","platinum-celebs","poker-chip",
            "poze","prescription","privacy assured","product for less",
            "products for less","protect yourself","psychic"
        };

    public string Phrase(int index)
    {
        if (index >= 0 && index < Phrases.Length)
            return Phrases[index];
        else
            return string.Empty;
    }
}
```

The SpamPhraseList class has a protected string array called Phrases. It also exposes the Phrase() method, which takes in an index and returns an element from the string array:

```
SpamPhraseList list = new SpamPhraseList();
Console.WriteLine(list.Phrase(17)); //---psychic---
```

Because the main purpose of the SpamPhraseList class is to return one of the phrases contained within it, it might be more intuitive to access it more like an array, like this:

```
SpamPhraseList list = new SpamPhraseList();
Console.WriteLine(list[17]); //---psychic---
```

In C#, you can use the indexer feature to make your class accessible just like an array. Using the SpamPhraseList class, you can use the this keyword to declare an indexer on the class:

```
public class SpamPhraseList
{
    protected string[] Phrases =
        new string[]{
            "pain relief","paxil","pharmacy","phendimetrazine",
            "phentamine","phentermine","pheramones","pherimones",
            "photos of singles","platinum-celebs","poker-chip",
            "poze","prescription","privacy assured","product for less",
            "products for less","protect yourself","psychic"
        };

    public string this[int index]
    {
        get
        {
            if (index >= 0 && index < Phrases.Length)
                return Phrases[index];
            else
                return string.Empty;
        }
        set
        {
            if (index >= 0 && index < Phrases.Length)
                Phrases[index] = value;
        }
    }
}
```

Once the indexer is added to the SpamPhraseList class, you can now access the internal array of string just like an array, like this:

```
SpamPhraseList list = new SpamPhraseList();
Console.WriteLine(list[17]); //---psychic---
```

Besides retrieving the elements from the class, you can also set a value to each individual element, like this:

```
list[17] = "psycho";
```

The indexer feature enables you to access the internal arrays of elements using array syntax, but you cannot use the foreach statement to iterate through the elements contained within it. For example, the following statements give you an error:

```
SpamPhraseList list = new SpamPhraseList();
foreach (string s in list) //---error---
    Console.WriteLine(s);
```

To ensure that your class supports the foreach statement, you need to use a feature known as *iterators*. Iterators enable you to use the convenient foreach syntax to step through a list of items in a class. To create an iterator for the SpamPhraseList class, you only need to implement the GetEnumerator() method, like this:

```
public class SpamPhraseList
{
    protected string[] Phrases =
        new string[]{
            "pain relief","paxil","pharmacy","phendimetrazine",
            "phentamine","phentermine","pheramones","pherimones",
            "photos of singles","platinum-celebs","poker-chip",
            "poze","prescription","privacy assured","product for less",
            "products for less","protect yourself","psychic"
        };

    public string this[int index]
    {
        get
        {
            if (index >= 0 && index < Phrases.Length)
                return Phrases[index];
            else
                return string.Empty;
        }
        set
        {
            if (index >= 0 && index < Phrases.Length)
                Phrases[index] = value;
        }
    }

    public IEnumerator<string> GetEnumerator()
    {
        foreach (string s in Phrases)
        {
            yield return s;
        }
    }
}
```

Within the GetEnumerator() method, you can use the foreach statement to iterate through all the elements in the Phrases array and then use the yield keyword to return individual elements in the array.

You can now iterate through the elements in a `SpamPhraseList` object using the `foreach` statement:

```
SpamPhraseList list = new SpamPhraseList();
foreach (string s in list)
    Console.WriteLine(s);
```

Implementing IEnumerable<T> and IEnumerator<T>

Besides using the iterators feature in your class to allow clients to step through its internal elements with `foreach`, you can make your class support the `foreach` statement by implementing the `IEnumerable` and `IEnumerator` interfaces. The generic equivalents of these two interfaces are `IEnumerable<T>` and `IEnumerator<T>`, respectively.

> **Use the generic versions because they are type safe.**

In .NET, all classes that enumerate objects must implement the `IEnumerable` (or the generic `IEnumerable<T>`) interface. The objects enumerated must implement the `IEnumerator` (or the generic `IEnumerable<T>`) interface, which has the following members:

- ❑ `Current` — Returns the current element in the collection
- ❑ `MoveNext()` — Advances to the next element in the collection
- ❑ `Reset()` — Resets the enumerator to its initial position

The `IEnumerable` interface has one member:

- ❑ `GetEnumerator()` — Returns the enumerator that iterates through a collection

> **All the discussions from this point onward use the generic versions of the `IEnumerable` and `IEnumerator` interfaces because they are type-safe.**

To understand how the `IEnumerable<T>` and `IEnumerator<T>` interfaces work, modify `SpamPhraseList` class to implement the `IEnumerable<T>` interface:

```
public class SpamPhraseList : IEnumerable<string>
{
    protected string[] Phrases =
        new string[]{
                "pain relief", "paxil", "pharmacy", "phendimetrazine",
                "phentamine", "phentermine", "pheramones", "pherimones",
                "photos of singles", "platinum-celebs", "poker-chip",
```

```
                              "poze","prescription","privacy assured","product for less",
                              "products for less","protect yourself","psychic"
               };

      //---for generic version of the class---
      public IEnumerator<string> GetEnumerator()
      {

      }


      //---for non-generic version of the class---
      System.Collections.IEnumerator System.Collections.IEnumerable.GetEnumerator()
      {

      }
   }
```

Notice that for the generic version of the IEnumerable interface, you need to implement two versions of the GetEnumerator() methods — one for the generic version of the class and one for the nongeneric version.

To ensure that the SpamPhraseList class can enumerate the strings contained within it, you define an enumerator class within the SpamPhraseList class:

```
public class SpamPhraseList : IEnumerable<string>
{
      private class SpamPhrastListEnum : IEnumerator<string>
      {
          private int index = -1;
          private SpamPhraseList spamlist;

          public SpamPhrastListEnum(SpamPhraseList sl)
          {
              this.spamlist = sl;
          }

          //---for generic version of the class---
          string IEnumerator<string>.Current
          {
              get
              {
                  return spamlist.Phrases[index];
              }
          }

          //---for non-generic version of the class---
          object System.Collections.IEnumerator.Current
          {
              get
```

(continued)

(continued)

```
            {
                return spamlist.Phrases[index];
            }
        }

        bool System.Collections.IEnumerator.MoveNext()
        {
            index++;
            return index < spamlist.Phrases.Length;
        }

        void System.Collections.IEnumerator.Reset()
        {
            index = -1;
        }

        void IDisposable.Dispose() { }
    }

    protected string[] Phrases =
        new string[]{
                "pain relief","paxil","pharmacy","phendimetrazine",
                "phentamine","phentermine","pheramones","pherimones",
                "photos of singles","platinum-celebs","poker-chip",
                "poze","prescription","privacy assured","product for less",
                "products for less","protect yourself","psychic"
            };

    public IEnumerator<string> GetEnumerator()
    {
        return new SpamPhrastListEnum(this);
    }

    //---for non-generic version of the class---
    System.Collections.IEnumerator System.Collections.IEnumerable.GetEnumerator()
    {
        return new SpamPhrastListEnum(this);
    }
}
```

In this example, the `SpamPhrastListEnum` class implements the `IEnumerator<string>` interface and provides the implementation for the `Current` property and the `MoveNext()` and `Reset()` methods.

To print out all the elements contained within a `SpamPhraseList` object, you can use the same statements that you used in the previous section:

```
SpamPhraseList list = new SpamPhraseList();
foreach (string s in list) //---error---
    Console.WriteLine(s);
```

Behind the scenes, the compiler is generating the following code for the `foreach` statement:

```
SpamPhraseList list = new SpamPhraseList();
IEnumerator<string> s = list.GetEnumerator();
while (s.MoveNext())
    Console.WriteLine((string)s.Current);
```

Implementing Comparison Using IComparer<T> and IComparable<T>

One of the tasks you often need to perform on a collection of objects is sorting. You need to know the order of the objects so that you can sort them accordingly. Objects that can be compared implement the `IComparable` interface (the generic equivalent of this interface is `IComparable<T>`). Consider the following example:

```
string[] Names = new string[] {
    "John", "Howard",
    "Margaret", "Brian" };

foreach (string n in Names)
    Console.WriteLine(n);
```

Here, `Names` is a string array containing four strings. This code prints out the following:

```
John
Howard
Margaret
Brian
```

You can sort the `Names` array using the `Sort()` method from the abstract static class `Array`, like this:

```
Array.Sort(Names);
foreach (string n in Names)
    Console.WriteLine(n);
```

Now the output is a sorted array of names:

```
Brian
Howard
John
Margaret
```

In this case, the reason the array of string can be sorted is because the `String` type itself implements the `IComparable` interface, so the `Sort()` method knows how to sort the array correctly. The same applies to other types such as `int`, `single`, `float`, and so on.

What if you have your own type and you want it to be sortable? Suppose that you have the `Employee` class defined as follows:

```csharp
public class Employee
{
    public string FirstName
    { get; set; }

    public string LastName
    { get; set; }

    public int Salary
    { get; set; }

    public override string ToString()
    {
        return FirstName + ", " + LastName +
            " $" + Salary;
    }
}
```

You can add several `Employee` objects to a `List` object, like this:

```csharp
List<Employee> employees = new List<Employee>();
employees.Add(new Employee()
{
    FirstName = "John",
    LastName = "Smith",
    Salary = 4000
});
employees.Add(new Employee()
{
    FirstName = "Howard",
    LastName = "Mark",
    Salary = 1500
});
employees.Add(new Employee()
{
    FirstName = "Margaret",
    LastName = "Anderson",
    Salary = 3000
});
employees.Add(new Employee()
{
    FirstName = "Brian",
    LastName = "Will",
    Salary = 3000
});
```

To sort a `List` object containing your `Employee` objects, you can use the following:

```csharp
employees.Sort();
```

However, this statement results in a runtime error (see Figure 13-4) because the Sort() method does not know how Employee objects should be sorted.

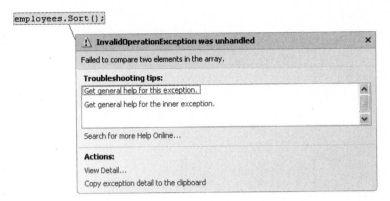

Figure 13-4

To solve this problem, the Employee class needs to implement the IComparable<T> interface and then implement the CompareTo() method:

```
public class Employee : IComparable<Employee>
{
    public string FirstName
    { get; set; }

    public string LastName
    { get; set; }

    public int Salary
    { get; set; }

    public override string ToString()
    {
        return FirstName + ", " + LastName +
            " $" + Salary;
    }

    public int CompareTo(Employee emp)
    {
        return this.FirstName.CompareTo(emp.FirstName);
    }
}
```

The CompareTo() method takes an Employee parameter, and you compare the current instance (represented by this) of the Employee class's FirstName property to the parameter's FirstName property. Here, you use the CompareTo() method of the String class (FirstName is of String type) to perform the comparison.

The return value of the `CompareTo(obj)` method has the possible values as shown in the following table.

Value	Meaning
Less than zero	The current instance is less than `obj`.
Zero	The current instance is equal to `obj`.
Greater than zero	The current instance is greater than `obj`.

Now, when you sort the `List` object containing `Employee` objects, the `Employee` objects will be sorted by first name:

```
employees.Sort();
foreach (Employee emp in employees)
    Console.WriteLine(emp.ToString());
```

These statements produce the following output:

```
Brian, Will $3000
Howard, Mark $1500
John, Smith $4000
Margaret, Anderson $3000
```

To sort the `Employee` objects using the `LastName` instead of `FirstName`, simply change the `CompareTo()` method as follows:

```
public int CompareTo(Employee emp)
{
    return this.LastName.CompareTo(emp.LastName);
}
```

The output becomes:

```
Margaret, Anderson $3000
Howard, Mark $1500
John, Smith $4000
Brian, Will $3000
```

Likewise, to sort by salary, you compare the `Salary` property:

```
public int CompareTo(Employee emp)
{
    return this.Salary.CompareTo(emp.Salary);
}
```

The output is now:

```
Howard, Mark $1500
Margaret, Anderson $3000
Brian, Will $3000
John, Smith $4000
```

Instead of using the `CompareTo()` method of the type you are comparing, you can manually perform the comparison, like this:

```
public int CompareTo(Employee emp)
{
    if (this.Salary < emp.Salary)
        return -1;
    else if (this.Salary == emp.Salary)
        return 0;
    else
        return 1;
}
```

How the `Employee` objects are sorted is fixed by the implementation of the `CompareTo()` method. If `CompareTo()` compares using the `FirstName` property, the sort is based on the `FirstName` property. To give users a choice of which field they want to use to sort the objects, you can use the `IComparer<T>` interface.

To do so, first declare a private class within the `Employee` class and call it `SalaryComparer`.

```
public class Employee : IComparable<Employee>
{
    private class SalaryComparer : IComparer<Employee>
    {
        public int Compare(Employee e1, Employee e2)
        {
            if (e1.Salary < e2.Salary)
                return -1;
            else if (e1.Salary == e2.Salary)
                return 0;
            else
                return 1;
        }
    }

    public string FirstName
    { get; set; }

    public string LastName
    { get; set; }

    public int Salary
```

(continued)

(continued)

```
        { get; set; }

        public override string ToString()
        {
            return FirstName + ", " + LastName +
                " $" + Salary;
        }

        public int CompareTo(Employee emp)
        {
            return this.FirstName.CompareTo(emp.FirstName);
        }
    }
```

The `SalaryComparer` class implements the `IComparer<T>` interface. `IComparer<T>` has one method — `Compare()` — that you need to implement. It compares the salary of two `Employee` objects.

To use the `SalaryComparer` class, declare the `SalarySorter` static property within the `Employee` class so that you can return an instance of the `SalaryComparer` class:

```
public class Employee : IComparable<Employee>
{
    private class SalaryComparer : IComparer<Employee>
    {
        public int Compare(Employee e1, Employee e2)
        {
            if (e1.Salary < e2.Salary)
                return -1;
            else if (e1.Salary == e2.Salary)
                return 0;
            else
                return 1;
        }
    }

    public static IComparer<Employee> SalarySorter
    {
        get { return new SalaryComparer(); }
    }

    public string FirstName
    { get; set; }

    public string LastName
    { get; set; }

    public int Salary
    { get; set; }

    public override string ToString()
    {
        return FirstName + ", " + LastName +
            " $" + Salary;
```

```
        }
        public int CompareTo(Employee emp)
        {
            return this.FirstName.CompareTo(emp.FirstName);
        }
    }
```

You can now sort the `Employee` objects using the default, or specify the `SalarySorter` property:

```
        employees.Sort(); //---sort using FirstName (default)---
        employees.Sort(Employee.SalarySorter); //---sort using Salary---
```

To allow the `Employee` objects to be sorted using the `LastName` property, you could define another class (say `LastNameComparer`) that implements the `IComparer<T>` interface and then declare the `SalarySorter` static property, like this:

```
public class Employee : IComparable<Employee>
{
    private class SalaryComparer : IComparer<Employee>
    {
        public int Compare(Employee e1, Employee e2)
        {
            if (e1.Salary < e2.Salary)
                return -1;
            else if (e1.Salary == e2.Salary)
                return 0;
            else
                return 1;
        }
    }

    private class LastNameComparer : IComparer<Employee>
    {
        public int Compare(Employee e1, Employee e2)
        {
            return e1.LastName.CompareTo(e2.LastName);
        }
    }

    public static IComparer<Employee> SalarySorter
    {
        get { return new SalaryComparer(); }
    }

    public static IComparer<Employee> LastNameSorter
    {
        get { return new LastNameComparer(); }
    }

    public string FirstName
    { get; set; }

    public string LastName
```

(continued)

(continued)

```
    { get; set; }

    public int Salary
    { get; set; }

    public override string ToString()
    {
        return FirstName + ", " + LastName +
            " $" + Salary;
    }

    public int CompareTo(Employee emp)
    {
        return this.FirstName.CompareTo(emp.FirstName);
    }
}
```

You can now sort by `LastName` using the `LastNameSorter` property:

```
employees.Sort(Employee.LastNameSorter); //---sort using LastName---
```

Dictionary

Most of you are familiar with the term *dictionary* — a reference book containing an alphabetical list of words with information about them. In computing, a dictionary object provides a mapping from a set of keys to a set of values. In .NET, this dictionary comes in the form of the `Dictionary` class (the generic equivalent is `Dictionary<T,V>`).

The following shows how you can create a new `Dictionary` object with type `int` to be used for the key and type `String` to be used for the values:

```
Dictionary<int, string> employees = new Dictionary<int, string>();
```

To add items into a `Dictionary` object, use the `Add()` method:

```
employees.Add(1001, "Margaret Anderson");
employees.Add(1002, "Howard Mark");
employees.Add(1003, "John Smith");
employees.Add(1004, "Brian Will");
```

Trying to add a key that already exists in the object produces an `ArgumentException` error:

```
//---ArgumentException; duplicate key---
employees.Add(1004, "Sculley Lawrence");
```

A safer way is to use the `ContainsKey()` method to check if the key exists before adding the new key:

```
if (!employees.ContainsKey(1005))
{
    employees.Add(1005, "Sculley Lawrence");
}
```

While having duplicate keys is not acceptable, you can have different keys with the same value:

```
employees.Add(1006, "Sculley Lawrence"); //---duplicate value is OK---
```

To retrieve items from the `Dictionary` object, simply specify the key:

```
Console.WriteLine(employees[1002].ToString()); //---Howard Mark---
```

When retrieving items from a `Dictionary` object, be certain that the key you specify is valid or you encounter a `KeyNotFoundException` error:

```
try
{
    //---KeyNotFoundException---
    Console.WriteLine(employees[1005].ToString());
}
catch (KeyNotFoundException ex)
{
    Console.WriteLine(ex.Message);
}
```

Rather than catching an exception when the specified key is not found, it's more efficient to use the `TryGetValue()` method:

```
string Emp_Name;
if (employees.TryGetValue(1005, out Emp_Name))
    Console.WriteLine(Emp_Name);
```

`TryGetValue()` takes in a key for the `Dictionary` object as well as an `out` parameter that will contain the associated value for the specified key. If the key specified does not exist in the `Dictionary` object, the `out` parameter (`Emp_Name`, in this case) contains the default value for the specified type (`string` in this case, hence the default value is `null`).

When you use the `foreach` statement on a `Dictionary` object to iterate over all the elements in it, each `Dictionary` object element is retrieved as a `KeyValuePair` object:

```
foreach (KeyValuePair<int, string> Emp in employees)
    Console.WriteLine("{0} - {1}", Emp.Key, Emp.Value);
```

Here's the output from these statements:

```
1001 - Margaret Anderson
1002 - Howard Mark
1003 - John Smith
1004 - Brian Will
```

To get all the keys in a `Dictionary` object, use the `KeyCollection` class:

```
//---get all the employee IDs---
Dictionary<int, string>.KeyCollection
    EmployeeID = employees.Keys;

foreach (int ID in EmployeeID)
    Console.WriteLine(ID);
```

These statements print out all the keys in the `Dictionary` object:

```
1001
1002
1003
1004
```

If you want all the employees' names, you can use the `ValueCollection` class, like this:

```
//---get all the employee names---
Dictionary<int, string>.ValueCollection
    EmployeeNames = employees.Values;

foreach (string emp in EmployeeNames)
    Console.WriteLine(emp);
```

You can also copy all the values in a `Dictionary` object into an array using the `ToArray()` method:

```
//---extract all the values in the Dictionary object
// and copy into the array---
string[] Names = employees.Values.ToArray();
foreach (string n in Names)
    Console.WriteLine(n);
```

To remove a key from a `Dictionary` object, use the `Remove()` method, which takes the key to delete:

```
if (employees.ContainsKey(1006))
{
    employees.Remove(1006);
}
```

To sort the keys in a `Dictionary` object, use the `SortedDictionary<K,V>` class instead of the `Dictionary<K,V>` class:

```
SortedDictionary<int, string> employees =
    new SortedDictionary<int, string>();
```

Stacks

A stack is a last in, first out (LIFO) data structure — the last item added to a stack is the first to be removed. Conversely, the first item added to a stack is the last to be removed.

In .NET, you can use the `Stack` class (or the generic equivalent of `Stack<T>`) to represent a stack collection. The following statement creates an instance of the `Stack` class of type `string`:

```
Stack<string> tasks = new Stack<string>();
```

To add items into the stack, use the `Push()` method. The following statements push four strings into the tasks stack:

```
tasks.Push("Do homework"); //---this item will be at the bottom of the stack
tasks.Push("Phone rings");
tasks.Push("Get changed");
tasks.Push("Go for movies"); //---this item will be at the top of the stack
```

To retrieve the elements from a stack, use either the `Peek()` method or the `Pop()` method.
`Peek()` returns the object at the top of the stack without removing it. `Pop()` removes and returns the object at the top of the stack:

```
Console.WriteLine(tasks.Peek()); //---Go for movies---
Console.WriteLine(tasks.Pop());  //---Go for movies---
Console.WriteLine(tasks.Pop());  //---Get changed---
Console.WriteLine(tasks.Pop());  //---Phone rings---
Console.WriteLine(tasks.Pop());  //---Do homework---
```

If a stack is empty and you try to call the `Pop()` method, an `InvalidOperationException` error occurs. For that reason, it is useful to check the size of the stack by using the `Count` property before you perform a `Pop()` operation:

```
if (tasks.Count > 0)
    Console.WriteLine(tasks.Pop());
else
    Console.WriteLine("Tasks is empty");
```

To extract all the objects within a `Stack` object without removing the elements, use a `foreach` statement, like this:

```
foreach (string t in tasks)
    Console.WriteLine(t);
```

Here's what prints out:

```
Go for movies
Get changed
Phone rings
Do homework
```

Queues

The queue is a first in, first out (FIFO) data structure. Unlike the stack, items are removed based on the sequence that they are added.

In .NET, you can use the `Queue` class (or the generic equivalent of `Queue<T>`) to represent a queue collection. The following statement creates an instance of the `Queue` class of type `string`:

```
Queue<string> tasks = new Queue<string>();
```

To add items into the queue, use the `Enqueue()` method. The following statement inserts four strings into the `tasks` queue:

```
tasks.Enqueue("Do homework");
tasks.Enqueue("Phone rings");
tasks.Enqueue("Get changed");
tasks.Enqueue("Go for movies");
```

To retrieve the elements from a queue, you can use either the `Peek()` method or the `Dequeue()` method. `Peek()` returns the object at the beginning of the queue without removing it. `Dequeue()` removes and returns the object at the beginning of the queue:

```
Console.WriteLine(tasks.Peek());       //---Do homework---
Console.WriteLine(tasks.Dequeue());    //---Do homework---
Console.WriteLine(tasks.Dequeue());    //---Phone rings---
Console.WriteLine(tasks.Dequeue());    //---Get changed---
Console.WriteLine(tasks.Dequeue());    //---Go for movies---
```

If a queue is empty and you try to call the `Dequeue()` method, an `InvalidOperationException` error occurs, so it is useful to check the size of the queue using the `Count` property before you perform a dequeue operation:

```
if (tasks.Count > 0)
    Console.WriteLine(tasks.Dequeue());
else
    Console.WriteLine("Tasks is empty");
```

To extract all the objects within a `Queue` object without removing the elements, use the `foreach` statement, like this:

```
foreach (string t in tasks)
    Console.WriteLine(t);
```

Here's what prints out:

```
Do homework
Phone rings
Get changed
Go for movies
```

Summary

This chapter explained how to manipulate data using arrays. In addition, it explored the `System.Collections` namespace, which contains the various interfaces that define basic collection functions. It also contains several useful data structures, such as a dictionary, stacks, and queues, that greatly simplify managing data in your application.

14

Language Integrated Query (LINQ)

One of the most exciting new features in the .NET Framework v3.5 is the Language Integrated Query (LINQ). LINQ introduces to developers a standard and consistent language for querying and updating data, which include objects (such as arrays and collections), databases, XML documents, ADO.NET DataSets, and so forth.

Today, most developers need to know a myriad of technologies to successfully manipulate data. For example, if you are dealing with databases, you have to understand Structured Query Language (SQL). If you are dealing with XML documents, you must understand technologies such as XPath, XQuery, and XSLT. And if you are working with ADO.NET DataSets, then you need to know the various classes and properties in ADO.NET that you can use.

A better approach would be to have a unified view of the data, regardless of its form and structure. That is the motivation behind the design of LINQ. This chapter provides the basics of LINQ and shows how you can use LINQ to access objects, DataSets, and XML documents, as well as SQL databases.

LINQ Architecture

Figure 14-1 shows the architecture of LINQ. The bottom layer contains the various data sources with which your applications could be working. On top of the data sources are the LINQ-enabled data sources: LINQ to Objects, LINQ to DataSet, LINQ to SQL, LINQ to Entities, and LINQ to XML. LINQ-enabled data sources are also known as LINQ providers; they translate queries expressed in Visual Basic or C# into the native language of the data source. To access all these data sources through LINQ, developers use either C# or Visual Basic and write LINQ queries.

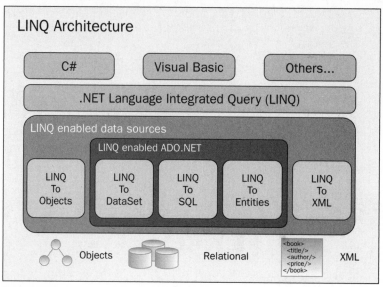

Figure 14-1

> LINQ to Entities is beyond the scope of this book. It was slated to be released later in 2008 and is not part of Visual Studio 2008.

So how does your application view the LINQ-enabled data sources?

❑ In LINQ to Objects, the source data is made visible as an `IEnumerable<T>` or `IQueryable<T>` collection.

❑ In LINQ to XML, the source data is made visible as an `IEnumerable<XElement>`.

❑ In LINQ to DataSet, the source data is made visible as an `IEnumerable<DataRow>`.

❑ In LINQ to SQL, the source data is made visible as an `IEnumerable` or `IQueryable` of whatever custom objects you have defined to represent the data in the SQL table.

LINQ to Objects

Let's start with LINQ to Objects. It enables you to use LINQ to directly query any `IEnumerable<T>` or `IQueryable<T>` collections (such as `string[]`, `int[]`, and `List<T>`) directly without needing to use an immediate LINQ provider or API such as the LINQ to SQL or LINQ to XML.

Say that you have a collection of data stored in an array, and you want to be able to retrieve a subset of the data quickly. In the old way of doing things, you write a loop and iteratively retrieve all the data that matches your criteria. That's time-consuming because you have to write all the logic to perform the comparison and so on. Using LINQ, you can declaratively write the condition using an SQL-like statement, and the compiler des the job of retrieving the relevant data for you.

Suppose that you have an array of type `string` that contains a list of names. The following program prints out all the names in the string array that start with the character G:

```csharp
using System;
using System.Collections.Generic;
using System.Linq;
using System.Text;

namespace LINQ
{
    class Program
    {
        static void Main(string[] args)
        {
            string[] allNames = new string[] {
                "Jeffrey", "Kirby", "Gabriel",
                "Philip", "Ross", "Adam",
                "Alston", "Warren", "Garfield"};

            foreach (string str in allNames)
            {
                if (str.StartsWith("G"))
                {
                    Console.WriteLine(str);
                }
            }

            Console.ReadLine();
        }
    }
}
```

Using LINQ to Objects, you can rewrite the program as follows:

```csharp
using System;
using System.Collections.Generic;
using System.Linq;
using System.Text;

namespace LINQ
{
    class Program
    {
        static void Main(string[] args)
        {
            string[] allNames = new string[] {
                "Jeffrey", "Kirby", "Gabriel",
                "Philip", "Ross", "Adam",
```

(continued)

(continued)

```
                    "Alston", "Warren", "Garfield"};

            IEnumerable<string> foundNames =
                from name in allNames
                where name.StartsWith("G")
                select name;

        foreach (string str in foundNames)
            Console.WriteLine(str);

        Console.ReadLine();
    }
  }
}
```

Notice that you have declared the `foundNames` variable to be of type `IEnumerable<string>`, and the expression looks similar to that of SQL:

```
        IEnumerable<string> foundNames =
            from name in allNames
            where name.StartsWith("G")
            select name;
```

The one important difference from SQL queries is that in a LINQ query the operator sequence is reversed. In SQL, you use the `select-from-where` format, while LINQ queries use the format `from-where-select`. This reversal in order allows IntelliSense to know which data source you are using so that it can provide useful suggestions for the `where` and `select` clauses.

The result of the query in this case is `IEnumerable<string>`. You can also use the new implicit typing feature in C# 3.0 to let the C# compiler automatically infer the type for you, like this:

```
        var foundNames =
            from name in allNames
            where name.StartsWith("G")
            select name;
```

When you now use a `foreach` loop to go into the `foundNames` variable, it will contain a collection of names that starts with the letter G. In this case, it returns `Gabriel`, `Garfield`.

The usefulness of LINQ is more evident when you have more complex filters. For example:

```
        var foundNames =
            from name in allNames
            where name.StartsWith("G") && name.EndsWith("l")
            select name;
```

In this case, only names that begin with G and end with "l" will be retrieved (`Gabriel`).

Here's an example where you have an array of integer values. You want to retrieve all the odd numbers in the array and sort them in descending order (that is, the bigger numbers come before the smaller numbers). Using LINQ, your code looks like this:

```
int[] nums = { 12, 34, 10, 3, 45, 6, 90, 22, 87, 49, 13, 32 };
var oddNums = from n in nums
              where (n % 2 == 1)
              orderby n descending
              select n;
foreach (int n in oddNums)
    Console.WriteLine(n);
```

And here's what the code will print out:

```
87
49
45
13
3
```

To find out the total number of odd numbers found by the query, you can use the Count() method from the oddNums variable (of type IEnumerable<int>):

```
int count = oddNums.Count();
```

You can also convert the result into an int array, like this:

```
int[] oddNumsArray = oddNums.ToArray();
```

Query Syntax versus Method Syntax and Lambda Expressions

The two LINQ queries in the previous section use the *query syntax*, which is written in a declarative manner, like this:

```
var oddNums = from n in nums
              where (n % 2 == 1)
              orderby n descending
              select n;
```

In addition to using the query syntax, you can also use the *method syntax*, which is written using method calls like Where and Select, like this:

```
int[] nums = { 12, 34, 10, 3, 45, 6, 90, 22, 87, 49, 13, 32 };
IEnumerable<int> oddNums = nums.Where(n => n % 2 == 1). OrderByDescending(n => n);
```

To find the total number of odd numbers in the array, you can also use the method syntax to query the array directly, like this:

```
int count = (nums.Where(n => n % 2 == 1).OrderBy(n => n)).Count();
```

Let's take a look at method syntax and how it works. First, the expression:

```
(n => n % 2 == 1)
```

is known as the lambda expression. The => is the lambda operator. You read it as "goes to," so this expression reads as "n goes to n modulus 2 equals to 1." Think of this lambda expression as a function that accepts a single input parameter, contains a single statement, and returns a value, like this:

```
static bool function(int n)
{
    return (n % 2 == 1);
}
```

The compiler automatically infers the type of n (which is int in this case because nums is an int array) in the lambda expression. However, you can also explicitly specify the type of n, like this:

```
IEnumerable<int> oddNums =
    nums.Where( (int n) => n % 2 == 1).OrderByDescending(n => n);
```

The earlier example of the string array can also be rewritten using the method syntax as follows:

```
string[] allNames = new string[] {
    "Jeffrey", "Kirby", "Gabriel",
    "Philip", "Ross", "Adam",
    "Alston", "Warren", "Garfield"};

var foundNames = allNames.Where(name = name.StartsWith("G") &&
                                name.EndsWith("l"));
```

Which syntax should you use? Here's some information regarding the two syntaxes:

- ❑ There is no performance difference between the method syntax and the query syntax.

- ❑ The query syntax is much more readable, so use it whenever possible.

- ❑ Use the method syntax for cases where there is no query syntax equivalent. For example, the Count and Max methods have no query equivalent syntax.

LINQ and Extension Methods

Chapter 4 explored extension methods and how you can use them to extend functionality to an existing class without needing to subclass it. One of the main reasons why the extension method feature was incorporated into the C# 3.0 language was because of LINQ.

Consider the earlier example where you have an array called allNames containing an array of strings. In .NET, objects that contain a collection of objects must implement the IEnumerable interface, so the allNames variable implicitly implements the IEnumerable interface, which only exposes one

```
using System;
using System.Collections.Generic;
using System.Linq;
using System.Text;

namespace ConsoleApplication5
{
    class Program
    {
        static void Main(string[] args)
        {

            int[] nums = { 12, 34, 10, 3, 45, 6, 90, 22, 87, 49, 13, 32 };
            var oddNums = nums.Where(n => n % 2 == 1).OrderByDescending(n => n);

            Console.WriteLine("First execution");
            Console.WriteLine("---------------");
            foreach (int n in oddNums)
                Console.WriteLine(n);

            //---add 20 to each number in the array---
            for (int i = 0; i < 11; i++)
                nums[i] += 20;

            Console.WriteLine("Second execution");
            Console.WriteLine("----------------");
            foreach (int n in oddNums)
                Console.WriteLine(n);

            Console.ReadLine();
        }
    }
}
```

The program prints out the following output:

```
First execution
---------------
87
49
45
13
3
Second execution
----------------
107
69
65
33
23
```

Because the output for the second foreach loop is different from the first, the program effectively proves that the query is not executed until it is accessed.

> Deferred execution works regardless of whether you are using the query or method syntax.

Forced Immediate Query Execution

One way to force an immediate execution of the query is to explicitly convert the query result into a `List` object. For example, the following query converts the result to a `List` object:

```
var oddNums = nums.Where
    (n => n % 2 == 1).OrderByDescending(n => n).ToList();
```

In this case, the query is executed immediately, as proven by the following program and its output:

```
using System;
using System.Collections.Generic;
using System.Linq;
using System.Text;

namespace ConsoleApplication5
{
    class Program
    {
        static void Main(string[] args)
        {
            int[] nums = { 12, 34, 10, 3, 45, 6, 90, 22, 87, 49, 13, 32 };
            var oddNums = nums.Where
                (n => n % 2 == 1).OrderByDescending(n => n).ToList();

            Console.WriteLine("First execution");
            Console.WriteLine("---------------");
            foreach (int n in oddNums)
                Console.WriteLine(n);

            //---add 20 to each number in the array---
            for (int i = 0; i < 11; i++)
                nums[i] += 20;

            Console.WriteLine("Second execution");
            Console.WriteLine("----------------");
            foreach (int n in oddNums)
                Console.WriteLine(n);

            Console.ReadLine();
        }
    }
}
```

Here's the program's output:

```
First execution
---------------
87
49
45
13
3
Second execution
---------------
87
49
45
13
3
```

The output of the first and second execution is the same, proving that the query is executed immediately after it's defined.

To force a LINQ query to execute immediately, you can use *aggregate functions* so that the query must iterate over the elements at once. An aggregate function takes a collection of values and returns a scalar value.

Aggregate functions are discussed in more detail later in this chapter.

Following is an example that uses the Count() aggregate function. The program selects all the odd numbers from an array and then counts the total number of odd numbers. Each number is then multiplied by two (which makes them all become even numbers).

```
static void Main(string[] args)
{
    int[] nums = { 12, 34, 10, 3, 45, 6, 90, 22, 87, 49, 13, 32 };
    var oddNumsCount = nums.Where
        (n => n % 2 == 1).OrderByDescending(n => n).Count();

    Console.WriteLine("First execution");
    Console.WriteLine("---------------");
    Console.WriteLine("Count: {0}", oddNumsCount);

    //---add 20 to each number in the array---
    for (int i = 0; i < 11; i++)
        nums[i] *= 2; //---all number should now be even---

    Console.WriteLine("Second execution");
    Console.WriteLine("----------------");
    Console.WriteLine("Count: {0}", oddNumsCount);

    Console.ReadLine();
}
```

The output shows that once the query is executed, its value does not change:

```
First execution
---------------
Count: 5
Second execution
---------------
Count: 5
```

LINQ and Anonymous Types

Although Chapter 4 explored anonymous types and how they allow you to define data types without having to formally define a class, you have not yet seen their real use. In fact, anonymous type is another new feature that Microsoft has designed with LINQ in mind.

Consider the following Contact class definition:

```
public class Contact
{
    public int id { get; set; }
    public string FirstName { get; set; }
    public string LastName { get; set; }
}
```

Suppose that you have a list containing Contact objects, like this:

```
List<Contact> Contacts = new List<Contact>() {
    new Contact() {id = 1, FirstName = "John", LastName = "Chen"},
    new Contact() {id = 2, FirstName = "Maryann", LastName = "Chen" },
    new Contact() {id = 3, FirstName = "Richard", LastName = "Wells" }
};
```

You can use LINQ to query all contacts with Chen as the last name:

```
IEnumerable<Contact> foundContacts = from c in Contacts
                                     where c.LastName == "Chen"
                                     select c;
```

The foundContacts object is of type IEnumerable<Contact>. To print out all the contacts in the result, you can use the foreach loop:

```
foreach (var c in foundContacts)
{
    Console.WriteLine("{0} - {1} {2}", c.id, c.FirstName, c.LastName);
}
```

The output looks like this:

```
1 - John Chen
2 - Maryann Chen
```

However, you can modify your query such that the result can be shaped into a custom class instead of type `Contact`. To do so, modify the query as the following highlighted code shows:

```
var foundContacts = from c in Contacts
                    where c.LastName == "Chen"
                    select new
                    {
                        id = c.id,
                        Name = c.FirstName + " " + c.LastName
                    };
```

Here, you reshape the result using the anonymous type feature new in C# 3.0. Notice that you now have to use the `var` keyword to let the compiler automatically infer the type of `foundContacts`. Because the result is an anoymous type that you are defining, the following generates an error:

```
IEnumerable<Contact> foundContacts = from c in Contacts
                                     where c.LastName == "Chen"
                                     select new
                                     {
                                         id = c.id,
                                         Name = c.FirstName + " " + c.LastName
                                     };
```

To print the results, use the `foreach` loop as usual:

```
foreach (var c in foundContacts)
{
    Console.WriteLine("{0} - {1}", c.id, c.Name);
}
```

Figure 14-4 shows that IntelliSense automatically knows that the result is an anonymous type with two fields — id and Name.

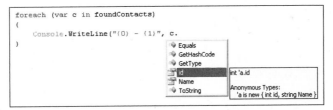

Figure 14-4

LINQ to DataSet

Besides manipulating data in memory, LINQ can also be used to query data stored in structures like DataSets and DataTables.

ADO.NET is the data access technology in .NET that allows you to manipulate data sources such as databases. If you are familiar with ADO.NET, you are familiar with the DataSet object, which represents an in-memory cache of data. Using LINQ to DataSet, you can use LINQ queries to access data stored in a DataSet object. Figure 14-5 shows the relationships between LINQ to DataSet and ADO.NET 2.0.

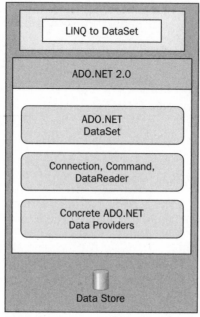

Figure 14-5

Notice that LINQ to DataSet is built on top of ADO.NET 2.0. You can continue using your ADO.NET code to access data stored in a DataSet, but using LINQ to DataSet will greatly simplify your tasks.

The best way to understand LINQ to DataSet is to look at an example and see how it can simplify your coding. The following code shows how, using ADO.NET, you can connect to the pubs sample database, retrieve all the authors from the Authors table, and then print their IDs and names to the output window:

Preparing the Sample Database

Because SQL Server 2005 Express does not come with any sample databases, you need to install the pubs database used in this section yourself.

You can install the pubs and Northwind databases by downloading the installation scripts at http://microsoft.com/downloads. Search for: "Northwind and pubs Sample Databases for SQL Server 2000."

Once the scripts are installed on your system, go to the Visual Studio 2008 Command Prompt (Start ⇨ Programs ⇨ Microsoft Visual Studio 2008 ⇨ Visual Studio Tools ⇨ Visual Studio 2008 Command Prompt) and change to the directory containing your installation scripts. Type in the following to install the two databases:

```
C:\SQL Server 2000 Sample Databases>sqlcmd -S .\SQLEXPRESS -i instpubs.sql
C:\SQL Server 2000 Sample Databases>sqlcmd -S .\SQLEXPRESS -i instnwnd.sql
```

```csharp
using System;
using System.Collections.Generic;
using System.ComponentModel;
using System.Data;
using System.Drawing;
using System.Linq;
using System.Text;
using System.Windows.Forms;
using System.Data.SqlClient;

namespace LINQtoDataset
{
    public partial class Form1 : Form
    {
        public Form1()
        {
            InitializeComponent();
        }

        private void Form1_Load(object sender, EventArgs e)
        {
            SqlConnection conn;
            SqlCommand comm;
            SqlDataAdapter adapter;
            DataSet ds = new DataSet();

            //---loads the Authors table into the dataset---
            conn = new SqlConnection(@"Data Source=.\SQLEXPRESS;" +
                    "Initial Catalog=pubs;Integrated Security=True");
            comm = new SqlCommand("SELECT * FROM Authors", conn);
            adapter = new SqlDataAdapter(comm);
```

(continued)

(continued)

```
                adapter.Fill(ds);

                foreach (DataRow row in ds.Tables[0].Rows)
                {
                    Console.WriteLine("{0} - {1} {2}",
                        row["au_id"], row["au_fname"], row["au_lname"]);
                }
            }
        }
    }
```

Observe that all the rows in the Authors table are now stored in the ds DataSet object (in ds.Tables[0]). To print only those authors living in CA, you would need to write the code to do the filtering:

```
            foreach (DataRow row in ds.Tables[0].Rows)
            {
                if (row["state"].ToString() == "CA")
                {
                    Console.WriteLine("{0} - {1} {2}",
                        row["au_id"], row["au_fname"], row["au_lname"]);
                }
            }
```

Using LINQ to DataSet, you can write a query that only retrieves authors living in CA:

```
            //---query for authors living in CA---
            EnumerableRowCollection<DataRow> authors =
                from author in ds.Tables[0].AsEnumerable()
                where author.Field<string>("State") == "CA"
                select author;
```

The result of the query is of type EnumerableRowCollection<DataRow>. Alternatively, you can also use the var keyword to let the compiler determine the correct data type:

```
            var authors =
                from author in ds.Tables[0].AsEnumerable()
                where author.Field<string>("State") == "CA"
                select author;
```

> To make use of LINQ to DataSet, ensure that you have a reference to System.Data.DataSetExtensions.dll in your project.

To display the result, you can either bind the result to a DataGridView control using the `AsDataView()` method:

```
//---bind to a datagridview control---
dataGridView1.DataSource = authors.AsDataView();
```

Or, iteratively loop through the result using a `foreach` loop:

```
foreach (DataRow row in authors)
{
    Console.WriteLine("{0} - {1}, {2}",
        row["au_id"], row["au_fname"], row["au_lname"]);
}
```

To query the authors based on their contract status, use the following query:

```
EnumerableRowCollection<DataRow> authors =
    from author in ds.Tables[0].AsEnumerable()
    where author.Field<Boolean>("Contract") == true
    select author;
```

Reshaping Data

Using the new anonymous types feature in C# 3.0, you can define a new type without needing to define a new class. Consider the following statement:

```
//---query for authors living in CA---
var authors =
    from author in ds.Tables[0].AsEnumerable()
    where author.Field<string>("State") == "CA"
    select new
    {
        ID = author.Field<string>("au_id"),
        FirstName = author.Field<string>("au_fname"),
        LastName = author.Field<string>("au_lname")
    };
```

Here, you select all the authors living in the CA state and at the same time create a new type consisting of three properties: `ID`, `FirstName`, and `LastName`. If you now type the word `authors`, IntelliSense will show you that `authors` is of type `EnumerableRowCollection <'a> authors`, and `'a` is an anonymous type containing the three fields (see Figure 14-6).

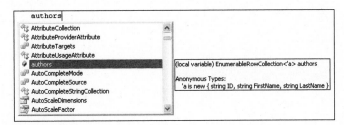

Figure 14-6

You can now print out the result using a `foreach` loop:

```
foreach (var row in authors)
{
    Console.WriteLine("{0} - {1}, {2}",
        row.ID, row.FirstName, row.LastName);
}
```

To databind to a DataGridView control, you first must convert the result of the query to a List object:

```
//---query for authors living in CA---
var authors =
    (from author in ds.Tables[0].AsEnumerable()
    where author.Field<string>("State") == "CA"
    select new
    {
        ID = author.Field<string>("au_id"),
        FirstName = author.Field<string>("au_fname"),
        LastName = author.Field<string>("au_lname")
    }).ToList();

//---bind to a datagridview control---
dataGridView1.DataSource = authors;
```

Aggregate Functions

In an earlier section, you used the following query to obtain a list of authors living in CA:

```
var authors =
    from author in ds.Tables[0].AsEnumerable()
    where author.Field<string>("State") == "CA"
    select author;
```

To get the total number of authors living in CA, you can use the `Count()` extension method (also known as an aggregate function), like this:

```
Console.WriteLine(authors.Count());
```

A much more efficient way would be to use the following query in method syntax:

```
var query =
    ds.Tables[0].AsEnumerable()
    .Count(a => a.Field<string>("State")=="CA");
Console.WriteLine(query);
```

LINQ supports the following standard aggregate functions:

Aggregate function	Description
Aggregate	Performs a custom aggregation operation on the values of a collection.
Average	Calculates the average value of a collection of values.
Count	Counts the elements in a collection, optionally only those elements that satisfy a predicate function.
LongCount	Counts the elements in a large collection, optionally only those elements that satisfy a predicate function.
Max	Determines the maximum value in a collection.
Min	Determines the minimum value in a collection.
Sum	Calculates the sum of the values in a collection.

For example, the following statements print out the largest odd number contained in the nums array:

```
int[] nums = { 12, 34, 10, 3, 45, 6, 90, 22, 87, 49, 13, 32 };
var maxOddNums = nums.Where
    (n => n % 2 == 1).OrderByDescending(n => n).Max();
Console.WriteLine("Largest odd number: {0}", maxOddNums); //---87---
```

The following statements print out the sum of all the odd numbers in nums:

```
int[] nums = { 12, 34, 10, 3, 45, 6, 90, 22, 87, 49, 13, 32 };
var sumOfOddNums = nums.Where
    (n => n % 2 == 1).OrderByDescending(n => n).Sum();
Console.WriteLine("Sum of all odd number: {0}", sumOfOddNums); //---197---
```

Joining Tables

So far you've been dealing with a single table. In real life, you often have multiple, related tables. A good example is the Northwind sample database, which contains a number of related tables, three of which are shown in Figure 14-7.

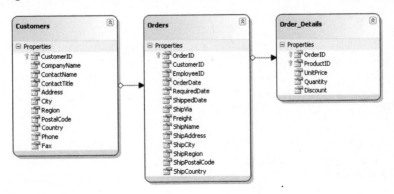

Figure 14-7

Here, the Customers table is related to the Orders table via the CustomerID field, while the Orders table is related to the Order_Details table via the OrderID field.

You can use LINQ to DataSet to join several tables stored in a DataSet. Here's how. First, load the three tables into the DataSet, using the following code:

```
conn = new SqlConnection(@"Data Source=.\SQLEXPRESS;" +
        "Initial Catalog=Northwind;Integrated Security=True");
comm = new SqlCommand("SELECT * FROM Customers; SELECT * FROM Orders;
SELECT * FROM [Order Details]", conn);
adapter = new SqlDataAdapter(comm);
adapter.Fill(ds);
```

The three tables loaded onto the DataSet can now be referenced using three DataTable objects:

```
DataTable customersTable = ds.Tables[0];      //---Customers---
DataTable ordersTable = ds.Tables[1];         //---Orders---
DataTable orderDetailsTable = ds.Tables[2];   //---Order Details---
```

The following LINQ query joins two DataTable objects — customersTable and ordersTable — using the query syntax:

```
//---using query syntax to join two tables - Customers and Orders---
var query1 =
    (from customer in customersTable.AsEnumerable()
     join order in ordersTable.AsEnumerable() on
     customer.Field<string>("CustomerID") equals
     order.Field<string>("CustomerID")
     select new
     {
         id = customer.Field<string>("CustomerID"),
         CompanyName = customer.Field<string>("CompanyName"),
         ContactName = customer.Field<string>("ContactName"),
         OrderDate = order.Field<DateTime>("OrderDate"),
         ShipCountry = order.Field<string>("ShipCountry")
     }).ToList();
```

As evident in the query, the Customers and Orders table are joined using the CustomerID field. The result is reshaped using an anonymous type and then converted to a List object using the ToList() extension method. You can now bind the result to a DataGridView control if desired. Figure 14-8 shows the result bound to a DataGridView control.

Figure 14-8

You can also rewrite the query using the method syntax:

```
//---using method syntax to join two tables - Customers and Orders---
var query1 =
    (customersTable.AsEnumerable().Join(ordersTable.AsEnumerable(),
     customer => customer.Field<string>("CustomerID"),
     order => order.Field<string>("CustomerID"),
     (customer, order) => new
     {
         id = customer.Field<string>("CustomerID"),
         CompanyName = customer.Field<string>("CompanyName"),
         ContactName = customer.Field<string>("ContactName"),
         OrderDate = order.Field<DateTime>("OrderDate"),
         ShipCountry = order.Field<string>("ShipCountry")
     })).ToList();
```

The following query joins three DataTable objects — customersTable, ordersTable, and orderDetailsTable — and sorts the result according to the OrderID field:

```
//---three tables join---
var query2 =
    (from customer in customersTable.AsEnumerable()
     join order in ordersTable.AsEnumerable() on
     customer.Field<string>("CustomerID") equals
     order.Field<string>("CustomerID")
     join orderDetail in orderDetailsTable.AsEnumerable() on
     order.Field<int>("OrderID") equals
     orderDetail.Field<int>("OrderID")
     orderby order.Field<int>("OrderID")
    select new
    {
        id = customer.Field<string>("CustomerID"),
        CompanyName = customer.Field<string>("CompanyName"),
        ContactName = customer.Field<string>("ContactName"),
        OrderDate = order.Field<DateTime>("OrderDate"),
        ShipCountry = order.Field<string>("ShipCountry"),
        OrderID = orderDetail.Field<int>("OrderID"),
        ProductID = orderDetail.Field<int>("ProductID")
    }).ToList();
```

445

As evident from the query, the `Customers` table is related to the `Orders` table via the `CustomerID` field, and the `Orders` table is related to the `Order Details` table via the `OrderID` field.

Figure 14-9 shows the result of the query.

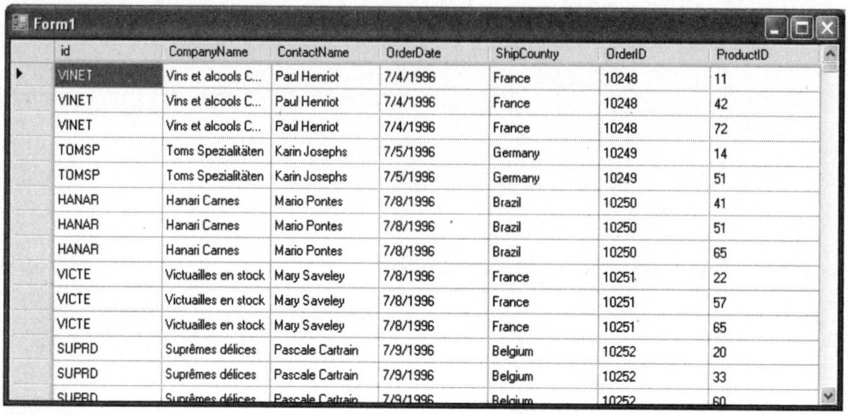

id	CompanyName	ContactName	OrderDate	ShipCountry	OrderID	ProductID
VINET	Vins et alcools C...	Paul Henriot	7/4/1996	France	10248	11
VINET	Vins et alcools C...	Paul Henriot	7/4/1996	France	10248	42
VINET	Vins et alcools C...	Paul Henriot	7/4/1996	France	10248	72
TOMSP	Toms Spezialitäten	Karin Josephs	7/5/1996	Germany	10249	14
TOMSP	Toms Spezialitäten	Karin Josephs	7/5/1996	Germany	10249	51
HANAR	Hanari Carnes	Mario Pontes	7/8/1996	Brazil	10250	41
HANAR	Hanari Carnes	Mario Pontes	7/8/1996	Brazil	10250	51
HANAR	Hanari Carnes	Mario Pontes	7/8/1996	Brazil	10250	65
VICTE	Victuailles en stock	Mary Saveley	7/8/1996	France	10251	22
VICTE	Victuailles en stock	Mary Saveley	7/8/1996	France	10251	57
VICTE	Victuailles en stock	Mary Saveley	7/8/1996	France	10251	65
SUPRD	Suprêmes délices	Pascale Cartrain	7/9/1996	Belgium	10252	20
SUPRD	Suprêmes délices	Pascale Cartrain	7/9/1996	Belgium	10252	33
SUPRD	Suprêmes délices	Pascale Cartrain	7/9/1996	Belgium	10252	60

Figure 14-9

Typed DataSet

So far you've used the `Field()` extension method to access the field of a `DataTable` object. For example, the following program uses LINQ to DataSet to query all the customers living in the USA. The result is then reshaped using an anonymous type:

```
SqlConnection conn;
SqlCommand comm;
SqlDataAdapter adapter;
DataSet ds = new DataSet();

conn = new SqlConnection(@"Data Source=.\SQLEXPRESS;" +
       "Initial Catalog=Northwind;Integrated Security=True");
comm = new SqlCommand("SELECT * FROM Customers", conn);
adapter = new SqlDataAdapter(comm);
adapter.Fill(ds, "Customers");

var query1 =
    (from customer in ds.Tables[0].AsEnumerable()
     where customer.Field<string>("Country") == "USA"
     select new
     {
         CustomerID = customer.Field<string>("CustomerID"),
         CompanyName = customer.Field<string>("CompanyName"),
         ContactName = customer.Field<string>("ContactName"),
         ContactTitle = customer.Field<string>("ContactTitle")
     }).ToList();

dataGridView1.DataSource = query1;
```

As your query gets more complex, the use of the `Field()` extension method makes the query unwieldy. A good way to resolve this is to use the typed DataSet feature in ADO.NET. A typed DataSet provides strongly typed methods, events, and properties and so this means you can access tables and columns by name, instead of using collection-based methods.

To add a typed DataSet to your project, first add a `DataSet` item to your project in Visual Studio 2008 (see Figure 14-10). Name it `TypedCustomersDataset.xsd`.

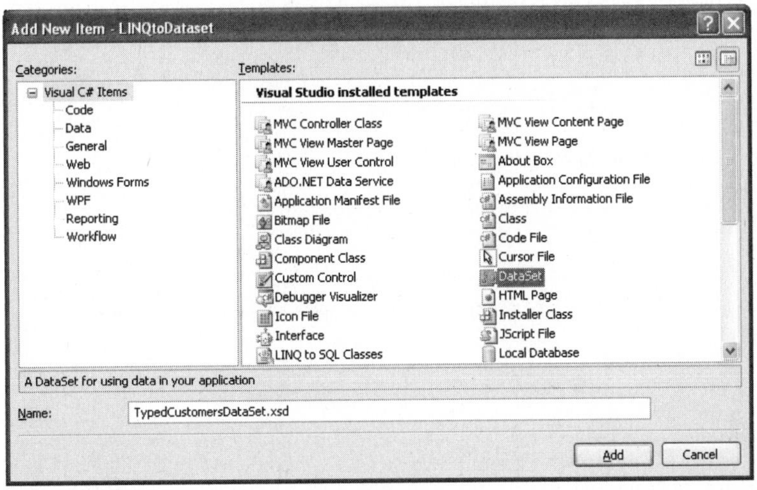

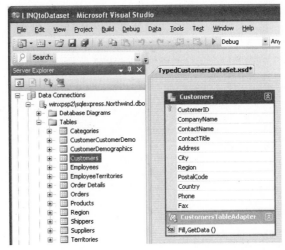

Figure 14-10

In the Server Explorer window, open a connection to the database you want to use (in this case it is the Northwind database) and drag and drop the `Customers` table onto the design surface of `TypedCustomersDataSet.xsd` (see Figure 14-11). Save the `TypedCustomersDataSet.xsd` file.

Figure 14-11

With the typed DataSet created, rewrite the query as follows:

```
SqlConnection conn;
SqlCommand comm;
SqlDataAdapter adapter;
TypedCustomersDataSet ds = new TypedCustomersDataSet();

conn = new SqlConnection(@"Data Source=.\SQLEXPRESS;" +
    "Initial Catalog=Northwind;Integrated Security=True");
comm = new SqlCommand("SELECT * FROM Customers", conn);
adapter = new SqlDataAdapter(comm);
adapter.Fill(ds, "Customers");

var query1 =
    (from customer in ds.Customers
    where customer.Country == "USA"
    select new
    {
        customer.CustomerID,
        customer.CompanyName,
        customer.ContactName,
        customer.ContactTitle
    }).ToList();

dataGridView1.DataSource = query1;
```

Notice that the query is now much clearer because there is no need to use the `Field()` extension method. Figure 14-12 shows the output.

	CustomerID	CompanyName	ContactName	ContactTitle
▶	GREAL	Great Lakes Foo...	Howard Snyder	Marketing Manager
	HUNGC	Hungry Coyote I...	Yoshi Latimer	Sales Represent...
	LAZYK	Lazy K Kountry S...	John Steel	Marketing Manager
	LETSS	Let's Stop N Shop	Jaime Yorres	Owner
	LONEP	Lonesome Pine ...	Fran Wilson	Sales Manager
	OLDWO	Old World Delicat...	Rene Phillips	Sales Represent...
	RATTC	Rattlesnake Can...	Paula Wilson	Assistant Sales R...
	SAVEA	Save-a-lot Markets	Jose Pavarotti	Sales Represent...
	SPLIR	Split Rail Beer & ...	Art Braunschweiger	Sales Manager
	THEBI	The Big Cheese	Liz Nixon	Marketing Manager
	THECR	The Cracker Box	Liu Wong	Marketing Assistant
	TRAIH	Trail's Head Gour...	Helvetius Nagy	Sales Associate
	WHITC	White Clover Mar...	Karl Jablonski	Owner

Figure 14-12

Detecting Null Fields

Using the same query used in the previous section, let's modify it so that you can retrieve all customers living in the WA region:

```
var query1 =
    (from customer in ds.Customers
    where customer.Region=="WA"
    select new
    {
        customer.CustomerID,
        customer.CompanyName,
        customer.ContactName,
        customer.ContactTitle
    }).ToList();
```

When you execute the query, the program raises an exception. That's because some of the rows in the Customers table have null values for the Region field. To prevent this from happening, you need to use the IsNull() method to check for null values, like this:

```
var query1 =
    (from customer in ds.Customers
    where !customer.IsNull("Region") &&  customer.Region == "WA"
    select new
    {
        customer.CustomerID,
        customer.CompanyName,
        customer.ContactName,
        customer.ContactTitle
    }).ToList();
```

Notice that LINQ uses short-circuiting when evaluating the conditions in the where statement, so the IsNull() method must be placed before other conditions.

Interestingly, the Field() extension method handles nullable types, so you do not have to explicitly check for null values if you are not using typed DataSets.

Saving the Result of a Query to a DataTable

The result of a LINQ query can be saved into a DataTable object by using the CopyToDataTable() method. The CopyToDataTable() method takes the result of a query and copies the data into a DataTable, which can then be used for data binding.

The following example shows a LINQ query using typed DataSet with the result copied to a DataTable object and then bound to a DataGridView control:

```
var query1 =
    from customer in ds.Customers
    where customer.Country == "USA"
    select customer;

DataTable USACustomers = query1.CopyToDataTable ();
dataGridView1.DataSource = USACustomers;
```

449

Note that the `CopyToDataTable()` method only operates on an `IEnumerable<T>` source where the generic parameter `T` is of type `DataRow`. Hence, it does not work for queries that project anonymous types or queries that perform table joins.

LINQ to XML

Also very cool is LINQ's capability to manipulate XML documents. In the past, you had to use XPath or XQuery whenever you need to manipulate XML documents. Using LINQ to XML, you can now query XML trees and documents using the familiar LINQ syntax.

> **To use the LINQ to XML, you must add a reference to the `System.Xml.Linq.dll` in your project and also import the `System.Xml.Linq` namespace.**

Creating XML Trees

To create an XML document tree in memory, use the `XDocument` object, which represents an XML document. To create an XML element, use the `XElement` class; for attributes, use the `XAttribute` class. The following code shows how to build an XML document using these objects:

```csharp
using System;
using System.Collections.Generic;
using System.Linq;
using System.Text;
using System.Xml.Linq;

namespace LINQtoXML
{
    class Program
    {
        static void Main(string[] args)
        {
            XDocument library = new XDocument(
                new XElement("Library",
                    new XElement("Book",
                        new XAttribute("published", "NYP"),
                        new XElement("Title", "C# 2008 Programmers' Reference"),
                        new XElement("Publisher", "Wrox")
                    ),
                    new XElement("Book",
                        new XAttribute("published", "Published"),
                        new XElement("Title", "Professional Windows Vista " +
                                    "Gadgets Programming"),
                        new XElement("Publisher", "Wrox")
                    ),
                    new XElement("Book",
```

```
                    new XAttribute("published", "Published"),
                    new XElement("Title", "ASP.NET 2.0 - A Developer's " +
                                "Notebook"),
                    new XElement("Publisher", "O'Reilly")
                ),
                new XElement("Book",
                    new XAttribute("published", "Published"),
                    new XElement("Title", ".NET 2.0 Networking Projects"),
                    new XElement("Publisher", "Apress")
                ),
                new XElement("Book",
                    new XAttribute("published", "Published"),
                    new XElement("Title", "Windows XP Unwired"),
                    new XElement("Publisher", "O'Reilly")
                )
            )
        );
        }
    }
}
```

The indentation gives you an overall visualization of the document structure.

To save the XML document to file, use the `Save()` method:

```
library.Save("Books.xml");
```

To print out the XML document as a string, use the `ToString()` method:

```
Console.WriteLine(library.ToString());
```

When printed, the XML document looks like this:

```
<Library>
  <Book published="NYP">
    <Title>C# 2008 Programmers' Reference</Title>
    <Publisher>Wrox</Publisher>
  </Book>
  <Book published="Published">
    <Title>Professional Windows Vista Gadgets Programming</Title>
    <Publisher>Wrox</Publisher>
  </Book>
  <Book published="Published">
    <Title>ASP.NET 2.0 - A Developer's Notebook</Title>
    <Publisher>O'Reilly</Publisher>
  </Book>
  <Book published="Published">
    <Title>.NET 2.0 Networking Projects</Title>
    <Publisher>Apress</Publisher>
  </Book>
  <Book published="Published">
    <Title>Windows XP Unwired</Title>
    <Publisher>O'Reilly</Publisher>
  </Book>
</Library>
```

To load an XML document into the XDocument object, use the `Load()` method:

```
XDocument LibraryBooks = new XDocument();
LibraryBooks = XDocument.Load("Books.xml");
```

Querying Elements

You can use LINQ to XML to locate specific elements. For example, to retrieve all books published by Wrox, you can use the following query:

```
var query1 =
    from book in LibraryBooks.Descendants("Book")
    where book.Element("Publisher").Value == "Wrox"
    select book.Element("Title").Value;

Console.WriteLine("------");
Console.WriteLine("Result");
Console.WriteLine("------");
foreach (var book in query1)
{
    Console.WriteLine(book);
}
```

This query generates the following output:

```
------
Result
------
C# 2008 Programmers' Reference
Professional Windows Vista Gadgets Programming
```

To retrieve all not-yet-published (NYP) books from Wrox, you can use the following query:

```
var query2 =
    from book in library.Descendants("Book")
    where book.Attribute("published").Value == "NYP" &&
          book.Element("Publisher").Value=="Wrox"
    select book.Element("Title").Value;
```

You can shape the result of a query as you've seen in earlier sections:

```
var query3 =
    from book in library.Descendants("Book")
    where book.Element("Publisher").Value == "Wrox"
    select new
    {
        Name = book.Element("Title").Value,
        Pub = book.Element("Publisher").Value
    };

Console.WriteLine("------");
```

```
        Console.WriteLine("Result");
        Console.WriteLine("------");
        foreach (var book in query3)
        {
            Console.WriteLine("{0} ({1})", book.Name, book.Pub);
        }
```

This code generates the following output:

```
------
Result
------
C# 2008 Programmers' Reference (Wrox)
Professional Windows Vista Gadgets Programming (Wrox)
```

Besides using an anonymous type to reshape the result, you can also pass the result to a non-anonymous type. For example, suppose that you have the following class definition:

```
public class Book
{
    public string Name { get; set; }
    public string Pub { get; set; }
}
```

You can shape the result of a query to the Book class, as the following example shows:

```
var query4 =
        from book in library.Descendants("Book")
        where book.Element("Publisher").Value == "Wrox"
        select new Book
        {
            Name = book.Element("Title").Value,
            Pub = book.Element("Publisher").Value
        };

    List<Book> books = query4.ToList();
```

An Example Using RSS

Let's now take a look at the usefulness of LINQ to XML. Suppose that you want to build an application that downloads an RSS document, extracts the title of each posting, and displays the link to each post.

Figure 14-13 shows an example of an RSS document.

Wrox All New Titles.xml

```xml
<?xml version="1.0" encoding="utf-8"?>
<?xml-stylesheet title="XSL_formatting" type="text/xsl" href="/WileyCDA/feed/RSS_WROX_ALLNEW.xsl"?>

<rss xmlns:dc="http://purl.org/dc/elements/1.1/" xmlns:rdf="http://www.w3.org/1999/02/22-rdf-syntax-ns#" xmlns:
  <channel>
    <title>Wrox: All New Titles</title>
    <link>http://www.wrox.com/</link>
    <description>New titles on Wrox.com &lt;!-- ckey="1E5F1C44" --&gt;</description>
    <copyright>Copyright &amp;copy; 2000-2008 by John Wiley &amp;amp; Sons, Inc. or related companies. All right
    <pubDate>Fri, 04 Apr 2008 14:22:23 GMT</pubDate>
    <dc:date>2008-04-04T14:22:23Z</dc:date>
    <dc:rights>Copyright &amp;copy; 2000-2008 by John Wiley &amp;amp; Sons, Inc. or related companies. All right
    <image>
      <title>Wrox: All New Titles</title>
      <url>http://media.wiley.com/assets/1103/76/wrox_logo_sm.gif</url>
      <link>http://www.wrox.com/</link>
    </image>
    <item>
      <title>Ivor Horton's Beginning Visual C++ 2008</title>
      <link>http://www.wrox.com/WileyCDA/WroxTitle/productCd-0470225904.html?cid=RSS_WROX_ALLNEW</link>
      <description>&lt;br&gt; &lt;table cellpadding="0" cellspacing="0"&gt; &lt;tr&gt; &lt;td valign="top"&gt;&
      <pubDate>Mon, 31 Mar 2008 04:00:00 GMT</pubDate>
      <guid>http://www.wrox.com/WileyCDA/WroxTitle/productCd-0470225904.html?cid=RSS_WROX_ALLNEW</guid>
      <dc:creator>Ivor Horton</dc:creator>
      <dc:date>2008-03-31T04:00:00Z</dc:date>
    </item>
    <item>
      <title>Migrating to LINQ to SQL in TheBeerHouse and ASP.NET 2.0 Website Programming Problem Design Solutic
      <link>http://www.wrox.com/WileyCDA/WroxTitle/productCd-0470375019.html?cid=RSS_WROX_ALLNEW</link>
      <description>&lt;br&gt; &lt;table cellpadding="0" cellspacing="0"&gt; &lt;tr&gt; &lt;td valign="top"&gt;&
      <pubDate>Mon, 31 Mar 2008 04:00:00 GMT</pubDate>
      <guid>http://www.wrox.com/WileyCDA/WroxTitle/productCd-0470375019.html?cid=RSS_WROX_ALLNEW</guid>
      <dc:creator>Doug Parsons</dc:creator>
      <dc:date>2008-03-31T04:00:00Z</dc:date>
```

Figure 14-13

To load an XML document directly from the Internet, you can use the `Load()` method from the `XDocument` class:

```csharp
XDocument rss =
XDocument.Load(@"http://www.wrox.com/WileyCDA/feed/RSS_WROX_ALLNEW.xml");
```

To retrieve the title of each posting and then reshape the result, use the following query:

```csharp
var posts =
    from item in rss.Descendants("item")
    select new
    {
        Title = item.Element("title").Value,
        URL = item.Element("link").Value
    };
```

In particular, you are looking for all the `<item>` elements and then for each `<item>` element found you would extract the values of the `<title>` and `<link>` elements.

```
<rss>
   <channel>
   ...
        <item>
           <title>...</title>
           <link>...</link>
           ...
        </item>

        <item>
           <title>...</title>
           <link>...</link>
           ...
        </item>

        <item>
           <title>...</title>
           <link>...</link>
           ...
        </item>

   ...
```

Finally, print out the title and URL for each post:

```
foreach (var post in posts)
{
    Console.WriteLine("{0}", post.Title);
    Console.WriteLine("{0}", post.URL);
    Console.WriteLine();
}
```

Figure 14-14 shows the output.

Figure 14-14

Query Elements with a Namespace

If you observe the RSS document structure carefully, you notice that the `<creator>` element has the dc namespace defined (see Figure 14-15).

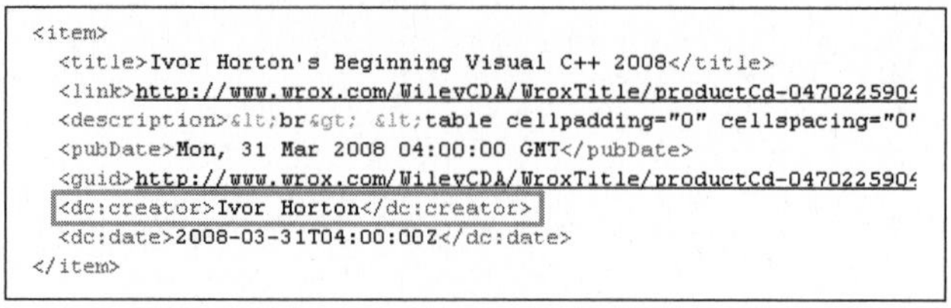

```
<item>
    <title>Ivor Horton's Beginning Visual C++ 2008</title>
    <link>http://www.wrox.com/WileyCDA/WroxTitle/productCd-0470225904
    <description>&lt;br&gt; &lt;table cellpadding="0" cellspacing="0'
    <pubDate>Mon, 31 Mar 2008 04:00:00 GMT</pubDate>
    <guid>http://www.wrox.com/WileyCDA/WroxTitle/productCd-0470225904
    <dc:creator>Ivor Horton</dc:creator>
    <dc:date>2008-03-31T04:00:00Z</dc:date>
</item>
```

Figure 14-15

The dc namespace is defined at the top of the document, within the `<rss>` element (see Figure 14-16).

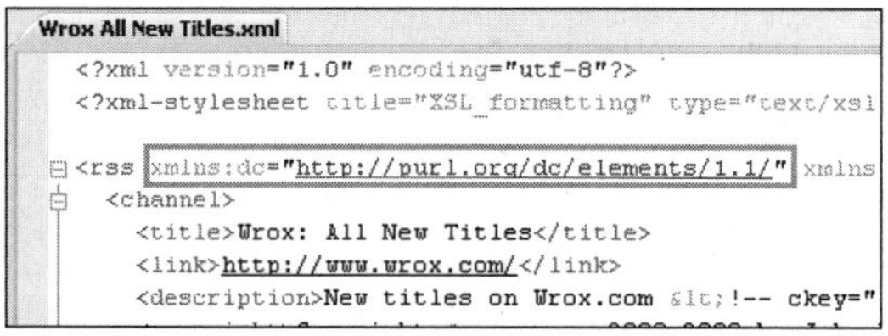

```
Wrox All New Titles.xml
    <?xml version="1.0" encoding="utf-8"?>
    <?xml-stylesheet title="XSL_formatting" type="text/xsl
  <rss xmlns:dc="http://purl.org/dc/elements/1.1/" xmlns
    <channel>
        <title>Wrox: All New Titles</title>
        <link>http://www.wrox.com/</link>
        <description>New titles on Wrox.com &lt;!-- ckey="
```

Figure 14-16

When using LINQ to XML to query elements defined with a namespace, you need to specify the namespace explicitly. The following example shows how you can do so using the XNamespace element and then using it in your code:

```
XDocument rss =
XDocument.Load(@"http://www.wrox.com/WileyCDA/feed/RSS_WROX_ALLNEW.xml");

XNamespace dcNamespace = "http://purl.org/dc/elements/1.1/";

var posts =
    from item in rss.Descendants("item")
    select new
    {
        Title = item.Element("title").Value,
        URL = item.Element("link").Value,
        Creator = item.Element(dcNamespace + "creator").Value
    };

foreach (var post in posts)
{
    Console.WriteLine("{0}", post.Title);
    Console.WriteLine("{0}", post.URL);
    Console.WriteLine("{0}", post.Creator);
    Console.WriteLine();
}
```

Figure 14-17 shows the query result.

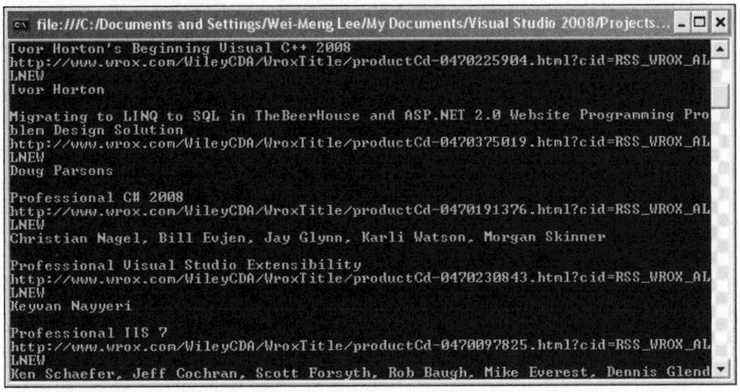

Figure 14-17

Retrieving Postings in the Last 10 Days

The <pubDate> element in the RSS document contains the date the posting was created. To retrieve all postings published in the last 10 days, you would need to use the Parse() method (from the DateTime class) to convert the string into a DateTime type and then deduct it from the current time. Here's how that can be done:

```
XDocument rss =
    XDocument.Load(
    @"http://www.wrox.com/WileyCDA/feed/RSS_WROX_ALLNEW.xml");

XNamespace dcNamespace = "http://purl.org/dc/elements/1.1/";

var posts =
    from item in rss.Descendants("item")
    where (DateTime.Now -
          DateTime.Parse(item.Element("pubDate").Value)).Days < 10
    select new
    {
        Title = item.Element("title").Value,
        URL = item.Element("link").Value,
        Creator = item.Element(dcNamespace + "creator").Value,
        PubDate = DateTime.Parse(item.Element("pubDate").Value)
    };

Console.WriteLine("Today's date: {0}",
                    DateTime.Now.ToShortDateString());
foreach (var post in posts)
{
    Console.WriteLine("{0}", post.Title);
    Console.WriteLine("{0}", post.URL);
    Console.WriteLine("{0}", post.Creator);
    Console.WriteLine("{0}", post.PubDate.ToShortDateString());
    Console.WriteLine();
}
```

LINQ to SQL

LINQ to SQL is a component of the .NET Framework (v3.5) that provides a runtime infrastructure for managing relational data as objects.

With LINQ to SQL, a relational database is mapped to an object model. Instead of manipulating the database directly, developers manipulate the object model, which represents the database. After changes are made to it, the object model is submitted to the database for execution.

Visual Studio 2008 includes the new Object Relational Designer (O/R Designer), which provides a user interface for creating LINQ to SQL entity classes and relationships. It enables you to easily model and visualize a database as a LINQ to SQL object model.

Using the Object Relational Designer

To see how LINQ to SQL works, create a new Windows application using Visual Studio 2008.

First, add a new LINQ to SQL Classes item to the project. Use the default name of `DataClasses1.dbml` (see Figure 14-18).

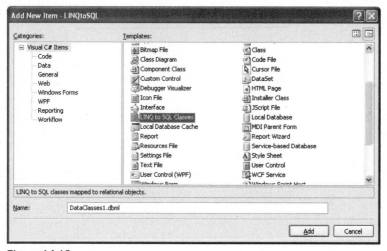

Figure 14-18

In Server Explorer, open a connection to the database you want to use. For this example, use the `pubs` sample database. Drag and drop the following tables onto the design surface of `DataClasses1.dbml`:

- ❑   `authors`
- ❑   `publishers`
- ❑   `titleauthor`
- ❑   `titles`

Figure 14-19 shows the relationships among these four tables.

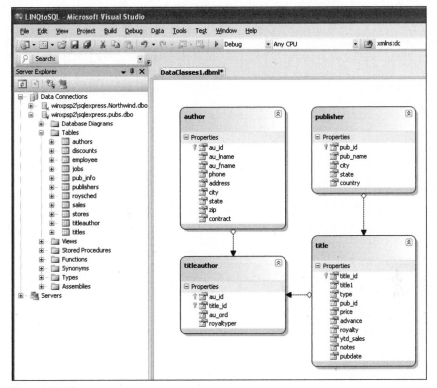

Figure 14-19

Now save the `DataClasses1.dbml` file, and Visual Studio 2008 will create the relevant classes to represent the tables and relationships that you just modeled. For every LINQ to SQL file you added to your solution, a `DataContext` class is generated. You can view this using the Class Viewer (View ➪ Class View; see Figure 14-20). In this case, the name of the `DataContext` class is `DataClasses1DataContext`. The name of this class is based on the name of the `.dbml` file; if you named the `.dbml` file `Pubs`, this class is named `PubsDataContext`.

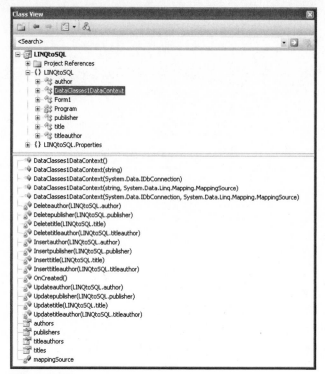

Figure 14-20

Querying

With the database modeled using the LINQ to SQL designer, it's time to write some code to query the database. First, create an instance of the DataClasses1DataContext class:

```
DataClasses1DataContext database = new DataClasses1DataContext();
```

To retrieve all the authors living in CA, use the following code:

```
var authors = from a in database.authors
              where (a.state == "CA")
              select new
              {
                  Name = a.au_fname + " " + a.au_lname
              };

foreach (var a in authors)
    Console.WriteLine(a.Name);
```

To retrieve all the titles in the `titles` table and at the same time print out the publisher name of each title, you first retrieve all the titles from the `titles` table:

```
var titles = from t in database.titles
             select t;
```

And then you retrieve each title's associated publisher:

```
foreach (var t in titles)
{
    Console.Write("{0} ", t.title1);
    var publisher = from p in database.publishers
                    where p.pub_id == t.pub_id
                    select p;
    if (publisher.Count() > 0)
        Console.WriteLine("({0})", publisher.First().pub_name);
}
```

The output looks something like this:

```
Cooking with Computers: Surreptitious Balance Sheets (Algodata Infosystems)
You Can Combat Computer Stress! (New Moon Books)
How to Motivate Your Employees Straight Talk About Computers (Algodata Infosystems)
Silicon Valley Gastronomic Treats (Binnet & Hardley)
The Gourmet Microwave (Binnet & Hardley)
The Psychology of Computer Cooking (Binnet & Hardley)
But Is It User Friendly? (Algodata Infosystems)
Secrets of Silicon Valley (Algodata Infosystems)
Net Etiquette (Algodata Infosystems)
Computer Phobic AND Non-Phobic Individuals: Behavior Variations (Binnet & Hardley)
Is Anger the Enemy? (New Moon Books)
Life Without Fear (New Moon Books)
Prolonged Data Deprivation: Four Case Studies (New Moon Books)
Emotional Security: A New Algorithm (New Moon Books)
Onions, Leeks, and Garlic: Cooking Secrets of the Mediterranean (Binnet & Hardley)
Fifty Years in Buckingham Palace Kitchens (Binnet & Hardley)
Sushi, Anyone? (Binnet & Hardley)
```

Inserting New Rows

To insert a row into a table, use the `InsertOnSubmit()` method. For example, the following code inserts a new author into the `authors` table:

```
DataClasses1DataContext database = new DataClasses1DataContext();

author a = new author()
{
    au_id = "789-12-3456",
    au_fname = "James",
    au_lname = "Bond",
    phone = "987654321"
};

//---record is saved to object model---
database.authors.InsertOnSubmit(a);
```

Note that the `InsertOnSubmit()` method only affects the object model; it does not save the changes back to the database. To save the changes back to the database, you need to use the `SubmitChanges()` method:

```
//---send changes to database---
database.SubmitChanges();
```

What happens when you need to insert a new book title from a new author? As you saw earlier, the `titles` table is related to the `titleauthors` via the `title_id` field, while the `authors` table is related to the `titleauthors` table via the `author_id` field. Therefore, if you insert a new row into the `titles` table, you need to insert a new row into the `authors` and `titleauthors` tables as well.

To do so, you first create a new `author` and `title` row:

```
DataClasses1DataContext database = new DataClasses1DataContext();
author a = new author()
{
    au_id = "123-45-6789",
    au_fname = "Wei-Meng",
    au_lname = "Lee",
    phone = "123456789"
};

title t = new title()
{
    title_id = "BU5555",
    title1 = "How to Motivate Your Employees",
    pubdate = System.DateTime.Now,
    type = "business"
};
```

Then, add a new `titleauthor` row by associating its `author` and `title` properties with the new `title` and `author` row you just created:

```
titleauthor ta = new titleauthor()
{
    author = a,
    title = t
};
```

Finally, save the changes to the object model and submit the changes to the database:

```
//---record is saved to object model---
database.titleauthors.InsertOnSubmit(ta);

//---send changes to database---
database.SubmitChanges();
```

Notice that you do not need to worry about indicating the `title_id` and `author_id` fields in the `titleauthors` table; LINQ to SQL does those for you automatically.

Updating Rows

Updating rows using LINQ to SQL is straightforward — you retrieve the record you need to modify:

```
DataClasses1DataContext database = new DataClasses1DataContext();
title bookTitle = (from t in database.titles
                   where (t.title_id == "BU5555")
                   select t).Single();
```

The Single() *method returns the only element of a sequence, and throws an exception if there is not exactly one element in the sequence.*

Modify the field you want to change:

```
bookTitle.title1 = "How to Motivate Your Staff";
```

And submit the changes using the SubmitChanges() method:

```
database.SubmitChanges();
```

The query can alternatively be written using the method syntax, like this:

```
title bookTitle = database.titles.Single(t => t.title_id == "BU5555");
```

Deleting Rows

To delete a row, you first retrieve the row to delete:

```
DataClasses1DataContext database = new DataClasses1DataContext();
//---find author ---
var author = from a in database.authors
             where a.au_id == "789-12-3456"
             select a;
```

Then, locate the row to delete by using the First() method, and finally call the DeleteOnSubmit() method to delete the row:

```
if (author.Count() > 0)
{
    database.authors.DeleteOnSubmit(author.First());
    database.SubmitChanges();
}
```

The First() *method returns the first element of a sequence.*

If you have multiple rows to delete, you need to delete each row individually, like this:

```
//---find author ---
var authors = from a in database.authors
              where a.au_id == "111-11-1111" ||
                    a.au_id == "222-22-1111"
              select a;

foreach (author a in authors)
{
    database.authors.DeleteOnSubmit(a);
}
database.SubmitChanges();
```

So far the deletion works only if the author to be deleted has no related rows in the `titleauthors` and `titles` tables. If the author has associated rows in the `titleauthors` and `titles` tables, these examples cause an exception to be thrown because the deletions violate the referential integrity of the database (see Figure 14-21).

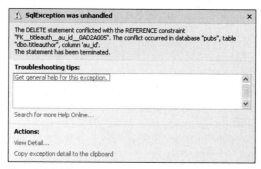

Figure 14-21

Because LINQ to SQL does not support cascade-delete operations, you need to make sure that rows in related tables are also deleted when you delete a row. The following code example shows how to delete a title from the `titles` and `titleauthors` tables:

```
DataClasses1DataContext database = new DataClasses1DataContext();
string titleid_to_remove = "BU5555";

//---find all associated row in Titles table---
var title = from t in database.titles
            where t.title_id == titleid_to_remove
            select t;

//---delete the row in the Titles table---
foreach (var t in title)
    database.titles.DeleteOnSubmit(t);

//---find all associated row in TitleAuthors table---
```

```
var titleauthor = from ta in database.titleauthors
                  where ta.title_id == titleid_to_remove
                  select ta;

//---delete the row in the TitleAuthors table---
foreach (var ta in titleauthor)
    database.titleauthors.DeleteOnSubmit(ta);

//---submit changes to database---
database.SubmitChanges();
```

Summary

This chapter, provides a quick introduction to the Language Integrated Query (LINQ) feature, which is new in .NET 3.5. It covered LINQ's four key implementations: LINQ to Objects, LINQ to XML, LINQ to Dataset, and LINQ to SQL. LINQ enables you to query various types of data sources, using a unified query language, making data access easy and efficient.

15

Assemblies and Versioning

In .NET, the basic unit deployable is called an assembly. Assemblies play an important part of the development process where understanding how they work is useful in helping you develop scalable, efficient .NET applications. This chapter explores:

- ❑ The components that make up a .NET assembly
- ❑ The difference between single-file and multi-file assemblies
- ❑ The relationships between namespaces and assemblies
- ❑ The role played by the Global Assembly Cache (GAC)
- ❑ How to develop a shared assembly, which can be shared by other applications

Assemblies

In .NET, an assembly takes the physical form of an EXE (known as a process assembly) or DLL (known as a library assembly) file, organized in the Portable Executable (PE) format. The PE format is a file format used by the Windows operating system for storing executables, object code, and DLLs. An assembly contains code in IL (Intermediate Language; compiled from a .NET language), which is then compiled into machine language at runtime by the Common Language Runtime (CLR) just-in-time compiler.

Structure of an Assembly

An assembly consists of the following four parts (see Figure 15-1).

Part	Description
Assembly metadata	Describes the assembly and its content
Type metadata	Defines all the types and methods exported from the assembly
IL code	Contains the MSIL code compiled by the compiler
Resources	Contains icons, images, text strings, as well as other resources used by your application

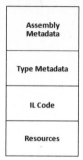

Figure 15-1

Physically, all four parts can reside in one physical file, or some parts of an assembly can be stored other *modules*. A module can contain type metadata and IL code, but it does not contain assembly metadata. Hence, a module cannot be deployed by itself; it must be combined with an assembly to be used. Figure 15-2 shows part of an assembly stored in two modules.

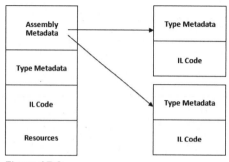

Figure 15-2

An assembly is the basic unit of installation. In this example, the assembly is made up of three files (one assembly and two modules). The two modules by themselves cannot be installed separately; they must accompany the assembly.

Examining the Content of an Assembly

As mentioned briefly in Chapter 1, you can use the MSIL Disassembler tool (`ildasm.exe`) to examine the content of an assembly. Figure 15-3 shows the tool displaying an assembly's content.

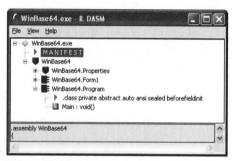

Figure 15-3

Among the various components in an assembly, the most important is the manifest (shown as MANIFEST in Figure 15-3), which is part of the assembly metadata. The manifest contains information such as the following:

❑ Name, version, public key, and culture of the assembly

❑ Files belonging to the assembly

❑ References assemblies (other assemblies referenced by this assembly)

❑ Permission sets

❑ Exported types

Figure 15-4 shows the content of the manifest of the assembly shown in Figure 15-3.

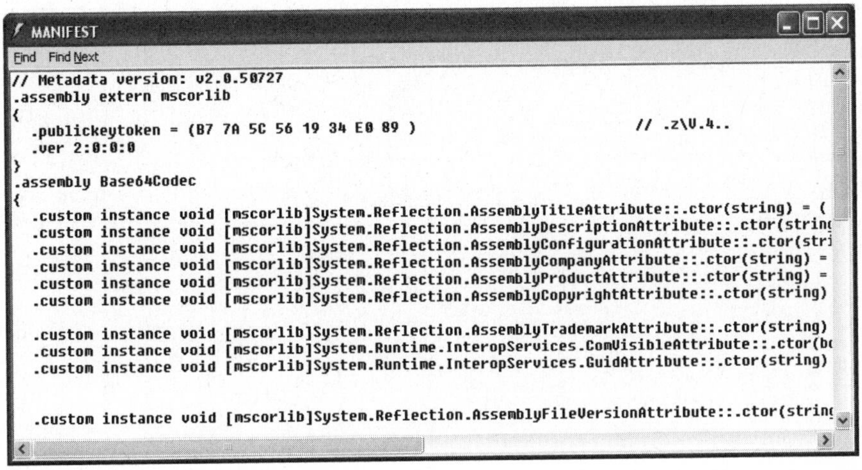

Figure 15-4

Single and Multi-File Assemblies

In Visual Studio, each project that you create will be compiled into an assembly (either EXE or DLL). By default, a single-file assembly is created. Imagine you are working on a large project with10 other programmers. Each one of you is tasked with developing part of the project. But how do you test the system as a whole? You could ask every programmer in the team to send you his or her code and then you could compile and test the system as a whole. However, that really isn't feasible, because you have to wait for everyone to submit his or her source code. A much better way is to get each programmer to build his or her part of the project as a standalone library (DLL). You can then get the latest version of each library and test the application as a whole. This approach has an added benefit — when a deployed application needs updating, you only need to update the particular library that needs updating. This is extremely useful if the project is large. In addition, organizing your project into multiple assemblies ensures that only the needed libraries (DLLs) are loaded during runtime.

To see the benefit of creating multi-file assemblies, let's create a new Class Library project, using Visual Studio 2008, and name it MathUtil. In the default Class1.cs, populate it with the following code:

```
using System;
using System.Collections.Generic;
using System.Linq;
using System.Text;

namespace MathUtil
{
    public class Utils
    {
        public int Fibonacci(int num)
        {
            if (num <= 1) return 2; //---should return 1; error on purpose---
            return Fibonacci(num - 1) + Fibonacci(num - 2);
        }
    }
}
```

This Utils class contains a method called Fibonacci(), which returns the nth number in the Fibonacci sequence (note that I have purposely injected an error into the code so that I can later show you how the application can be easily updated by replacing the DLL). Figure 15-5 shows the first 20 numbers in the correct Fibonacci sequence.

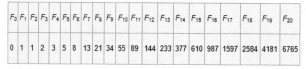

Figure 15-5

Build the Class Library project (right-click on the project's name in Solution Explorer, and select Build) so that it will compile into a DLL — MathUtil.dll.

Add a Windows Application project to the current solution, and name it WindowsApp-Util. This application will use the Fibonacci() method defined in MathUtil.dll. Because the MathUtil.dll assembly is created in the same solution as the Windows project, you can find it in the Projects tab of the Add Reference dialog (see Figure 15-6). Select the assembly, and click OK.

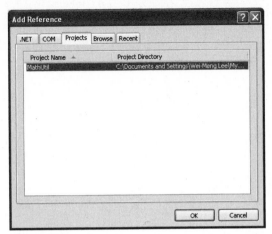

Figure 15-6

The `MathUtil.dll` assembly will now be added to the project. Observe that the `Copy Local` property for the `MathUtil.dll` assembly is set to `True` (see Figure 15-7). This means that a copy of the assembly will be placed in the project's output directory (that is, the bin\Debug folder).

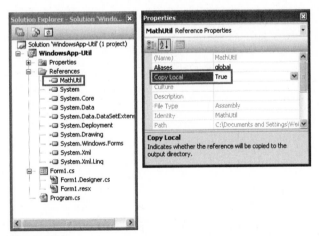

Figure 15-7

> When you add a reference to one of the classes in the .NET class library, the Copy Local property for the added assembly will be set to False. That's because the .NET assembly is in the Global Assembly Cache (GAC), and all computers with the .NET Framework installed have the GAC. The GAC is discussed later in this chapter.

Switch to the code-behind of the default `Form1` and code the following statements:

```csharp
namespace WindowsApp_Util
{
    public partial class Form1 : Form
    {
        public Form1()
        {
            InitializeComponent();
        }

        private void Form1_Load(object sender, EventArgs e)
        {
            CallUtil();
        }

        private void CallUtil()
        {
            MathUtil.Utils util = new MathUtil.Utils();
            MessageBox.Show(util.Fibonacci(7).ToString());
        }
    }
}
```

Set a breakpoint at the `CallMathUtil()` method (see Figure 15-8).

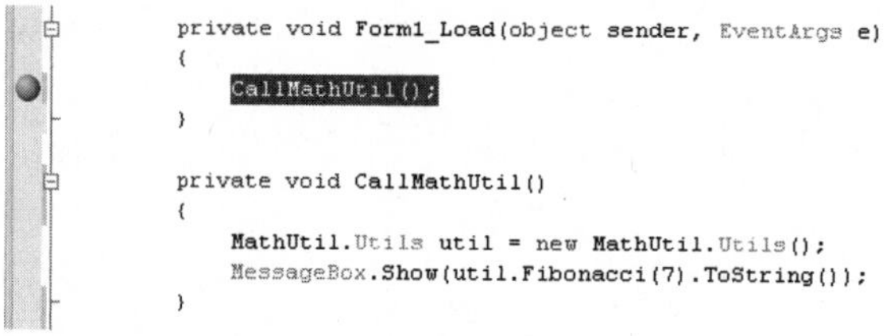

```csharp
private void Form1_Load(object sender, EventArgs e)
{
    CallMathUtil();
}

private void CallMathUtil()
{
    MathUtil.Utils util = new MathUtil.Utils();
    MessageBox.Show(util.Fibonacci(7).ToString());
}
```

Figure 15-8

Right-click on the `WindowsApp-Util` project name in Solution Explorer, and select Start as Startup Project. Press F5 to debug the application. When the application stops at the breakpoint, view the modules loaded into memory by selecting Debug ⇨ Windows ⇨ Modules (see Figure 15-9).

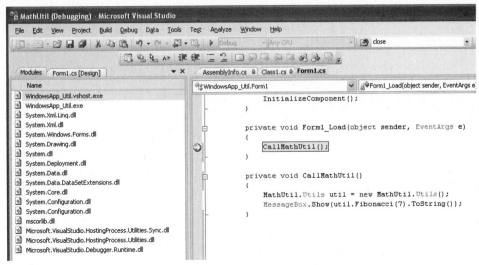

Figure 15-9

Observe that `MathUtil.dll` library has not been loaded yet. Press F11 to step into the `CallMathUtil()` function (see Figure 15-10). The `MathUtil.dll` library is now loaded into memory.

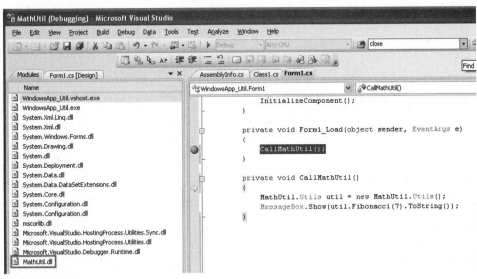

Figure 15-10

Press F5 to continue the execution. You should see a message box displaying the value 42. In the bin\ Debug folder of the Windows application project, you will find the EXE assembly as well as the DLL assembly (see Figure 15-11).

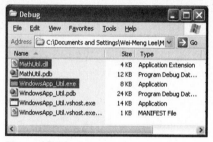

Figure 15-11

Updating the DLL

The `Fibonacci()` method defined in the `MathUtil` project contains a bug. When `num` is less than or equal to 1, the method should return 1 and not 2. In the real world, the application and the DLL may already been deployed to the end user's computer. To fix this bug, you simply need to modify the `Utils` class, recompile it, and then update the user's computer with the new DLL:

```csharp
namespace MathUtil
{
    public class Utils
    {
        public int Fibonacci(int num)
        {
            if (num <= 1) return 1; //---fixed!---
            return Fibonacci(num - 1) + Fibonacci(num - 2);
        }
    }
}
```

Copy the recompiled `MathUtil.dll` from the bin\Debug folder of the `MathUtil` project, and overwrite the original `MathUtil.dll` located in the bin\Debug folder of the Windows project. When the application runs again, it will display the correct value, 21 (previously it displayed 42).

> *Because the `MathUtil.dll` assembly is not digitally signed, a hacker could replace this assembly with one that contains malicious code, and the client of this assembly (which is the WindowsApp-Util application in this case) would not know that the assembly has been tampered with. Later in this chapter, you will see how to give the assembly a unique identity using a strong name.*

Modules and Assemblies

An application using a library loads it only when necessary — the entire library is loaded into memory during runtime. If the library is large, your application uses up more memory and takes a longer time to load. To solve this problem, you can split an assembly into multiple modules and then compile each individually as a module. The modules can then be compiled into an assembly.

To see how you can use a module instead of an assembly, add a new Class Library project to the solution used in the previous section. Name the Class Library project `StringUtil`. Populate the default `Class1` `.cs` file as follows:

```
using System.Text.RegularExpressions;
namespace StringUtil
{
    public class Utils
    {
        public bool ValidateEmail(string email)
        {
            string strRegEx = @"^([a-zA-Z0-9_\-\.]+)@((\[[0-9]{1,3}" +
                @"\.[0-9]{1,3}\.[0-9]{1,3}\.)|(([a-zA-Z0-9\-]+\" +
                @".)+))([a-zA-Z]{2,4}|[0-9]{1,3})(\]?)$";
            Regex regex = new Regex(strRegEx);
            if (regex.IsMatch(email))
                return (true);
            else
                return (false);
        }
    }
}
```

Instead of using Visual Studio 2008 to build the project into an assembly, use the C# compiler to manually compile it into a module.

To use the C# compiler, launch the Visual Studio 2008 Command Prompt (Start ⇨ Programs ⇨ Microsoft Visual Studio 2008 ⇨ Visual Studio Tools ⇨ Visual Studio 2008 Command Prompt).

Navigate to the folder containing the StringUtil project, and type in the following command to create a new module:

```
csc /target:module /out:StringUtil.netmodule Class1.cs
```

When the compilation is done, the StringUtil.netmodule file is created (see Figure 15-12).

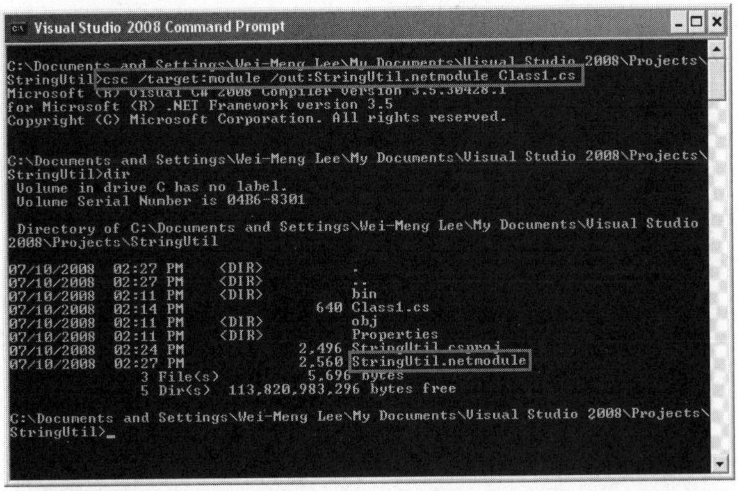

Figure 15-12

Do the same for the `MathUtil` class that you created earlier (see Figure 15-13):

```
csc /target:module /out:MathUtil.netmodule Class1.cs
```

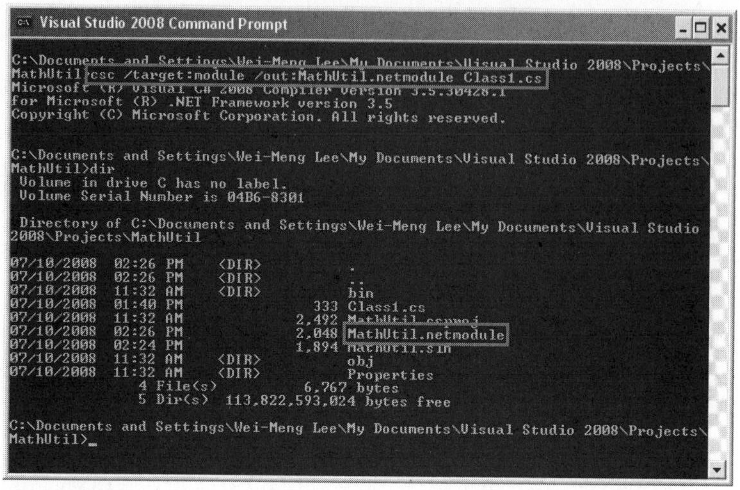

Figure 15-13

Copy the two modules that you have just created — `StringUtil.netmodule` and `MathUtil` `.netmodule` — into a folder, say C:\Modules\. Now to combine these two modules into an assembly, type the following command:

```
csc /target:library /addmodule:StringUtil.netmodule /addmodule:MathUtil.netmodule
/out:Utils.dll
```

This creates the `Utils.dll` assembly (see Figure 15-14).

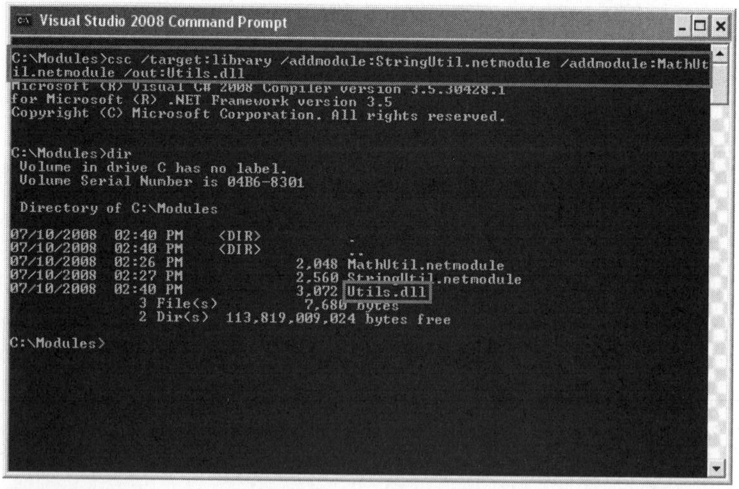

Figure 15-14

In the `WindowsApp-Utils` project, remove the previous versions of the `MathUtil.dll` assembly and add a reference to the `Utils.dll` assembly that you just created (see Figure 15-15). You can do so via the Browse tab of the Add Reference dialog (navigate to the directory containing the modules and assembly, C:\Modules). Click OK.

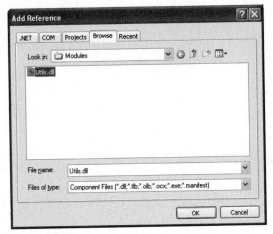

Figure 15-15

In the code-behind of `Form1`, modify the following code as shown:

```
namespace WindowsApp_Util
{
    public partial class Form1 : Form
    {
        public Form1()
        {
            InitializeComponent();
        }

        private void Form1_Load(object sender, EventArgs e)
        {
            CallMathUtil();
            CallStringUtil();
        }

        private void CallMathUtil()
        {
            MathUtil.Utils util = new MathUtil.Utils();
            MessageBox.Show(util.Fibonacci(7).ToString());
        }

        private void CallStringUtil()
        {
            StringUtil.Utils util = new StringUtil.Utils();
            MessageBox.Show(util.ValidateEmail(
                "weimenglee@learn2develop.net").ToString());
        }
    }
}
```

477

The `CallMathUtil()` function invokes the method defined in the `MathUtil` module. The `CallStringUtil()` function invokes the method defined in the `StringUtil` module.

Set a break point in the `Form1_Load` event handler, as shown in Figure 15-16, and press F5 to debug the application.

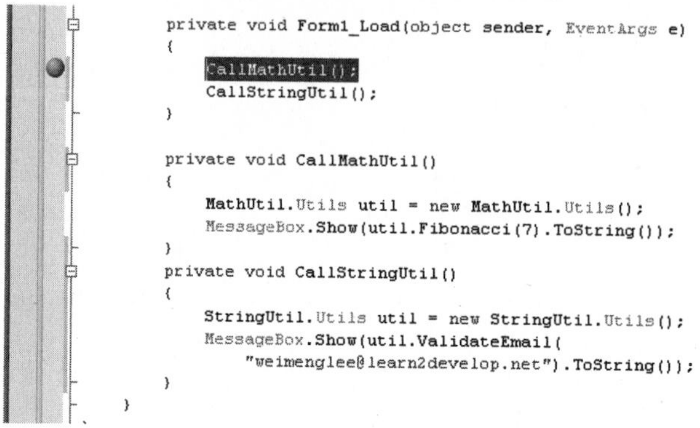

```
private void Form1_Load(object sender, EventArgs e)
{
    CallMathUtil();
    CallStringUtil();
}

private void CallMathUtil()
{
    MathUtil.Utils util = new MathUtil.Utils();
    MessageBox.Show(util.Fibonacci(7).ToString());
}
private void CallStringUtil()
{
    StringUtil.Utils util = new StringUtil.Utils();
    MessageBox.Show(util.ValidateEmail(
        "weimenglee@learn2develop.net").ToString());
}
```

Figure 15-16

When the breakpoint is reached, view the Modules window (Debug ⇨ Windows ⇨ Modules), and note that the `Utils.dll` assembly has not been loaded yet (see Figure 15-17).

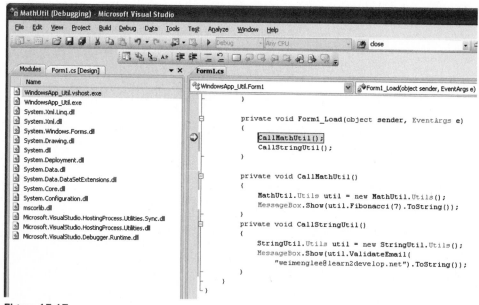

Figure 15-17

Press F11 to step into the `CallMathUtil()` function, and observe that the `Utils.dll` assembly is now loaded, together with the `MathUtil.netmodule` (see Figure 15-18).

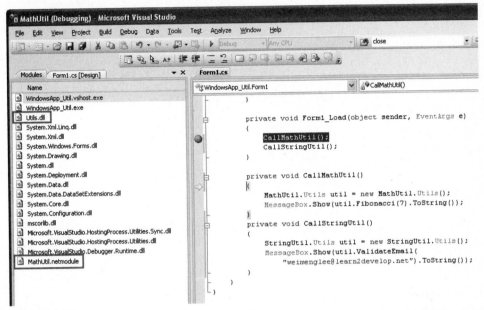

Figure 15-18

Press F11 a few times to step out of the `CallMathUtil()` function until you step into `CallStringUtil()`. See that the `StringUtil.netmodule` is now loaded (see Figure 15-19).

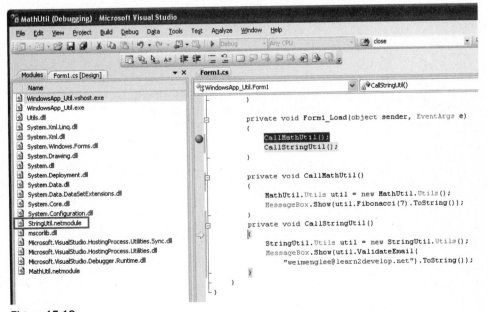

Figure 15-19

This example proves that modules in an assembly are loaded only as and when needed. Also, when deploying the application, the `Util.dll` assembly and the two modules must be in tandem. If any of the modules is missing during runtime, you will encounter a runtime error, as shown in Figure 15-20.

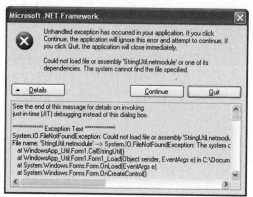

Figure 15-20

Understanding Namespaces and Assemblies

As you know from Chapter 1, the various class libraries in the .NET Framework are organized using namespaces. So how do namespaces relate to assemblies? To understand the relationship between namespaces and assemblies, it's best to take a look at an example.

Create a new Class Library project in Visual Studio 2008, and name it `ClassLibrary1`. In the default `Class1.cs`, populate it with the following:

```
using System;
using System.Collections.Generic;
using System.Linq;
using System.Text;

namespace Learn2develop.net
{
    public class Class1
    {
        public void DoSomething()
        {
        }
    }
}
```

Observe that the definition of Class1 is enclosed within the Learn2develop.net namespace. The class also contains the DoSomething() method.

Add a new class to the project by right-clicking on the project's name in Solution Explorer and selecting Add ⇨ Class (see Figure 15-21).

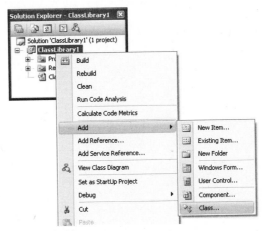

Figure 15-21

Use the default name of Class2.cs. In the newly added Class2.cs, code the following:

```
using System;
using System.Collections.Generic;
using System.Linq;
using System.Text;

namespace Learn2develop.net
{
    public class Class2
    {
        public void DoSomething()
        {
        }
    }
}
```

Class2 is enclosed within the same namespace — Learn2develop.net, and it also has a DoSomething() method. Compile the ClassLibrary1 project so that an assembly is generated in the bin\Debug folder of the project — ClassLibrary1.dll. Add another Class Library project to the current solution and name the project ClassLibrary2 (see Figure 15-22).

Figure 15-22

Populate the default Class1.cs as follows:

```
using System;
using System.Collections.Generic;
using System.Linq;
using System.Text;

namespace Learn2develop.net
{
    public class Class3
    {
        public void DoSomething()
        {
        }
    }
}

namespace CoolLabs.net
{
    public class Class5
    {
        public void DoSomething()
        {
        }
    }
}
```

This file contains two namespaces — Learn2develop.net and CoolLabs.net — each containing a class and a method.

Compile the ClassLibrary2 project so that an assembly is generated in the bin\Debug folder of the project — ClassLibrary2.dll.

Now, add another Class Library project to the current solution, and this time use the Visual Basic language. Name the project ClassLibrary3 (see Figure 15-23).

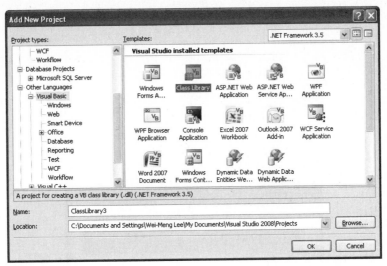

Figure 15-23

In the Properties page of the `ClassLibrary3` project, set its root namespace to `Learn2develop.net` (see Figure 15-24).

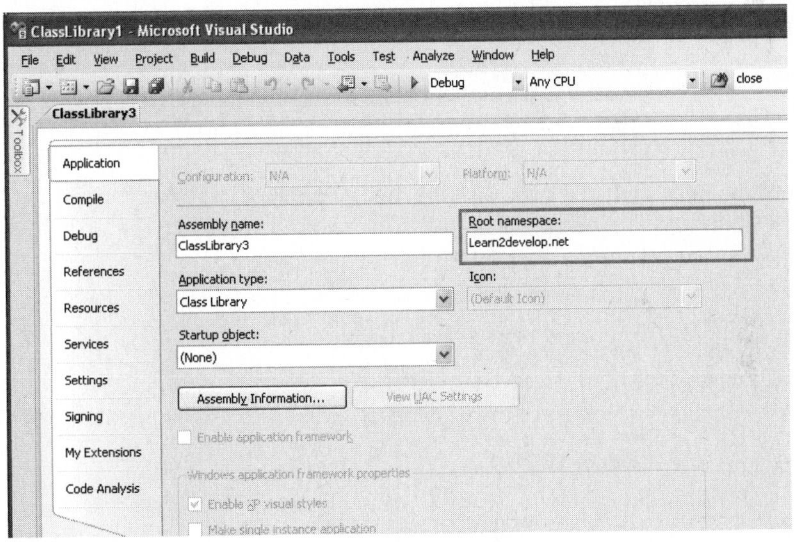

Figure 15-24

In the default `Class1.vb`, define `Class4` and add a method to it:

```
Public Class Class4
    Public Sub DoSomething()
    End Sub
End Class
```

483

Compile the ClassLibrary3 project so that an assembly is generated in the bin\Debug folder of the project — ClassLibrary3.dll.

Now add a new Windows application project (name it WindowsApp) to the current solution so that you can use the three assemblies (ClassLibrary1.dll, ClassLibrary2.dll, and ClassLibrary3.dll) that you have created.

To use the three assemblies, you need to add a reference to all of them. Because the assemblies are created in the same solution as the current Windows project, you can find them in the Projects tab of the Add Reference dialog (see Figure 15-25).

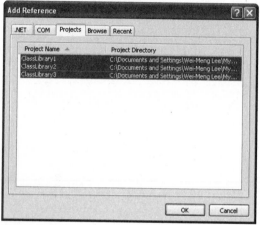

Figure 15-25

In the code-behind of the default Form1, type the Learn2develop.net namespace, and IntelliSense will show that four classes are available (see Figure 15-26).

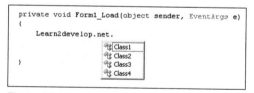

Figure 15-26

Even though the classes are located in different assemblies, IntelliSense still finds them because all these classes are grouped within the same namespace. You can now use the classes as follows:

```
Learn2develop.net.Class1 c1 = new Learn2develop.net.Class1();
c1.DoSomething();

Learn2develop.net.Class2 c2 = new Learn2develop.net.Class2();
c2.DoSomething();
```

```
Learn2develop.net.Class3 c3 = new Learn2develop.net.Class3();
c3.DoSomething();

Learn2develop.net.Class4 c4 = new Learn2develop.net.Class4();
c4.DoSomething();
```

For `Class5`, you need to use the `CoolLabs.net` namespace. If you don't, IntelliSense will check against all the referenced assemblies and suggest an appropriate namespace (see Figure 15-27).

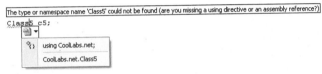

Figure 15-27

You can use `Class5` as follows:

```
CoolLabs.net.Class5 c5 = new CoolLabs.net.Class5();
c5.DoSomething();
```

Namespace Alias

There are times when you want to specify the fully qualified name of a class so that your code is easier to understand. For example, you usually import the namespace of a class and use the class like this:

```
using CoolLabs.net;
//...
    Class5 c5 = Class5();
    c5.DoSomething();
```

However, you might want to use the fully qualified name for `Class5` to make it clear that `Class5` belongs to the `CoolLabs.net` namespace. To do so, you can rewrite your code like this:

```
CoolLabs.net.Class5 c5 = new CoolLabs.net.Class5();
c5.DoSomething();
```

But the `CoolLabs.net` namespace is quite lengthy and may make your code look long and unwieldy. To simplify the coding, you can give an alias to the namespace, like this:

```
using cl = CoolLabs.net;
//...
    cl.Class5 c5 = cl.Class5();
    c5.DoSomething();
```

Then, instead of using the full namespace, you can simply refer to the `CoolLabs.net` namespace as `cl`.

To summarize, this example shows that:

❑ Classes belonging to a specific namespace can be located in different assemblies.

❑ An assembly can contain one or more namespaces.

❑ Assemblies created using different languages are transparent to each other.

Private versus Shared Assemblies

So far, all the assemblies you have seen and created are all private assemblies — that is, they are used specifically by your application and nothing else. As private assemblies, they are stored in the same folder as your executable and that makes deployment very easy — there is no risk that someone else has another assembly that overwrites yours particular and thus breaks your application.

DLL Hell

If you programmed prior to the .NET era, you've no doubt heard of (maybe even experienced) the phrase DLL Hell. Suppose that you have installed an application on your customer's computer and everything works fine until one day your customer calls and says that your application has suddenly stopped working. Upon probing, you realize that the customer has just downloaded and installed a new application from another vendor. Your application stopped working because one of the libraries (DLLs) that you have been using in your application has been overwritten by the application from the other vendor. And because your application could no longer find the particular DLL that it needs, it ceases to work.

.NET eliminates this nightmare by ensuring that each application has its own copy of the libraries it needs.

But assemblies can also be shared — that is, used by more than one application running on the computer. Shared assemblies are useful if they provide generic functionalities needed by most applications. To prevent DLL Hell, Microsoft has taken special care to make sure that shared assemblies are well protected. First, all shared assemblies are stored in a special location known as the Global Assembly Cache (GAC). Second, each shared assembly must have a strong name to uniquely identify itself so that no other assemblies have the same name.

A strong name comprises the following:

❑ Name of the assembly
❑ Version number
❑ Public key
❑ Culture

Understanding Cryptography

In the world of cryptography, there are two main types of encryption and encryption algorithms — symmetric and asymmetric.

Symmetric encryption is also sometimes known as private key encryption. With private key encryption, you encrypt a secret message using a key that only you know. To decrypt the message, you need to use the same key. Private key encryption is effective only if the key can be kept a secret. If too many people know the key, its effectiveness is reduced.

Imagine that you are trying to send a secret message to your faraway friend, Susan, using a private key. For Susan to decrypt the secret message, she must know the private key. So you need to send it to her. But if the secrecy of the key is compromised somehow (such as through people eavesdropping on your conversation), then the message is no longer secure. Moreover, if Susan tells another friend about the private key, her friend can then also decrypt the message. Despite the potential weakness of private key encryption, it is very easy to implement and, computationally, it does not take up too many resources.

Private key encryption requires that the key used in the encryption process be kept a secret. A more effective way to transport secret messages to your intended recipient is to use asymmetric encryption (also known as public key encryption). In public key encryption, there is a pair of keys involved. This pair, consisting of a private key and a public key, is related mathematically such that messages encrypted with the public key can only be decrypted with the corresponding private key. The contrary is true; messages encrypted with the private key can only be decrypted with the public key. Let's see an example for each scenario.

Before you send a message to Susan, Susan needs to generate the key pair containing the private key and the public key. Susan then freely distributes the public key to you (and all her other friends) but keeps the private key to herself. When you want to send a message to Susan, you use her public key to encrypt the message and then send it to her. Upon receiving the encrypted message, Susan proceeds to decrypt it with her private key. In this case, Susan is the only one who can decrypt the message because the key pair works in such a way that only messages encrypted with the public key can be decrypted with the private key. Also, there is no need to exchange secret keys, thus eliminating the risk of compromising the secrecy of the key.

The reverse can happen. Suppose Susan now sends a message encrypted with her private key to you. To decrypt the message, you need the public key. The scenario may seem redundant because the public key is not a secret; everyone knows it. But using this method guarantees that the message has not been tampered with and that it indeed comes from Susan. If the message had been modified, you would not be able to decrypt it. The fact that you can decrypt the message using the public key proves that the message has not been modified.

In computing, public key cryptography is a secure way to encrypt information. However, it is computationally expensive, because it is time-consuming to generate the key pairs and to perform encryption and decryption. It is usually used for encrypting a small amount of sensitive information.

To deploy an assembly as a shared assembly, you need to create a signature for your assembly by performing the following steps:

1. Generate a key pair containing a private key and a public key.

2. Write the public key to the manifest of the assembly.

3. Create a hash of all files belonging to the assembly.

4. Sign the hash with the private key (the private key is not stored within the assembly).

These steps guarantee that the assembly cannot be altered in any way, ensuring that the shared assembly you are using is the authentic copy provided by the vendor. The signature can be verified using the public key.

The following sections will show you how to perform each of these steps.

For the client application using the shared assembly, the compiler writes the public key of the shared assembly to the manifest of the client so that it can unique identify the shared assembly (only the last 8 bytes of a hash of a public key are stored; this is known as the public key token and is always unique). When an application loads the shared assembly, it uses the public key stored in the shared assembly to decrypt the encrypted hash and match it against the hash of the shared assembly to ensure that the shared assembly is authentic.

Creating a Shared Assembly

You'll better understand how to create a shared assembly by actually creating one. In this example, you create a library to perform Base64 encoding and decoding. Basically, Base64 encoding is a technique to encode binary data into a text-based representation so that it can be easily transported over networks and Web Services. A common usage of Base64 is in emails.

Using Visual Studio 2008, create a new Class Library project and name it `Base64Codec`. In the default `Class1.cs`, define the `Helper` class containing two methods — `Decode()` and `Encode()`:

```
using System;
using System.Collections.Generic;
using System.Linq;
using System.Text;

namespace Base64Codec
{
    public class Helper
    {
        public byte[] Decode(string base64string)
        {
            byte[] binaryData;
            try
            {
                binaryData =
                    Convert.FromBase64String(base64string);
                return binaryData;
            }
```

```
            catch (Exception)
            {
                return null;
            }
        }

        public string Encode(byte[] binaryData)
        {
            string base64String;
            try
            {
                base64String =
                    Convert.ToBase64String(
                    binaryData, 0, binaryData.Length);
                return base64String;
            }
            catch (Exception)
            {
                return string.Empty;
            }
        }
    }
}
```

Creating a Strong Name

To create a strong name for the assembly, you need to sign it. The easiest way is to use the Properties page of the project in Visual Studio 2008. Right-click on the project name in Solution Explorer, and select Properties. Select the Signing tab (see Figure 15-28), and check the Sign The Assembly checkbox. Select <New> from the Choose A Strong Name Key File dropdown list to specify a name for the strong name file.

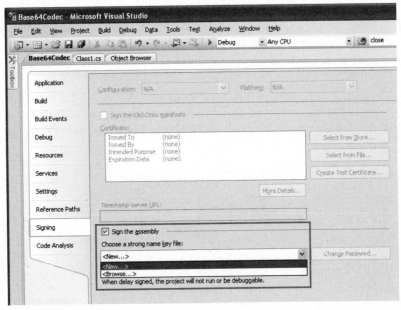

Figure 15-28

In the Create Strong Name Key dialog (see Figure 15-29), specify a name to store the pair of keys (`KeyFile.snk`, for instance). You also have the option to protect the file with a password. Click OK.

An SNK file is a binary file containing the pair of public and private keys.

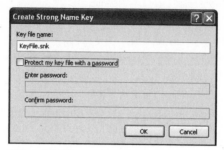

Figure 15-29

A strong name file is now created in your project (see Figure 15-30).

Figure 15-30

Alternatively, you can also use the command line to generate the strong name file:

```
sn -k KeyFile.snk
```

Versioning

With .NET, you can create different versions of the same assembly and share them with other applications. To specify version information, you can edit the `AssemblyInfo.cs` file, located under the Properties item in Solution Explorer (see Figure 15-31).

Figure 15-31

In the `AssemblyInfo.cs` file, locate the following lines:

```
...
// You can specify all the values or you can default the Build and Revision Numbers
// by using the '*' as shown below:
// [assembly: AssemblyVersion("1.0.*")]
[assembly: AssemblyVersion("1.0.0.0")]
[assembly: AssemblyFileVersion("1.0.0.0")]
```

The version number of an assembly is specified using the following format:

```
[Major Version, Minor Version, Build Number, Revision]
```

The `AssemblyVersion` attribute is used to identify the version number of an assembly. Applications that use this particular assembly reference this version number. If this version number is changed, applications using this assembly will not be able to find it and will break.

The `AssemblyFileVersion` attribute is used to specify the version number of the assembly, and it shows up in the properties page of the assembly (more on this in a later section).

Building the Assembly

Build the Class Library project so that Visual Studio 2008 will now generate the shared assembly and sign it with the strong name. To examine the shared assembly created, navigate to the bin\Debug folder of the project and type in the following command:

```
ildasm Base64Codec.dll
```

Figure 15-32 shows the public key stored in the manifest of the shared assembly.

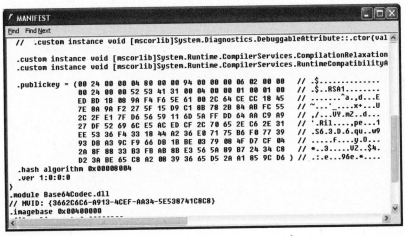

Figure 15-32

You can obtain the public key token of the shared assembly by using the following command:

```
sn -T Base64Codec.dll
```

Figure 15-33 shows the public key token displayed in the console window. Note this number because you will use it for comparison later.

Figure 15-33

The Global Assembly Cache

Now that you have created a shared assembly, the next task is to put it into the GAC. The GAC is a central repository of .NET assemblies that can be shared by all applications. There are several reasons why you should put your shared assembly into the GAC, some of which are:

❑ **Security** — Assemblies stored in the GAC are required to be signed with a cryptographic key. This makes it difficult for others to tamper with your assembly, such as replacing or injecting your shared assembly with malicious code.

❑ **Version management** — Multiple versions of the same assembly can reside in the GAC so that each application can find and use the version of your assembly to which it was compiled. This helps to avoid DLL Hell, where applications compiled to different versions of your assembly can potentially break because they are all forced to use a single version of your assembly.

❑ **Faster loading** — Assemblies are verified when they are first installed in the GAC, eliminating the need to verify an assembly each time it is loaded from the GAC. This improves the startup speed of your application if you load many shared assemblies.

The GAC is located in <windows_directory>\Assembly. In most cases, it is C:\Windows\Assembly. When you navigate to this folder by using Windows Explorer, the Assembly Cache Viewer launches to display the list of assemblies stored in it (see Figure 15-34).

Assembly Name	Version	Culture	Public Key Token	Proces...
System	2.0.0.0		b77a5c561934e089	MSIL
System.AddIn	3.5.0.0		b77a5c561934e089	MSIL
System.AddIn.Contract	2.0.0.0		b03f5f7f11d50a3a	MSIL
System.ComponentModel.DataAnnotations	3.5.0.0		31bf3856ad364e35	MSIL
System.Configuration	2.0.0.0		b03f5f7f11d50a3a	MSIL
System.Configuration.Install	2.0.0.0		b03f5f7f11d50a3a	MSIL
System.Core	3.5.0.0		b77a5c561934e089	MSIL
System.Data	2.0.0.0		b77a5c561934e089	x86
System.Data.DataSetExtensions	3.5.0.0		b77a5c561934e089	MSIL
System.Data.Entity	3.5.0.0		b77a5c561934e089	MSIL
System.Data.Entity.Design	3.5.0.0		b77a5c561934e089	MSIL
System.Data.Linq	3.5.0.0		b77a5c561934e089	MSIL
System.Data.OracleClient	2.0.0.0		b77a5c561934e089	x86
System.Data.Services	3.5.0.0		b77a5c561934e089	MSIL
System.Data.Services.Client	3.5.0.0		b77a5c561934e089	MSIL

Figure 15-34

Putting the Shared Assembly into GAC

To put the shared assembly that you have just built into the GAC, drag and drop it onto the Assembly Cache Viewer. Alternatively, you can also use the `gacutil.exe` utility to install the shared assembly into the GAC (see Figure 15-35):

```
gacutil /i Base64Codec.dll
```

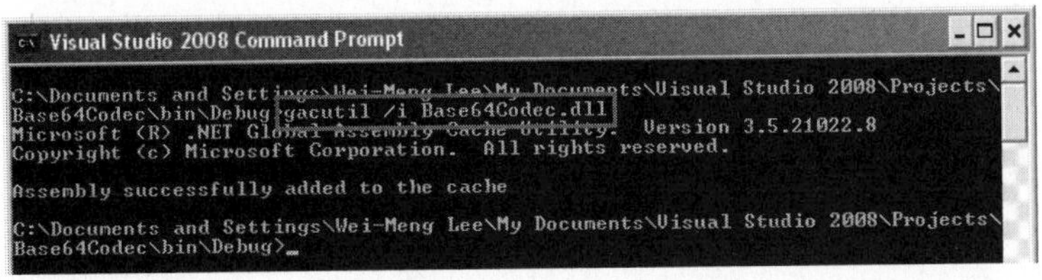

Figure 15-35

> If you are using Windows Vista, make sure to run the command prompt as Administrator.

If the installation is successful, you will see the shared assembly in the Assembly Cache Viewer (see Figure 15-36).

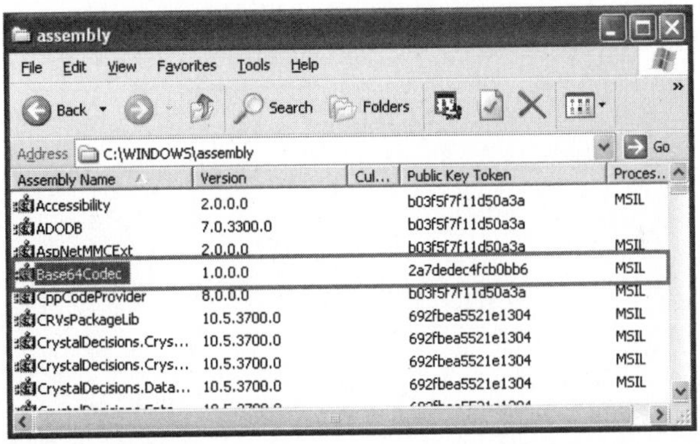

Figure 15-36

The version number displayed next to the DLL is specified by using the `AssemblyVersion` attribute in the `AssemblyInfo.cs` file (as discussed earlier). Select the Base64Codec DLL, and click the Properties button (the button with the tick icon) to see the Properties page as shown in Figure 15-37.

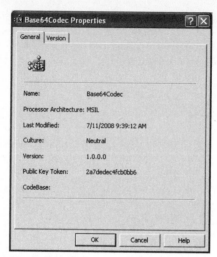

Figure 15-37

The version number displayed in this page is specified using the `AssemblyFileVersion` attribute.

To install different versions of the same assembly to the GAC, simply modify the version number in `AssemblyInfo.cs` *(via the* `AssemblyVersion` *attribute), recompile the assembly, and install it into the GAC.*

Physically, the shared assembly is copied to a folder located under the `GAC_MSIL` subfolder of the GAC, in the following format:

```
<Windows_Directory>\assembly\GAC_MSIL\<Assembly_Name>\<Version>_<Public_Key_Token>
```

In this example, it is located in:

```
C:\Windows\assembly\GAC_MSIL\Base64Codec\1.0.0.0_2a7dec4fb0bb6
```

Figure 15-38 shows the physical location of the `Base64Codec.dll` assembly.

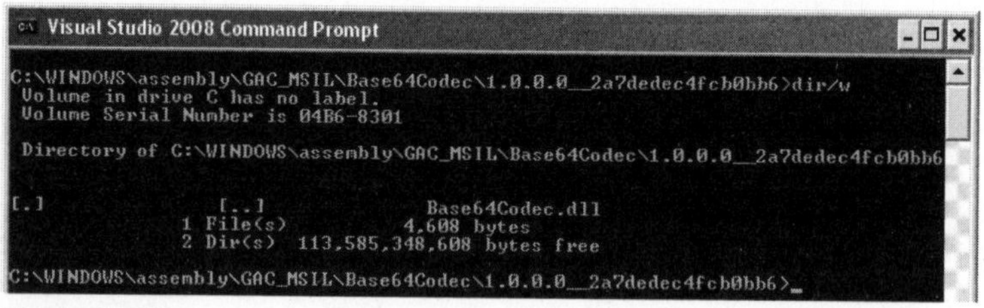

```
Visual Studio 2008 Command Prompt                                        _□×
C:\WINDOWS\assembly\GAC_MSIL\Base64Codec\1.0.0.0__2a7dedec4fcb0bb6>dir/w
Volume in drive C has no label.
Volume Serial Number is 04B6-8301

Directory of C:\WINDOWS\assembly\GAC_MSIL\Base64Codec\1.0.0.0__2a7dedec4fcb0bb6

[.]             [..]            Base64Codec.dll
         1 File(s)          4,608 bytes
         2 Dir(s)  113,585,348,608 bytes free

C:\WINDOWS\assembly\GAC_MSIL\Base64Codec\1.0.0.0__2a7dedec4fcb0bb6>_
```

Figure 15-38

Making the Shared Assembly Visible in Visual Studio

By default, adding a shared assembly into the GAC does not make it appear automatically in Visual Studio's Add Reference dialog. You need to add a registry key for that to happen. Here's how to handle that.

First, launch the registry editor by typing `regedit` in the Run command box.

> **If you are using Windows Vista, make sure to run regedit as Administrator.**

Navigate to the `HKEY_LOCAL_MACHINE\SOFTWARE\Microsoft\.NETFramework\AssemblyFolders` key. Right-click on the AssemblyFolders key and select New ⇨ Key (see Figure 15-39).

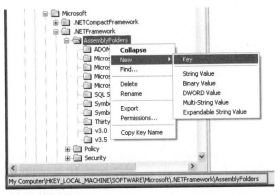

Figure 15-39

Name the new key `Base64Codec`. Double-click on the key's (`Default`) value, and enter the full path of the shared assembly (for example, `C:\Documents and Settings\Wei-Meng Lee\My Documents\Visual Studio 2008\Projects\Base64Codec\bin\Debug`; see Figure 15-40).

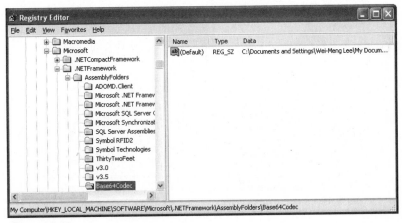

Figure 15-40

Then restart Visual Studio 2008, and the assembly should appear in the Add Reference dialog.

Using the Shared Assembly

Let's now create a new Windows application project to use the shared assembly stored in the GAC. Name the project `WinBase64`.

To use the shared assembly, add a reference to the DLL. In the Add Reference dialog, select the `Base64Codec` assembly, as shown in Figure 15-41, and click OK.

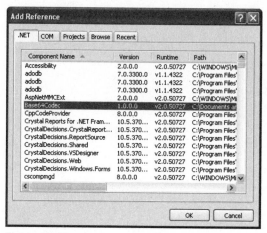

Figure 15-41

Note in the Properties window that the Copy Local property of the `Base64Codec` is set to `False` (see Figure 15-42), indicating that the assembly is in the GAC.

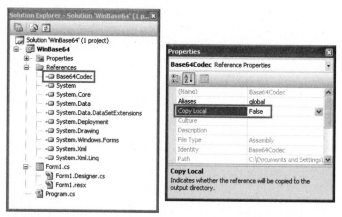

Figure 15-42

Populate the default `Form1` with the controls shown in Figure 15-43 (load the `pictureBox1` with a JPG image).

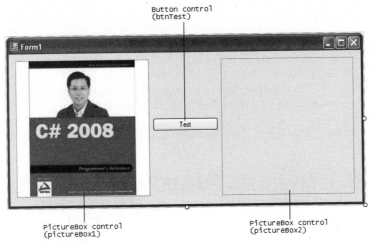

Figure 15-43

In the code-behind of `Form1`, define the two helper functions as follows:

Remember to import the `System.IO` namespace for these two helper functions.

```csharp
public byte[] ImageToByteArray(Image img)
{
    MemoryStream ms = new MemoryStream();
    img.Save(ms, System.Drawing.Imaging.ImageFormat.Jpeg);
    return ms.ToArray();
}

public Image ByteArrayToImage(byte[] data)
{
    MemoryStream ms = new MemoryStream(data);
    Image img = new Bitmap(ms);
    return img;
}
```

Code the Test button as follows:

```csharp
private void btnTest_Click(object sender, EventArgs e)
{
    //---create an instance of the Helper class---
    Base64Codec.Helper codec = new Base64Codec.Helper();

    //---convert the image in pictureBox1 to base64---
```

(continued)

(continued)

```
        string base64string =
            codec.Encode(ImageToByteArray(pictureBox1.Image));

        //---decode the base64 to binary and display in pictureBox2---
        pictureBox2.Image = ByteArrayToImage(codec.Decode(base64string));
    }
```

Here you are creating an instance of the `Helper` class defined in the shared assembly. To test that the methods defined in the `Helper` class are working correctly, encode the image displayed in `pictureBox1` to base64, decode it back to binary, and then display the image in `pictureBox2`.

Press F5 to test the application. When you click the Test button, an identical image should appear on the right (see Figure 15-44).

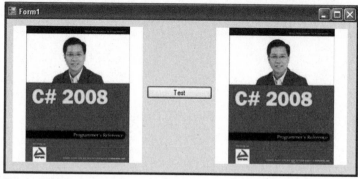

Figure 15-44

Examine the manifest of the `WinBase64.exe` assembly to see the reference to the Base64Codec assembly (see Figure 15-45). Observe the public key token stored in the manifest — it is the public key token of the shared assembly.

```
/ MANIFEST
Find   Find Next
{
  .publickeytoken = (B7 7A 5C 56 19 34 E0 89 )                        // .z
  .ver 2:0:0:0
}
.assembly extern System.Drawing
{
  .publickeytoken = (B0 3F 5F 7F 11 D5 0A 3A )                        // .?
  .ver 2:0:0:0
}
.assembly extern Base64Codec
{
  .publickeytoken = (2A 7D ED EC 4F CB 0B B6 )                        // *}
  .ver 1:0:0:0
}
.assembly WinBase64
{
  .custom instance void [mscorlib]System.Reflection.AssemblyConfigurationAtt
  .custom instance void [mscorlib]System.Reflection.AssemblyCompanyAttribute
  .custom instance void [mscorlib]System.Runtime.CompilerServices.RuntimeCom

  .custom instance void [mscorlib]System.Reflection.AssemblyTrademarkAttribu
  .custom instance void [mscorlib]System.Runtime.CompilerServices.Compilatio
```

Figure 15-45

Summary

This chapter explained the parts that make up a .NET assembly. Splitting your application into multiple assemblies and modules will make your application easier to manage and update. At the same time, the CLR will only load the required assembly and modules, thereby making your application more efficient. If you have a shared assembly that can be used by other applications, consider deploying it into the Global Assembly Cache (GAC).

Part II
Application Development Using C#

16

Developing Windows Applications

Chapters 16–19 show how you can use the C# language to create a different type of application. This chapter tackles Windows application development. The best way to learn a language is to actually work on a real project from the beginning to deployment. So, this chapter leads you through creating a Windows application that performs some useful tasks and then shows you how to deploy it using a technique in Visual Studio known as ClickOnce.

Specifically, the Windows application you build in this chapter demonstrates how to:

❑   Programmatically access FTP servers using the `FtpWebRequest` and `FtpWebResponse` classes (both derived from the `WebRequest` and `WebResponse` classes in the `System.Net` namespace)

❑   Incorporate printing capability in your Windows application using the `PrintDocument` class (located in the `System.Drawing.Printing` namespace)

❑   Deploy a Windows application using ClickOnce. You will also see how to programmatically cause an application to update itself.

The Project

The project in this chapter is a photo viewer Windows application that accesses an FTP server. Using this application, users can upload photos to an FTP server and also download and view images stored on the FTP server. The application is useful for companies that may need to access images uploaded by their partners. Insurance companies, for instance, may need to access photographs of car damage taken by auto body shop mechanics to facilitate estimating the cost of repair. Rather than build a complex web application, the shops and insurance companies can simply use this application to quickly upload and view photos. Users can also print the photos directly from the application.

Figure 16-1 shows how the application will look like when it is completed.

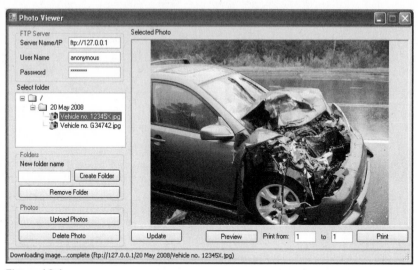

Figure 16-1

Configuring the FTP Server

Before you start writing the code of this application, you first need to configure FTP service for your computer. For this project, use the FTP service on your development machine.

> By default, FTP service is not installed in Windows (note that FTP service is not available on Windows Vista Home editions). To add FTP Service to your computer, select Control Panel ⇨ Add or Remove Programs. Click the Add/Remove Windows Component tab, select Internet Information Services (IIS), and click the Details button. Select File Transfer Protocol (FTP) Service, and click OK.

To configure the FTP service on your computer, launch the Internet Information Services management console window by typing the command −inetmgr in the Run window. Your FTP site should look like Figure 16-2.

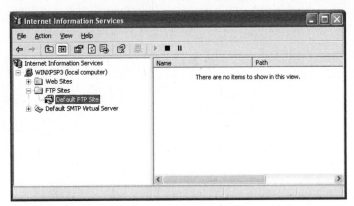

Figure 16-2

Right-click the Default FTP Site item, and select Properties. Click the Security Accounts tab. Ensure that the Allow Anonymous Connections checkbox is checked (see Figure 16-3) to enable an anonymous user to log in to your FTP service.

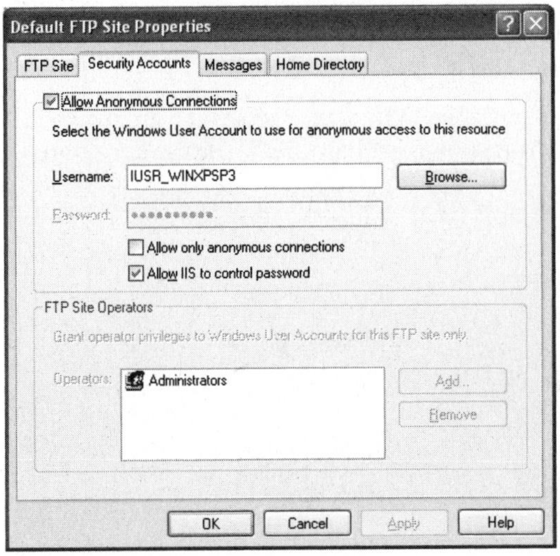

Figure 16-3

Next, click on the Home Directory tab, and check the Write checkbox (see Figure 16-4). This allows users to your FTP service to upload files and create directories on the FTP server.

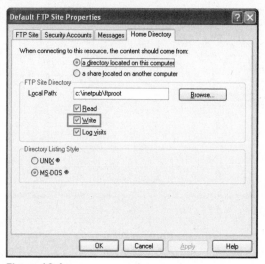

Figure 16-4

Click OK to finish the configuration of the FTP service.

Creating the Application

Using Visual Studio 2008, create a new Windows application and name it `PhotoViewer`. Populate the default `Form1` with the controls shown in Figure 16-5. These controls are:

Control	Text	Name
Button controls (4)	Create Folder	btnCreateFolder
	Remove Folder	btnRemoveFolder
	Upload Photos	btnUploadPhotos
	Delete Photo	btnDeletePhoto
GroupBox controls (3)	FTP Server	
	Folders	
	Photos	
Label controls (6)	Server Name/IP	
	User Name	
	Password	
	Select folder	
	New folder name	
	Selected Photo	

Control	Text	Name
PictureBox		PictureBox1
TextBox controls (4)		txtFTPServer
		txtUserName
		txtPassword
		txtNewFolderName
ToolStripStatusLabel	ToolStripStatusLabel1	ToolStripStatusLabel1
TreeView		TreeView1

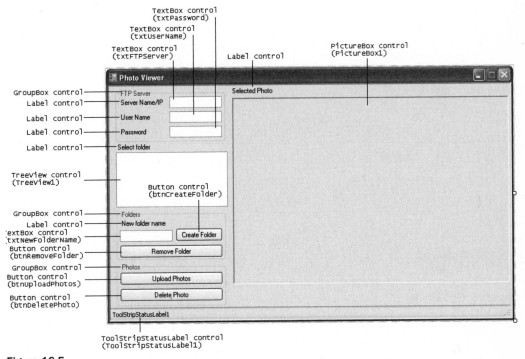

Figure 16-5

The source code for this project can be downloaded from Wrox's web site at www.wrox.com.

You'll also need to add an ImageList control (ImageList1) to Form1 to contain three images representing an opened folder, a closed folder, and an image file. You can specify these images in the control's Image property (see Figure 16-6).

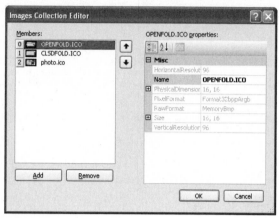

Figure 16-6

Set the control properties in the following table.

Control	Property	Value
TreeView1	ImageList	ImageList1
PictureBox1	SizeMode	Zoom
txtPassword	PasswordChar	"*"

Using Application Settings

When users launch the PhotoViewer application, they need to supply three pieces of information to access the FTP Server:

❑ FTP Server name/IP address

❑ Username

❑ Password

Because this information is needed every time the user uses the application, it would be helpful to save it somewhere persistently so that the next time the user launches the application, it's available without his needing to type it in again.

In Windows Forms, a feature known as *application settings* allows you to store information persistently in a structured manner without resorting to using a database or forcing you to manually save it to a file. So let's see how application settings can help you in this instance.

Right-click on the `PhotoViewer` project in Solution Explorer and select Properties. In the Properties page, click on the Settings tab and enter the three application settings in the following table (see Figure 16-7).

Name	Type	Scope	Value
FTP_SERVER	string	User	ftp://127.0.0.1
UserName	string	User	anonymous
Password	string	User	password

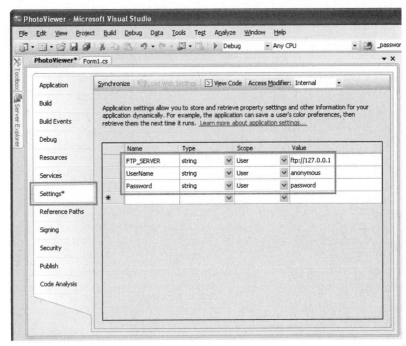

Figure 16-7

As their names suggest, `FTP_Server` stores the name or IP address of the FTP server, `UserName` stores the username used to log in to the FTP server, and `Password` stores the password used to log in to the FTP server.

Notice the following:

❑ The type of each application setting is `string`. You can also specify other .NET types for each application setting.

❑ The scope for each application setting is User. Application settings can be either user-scoped or application-scoped. Application-scoped settings are not discussed because they are beyond the scope of this book.

❑ The default value for each application setting is also specified here.

Save the solution in Visual Studio 2008 so that the application settings can be saved.

Let's examine the project a little closer to see how the application settings work. Figure 16-8 shows the three files in Solution Explorer that are used to maintain your application settings (you need to click the Show All Files button in Solution Explorer to view all these files).

Figure 16-8

The `Settings.settings` file refers to the Settings page that you have been using to add the application settings. The `Settings.Designer.cs` file is a compiler-generated file that contains the data types of the various settings that you have defined. Here are the definitions for the various application settings:

```
namespace PhotoViewer.Properties
{
    [global::System.Runtime.CompilerServices.CompilerGeneratedAttribute()]
    [global::System.CodeDom.Compiler.GeneratedCodeAttribute(
        "Microsoft.VisualStudio.Editors.SettingsDesigner
.SettingsSingleFileGenerator", "9.0.0.0")]
    internal sealed partial class Settings :
        global::System.Configuration.ApplicationSettingsBase
    {

        private static Settings defaultInstance =
            ((Settings)(global::System.Configuration
            .ApplicationSettingsBase.Synchronized(new Settings())));

        public static Settings Default
        {
```

```
        get
        {
            return defaultInstance;
        }
    }

    [global::System.Configuration.UserScopedSettingAttribute()]
    [global::System.Diagnostics.DebuggerNonUserCodeAttribute()]
    [global::System.Configuration.DefaultSettingValueAttribute(
        "ftp://127.0.0.1")]
    public string FTP_SERVER
    {
        get
        {
            return ((string)(this["FTP_SERVER"]));
        }
        set
        {
            this["FTP_SERVER"] = value;
        }
    }

    [global::System.Configuration.UserScopedSettingAttribute()]
    [global::System.Diagnostics.DebuggerNonUserCodeAttribute()]
    [global::System.Configuration.DefaultSettingValueAttribute("anonymous")]
    public string UserName
    {
        get
        {
            return ((string)(this["UserName"]));
        }
        set
        {
            this["UserName"] = value;
        }
    }

    [global::System.Configuration.UserScopedSettingAttribute()]
    [global::System.Diagnostics.DebuggerNonUserCodeAttribute()]
    [global::System.Configuration.DefaultSettingValueAttribute("password")]
    public string Password
    {
        get
        {
            return ((string)(this["Password"]));
        }
        set
        {
            this["Password"] = value;
        }
    }
}
}
```

The `app.config` file is an XML File containing the default values of your application settings. Its content is:

```xml
<?xml version="1.0" encoding="utf-8" ?>
<configuration>
    <configSections>
        <sectionGroup name="userSettings" type="System.Configuration.UserSettingsGroup,
System, Version=2.0.0.0, Culture=neutral, PublicKeyToken=b77a5c561934e089" >
            <section name="PhotoViewer.Properties.Settings"
type="System.Configuration.ClientSettingsSection, System, Version=2.0.0.0,
Culture=neutral, PublicKeyToken=b77a5c561934e089" allowExeDefinition="MachineToLocalUser"
requirePermission="false" />
        </sectionGroup>
    </configSections>
    <userSettings>
        <PhotoViewer.Properties.Settings>
            <setting name="FTP_SERVER" serializeAs="String">
                <value>ftp://127.0.0.1</value>
            </setting>
            <setting name="UserName" serializeAs="String">
                <value>anonymous</value>
            </setting>
            <setting name="Password" serializeAs="String">
                <value>password</value>
            </setting>
        </PhotoViewer.Properties.Settings>
    </userSettings>
</configuration>
```

The highlighted code shows the settings that you added earlier and their default values. When the project is compiled, this `app.config` file will be named `<assembly_name>.exe.config` and stored in the bin\Debug (or bin\Release) folder of the project. For this project, the filename will be `PhotoViewer.exe.config`.

During runtime, any changes made to the application settings' values will cause a `user.config` file to be created in the following folder:

```
C:\Documents and Settings\<user_name>\Local Settings\Application Data\<application_
name>\<application_name>.vshost.exe_Url_iwwpinbgs0makur33st4vnin2nkwxgq1\
<version_no>\
```

Notice the long string of random characters in the path. The folder name is generated by the system, and each time you have a different folder name.

For this project, the `user.config` file will be stored in a folder with a name like this:

```
C:\Documents and Settings\Wei-Meng Lee\Local Settings\Application Data\PhotoViewer\
PhotoViewer.vshost.exe_Url_iwwpinbgs0makur33st4vnin2nkwxgq1\1.0.0.0
```

The content of the user.config file looks like this:

```xml
<?xml version="1.0" encoding="utf-8"?>
<configuration>
    <userSettings>
        <PhotoViewer.Properties.Settings>
            <setting name="FTP_SERVER" serializeAs="String">
                <value>ftp://127.0.0.1</value>
            </setting>
            <setting name="UserName" serializeAs="String">
                <value>anonymous1</value>
            </setting>
            <setting name="Password" serializeAs="String">
                <value>password</value>
            </setting>
        </PhotoViewer.Properties.Settings>
    </userSettings>
</configuration>
```

Each user (of your computer) will maintain his own copy of the user.config file.

Coding the Application

Now to code the application. Switching to the code-behind of Form1, import the following namespaces:

```csharp
using System.Net;
using System.IO;
```

Define the WebRequestMethod enumeration:

```csharp
namespace PhotoViewer
{
    enum WebRequestMethod
    {
        MakeDirectory,
        DownloadFile,
        ListDirectoryDetails,
        RemoveDirectory,
        DeleteFile
    }
```

Declare the following constants and member variables:

```csharp
public partial class Form1 : Form
{
    //---constants for the icon images---
    const int ico_OPEN = 0;
    const int ico_CLOSE = 1;
    const int ico_PHOTO = 2;
```

In Form1, select the three TextBox controls (you can Ctrl+click each of them) that ask for the FTP server name, user name, and password (see Figure 16-9). In the Properties window, double-click the Leave property to generate an event handler stub for the Leave event.

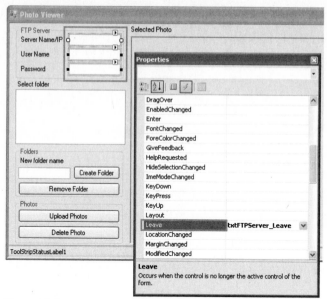

Figure 16-9

Visual Studio 2008 then generates the `txtFtpServer_Leave` event handler:

```
private void txtFTPServer_Leave(object sender, EventArgs e)
{

}
```

The event handler is invoked whenever the focus leaves one of the three `TextBox` controls you have selected. This is where you can save the information entered by the user into the application settings you have created in the previous section.

Code the event handler as follows:

```
private void txtFTPServer_Leave(object sender, EventArgs e)
{
    //---save the values in the textbox controls
    // into the application settings---
    Properties.Settings.Default.FTP_SERVER = txtFTPServer.Text;
    Properties.Settings.Default.UserName = txtUserName.Text;
    Properties.Settings.Default.Password = txtPassword.Text;
    Properties.Settings.Default.Save();
}
```

You access the various application settings using the `Properties.Settings.Default` class (as generated in the `Settings.Designer.cs` file). Once the application settings are assigned a value, you need to persist them using the `Save()` method.

Building the Directory Tree and Displaying Images

When the form is loaded, you first load the values of the application settings into the `TextBox` controls, and then display a node representing the root directory of the FTP server in the `TreeView` control:

```
private void Form1_Load(object sender, EventArgs e)
{
    try
    {
        //---load the application settings values
        // into the textbox controls---
        txtFTPServer.Text = Properties.Settings.Default.FTP_SERVER;
        txtUserName.Text = Properties.Settings.Default.UserName;
        txtPassword.Text = Properties.Settings.Default.Password;

        //---create the root node for the TreeView---
        TreeNode node = new TreeNode();
        node.ImageIndex = ico_CLOSE;
        node.SelectedImageIndex = ico_OPEN;
        node.Text = @"/";

        //---add the root node to the control---
        TreeView1.Nodes.Add(node);

        //---add the dummy child node to the root node---
        node.Nodes.Add("");

        //---select the root node---
        TreeView1.SelectedNode = node;
    }
    catch (Exception ex)
    {
        MessageBox.Show(ex.ToString());
    }
}
```

You will always add a dummy node in the `TreeView` control after a node is created to ensure that the current node can be expanded to reveal subdirectories (even if there are none). This is shown in Figure 16-10.

Figure 16-10

When a node is expanded (by clicking on the + symbol), the `TreeView1_BeforeExpand` event is fired. You have to write code that checks to see if the current node is a leaf node (meaning that it is not a directory but a file). If it is a leaf node, exit the method. Otherwise, you need to display its subdirectories (if any).

You should also change the current node icon to "open" if the node is selected and "closed" if the node is not selected. Here's the code for expanding folders and displaying the proper icon at each node:

```csharp
private void TreeView1_BeforeExpand(
    object sender, TreeViewCancelEventArgs e)
{
    //---if leaf node (photo) then exit---
    if (e.Node.ImageIndex == ico_PHOTO) return;

    //---remove the dummy node and display the subdirectories and files---
    try
    {
        //---clears all the nodes and...---
        e.Node.Nodes.Clear();

        //---create the nodes again---
        BuildDirectory(e.Node);
    }
    catch (Exception ex)
    {
        ToolStripStatusLabel1.Text = ex.ToString();
    }

    //---change the icon for this node to open---
    if (e.Node.GetNodeCount(false) > 0)
    {
        e.Node.ImageIndex = ico_CLOSE;
        e.Node.SelectedImageIndex = ico_OPEN;
    }
}
```

The `BuildDirectory()` function displays all the files and subdirectories within the current directory in the `TreeView` control. Before you look at the definition of the `BuildDirectory()` function, you define the `GetDirectoryListing()` function, whose main job is to request from the FTP server the directory listing of a specified path:

```csharp
//---Get the file/dir listings and return them as a string array---
private string[] GetDirectoryListing(string path)
{
    try
    {
        //---get the directory listing---
        FtpWebResponse FTPResp = PerformWebRequest(
            path, WebRequestMethod.ListDirectoryDetails);

        //---get the stream containing the directory listing---
        Stream ftpRespStream = FTPResp.GetResponseStream();
        StreamReader reader =
```

```
                    new StreamReader(ftpRespStream, System.Text.Encoding.UTF8);

            //---obtain the result as a string array---
            string[] result = reader.ReadToEnd().Split(
                Environment.NewLine.ToCharArray(),
                StringSplitOptions.RemoveEmptyEntries);
            FTPResp.Close();
            return result;
        }
        catch (Exception ex)
        {
            MessageBox.Show(ex.ToString());
            return null;
        }
    }
```

To view the directory listing of an FTP server, you make use of the `PerformWebRequest()` helper function, which is defined as follows:

```
private FtpWebResponse PerformWebRequest(
    string path, WebRequestMethod method)
{
    //---display the hour glass cursor---
    Cursor.Current = Cursors.WaitCursor;

    FtpWebRequest ftpReq = (FtpWebRequest)WebRequest.Create(path);
    switch (method)
    {
        case WebRequestMethod.DeleteFile:
            ftpReq.Method = WebRequestMethods.Ftp.DeleteFile;
            break;
        case WebRequestMethod.DownloadFile:
            ftpReq.Method = WebRequestMethods.Ftp.DownloadFile;
            break;
        case WebRequestMethod.ListDirectoryDetails:
            ftpReq.Method = WebRequestMethods.Ftp.ListDirectoryDetails;
            break;
        case WebRequestMethod.MakeDirectory:
            ftpReq.Method = WebRequestMethods.Ftp.MakeDirectory;
            break;
        case WebRequestMethod.RemoveDirectory:
            ftpReq.Method = WebRequestMethods.Ftp.RemoveDirectory;
            break;
    }
    ftpReq.Credentials = new NetworkCredential(
        Properties.Settings.Default.UserName,
        Properties.Settings.Default.Password);

    FtpWebResponse ftpResp = (FtpWebResponse)ftpReq.GetResponse();

    //---change back the cursor---
    Cursor.Current = Cursors.Default;
    return ftpResp;
}
```

The `PerformWebRequest()` function contains two parameters:

- ❏ A path representing the full FTP path
- ❏ A `WebRequestMethod` enumeration representing the type of request you are performing

In the `PerformWebRequest()` function, you perform the following:

- ❏ Create an instance of the `FtpWebRequest` class, using the `WebRequest` class's `Create()` method. `Create()` takes in a URI parameter (containing the full FTP path).
- ❏ Set the command to be sent to the FTP server, using the `Method` property of the `FtpWebRequest` object.
- ❏ Specify the login credential to the FTP server, using the `NetWorkCredential` class.
- ❏ Obtain the response from the FTP server, using the `GetResponse()` method from the `FtpWebRequest` class.

The `PerformWebRequest()` function returns a `FtpWebResponse` object.

Back in the `GetDirectoryListing()` function, after the call to `PerformWebRequest()` returns, you retrieve the stream containing the response data sent by the FTP server, using the `GetResponseStream()` method from the `FtpWebResponse` class. You then use a `StreamReader` object to read the directory listing:

```
//---Get the file/dir listings and return them as a string array---
private string[] GetDirectoryListing(string path)
{
    try
    {
        //---get the directory listing---
        FtpWebResponse FTPResp = PerformWebRequest(
            path, WebRequestMethod.ListDirectoryDetails);

        //---get the stream containing the directory listing---
        Stream ftpRespStream = FTPResp.GetResponseStream();
        StreamReader reader =
            new StreamReader(ftpRespStream, System.Text.Encoding.UTF8);

        //---obtain the result as a string array---
        string[] result = reader.ReadToEnd().Split(
            Environment.NewLine.ToCharArray(),
            StringSplitOptions.RemoveEmptyEntries);
        FTPResp.Close();
        return result;
    }
    catch (Exception ex)
    {
        MessageBox.Show(ex.ToString());
        return null;
    }
}
```

The directory listing is split into a string array. The directory listings are separated by newline characters. If your FTP server is configured with an MS-DOS directory listing style (see Figure 16-11), the directory listing will look something like this:

```
12-11-06   10:54PM                    2074750 DSC00098.JPG
12-11-06   10:54PM                    2109227 DSC00099.JPG
12-11-06   10:49PM        <DIR>               George
12-11-06   10:49PM        <DIR>               James
12-11-06   10:58PM        <DIR>               Wei-Meng Lee
```

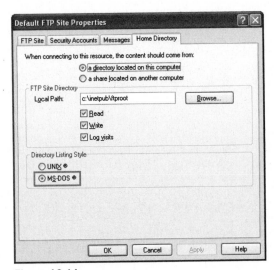

Figure 16-11

Because all subdirectories have the <DIR> field, you can easily differentiate subdirectories from files in the BuildDirectory() function by looking for <DIR> in each line:

```
//---Build the directory in the TreeView control---
private void BuildDirectory(TreeNode ParentNode)
{
    string[] listing = GetDirectoryListing(
        Properties.Settings.Default.FTP_SERVER +
        ParentNode.FullPath);
    foreach (string line in listing)
    {
        if (line == String.Empty) break;

        TreeNode node = new TreeNode();
        if (line.Substring(24, 5) == "<DIR>")
        {
```

(continued)

(continued)

```
                            //---this is a directory; create a new node to be added---
                            node.Text = line.Substring(39);
                            node.ImageIndex = ico_CLOSE;
                            node.SelectedImageIndex = ico_OPEN;

                            //---add the dummy child node---
                            node.Nodes.Add("");
                            ParentNode.Nodes.Add(node);
                        }
                        else
                        {
                            //---this is a normal file; create a new node to be added---
                            node.Text = line.Substring(39);
                            node.ImageIndex = ico_PHOTO;
                            node.SelectedImageIndex = ico_PHOTO;
                            ParentNode.Nodes.Add(node);
                        }
                    }
                }
```

When a node is selected, you first obtain its current path and then display that path in the status bar if it is a folder. If it is an image node, download and display the photo, using the `DownloadImage()` function. All these are handled in the `TreeView1_AfterSelect` event. Here's the code:

```
        private void TreeView1_AfterSelect(object sender, TreeViewEventArgs e)
        {
            //---always ignore the first "/" char---
            string FullPath =
                Properties.Settings.Default.FTP_SERVER +
                e.Node.FullPath.Substring(1).Replace("\r", "");

            //---display the current folder selected---
            if (e.Node.ImageIndex != ico_PHOTO)
            {
                ToolStripStatusLabel1.Text = FullPath;
                return;
            }

            //---download image---
            DownloadImage(FullPath);
        }
```

The `DownloadImage()` function downloads an image from the FTP server and displays the image in a PictureBox control:

```
//---Download the image from the FTP server---
private void DownloadImage(string path)
{
    try
    {
        ToolStripStatusLabel1.Text = "Downloading image..." + path;
        Application.DoEvents();

        //---download the image---
        FtpWebResponse FTPResp =
            PerformWebRequest(path,
            WebRequestMethod.DownloadFile);

        //---get the stream containing the image---
        Stream ftpRespStream = FTPResp.GetResponseStream();

        //---display the image---
        PictureBox1.Image = Image.FromStream(ftpRespStream);
        FTPResp.Close();

        ToolStripStatusLabel1.Text =
            "Downloading image...complete (" + path + ")";
    }
    catch (Exception ex)
    {
        MessageBox.Show(ex.Message);
    }
}
```

To download an image file using FTP and then bind it to a `PictureBox` control:

❑ Call the `PerformWebRequest()` helper function you defined earlier.

❑ Retrieve the stream that contains response data sent from the FTP server, using the `GetResponseStream()` method from the `FtpWebResponse` class.

To set the `PictureBox` control to display the downloaded image, use the `FromStream()` method from the `Image` class to convert the response from the FTP server (containing the image) into an image.

Creating a New Directory

The user can create a new directory on the FTP server by clicking the Create Folder button. To create a new directory, select a node (by clicking on it) to add the new folder, and then call the `PerformWebRequest()` helper function you defined earlier. This is accomplished by the Create Folder button:

```
//---Create a new folder---
private void btnCreateFolder_Click(object sender, EventArgs e)
{
    //---ensure user selects a folder---
    if (TreeView1.SelectedNode.ImageIndex == ico_PHOTO)
    {
        MessageBox.Show("Please select a folder first.");
        return;
    }

    try
    {
        //---formulate the full path for the folder to be created---
        string folder = Properties.Settings.Default.FTP_SERVER +
            TreeView1.SelectedNode.FullPath.Substring(1).Replace
            ("\r", "") + @"/" + txtNewFolderName.Text;

        //---make the new directory---
        FtpWebResponse ftpResp =
            PerformWebRequest(folder, WebRequestMethod.MakeDirectory);
        ftpResp.Close();

        //---refresh the newly added folder---
        RefreshCurrentFolder();

        //---update the statusbar---
        ToolStripStatusLabel1.Text =
            ftpResp.StatusDescription.Replace("\r\n",string.Empty);
    }
    catch (Exception ex)
    {
        MessageBox.Show(ex.ToString());
    }
}
```

When a new folder is created, you update the `TreeView` control to reflect the newly added folder. This is accomplished by the `RefreshCurrentFolder()` function:

```
private void RefreshCurrentFolder()
{
    //---clears all the nodes and...---
    TreeView1.SelectedNode.Nodes.Clear();

    //---...create the nodes again---
    BuildDirectory(TreeView1.SelectedNode);
}
```

Removing a Directory

To remove (delete) a directory, a user first selects the folder to delete and then clicks the Remove Folder button. To delete a directory, you call the `PerformWebRequest()` helper function you defined earlier. This is accomplished with the Remove Folder button:

```
//---Remove a folder---
private void btnRemoveFolder_Click(object sender, EventArgs e)
{
    if (TreeView1.SelectedNode.ImageIndex == ico_PHOTO)
    {
        MessageBox.Show("Please select a folder to delete.");
        return;
    }

    try
    {
        string FullPath =
            Properties.Settings.Default.FTP_SERVER +
            TreeView1.SelectedNode.
            FullPath.Substring(1).Replace("\r", "");

        //---remove the folder---
        FtpWebResponse ftpResp =
            PerformWebRequest(FullPath, WebRequestMethod.RemoveDirectory);

        //---delete current node---
        TreeView1.SelectedNode.Remove();

        //---update the statusbar---
        ToolStripStatusLabel1.Text =
            ftpResp.StatusDescription.Replace("\r\n", string.Empty);
    }
    catch (Exception ex)
    {
        MessageBox.Show(ex.ToString());
    }
}
```

If a directory is not empty (that is, if it contains files and subdirectories), the deletion process will fail. The user will have to remove its content before removing the directory.

Uploading Photos

To upload photos to the FTP server, you first select a folder to upload the photos to and then use the `OpenFileDialog` class to ask the user to select the photo(s) he wants to upload. Finally, you upload the photos individually, using the `UploadImage()` function:

```csharp
private void btnUploadPhotos_Click(object sender, EventArgs e)
{
    //---ensure user selects a folder---
    if (TreeView1.SelectedNode.ImageIndex == ico_PHOTO)
    {
        MessageBox.Show("Please select a folder to upload the photos.");
        return;
    }

    OpenFileDialog openFileDialog1 = new OpenFileDialog()
    {
        Filter = "jpg files (*.jpg)|*.jpg",
        FilterIndex = 2,
        RestoreDirectory = true,
        Multiselect = true
    };

    //---formulate the full path for the folder to be created---
    string currentSelectedPath =
        Properties.Settings.Default.FTP_SERVER +
        TreeView1.SelectedNode.FullPath.Substring(1).Replace("\r", "");

    //---let user select the photos to upload---
    if (openFileDialog1.ShowDialog() ==
        System.Windows.Forms.DialogResult.OK)
    {
        //---upload each photo individually---
        for (int i = 0; i <= openFileDialog1.FileNames.Length - 1; i++)
        {
            UploadImage(currentSelectedPath + "/" +
                openFileDialog1.FileNames[i].Substring(
                openFileDialog1.FileNames[i].LastIndexOf(@"\") + 1),
                openFileDialog1.FileNames[i]);
        }
    }

    //---refresh the folder to show the uploaded photos---
    RefreshCurrentFolder();
}
```

The `UploadImage()` function uploads a photo from the hard disk to the FTP server:

❑ First, create a new instance of the `WebClient` class.

❑ Specify the login credential to the FTP server.

❑ Upload the file to the FTP server, using the `UploadFile()` method from the `WebClient` class. Note that the full pathname of the file to be uploaded to the FTP server must be specified.

```
//---upload a photo to the FTP server---
private void UploadImage(string path, string filename)
{
    try
    {
        WebClient client = new WebClient();
        client.Credentials = new NetworkCredential(
            Properties.Settings.Default.UserName,
            Properties.Settings.Default.Password);

        //---upload the photo---
        client.UploadFile(path, filename);

        //---update the statusbar---
        ToolStripStatusLabel1.Text = filename + " uploaded!";
    }
    catch (Exception ex)
    {
        Console.WriteLine(ex.ToString());
    }
}
```

Deleting a Photo

To delete a photo, the user first selects a photo to delete and then you call the `PerformWebRequest()` helper function you have defined earlier:

```
private void btnDeletePhoto_Click(object sender, EventArgs e)
{
    if (TreeView1.SelectedNode.ImageIndex != ico_PHOTO)
    {
        MessageBox.Show("Please select a photo to delete.");
        return;
    }
    try
    {
        string FullPath = Properties.Settings.Default.FTP_SERVER +
            TreeView1.SelectedNode.FullPath.Substring(1).Replace("\r", "");

        //---delete the photo---
        FtpWebResponse ftpResp =
            PerformWebRequest(FullPath, WebRequestMethod.DeleteFile);

        //---delete the current node---
        TreeView1.SelectedNode.Remove();

        //---update the statusbar---
        ToolStripStatusLabel1.Text =
            ftpResp.StatusDescription.Replace("\r\n", string.Empty);
    }
    catch (Exception ex)
    {
        MessageBox.Show(ex.ToString());
    }
}
```

Once the photo is removed from the FTP server, you also need to delete its node in the `TreeView` control.

Testing the Application

That's it! You can now test the application by pressing F5. Ensure that the credentials for logging in to the FTP server are correct. If the login is successful, you should be able to create a new folder on the FTP server and then upload photos. Figure 16-12 shows the complete application.

Figure 16-12

Adding Print Capability

The .NET Framework contains classes that make it easy for you to support printing in your applications. In this section, you add printing support to the `PhotoViewer` application so that you can print the photos. You'll explore the basics of printing in .NET and see how to configure page setup, print multiple pages, and preview a document before it is printed, as well as let users select a printer with which to print.

Basics of Printing in .NET

In .NET, all the printing functionality is encapsulated within the `PrintDocument` control/class, which can be found in the Toolbox (see Figure 16-13). The `PrintDocument` control defines the various methods that allow you to send output to the printer.

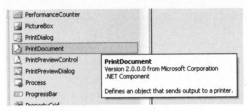

Figure 16-13

To incorporate printing functionality into your Windows application, you can either drag and drop the `PrintDocument` control onto your form or create an instance of the `PrintDocument` class at runtime. This example uses the latter approach.

To start the printing process, you use the `Print()` method of the `PrintDocument` class. To customize the printing process using the `PrintDocument` object, there are generally three events with which you need to be acquainted:

❏ `BeginPrint` — Occurs when the `Print()` method is called and before the first page of the document prints. Typically, you use this event to initialize fonts, file streams, and other resources used during the printing process.

❏ `PrintPage` — Occurs when the output to print for the current page is needed. This is the main event to code the logic required for sending the outputs to the printer.

❏ `EndPrint` — Occurs when the last page of the document has printed. Typically, you use this event to release fonts, file streams, and other resources used during the printing process.

Adding Print Support to the Project

To add print support to the `PhotoViewer` application, first add the controls (see Figure 16-14) in the following table.

Control	Text	Name
Label controls (2)	Print from:	
	to	
TextBox controls (2)		txtFrom
		txtTo
Button controls (2)	Preview	btnPreview
	Print	btnPrint

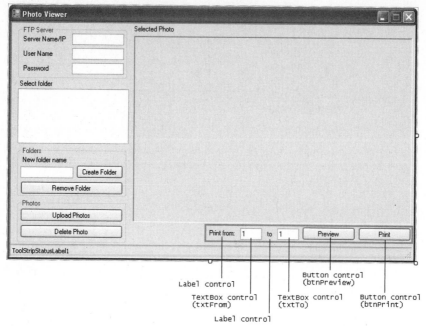

Figure 16-14

Switch to the code-behind of Form1, and import the following namespace:

```
using System.Drawing.Printing;
```

Declare the following member variables:

```
public partial class Form1 : Form
{
    //---constants for the icon images---
    const int ico_OPEN = 0;
    const int ico_CLOSE = 1;
    const int ico_PHOTO = 2;

    //---font variables---
    Font f_title;
    Font f_body;

    //---page counter---
    int pagecounter;

    //---PrintDocument variable---
    PrintDocument printDoc;
```

When the form is loaded during runtime, create an instance of the `PrintDocument` class, and wire up the three main event handlers described earlier:

```
private void Form1_Load(object sender, EventArgs e)
{
    printDoc = new PrintDocument()
    {
        DocumentName = "Printing from Photo Viewer"
    };
    printDoc.BeginPrint += new PrintEventHandler(printDoc_BeginPrint);
    printDoc.PrintPage += new PrintPageEventHandler(printDoc_PrintPage);
    printDoc.EndPrint += new PrintEventHandler(printDoc_EndPrint);

    try
    {
        //---load the application settings values
        // into the textbox controls---
        ...
```

In the event handler for the `BeginPrint` event, initialize the page counter as well as the fonts of the text to be used for printing the page:

```
void printDoc_BeginPrint(object sender, PrintEventArgs e)
{
    //---initialize the page counter---
    pagecounter = int.Parse(txtFrom.Text);

    //---initialize the fonts---
    f_title = new Font("Arial", 16, FontStyle.Bold);
    f_body = new Font("Times New Roman", 10);
}
```

In the `EndPrint` event handler, dereference the font variables used:

```
void printDoc_EndPrint(object sender, PrintEventArgs e)
{
    //---de-reference the fonts---
    f_title = null;
    f_body = null;
}
```

Finally, the event handler for `PrintPage` is the place where you do the bulk of the work of sending the output to the printer. Basically, you use the `Graphics` object in the `PrintPageEventArgs` class to specify the output you want to print. For example, to draw a rectangle you would use the `e.Graphics.DrawRectangle()` method (where e is an instance of the `PrintPageEventArgs` class). To print a string, you use the `e.Graphics.DrawString()` method. After printing, you increment the page count and determine if there are any more pages to print. If there are, setting the `HasMorePages` property of the `PrintPageEventArgs` class to `true` will cause the `printDoc_PrintPage` event handler fire one more time. Once there are no more pages left to print, set the `HasMorePages` property to `false`:

```csharp
void printDoc_PrintPage(object sender, PrintPageEventArgs e)
{
    Graphics g = e.Graphics;

    //---draws the title---
    g.DrawString(TreeView1.SelectedNode.Text,
        f_title, Brushes.Black, 20, 30);

    //---draws a border...---
    Rectangle border =
        new Rectangle(10, 10,
            PictureBox1.Width + 20, PictureBox1.Height + 60);

    //---...using a thick pen---
    Pen thickPen = new Pen(Color.Black, 3);
    g.DrawRectangle(thickPen, border);

    //---draws the picture---
    if (PictureBox1.Image != null)
    {
        g.DrawImage(PictureBox1.Image, 20, 60,
        PictureBox1.Size.Width,
        PictureBox1.Size.Height);
    }

    //---draws the page count---
    g.DrawString("Page " + pagecounter,
        f_body, Brushes.Black,
        20, 420);

    //---increments the page counter---
    pagecounter += 1;

    //---determine if you have more pages to print---
    if (pagecounter <= int.Parse(txtTo.Text))
        e.HasMorePages = true;
    else
        e.HasMorePages = false;
}
```

To let the user preview the output before the image is sent to the printer for printing, use the
`PrintPreviewDialog()` class:

```
private void btnPreview_Click(object sender, EventArgs e)
{
    //---show preview---
    PrintPreviewDialog dlg = new PrintPreviewDialog()
    {
        Document = printDoc
    };
    dlg.ShowDialog();
}
```

This code previews the output in a separate window (see Figure 16-15). The user can click the printer
icon to send the output to the printer. The user can also choose to enlarge the page or view multiple
pages on one single screen.

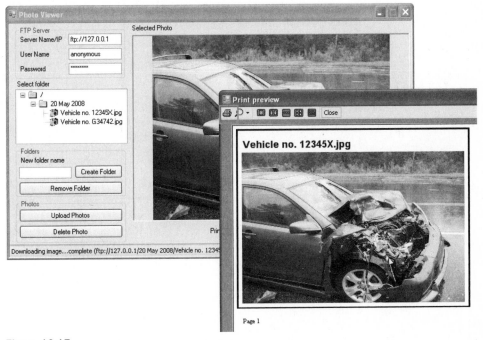

Figure 16-15

To print the image to a printer, use the `PrintDialog` class to let the user choose the desired printer (see Figure 16-16) instead of sending the output directly to the default printer:

```csharp
private void btnPrint_Click(object sender, EventArgs e)
{
    //---let user select a printer to print---
    PrintDialog pd = new PrintDialog()
    {
        Document = printDoc,
        AllowSomePages = true
    };

    DialogResult result = pd.ShowDialog();
    if (result == DialogResult.OK)
        printDoc.Print();
}
```

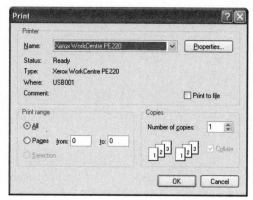

Figure 16-16

Figure 16-17 shows the output if the user indicated that he wanted to print from page 1 to 3 (in `Form1`). Note the page number displayed below the image.

Figure 16-17

Deploying the Application

Now the application is ready to be deployed to your customers. One of the most challenging tasks faced by Windows application developers today is the deployment of their applications on the client machines. Once an application is deployed, any change to or maintenance of the application requires redeployment. Worse, with so many different client configurations, updating a Windows application is always fraught with unknowns.

Beginning with Visual Studio 2005, Microsoft rolled out a new deployment technology known as ClickOnce, which makes such deployments and even updates extremely easy and painless. ClickOnce was designed specifically to ease the deployment of Windows applications, in particular *smart clients*. A smart client is basically a Windows application that leverages local resources and intelligently connects to distributed data sources (such as Web Services) as and when needed. While a lot of companies are deploying web applications (due to the web's ubiquitous access) today, network latencies and server delays are some of the problems that prevent developers from reaping the full benefits of the web. Common frustrations over web applications include slow response time from web sites and limited functionality (due to the stateless nature of the HTTP protocol). A smart client aims to reap the benefit of the rich functionality of the client (Windows), while at the same time utilizing the power of Web Services in the backend.

Using ClickOnce, a Windows application can be deployed through the convenience of a web server, file servers, or even CDs. Once an application is installed using ClickOnce, it can automatically check for new updates to the application from the publisher, saving a lot of effort in maintenance and application upgrades. On the security front, ClickOnce applications run within a secure sandbox and are configured using the Code Access Security model.

Publishing the Application Using ClickOnce

Deploying your application using ClickOnce is very straightforward. In Visual Studio 2008, select Build ⇨ Publish PhotoViewer (see Figure 16-18).

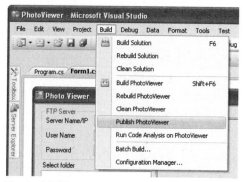

Figure 16-18

The Publish Wizard (see Figure 16-19) opens. By default, your application will be published to the local web server (IIS) using the path shown in the textbox. However, you can also publish your application using a disk path, file share, FTP, or an external web server. For this example, use the default and click Next.

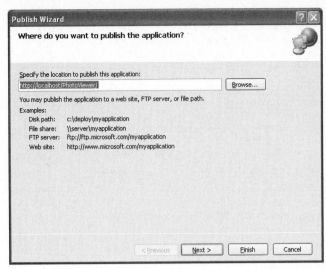

Figure 16-19

In the next page, indicate if the application is available both online and offline or available online only. Accept the default selection, and click Next to proceed to the next step.

In the next page, click Finish to complete the wizard and start the publishing process. When publishing is completed, a web page (publish.htm) appears; it contains a link to install the application (see Figure 16-20).

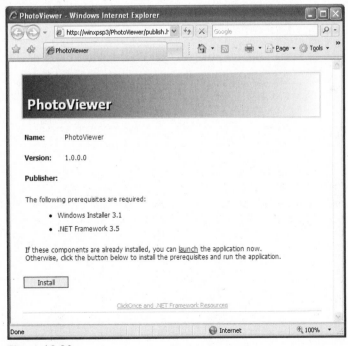

Figure 16-20

The `Publish.htm` page lists the following:

❑ Name, Version, and Publisher information

❑ Prerequisites required for your application (automatically generated based on the application you are deploying)

> **The URL** `http://<server_name>/PhotoViewer/publish.htm` **is the deployment location of your application. Users who want to install this application through ClickOnce simply need to go to this URL, using their web browser. You provide the URL to your users through email, brochures, and so on.**

To install the application, click the Install button. You are presented with:

❑ **File Download dialog** — Security Warning prompt. Click Run to download the application.

❑ **Internet Explorer dialog** — Security Warning. Click Run to proceed with the installation.

❑ **Application Install dialog** — Security Warning. Click Install to install the application (see Figure 16-21).

Figure 16-21

Once installed, the application is launched automatically. You can also launch the application from Start ➪ Programs ➪ PhotoViewer ➪ PhotoViewer.

Updating the Application

Let's now update the application so that you can republish the application and see how the changes can be updated on the client side. For simplicity, move the Preview button to the left of the `Print from` label control as shown in Figure 16-22. This will enable you to verify that the application has been updated after it is republished.

Figure 16-22

To republish the application, simply select Build ⇨ Publish PhotoViewer again. When the Publish Wizard appears, click Finish so that it can publish the application using the default settings.

Each time you publish the application, the version number of the application is incremented automatically. That's controlled by the Publish settings page in the project's properties page (see Figure 16-23).

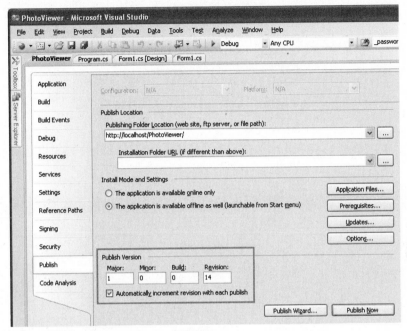

Figure 16-23

In addition, the Publish settings page also contains the Updates button, which enables you to specify how and when the application should check for updates (see Figure 16-24).

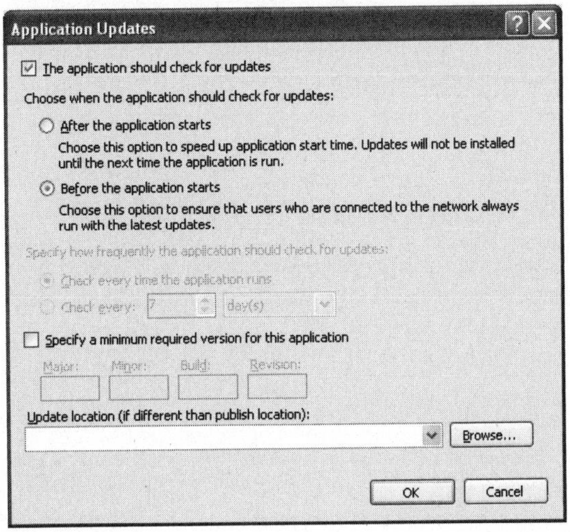

Figure 16-24

By default, the application checks for updates every time before it starts.

When the user closes and then relaunches the PhotoViewer application, he gets a prompt, as shown in Figure 16-25.

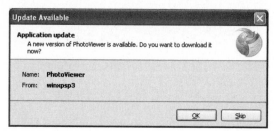

Figure 16-25

The user can click OK to download the updated application, or click Skip if he doesn't want to update the application now. The updated application will look like Figure 16-26.

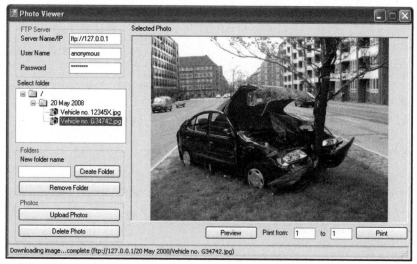

Figure 16-26

Programmatically Updating the Application

Instead of the application checking for updates before it starts, it would be a good idea for users to be able to choose when they want to check for updates. For that, add a new button to the form, as shown in Figure 16-27.

Figure 16-27

538

Import the following namespace:

```
using System.Deployment.Application;
```

Code the Update button like this:

```
private void btnUpdate_Click(object sender, EventArgs e)
{
    //---check if the application is deployed by ClickOnce---
    if (ApplicationDeployment.IsNetworkDeployed)
    {
        //---Get an instance of the deployment---
        ApplicationDeployment deployment =
            ApplicationDeployment.CurrentDeployment;

        //---if there is any update---
        if (deployment.CheckForUpdate())
        {
            DialogResult response =
                MessageBox.Show(("A new version of the " +
                "application is available. " +
                "Do you want to update application?"),
                ("Application Updates"),
                MessageBoxButtons.YesNo);

            //---if user wants to update---
            if (response == DialogResult.Yes)
            {
                Cursor.Current = Cursors.WaitCursor;

                //---update the application---
                deployment.Update();

                //---prompt the user to restart---
                MessageBox.Show("Update completed. You need to restart" +
                    " the application.",
                    ("Update Completed"), MessageBoxButtons.OK,
                    MessageBoxIcon.Information);

                //---restart the application---
                Application.Restart();
            }
        }
        else
        {
            //---application is up-to-date---
            MessageBox.Show(("Application is up-to-date."), "Update",
                MessageBoxButtons.OK, MessageBoxIcon.Information);
        }
    }
    else
```

(continued)

(continued)

```
        {
                //---application is not installed using ClickOnce---
                MessageBox.Show(("Application is not installed " +
                    "using ClickOnce"),
                    ("Updates not available"),
                    MessageBoxButtons.OK, MessageBoxIcon.Information);
        }
    }
```

You first check to see if the application is deployed using ClickOnce. This can be done by using the `IsNetworkDeployed` property from the `ApplicationDeployment` static class. If the application is indeed deployed using ClickOnce, you proceed to obtain an instance of the deployment using the `currentDeployment` property of the `ApplicationDeployment` class. Using this instance of the deployment, you call the `CheckForUpdate()` method to check whether there is a newer version of the application available from the publishing server. If there is, you prompt the user by asking if he wants to update the application. If he does, you update the application, using the `Update()` method. After that, you force the user to restart the application, using the `Restart()` method.

To test the update, first run an instance of the PhotoViewer application by launching it from the Start menu. Next, republish the application in Visual Studio 2008. Click the Update button to see if an update is available. You should see the prompt shown in Figure 16-28. Click Yes, and the application will be updated.

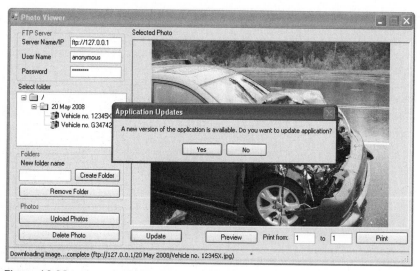

Figure 16-28

Rolling Back

Once an application is updated, the user has a choice to roll it back to its previous version. To do so, go to the Control Panel and run the Add or Remove Programs application. Locate the application (in this case, PhotoViewer) and click on the Change/Remove button. You have two choices — restore the application to its previous state or remove the application from the computer (see Figure 16-29).

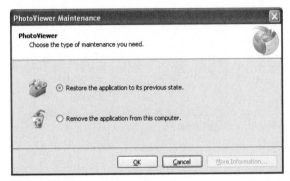

Figure 16-29

An application can be rolled back only to its previous version. If it's been updated several times, it only rolls back to the version preceding the last update.

Under the Hood: Application and Deployment Manifests

When you use the Publish Wizard to publish your application using ClickOnce, Visual Studio 2008 publishes your application to the URL that you have indicated. For example, if you specified `http://localhost/PhotoViwer/` as the publishing directory and your web publishing directory is C:\Inetpub\wwwroot\, then the virtual directory `PhotoViewer` will be mapped to the local path C:\Inetpub\wwwroot\PhotoViewer\.

Two types of files will be created under the C:\Inetpub\wwwroot\PhotoViewer directory:

❑   Application Manifest

❑   Deployment Manifest

The next two sections take a closer look at these two types of files.

Application Manifest

When you publish your application, three files and a folder are created in the publishing directory (see Figure 16-30):

❑   **Application Files** — Folder containing the deployment files.

❑   **A `publish.htm` web page** — This contains instructions on how to install the application.

❑ **Application manifest** — `PhotoViewer.application`. This is the file that is referenced by the `publish.htm` file. An application manifest is an XML file that contains detailed information about the current application as well as its version number. Chapter 15 has more about application manifests.

❑ `setup.exe` — A setup application that installs the application onto the target computer.

Figure 16-30

The Application Files folder contains the various versions of the application that have been published (see Figure 16-31).

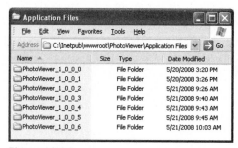

Figure 16-31

When you republish your application using ClickOnce, the content of `PhotoViewer.application`, `publish.htm`, and `setup.exe` are modified, and one new application manifest is created inside a new folder (for instance, `PhotoViewer_1_0_0_6`; located within the Application Files folder), containing the new version of deployment files, will be created.

As mentioned, the `PhotoViewer.application` application manifest is an XML file that contains detailed information about the current application as well as its version number. It allows the client to know if he needs to update his application.

Deployment Manifest

The deployment manifest — `PhotoViewer.exe.manifest`, in this example — is located in the C:\Inetpub\wwwroot\PhotoViewer\Application Files\PhotoViewer_1_0_0_6 directory (assuming that the latest version published is 1.0.0.6; see Figure 16-32). It contains detailed information about the application (such as dependencies and attached files).

The `PhotoViewer.exe.deploy` file is the executable of your application. Other files in the same directory may include files/databases used by your application. During installation these files will be deployed (downloaded) onto the user's machine.

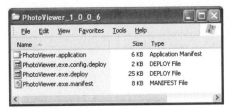

Figure 16-32

Where Are the Files Installed Locally?

When the user installs an application onto his computer via ClickOnce, he does not have a choice of where to store the application. In fact, the application is stored on a per-user basis, and different versions of the application are stored in different folders. For example, when I installed the example application on my computer, the application files were stored in:

```
C:\Documents and Settings\Wei-Meng Lee\Local Settings\Apps\2.0\JGEG6REQ.YQK\
C2N9O65K.16D\phot..tion_4f46313378dcdeb5_0001.0000_ff3a6bf346a40e4d
```

Generally, application files are stored in subdirectories under the C:\Documents and Settings\<*User Name*>\Local Settings\Apps\2.0 folder. To find this directory programmatically during runtime, use the following code snippet:

```
//---ExecutablePath includes the executable name---
string path = Application.ExecutablePath;
//---Strip away the executable name---
path = path.Substring(0, path.LastIndexOf(@"\"));
```

Summary

This chapter explained how to develop a Windows application to upload and download pictures to and from an FTP server. Several Windows Forms controls were used to build the application's user interface, and you saw how to use the application settings feature in .NET to preserve the status of an application even after it has exited. Finally, the application was deployed using the ClickOnce, which allows applications to be easily updated after they have been deployed.

17

Developing ASP.NET Web Applications

ASP.NET (Active Server Pages .NET) is a web development technology from Microsoft. Part of the .NET Framework, ASP.NET enables developers to build dynamic web applications and Web Services using compiled languages like VB.NET and C#. Developers can use Visual Studio 2008 to develop compelling web applications using ASP.NET, with the ease of drag-and-drop server controls. The latest version of ASP.NET is version 3.5.

This chapter explains how to:

❑   Display database records using a server control call `GridView`

❑   Perform data binding in an ASP.NET application using the new `LinqDataSource` control

❑   AJAX-enable your application by using the new AJAX framework in ASP.NET 3.5 and the AJAX Control Toolkit

❑   Deploy your web application to a web server

About ASP.NET

In the early days of the web, the contents of web pages were largely static. Pages needed to be constantly — and manually — modified. To create web sites that were dynamic and would update automatically, a number of server-side technologies sprouted up, including Microsoft's Active Server Pages (ASP). ASP executed on the server side, with its output sent to the user's web browser, thus allowing the server to generate dynamic web pages based on the actions of the user.

These server-side technologies are important contributions to the development of the web. Without them, web applications that users are accustomed to today, such as Amazon.com and eBay.com, would not be possible.

Microsoft ASP began as a public beta (v1.0) in October 1996 as an upgrade to Internet Information Server (IIS) 2.0. In the initial three versions, ASP used a scripting language, VBScript, as the default language. Using a scripting language had its flaws — code is interpreted rather than compiled, and using VBScript as the default language turned some people off (although technically you could configure ASP to use other languages such as JScript and Perl, but this was not commonly done). This interpreted code model of ASP seriously limited performance.

In early 2000, Microsoft introduced the.NET Framework and, together with it, the upgrade of ASP: ASP.NET 1.0 (previously known as ASP+). Over the last few years, ASP.NET has evolved to ASP.NET 3.5.

In ASP.NET, you are not limited to scripting languages; you can use the following .NET languages:

- ❑ C#
- ❑ VB.NET

How ASP.NET Works

When a web browser requests a page from a web server, the web server (IIS) first checks whether the request is for an HTML page. If it is, the request is filled by fetching the files from the hard drive and returning them to the client (web browser). If the client is requesting an ASP.NET page, IIS passes the request to the ASP.NET runtime, which then processes the application and returns the output to the client.

ASP.NET pages use the `.aspx` extension, which ensures that ASP.NET can run side by side with classic ASP, which uses the extension `.asp`.

One of the inherent problems with the HTTP protocol is its stateless nature. Put simply, a request made by a user is loaded into memory, fulfilled, and then unloaded. Subsequent requests by the same user are treated just like any other request; the server makes no attempt to remember what the user has previously requested. This stateless nature makes writing web applications a challenge because the application developer must explicitly devise mechanisms to enable the server to remember the previous state of the application. Several mechanisms have been devised over the years, including cookies and query strings for passing information to and from the server and the client.

In classic ASP, you typically need to write pages of code to preserve the state of the page after the user has posted a value back to the server. In ASP.NET, all of these mundane tasks (collectively known as state management) are accomplished by the ASP.NET runtime.

What Do You Need to Run ASP.NET?

ASP.NET is supported on the following operating systems:

- ❑ Microsoft Windows 2000 Professional and Server (SP 2 recommended)
- ❑ Microsoft Windows XP Professional
- ❑ Microsoft Windows Server 2003/2008
- ❑ Microsoft Windows Vista

To run ASP.NET applications, you need to install IIS on your computer (IIS is not installed by default; you can install IIS on your computer by running the Add or Remove Programs application in the Control Panel and then selecting the Add/Remove Windows Components tab). To obtain the ASP.NET runtime, you must install the .NET Framework on your machine. You can obtain the latest .NET Framework from the following site: `http://microsoft.com/downloads`.

Data Binding

One of the most common tasks a web application does is display records from a database. For example, you may have an inventory web application with which your staff can check the latest pricing information and stock availability. This chapter explains how to retrieve records from a database and use data binding in ASP.NET to display them on a page. In addition, it shows how to use the new `LinqDataSource` control, which enables you to use LINQ to talk to databases without needing to write complex SQL queries.

To start, launch Visual Studio 2008 and create a new ASP.NET Web Site project (see Figure 17-1).

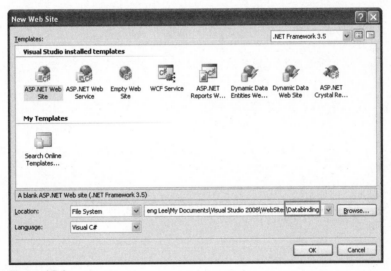

Figure 17-1

The default location is File System (see Figure 17-2), which means that you can save your ASP.NET project in any folder on your local drive so that during debugging a built-in web server is automatically launched to host your ASP.NET application. Alternatively, you can choose the HTTP option, which means that your ASP.NET application will be hosted by a web server (most commonly the local IIS), or the FTP option, which uses an FTP Server. For this example, use File System, the default option.

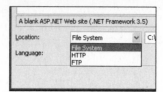

Figure 17-2

Modeling Databases Using LINQ to SQL

The example web application will display records from two tables in the pubs sample database. Because you are going to use LINQ to access the database, you do not connect to the database directly. Instead, you generate classes that represent the database and its tables and then use those classes to interact with the data. To begin, add a new item to the project and select the LINQ to SQL Classes template (see Figure 17-3).

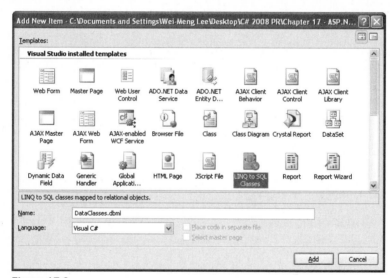

Figure 17-3

Use the default name of DataClasses.dbml. When prompted to save the item in the App_Code folder, click Yes. The DataClasses.dbml file is created in the App_Code folder of your project (see Figure 17-4).

Figure 17-4

The Object Relational Designer (O/R Designer) then launches so that you can visually edit the databases and tables you want to use. Open the Server Explorer window, and connect to the `pubs` sample database. Drag and drop the `publisher` and `title` tables onto the design surface of `DataClasses.dbml` (see Figure 17-5).

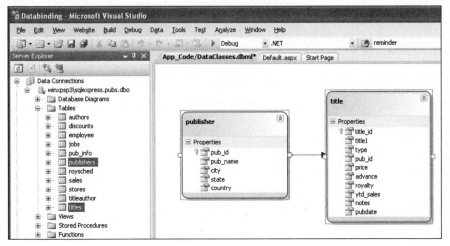

Figure 17-5

Save the `DataClasses.dbml` file by pressing Ctrl+S. When you save the file, Visual Studio 2008 persists out .NET classes that represent the entities and database relationships that you have just added. For each LINQ to SQL designer file you add to your solution, a custom `DataContext` class is generated. It is the main object that you use to manipulate the table. In this example, the `DataContext` class is named `DataClassesDataContext`.

Be sure to save `DataClasses.dbml` before proceeding.

Data Binding Using the GridView Control

To display the records from a table, you can use the `GridView` control, which displays the values of a data source in a table where each column represents a field and each row represents a record. Drag the `GridView` control from the Toolbox and drop it onto the design surface of `Default.aspx`. In the SmartTag of the `GridView` control, select <New data source . . . > in the Choose Data Source dropdown list (see Figure 17-6).

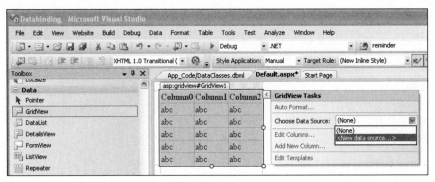

Figure 17-6

In the Data Source Configuration Wizard (see Figure 17-7), select LINQ and click OK. Use the default name of `LinqDataSource1`. Click OK.

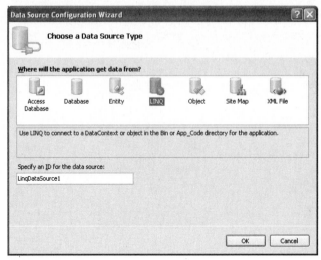

Figure 17-7

For those of you familiar with the various data source controls (such as `SqlDataSource` and `ObjectDataSource`) in ASP.NET 2.0, the `LinqDataSource` control works much like them. What is special about the `LinqDataSource` control is that instead of binding directly to a database (as with the `SqlDataSource`), it binds to a LINQ-enabled data model. The beauty of this is that you need not write the various complex SQL queries (such as `insert`, `delete`, and `modify`) to use it. Instead, you just need to specify the data model you are working with, and the type of operations you want to perform on it (such as `delete`, `insert`, or `update`) and then the control takes care of performing those operations by itself.

The `DataClassesDataContext` object that you generated earlier is automatically selected for you (see Figure 17-8). Click Next.

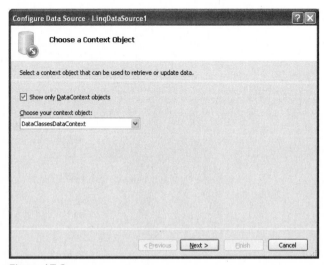

Figure 17-8

Select the `titles` table, and click the * checkbox to select all fields (see Figure 17-9).

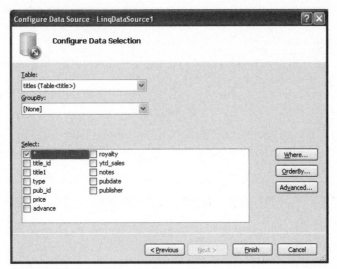

Figure 17-9

Click the Advanced button and check all the checkboxes. Click OK (see Figure 17-10) and then click Finish.

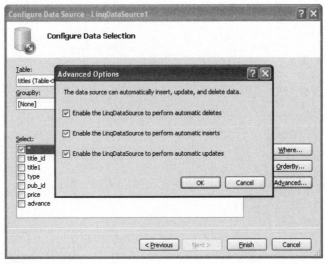

Figure 17-10

Switch to the source view of Default.aspx page, and observe the <asp:LinqDataSource> element:

```
<asp:LinqDataSource
    ID="LinqDataSource1"
    runat="server"
    ContextTypeName="DataClassesDataContext"
    EnableDelete="True"
    EnableInsert="True"
    EnableUpdate="True"
    TableName="titles">
</asp:LinqDataSource>
```

Select the GridView control's SmartTag, and check the five checkboxes (see Figure 17-11).

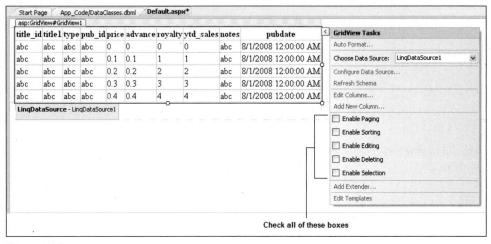

Figure 17-11

This makes the GridView look like Figure 17-12. The column names are now clickable and that new column containing Edit, Delete, and Select is added to the GridView control. Also, paging is now enabled (located at the bottom of the GridView control).

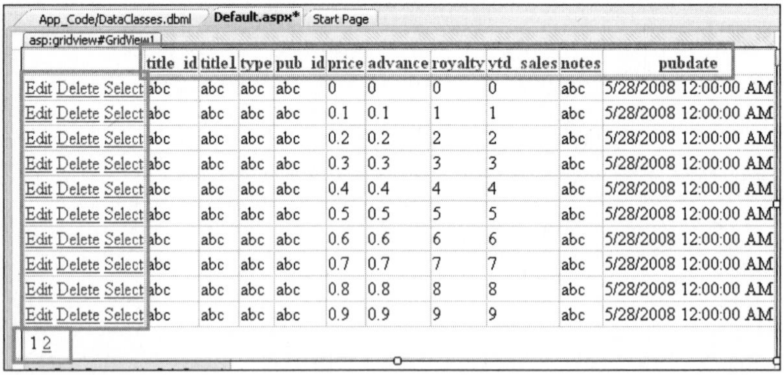

Figure 17-12

Click the Auto Format link in the SmartTag of the `GridView` control, and select the Sand and Sky scheme.

The `GridView` control contains all the fields of the `titles` table, but there are some that you don't really need. So select the `notes` column, and remove it by choosing Remove Column from GridView Tasks (see Figure 17-13). Delete the `advance`, `royalty`, and `ytd_sales` columns as well.

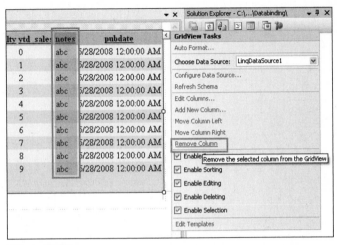

Figure 17-13

The `GridView` control should now look like Figure 17-14.

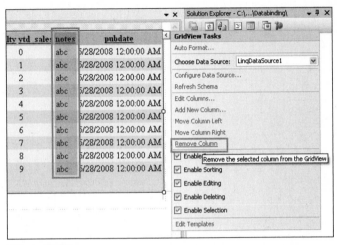

Figure 17-14

Now, to debug the application, press F5. You are asked to modify the `Web.config` file for debugging; click OK. You also are prompted that script debugging is disabled in Internet Explorer; click Yes to continue debugging.

Figure 17-15 shows the `GridView` control displaying the rows in the titles table. You can sort the rows by clicking on the column headers, and edit and delete records.

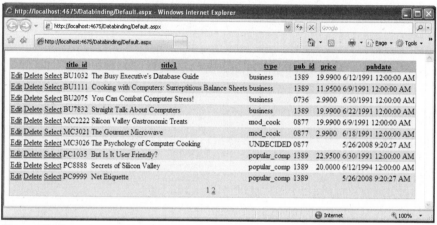

Figure 17-15

Displaying Publisher's Name

As Figure 17-15 shows, the publisher's ID appears in the `GridView` control under the `pub_id` field. It would be helpful to the user if the publisher's name displayed instead of its ID. To do that, switch to the source view of `Default.aspx` and within the `<asp:GridView>` element, replace the following element:

```
<asp:BoundField
    DataField="pub_id"
    HeaderText="pub_id"
    SortExpression="pub_id" />
```

with this:

```
<asp:TemplateField
    HeaderText="Publisher">
    <ItemTemplate>
        <%#Eval("publisher.pub_name")%>
    </ItemTemplate>
</asp:TemplateField>
```

Essentially, this changes the header for the publisher column in the GridView to `Publisher`, and the values are now derived from the `publisher.pub_name` property of the `DataClassesDataContext` class.

Press F5 to debug the application again to see the publishers' names instead of the publishers' IDs (see Figure 17-16).

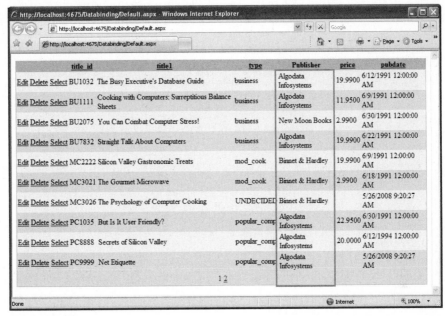

Figure 17-16

Displaying Titles from a Selected Publisher

So far, all the titles in the `titles` table are displayed in the `GridView` control. You might want to restrict the titles displayed to a particular selected publisher. To do so, insert another `LinqDataSource` control to the `Default.aspx` page by adding the following highlighted code:

```
<asp:LinqDataSource
    ID="LinqDataSource1"
    runat="server"
    ContextTypeName="DataClassesDataContext"
    EnableDelete="True"
    EnableInsert="True"
    EnableUpdate="True"
    TableName="titles">
</asp:LinqDataSource>
```

```
<asp:LinqDataSource
    ID="LinqDataSource2"
    runat="server"
    ContextTypeName="DataClassesDataContext"
    OrderBy="pub_name"
    Select="new (pub_name, pub_id)"
    TableName="publishers">
</asp:LinqDataSource>
```

Notice that the second `LinqDataSource` control has the `Select` attribute where you can specify the name of the fields you want to retrieve (`pub_name` and `pub_id`, in this example).

Add a `DropDownList` control to the top of the page by adding the following highlighted code:

```
<body>
    <form id="form1" runat="server">
    <div>
        Display titles by publisher:
        <asp:DropDownList
            ID="DropDownList1"
            runat="server"
            DataSourceID="LinqDataSource2"
            DataTextField="pub_name"
            DataValueField="pub_id"
            AutoPostBack="True">
        </asp:DropDownList>

        <asp:GridView ID="GridView1" runat="server"
        . . .
        . . .
```

This addition binds a `DropDownList` control to the `LinqDataSource` control. The `DropDownList` control will display the list of publisher names (`pub_name`), and each publisher's name has the `pub-id` as its value.

`Default.aspx` should now look like Figure 17-17 in design view. You will see the text "Display titles by publisher:" as well as a dropdown list control.

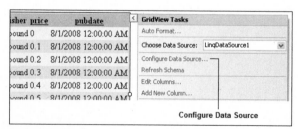

Figure 17-17

To configure the first `LinqDataSource` control so that the GridView control will only display titles from the selected publisher, click on the SmartTag of the `GridView` control, and click the Configure Data Source link (see Figure 17-18).

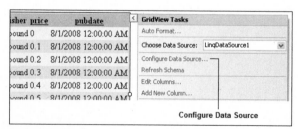

Figure 17-18

Click Next, and then click the Where button. Enter the following values in the dialog (see Figure 17-19).

Condition	Value
Column	pub_id
Operator	==
Source	Control
Control ID	DropDownList1

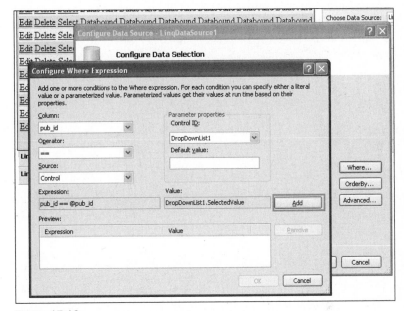

Figure 17-19

Click Add, OK, and then Finish. Visual Studio 2008 will ask if you want to regenerate the GridView columns fields and data keys. Click No.

This will make the GridView control display titles whose pub_id file match the pub-id value of the selected publisher in the DropDownList1 control.

The source of the `LinqDataSource` control now looks like this:

```
<asp:LinqDataSource
    ID="LinqDataSource1"
    runat="server"
    ContextTypeName="DataClassesDataContext"
    EnableDelete="True"
    EnableInsert="True"
    EnableUpdate="True"
    TableName="titles"
    Where="pub_id == @pub_id">

    <WhereParameters>
        <asp:ControlParameter
            ControlID="DropDownList1"
            Name="pub_id"
            PropertyName="SelectedValue"
            Type="String" />
    </WhereParameters>

</asp:LinqDataSource>
```

Press F5 to debug the application. When you select a publisher now, all books published by that publisher are displayed in the `GridView` control (see Figure 17-20).

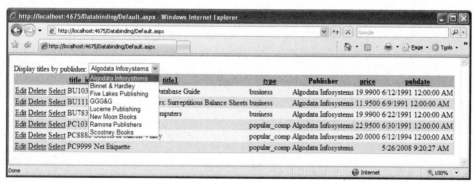

Figure 17-20

Making the Publisher Field Editable

Now select a record, and click the Edit link. Notice that the publisher is not editable (see Figure 17-21).

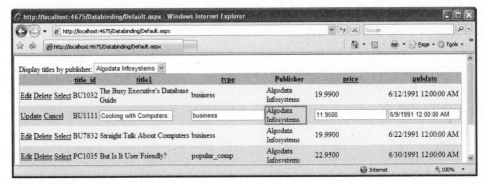

Figure 17-21

Here's how to make the publisher field editable. In the source view of `Default.aspx`, insert the following highlighted code:

```
<asp:TemplateField HeaderText="Publisher">
    <ItemTemplate>
    <%#Eval("publisher.pub_name")%>
    </ItemTemplate>

    <EditItemTemplate>
        <asp:DropDownList
            ID="DropDownList2"
            DataSourceID="LinqDataSource2"
            DataTextField="pub_name"
            DataValueField="pub_id"
            SelectedValue='<%#Bind("pub_id")%>'
            runat="server">
        </asp:DropDownList>
    </EditItemTemplate>

</asp:TemplateField>
```

This creates a dropdown list within the `GridView` control (under the `Publisher` column) and displays a list of publishers available.

Press F5 to debug the application again. A title's publisher can now be changed (see Figure 17-22).

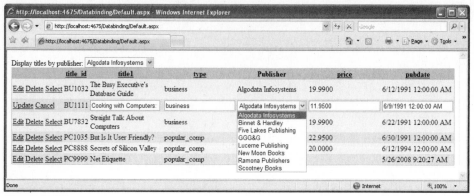

Figure 17-22

Building Responsive Applications Using AJAX

One of the challenges developers face in building appealing web applications is overcoming the constant need to refresh entire web pages to update just portions of their content. In the real world, network latencies prevent web applications from refreshing as often as you might want. Typically, when a user submits a request to a web server, the entire page must be refreshed and the user is forced to wait while it makes a round trip to the server even when only a fraction of the page has to be changed. Clearly, this is a key usability issue that developers want to put behind them in their quest to build applications that are more desktop-like in their responsiveness.

Enter AJAX, originally an acronym for Asynchronous JavaScript and XML but increasingly a term that embraces a collection of techniques for creating more responsive and feature-rich web applications. Instead of waiting for web pages to refresh, AJAX-enabled web sites dynamically and asynchronously update portions of the pages, thus providing a much more responsive experience to the user. What's more, with AJAX you can now develop richer applications that draw on the JavaScript and CSS support found in modern web browsers such as Firefox and Internet Explorer (IE) 6 and later. A quick look at the Windows Live Local site (see `http://maps.live.com`) or Google Spreadsheets (see `http://spreadsheets.google.com`) should be enough to convince you of the wonders that AJAX can deliver to a user experience.

AJAX is not a product but rather a collection of client-empowering web technologies, including XML, JavaScript, HTTP, the DOM, JSON, and CSS. Writing AJAX-style applications is not easy and has traditionally required that you have an intimate knowledge of client-side scripting languages, most notably JavaScript.

With ASP.NET 3.5, Microsoft has built-in support for AJAX. In the Toolbox, you can find a new tab called AJAX Extensions (see Figure 17-23) containing the various AJAX controls.

Figure 17-23

AJAX Control Toolkit

While ASP.NET 3.5 comes with a built-in set of controls you can use to create AJAX-style web applications, one of the greatest benefits of AJAX is that its framework is extensible, which allows you and other developers to create your own AJAX controls by extending those that already exist. Microsoft encourages this activity and sponsors an open-source-style project — the AJAX Control Toolkit that makes available a set of controls developed by Microsoft and seeks to involve the community in creating more elements to extend the functionality of AJAX. The AJAX Control Toolkit gives you access to a growing collection of robust controls that give you additional AJAX-style functionality beyond that provided by the basic AJAX framework.

You can download the AJAX Control Toolkit from: `http://codeplex.com/AtlasControlToolkit/Release/ProjectReleases.aspx?ReleaseId=11121`.

You have a choice of two files to download:

❑   `AjaxControlToolkit-Framework3.5.zip` is the full release package with complete source code to all controls, the test framework, VSI, and more.

❑   `AjaxControlToolkit-Framework3.5-NoSource.zip` contains only the sample web site and VSI, and is for people who don't need or want the source code for the controls.

The AJAX Control Toolkit comes with a set of AJAX Extender controls. Unlike the AJAX controls that come with ASP.NET 3.5, you need to manually add these to the Toolbox in Visual Studio 2008. To do so, add a new tab in Toolbox (see Figure 17-24), and name it AJAX Control Toolkit.

Figure 17-24

Extract the `AjaxControlToolkit-Framework3.5-NoSource.zip` file (assuming that you downloaded the version without source code) into a folder (C:\AJAXControlToolkit\, for instance). Inside the new folder is a folder named SampleWebSite\Bin. Drag and drop the `AjaxControlToolkit.dll` library from that Bin folder onto the new AJAX Control Toolkit tab. The set of AJAX Control Toolkit Extender controls appears, as shown in Figure 17-25.

Figure 17-25

AJAX-Enabling a Page Using the ScriptManager Control

Now let's use some of the core AJAX controls in ASP.NET 3.5 to AJAX-enable the sample project created earlier in this chapter.

The first step toward AJAX-enabling an ASP.NET web page is to add the `ScriptManager` control to the page. That's the control that manages all the AJAX functionality on your page. It should be placed before any AJAX controls, so it's a good idea to place it at the top of the page, like this:

```
<body>
    <form id="form1" runat="server">
    <div>
        <asp:ScriptManager ID="ScriptManager1" runat="server">
        </asp:ScriptManager>
        Display titles by publisher:
        <asp:DropDownList ID="DropDownList1" runat="server"
            DataSourceID="LinqDataSource2"
            DataTextField="pub_name"
            DataValueField="pub_id"
            AutoPostBack="True">
        </asp:DropDownList>
        ...
```

To place the `ScriptManager` control on the page, you can either type it manually or drag the `ScriptManager` control from the Toolbox and drop it onto the code editor.

Using the UpdatePanel Control

To delineate the part of the page you want to update without causing the entire page to refresh, drag and drop an `UpdatePanel` control from the AJAX Extensions tab of the Toolbox onto the `Default.aspx` page, like this:

```
<body>
    <form id="form1" runat="server">
    <div>
        <asp:ScriptManager ID="ScriptManager1" runat="server">
        </asp:ScriptManager>
        Display titles by publisher:
        <asp:DropDownList ID="DropDownList1" runat="server"
            DataSourceID="LinqDataSource2"
            DataTextField="pub_name"
            DataValueField="pub_id"
            AutoPostBack="True">
        </asp:DropDownList>

        <asp:UpdatePanel ID="UpdatePanel1" runat="server">
            <ContentTemplate>

            </ContentTemplate>
        </asp:UpdatePanel>
    ...
```

The <asp:UpdatePanel> control divides a web page into regions — each region can be updated without refreshing the entire page. The <ContentTemplate> element sets the template that defines the contents of the <asp:UpdatePanel> control.

Now, move a GridView control into the <ContentTemplate> element so that the content of the GridView can be updated without causing a postback to the server:

```
<asp:UpdatePanel ID="UpdatePanel1" runat="server">
    <ContentTemplate>
        <asp:GridView ID="GridView1" runat="server" AllowPaging="True"
            AllowSorting="True"
            AutoGenerateColumns="False" BackColor="LightGoldenrodYellow"
            BorderColor="Tan"
            ...
        </asp:GridView>
    </ContentTemplate>
</asp:UpdatePanel>
```

Press F5 to test the application again. This time, edit the record by clicking the Edit link (see Figure 17-26). Notice that, as you click on the links (Edit, Update, Cancel, and Select), the page does not reload. Instead, all the changes happen inside the GridView control.

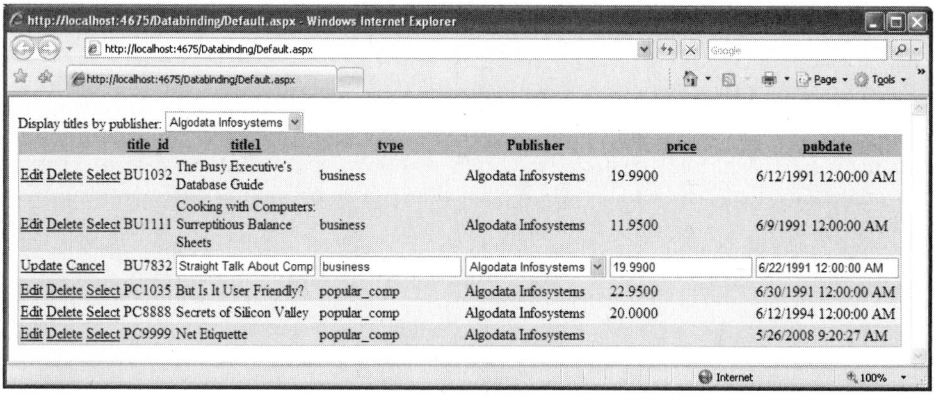

Figure 17-26

Using Triggers to Cause an Update

So far, you have used the <asp:UpdatePanel> control to enclose controls to ensure that changes in this control do not cause a postback to the server. If you select a publisher from the dropdown list, though, you will realize that the entire page is refreshed. By adding a *trigger* to the page, you can specify a control (and, optionally, its event) that causes an <asp:UpdatePanel> control to refresh. The trigger <asp:AsyncPostBackTrigger> causes an update when the specified control raises an event. In other words, when a control specified by a trigger causes an update to a control located with an <asp:UpdatePanel> control, only the control is updated and not the entire page.

Here's the markup you need to add a trigger to an `<asp:UpdatePanel>` control:

```
<asp:UpdatePanel ID="UpdatePanel1" runat="server">
    <Triggers>
        <asp:AsyncPostBackTrigger ControlID="DropDownList1" />
    </Triggers>
    <ContentTemplate>
    ...
```

Here, the `<asp:UpdatePanel>` control will refresh whenever the value of `DropDownList1` changes.

Press F5 to test the application. Now selecting a publisher from the dropdown list updates the `GridView` control without causing a refresh in the page.

Displaying Progress Using the UpdateProgress Control

The refreshing of the `GridView` control may happen very quickly on your computer because your web server is running locally. In the real world, there is network latency, and users may experience a delay but not be aware that a control is in the midst of a refresh. Therefore, it's important to give visual cues to users to let them know when an update is in progress.

You can display a progress report while an `<asp:updatePanel>` is being refreshed by using the `<asp:UpdateProgress>` control. Add the following to the source view of `Default.aspx`:

```
<body>
    <form id="form1" runat="server">
    <div>
        <asp:ScriptManager ID="ScriptManager1" runat="server">
        </asp:ScriptManager>
        Display titles by publisher:
        <asp:DropDownList ID="DropDownList1" runat="server"
            DataSourceID="LinqDataSource2"
            DataTextField="pub_name" DataValueField="pub_id" AutoPostBack="True">
        </asp:DropDownList>
        <asp:UpdatePanel ID="UpdatePanel1" runat="server">
            <Triggers>
                <asp:AsyncPostBackTrigger ControlID="DropDownList1" />
            </Triggers>
            <ContentTemplate>
                <asp:UpdateProgress ID="UpdateProgress1" runat="server">
                    <ProgressTemplate>
                        <asp:Label ID="Label1" runat="server" Text="Label">
                            Displaying titles...Please wait.
                        </asp:Label>
                    </ProgressTemplate>
                </asp:UpdateProgress>
                <asp:GridView ID="GridView1" runat="server" AllowPaging="True"
                    AllowSorting="True"
                    AutoGenerateColumns="False" BackColor="LightGoldenrodYellow"
                    BorderColor="Tan"
                ...
```

To inject a delay, double-click on the dropdown list control and use the `Sleep()` method to insert a two-second delay:

```
protected void DropDownList1_SelectedIndexChanged(object sender, EventArgs e)
{
    System.Threading.Thread.Sleep(2000);
}
```

Within the `<ProgressTemplate>` element, you can embed a control such as an `<asp:Label>` control or an `<asp:img>` control containing an animated GIF image to display some information to inform the user. Here, you display the message "Displaying titles . . . Please wait" (see Figure 17-27) to let the user know that the `GridView` control is updating.

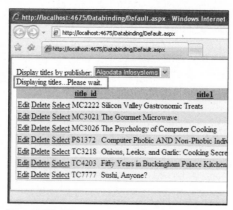

Figure 17-27

Press F5 to test the application.

Displaying a Modal Dialog Using the ModalPopupExtender Control

One problem with the current example is that when the user clicks the Delete link, the record in the `GridView` control is deleted straightaway. When you delete a record in the real world, it is always good to confirm the action with the user. In the Windows world, you can easily display a message box to let the user confirm the action. However, in a web application, it is slightly tricky.

The solution to this problem is to use the `ModalPopupExtender` control available in the AJAX Control Toolkit. The `ModalPopupExtender` control uses a popup to display content to the user in a modal fashion and prevents users from interacting with the rest of the page.

Let's modify the application to show a modal popup whenever the user tries to delete a record. Figure 17-28 shows the end result.

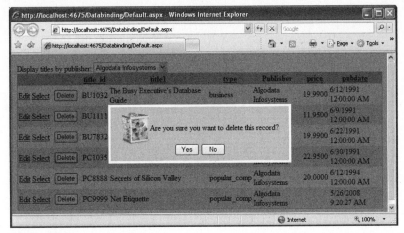

Figure 17-28

First, define the following CSS styles in the source view of the `Default.aspx` page:

```
<head runat="server">
    <title></title>

    <style type="text/css">
        .modalBackground {
            background-color:Blue;
            filter:alpha(opacity=50);
            opacity:0.5;
        }

        .dialog
        {
            border-left:5px solid #fff; border-right:5px solid #fff;
            border-top:5px solid #fff; border-bottom:5px solid #fff;
            background:#ccc;
            padding: 10px;
            width: 350px;
        }
    </style>

...
```

The `.modalBackground` style defines the background color of the modal popup. In this case, it is used to block off the rest of the page and prevent the user from interacting with that content. The `.dialog` style defines the shape and color of the popup itself. Here it has a rectangular border of 5px and a width of 350px.

Next, add a `<asp:Template>` control to the GridView control to display a Delete button:

```
<asp:GridView ID="GridView1" runat="server" AllowPaging="True"
     AllowSorting="True"
     AutoGenerateColumns="False" BackColor="LightGoldenrodYellow"
     BorderColor="Tan"
     BorderWidth="1px" CellPadding="2" DataKeyNames="title_id"
     DataSourceID="LinqDataSource1"
     ForeColor="Black" GridLines="None">
<Columns>
     <asp:CommandField ShowDeleteButton="True"
          ShowEditButton="True" ShowSelectButton="True" />
     <asp:TemplateField ControlStyle-Width="50px"
          HeaderStyle-Width="60px"
          ItemStyle-HorizontalAlign="Center">
          <ItemTemplate>
               <asp:Button ID="btnDelete"
                    runat="server"
                    OnClick="btnDelete_Click"
                    OnClientClick="displayPopup(this); return false;"
                    Text="Delete" />
          </ItemTemplate>
     </asp:TemplateField>
     <asp:BoundField DataField="title_id" HeaderText="title_id"
          ReadOnly="True" SortExpression="title_id" />
     <asp:BoundField DataField="title1" HeaderText="title1"
          SortExpression="title1" />
     ...
```

Notice that the Delete button has two events defined: `OnClick` and `OnClientClick`. In this example, when the user clicks the button, the JavaScript function named `displayPopup()` (which you will define shortly) is called. You insert the `return false;` statement to prevent a postback from occurring while the dialog is being displayed.

You also need to disable the Delete link in the GridView control because you now have the Delete button. Set the `ShowDeleteButton` attribute in the `<asp:CommandField>` element to `False`:

```
<asp:CommandField
     ShowDeleteButton="False"
     ShowEditButton="True"
     ShowSelectButton="True" />
```

The `Default.aspx` page now looks like Figure 17-29.

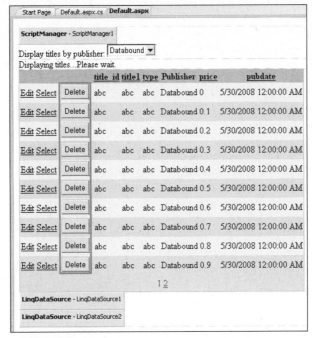

Figure 17-29

Create a new folder in the project and name it `images`. Add an image called `delete.png` into the `images` folder (see Figure 17-30).

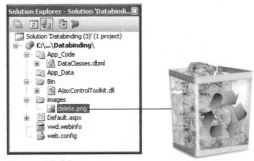

Figure 17-30

You will now use a `<div>` element to define the content of the popup that you want to display:

```
<div id="divDialog" runat="server" class="dialog" style="display: none">
    <center>
        <img style="vertical-align: middle"
            src="images/delete.png" width="60" />
        Are you sure you want to delete this record?<br />
```

(continued)

(continued)

```
            <asp:Button ID="btnOK" runat="server" Text="Yes" Width="50px" />
            <asp:Button ID="btnNO" runat="server" Text="No" Width="50px" />
        </center>
      </div>

    </form>
  </body>
</html>
```

This block of code defines the popup shown in Figure 17-31.

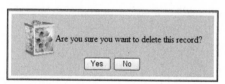

Figure 17-31

To display the `<div>` element as a modal popup, use the `ModalPopupExtender` control:

```
<cc1:ModalPopupExtender
    ID="popupDialog"
    runat="server"
    TargetControlID="divDialog"
    PopupControlID="divDialog"
    OkControlID="btnOK"
    CancelControlID="btnNO"
    OnOkScript="OK_Click();"
    OnCancelScript="No_Click();"
    BackgroundCssClass="modalBackground">
</cc1:ModalPopupExtender>

    </form>
  </body>
</html>
```

The `ModalPopupExtender` control has the attributes described in the following table.

Attribute	Description
ID	Identifies the `ModalPopupExtender` control
TargetControlID	Specifies the control that activates the `ModalPopupExtender` control
PopupControlID	Specifies the control to display as a modal popup
OkControlID	Specifies the control that dismisses the modal popup

Attribute	Description
CancelControlID	Specifies the control that cancels the modal popup
OnOkScript	Specifies the script to run when the modal popup is dismissed with the OkControlID
OnCancelScript	Specifies the script to run when the modal popup is canceled with the CancelControlID
BackgroundCssClass	Specifies the CSS class to apply to the background when the modal popup is displayed

Finally, insert the JavaScript functions into the source view of Default.aspx:

```
<script type="text/javascript">
    var _source;
    var _popup;

    function displayPopup(source) {
        _source = source;
        _popup = $find('popupDialog');
        //---display the popup dialog---
        _popup.show();
    }

    function OK_Click() {
        //---hides the popup dialog---
        _popup.hide();
        //---posts back to the server---
        __doPostBack(_source.name, '');
    }

    function No_Click() {
        //---hides the popup---
        _popup.hide();
        //---clears the event sourcesss
        _source = null;
        _popup = null;
    }
</script>
</head>
<body>
```

The displayPopup() function looks for the ModalPopupExtender control in the page and displays the modal popup. The OK_Click() function is called when the user decides to proceed with the deletion. It hides the modal popup and initiates a postback to the server. The No_Click() function is called when the user cancels the deletion. It hides the modal popup.

That's it! Press F5 to test the application.

In this particular example, you will get a runtime error if you proceed with the deletion. That's because the `titles` table is related to the `titleauthor` table (also part of the `pubs` database), and deleting a record in the `titles` table violates the reference integrity of the database.

Summary

This chapter developed a simple ASP.NET web application that displays data stored in a database. One of the new features in ASP.NET 3.5 is the `LinqDataSource` control that enables you to bind directly against a LINQ-enabled data model instead of a database, so instead of specifying SQL statements for querying data, you can use LINQ queries. You also saw how to use the built-in AJAX support in ASP.NET 3.5 to create responsive AJAX applications.

18

Developing Windows Mobile Applications

The mobile application platform has gained a lot of interest among enterprise developers in recent years. With so many mobile platforms available, customers are spoiled for choice. However, at the front of developers' minds are the various criteria that they need to evaluate before deciding on the platform to support. These factors are:

❑ Size of device install base

❑ Ease of development and support for widely known/used programming languages

❑ Capability to run one version of an application on a large number of devices

One mobile platform of choice among developers is the Microsoft Windows Mobile platform, now into its sixth generation. Today, the Windows Mobile platform is one of the most successful mobile device platforms in the market, with several handset manufacturers (such as HP, Asus, HTC, and even Sony Ericsson and Palm) supporting it.

This chapter presents the basics of Windows Mobile. It shows you how to create an RSS Reader application and then how to test and deploy the application to a real device. In particular, you will:

❑ Examine the basics of the Windows Mobile platform

❑ Learn how to download and install the various Software Development Kits (SDKs) to target the different platforms

❑ Create an RSS Reader application that allows users to subscribe to RSS feeds

❑ Explore various ways to deploy your Windows Mobile applications

❑ Create a professional-looking setup application to distribute your Windows Mobile applications

The Windows Mobile Platform

The Windows Mobile platform defines a device running the Windows CE operating system customized with a standard set of Microsoft-designed user interface shells and applications. Devices that use the Windows Mobile platform include:

❑ Pocket PCs

❑ Smartphones

❑ Portable Media Centers

❑ Automobile computing devices

For this chapter, the discussion is restricted to the first two categories — Pocket PCs and Smartphones. (The latter two categories use a different shell and are not widely used in today's market.)

The latest version of the Windows Mobile platform at the time of writing is Windows Mobile 6.1. With this new release, there are some new naming conventions. Here's a list of the Pocket PC and Smartphone names used by Microsoft over the years.

Pocket PCs	Smartphones
Pocket PC 2000/Pocket PC 2000 Phone Edition	
Pocket PC 2002/Pocket PC 2002 Phone Edition	Smartphone 2002
Windows Mobile 2003 for Pocket PC/Windows Mobile 2003 for Pocket PC Phone Edition	Windows Mobile 2003 for Smartphone
Windows Mobile 2003 SE (Second Edition) for Pocket PC/Windows Mobile 2003 SE (Second Edition) for Pocket PC Phone Edition	Windows Mobile 2003 SE for Smartphone
Windows Mobile 5.0 for Pocket PC/Windows Mobile 5.0 for Pocket PC Phone Edition	Windows Mobile 5.0 for Smartphone
Windows Mobile 6 Classic/Windows Mobile 6 Professional	Windows Mobile 6 Standard

Beginning with Windows Mobile 6, Microsoft defines a device with a touch screen but without phone capability as a Windows Mobile 6 Classic device (previously known as Pocket PC or Windows Mobile). Figure 18-1 shows a Windows Mobile 6 Classic device (the iPaq 211).

Figure 18-1

Touch-screen devices with phone functionality are now known as Windows Mobile 6 Professional (previously Windows Mobile Phone Edition). Figure 18-2 shows such a device (the HTC Touch Cruise).

Figure 18-2

Devices that do not support touch screens are now known as Windows Mobile 6 Standard (previously Smartphones). One is the Moto Q9h, shown in Figure 18-3.

Figure 18-3

Developing Windows Mobile Applications Using the .NET Compact Framework

The easiest way to develop for the Windows Mobile platform is to use the Microsoft .NET Compact Framework (.NET CF). The .NET CF is a scaled-down version of the .NET Framework and is designed to work on Windows CE (a scaled-down version of the Windows OS supporting a subset of the Win32 APIs) based devices. The .NET CF contains a subset of the class libraries available on the desktop version of the .NET Framework and includes a few new libraries designed specifically for mobile devices.

At the time of writing, the latest version of .NET CF is version 3.5. Following is a list of the various version names of the .NET CF and their corresponding version numbers:

Version Name	Version Number
1.0 RTM	1.0.2268.0
1.0 SP1	1.0.3111.0
1.0 SP2	1.0.3316.0
1.0 SP3	1.0.4292.0
2.0 RTM	2.0.5238.0
2.0 SP1	2.0.6129.0
2.0 SP2	2.0.7045.0
3.5 Beta 1	3.5.7066.0
3.5 Beta 2	3.5.7121.0
RTM	3.5.7283.0

Source: http://en.wikipedia.org/wiki/
.NET_vCompact_Framework

Knowing the version number of the .NET CF installed in your device is useful at development time because it helps you determine the exact version of the .NET CF installed on the target device/emulator.

As a developer, you can use either the C# or VB.NET language to write applications for the Windows Mobile platform. All the functionalities required by your applications can be satisfied by:

❑ The class libraries in the .NET CF, and/or

❑ APIs at the OS level via Platform Invoke (P/Invoke), and/or

❑ Alternative third-party class libraries such as the OpenNetCF's Smart Device Extension (SDE)

You can determine the versions of the .NET Compact Framework currently installed on your Windows Mobile device by going to Start ⇨ File Explorer and launching the cgacutil.exe utility located in \Windows.

Figure 18-4 shows the version of the .NET CF installed on a Windows Mobile emulator (more on this later).

Figure 18-4

Windows Mobile 5.0 devices comes with the .NET CF 1.0 preinstalled in ROM, whereas the newer Windows Mobile 6 devices come with the .NET CF 2.0 preinstalled in ROM. If your application uses the newer .NET CF v3.5, you will need to install it onto the device before applications based on it can execute.

Obtaining the Appropriate SDKs and Tools

To develop Windows Mobile applications using the .NET CF, you need to download the SDK for each platform. Here are the SDKs you need:

- ❑ Windows Mobile 5.0 SDK for Pocket PC
- ❑ Windows Mobile 5.0 SDK for Smartphone
- ❑ Windows Mobile 6 Professional and Standard Software Development Kits Refresh

You can download the SDKs from Microsoft's web site (http:// microsoft.com/downloads) at no cost. The best tool to develop Windows Mobile applications using the .NET CF is to use the Visual Studio IDE, using Visual Studio 2005 Professional or above.

If you are using Visual Studio 2005, you need to download the Windows Mobile 5.0 SDK for Pocket PC and Smartphone (as described earlier). If you are using Visual Studio 2008, the Windows Mobile 5.0 SDKs for Pocket PC and Smartphone are already installed by default. For both versions, you need to download the Windows Mobile 6 SDKs to develop applications for Windows Mobile 6 devices.

With the relevant SDKs installed, the first step toward Windows Mobile development is to launch Visual Studio 2008 and create a new project. Select the Smart Device project type, and then select the Smart Device Project template (see Figure 18-5).

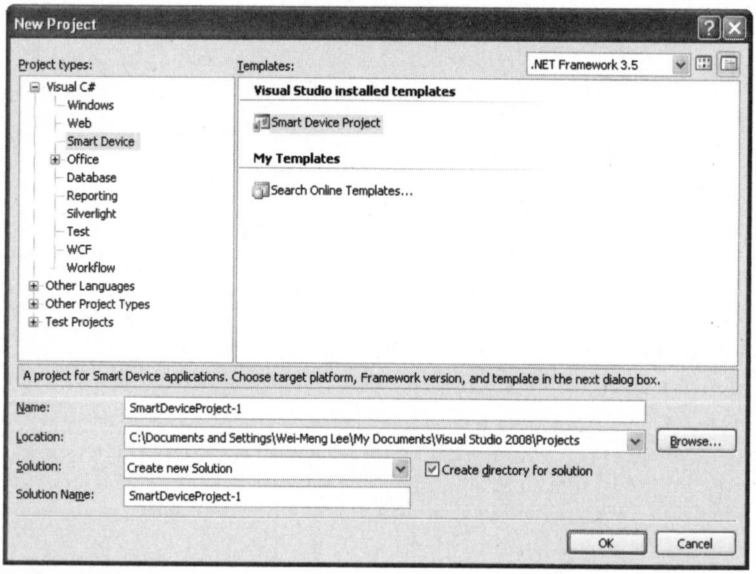

Figure 18-5

The Add New Smart Device Project dialog opens. You can select the target platform as well as the version of the .NET CF you want to use (see Figure 18-6).

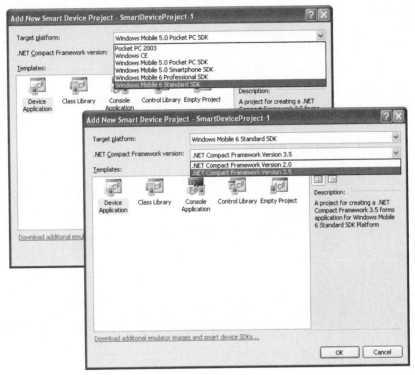

Figure 18-6

You are now ready to start developing for Windows Mobile. Figure 18-7 shows the design view of a Windows Mobile Form in Visual Studio 2008 designer.

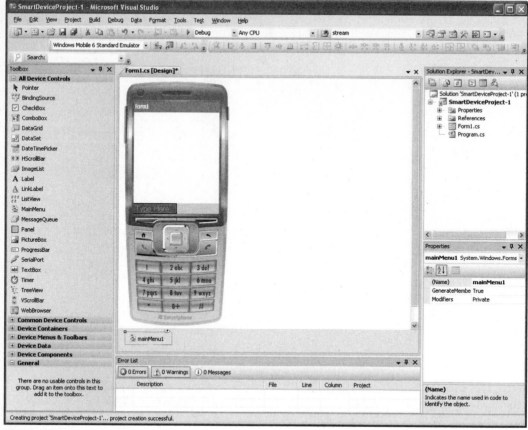

Figure 18-7

Building the RSS Reader Application

With the recent introduction of the Windows Mobile 6 platforms, we are now beginning to see a proliferation of new devices supporting Windows Mobile 6 Standard (aka Smartphone). As Windows Mobile 6 Standard devices do not have touch screens, they pose certain challenges when developing applications to run on them. Hence, in this section you will learn how to develop a Windows Mobile 6 Standard application that allows users to subscribe to RSS feeds.

The RSS Reader application has the following capabilities:

❑ Can subscribe to RSS feeds as well as unsubscribe from feeds

❑ Can cache the feeds as XML files on the device so that if the device goes offline the feeds are still available

❑ Uses a web browser to view the content of a post

Building the User Interface

To get started, launch Visual Studio 2008 and create a new Windows Mobile 6 Standard application using .NET CF 3.5. Name the application `RSSReader`.

Don't forget to download the free Windows Mobile 6 Standard SDK (`http://microsoft.com/ downloads`). You need it to create the application detailed in this chapter.

The default Form1 uses the standard form factor of 176x180 pixels. As this application is targeted at users with wide-screen devices, change the `FormFactor` property of `Form1` to `Windows Mobile 6 Landscape QVGA`.

Populate the default `Form1` with the following controls (see also Figure 18-8):

❑   One `TreeView` control

❑   Four `MenuItem` controls

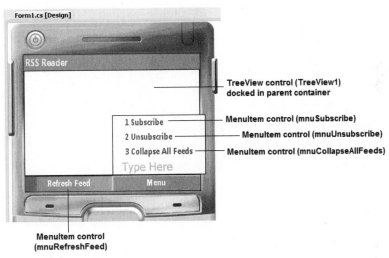

Figure 18-8

Add an `ImageList` control to `Form1` and add three images to its `Images` property (see Figure 18-9).

You can download the images from this book's source code at its Wrox web site.

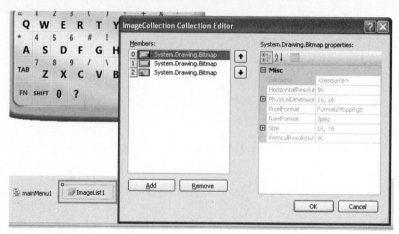

Figure 18-9

These images will be used by the `TreeView` control to display its content when the tree is expanded or closed. Hence, associate the `ImageList` control to the `TreeView` control by setting the `ImageList` property of the `TreeView` control to `ImageList1`.

Add a new Windows Form to the project, and populate it with a `WebBrowser` and `MenuItem` control (see Figure 18-10). The `WebBrowser` control will be used to view the content of a posting.

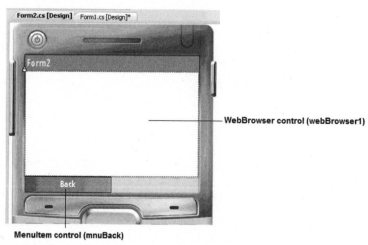

Figure 18-10

Set the `Modifiers` property of the `WebBrowser` control to `Internal` so that the control is accessible from other forms. Specifically, you want to set the content of the control from within `Form1`.

Switch to the code behind of `Form1`, and import the following namespaces:

```
using System.IO;
using System.Net;
using System.Xml;
using System.Text.RegularExpressions;
```

Declare the following constants and variable:

```
namespace RSSReader
{
    public partial class Form1 : Form
    {
        //---constants for icons---
        const int ICO_OPEN = 0;
        const int ICO_CLOSE = 1;
        const int ICO_POST = 2;

        //---file containing the list of subscribed feeds---
        string feedsList = @"\Feeds.txt";

        //---app's current path---
        string appPath = string.Empty;

        //---the last URL entered (subscribe)---
        string lastURLEntered = string.Empty;

        //---used for displaying a wait message panel---
        Panel displayPanel;

        //---for displaying individual post---
        Form2 frm2 = new Form2();
```

Creating the Helper Methods

When RSS feeds are being downloaded, you want to display a message on the screen to notify the user that the application is downloading the feed (see Figure 18-11).

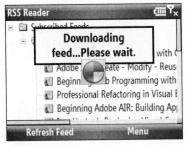

Figure 18-11

For this purpose, you can improvise with the aid of the Panel and Label controls. Define the CreatePanel() function so that you can dynamically create the message panel using a couple of Panel controls and a Label control:

```csharp
//---create a Panel control to display a message---
private Panel CreatePanel(string str)
{
    //---background panel---
    Panel panel1 = new Panel()
    {
        BackColor = Color.Black,
        Location = new Point(52, 13),
        Size = new Size(219, 67),
        Visible = false,
    };
    panel1.BringToFront();

    //---foreground panel---
    Panel panel2 = new Panel()
    {
        BackColor = Color.LightYellow,
        Location = new Point(3, 3),
        Size = new Size(panel1.Size.Width - 6, panel1.Size.Height - 6)
    };

    //---add the label to display text---
    Label label = new Label()
    {
        Font = new Font(FontFamily.GenericSansSerif, 12, FontStyle.Bold),
        TextAlign = ContentAlignment.TopCenter,
        Location = new Point(3, 3),
        Size = new Size(panel2.Size.Width - 6, panel2.Size.Height - 6),
        Text = str
    };

    //---adds the label to Panel2---
    panel2.Controls.Add(label);

    //---adds the Panel2 to Panel1---
    panel1.Controls.Add(panel2);
    return panel1;
}
```

For simplicity, you are hardcoding the location of panel1 (assuming that this application is running on a wide-screen device). Figure 18-12 shows the various controls forming the display panel.

Figure 18-12

Next, define the `IsConnected()` function to test whether the user is connected to the Internet:

```
//---check if you are connected to the Internet---
private bool IsConnected()
{
    try
    {
        string hostName = Dns.GetHostName();
        IPHostEntry curhost = Dns.GetHostEntry(hostName);
        return (curhost.AddressList[0].ToString() !=
            IPAddress.Loopback.ToString());
    }
    catch (Exception)
    {
        return false;
    }
}
```

`Dns` is a static class that provides simple domain name resolution. The `GetHostName()` method gets the host name of the local computer, which is then passed to the `GetHostEntry()` method of the `Dns` class to obtain an `IPHostEntry` object. `IPHostEntry` is a container class for Internet host address information. Using this object, you can access its `AddressList` property to obtain the list of IP addresses associated with it. If the first member of the `AddressList` property array is not the loopback address (`127.0.0.1`; represented by `IPAddress.Loopback`), it is assumed that there is Internet connectivity.

Next, define the `DownloadFeed()` function, which takes in the URL for the feed you want to download and a title argument (to return the title of the feed). Each post title and its corresponding description is appended to a string and returned to the calling function:

```
//---download feed and extract Title and Description for each post---
private string DownloadFeed(string feedURL, ref string title)
{
    XmlDocument xml = new XmlDocument();

    //---always load from storage first---
    string FileName =
        appPath + @"\" + RemoveSpecialChars(feedURL) + ".xml";

    if (File.Exists(FileName))
    {
        xml.Load(FileName);
    }
    else
    {
        //---check if there is network connectivity---
        if (IsConnected())
        {
            WebRequest ftpReq = null;
            WebResponse ftpResp = null;
            Stream ftpRespStream = null;
            StreamReader reader = null;
            bool getRSSFeedFailed = false;
```

(continued)

(continued)

```
                    try
                    {
                        //---download the RSS document---
                        ftpReq = WebRequest.Create(feedURL);
                        ftpResp = ftpReq.GetResponse();
                        ftpRespStream = ftpResp.GetResponseStream();
                        reader = new StreamReader(ftpRespStream,
                            System.Text.Encoding.UTF8);

                        //---load the RSS document into an XMLDocument object---
                        xml.Load(reader);

                        //---save a local copy of the feed document---
                        xml.Save(FileName);
                    }
                    catch (Exception ex)
                    {
                        MessageBox.Show(ex.Message);
                        getRSSFeedFailed = true;
                    }
                    finally
                    {
                        if (ftpRespStream != null)
                        {
                            ftpRespStream.Dispose();
                            ftpRespStream.Close();
                        };
                        if (ftpResp != null) ftpResp.Close();
                    }
                    if (getRSSFeedFailed) return String.Empty;
                }
                else
                {
                    return String.Empty;
                }
            }

            //---get the title of the feed---
            XmlNode titleNode = xml.SelectSingleNode(@"rss/channel/title");
            title = titleNode.InnerText;

            //---select all <rss><channel><item> elements---
            XmlNodeList nodes = xml.SelectNodes("rss/channel/item");

            string result = String.Empty;
            foreach (XmlNode node in nodes)
            {
                //---select each post's <title> and <description> elements---
                result += node.SelectSingleNode("title").InnerText + ((char)3);
                result += node.SelectSingleNode("description").InnerText +
                    ((char)12);
            }
            return result;
        }
```

To download the RSS feed XML documents, you use the `WebRequest` and `WebResponse` classes. The document is then read using a `StreamReader` object and loaded into an `XmlDocument` object. Each post title and its description are separated by the ASCII character 3, and each posting is separated by the ASCII character 12, like this:

```
Post_Title<3>Post_Description<12>Post_Title<3>Post_Description<12>
Post_Title<3>Post_Description<12>Post_Title<3>Post_Description<12>
Post_Title<3>Post_Description<12>...
```

Notice that after the XML feed for an URL is downloaded, it is saved onto storage. This ensures that the application continues to work in offline mode (when user disconnects from the Internet). The URL of the feed is used as the filename, minus all the special characters within the URL, with the `.xml` extension appended. For example, if the feed URL is `http://www.wrox.com/WileyCDA/feed/RSS_WROX_ALLNEW.xml`, then the filename would be `httpwwwwroxcomWileyCDAfeedRSSWROXALLNEWxml.xml`. To strip off all the special characters in the URL, define the `RemoveSpecialChars()` function as follows:

```
//---removes special chars from an URL string---
private string RemoveSpecialChars(string str)
{
    string NewString = String.Empty;
    Regex reg = new Regex("[A-Z]|[a-z]");

    MatchCollection coll = reg.Matches(str);
    for (int i = 0; i <= coll.Count - 1; i++)
        NewString = NewString + coll[i].Value;

    return NewString;
}
```

You use the `Regex` (regular expression) class to extract all the alphabets from the URL and append them into a string, which will be returned to the calling function to use as a filename.

Next, define the `SubscribeFeed()` function to subscribe to a feed, and then add each post to the `TreeView` control (see Figure 18-13):

```
//---returns true if subscription is successful---
private bool SubscribeFeed(string URL)
{
    bool succeed = false;
    try
    {
        //---display the wait message panel---
        if (displayPanel == null)
        {
            displayPanel = CreatePanel("Downloading feed...Please wait.");
            this.Controls.Add(displayPanel);
        }
        else
        {
            displayPanel.BringToFront();
            displayPanel.Visible = true;
```

(continued)

587

(continued)

```
                            Cursor.Current = Cursors.WaitCursor;
                            //---update the UI---
                            Application.DoEvents();
                    }

                    //---download feed---
                    string title = String.Empty;
                    string[] posts = DownloadFeed(URL, ref title).Split((char)12);
                    if (posts.Length > 0 && posts[0] != String.Empty)
                    {
                        //---always add to the root node---
                        TreeNode FeedTitleNode = new TreeNode()
                        {
                            Text = title,
                            Tag = URL,  //---stores the Feed URL---
                            ImageIndex = ICO_CLOSE,
                            SelectedImageIndex = ICO_OPEN
                        };

                        //---add the feed title---
                        TreeView1.Nodes[0].Nodes.Add(FeedTitleNode);

                        //---add individual elements (posts)---
                        for (int i = 0; i <= posts.Length - 2; i++)
                        {
                            //---extract each post as "title:description"---
                            string[] str = posts[i].Split((char)3);

                            TreeNode PostNode = new TreeNode()
                            {
                                Text = str[0], //---title---
                                Tag = str[1],  //---description---
                                ImageIndex = ICO_POST,
                                SelectedImageIndex = ICO_POST
                            };

                            //---add the posts to the tree---
                            TreeView1.Nodes[0].Nodes
                                [TreeView1.Nodes[0].Nodes.Count - 1].
                                Nodes.Add(PostNode);
                        }
                        //---subscription is successful---
                        succeed = true;

                        //---highlight the new feed and expand its post---
                        TreeView1.SelectedNode = FeedTitleNode;
                    }
                    else
                        succeed = false;
            }
            catch (Exception ex)
            {
                MessageBox.Show(ex.Message);
```

```
            //---subscription is not successful---
            succeed = false;
        }
        finally
        {
            //---clears the panel and cursor---
            Cursor.Current = Cursors.Default;
            displayPanel.Visible = false;

            //---update the UI---
            Application.DoEvents();
        }
        return succeed;
    }
```

Figure 18-13

For each TreeView node representing a feed title (such as Wrox: All New Titles), the Text property is set to the feed's title and its URL is stored in the Tag property of the node. For each node representing a posting (.NET Domain-Driven Design and so forth), the Text property is set to the posting's title and its description is stored in the Tag property.

Wiring All the Event Handlers

With the helper functions defined, let's wire up all the event handlers for the various controls. First, code the Form1_Load event handler as follows:

```
private void Form1_Load(object sender, EventArgs e)
{
    //---find out the app's path---
    appPath = Path.GetDirectoryName(
        System.Reflection.Assembly.GetExecutingAssembly().
        GetName().CodeBase);

    //---set the feed list to be stored in the app's folder---
    feedsList = appPath + feedsList;

    try
    {
        //---create the root node---
```

(continued)

(continued)

```
                    TreeNode node = new TreeNode()
                    {
                        ImageIndex = ICO_CLOSE,
                        SelectedImageIndex = ICO_OPEN,
                        Text = "Subscribed Feeds"
                    };

                    //---add the node to the tree---
                    TreeView1.Nodes.Add(node);
                    TreeView1.SelectedNode = node;
                }
                catch (Exception ex)
                {
                    MessageBox.Show(ex.Message);
                    return;
                }

                try
                {
                    //---load all subscribed feeds---
                    if (File.Exists(feedsList))
                    {
                        TextReader textreader = File.OpenText(feedsList);

                        //---read URLs of all the subscribed feeds---
                        string[] feeds = textreader.ReadToEnd().Split('|');
                        textreader.Close();

                        //---add all the feeds to the tree---
                        for (int i = 0; i <= feeds.Length - 2; i++)
                            SubscribeFeed(feeds[i]);
                    }
                    else
                    {
                        //---pre-subscribe to a few feed(s)---
                        SubscribeFeed(
                            "http://www.wrox.com/WileyCDA/feed/RSS_WROX_ALLNEW.xml");
                    }
                }
                catch (Exception ex)
                {
                    MessageBox.Show(ex.Message);
                }
            }
```

When the form is first loaded, you have to create a root node for the `TreeView` control and load all the existing feeds. All subscribed feeds are saved in a plain text file (`Feeds.txt`), in the following format:

```
Feed URL|Feed URL|Feed URL|
```

An example is:

```
http://news.google.com/?output=rss|http://rss.cnn.com/rss/cnn_topstories.rss|
```

If there are no existing feeds (that is, if Feeds.txt does not exist), subscribe to at least one feed.

In the Click event handler of the Subscribe MenuItem control, prompt the user to input a feed's URL, and then subscribe to the feed. If the subscription is successful, save the feed URL to file:

```csharp
private void mnuSubscribe_Click(object sender, EventArgs e)
{
    if (!IsConnected())
    {
        MessageBox.Show("You are not connected to the Internet.");
        return;
    }

    //---add a reference to Microsoft.VisualBasic.dll---
    string URL = Microsoft.VisualBasic.Interaction.InputBox(
        "Please enter the feed URL", "Feed URL", lastURLEntered, 0, 0);

    if (URL != String.Empty)
    {
        lastURLEntered = URL;

        //---if feed is subscribed successfully---
        if (SubscribeFeed(URL))
        {
            //---save in feed list---
            TextWriter textwriter = File.AppendText(feedsList);
            textwriter.Write(URL + "|");
            textwriter.Close();
        }
        else
        {
            MessageBox.Show("Feed not subscribed. " +
            "Please check that you have entered " +
            "the correct URL and that you have " +
            "Internet access.");
        }
    }
}
```

C# does not include the InputBox() function that is available in VB.NET to get user's input (see Figure 18-14). Hence, it is a good idea to add a reference to the Microsoft.VisualBasic.dll library and use it as shown in the preceding code.

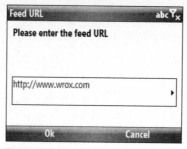

Figure 18-14

Whenever a node in the `TreeView` control is selected, you should perform a check to see if it is a posting node and enable/disable the MenuItem controls appropriately (see Figure 18-15):

```
//---fired after a node in the TreeView control is selected---
private void TreeView1_AfterSelect(object sender, TreeViewEventArgs e)
{
    //---if a feed node is selected---
    if (e.Node.ImageIndex != ICO_POST && e.Node.Parent != null)
    {
        mnuUnsubscribe.Enabled = true;
        mnuRefreshFeed.Enabled = true;
    }
    else
    {   //---if a post node is selected---
        mnuUnsubscribe.Enabled = false;
        mnuRefreshFeed.Enabled = false;
    }
}
```

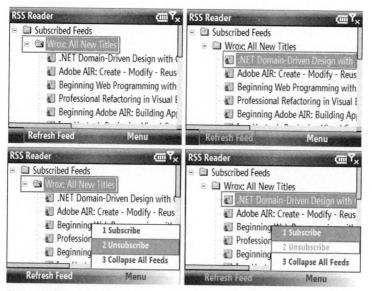

Figure 18-15

When the user selects a post using the Select button on the navigation pad, Form2 containing the WebBrowser control is loaded and its content set accordingly (see Figure 18-16). This is handled by the KeyDown event handler of the TreeView control:

```
//---fired when a node in the TreeView is selected
// and the Enter key pressed---
private void TreeView1_KeyDown(object sender, KeyEventArgs e)
{
    TreeNode node = TreeView1.SelectedNode;
    //---if the Enter key was pressed---
    if (e.KeyCode == System.Windows.Forms.Keys.Enter)
    {
        //---if this is a post node---
        if (node.ImageIndex == ICO_POST)
        {
            //---set the title of Form2 to title of post---
            frm2.Text = node.Text;

            //---modifier for webBrowser1 in Form2 must be set to
            // Internal---
            //---set the webbrowser control to display the post content---
            frm2.webBrowser1.DocumentText = node.Tag.ToString();

            //---show Form2---
            frm2.Show();
        }
    }
}
```

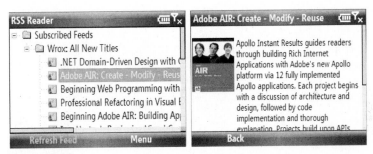

Figure 18-16

To unsubscribe a feed, you remove the feed's URL from the text file and then remove the feed node from the TreeView control. This is handled by the Unsubscribe MenuItem control:

```csharp
//---Unsubscribe a feed---
private void mnuUnsubscribe_Click(object sender, EventArgs e)
{
    //---get the node to unsubscribe---
    TreeNode CurrentSelectedNode = TreeView1.SelectedNode;

    //---confirm the deletion with the user---
    DialogResult result =
        MessageBox.Show("Remove " + CurrentSelectedNode.Text + "?",
        "Unsubscribe", MessageBoxButtons.YesNo,
        MessageBoxIcon.Question,
        MessageBoxDefaultButton.Button1);

    try
    {
        if (result == DialogResult.Yes)
        {
            //---URL To unsubscribe---
            string urlToUnsubscribe = CurrentSelectedNode.Tag.ToString();

            //---load all the feeds from feeds list---
            TextReader textreader = File.OpenText(feedsList);
            string[] feeds = textreader.ReadToEnd().Split('|');
            textreader.Close();

            //---rewrite the feeds list omitting the one to be
            // unsubscribed---
            TextWriter textwriter = File.CreateText(feedsList);
            for (int i = 0; i <= feeds.Length - 2; i++)
            {
                if (feeds[i] != urlToUnsubscribe)
                {
                    textwriter.Write(feeds[i] + "|");
                }
            }
            textwriter.Close();

            //---remove the node from the TreeView control---
            CurrentSelectedNode.Remove();
            MessageBox.Show("Feed unsubscribed!");
        }
    }
    catch (Exception ex)
    {
        MessageBox.Show(ex.Message);
    }
}
```

When the user needs to refresh a feed, first make a backup copy of the feed XML document and proceed to subscribe to the same feed again. If the subscription is successful, remove the node containing the old feed. If the subscription is not successful (for example, when a device is disconnected from the Internet), restore the backup feed XML document. This is handled by the `Refresh Feed MenuItem` control:

```
//---refresh the current feed---
private void mnuRefreshFeed_Click(object sender, EventArgs e)
{
    //---if no Internet connectivity---
    if (!IsConnected())
    {
        MessageBox.Show("You are not connected to the Internet.");
        return;
    }

    //---get the node to be refreshed---
    TreeNode CurrentSelectedNode = TreeView1.SelectedNode;
    string url = CurrentSelectedNode.Tag.ToString();

    //---get the filename of the feed---
    string FileName =
        appPath + @"\" + RemoveSpecialChars(url) + ".xml";

    try
    {
        //---make a backup copy of the current feed---
        File.Copy(FileName, FileName + "_Copy", true);

        //---delete feed from local storage---
        File.Delete(FileName);

        //---load the same feed again---
        if (SubscribeFeed(url))
        {
            //---remove the node to be refreshed---
            CurrentSelectedNode.Remove();
        }
        else //---the subscription(refresh) failed---
        {
            //---restore the deleted feed file---
            File.Copy(FileName + "_Copy", FileName, true);
            MessageBox.Show("Refresh not successful. Please try again.");
        }

        //---delete the backup file---
        File.Delete(FileName + "_Copy");
    }
    catch (Exception ex)
    {
        MessageBox.Show("Refresh failed (" + ex.Message + ")");
    }
}
```

In the `Click` event handler for the `Collapse All Feeds MenuItem` control, use the `CollapseAll()` method from the `TreeView` control to collapse all the nodes:

```
private void mnuCollapseAllFeeds_Click(object sender, EventArgs e)
{
    TreeView1.CollapseAll();
}
```

Finally, code the `Click` event handler in the `Back MenuItem` control in `Form2` as follows:

```
private void mnuBack_Click(object sender, EventArgs e)
{
    this.Hide();
}
```

That's it! You are now ready to test the application.

Testing Using Emulators

The SDKs for the various platforms include various emulators for you to test your Windows Mobile applications without needing to use a real device. For example, if your project is targeting the Windows Mobile 6 platform, you would see a list of emulators available for your testing (see Figure 18-17).

Figure 18-17

Once you have selected an emulator to use, click the Connect to Device button to launch it. To test your application, cradle the emulator to ActiveSync first so that you have Internet connectivity on the emulator. To cradle the emulator to ActiveSync, select Tools ⇨ Device Emulator Manager in Visual Studio 2008; right-click the emulator that has been launched (the one with the green arrow next to it); and select Cradle (see Figure 18-18).

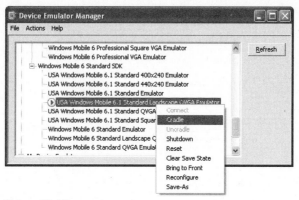

Figure 18-18

Now press F5 in Visual Studio 2008 to deploy the application onto the emulator for testing.

Testing Using Real Devices

While most of the testing can be performed on the emulators, it is always helpful to use a real device to fully test your application. For example, you will find out the true usability of your application when users have to type using the small keypad on the phone (versus typing using a keyboard when testing on an emulator). For this purpose, you can test your application on some of the devices running the Windows Mobile 6 Standard platform, such as the Samsung Black II (see Figure 18-19).

Figure 18-19

Testing your Windows Mobile application on real devices could not be easier. All you need is to:

1.   Connect your device to your development machine using ActiveSync.

2.   Select Windows Mobile 6 Standard Device (see Figure 18-20) in Visual Studio 2008.

Figure 18-20

3.   Press F5.

The application is now deployed onto the device.

Deploying the Application

Once the testing and debugging process is over, you need to package the application nicely so that you have a way to get it installed on your users' devices.

The following sections show how to create a CAB (cabinet) file — a library of compressed files stored as a single file — so that you can easily distribute your application. Subsequent sections explain how to create an MSI (Microsoft Installer) file to automate the installation process.

Creating a CAB File

An easy way to package your Windows Mobile application is to create a CAB file so that you can transfer it onto the end user's device (using emails, web browser, memory card, and so on). The following steps show you how:

1.   Add a new project to the current solution in Visual Studio 2008 (see Figure 18-21).

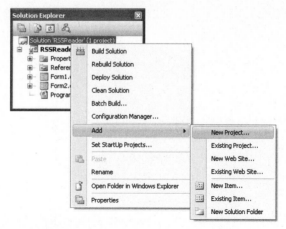

Figure 18-21

2. Choose the Setup and Deployment project type, and select the Smart Device CAB Project template (see Figure 18-22). Use the default name of SmartDeviceCab1, and click OK.

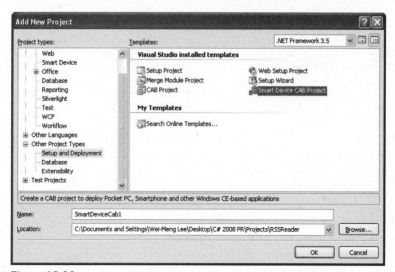

Figure 18-22

3. In the File System tab, right-click on Application Folder, and select Add ⇨ Project Output (see Figure 18-23).

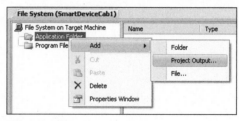

Figure 18-23

4. Select the `RSSReader` project, and click Primary output (see Figure 18-24). Click OK. This adds the output of the `RSSReader` project (which is your executable application) to the current project.

Figure 18-24

5. Right-click on the output item shown on the right-side of the File System tab, and create a shortcut to it (see Figure 18-25). Name the shortcut `RSSReader`.

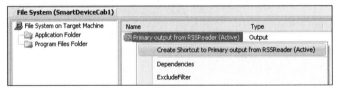

Figure 18-25

6. Right-click the File System on Target Machine item, and select Add Special Folder ⇨ Start Menu Folder (see Figure 18-26).

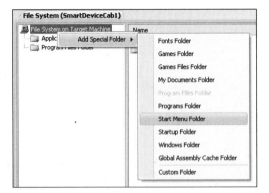

Figure 18-26

7. Drag and drop the RSSReader shortcut onto the newly added Start Menu Folder (see Figure 18-27). This ensures that when the CAB file is installed on the device, a shortcut named RSS Reader appears in the Start menu.

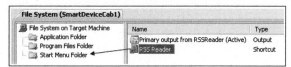

Figure 18-27

8. Right-click on the SmartDeviceCab1 project name in Solution Explorer, and select Properties. Change the Configuration from `Debug` to `Release`. Also, name the output file `Release\RSSReader.cab` (see Figure 18-28).

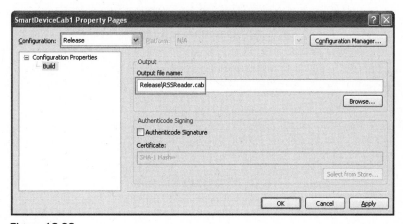

Figure 18-28

9. In Visual Studio 2008, change the configuration from `Debug` to `Release` (see Figure 18-29).

Figure 18-29

10. Finally, set the properties of the `SmartDeviceCab1` project as shown in the following table (see Figure 18-30).

Property	Value
Manufacturer	Developer Learning Solutions
ProductName	RSS Reader v1.0

Figure 18-30

That's it! Right-click on the `SmartDeviceCab1` project name in Solution Explorer and select Build. You can find the CAB file located in the `\Release` folder of the `SmartDeviceCab1` project (see Figure 18-31).

Figure 18-31

Now you can distribute the CAB file to your customers using various media such as FTP, web hosting, email, and so on. When the user clicks on the RSSReader CAB file in File Explorer (on the device; see Figure 18-32), the application will ask if he wants to install it onto the device, or onto the storage card (if available).

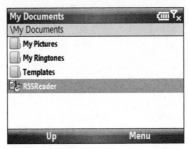

Figure 18-32

When the application is installed, the RSS Reader shortcut is in the Start menu (see Figure 18-33).

Figure 18-33

Creating a Setup Application

Although you can deploy CAB files directly to your users, you might want to use a more user-friendly way using the traditional setup application that most Windows users are familiar with — users simply connect their devices to their computers and then run a setup application, which then installs the application automatically on their devices through ActiveSync.

Creating a setup application for a Windows Mobile application is more involved than for a conventional Windows application because you have to activate ActiveSync to install it. Figure 18-34 shows the steps in the installation process.

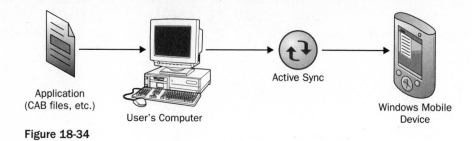

Figure 18-34

First, the application containing the CAB files (and other relevant files) must be installed on the user's computer. Then ActiveSync needs to install the application onto the user's device.

The following sections detail how to create an MSI file to install the application onto the user's computer and then onto the device.

Creating the Custom Installer

The first component you will build is the custom installer that will invoke ActiveSync to install the application onto the user's device. For this, you will use a Class Library project.

Add a new project to your current solution by going to File ⇨ Add ⇨ New Project. Select the Windows project type and select the Class Library template. Name the project RSSReaderInstaller (see Figure 18-35). Click OK.

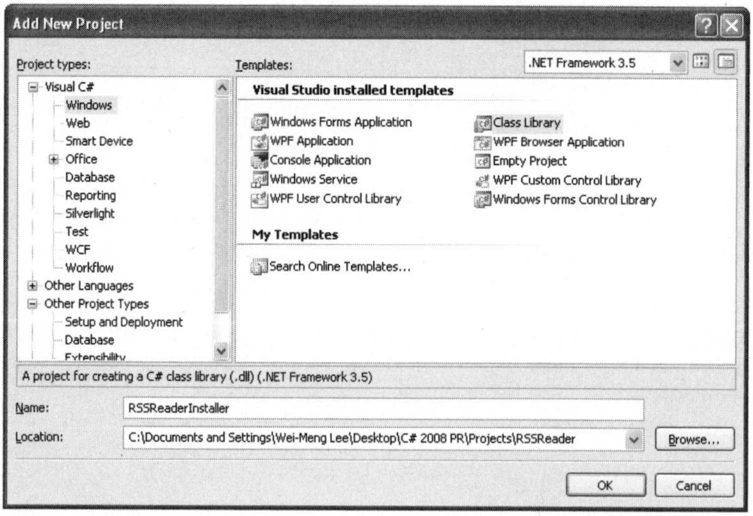

Figure 18-35

Delete the default `Class1.cs` file and add a new item to the project. In the Add New Item dialog, select the Installer Class template, and name the file `RSSReaderInstaller.cs` (see Figure 18-36).

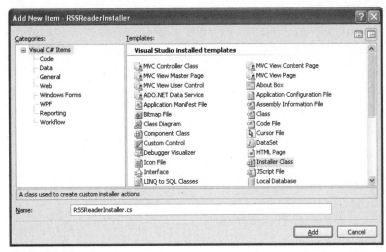

Figure 18-36

Add two references to the project: `System.Configuration.Install` and `System.Windows.Forms` (see Figure 18-37).

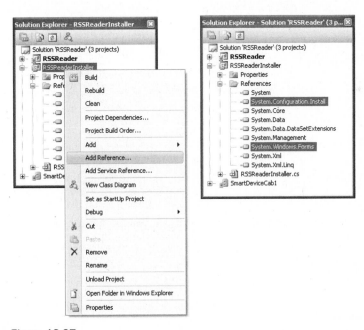

Figure 18-37

Switch to the code view of the `RSSReaderInstaller.cs` file and import the following namespaces:

```
using Microsoft.Win32;
using System.IO;
using System.Diagnostics;
using System.Windows.Forms;
```

Within the `RSSReaderInstaller` class, define the `INI_FILE` constant. This constant holds the name of the `.ini` file that will be used by ActiveSync for installing the CAB file onto the target device.

```
namespace RSSReaderInstaller
{
    [RunInstaller(true)]
    public partial class RSSReaderInstaller : Installer
    {

        const string INI_FILE = @"setup.ini";
```

In the constructor of the `RSSReaderInstaller` class, wire the `AfterInstall` and `Uninstall` events to their corresponding event handlers:

```
        public RSSReaderInstaller()
        {
            InitializeComponent();

            this.AfterInstall += new
                InstallEventHandler(RSSReaderInstaller_AfterInstall);
            this.AfterUninstall += new
                InstallEventHandler(RSSReaderInstaller_AfterUninstall);

        }

        void RSSReaderInstaller_AfterInstall(object sender, InstallEventArgs e)
        {
        }

        void RSSReaderInstaller_AfterUninstall(object sender, InstallEventArgs e)
        {
        }
```

The `AfterInstall` event is fired when the application (CAB file) has been installed onto the user's computer. Similarly, the `AfterUninstall` event fires when the application has been uninstalled from the user's computer.

When the application is installed on the user's computer, you use Windows CE Application Manager (`CEAPPMGR.EXE`) to install the application onto the user's device.

The Windows CE Application Manager is installed automatically when you install ActiveSync on your computer.

To locate the Windows CE Application Manager, define the following function named
GetWindowsCeApplicationManager():

```
private string GetWindowsCeApplicationManager()
{
    //---check if the Windows CE Application Manager is installed---
    string ceAppPath = KeyExists();
    if (ceAppPath == String.Empty)
    {
        MessageBox.Show("Windows CE App Manager not installed",
        "Setup", MessageBoxButtons.OK,
                        MessageBoxIcon.Error);
        return String.Empty;
    }
    else
        return ceAppPath;
}
```

This function locates the Windows CE Application Manager by checking the registry of the computer
using the KeyExists() function, which is defined as follows:

```
private string KeyExists()
{
    //---get the path to the Windows CE App Manager from the registry---
    RegistryKey key =
      Registry.LocalMachine.OpenSubKey(
      @"SOFTWARE\Microsoft\Windows\CurrentVersion\App Paths\CEAPPMGR.EXE");
    if (key == null)
        return String.Empty;
    else
        return key.GetValue(String.Empty, String.Empty).ToString();
}
```

The location of the Windows CE Application Manager can be obtained via the registry key: "SOFTWARE\
Microsoft\Windows\CurrentVersion\App Paths\CEAPPMGR.EXE", so querying the value of this
key provides the location of this application.

The next function to define is GetIniPath(), which returns the location of the .ini file that is needed
by the Windows CE Application Manager:

```
private string GetIniPath()
{
    //---get the path of the .ini file---
    return "\"" +
        Path.Combine(Path.GetDirectoryName(
        System.Reflection.Assembly.
        GetExecutingAssembly().Location), INI_FILE) + "\"";
}
```

By default, the .ini file is saved in the same location as the application (you will learn how to
accomplish this in the next section). The GetIniPath() function uses reflection to find the location of
the custom installer, and then return the path of the .ini file as a string, enclosed by a pair of double
quotation marks (the Windows CE Application requires the path of the .ini file to be enclosed by a pair
of double quotation marks).

Finally, you can now code the `AfterInstall` event handler, like this:

```
void RSSReaderInstaller_AfterInstall(object sender, InstallEventArgs e)
{
    //---to be executed when the application is installed---
    string ceAppPath = GetWindowsCeApplicationManager();
    if (ceAppPath == String.Empty)
        return;
    Process.Start(ceAppPath, GetIniPath());
}
```

Here, you get the location of the Windows CE Application Manager and then use the `Process.Start()` method to invoke the Windows CE Application Manager, passing it the path of the `.ini` file.

Likewise, when the application has been uninstalled, you simply invoke the Windows CE Application Manager and let the user choose the application to remove from the device. This is done in the `AfterUninstall` event handler:

```
void RSSReaderInstaller_AfterUninstall(object sender, InstallEventArgs e)
{
    //---to be executed when the application is uninstalled---
    string ceAppPath = GetWindowsCeApplicationManager();
    if (ceAppPath == String.Empty)
        return;
    Process.Start(ceAppPath, String.Empty);
}
```

The last step in this section is to add the `setup.ini` file that the Windows CE Application Manager needs to install the application onto the device. Add a text file to the project and name it `setup.ini`. Populate the file with the following:

```
[CEAppManager]
Version      = 1.0
Component    = RSSReader

[RSSReader]
Description  = RSSReader Application
Uninstall    = RSSReader
CabFiles     = RSSReader.cab
```

For more information about the various components in an `.ini` *file, refer to the documentation at* `http://msdn.microsoft.com/en-us/library/ms889558.aspx`.

To build the project, right-click on RSSReaderInstaller in Solution Explorer and select Build.

Set the `SmartDeviceCab1` project's properties as shown in the following table.

Property	Value
Manufacturer	Developer Learning Solutions
ProductName	RSS Reader v1.0

Creating a MSI File

You can now create the MSI installer to install the application onto the user's computer and then invoke the custom installer built in the previous section to instruct the Windows CE Application Manager to install the application onto the device.

Using the same solution, add a new Setup Project (see Figure 18-38). Name the project RSSReaderSetup.

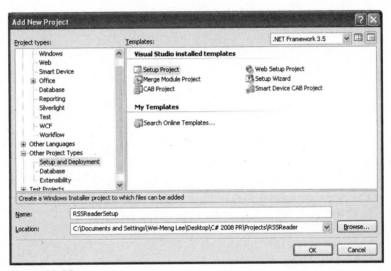

Figure 18-38

Using the newly created project, you can now add the various components and files that you have been building in the past few sections. Right-click on the RSSReaderSetup project in Solution Explorer, and select Add ➪ File (see Figure 18-39).

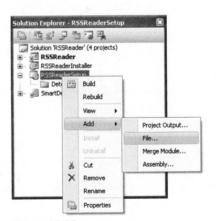

Figure 18-39

Add the following files (see Figure 18-40):

- ❏ SmartDeviceCab1\Release\RSSReader.CAB

- ❏ RSSReaderInstaller\bin\Release\RSSReaderInstaller.dll

- ❏ RSSReaderInstaller\setup.ini

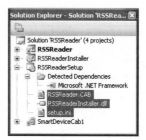

Figure 18-40

These three files will be copied to the user's computer during the installation.

The next step is to configure the MSI installer to perform some custom actions during the installation stage. Right-click the RSSReaderSetup project in Solution Explorer, and select View ➪ Custom Actions (see Figure 18-41).

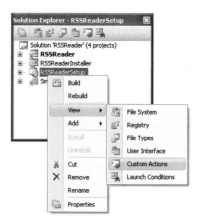

Figure 18-41

The Custom Actions tab displays. Right-click on Custom Actions, and select Add Custom Action (see Figure 18-42).

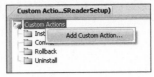

Figure 18-42

Select Application Folder, select the RSSReaderInstall.dll file (see Figure 18-43), and click OK.

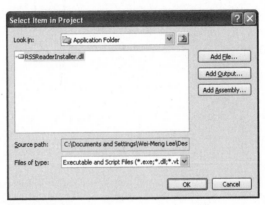

Figure 18-43

The Custom Actions tab should now look like Figure 18-44.

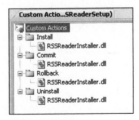

Figure 18-44

Set the various properties of the RSSReaderSetup project as shown in the following table (see Figure 18-45).

Property	Value
Author	Wei-Meng Lee
Manufacturer	Developer Learning Solutions
ProductName	RSSReader

Figure 18-45

The last step is to build the project. Right-click on the RSSReaderSetup project in Solution Explorer, and select Build.

The MSI installer is now in the \Release subfolder of the folder containing the RSSReaderSetup project (see Figure 18-46).

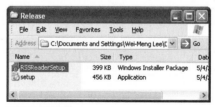

Figure 18-46

Testing the Setup

To test the MSI installer, ensure that your emulator (or real device) is connected to ActiveSync. Double-click the RSSReaderSeup.msi application, and the installation process begins (see Figure 18-47).

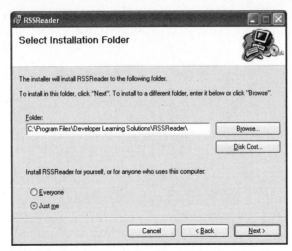

Figure 18-47

Follow the instructions on the dialog. At the end, an Application Downloading Complete message displays (see Figure 18-48).

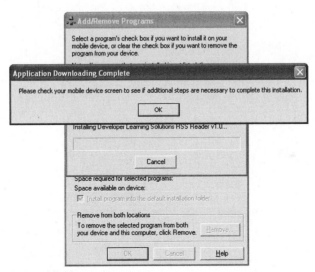

Figure 18-48

Check your emulator (or real device) to verify that the application is successfully installed (see Figure 18-49).

Figure 18-49

To uninstall the application, double-click the `RSSReaderSeup.msi` application again. This time, you see the dialog shown in Figure 18-50.

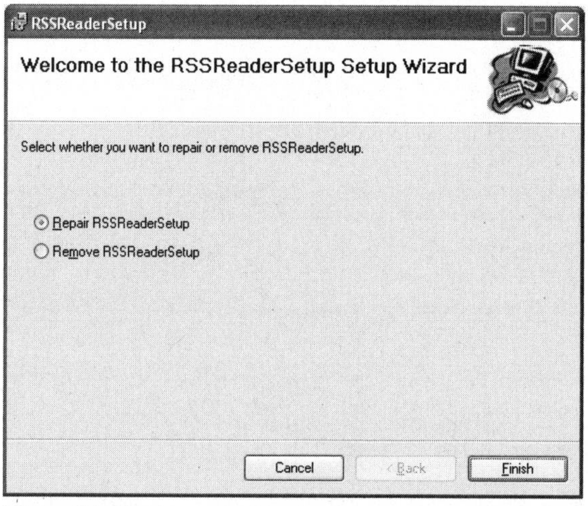

Figure 18-50

If you choose to remove the application, the Windows CE Application Manager displays the list of programs that you have installed through ActiveSync (see Figure 18-51). To uninstall the RSS Reader application, uncheck the application and click OK. The application is removed.

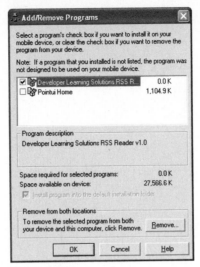

Figure 18-51

Installing the Prerequisites — .NET Compact Framework 3.5

One problem you will likely face when deploying your application to real devices is that the target device does not have the required version of the .NET Compact Framework (version 3.5 is needed). Hence, you need to ensure that the user has a means to install the right version of the .NET Compact Framework. There are two ways of doing this:

❑ Distribute a copy of the .NET Compact Framework 3.5 Redistributable to your client. You can download a copy from `http://microsoft.com/downloads`. Users can install the .NET Compact Framework before or after installing your application. This is the easiest approach, but requires the user to perform the extra step of installing the .NET Compact Framework.

❑ Programmatically install the .NET Compact Framework during installation, using the custom installer. Earlier, you saw how you can invoke the Windows CE Application Manager from within the custom installer class by using the `.ini` file. In this case, you simply need to create another `.ini` file, this time to install the CAB file containing the .NET Compact Framework. The various CAB files for the .NET Compact Framework 3.5 can be found on your local drive in the following directory: `C:\Program Files\Microsoft.NET\SDK\CompactFramework\v3.5\WindowsCE`. Figure 18-52 shows the various CAB files for each processor type (ARM, MIPS, SH4, X86, and so on). To install the .NET Compact Framework 3.5 on Windows Mobile 6 Standard devices, you just need to add the `NETCFv35.wm.armv4i.cab` file to the `RSSReaderInstaller` project, together with its associated `.ini` file.

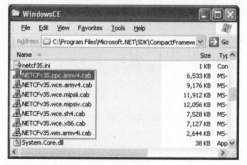

Figure 18-52

Summary

This chapter explored developing applications for the Windows Mobile 6 platform, using the .NET Compact Framework. Using that framework, you can leverage your familiarity with the .NET Framework to develop compelling mobile applications. The RSS application is an example of a useful application that you can use on a daily basis. The chapter also explained how to package an application into a CAB file and then into a MSI package so that you can distribute it to your users easily.

19

Developing Silverlight Applications

Over the years, we have all seen the proliferation of web applications. In the early days, web sites consisted of sets of static HTML pages with nice graphics and lots of information. Then, server-side technologies like CGI, ASP, and JSP made web applications possible, and suddenly users could do a lot of things on the web, including buying products and making reservations online. Client-side innovations such as JavaScript helped improve the user experience of web applications, making them feel much more responsive. Although AJAX's underlying technologies had been available for several years, it wasn't really until the last couple of years that people really started spending more time AJAX-enabling their web applications. All this boils down to one important goal of web developers — making web applications much more interactive and responsive.

Today, a new term has been coined: RIA — Rich Internet Application. To Microsoft, RIA really stands for Rich Interactive Application. And it was with that in mind that Microsoft recently launched a new technology/product called Silverlight. Previously known as Windows Presentation Foundation/Everywhere (WPF/E), Microsoft Silverlight is a browser plug-in that enables developers to host RIAs that feature animation and vector graphics, as well as video playback.

This chapter will help you get started with Silverlight and provides an opportunity for you to get a feel for how Silverlight development works.

The State of Silverlight

At the time of writing, there are two versions of Silverlight — 1.0 and 2 (previously known as version 1.1), the main difference being the support of .NET languages in version 2. For Silverlight version 1.0, you have to use JavaScript for writing your application logic. In version 2, in addition to JavaScript you can also use either C# or Visual Basic for your application logic, which is then executed by a version of the CLR built within the runtime.

At the time of writing, Silverlight 2 is in Beta 1.

The Silverlight runtimes currently support the following browsers:

- ❑   Internet Explorer 6/7
- ❑   Firefox 1.5/2.0
- ❑   Safari 2.0

The following table compares the feature set of Silverlight 1.0 and Silverlight 2 Beta 1.

Features	Silverlight 1.0	Silverlight 2 Beta 1
2D Vector Animation/Graphics	X	X
AJAX Support	X	X
Cross-Browser (Firefox, IE, Safari)	X	X
Cross-Platform (Windows, Mac)	X	X
Framework Languages(Visual Basic, Visual C#, IronRuby, Ironpython)		X
HTML DOM Integration	X	X
HTTP Networking	X	X
Isolated Storage		X
JavaScript Support	X	X
JSON, REST, SOAP/WS-*, POX, and RSS Web Services (as well as support for Sockets)		X
Cross Domain Network Access		X
LINQ to Objects		X
Canvas Layout Support	X	X
StackPanel, Grid and Panel Layout Support		X
Managed Control Framework		X
Full suite of Controls (TextBox, RadioButton, Slider, Calendar, DatePicker, DataGrid, ListBox, and others)		X
Deep Zoom Technology		X
Managed HTML Bridge		X
Managed Exception Handling		X
Media — Content Protection		X
Media — 720P High Definition (HD) Video	X	X

Features	Silverlight 1.0	Silverlight 2 Beta 1
Media — Audio/Video Support (VC-1, WMV, WMA, MP3)	X	X
Media — Image Support (JPG, PNG)	X	X
Media Markers	X	X
Rich Core Framework (e.g. Generics, collections)		X
Security Enforcement		X
Silverlight ASP.NET Controls (asp:media, asp:xaml)	X	X
Type Safety Verification		X
Windows Media Server Support	X	X
XAML Parser (based on WPF)	X	X
XMLReader/Writer		X

Obtaining the Tools

To view Silverlight applications on your browser, you need to download one or all of the following runtimes:

- ❑ Microsoft Silverlight 1.0 for Mac
- ❑ Microsoft Silverlight 1.0 for Windows
- ❑ Microsoft Silverlight 2 for Mac
- ❑ Microsoft Silverlight 2 for Windows

> **When your web browser encounters a Silverlight application and there is no runtime installed, click on the Silverlight icon to download the required version of the runtime.**

For developing Silverlight 1.0 applications, you need to download the Silverlight 1.0 SDK from `www.microsoft.com/downloads`.

For Silverlight 2 applications, the easiest way to get started is to use Visual Studio 2008. In addition to Visual Studio 2008, you also need to download Microsoft Silverlight Tools Beta 1 for Visual Studio 2008 (www.microsoft.com/downloads), which will install the following components:

- ❏ Silverlight 2 Beta 1 runtime

- ❏ Silverlight 2 SDK Beta 1

- ❏ KB949325 for Visual Studio 2008

- ❏ Silverlight Tools Beta 1 for Visual Studio 2008

You can also purchase one or more of the following professional tools to help design your Silverlight applications:

- ❏ **Expression Blend 2** — A professional design tool to create Silverlight applications.

- ❏ **Expression Media Encoder Preview Update** — A feature that will be part of Microsoft Expression Media, a commercial digital asset management (DAM) cataloging program. It enables you to create and enhance video.

- ❏ **Expression Design** — A professional illustration and graphic design tool to create Silverlight assets.

Architecture of Silverlight

Figure 19-1 shows the architecture for Silverlight 1.0 and 2.

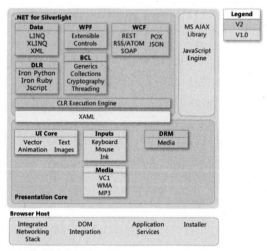

Figure 19-1
Used by permission of Microsoft Corporation

The Presentation Core handles all the interactions with the user (through keyboard, mouse, and so on) as well as the rendering of UI elements such as media and controls. The XAML (Extensible Application Markup Language) component provides a parser for XAML markup (more about this in the next section), which is used as the UI of a Silverlight application. For Silverlight 1.0 applications, the primary means to program the application is JavaScript. In Silverlight 2, you can use either C# or VB.NET. During runtime, the application will be executed by the CLR Execution Engine. Notice that the various features available in the desktop version of the .NET Framework is also available for Silverlight — LINQ, WPF, WCF, BCL, and so forth.

Building a Silverlight UI Using XAML

A typical Silverlight project has four files:

❑ An HTML file that hosts the Silverlight plug-in instance

❑ A Silverlight.js file that contains all the necessary plumbing code required by Silverlight

❑ An XAML file that contains the UI elements that make up a Silverlight application

❑ A JavaScript file that contains the logic of your Silverlight application

The following sections show how to build a Silverlight application while presenting the basics of XAML, the UI language of Silverlight applications.

Creating a Bare-Bones Silverlight Application

Let's create a bare-bones Silverlight application by referencing all the necessary files required in a Silverlight application. First, remember to download the Silverlight 1.0 SDK from http://www.microsoft.com/downloads.

Once the SDK is downloaded, double-click on the Silverlightv1.0SDK.msi file to install the files onto your local computer (use the default directory).

Create a new folder in C:\ and name it Silverlight.

Copy the Silverlight.js file located in the C:\Program Files\Microsoft Silverlight 1.0 SDK\Tools\ Silverlight.js\ folder into C:\Silverlight\.

Using Notepad, create the following HTML file; name it Default.html, and save it in the C:\ Silverlight\ folder:

```
<!DOCTYPE html PUBLIC "-//W3C//DTD XHTML 1.0 Transitional//EN" "http://www.w3.org/
TR/xhtml1/DTD/xhtml1-transitional.dtd">
<html xmlns="http://www.w3.org/1999/xhtml" xml:lang="en">
  <head>
    <title>Our First Silverlight Application</title>
    <script type="text/javascript" src="Silverlight.js"></script>
    <script type="text/javascript" src="MySilverlight.js"></script>
  </head>
  <body>

    <!-- location for the Silverlight plug-in-->
    <div id="SilverlightPluginHost">
    </div>

    <script type="text/javascript">
```

(continued)

(continued)

```
            // Retrieve the div element you created in the previous step.
            var parentElement =
                document.getElementById("SilverlightPluginHost");

            // creates the Silverlight plug-in.
            createSilverlightPlugin();
        </script>

    </body>
</html>
```

This HTML file is the page that will host the Silverlight plug-in. Notice that it references two JavaScript files:

❑   Silverlight.js

❑   MySilverlight.js

You've already added the first one. Now, using Notepad, create the following JavaScript file; name it MySilverlight.js, and save it in C:\Silverlight\.

```
function createSilverlightPlugin()
{
    Silverlight.createObject(
      "UI.xaml",                    // Source property value.
      parentElement,                // DOM reference to hosting DIV tag.
      "mySilverlightPlugin",        // Unique plug-in ID value.
      {                             // Per-instance properties.
        width:'300',                // Width of rectangular region of
                                    // plug-in area in pixels.
        height:'300',               // Height of rectangular region of
                                    // plug-in area in pixels.
        inplaceInstallPrompt:false, // Determines whether to display
                                    // in-place install prompt if
                                    // invalid version detected.
        background:'#D6D6D6',       // Background color of plug-in.
        isWindowless:'false',       // Determines whether to display
                                    // plug-in in Windowless mode.
        framerate:'24',             // MaxFrameRate property value.
        version:'1.0'               // Silverlight version to use.
      },
      {
        onError:null,               // OnError property value --
                                    // event handler function name.
        onLoad:null                 // OnLoad property value --
                                    // event handler function name.
      },
      null);                        // Context value -- event handler
                                    // function name.
}
```

This JavaScript file contains the logic behind your Silverlight application. It loads the Silverlight plug-in as well as the XAML file (UI.xaml, which is defined in the next section).

Double-click on `Default.html` now to load it in Internet Explorer. You will see the message shown in Figure 19-2 if your web browser does not have the Silverlight plug-in installed.

Figure 19-2

To install the Silverlight plug-in, click on the Get Microsoft Silverlight logo and follow the onscreen instructions. Once the plug-in is installed, refresh the page and you should see a gray box (there is nothing displayed yet, thus just a gray box). Right-click on the gray box and select Silverlight Configuration to verify the version of the plug-in installed (see Figure 19-3).

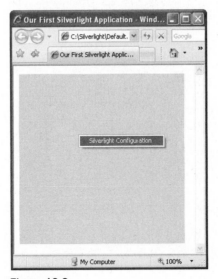

Figure 19-3

Understanding XAML

In this section, you see how to create the user interface of a Silverlight application using the Extensible Application Markup Language (XAML).

Using Notepad, create the following XAML file; name it UI.xaml and save it in C:\Silverlight\.

```xaml
<Canvas
    xmlns="http://schemas.microsoft.com/client/2007"
    xmlns:x="http://schemas.microsoft.com/winfx/2006/xaml">

    <Ellipse
        Height="200" Width="200"
        Stroke="Black"
        StrokeThickness="10"
        Fill="Yellow" />

    <Rectangle
        Canvas.Left="80" Canvas.Top="80"
        Height="200" Width="200"
        Stroke="Black"
        StrokeThickness="10"
        Fill="LightBlue"/>

</Canvas>
```

Double-click on Default.html now to load it in the web browser. Figure 19-4 shows the output.

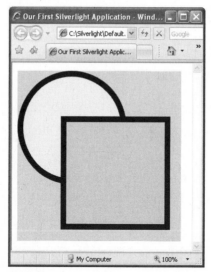

Figure 19-4

This XAML file contains two elements, `<Ellipse>` and `<Rectangle>`, which display an ellipse and a rectangle, respectively, on the page. Both elements are embedded within a Canvas control.

The Canvas Control

The Canvas control (every Silverlight application has at least one Canvas control) is designed to contain and position other controls and elements.

To define the positioning of controls within the `Canvas` control, you use the `Canvas.Left` and `Canvas.Top` attributes. The z order of objects embedded within a `Canvas` object is determined by the sequence in which they are declared. As the previous section shows, the `<Rectangle>` element is defined after the `<Ellipse>` element, and hence it overlaps the `<Ellipse>` element. However, you can override this default ordering by specifying the `ZIndex` attribute, as the following example shows.

Edit the `UI.xaml` file created in the previous section, and add the `Canvas.ZIndex` attribute for both the `<Ellipse>` and `<Rectangle>` elements:

```
<Canvas
    xmlns="http://schemas.microsoft.com/client/2007"
    xmlns:x="http://schemas.microsoft.com/winfx/2006/xaml">

    <Ellipse
        Canvas.ZIndex="2"
        Height="200" Width="200"
        Stroke="Black"
        StrokeThickness="10"
        Fill="Yellow" />

    <Rectangle
        Canvas.ZIndex="1"
        Canvas.Left="80" Canvas.Top="80"
        Height="200" Width="200"
        Stroke="Black"
        StrokeThickness="10"
        Fill="LightBlue"/>

</Canvas>
```

Reload the `Default.html` file in the web browser, and notice that the ellipse is now on top of the rectangle (see Figure 19-5).

Figure 19-5

You can also nest `Canvas` controls within one another. Edit the `UI.xaml` file created earlier and replace its content with the following:

```
<Canvas
    xmlns="http://schemas.microsoft.com/client/2007"
    xmlns:x="http://schemas.microsoft.com/winfx/2006/xaml">

    <Canvas
        Canvas.Left="80" Canvas.Top="80"
        Height="250" Width="250"
        Background="lightgreen">

        <Ellipse
            Canvas.ZIndex="2"
            Canvas.Left="10" Canvas.Top="10"
            Height="200" Width="200"
            Stroke="Black"
            StrokeThickness="10"
            Fill="Yellow" />

    </Canvas>

</Canvas>
```

Reload the `Default.html` file in the web browser, and observe the changes (see Figure 19-6).

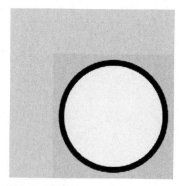

Figure 19-6

The positions specified by the `Canvas.Left` and `Canvas.Top` attributes of each element or control are relative to its parent control, and not the root control.

Drawing Shapes

One of the key capabilities of Silverlight is the support for drawing objects of different shapes and sizes. Silverlight provides the following basic shape elements:

- ❑   Rectangle
- ❑   Ellipse
- ❑   Line
- ❑   Polygon
- ❑   Polyline

Rectangle

A `<Rectangle>` element draws a rectangle (or square) with optional rounded corners. To specify rounded corners, use the `RadiusX` and `RadiusY` attributes. Edit the `UI.xaml` file created in the previous section and replace its content with the following:

```
<Canvas
    xmlns="http://schemas.microsoft.com/client/2007"
    xmlns:x="http://schemas.microsoft.com/winfx/2006/xaml">

    <Rectangle
        Canvas.Left="10" Canvas.Top="10"
        Height="100" Width="200"
        Stroke="Black"
        StrokeThickness="10"
        Fill="Yellow"
        RadiusX="10" RadiusY="10" />

    <Rectangle
        Canvas.Left="60" Canvas.Top="60"
        Height="200" Width="180"
        Stroke="Black"
        StrokeThickness="10"
        Fill="LightBlue"
        RadiusX="30" RadiusY="30" />

</Canvas>
```

Reload `Default.html` in the web browser. Figure 19-7 shows the output.

Figure 19-7

Line

A `<Line>` element draws a line on the `Canvas` control. Edit the `UI.xaml` file created in the previous section and replace its content with the following:

```
<Canvas
    xmlns="http://schemas.microsoft.com/client/2007"
    xmlns:x="http://schemas.microsoft.com/winfx/2006/xaml">

    <Line X1="10" Y1="10" X2="100" Y2="180"
        Stroke="black" StrokeThickness="5"/>

    <Line X1="100" Y1="10" X2="10" Y2="180"
        Stroke="red" StrokeThickness="10"/>

</Canvas>
```

Reload the `Default.html` file in the web browser, and observe the output (see Figure 19-8).

Figure 19-8

Ellipse

An `<Ellipse>` element draws a circle (or oval) on the `Canvas` control. Edit the `UI.xaml` file created in the previous section, and replace its content with the following:

```
<Canvas
    xmlns="http://schemas.microsoft.com/client/2007"
    xmlns:x="http://schemas.microsoft.com/winfx/2006/xaml">

    <Ellipse
        Canvas.Left="30" Canvas.Top="30"
        Height="60" Width="60"
        Stroke="Black" StrokeThickness="10"
        Fill="Pink"/>

    <Ellipse
        Canvas.Left="200" Canvas.Top="30"
        Height="60" Width="60"
        Stroke="Black" StrokeThickness="10"
        Fill="LightBlue"/>

    <Ellipse
        Canvas.Left="20" Canvas.Top="100"
        Height="70" Width="250"
        Stroke="Black" StrokeThickness="10"
        Fill="LightGreen"/>

</Canvas>
```

Reload `Default.html` in the web browser. Figure 19-9 shows the output.

Figure 19-9

Polygon

A `<Polygon>` element draws a shape with arbitrary number of sides. Edit `UI.xaml` again, replacing its content with the following:

```
<Canvas
    xmlns="http://schemas.microsoft.com/client/2007"
    xmlns:x="http://schemas.microsoft.com/winfx/2006/xaml">

    <Polygon Points="100,10 10,160 190,160"
        Stroke="Yellow" Strok eThickness="5" Fill="Red"/>

</Canvas>
```

Reload `Default.html` in the web browser to see the result (see Figure 19-10).

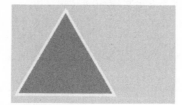

Figure 19-10

Polyline

A `<Polyline>` element draws a series of connected lines. Edit the `UI.xaml` file and replace its content with the following:

```
<Canvas
    xmlns="http://schemas.microsoft.com/client/2007"
    xmlns:x="http://schemas.microsoft.com/winfx/2006/xaml">

    <Polyline Points="100,10 10,160 210,160 120,10"
        Stroke="Black" StrokeThickness="8"/>

</Canvas>
```

Reload `Default.html` in the web browser, and observe the output (see Figure 19-11).

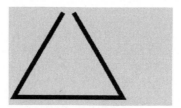

Figure 19-11

Painting Shapes

The `Fill` attribute that you have seen in many of the previous examples fills (paints) a shape with a solid color. However, the fill is not restricted to solid colors. Silverlight supports various ways to paint a shape:

- ❑ `SolidColorBrush`
- ❑ `LinearGradientBrush`
- ❑ `RadialGradientBrush`
- ❑ `ImageBrush`

Using *SolidColorBrush*

The `<SolidColorBrush>` element paints an area with a solid color. Edit the `UI.xaml` file created in the previous section, and replace its content with the following:

```xml
<Canvas
    xmlns="http://schemas.microsoft.com/client/2007"
    xmlns:x="http://schemas.microsoft.com/winfx/2006/xaml">

    <Ellipse
        Canvas.Left="10" Canvas.Top="10"
        Height="100" Width="100"
        Stroke="Black"
        StrokeThickness="10"
        Fill="Yellow" />

    <Ellipse
        Canvas.Left="120" Canvas.Top="10"
        Height="100" Width="100"
        Stroke="Black"
        StrokeThickness="10"
        Fill="#A3FC96" /> <!-- 6-digit hexadecimal -->

    <Ellipse
        Canvas.Left="10" Canvas.Top="120"
        Height="100" Width="100"
        Stroke="Black"
        StrokeThickness="10"
        Fill="#A3FC96FF" />
        <!-- 6-digit hexadecimal + 2-digit for alpha/opacity value -->

    <Ellipse
        Canvas.Left="120" Canvas.Top="120"
        Height="100" Width="100"
        Stroke="Black"
        StrokeThickness="10">
        <Ellipse.Fill>
            <SolidColorBrush Color="LightBlue"/>
        </Ellipse.Fill>
    </Ellipse>

</Canvas>
```

In this example, the `Fill` attribute specifies the solid color to use to fill up the particular element. Reload the `Default.html` file in the web browser, and observe the output in your browser (see Figure 19-12).

Figure 19-12

Using LinearGradientBrush

The `<LinearGradientBrush>` element paints an area with a linear gradient. Edit the `UI.xaml` file again, replacing its content with the following:

```
<Canvas
    xmlns="http://schemas.microsoft.com/client/2007"
    xmlns:x="http://schemas.microsoft.com/winfx/2006/xaml">

    <Ellipse
        Canvas.Left="10" Canvas.Top="10"
        Height="100" Width="100"
        Stroke="Black"
        StrokeThickness="10">
        <Ellipse.Fill>
            <LinearGradientBrush> <!-- fill is diagonal by default -->
                <GradientStop Color="Yellow" Offset="0.25" />
                <GradientStop Color="Red" Offset="0.5" />
                <GradientStop Color="Blue" Offset="0.75" />
            </LinearGradientBrush>
        </Ellipse.Fill>
    </Ellipse>

    <Ellipse
        Canvas.Left="120" Canvas.Top="10"
        Height="100" Width="100"
        Stroke="Black"
        StrokeThickness="10">
        <Ellipse.Fill>
            <!-- fill is horizontal -->
            <LinearGradientBrush StartPoint="0,0" EndPoint="1,0">
                <GradientStop Color="Yellow" Offset="0.25" />
                <GradientStop Color="Red" Offset="0.5" />
                <GradientStop Color="Blue" Offset="0.75" />
            </LinearGradientBrush>
        </Ellipse.Fill>
    </Ellipse>

</Canvas>
```

Here you used the `<Ellipse.Fill>` element to fill the each ellipse shapes with a `<LinearGradientBrush>` element. Reload the `Default.html` file in the web browser. Figure 19-13 shows the output.

Figure 19-13

Using RadialGradientBrush

The `<RadialGradientBrush>` element paints an area with a radial gradient. Edit the `UI.xaml` file, and replace its content with the following:

```
<Canvas
    xmlns="http://schemas.microsoft.com/client/2007"
    xmlns:x="http://schemas.microsoft.com/winfx/2006/xaml">

    <Ellipse
        Canvas.Left="10" Canvas.Top="10"
        Height="100" Width="100"
        Stroke="Black"
        StrokeThickness="10">
        <Ellipse.Fill>
            <RadialGradientBrush>
                <GradientStop Color="Yellow" Offset="0.25" />
                <GradientStop Color="Red" Offset="0.5" />
                <GradientStop Color="Blue" Offset="0.75" />
            </RadialGradientBrush>
        </Ellipse.Fill>
    </Ellipse>

    <Ellipse
        Canvas.Left="120" Canvas.Top="10"
        Height="100" Width="100"
        Stroke="Black"
        StrokeThickness="10">
        <Ellipse.Fill>
            <RadialGradientBrush GradientOrigin="0.5,0">
                <GradientStop Color="Yellow" Offset="0.25" />
                <GradientStop Color="Red" Offset="0.5" />
                <GradientStop Color="Blue" Offset="0.75" />
            </RadialGradientBrush>
        </Ellipse.Fill>
    </Ellipse>

</Canvas>
```

Reload the `Default.html` file in the web browser, and observe the output (see Figure 19-14).

Figure 19-14

Using ImageBrush

The <ImageBrush> element paints an area with an image. Assuming that you have the image shown in Figure 19-15 saved as C:\Silverlight\USFlag.jpg, edit the UI.xaml file created, and replace its content with the following:

Figure 19-15

```
<Canvas
    xmlns="http://schemas.microsoft.com/client/2007"
    xmlns:x="http://schemas.microsoft.com/winfx/2006/xaml">

    <Ellipse
        Canvas.Left="10" Canvas.Top="10"
        Height="100" Width="100"
        Stroke="Black"
        StrokeThickness="10">
        <Ellipse.Fill>
            <ImageBrush ImageSource="USFlag.jpg"/>
        </Ellipse.Fill>
    </Ellipse>

    <Ellipse
        Canvas.Left="120" Canvas.Top="10"
        Height="100" Width="100"
        Stroke="Black"
        StrokeThickness="10">
        <Ellipse.Fill>
            <ImageBrush ImageSource="USFlag.jpg" Stretch="Uniform"/>
        </Ellipse.Fill>
    </Ellipse>

</Canvas>
```

Reload Default.html in the web browser to view the output (see Figure 19-16).

Figure 19-16

Crafting XAML Using Expression Blend 2

While you can code the UI by hand, an easier way is to use a designer tool to design and create the UI graphically.

Microsoft Expression Blend 2 is the professional design tool to create engaging web-connected experiences for Windows and Silverlight. Currently in version 2, you can download a 30-day trial edition of Expression Blend 2 from www.microsoft.com/downloads.

This section explains how to use Expression Blend 2 to build a Silverlight application and programmatically interact with the content of a Silverlight application using JavaScript.

Using Expression Blend 2

Launch Expression Blend 2 by selecting Start ➪ Programs ➪ Microsoft Expression ➪ Microsoft Expression Blend 2. Create a new project by selecting the New Project item.

In the New Project dialog, select the Silverlight 1 Site project type and name the project RoundButton (see Figure 19-17). Click OK.

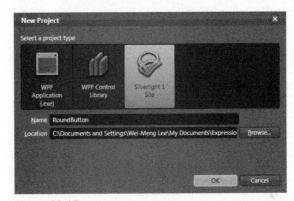

Figure 19-17

In the design view, double-click on the Canvas control to insert one onto the page (see Figure 19-18).

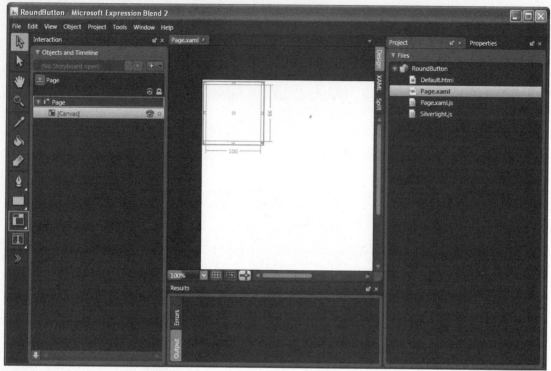

Figure 19-18

Right-click on the Rectangle control in the Toolbox, and select the Ellipse (see Figure 19-19).

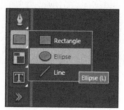

Figure 19-19

Double-click on the Ellipse element to add it to the page. Move the Ellipse object into the Canvas control by dragging it onto the Canvas object in the Objects and Timeline window (see Figure 19-20).

Figure 19-20

The page now looks like Figure 19-21.

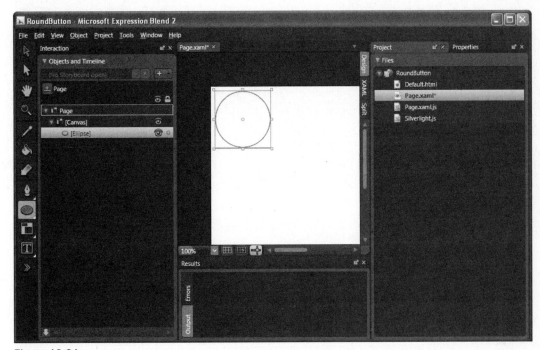

Figure 19-21

With the `Ellipse` object selected, select the Properties inspector, and click (see Figure 19-22):

❑ Stroke

❑ Solid Color Brush

❑ Specify 5 for StrokeThickness

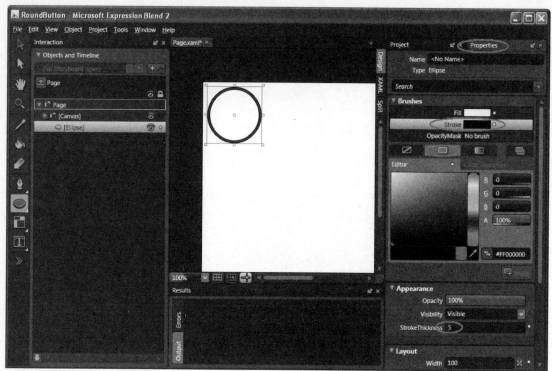

Figure 19-22

Next, click the following (see Figure 19-23):

❑ Fill

❑ Gradient Brush

❑ Specify 180 for B, 248 for G, 8 for B, and 100% for A

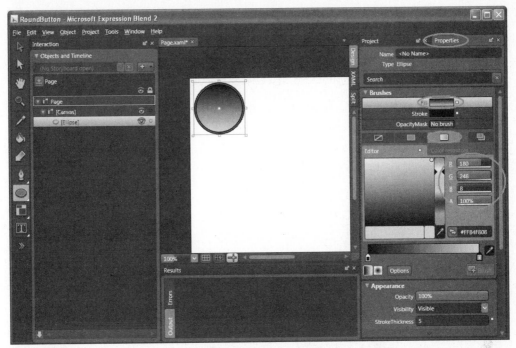

Figure 19-23

Click on the Brush Transform tool, and observe the arrow on the Ellipse element (see Figure 19-24).

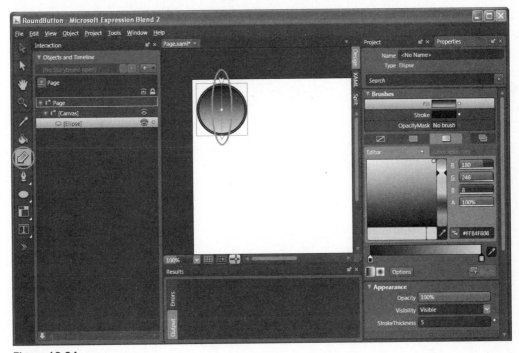

Figure 19-24

Move the arrow 135 degrees counterclockwise, as shown in Figure 19-25.

Figure 19-25

Make a copy of the Ellipse element (right-click on the Ellipse element in the Objects and Timeline window and select Copy, then paste it onto the page and move it into the Canvas control again).

For the new Ellipse control, gradient-fill it in the opposite direction by reversing the direction of the arrow (see Figure 19-26).

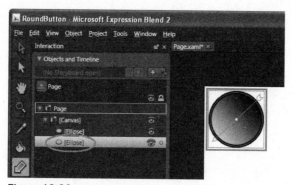

Figure 19-26

Select the Properties inspector, and set its properties as follows (see Figure 19-27):

Property	Value
Name	EllipsePressed
Opacity	0%

Figure 19-27

Double-click on the `TextBlock` element to add it to the page. As usual, move it into the `Canvas` control and type OK into the `TextBlock` element (see Figure 19-28).

Figure 19-28

With the `TextBlock` object selected, select the Properties inspector, and click (see Figure 19-29):

❑ Foreground

❑ Solid Color Brush

❑ Specify 251 for B, 219 for G, 8 for B, and 100% for A

Figure 19-29

Set the TextBlock's font size to 18 and Bold (see Figure 19-30).

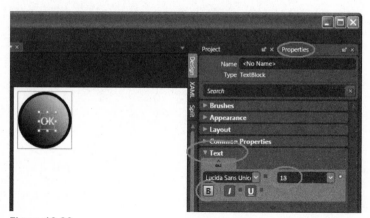

Figure 19-30

Control-click the following controls in the Objects and Timeline window and right-click on them and then select Group Into ⇨ Canvas (see Figure 19-31):

- ❏ Ellipse
- ❏ EllipsePressed
- ❏ TextBlock

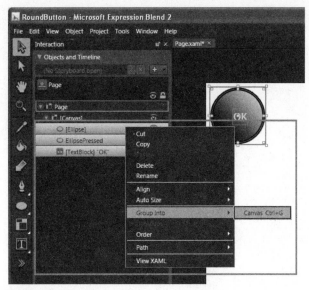

Figure 19-31

All the selected controls are now grouped into one. Name the new composite control `RoundButton` (see Figure 19-32).

Figure 19-32

Switch to the XAML view of the project (see Figure 19-33).

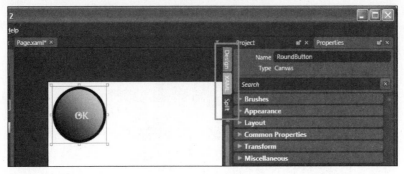

Figure 19-33

Scripting the UI Using JavaScript

Insert the following highlighted code into the RoundButton Canvas control:

```
<Canvas
    xmlns="http://schemas.microsoft.com/client/2007"
    xmlns:x="http://schemas.microsoft.com/winfx/2006/xaml"
    Width="640" Height="480"
    Background="White"
    x:Name="Page">
    <Canvas Width="100" Height="100" Canvas.Top="8" Canvas.Left="8">
      <Canvas Width="100" Height="100" x:Name="RoundButton"
              MouseLeftButtonDown="ButtonClicked"
              MouseLeftButtonUp="ButtonReleased"
              MouseLeave="ButtonReleased">
```

In the Project window, double-click the Page.xaml.js file. Append the following block of code to the end of the file:

```
function ButtonClicked(sender, eventArgs)
{
    if(sender.name == "RoundButton")
    {
      //---Get a reference to the ellipse---
      var pressedEllipse = sender.findName("EllipsePressed");
      pressedEllipse.opacity = 1;
    }
}

function ButtonReleased(sender, eventArgs)
{
    if(sender.name == "RoundButton")
    {
      //---Get a reference to the ellipse---
      var pressedEllipse = sender.findName("EllipsePressed");
      pressedEllipse.opacity = 0;
    }
}
```

Finally, press F5 to test the application. Click the button and observe the effect (see Figure 19-34).

Figure 19-34

Silverlight 1.0

Animation is one of the core capabilities of Silverlight. The following sections describe how to perform simple animations in Silverlight 1.0.

Animation — Part 1

You can use the `Timeline` object to perform some simple animation. Figure 19-35 shows the page displaying an image. When the mouse hovers over the image, the image will expand. When you move the mouse away, the image returns to its original size.

Figure 19-35

Using Expression Blend 2, create a new Silverlight project and name it `Animations`. Add an `Image` element to the page (see Figure 19-36).

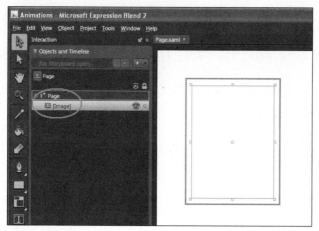

Figure 19-36

The XAML source of the page looks like this:

```
<Canvas
    xmlns="http://schemas.microsoft.com/client/2007"
    xmlns:x="http://schemas.microsoft.com/winfx/2006/xaml"
    Width="640" Height="480"
    Background="White"
    x:Name="Page">

    <Image Width="165" Height="220" Canvas.Top="70" Canvas.Left="71"/>

</Canvas>
```

Set the `Source` property of the `Image` control to reference an image (see Figure 19-37).

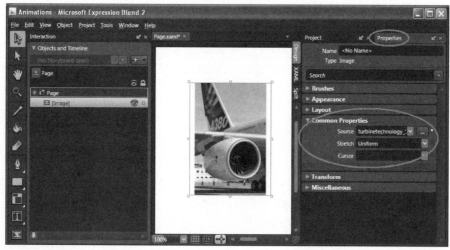

Figure 19-37

In the Objects and Timeline window, click the + button (see Figure 19-38), use the default name of StoryBoard1, and click OK.

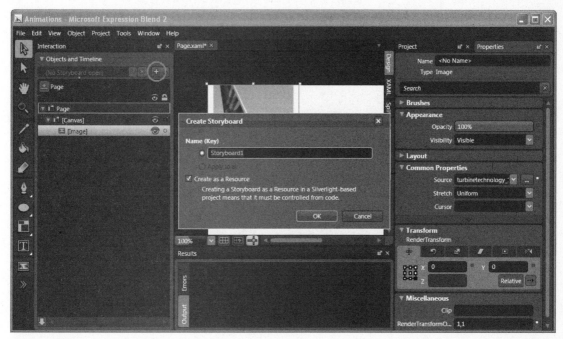

Figure 19-38

Click the Record Keyframe button (see Figure 19-39).

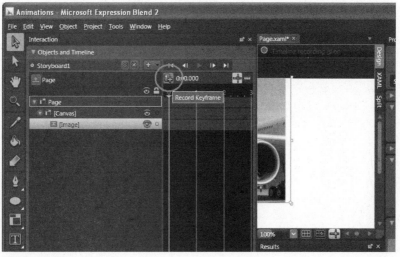

Figure 19-39

Move the yellow timeline (see Figure 19-40) to the 0:00.200 position and click the Record Keyframe button again.

If you like, you can magnify the timeline by setting the Timeline zoom to 500%.

Figure 19-40

With the Image element selected, select the Properties Inspector and expand the Transform section. Click on the Scale tab. Set both X and Y to 1.5 (see Figure 19-41).

Figure 19-41

Add a second timeline to the project, and use its default name of StoryBoard2.

Click the Record Keyframe button, and then in the Properties Inspector's Transform section, click on the Scale tab again. Set both X and Y to 1.5.

Move the yellow timeline to the 0:00.200 position and click the Record Keyframe button again.

In the Properties Inspector's Transform section, click the Scale tab. This time set both X and Y to 1.

Switch the project to XAML view, and add the following highlighted code:

```
<Image Width="165" Height="220" RenderTransformOrigin="1,1"
    Source="turbinetechnology_1.jpg" x:Name="image"
    MouseEnter="MouseEnter"
    MouseLeave="MouseLeave" >
        <Image.RenderTransform>
            <TransformGroup>
                <ScaleTransform ScaleX="1" ScaleY="1"/>
                <SkewTransform AngleX="0" AngleY="0"/>
                <RotateTransform Angle="0"/>
                <TranslateTransform X="0" Y="0"/>
            </TransformGroup>
        </Image.RenderTransform>
    </Image>
```

Append the following block of code to Page.xaml.js:

```
function MouseEnter (sender, eventArgs)
{
    var obj = sender.findName("Storyboard1");
    obj.Duration="00:00:00.2000000";
    obj.begin();
}

function MouseLeave (sender, eventArgs)
{
    var obj = sender.findName("Storyboard2");
    obj.Duration="00:00:00.2000000";
    obj.begin();
}
```

Press F5 to test the application. When the mouse now hovers over the image, the MouseEnter event is fired, and the Storyboard1 timeline object is executed for a duration of 0.2 second. The Storyboard1 timeline object basically scales the image horizontally and vertically by 1.5 times. When the mouse leaves the image, the MouseLeave event is fired, and the Storyboard2 timeline object is executed. It scales the image from 1.5 times down to its original size (within 0.2 second; see Figure 19-42).

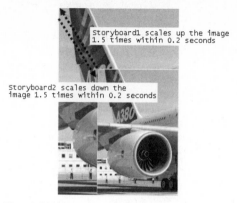

Figure 19-42

Animations — Part 2

Of course, you can perform more complex animation. This section shows you how to make the animation real-life using a KeySpline.

Using Expression Blend 2, create a new Silverlight project and name it `Animations2`.

Add an Image element to the page, and set it to display an image (see Figure 19-43).

Figure 19-43

Add a `Timeline` object to the project and use its default name of `Storyboard1`.

Add two keyframes to time `0:00.000` and `0:01.000`, respectively.

At time 0:01.000, click the Translate tab in the Transform section of the Properties Inspector. Set X to `0` and set Y to `250` (see Figure 19-44).

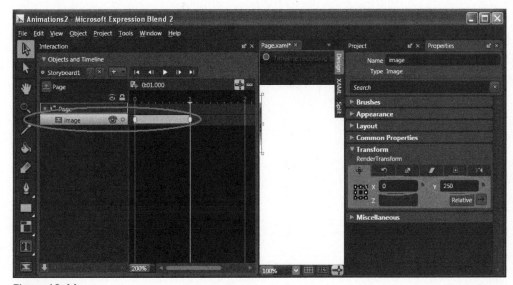

Figure 19-44

This will move the image vertically from the top to the bottom.

In the Rotate tab, set the Angle to 360 (see Figure 19-45).

Figure 19-45

This will cause the image to rotate 360 degrees clockwise.

In the XAML view, add the `Loaded` attribute to the `<Canvas>` element:

```
<Canvas Loaded="onLoad"
        xmlns="http://schemas.microsoft.com/client/2007"
        xmlns:x="http://schemas.microsoft.com/winfx/2006/xaml"
        Width="640" Height="480"
        Background="White"
        x:Name="Page">
```

Append the following block of code to `Page.xaml.js`:

```
function onLoad (sender, eventArgs)
{
    var obj = sender.findName("Storyboard1");
    obj.begin();
}
```

Press F5 to test the application. Notice that when the page is loaded, the image drops to the bottom of the page, while rotating clockwise (see Figure 19-46).

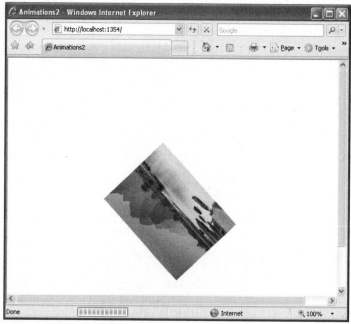

Figure 19-46

Slowing the Rate of Fall

To slow down the rate of all, you can increase the duration of the timeline object. In `Storyboard1`, move the second keyframe from time `0:01.000` to `0:02.500` (see Figure 19-47).

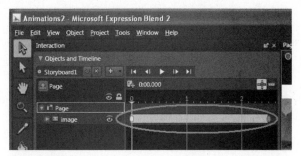

Figure 19-47

Press F5 to test again. Notice that this time the image falls is longer compared to the previous instance.

Varying the Rate of Fall

In the previous section, the image drops at a uniform speed. That isn't very realistic, because in real life an object accelerates as it falls. You need to tweak the properties a little to make it more lifelike.

Select the second keyframe (at time `0:02.500`) and select the Properties Inspector.

In the Easing section, modify the KeySpline by dragging the yellow dot from the top to the bottom (see Figure 19-48).

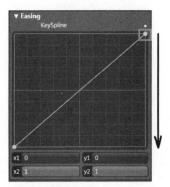

Figure 19-48

A KeySpline is used to define the progress of an animation. The x-axis of the KeySpline represents time and the y-axis represents value. The KeySpline should now look like Figure 19-49.

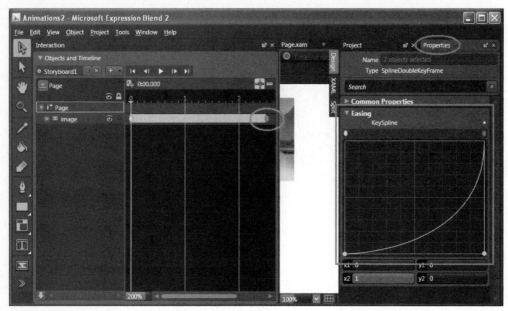

Figure 19-49

The modified KeySpline means "as time progresses, increase the rate of change." In this example, it means that as the falling image approaches the bottom, it will drop faster.

Press F5 to test again, and you'll see that the image accelerates as it nears the bottom. The animation is now more realistic, simulating free-fall.

Playing Media

One of Silverlight's key capabilities is a rich media experience. This section examines how to embed a Windows media file in your Silverlight application and how to control its playback. In addition, it also explains how to create simple effects on the video.

Creating the Silverlight Project

Using Expression Blend 2, create a Silverlight project and name it `Media`.

In the Project window, right-click on the project name (`Media`) and select Add Existing Item. Select a Windows Media file (`WindowsMedia.wmv`, for this example; it's included in the book's code download). After this, the WindowsMedia.wmv file will be added to the project.

Double-click `WindowsMedia.wmv` in the Project window to add it to the page (see Figure 19-50).

Figure 19-50

You need Windows Media Player 10 or later for this project to work.

The `WindowsMedia.wmv` file in now contained within a `MediaElement` control (see also Figure 19-51):

```
<Canvas
    xmlns="http://schemas.microsoft.com/client/2007"
    xmlns:x="http://schemas.microsoft.com/winfx/2006/xaml"
    Width="640" Height="480"
    Background="White"
    x:Name="Page">
    <MediaElement x:Name="WindowsMedia_wmv"
        Width="320" Height="240"
        Source="WindowsMedia.wmv"
        Stretch="Fill"
        Canvas.Top="8" Canvas.Left="8"
        AutoPlay="True"v
    />
</Canvas>
```

Figure 19-51

Press F5 to test the page. The video automatically starts to play when the page has finished loading (see Figure 19-52).

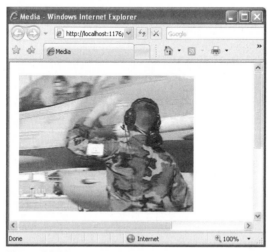

Figure 19-52

Disabling Auto-Play

While automatically playing a video is a useful feature, sometimes you might want to disable this. For example, if you have multiple videos embedded in a page, this feature is actually more nuisance than helpful. To disable the auto-play feature, just set the AutoPlay attribute in the <MediaElement> element to False, like this:

```
<Canvas
    xmlns="http://schemas.microsoft.com/client/2007"
    xmlns:x="http://schemas.microsoft.com/winfx/2006/xaml"
    Width="640" Height="480"
    Background="White"
    x:Name="Page">
    <MediaElement x:Name="WindowsMedia_wmv"
        Width="320" Height="240"
        Source="WindowsMedia.wmv"
        Stretch="Fill"
        Canvas.Top="8" Canvas.Left="8"
        AutoPlay="False"
    />
</Canvas>
```

So how and when do you get it to play? You can programmatically play the video when the user's mouse enters the video and pause it when the mouse leaves the video. Also, if the user clicks on the video, the video can stop and return to the beginning. To do so, set the following highlighted attributes:

```
<Canvas
    xmlns="http://schemas.microsoft.com/client/2007"
    xmlns:x="http://schemas.microsoft.com/winfx/2006/xaml"
    Width="640" Height="480"
    Background="White"
    x:Name="Page">
    <MediaElement x:Name="WindowsMedia_wmv"
    Width="320" Height="240"
    Source="WindowsMedia.wmv"
    Stretch="Fill"
    Canvas.Top="8" Canvas.Left="8"
    AutoPlay="False"
    MouseEnter="MouseEnter"
    MouseLeave="MouseLeave"
    MouseLeftButtonDown="MouseClick"
    />
</Canvas>
```

Basically, you are setting the event handlers for the various events handled by the <MediaElement> element. To write the event handler, go to the Project window and double-click on the Page.xaml.js file.

Append the `Page.xaml.js` file with the following code:

```
function MouseEnter (sender, eventArgs)
{
    var obj = sender.findName("WindowsMedia_wmv");
    obj.play();
}

function MouseLeave (sender, eventArgs)
{
    var obj = sender.findName("WindowsMedia_wmv");
    obj.pause();
}

function MouseClick (sender, eventArgs)
{
    var obj = sender.findName("WindowsMedia_wmv");
    obj.stop();
}
```

The `findName()` method allows you to programmatically get a reference to the specified element (via its `x:Name` attribute) on the Silverlight page. In this case, you are referencing an instance of the `MediaElement` element. This object supports the `play`, `pause`, and `stop` methods.

Press F5 to test the application again. This time, the video will start to play when the mouse hovers over it and pauses when the mouse leaves it. To restart the video to the beginning, simply click on the video.

Creating the Mirror Effect

One interesting thing you can do with a video is to create a mirror effect. For example, Figure 19-53 shows a video playing with a mirror image at the bottom of it.

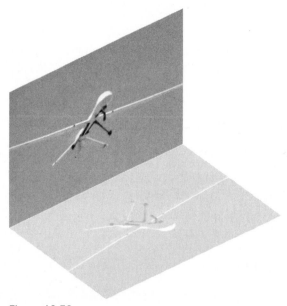

Figure 19-53

Modify the original `Canvas` control by switching the page to XAML view and adding the following highlighted code:

```xaml
<Canvas
    xmlns="http://schemas.microsoft.com/client/2007"
    xmlns:x="http://schemas.microsoft.com/winfx/2006/xaml"
    Width="640" Height="480"
    Background="White"
    x:Name="Page">
    <MediaElement x:Name="WindowsMedia_wmv"
        Width="238" Height="156"
        Source="WindowsMedia.wmv"
        Stretch="Fill"
        Canvas.Top="124" Canvas.Left="8"
        AutoPlay="False"
        MouseEnter="MouseEnter"
        MouseLeave="MouseLeave"
        MouseLeftButtonDown="MouseClick">
        <MediaElement.RenderTransform>
            <TransformGroup>
                <ScaleTransform ScaleX="1" ScaleY="1"/>
                <SkewTransform AngleX="0" AngleY="-25"/>
                <RotateTransform Angle="0"/>
                <TranslateTransform X="0" Y="0"/>
            </TransformGroup>
        </MediaElement.RenderTransform>
    </MediaElement>
</Canvas>
```

This transforms the video into the shape shown in Figure 19-54.

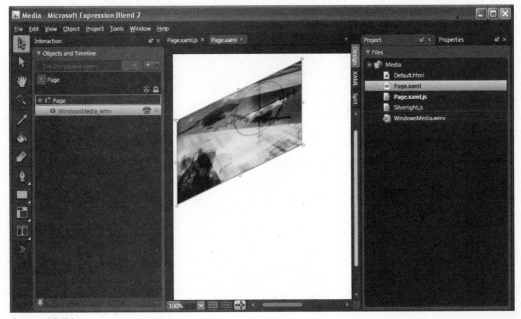

Figure 19-54

Add another `<MediaElement>` element (highlighted code) to simulate the mirror effect:

```xml
<Canvas
    xmlns="http://schemas.microsoft.com/client/2007"
    xmlns:x="http://schemas.microsoft.com/winfx/2006/xaml"
    Width="640" Height="480"
    Background="White"
    x:Name="Page">
    <MediaElement x:Name="WindowsMedia_wmv"
        Width="238" Height="156"
        Source="WindowsMedia.wmv"
        Stretch="Fill"
        Canvas.Top="124" Canvas.Left="8"
        AutoPlay="False"
        MouseEnter="MouseEnter"
        MouseLeave="MouseLeave"
        MouseLeftButtonDown="MouseClick">
        <MediaElement.RenderTransform>
            <TransformGroup>
                <ScaleTransform ScaleX="1" ScaleY="1"/>
                <SkewTransform AngleX="0" AngleY="-25"/>
                <RotateTransform Angle="0"/>
                <TranslateTransform X="0" Y="0"/>
            </TransformGroup>
        </MediaElement.RenderTransform>
    </MediaElement>

    <MediaElement x:Name="WindowsMedia_wmv1"
        AutoPlay="False"
        MouseEnter="MouseEnter"
        MouseLeave="MouseLeave"
        MouseLeftButtonDown="MouseClick"
        Width="238.955" Height="99.454"
        Source="WindowsMedia.wmv"
        Stretch="Fill" Canvas.Left="149.319" Canvas.Top="379.884">
        <MediaElement.RenderTransform>
            <TransformGroup>
                <ScaleTransform ScaleX="1" ScaleY="-1"/>
                <SkewTransform AngleX="55" AngleY="-25"/>
                <TranslateTransform X="0" Y="0"/>
            </TransformGroup>
        </MediaElement.RenderTransform>
    </MediaElement>

</Canvas>
```

You now have two videos with the second video mirroring the first (see Figure 19-55).

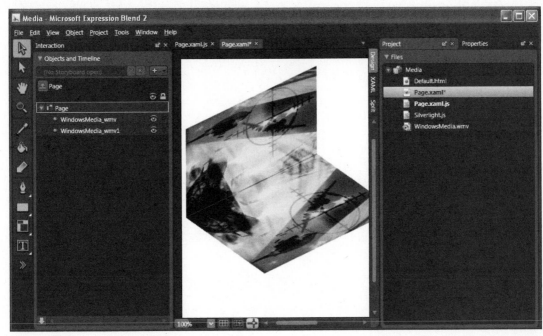

Figure 19-55

To create the translucent effect for the mirror image, set the Opacity attribute to a value between 0 and 1 (in this case it's set to 0.3):

```
<MediaElement x:Name="WindowsMedia_wmv1"
    AutoPlay="False"
    MouseEnter="MouseEnter"
    MouseLeave="MouseLeave"
    MouseLeftButtonDown="MouseClick"
    Width="238.955" Height="99.454"
    Source="WindowsMedia.wmv"
    Stretch="Fill" Canvas.Left="149.319" Canvas.Top="379.884"
    Opacity="0.3">
```

Modify the following block of code in `Page.xaml.js` highlighted here:

```javascript
//---make these variables global---
var obj, obj1;

if (!window.Media)
    Media = {};

Media.Page = function()
{
}

Media.Page.prototype =
{
    handleLoad: function(control, userContext, rootElement)
    {
        this.control = control;

        // Sample event hookup:
        rootElement.addEventListener("MouseLeftButtonDown", Silverlight.
createDelegate(this, this.handleMouseDown));

        //---the original video---
        obj = this.control.content.findName("WindowsMedia_wmv");

        //---the reflected video---
        obj1 = this.control.content.findName("WindowsMedia_wmv1");
    },

    // Sample event handler
    handleMouseDown: function(sender, eventArgs)
    {
        // The following line of code shows how to find an element by name and
call a method on it.
        // this.control.content.findName("Storyboard1").Begin();
    }
}

function MouseEnter (sender, eventArgs)
{
    //---mute the reflected video---
    obj1.volume=0;

    //---play the 2 videos---
    obj.play();
    obj1.play();
}

function MouseLeave (sender, eventArgs)
{
    //---pause the 2 videos---
```

```
        obj.pause();
        obj1.pause();
    }

    function MouseClick (sender, eventArgs)
    {
        //---stop the 2 videos---
        obj.stop();
        obj1.stop();
    }
```

Notice that instead of programmatically finding the media object — using the `findName()` method — in each event handler, you can also locate it via the `handleLoad()` function. Also, because there are two identical videos in the page, you do not need the audio playback in the mirroring video. Hence, you turn off its volume by setting its `volume` property to 0 (valid values are from 0 to 1).

Press F5 to test the page. Both videos start to play when the mouse hovers over either of the two videos (see Figure 19-56).

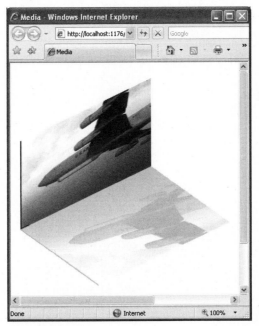

Figure 19-56

Creating Your Own Media Player

The `MediaElement` element is a bare-bones control that simply plays back a media file — it does not have visual controls for you to pause or advance the media (although you can programmatically do that). In this section, you build a Silverlight application that resembles the YouTube player, allowing you to visually control the playback of the media as well as customize its look and feel. Figure 19-57 shows the end product.

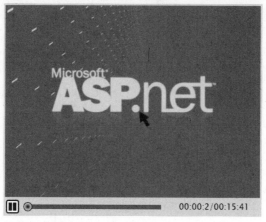

Figure 19-57

Creating the Project

Using Expression Blend 2, create a new Silverlight project and name it `MediaPlayer`.

Add a Windows Media file (`.wmv`) file to the project by right-clicking on the project name and selecting Add Existing Item. For this project, use the same file as in the previous example, `WindowsMedia.wmv`.

Designing the User Interface

The first step is to design the user interface of the media player. Figure 19-58 shows the various controls that you will add to the page. The outline is used to identify the major parts of the player.

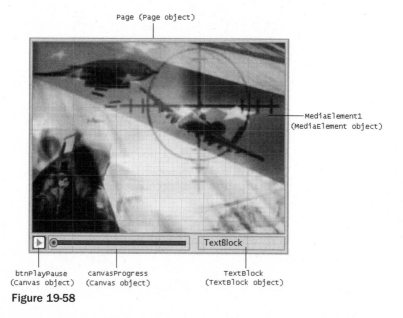

Figure 19-58

Figure 19-59 shows the organization and hierarchy of the various controls. Those controls correspond to the controls listed in Figure 19-58.

Figure 19-59

The most delicate part of the media player is the slider used to indicate the progress of the media playback. As shown in Figure 19-60, the slider (canvasProgress) consists of two Rectangle elements and an Ellipse element. The first Rectangle element (rectProgressWell) represents the entire duration of the movie. This control also forms the path that the marker (ellMarker, an Ellipse element) slides on. The second Rectangle control (rectDownloadProgress) is used to indicate the percentage of the media downloaded from the remote server. The lower part of Figure 19-60 shows this control in action (partially filled).

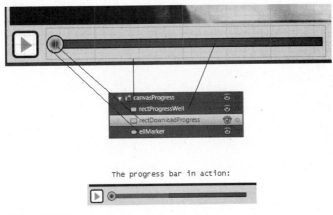

Figure 19-60

Here's the complete XAML code for the media player:

```xml
<Canvas
    xmlns="http://schemas.microsoft.com/client/2007"
    xmlns:x="http://schemas.microsoft.com/winfx/2006/xaml"
    Width="472" Height="376"
    Background="#FFD6D4C8"
    x:Name="Page" >

    <MediaElement x:Name="MediaElement1" Width="466" Height="340"
        Stretch="Fill" Canvas.Left="3" Canvas.Top="3"
        AutoPlay="false"
        Source="WindowsMedia.wmv" />

    <Canvas Width="24" Height="24" Canvas.Left="5" Canvas.Top="348"
        x:Name="btnPlayPause">
        <Canvas Width="24" Height="24" x:Name="canvasPlay" >
            <Rectangle Width="24" Height="24" Fill="#FFFFFFFF"
                Stroke="#FF000000" RadiusX="3" RadiusY="3" x:Name="RectPlay"
                StrokeThickness="2"/>
            <Polygon Points="8,5 8,19 18,13" StrokeThickness="5" Fill="Red"
                Width="24" Height="24"/>
        </Canvas>

        <Canvas Width="24" Height="24" x:Name="canvasPause"
            MouseEnter="PauseButtonMouseEnter"
            MouseLeave="PauseButtonMouseLeave" Opacity="0">
            <Rectangle Width="24" Height="24" Fill="#FFFFFFFF"
                Stroke="#FF000000" RadiusX="3" RadiusY="3" x:Name="RectPause"
                StrokeThickness="2"/>
            <Rectangle Width="6" Height="14" Fill="#FF141414" Stroke="#FF000000"
                Canvas.Left="13" Canvas.Top="5" x:Name="rectPauseBar1"/>
            <Rectangle Width="6" Height="14" Fill="#FF141414" Stroke="#FF000000"
                Canvas.Left="5" Canvas.Top="5" x:Name="rectPauseBar2"/>
        </Canvas>
    </Canvas>

    <Canvas Width="255" Height="27" Canvas.Left="36" Canvas.Top="346"
        x:Name="canvasProgress">
        <Rectangle Width="244" Height="8" Fill="#FF414141" Stroke="#FF000000"
            Canvas.Top="10"
            x:Name="rectProgressWell"
            Canvas.Left="8.5" />

        <Rectangle Width="3" Height="8" Fill="#FF9D0808" Stroke="#FF000000"
            Canvas.Top="10" x:Name="rectDownloadProgress" StrokeThickness="0"
            Canvas.Left="8.5"/>

        <Ellipse Width="16" Height="16" Stroke="#FF000000" Canvas.Top="6"
            Canvas.Left="0"
            x:Name="ellMarker">
            <Ellipse.Fill>
                <RadialGradientBrush>
                    <GradientStop Color="#FF000000" Offset="0"/>
                    <GradientStop Color="#FFF6F6EC" Offset="1"/>
                </RadialGradientBrush>
```

```
        </Ellipse.Fill>
      </Ellipse>
    </Canvas>

    <TextBlock Width="148" Height="21" Text="TextBlock" TextWrapping="Wrap"
        Canvas.Left="321" Canvas.Top="348" x:Name="TextBlock"/>

  </Canvas>
```

Wiring All the Controls

With the UI created and ready for coding, you're ready to wire up all the controls so that they will function as one. You'll define the event handlers in the following table.

Event Handler	Description
DownloadProgressChanged()	Continuously invoked when the MediaElement control downloads the media from the remote server. It is used to update the red progress bar indicating the progress of the download.
EllMarkerMouseDown()	Invoked when the user clicks on the marker using the left mouse button.
EllMarkerMouseUp()	Invoked when the user releases the left mouse button.
MediaPlayerMouseMove()	Invoked when the mouse moves across the Silverlight page.
MediaPlayerMouseLeave()	Invoked when the mouse leaves the Silverlight page.
MediaEnded()	Invoked when the media has finished playing. The media will be reset to its starting position (so is the marker).
PlayPauseButtonUp()	Invoked when the user clicks on the Play/Pause button.

First, assign the various event handlers to the elements as shown in the following highlighted code:

```
<Canvas
    xmlns="http://schemas.microsoft.com/client/2007"
    xmlns:x="http://schemas.microsoft.com/winfx/2006/xaml"
    Width="472" Height="376"
    Background="#FFD6D4C8"
    x:Name="Page"
    MouseMove="MediaPlayerMouseMove"
    MouseLeave="MediaPlayerMouseLeave"
    MouseLeftButtonUp="EllMarkerMouseUp" >

    <MediaElement x:Name="MediaElement1" Width="466" Height="340"
        Stretch="Fill" Canvas.Left="3" Canvas.Top="3"
        AutoPlay="false"
        Source="WindowsMedia.wmv"
        MediaEnded="MediaEnded"
        DownloadProgressChanged="DownloadProgressChanged" />

    <Canvas Width="24" Height="24" Canvas.Left="5" Canvas.Top="348"
```

(continued)

(continued)

```xml
                x:Name="btnPlayPause"
                MouseLeftButtonUp="PlayPauseButtonUp" >
                <Canvas Width="24" Height="24" x:Name="canvasPlay" >
                    <Rectangle Width="24" Height="24" Fill="#FFFFFFFF"
                        Stroke="#FF000000" RadiusX="3" RadiusY="3" x:Name="RectPlay"
                        StrokeThickness="2"/>
                    <Polygon Points="8,5 8,19 18,13" StrokeThickness="5" Fill="Red"
                        Width="24" Height="24"/>
                </Canvas>

                <Canvas Width="24" Height="24" x:Name="canvasPause"
                    MouseEnter="PauseButtonMouseEnter"
                    MouseLeave="PauseButtonMouseLeave" Opacity="0">
                    <Rectangle Width="24" Height="24" Fill="#FFFFFFFF"
                        Stroke="#FF000000" RadiusX="3" RadiusY="3" x:Name="RectPause"
                        StrokeThickness="2"/>
                    <Rectangle Width="6" Height="14" Fill="#FF141414" Stroke="#FF000000"
                        Canvas.Left="13" Canvas.Top="5" x:Name="rectPauseBar1"/>
                    <Rectangle Width="6" Height="14" Fill="#FF141414" Stroke="#FF000000"
                        Canvas.Left="5" Canvas.Top="5" x:Name="rectPauseBar2"/>
                </Canvas>
            </Canvas>

            <Canvas Width="255" Height="27" Canvas.Left="36" Canvas.Top="346"
                x:Name="canvasProgress">
                <Rectangle Width="244" Height="8" Fill="#FF414141" Stroke="#FF000000"
                    Canvas.Top="10"
                    x:Name="rectProgressWell"
                    Canvas.Left="8.5" />

                <Rectangle Width="3" Height="8" Fill="#FF9D0808" Stroke="#FF000000"
                    Canvas.Top="10" x:Name="rectDownloadProgress" StrokeThickness="0"
                    Canvas.Left="8.5"/>

                <Ellipse Width="16" Height="16" Stroke="#FF000000" Canvas.Top="6"
                    Canvas.Left="0"
                    x:Name="ellMarker"
                    MouseLeftButtonDown="EllMarkerMouseDown"
                    MouseLeftButtonUp="EllMarkerMouseUp" >
                    <Ellipse.Fill>
                        <RadialGradientBrush>
                            <GradientStop Color="#FF000000" Offset="0"/>
                            <GradientStop Color="#FFF6F6EC" Offset="1"/>
                        </RadialGradientBrush>
                    </Ellipse.Fill>
                </Ellipse>
            </Canvas>

            <TextBlock Width="148" Height="21" Text="TextBlock" TextWrapping="Wrap"
                Canvas.Left="321" Canvas.Top="348" x:Name="TextBlock"/>

        </Canvas>
```

Now double-click on the `Page.xaml.js` file in the Project window to open it. Declare the following global variables at the top of the file:

```
//---global variables---
var playing = false;
var markerClicked = false;
var duration=0;
var intervalID;

//---all the major elements on the page---
var ellMarker;
var MediaElement1;
var textblock;
var rectProgressWell;
var rectDownloadProgress;
//--------------------------------
```

When the page is loaded, get a reference to all the major controls on the page:

```
MediaPlayer.Page.prototype =
{
    handleLoad: function(control, userContext, rootElement)
    {
        this.control = control;

        //---get a reference to all the major controls on the page---
        MediaElement1 = rootElement.findName("MediaElement1");
        ellMarker = rootElement.findName("ellMarker");
        textblock = rootElement.findName("TextBlock");
        rectProgressWell = rootElement.findName("rectProgressWell");
        rectDownloadProgress =
            rootElement.findName("rectDownloadProgress");
        textblock = rootElement.findName("TextBlock");
        //-----------------------------------------------------

        // Sample event hookup:
        rootElement.addEventListener("MouseLeftButtonDown",
            Silverlight.createDelegate(this, this.handleMouseDown));
    },

    // Sample event handler
    handleMouseDown: function(sender, eventArgs)
    {
        // The following line of code shows how to find an element by
        //   name and call a method on it.
        // this.control.content.findName("Timeline1").Begin();
    }
}
```

Creating the Helper Functions

Two helper functions — `ConvertToTimeSpan()` and `DisplayCurrentPlayBack()` — need to be defined.

The `ConvertToTimeSpan()` function converts value in seconds to the `TimeSpan` format of `hh:mm:ss`. For example, 61 seconds converts to `00:01:01`. You need this function because the `Position` property of the `MediaElement` control accepts only values of the `TimeSpan` type. The `ConvertToTimeSpan()` function is defined as follows:

```
//---convert time in seconds to "hh:mm:ss"---
function ConvertToTimeSpan(timeinseconds)
{
    if (timeinseconds<0) {
        return ("00:00:00");
    }
    else
    if (timeinseconds<60) {
        return ("00:00:" + Math.floor(timeinseconds));
    }
    else
    if (timeinseconds<3600)
    {
        var mins = Math.floor(timeinseconds / 60);
        var seconds = Math.floor(timeinseconds - (mins * 60));
        return ("00:" + mins + ":" + seconds);
    }
    else
    {
        var hrs = Math.floor(timeinseconds / 3600);
        var mins = timeinseconds - (hrs * 3600)
        var seconds = Math.floor(timeinseconds - (hrs * 3600) - (mins * 60));
        return (hrs + mins + ":" + seconds);
    }
}
```

The `DisplayCurrentPlayBack()` function is used to display the current status of the media playback. It displays the elapsed time versus the total time of the media. For example, if the media (total duration two minutes) is into its 30th second, the `DisplayCurrentPlayBack()` function displays `00:00:30 / 00:02:00`. In addition, the function is also responsible for synchronizing the marker as the media is played. To ensure that the status of the playback is updated constantly, you call `DisplayCurrentPlayBack()` repeatedly, using the `setInterval()` JavaScript function (more on this later). The `DisplayCurrentPlayBack()` function is defined as follows:

```
//---shows the current playback -- marker and position---
function DisplayCurrentPlayBack()
{
    //---find duration of movie---
    if (duration==0)
        duration = Math.round(MediaElement1.NaturalDuration.Seconds * 100) /
                   100;

    //---find current position---
    var position = MediaElement1.Position.Seconds;

    //---move the marker---
```

```
ellMarker["Canvas.Left"] = Math.round((position / duration) *
                           rectProgressWell.width);

//---format - elapsed time/total time---
var str =  ConvertToTimeSpan(position) + "/" +
           ConvertToTimeSpan(duration);

textblock.Text = str;
}
```

Defining the Event Handlers

Finally you define the various event handlers.

The `DownloadProgressChanged` event handler is continuously fired when the `MediaElement` control is downloading the media from the remote server. In this event handler, you first obtain the progress value (from 0 to 1) and then display the downloaded percentage on the `TextBlock` control. In addition, you adjust the width of the `rectProgressWell` control so that as the media is downloaded, its width expands (see Figure 19-61). Here's the code:

```
//---fired while the movie is being downloaded---
function DownloadProgressChanged(sender, eventArgs)
{
    //---get the progress value from 0 to 1---
    var progress = MediaElement1.DownloadProgress;

    //---display the download in percentage---
    textblock.Text = Math.round(progress*100).toString() + "%";

    //---adjust the width of the progress bar---
    var progressWidth = progress * rectProgressWell.width;
    rectDownloadProgress.width = Math.round(progressWidth);
}
```

Figure 19-61

The `EllMarkerDown` event handler is fired when the user clicks on the marker (the Ellipse element). Here, you set the `markerClicked` variable to `true` to indicate that the marker has been clicked:

```
//---marker is clicked---
function EllMarkerMouseDown(sender, eventArgs)
{
    markerClicked = true;
}
```

When the user releases the mouse button, the `EllMarkerMouseUp` event handler is fired. You first need to check if the user releases the button on the main canvas itself or on the marker. If the marker was previously clicked, you need to move the marker to the current location of the mouse and set the media to the new position. The new position of the movie is determined by multiplying the duration of the media and the ratio of the position of the marker with respect to the width of the progress well. Here's the code:

```
//---marker is released---
function EllMarkerMouseUp(sender, eventArgs)
{
    //---only execute this function if the user is moving the marker---
    if (markerClicked) {
        markerClicked=false;

        //---find duration of movie---
        duration = Math.round(MediaElement1.NaturalDuration.Seconds *
                100)/100;

        //---get the position of the marker w.r.t. to the Well---
        position = ((ellMarker["Canvas.Left"]) / rectProgressWell.width) *
                duration;

        //---get integer part---
        position = Math.floor(position);

        //---end of the media---
        if (ellMarker["Canvas.Left"]==rectProgressWell.width) {
            //---move the movie to the last frame---
            MediaElement1.Position = ConvertToTimeSpan(duration);
        }
        else
        {
            //---move the movie to the new position---
            MediaElement1.Position = ConvertToTimeSpan(position);
        }
    }
}
```

The `MediaPlayerMouseMove` event handler is continuously fired when the mouse moves over the page. You need to determine if the marker is clicked when the mouse is moving. If it is, that means that the user is moving the marker, and you need to reposition the marker. Here's the code:

```
//---mouse moves inside the Silverlight media player control---
function MediaPlayerMouseMove(sender, eventArgs)
{
    //---user clicks marker and drags it---
    if (markerClicked)
    {
        //---find duration of movie---
        if (duration==0)
            duration = Math.round(MediaElement1.NaturalDuration.Seconds * 100)
                    / 100;

        clearInterval(intervalID);

        //---get the position of the mouse with respect to the progress Well---
```

```
var pt = eventArgs.getPosition(rectProgressWell);

//---marker not allowed to stray outside the well---
if (pt.x > 0 && pt.x < rectProgressWell.width)
{
    //---moves the marker---
    ellMarker["Canvas.Left"] = pt.x;

    //---display the new time---
    textblock.Text = ConvertToTimeSpan((pt.x / rectProgressWell.width)
                    * duration).toString();
}
else
if (pt.x <= 0)  //---move to the beginning---
{
    //---moves the marker---
    ellMarker["Canvas.Left"] = 0;

    //---display the new time---
    textblock.Text = "00:00:00";
}
else
if (pt.x >= rectProgressWell.width) //---move to the end---
{
    //---moves the marker---
    ellMarker["Canvas.Left"] = rectProgressWell.width;

    //---display the new time---
    textblock.Text = ConvertToTimeSpan(duration);
}

if (playing)
    intervalID = window.setInterval("DisplayCurrentPlayBack()", 500);
}
}
```

The MediaPlayerMouseLeave event handler is fired when the mouse leaves the Silverlight page. In this case, you set the markerClicked variable to false:

```
//---mouse leaves the entire Silverlight media player control
function MediaPlayerMouseLeave(sender, eventArgs)
{
    markerClicked=false;
}
```

The MediaEnded event handler is fired when the media has finished playing. You have to make the Play button visible again and hide the Pause button. In addition, you have to move the marker to the beginning and reset the media to the beginning. Here's the code:

```
//---movie has finished playing---
function MediaEnded(sender, eventArgs)
{
    var btnPlay = sender.findName("canvasPlay");
    var btnPause = sender.findName("canvasPause");

    playing = false;
    clearInterval(intervalID);    //---clear the progress updating---
    btnPlay.opacity = 1;          //---show the Play button---
    btnPause.opacity = 0;         //---hide the Pause button---

    //---move the marker to the beginning---
    ellMarker["Canvas.Left"] = -2;
    MediaElement1.Position="00:00:00"; //---reset the movie position---
}
```

The PlayPauseButtonUp button is fired when the user clicks on the Play/Pause button and releases the mouse. When the media has started playing, you use the setInterval() JavaScript function to display the media progress every half second:

```
function PlayPauseButtonUp(sender, eventArgs)
{
    var btnPlay = sender.findName("canvasPlay");
    var btnPause = sender.findName("canvasPause");

    //---if currently playing and now going to pause---
    if (playing==true) {
        MediaElement1.pause();      //---pause the movie---
        clearInterval(intervalID);  //---stop updating the marker---
        playing = false;
        btnPlay.opacity = 1;        //---show the Play button---
        btnPause.opacity = 0;       //---hide the Pause button---
    }
    else
    {
        MediaElement1.play();       //---play the movie---
        playing = true;
        btnPlay.opacity = 0;        //---hide the Play button---
        btnPause.opacity = 1;       //---show the Pause button---

        //---update the progress of the movie---
        intervalID = window.setInterval("DisplayCurrentPlayBack()", 500);
    }
}
```

That's it! Press F5 in Expression Blend 2, and you should be able to use the new media player (see Figure 19-62)!

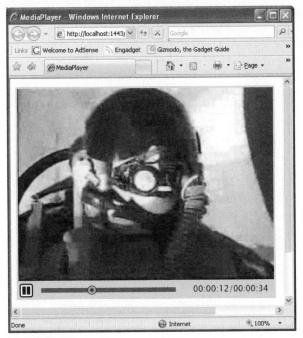

Figure 19-62

Silverlight 2.0

One of the key strengths of Silverlight is its rich interactive capabilities. Apart from performing cool animations and transformations on graphics and videos, one good use of Silverlight is to develop applications that could not easily be achieved using conventional web applications (even when using ASP.NET and AJAX). A good example is capturing signatures. Often, when you sign for an online service (such as applying for a Google AdSense account) you need to sign a contractual agreement. In place of the traditional signature, you are often requested to provide some sort of personal information (such as your birth date or mother's maiden name) to prove that you are who are say you are. That's because there is no way you could sign (literally) on the web page, unless you print out the form, sign it, and fax it back to the service provider.

With Silverlight, you can develop an application that allows users to sign on the page itself. And with more and more people using Tablet PCs (or having access to a pen tablet such as the Wacom Intuos Pen Tablet), pen input is no longer a dream. This section shows you how to create a Silverlight 2 application that captures the user's signature. In addition, you'll see how the signature can be sent back to a Web Service for archival.

> Remember to download the Microsoft Silverlight Tools Beta 1 for Visual Studio 2008 tool from www.microsoft.com/downloads before you start the project.

Creating the Project Using Visual Studio 2008

Using Visual Studio 2008, create a new Silverlight project using C# and name it `Signature` (see Figure 19-63).

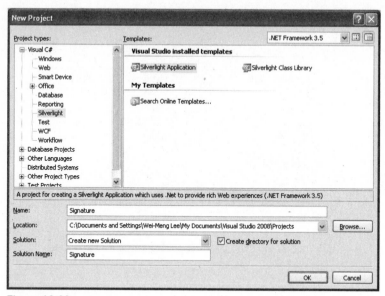

Figure 19-63

> If you have installed the Microsoft Silverlight Tools Beta 1 for Visual Studio 2008 tool, you should see Silverlight in the Project Types list in the New Project dialog.

You will be asked how you want to host your application. Select the second option (Generate an HTML test page to host Silverlight within this project), and click OK (see Figure 19-64).

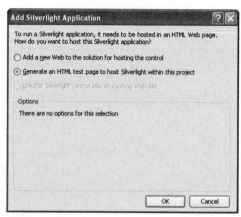

Figure 19-64

Populate `Page.xaml` as follows:

```
<UserControl x:Class="Signature.Page"
    xmlns="http://schemas.microsoft.com/client/2007"
    xmlns:x="http://schemas.microsoft.com/winfx/2006/xaml"
    Width="400" Height="300">

    <Canvas>
        <Canvas x:Name="SigPad" Width="404" Height="152"
            Canvas.Left="8" Canvas.Top="9" Background="#FFF4F60C" >
            <Rectangle Width="404" Height="152" Fill="#FFF1F8DB"
                Stroke="#FF000000" StrokeThickness="3"/>
        </Canvas>
    </Canvas>

</UserControl>
```

The page should now look like Figure 19-65.

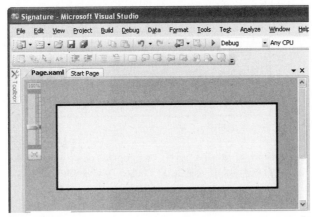

Figure 19-65

Capturing the Signature

As the user uses the mouse (or stylus if he/she is using a tablet PC) to write on the control, the series of points it makes on the control will be saved. There will be three events of concern to you:

❑ `MouseLeftButtonDown` — Fired when the left mouse button is clicked

❑ `MouseMove` — Fired when the mouse moves

❑ `MouseLeftButtonUp` — Fired when the left mouse button is released

Figure 19-66 shows what happens when you write the character "C". When the left mouse button is clicked, the `MouseLeftButtonDown` event is fired, followed by a series of `MouseMove` events as the mouse moves counterclockwise, and then finally the `MouseLeftButtonUp` event is fired when the mouse's left button is released. As the mouse moves, the series of points made by it are joined together.

677

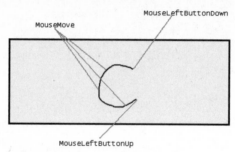

Figure 19-66

The points touched by the mouse between the `MouseLeftButtonDown` and `MouseLeftButtonUp` events are saved as a series of continuous points (called a line). For example, the character "C" is made up of one line (assuming that you did not release the left mouse button while drawing it), while the character "t" is made up of two lines — one horizontal and one vertical (see Figure 19-67).

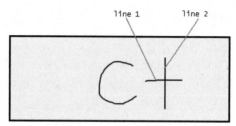

Figure 19-67

The points making up an individual line are saved in a generic `List` object. The individual lines in each character are also saved in a generic `List` object, as Figure 19-68 shows.

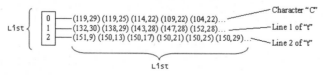

Figure 19-68

Coding the Application

In `Page.xaml.cs` (see Figure 19-69), declare the following member variables:

Figure 19-69

```
public partial class Page : UserControl
{
        private bool MouseDown = false;
        private Point _previouspoint;
        private List<Point> _points;
        private List<List<Point>> _lines = new List<List<Point>>();
```

Add the following highlighted lines to the Page() constructor:

```
public Page()
{
    InitializeComponent();

    //---wire up the event handlers---
    SigPad.MouseLeftButtonDown += new
        MouseButtonEventHandler(SigPad_MouseLeftButtonDown);
    SigPad.MouseLeftButtonUp += new
        MouseButtonEventHandler(SigPad_MouseLeftButtonUp);
    SigPad.MouseMove += new
        MouseEventHandler(SigPad_MouseMove);
}
```

The MouseLeftButtonDown event is fired when the user clicks on the left mouse button. Here you interpret it as the beginning of the signature signing process. Code the MouseLeftButtonDown event handler of SigPad as follows:

```
//---fired when the user clicks on the Signature pad---
void SigPad_MouseLeftButtonDown(
    object sender, MouseButtonEventArgs e)
{
    //---record that the mouse left button is pressed---
    MouseDown = true;

    //---create a new instance of _points and _lines to
    // record all the points drawn---
    _points = new List<Point>();

    //---save the current point for later use---
    _previouspoint = e.GetPosition(SigPad);

    //---add the point---
    _points.Add(_previouspoint);
}
```

The MouseLeftButtonUp event is fired when the user releases the left mouse button. You interpret that as the end of the signature signing process. Code the MouseLeftButtonUp event handler of SigPad as follows:

```
//---fired when the user let go of the left mouse button---
void SigPad_MouseLeftButtonUp(
    object sender, MouseButtonEventArgs e)
{
    //---user has let go of the left mouse button---
    MouseDown = false;

    //---add the list of points to the current line---
    _lines.Add(_points);
}
```

The MouseMove event is fired continuously when the user moves the mouse. Here, you draw a line connecting the previous point with the current point. Code the MouseMove event handler of SigPad as follows:

```
//---fired when the left mouse button is moved---
void SigPad_MouseMove(object sender, MouseEventArgs e)
{
    //---if left mouse button is pressed...---
    if (MouseDown)
    {
        //---add the current point---
        var currentPoint = e.GetPosition(SigPad);
        _points.Add(currentPoint);

        //---draws a line connecting the previous
        // point and the current point---
        Line line = new Line()
        {
            X1 = _previouspoint.X,
            Y1 = _previouspoint.Y,
            X2 = currentPoint.X,
            Y2 = currentPoint.Y,
            StrokeThickness = 2,
            Stroke = new SolidColorBrush(Colors.Black)
        };

        //---add the line to the signature pad---
        SigPad.Children.Add(line);

        //---saves the current point for later use---
        _previouspoint = currentPoint;
    }
}
```

Press F5 to test the application. Use your mouse to draw on the web page (see Figure 19-70).

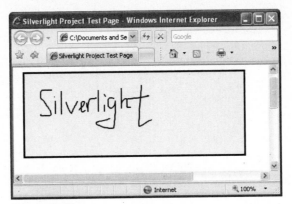

Figure 19-70

Saving the Signature to Isolated Storage

This section explains how to store the coordinates of the signature using isolated storage. This technique is useful if you need to persist information on the client side, such as backing up the signature that the user has signed.

Using the same project created in the previous section, add the following highlighted code to Page.xaml:

```
<UserControl x:Class="Signature.Page"
    xmlns="http://schemas.microsoft.com/client/2007"
    xmlns:x="http://schemas.microsoft.com/winfx/2006/xaml"
    Width="400" Height="300">
    <Canvas>

        <Canvas x:Name="SigPad" Width="404" Height="152"
            Canvas.Left="8" Canvas.Top="9" Background="#FFF4F60C" >
            <Rectangle Width="404" Height="152" Fill="#FFF1F8DB"
                Stroke="#FF000000" StrokeThickness="3"/>
        </Canvas>

        <Canvas>
            <Canvas x:Name="btnSave" Width="97" Height="26"
                Canvas.Left="315" Canvas.Top="168">
                <Rectangle Width="96" Height="25" Stroke="#FF000000"
                    Fill="#FFE6EBFF" RadiusX="3" RadiusY="3"
                    StrokeThickness="3"/>
                <TextBlock Width="34" Height="20" TextWrapping="Wrap"
                    Canvas.Left="32" Canvas.Top="1" Text ="Save" />
            </Canvas>

            <Canvas x:Name="btnLoad" Width="97" Height="26"
                Canvas.Left="214" Canvas.Top="168">
                <Rectangle Width="96" Height="25" Stroke="#FF000000"
                    Fill="#FFE6EBFF" RadiusX="3" RadiusY="3"
                    StrokeThickness="3"/>
```

(continued)

(continued)

```xaml
                <TextBlock Width="37" Height="20" TextWrapping="Wrap"
                    Canvas.Left="30" Canvas.Top="1" Text="Load"/>
            </Canvas>

            <Canvas x:Name="btnClear" Width="97" Height="26"
                Canvas.Left="113" Canvas.Top="168">
                <Rectangle Width="96" Height="25" Stroke="#FF000000"
                    Fill="#FFE6EBFF" RadiusX="3" RadiusY="3"
                    StrokeThickness="3"/>
                <TextBlock Width="37" Height="20" TextWrapping="Wrap"
                    Canvas.Left="30" Canvas.Top="1" Text="Clear" />
            </Canvas>

            <TextBlock Width="404" Height="20" Text="[Status]"
                TextWrapping="Wrap" Canvas.Left="8" Canvas.Top="198"
                OpacityMask="#FF000000" x:Name="txtStatus"/>

        </Canvas>

    </Canvas>

</UserControl>
```

`Page.xaml` should now look like Figure 19-71.

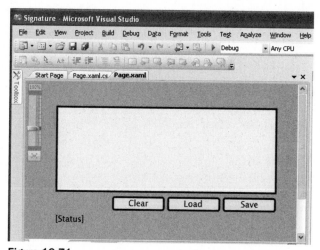

Figure 19-71

In `Page.xaml.cs`, import the following namespaces:

```
using System.IO.IsolatedStorage;
using System.IO;
```

Add the following lines to the `Page()` constructor:

```
public Page()
{
    InitializeComponent();

    //---wire up the event handlers---
    SigPad.MouseLeftButtonDown += new
        MouseButtonEventHandler(SigPad_MouseLeftButtonDown);
    SigPad.MouseLeftButtonUp += new
        MouseButtonEventHandler(SigPad_MouseLeftButtonUp);
    SigPad.MouseMove += new
        MouseEventHandler(SigPad_MouseMove);

    //---wire up the event handlers---
    btnSave.MouseLeftButtonDown += new
        MouseButtonEventHandler(btnSave_MouseLeftButtonDown);
    btnLoad.MouseLeftButtonDown += new
        MouseButtonEventHandler(btnLoad_MouseLeftButtonDown);
    btnClear.MouseLeftButtonDown += new
        MouseButtonEventHandler(btnClear_MouseLeftButtonDown);
}
```

Define the `GetSignatureLines()` function so that the coordinates of the signature can be converted from a List object to a string:

```
//---returns the signature as a series of lines---
private string GetSignatureLines()
{
    System.Text.StringBuilder sb = new
        System.Text.StringBuilder();
    //---for each line---
    for (int i = 0; i <= _lines.Count - 1; i++)
    {
        //---for each point---
        foreach (Point pt in _lines[i])
        {
            sb.Append(pt.X + "," + pt.Y + "|");
        }
        sb.Append("\n");
    }
    return sb.ToString();
}
```

Code the `MouseLeftButtonDown` event handler for the Save button so that the signature can be saved to isolated storage:

```
//---Save button---
void btnSave_MouseLeftButtonDown(
    object sender, MouseButtonEventArgs e)
{
    //---save into isolated storage---
    IsolatedStorageFile isoStore =
        IsolatedStorageFile.GetUserStoreForApplication();

    IsolatedStorageFileStream isoStream =
        new IsolatedStorageFileStream("IsoStoreFile.txt",
            FileMode.Create, isoStore);

    StreamWriter writer = new StreamWriter(isoStream);
    //---writes the lines to file---
    writer.Write(GetSignatureLines());
    txtStatus.Text = "Signature saved!";

    writer.Close();
    isoStream.Close();
}
```

Define the `DrawSignature()` subroutine so that the signature can be reproduced from a string representing a collection of lines:

```
//---draws the signature---
private void DrawSignature(string value)
{
    _lines = new List<List<Point>>();

    //---split into individual lines---
    string[] lines = value.Split('\n');

    //---for each individual line---
    for (int i = 0; i <= lines.Length - 2; i++)
    {
        //---split into individual points---
        string[] ps = lines[i].Split('|');
        _points = new List<Point>();

        //---for each point---
        for (int j = 0; j <= ps.Length - 2; j++)
        {
            string[] xy = ps[j].Split(',');
            _points.Add(new Point(
                (Convert.ToDouble(xy[0])),
                 Convert.ToDouble(xy[1])));
        }
```

```
            _lines.Add(_points);
        }

        //---draws the signature---
        for (int line = 0; line <= _lines.Count - 1; line++)
        {
            _points = (List<Point>)_lines[line];
            for (int i = 1; i <= _points.Count - 1; i++)
            {
                Line sline = new Line()
                {
                    X1 = _points[i - 1].X,
                    Y1 = _points[i - 1].Y,
                    X2 = _points[i].X,
                    Y2 = _points[i].Y,
                    StrokeThickness = 2,
                    Stroke = new SolidColorBrush(Colors.Black)
                };
                SigPad.Children.Add(sline);
            }
        }
    }
```

Code the MouseLeftButtonDown event handler for the Load button so that the series of signature lines can be loaded from isolated storage:

```
//---Load button---
void btnLoad_MouseLeftButtonDown(
    object sender, MouseButtonEventArgs e)
{
    IsolatedStorageFile isoStore =
        IsolatedStorageFile.GetUserStoreForApplication();

    IsolatedStorageFileStream isoStream =
        new IsolatedStorageFileStream("IsoStoreFile.txt",
            FileMode.Open, isoStore);

    StreamReader reader = new StreamReader(isoStream);
    //---read all lines from the file---
    string lines = reader.ReadToEnd();

    //---draws the signature---
    DrawSignature(lines);
    txtStatus.Text = "Signature loaded!";

    reader.Close();
    isoStream.Close();
}
```

Code the `MouseLeftButtonDown` event handler for the `Clear` button so that the signature can be cleared from the drawing pad:

```
//---Clear button---
void btnClear_MouseLeftButtonDown(
    object sender, MouseButtonEventArgs e)
{
    _lines = new List<List<Point>>();
    _points = new List<Point>();

    //---iteratively clear all the signature lines---
    int totalChild = SigPad.Children.Count - 2;
    for (int i = 0; i <= totalChild; i++)
    {
        SigPad.Children.RemoveAt(1);
    }

    txtStatus.Text = "Signature cleared!";
}
```

Press F5 to test the application. You can now sign and then save the signature. You can also load the saved signature (see Figure 19-72).

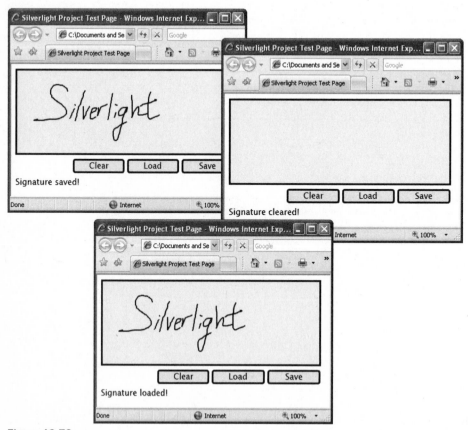

Figure 19-72

Saving the Signature to Web Services

One of these signatures isn't a lot of good unless you can send it to a Web Service. This section shows you how to do that.

Using the same project created in the previous section, add a new Web Site project to the current solution (see Figure 19-73).

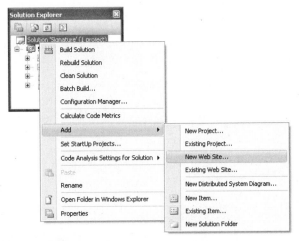

Figure 19-73

Select ASP.NET Web Site, and name the project `SignatureWebSite`.

Add a new Web Service item to the Web Site project, and use its default name of `WebService.asmx` (see Figure 19-74).

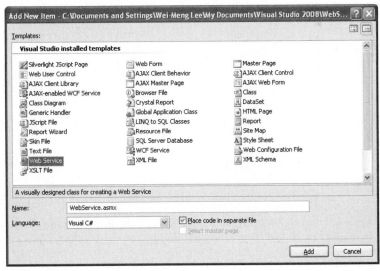

Figure 19-74

In the `WebService.cs` file, add the following lines:

```
using System;
using System.Collections;
using System.Linq;
using System.Web;
using System.Web.Services;
using System.Web.Services.Protocols;
using System.Xml.Linq;

using System.IO;
using System.Web.Script.Services;
/// <summary>
/// Summary description for WebService
/// </summary>
[WebService(Namespace = "http://tempuri.org/")]
[WebServiceBinding(ConformsTo = WsiProfiles.BasicProfile1_1)]
[System.Web.Script.Services.ScriptService]
public class WebService : System.Web.Services.WebService
{
    ...
    ...
}
```

Define the following two web methods:

```
[WebMethod]
public bool SaveSignature(string value)
{
    try
    {
        File.WriteAllText(Server.MapPath(".") +
            @"\Signature.txt", value);
        return true;
    }
    catch (Exception ex)
    {
        return false;
    }
}

[WebMethod]
public string GetSignature()
{
    string fileContents;
    fileContents = File.ReadAllText(
        Server.MapPath(".") + @"\Signature.txt");
    return fileContents;
}
```

The `SaveSignature()` function saves the values of the signature into a text file. The `GetSignature()` function reads the content of the text file and returns the content to the caller.

In the `Signature` project, add a service reference (see Figure 19-75).

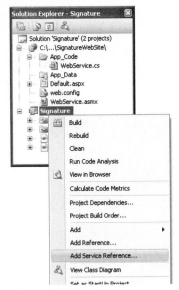

Figure 19-75

Click the Discover button and then OK (see Figure 19-76).

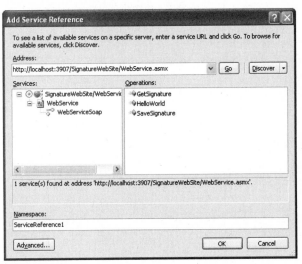

Figure 19-76

In `Page.xaml.cs`, modify the Save button as follows:

```
//---Save button---
void btnSave_MouseLeftButtonDown(
    object sender, MouseButtonEventArgs e)
{
    try
    {
        ServiceReference1.WebServiceSoapClient ws = new
            Signature.ServiceReference1.WebServiceSoapClient();

        //---wire up the event handler when the web service returns---
        ws.SaveSignatureCompleted += new
            EventHandler<Signature.ServiceReference1.
            SaveSignatureCompletedEventArgs>(ws_SaveSignatureCompleted);

        //---calls the web service method---
        ws.SaveSignatureAsync(GetSignatureLines());
    }

    catch (Exception ex)
    {
        txtStatus.Text = ex.ToString();
    }
}
```

Here, you send the signature to the Web service asynchronously. When the Web Service call returns, the `ws_SaveSignatureCompleted` event handler will be called.

Code the `ws_SaveSignatureCompleted` event handler as follows:

```
void ws_SaveSignatureCompleted(
    object sender,
    Signature.ServiceReference1.SaveSignatureCompletedEventArgs e)
{
    txtStatus.Text = "Signature sent to WS!";
}
```

In `Page.xaml.cs`, code the Load button as follows:

```
//---Load button---
void btnLoad_MouseLeftButtonDown(
    object sender, MouseButtonEventArgs e)
{
    try
    {
        ServiceReference1.WebServiceSoapClient ws = new
            Signature.ServiceReference1.WebServiceSoapClient();

        //---wire up the event handler when the web service
        // returns---
```

```
                    ws.GetSignatureCompleted +=
                        new EventHandler<Signature.ServiceReference1.
                        GetSignatureCompletedEventArgs>(ws_GetSignatureCompleted);

                    //---calls the web service method---
                    ws.GetSignatureAsync();
                }
                catch (Exception ex)
                {
                    txtStatus.Text = ex.ToString();
                }
            }
```

Here, you call the Web service to retrieve the saved signature. When the Web Service call returns, the `ws_ GetSignatureCompleted` event handler will be called.

Code the `ws_GetSignatureCompleted` event handler as follows:

```
            void ws_GetSignatureCompleted(
                object sender,
                Signature.ServiceReference1.GetSignatureCompletedEventArgs e)
            {
                txtStatus.Text = "Signature loaded from WS!";
                DrawSignature(e.Result);
            }
```

Save the `Signature` project. In Solution Explorer, right-click on the `SignatureWebSite` project and select Add Silverlight Link (see Figure 19-77).

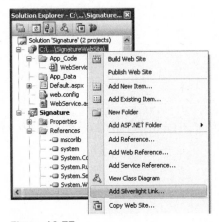

Figure 19-77

This causes Visual Studio 2008 to copy the relevant files from the Silverlight project onto the current project. Use the default values populated and click Add (see Figure 19-78).

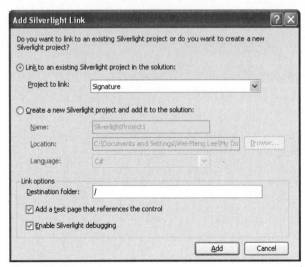

Figure 19-78

Notice that a new folder named ClientBin, containing the `Signature.xap` file, is added to the project (see Figure 19-79).

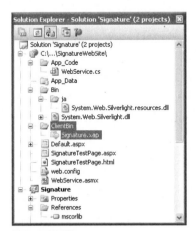

Figure 19-79

In Solution Explorer, right-click the `SignatureWebSite` project and select Set as Startup Project (see Figure 19-80).

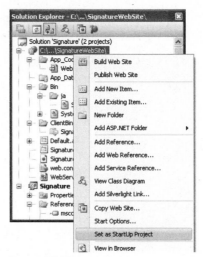

Figure 19-80

Select `SignatureTestPage.aspx`, and press F5 to test the project. You can now save the signature to the Web Service as well as load the saved signature from the Web Service (see Figure 19-81).

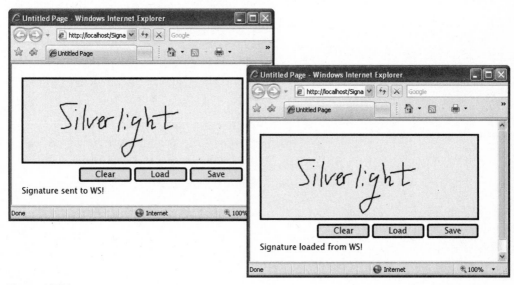

Figure 19-81

Summary

This chapter has demonstrated how you can use Silverlight to build Rich Interactive Applications (RIAs). At the time of writing, there are two versions of Silverlight — 1.0 and 2 — the key difference being the integration of the .NET Framework in Silverlight 2. To build the user interface of a Silverlight application, you can use the Microsoft Expression suite of applications, while the coding can be done using Visual Studio 2008.

20

Windows Communication Foundation

Windows Communication Foundation (WCF) is Microsoft's unified programming model for building service oriented applications (SOA). Parts of a service-oriented application can be exposed as a service that other applications can access.

WCF is a big topic, and it cannot be fully covered in a single chapter. However, this chapter provides a quick introduction to this new technology and shows how it addresses some of the limitations of today's technology. While most books and conference focused heavily on the theory behind WCF, this chapter shows you how to build WCF services and then explains the theory behind them.

In short, this chapter explores:

❑ How traditional ASMX Web Services differ from WCF

❑ The ABCs of WCF

❑ Building different types of WCF services

What Is WCF?

To understand the rationale behind WCF, it is important to understand the offerings that are available today. In previous versions of Visual Studio (Visual Studio 2005 and Visual Studio .NET 2003), you use the ASP.NET application model to you create ASMX XML Web Services that expose functionalities to clients who want to use them.

ASMX Web Services are still supported in Visual Studio 2008 for backward compatibility, but going forward Microsoft recommends that developers use WCF when building services.

To compare WCF and ASMX Web Services, let's first use Visual Studio 2008 to create a new ASP.NET Web Service Application project. Name the project StocksWS.

Populate the default `Service1.asmx.cs` file as follows:

```
using System;
using System.Collections;
using System.ComponentModel;
using System.Data;
using System.Linq;
using System.Web;
using System.Web.Services;
using System.Web.Services.Protocols;
using System.Xml.Linq;

namespace StocksWS
{
    [WebService(Namespace = "http://tempuri.org/")]
    [WebServiceBinding(ConformsTo = WsiProfiles.BasicProfile1_1)]
    [ToolboxItem(false)]
    public class Service1 : System.Web.Services.WebService
    {
        [WebMethod]
        public float GetStockPrice(string symbol)
        {
            switch (symbol)
            {
                case "MSFT": return 29.91f;
                case "AAPL": return 180.21f;
                case "YHOO": return 23.93f;
                default: return 0;
            }
        }
    }
}
```

This Web Service contains a web method to let users query the price of a stock. For simplicity, you will hardcode the stock prices of a few stocks.

To host this Web Service, you need to publish this project to a web server (IIS, for instance), or use the ASP.NET Web Development server that ships with Visual Studio. Figure 20-1 shows the ASP.NET Web Development Server hosting the service after you press F5.

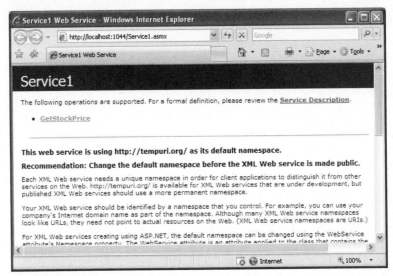

Figure 20-1

For a client to use this Web Service, you need to add a web reference. So add a Windows Forms Application project to the current solution to consume this service. Name the project `StockPriceChecker`.

Populate the default `Form1` with the controls shown in Figure 20-2.

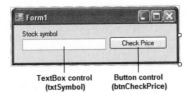

Figure 20-2

To add a reference to the Web Service, right-click the project name in Solution Explorer and select Add Service Reference (see Figure 20-3).

Figure 20-3

In the Add Service Reference dialog, enter the URL for the Web Service that you created earlier (see Figure 20-4). Because the Web Service is in the current solution, you can also click the Discover button to locate the Web Service.

> In Visual Studio 2008, the Add Service Reference option replaces the Add Web Reference option. That's because WCF is the preferred way to write your services in Visual Studio 2008. The exception to this is when developing Windows Mobile applications — for those, the Add Web Reference option is available, but the Add Service Reference item is not.

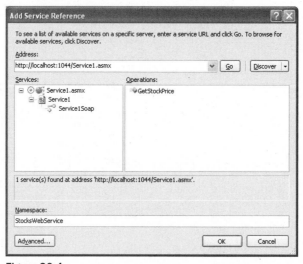

Figure 20-4

Give a name to the Web Service (say, `StocksWebService`), and click OK. A reference to the Web Service is added to the project (see Figure 20-5).

Figure 20-5

The `StocksWebService` is a proxy class generated by Visual Studio 2008 to handle all the work of mapping parameters to XML elements and then sending the SOAP messages over the network to the Web Service. Behind the scenes, Visual Studio has actually downloaded the WSDL (Web Services Description Language) document from the Web Service so that it knows exactly what the service offers and requires. You can view the WSDL document of the document by appending `?WSDL` to the end of the Web Services URL, like this:

```
http://localhost:1044/Service1.asmx?WSDL
```

To access the services provided by the Web Service, you programmatically create an instance of the proxy class and then call the appropriate methods. Here's the code for the Check Price button:

```
private void btnCheckPrice_Click(object sender, EventArgs e)
{
    StocksWebService.Service1SoapClient ws =
        new StocksPriceChecker.StocksWebService.Service1SoapClient();
    MessageBox.Show("Price for " + txtSymbol.Text +
        " is " + ws.GetStockPrice(txtSymbol.Text));
}
```

Set the `StocksPriceChecker` project as the startup project in Visual Studio 2008, and press F5 to debug the application. When you enter a stock symbol and click Check Price, the Web Service returns the price of the specified stock (see Figure 20-6).

Figure 20-6

From this very simple example, you want to note the following:

❑   You need to host even a simple ASMX Web Service on a web server such as IIS.

❑   To access the Web Service, clients use HTTP, a stateless protocol, which means that every request is treated like a new one. If you want to write an application that requires the Web Service to remember its previous state, you need to implement your own "stateful" mechanism.

❑   The ASMX Web Service uses a request/response communication model. The Web Service only responds when requested by the client. In this example, if you need to monitor the price of a stock and want to be notified whenever a stock falls below a certain price, you must constantly poll the Web Service to retrieve the latest price. A better way would be to have a service that can automatically invoke the client when specific events happen on the service's end. You'll see how this can be done with WCF later in this chapter.

Comparing WCF with ASMX Web Services

Now that you've created a traditional ASMX Web Service, let's compare ASMX and WCF and see how they differ:

❑   ASMX Web Services use web methods that are exposed to the world. Web methods use the request/response communication models. In WCF, these web methods are known as *operations*, and you can use any one of the three different types of communication models: one-way transaction, request/response, and full-duplex.

❑   Web services use the Simple Object Access Protocol (SOAP) messaging transported over HTTP. WCF can utilize different protocols for messaging — SOAP, Plain Old XML (POX), and so on — transported over a wide variety of communication protocols, including TCP and HTTP.

❑   Web services listen at a particular port number (such as port 80); WCF can have multiple endpoints listening at different port numbers.

❑   Web services are hosted by web servers (such as IIS); WCF can be hosted in different forms, such as Windows services, Windows applications, or just processes.

Your First WCF Service

Developing a WCF service using Visual Studio 2008 will be helpful in comparing it with the traditional ASMX Web Services.

Using Visual Studio 2008, create a new WCF Service Library application, and name it `WcfServiceLibraryTest` (see Figure 20-7).

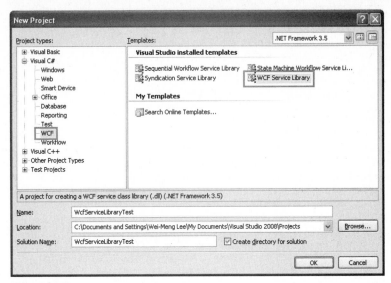

Figure 20-7

Notice the two files created in the project (see Figure 20-8):

❑ IService1.cs contains the service contract as well as the data contract.

❑ Service1.cs contains the implementation of the contract defined in the IService1.cs file.

Figure 20-8

Here's the content of the `IService1.cs` file:

```csharp
using System;
using System.Collections.Generic;
using System.Linq;
using System.Runtime.Serialization;
using System.ServiceModel;
using System.Text;

namespace WcfServiceLibraryTest
{
    // NOTE: If you change the interface name "IService1" here, you must also
    // update the reference to "IService1" in App.config.
    [ServiceContract]
    public interface IService1
    {
        [OperationContract]
        string GetData(int value);

        [OperationContract]
        CompositeType GetDataUsingDataContract(CompositeType composite);

        // TODO: Add your service operations here
    }

    // Use a data contract as illustrated in the sample below to add composite
    // types to service operations
    [DataContract]
    public class CompositeType
    {
        bool boolValue = true;
        string stringValue = "Hello ";

        [DataMember]
        public bool BoolValue
        {
            get { return boolValue; }
            set { boolValue = value; }
        }

        [DataMember]
        public string StringValue
        {
            get { return stringValue; }
            set { stringValue = value; }
        }
    }
}
```

Here, there is an interface (IService1) and a class (CompositeType) defined. The IService1 interface is set with the [ServiceContract] attribute to indicate that this is a service contract and contains signatures of operations exposed by the service. Within this interface are signatures of methods that you will implement in the Service1.cs file. Each method is set with the [OperationContract] attribute to indicate that it is an operation. If you have additional operations to add, you can add them here.

The CompositeType class is prefixed with the [DataContract] attribute. This class defines the various composite data types required by your service.

The Service1.cs file contains the implementation for the operations defined in the IService1 interface in the IService1.cs file:

```
using System;
using System.Collections.Generic;
using System.Linq;
using System.Runtime.Serialization;
using System.ServiceModel;
using System.Text;

namespace WcfServiceLibraryTest
{
    // NOTE: If you change the class name "Service1" here, you must also update the
    // reference to "Service1" in App.config.
    public class Service1 : IService1
    {
        public string GetData(int value)
        {
            return string.Format("You entered: {0}", value);
        }

        public CompositeType GetDataUsingDataContract(CompositeType composite)
        {
            if (composite.BoolValue)
            {
                composite.StringValue += "Suffix";
            }
            return composite;
        }
    }
}
```

For now, use the default implementation provided by Visual Studio 2008 and examine how the service works.

Press F5 to debug the service. A WCF Test Client window will be displayed (see Figure 20-9). This is a test client shipped with Visual Studio 2008 to help you test your WCF service.

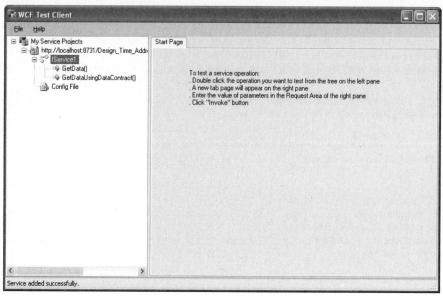

Figure 20-9

Expand the IService1 item, and select the GetData() method. In the right of the window, enter 5 for the value and click the Invoke button (see Figure 20-10).

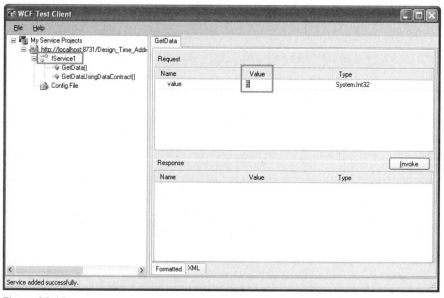

Figure 20-10

When you see a security warning dialog, click OK. The service returns its result in the Response pane (see Figure 20-11).

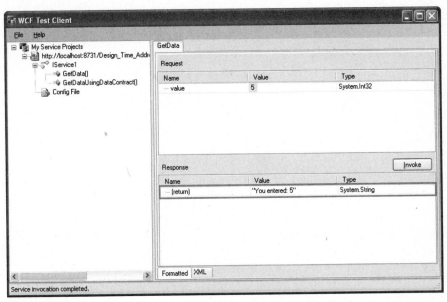

Figure 20-11

Also, try the `GetDataUsingDataContract()` operation and enter some values as shown in Figure 20-12. Click Invoke, and observe the results returned.

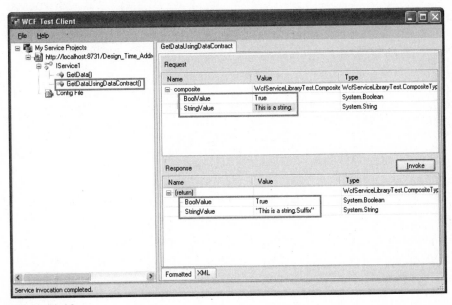

Figure 20-12

You can also see the SOAP messages exchanged between the test client and the service by clicking on the XML tab (see Figure 20-13).

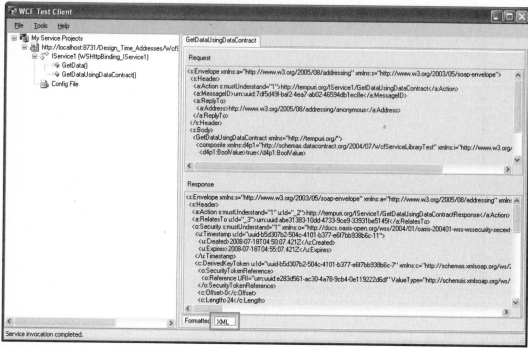

Figure 20-13

Notice that the SOAP messages contain a lot more information than a traditional ASMX Web Service SOAP packet. This is because WCF services, by default, use wsHttpBinding, which ensures that information exchanged between the client and the service is encrypted automatically.

You'll see more about wsHttpBinding later in this chapter.

Close the WCF Test Client window. Back in Visual Studio 2008, edit the IService1.cs file, adding the getAge() function signature to the IService1 interface:

```
[ServiceContract]
public interface IService1
{
    [OperationContract]
    string GetData(int value);

    [OperationContract]
```

```
CompositeType GetDataUsingDataContract(CompositeType composite);
```

```
[OperationContract]
int getAge(Contact c);
```
```
}
```

By default, the [OperationContract] attribute specifies a request/response messaging pattern for the operation.

After the class definition for CompositeType, define the following data contract called Contact:

```
[DataContract]
public class CompositeType
{
    //...
}
```

```
[DataContract]
public class Contact
{
    [DataMember]
    public string Name { get; set; }

    [DataMember]
    public int YearofBirth { get; set; }
}
```

In Service1.cs, define the getAge() function as follows:

```
public class Service1 : IService1
{
    //...
    //...
```

```
    public int getAge(Contact c)
    {
        return (DateTime.Now.Year - c.YearofBirth);
    }
```
```
}
```

Press F5 to test the application again. This time, select the getAge() method, enter your name and year of birth, and then click Invoke (see Figure 20-14). Observe the result returned by the service.

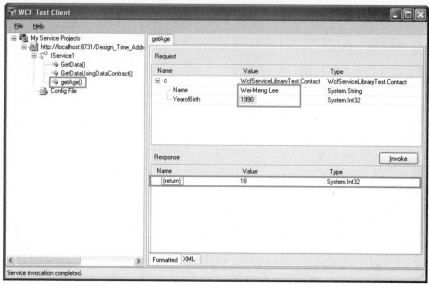

Figure 20-14

Consuming the WCF Service

The example you just created is a WCF Service Library. The useful aspect of the project is that it includes the WCF Test Client, which enables you to test your WCF easily without needing to build your own client. In this section, you build a Windows application to consume the service.

Add a Windows Forms Application project to the current solution, and name it `ConsumeWCFService`.

Add a service reference to the WCF service created in the previous section. Because the WCF Service is in the same solution as the Windows Forms application, you can simply click the Discover button in the Add Service Reference dialog to locate the service (see Figure 20-15).

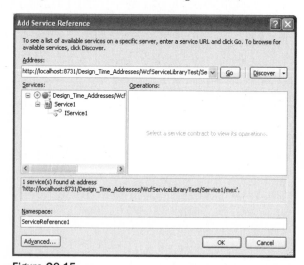

Figure 20-15

Use the default `ServiceReference1` name, and click OK. Visual Studio 2008 automatically adds the two libraries — `System.Runtime.Serialization.dll` and `System.ServiceModel.dll` — to your project (see Figure 20-16). The proxy class `ServiceReference1` is the reference to the WCF service.

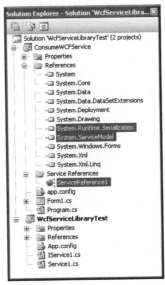

Figure 20-16

Double-click on `Form1`, and in the `Form1_Load` event handler, code the following:

```csharp
private void Form1_Load(object sender, EventArgs e)
{
    //---create an instance of the service---
    ServiceReference1.Service1Client client =
        new ConsumeWCFService.ServiceReference1.Service1Client();

    //---create an instance of the Contact class---
    ServiceReference1.Contact c =
        new ConsumeWCFService.ServiceReference1.Contact()
        {
            Name = "Wei-Meng Lee",
            YearofBirth = 1990
        };

    //---calls the service and display the result---
    MessageBox.Show(client.getAge(c).ToString());

    //---close the client---
    client.Close();
}
```

Calling the WCF service is very similar to consuming an ASMX Web Service — create an instance of the proxy class, call the service's operation, pass in the required parameters, and wait for the result from the service.

Set the Windows Forms application as the startup project, and press F5. A message box appears, displaying 18.

Understanding How WCF Works

Now that you have built your first WCF service, let's take a more detailed look at the innards of WCF.

WCF Communication Protocols

As mentioned earlier, WCF can use a wide variety of transport protocols to transport its messages. Here are just some of the common ones that you can use:

- ❑ **HTTP** — Much like the traditional ASMX Web Services
- ❑ **TCP** — Much more flexible and efficient than HTTP; more complex to configure (you'll see an example of this later in this chapter)
- ❑ **Named Pipe** — Used to communicate with WCF services on the same machine but residing in different processes
- ❑ **MSMQ** — Uses queuing technology; inherently asynchronous

The ABCs of WCF

Figure 20-17 shows the ABCs of WCF — address, binding, and contract.

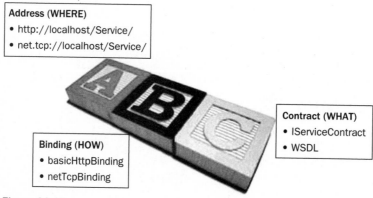

Address (WHERE)
- http://localhost/Service/
- net.tcp://localhost/Service/

Contract (WHAT)
- IServiceContract
- WSDL

Binding (HOW)
- basicHttpBinding
- netTcpBinding

Figure 20-17

❑ **Address** — The address that the service is listening at. This indicates *where* the service can be located and used. The address for a WCF service is dependent on the communication protocol used.

❑ **Binding** — The type of binding that you will use to communicate with the service. The binding used determines the security requirements for the communication and *how* clients will connect to the service.

❑ **Contract** — The contract defines *what* the service offers.

The following sections discuss each of these points in detail.

Addresses and Endpoints

Every WCF service has an address and endpoints in which it listens for incoming connections. Figure 20-18 shows a WCF service with two endpoints exposed. A client wanting to use the service just needs to send messages to the appropriate endpoint.

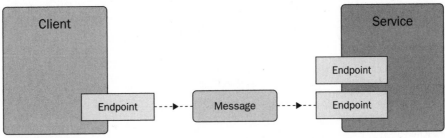

Figure 20-18

The address of a WCF service depends on the protocols used for the service. For example, if a WCF service uses the HTTP protocol, then its address may be:

❑   `http://<server>:<port>/<service>`

❑   `https://<server>:<port>/<service>`

❑   `https://<server>:<port>/<service>.svc`

If a WCF service uses TCP as the protocol, its address is in this format: `net.tcp://<server>:<port>/<service>`.

For Named Pipes, the address is `net.pipe://<server>/<service>`.

A service may have an operation that uses any of the protocols (or all). For example, a service may listen at port 80 (endpoint number 1) using HTTP as well as listen at port 5000 (endpoint number 2) using TCP.

Bindings

The bindings of a WCF not only specify the protocols used but also the security requirements for communication. The following table describes the available bindings:

Binding	Description
BasicHttpBinding	Most basic; limited security and no transactional support. Compatible with traditional ASMX Web Services.
WSHttpBinding	More advanced HTTP with WSE security.
WSDualHttpBinding	Extends WSHttpBinding and includes duplex communications.
WSFederationHttpBinding	Extends WSHttpBinding and includes federation capabilities.
NetTcpBinding	Used for TCP communication; supports security, transaction, and so on.
NetNamedPipeBinding	Used for named pipe communication; supports security, transaction, and so on.
NetPeerTcpBinding	Supports broadcast communication.
MexHttpBinding	Publishes the metadata for the WCF service.
NetMsmqBinding	Used for MSMQ.
MsmqIntegrationBinding	Used for MSMQ.

The bindings of a WCF determine how a client can communicate with the service.

How to use BasicHttpBinding, WSHttpBinding, and NetTcpBinding bindings is shown later in this chapter.

Contracts

Contracts define what a WCF service offers. The types of available contracts are explained in the following table.

Contract	Defines
Service	All the operations contained in a service.
Operation	All the methods, parameters, return types, and so on.
Message	How messages are formatted. For instance, data should be included in SOAP header or SOAP message body, and so on.
Fault	Faults an operation may return.
Data	The type of data used and required by the service.

Messaging Patterns

Traditional ASMX Web Services use the request/response communication model. This model has some disadvantages. In some cases, the client might want to call the service without waiting for a response from the service. For example, you might want to call a service rapidly to turn on and off a switch and you do not need a response from the service. Using the request/response model, all requests made by the client have to wait for a reply from the service (even if the request does not return a result). The result is unnecessary blocking on the client side, especially if there are many queued requests on the service's end.

WCF supports three communication models (also known as *messaging patterns*):

❑ Request/response

❑ One-way (simplex)

❑ Two-way (duplex)

The one-way messaging pattern allows clients to fire off a request and forget about it; no response is needed from the service. The two-way messaging pattern allows both the service and the client to send and receive messages.

Hosting Web Services

As mentioned earlier, WCF services can be hosted using different forms:

❑ **Web Servers** — IIS; similar to Web Services

❑ **Executable** — Console application, Windows Forms, WPF, and so on

❑ **Windows Service** — Runs in the background

❑ **Windows Activation Service (WAS)** — Simpler version of IIS

In the earlier example, the WCF service is hosted by the WCF Service Host (see Figure 20-19), a utility provided by Visual Studio 2008.

Figure 20-19

If you host a WCF service using an executable or Windows service, that WCF service is said to be self-hosted.

Building WCF Services

This section explores more sophisticated WCF services that illustrate the various theories presented earlier. Let's start off with creating a WCF that exposes multiple endpoints.

Exposing Multiple Endpoints

A WCF service can expose multiple endpoints. Follow along to build a WCF service that exposes endpoints using two different bindings: `WSHttpBinding` and `BasicHttpBinding`.

Creating the WCF Service

Using Visual Studio 2008, create a new WCF Service Application and name it `MultipleEndpointsService` (see Figure 20-20).

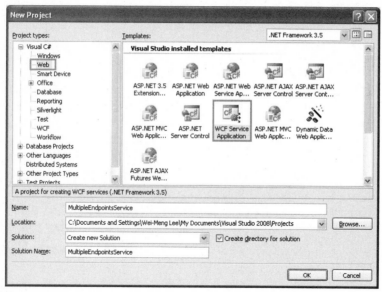

Figure 20-20

In this example, the WCF service is hosted by the ASP.NET Development Server, a web server shipped with Visual Studio 2008. Because the service is hosted by a web server, the `NetTcpBinding` binding is not supported.

Edit the `Web.config` file by right-clicking it in Solution Explorer and selecting Edit WCF Configuration. (You can also launch the WCF Service Configuration Editor by selecting Tools ⇨ WCF Service Configuration Editor.)

Expand the Endpoints node, and select the first endpoint. Name it WS (see Figure 20-21).

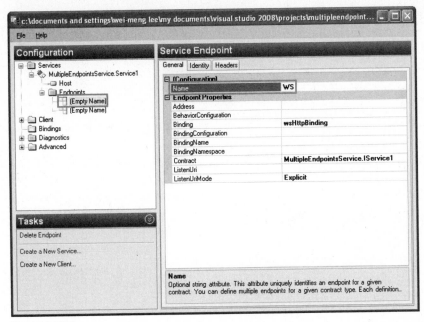

Figure 20-21

Right-click on the Endpoints node, and select New Service Endpoint to add a new endpoint to the service (see Figure 20-22).

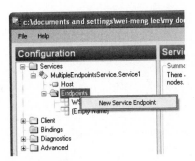

Figure 20-22

Name the new endpoint BASIC, and set its various properties as indicated (see Figure 20-23).

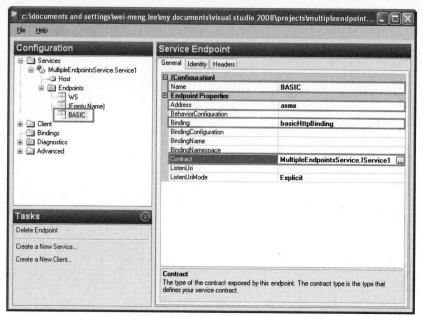

Figure 20-23

Property	Value
Address	asmx
Binding	basicHttpBinding
Contract	MultipleEndpointsService.IService1

Save and close the `Web.config` file. Build the `MultipleEndpointsService` project.

The WCF service now has three endpoints as shown in the following table.

Name	Binding	Description
WS	wsHttpBinding	The wsHttpBinding: Uses the WS-* protocols. Security is at the message level. Uses additional handshake messaging. Supports reliable session. Messages exchanged between the client and the server are encrypted.

Name	Binding	Description
[Empty Name]	`mexHttpBinding`	Publishes the metadata for the WCF service, allowing clients to retrieve the metadata using a `WS-Transfer GET` request or an `HTTP/GET` request using the `?wsdl` query string. By default, every WCF service created using Visual Studio 2008 has this endpoint to allow clients to request the service's metadata.
BASIC	`basicHttpBinding`	The `basicHttpBinding`: Supports old ASMX-style (based on `WS-BasicProfile1.1`) Web Services call. Does not support secure messaging (no WS enhancements). Does not support reliability and ordered delivery. Calls may be lost and the client simply time out. Calls may not be ordered correctly. Security is at the transport layer (SSL, for instance). Allows compatibility with ASMX Web Services and clients.

Creating the Client

Now add a new project to the current solution so that you can consume the WCF service created. Add a new Windows Forms Application project to the current solution and use its default name, `WindowsFormsApplication1`.

Populate the default `Form1` with the two Button controls shown in Figure 20-24.

Figure 20-24

Add a Service reference to the `WindowsFormApplication1` project, and click the Discover button to locate the WCF service in your solution. When the service is found, click OK (see Figure 20-25).

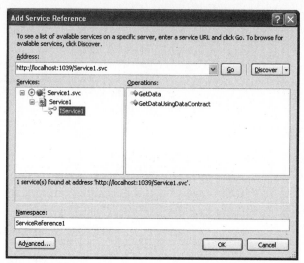

Figure 20-25

To inform clients of your service, you simply need to inform them of this URL: `http://localhost:1039/Service1.svc`. Because the WCF service is hosted by the ASP.NET Development server, the port number is dynamically chosen. The port number you will see is likely to be different from that shown.

Add another service reference to the `WindowsFormApplication1` project. This time, click the Advanced button at the bottom left of the Add Service Reference dialog, and then click the Add Web Reference button at the bottom left of the Service Reference Settings dialog (see Figure 20-26).

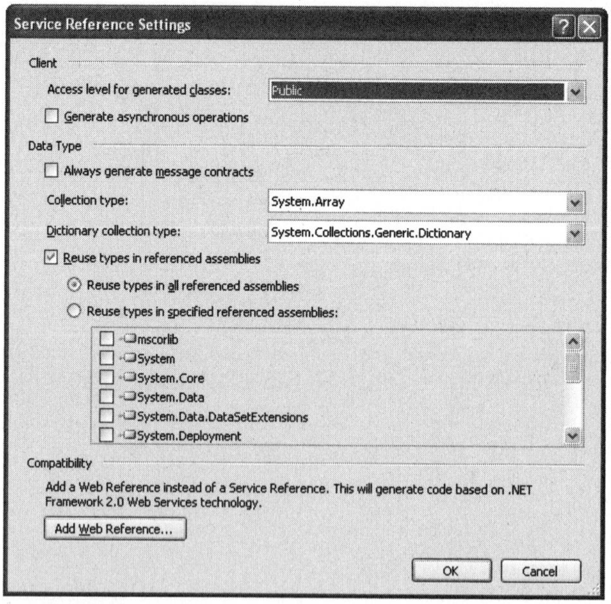

Figure 20-26

In the Add Web Reference dialog, click the Web services In the This Solution link and click Service1. Use the default name of `localhost`, and click the Add Reference button to add a web reference to the project (see Figure 20-27).

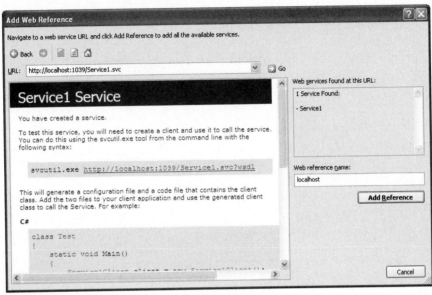

Figure 20-27

Double-click the Use wsHttpBinding button in Form1, and code it as follows:

```csharp
private void btnwsHttpBinding_Click(object sender, EventArgs e)
{
    ServiceReference1.Service1Client client =
        new ServiceReference1.Service1Client("WS");
    MessageBox.Show("Using wsHttpBinding: " +
        client.GetData(5));
    client.Close();
}
```

Double-click the Use basicHttpBinding button, and code it as follows:

```csharp
private void btnBasicHttpBinding_Click(object sender, EventArgs e)
{
    localhost.Service1 ws = new localhost.Service1();
    MessageBox.Show("Using basicHttpBinding: " +
        ws.GetData(6, true));
}
```

Set the `WindowsFormApplication1` project as the startup project, and press F5 to test it. Click both buttons (see Figure 20-28) to access the WCF service using `WSHttpBinding` and `BasicHTTPBinding`.

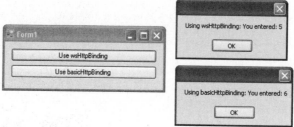

Figure 20-28

This example shows that you can have one WCF service exposed via different endpoints — traditional ASMX Web Service clients can connect to the service using the `basicHttpBinding` binding, while the rest can connect using the `wsHttpBinding` binding.

Creating Self-Hosted WCF Service

So far, all the WCF services you have seen are hosted using either a web server or the WCF Service Host. This section shows how you can host a WCF service right from within a Windows Forms application. This example can also be used with the `netTCPBinding` binding.

The example application is a simple message server that allows clients to send messages to it. Messages received by the service are displayed in a Windows Form.

Creating the WCF Service

Launch Visual Studio 2008 and create a new Windows Forms Application project. Name the project `MessageServer`.

Populate the default Form1 with a `TextBox` control, and set its `MultiLine` property to `true` (see Figure 20-29).

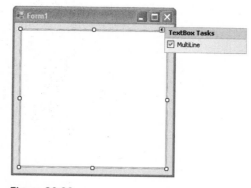

Figure 20-29

Add a new item to the project. Select the WCF Service template, and name it `MessageService.cs` (see Figure 20-30).

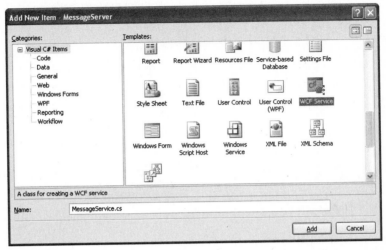

Figure 20-30

In the code-behind of `Form1`, import the following namespace:

```
using System.ServiceModel;
```

Declare the following objects:

```
public partial class Form1 : Form
{
    private MessageService service;
    private ServiceHost host;
```

The `ServiceHost` class is used to host a WCF service. In the `Form1_Load` event handler, code the following:

```
private void Form1_Load(object sender, EventArgs e)
{
    //---host the service---
    service = new MessageService(this);
    host = new ServiceHost(service);
    host.Open();
}
```

In the design view of Form1, create an event handler for the FormClosing event of Form1 by using the Properties window (see Figure 20-31).

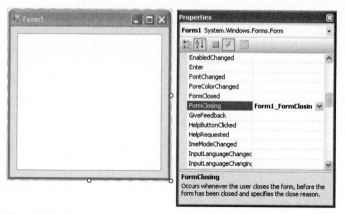

Figure 20-31

Code the Form1_FormClosing event handler as follows:

```
private void Form1_FormClosing(
object sender, FormClosingEventArgs e)
{
    //---end the hosting of the service---
    host.Close();
}
```

This code simply ends the hosting of the WCF service when the window is closed.

Define the DisplayMessage() function within the Form1 class as follows:

```
//---display a message on the TextBox control---
internal void DisplayMessage(string msg)
{
    textBox1.Text += msg + Environment.NewLine;
}
```

In the IMessageService.cs file, define the operation contract SetMessage, highlighted here:

```
namespace MessageServer
{
    [ServiceContract]
    public interface IMessageService
    {
        [OperationContract]
        void DoWork();

        [OperationContract(IsOneWay = true)]
        void SetMessage(string msg);
    }
}
```

The `SetMessage()` *operation uses the one-way messaging pattern because clients simply send messages to the sender and do not need to wait for a response from the server.*

This operation allows clients to send a message to the WCF service.

In the `MessageService.cs` file, add the following highlighted code:

```
using System;
using System.Collections.Generic;
using System.Linq;
using System.Runtime.Serialization;
using System.ServiceModel;
using System.Text;

namespace MessageServer
{
    [ServiceBehavior(InstanceContextMode=InstanceContextMode.Single)]
    public class MessageService : IMessageService
    {
        private Form1 hostApp;

        public void DoWork()
        {
        }

        //---constructor---
        public MessageService(Form1 hostApp)
        {
            //---set which host is hosting this service---
            this.hostApp = hostApp;
        }

        //---called by clients sending a message to the service---
        public void SetMessage(string msg)
        {
            //---display the message in Form1---
            hostApp.DisplayMessage(msg);
        }
    }
}
```

Notice that the `MessageService` class is prefixed with the `[ServiceBehavior]` attribute. It contains the `InstanceContextMode` property, which is set to `Single`.

Service Behaviors: InstanceContextMode

When a WCF Service receives a message, the message is dispatched to an object's instance methods:

- ❏ A single instance of the receiver may be created for *all* clients, or

- ❏ A single instance of the receiver may be created for *each* client.

The `InstanceContextMode` property specifies the number of service instances available for handling calls that are contained in incoming messages. It can be one of the following:

- ❏ `Single` — Every received message is dispatched to the same object (a singleton).

- ❏ `Percall` — Every received message is dispatched to a newly created object. This is the default.

- ❏ `PerSession` — Messages received within a session (usually a single sender) are dispatched to the same object.

- ❏ `Shareable` — Messages received within a session (can be one or more senders) are dispatched to the same object.

Edit the `App.config` file, using the WCF Service Configuration Editor (you can also select it from Tools ⇨ WCF Service Configuration Editor).

Set the following details for the first endpoint (see Figure 20-32).

Property	Value
Address	`net.tcp://localhost:1234/MessageService`
Binding	`netTcpBinding`

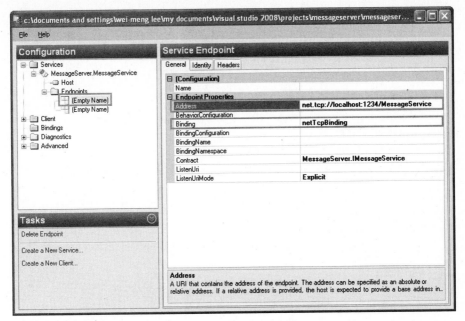

Figure 20-32

Save the file and close the editor.

Basically, you set the endpoint to use the netTcpbinding binding. Examine the App.config file now, and you'll see that the following highlighted code has been added:

```xml
<?xml version="1.0" encoding="utf-8" ?>
<configuration>
    ...
        <services>
            <service behaviorConfiguration="MessageServer.MessageServiceBehavior"
                name="MessageServer.MessageService">
                <endpoint address="net.tcp://localhost:1234/MessageService"
                    binding="netTcpBinding"
                    bindingConfiguration=""
                    contract="MessageServer.IMessageService">
                <identity>
                    <dns value="localhost" />
                </identity>
                </endpoint>
                <endpoint address="mex" binding="mexHttpBinding"
                    contract="IMetadataExchange" />
                <host>
                    <baseAddresses>
                        <add baseAddress="http://localhost:8731/Design_Time_
Addresses/MessageServer/MessageService/" />
                    </baseAddresses>
```

(continued)

(continued)

```
            </host>
          </service>
        </services>
      </system.serviceModel>
    </configuration>
```

Notice the base address contained in the `app.config` file:

```
http://localhost:8731/Design_Time_Addresses/MessageServer/MessageService/
```

This is the address that clients can use to add a service reference to your WCF service.

Press F5 to test the application now. When prompted with the Windows Security Alert dialog, click Unblock (see Figure 20-33).

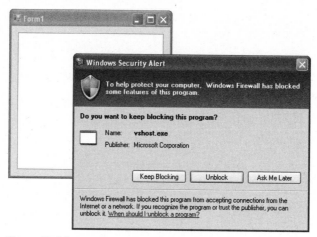

Figure 20-33

In this example, the WCF service is hosted by the Windows Form application, at port 1234, using the TCP protocol.

Creating the Client

Launch another instance of Visual Studio 2008, and create a new Windows Forms Application project. Name it `MessageClient`.

Populate the default `Form1` with the controls shown in Figure 20-34.

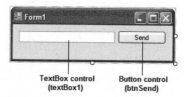

TextBox control   Button control
(textBox1)   (btnSend)

Figure 20-34

Add a service reference to the WCF service created earlier (see Figure 20-35). Enter the base address URL (`http://localhost:8731/Design_Time_Addresses/MessageServer/MessageService`) that you have observed in the `app.config` file.

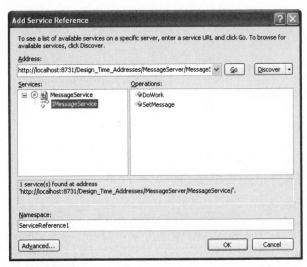

Figure 20-35

Switch to the code-behind of `Form1`, and import the following namespace:

```
using System.ServiceModel;
```

Declare the following member variable:

```
public partial class Form1 : Form
{
    ServiceReference1.MessageServiceClient client;
```

Double-click the Send button, and code the `button1_Click` event handler as follows:

```
private void btnSend_Click(object sender, EventArgs e)
{
    client = new
        MessageClient.ServiceReference1.MessageServiceClient();
    client.SetMessage(textBox1.Text);
    client.Close();
}
```

That's it! Press F5 and you can now send a message to the server using the WCF service (see Figure 20-36).

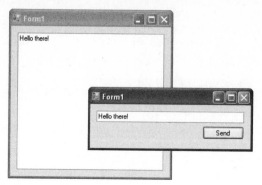

Figure 20-36

Implementing WCF Callbacks

One of the limitations of a traditional ASMX Web Service call lies in its request/response communication model. ASMX Web Services calls are passive and return results only when called upon. For instance, say that a particular cinema operator deploys a Web Service to allow online purchasing of tickets. The cinema's branches have systems that are connected to the Web Service to obtain the latest status of seat allocation and that sell tickets to cinema goers. In this case, the systems have to keep polling the Web Service at regular intervals to obtain the latest seats status. Moreover, it is very likely that a few branches may be booking the same seat(s) at the same time.

A better approach would be for the Web Service to notify all the branches about the changes in seat status as and when a seat has been reserved. This way, all branches have the latest seat information, and there is no need to poll the Web Service at regular intervals, thereby relieving the Web Service of the additional load. To accomplish this, you need a communication model in which the client is always connected to the service and is notified when an event occurs. Using WCF, this communication model can be implemented by using *callbacks*. A callback allows a service to call back its clients. The roles of the service and the client are now duplicated — the client is also the service, and the service is also the client.

This section of the chapter leads you through building a WCF ticketing service that allows clients to book tickets. When multiple clients are connected to the service, a seat booked by one client is broadcast to all the connected clients. Figure 20-37 illustrates the flow of the system. It shows four cinema branches using the client to connect to the WCF ticketing service. Once seats are selected (represented by the yellow buttons), a client will click on the Book Seats button to send the reservation to the WCF service. The WCF service will then broadcast the booked seats to all connected clients, which will then set the booked seats in red.

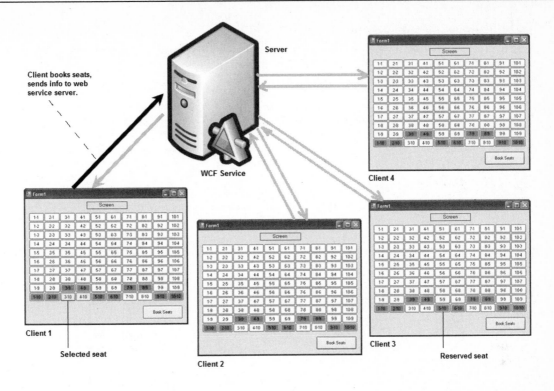

Client books seats, sends info to web service server.

Server

WCF Service

Client 4

Client 1

Selected seat

Client 2

Client 3

Reserved seat

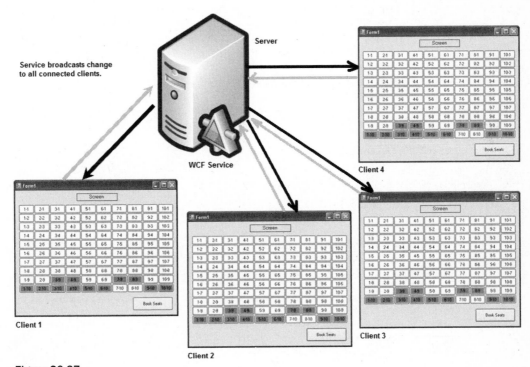

Service broadcasts change to all connected clients.

Server

WCF Service

Client 4

Client 1

Client 2

Client 3

Figure 20-37

Building the Service

The WCF service that allows clients to book cinema tickets needs to come first. Launch Visual Studio 2008 and create a new WCF Service Library project. Name the project WcfTicketingService (see Figure 20-38).

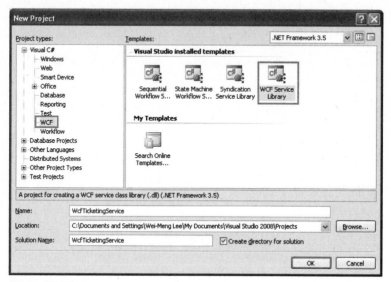

Figure 20-38

In this example, the WCF service will be hosted by the WCF Service Host, a utility provided by Visual Studio 2008.

In the IService1.cs file, define the following service and data contracts:

```
using System;
using System.Collections.Generic;
using System.Linq;
using System.Runtime.Serialization;
using System.ServiceModel;
using System.Text;

namespace WcfTicketingService
{
```

```
    [ServiceContract(
        Name = "TicketingService",
        Namespace = "http://www.learn2develop.net/",
        CallbackContract = typeof(ITicketCallBack),
        SessionMode = SessionMode.Required)]
    public interface ITicketService
    {
        [OperationContract(IsOneWay = true)]
        void SetSeatStatus(string strSeats);
```

```
        [OperationContract(IsOneWay = true)]
        void RegisterClient(Guid id);

        [OperationContract(IsOneWay = true)]
        void UnRegisterClient(Guid id);
    }

    public interface ITicketCallBack
    {
        [OperationContract(IsOneWay = true)]
        void SeatStatus(string message);
    }

    //---each client connected to the service has a GUID---
    [DataContract]
    public class Client
    {
        [DataMember]
        public Guid id { get; set; }
    }

}
```

The ITicketService interface defines three operations, which are described in the following table.

Operation	Description
SetSeatStatus	Allows clients to book seats. Takes in a string containing the seats to be booked.
RegisterClient	Registers a client when it connects to the service. Takes in a GUID so that the service can uniquely identify a client.
UnRegisterClient	Unregisters a client when it disconnects from the service. Takes in the client's GUID.

The ITicketService interface is also prefixed with the [ServiceContract] attribute. Specifically, note the CallbackContract property, which specifies the interface that defines the callback operation. The SessionMode property is set to Required, indicating that state must be maintained between the service and client.

The ITicketCallBack interface contains one operation — SeatStatus, which allows the service to initiate a callback to the client, thereby updating the client about the latest seat status (that is, which seats have been booked by other clients).

The Client class defines the data contract. It contains the GUID of a client connecting to the service.

All the operations in these two interfaces are defined as one-way operations. To understand why this is so, assume that all the operations use the default request/response model. When the SetSeatStatus() method is called to book seats, it waits for a response from the service. However, the service now invokes the SeatStatus callback on the client (the service informs all clients about the seats booked) and waits for a reply from the client. A deadlock occurs because the client is waiting for a response from the service while the service is waiting for a response from the client after invoking the callback. By defining the operations as one-way, the service can invoke the callback on the client without waiting for a reply from the client, preventing a deadlock from happening.

In the `Service1.cs` file, define the `SeatStatus` class:

```
using System;
...
using System.Text;
using System.Timers;

namespace WcfTicketingService
{
    //...
}
```

```
public class SeatStatus
{
    //---a string representing the seats booked by a client---
    public string Seats { get; set; }
}
```

The `SeatStatus` class contains `Seats`, a property for storing the seats booked by a client.

In the `Service1.cs` file, define the `Ticketing` class that implements the `ITicketingService` service contract:

```
using System;
using System.Collections.Generic;
using System.Linq;
using System.Runtime.Serialization;
using System.ServiceModel;
using System.Text;

using System.Collections;

namespace WcfTicketingService
{
    [ServiceBehavior(InstanceContextMode =
        InstanceContextMode.Single,
        ConcurrencyMode = ConcurrencyMode.Multiple)]
    public class Ticketing : ITicketService
    {
        //---used for locking---
        private object locker = new object();

        private SeatStatus _seatStatus = null;

        //---for storing all the clients connected to the service---
        private Dictionary<Client, ITicketCallBack> clients =
            new Dictionary<Client, ITicketCallBack>();

        public Ticketing() { }
```

```
        //---add a newly connected client to the dictionary---
        public void RegisterClient(Guid guid)
        {
            ITicketCallBack callback =
                OperationContext.Current.GetCallbackChannel
                <ITicketCallBack>();

            //---prevent multiple clients adding at the same time---
            lock (locker)
            {
                clients.Add(new Client { id = guid }, callback);
            }
        }

        //---unregister a client by removing its GUID from
        // dictionary---
        public void UnRegisterClient(Guid guid)
        {
            var query = from c in clients.Keys
                        where c.id == guid
                        select c;
            clients.Remove(query.First());
        }

        //---called by clients when they want to book seats---
        public void SetSeatStatus(string strSeats)
        {
            _seatStatus = new SeatStatus
            {
                //---stores the seats to be booked by a client---
                Seats = strSeats
            };

            //---get all the clients in dictionary---
            var query = (from c in clients
                         select c.Value).ToList();

            //---create the callback action delegate---
            Action<ITicketCallBack> action =
                delegate(ITicketCallBack callback)
                {
                    //---callback to pass the seats booked
                    // by a client to all other clients---
                    callback.SeatStatus(_seatStatus.Seats);
                };

            //---for each connected client, invoke the callback---
            query.ForEach(action);
        }
    }
}
```

Within the `Ticketing` class are the implementations for the three operations defined in the `ITicketService` interface:

❑ `RegisterClient()` — Called when clients are connected to the service for the first time. Clients are stored in a generic `Dictionary<K,V>` object. The key used for storing a client is its GUID, and its callback handler is stored as the value.

❑ `UnRegisterClient()` — Called when a client is disconnected from the service; its entry in the `Dictionary` object is removed.

❑ `SetSeatStatus()` — Called when clients want to book seats. The seats to be booked are stored in a `SeatStatus` object and then you create an `Action` delegate to invoke the callback of a client to pass the seats that have been booked by a client. Because all connected clients need to be notified, you invoke the callback for each client.

The `[ServiceBehavior]` attribute specifies the `InstanceContextMode` to be `Single` and the `ConcurrencyMode` property to be `Multiple`.

Service Behaviors — ConcurrencyMode

When messages are received by a WCF service, you can set how threads are used to manage all received messages:

❑ One thread can be used to access the receiver object(s) at a time, or

❑ Multiple threads can be used to access the receiver object(s) concurrently.

How you handle all incoming messages is specified using the `ConcurrencyMode` property of the `[ServiceBehavior]` attribute, which can assume one of the following values:

❑ `Single` (default) — Only one thread can access the receiver object at a time.

❑ `Multiple` — Multiple threads can access the receiver object(s) concurrently.

❑ `Reentrant` — Only one thread can access the receiver object at a time, but callbacks can reenter that object on another thread.

When you use the `Multiple` mode on the service, take special care to make sure that threads are synchronized properly and that critical regions are locked when a threading is accessing it.

For simplicity of demonstration, the following shortcuts are made:

❑ The seats booked by a client are simply broadcast to all connected clients. In real life, they would also be saved in database or array.

❑ When new clients connect to the server, the current seat allocation status (which seats are booked and which are not) is not sent to them.

Next, double-click on the `App.config` file in Solution Explorer. Change the following highlighted attributes values:

```
<system.serviceModel>
  <services>
    <service name="WcfTicketingService.Ticketing"
             behaviorConfiguration=
             "WcfTicketingService.Service1Behavior">
      <host>
        <baseAddresses>
          <add baseAddress =
"http://localhost:8731/Design_Time_Addresses/WcfTicketingService/Service1/" />
        </baseAddresses>
      </host>
      <!-- Service Endpoints -->
      <!-- Unless fully qualified, address is relative to base address
           supplied above -->
      <endpoint address ="" binding="wsHttpBinding"
                contract="WcfTicketingService.ITicketService">
        ...
```

Right-click on the `App.config` file, and select Edit WCF Configuration. Expand the `EndPoints` node (see Figure 20-39), and select the first `[Empty Name]` node. Set its properties as follows:

Property	Value
Address	net.tcp://localhost:5000/TicketingService
Binding	NetTcpBinding

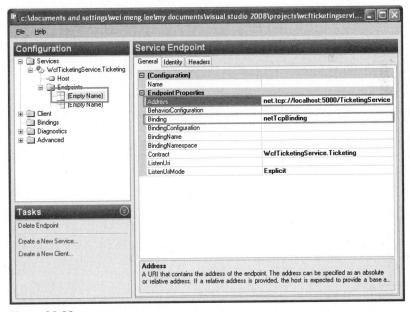

Figure 20-39

TCP is the transport protocol.

Save the `app.config` file and close the configuration window. Press F5 to debug the service. In the WCF Test Client, you will see something like Figure 20-40. The error icons (represented by the exclamation symbols) are normal.

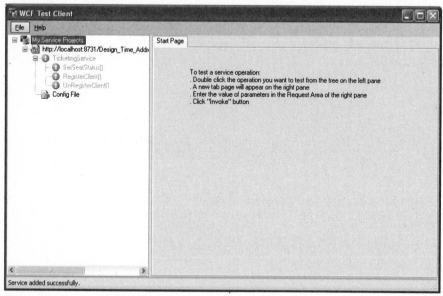

Figure 20-40

Building the Client

The WCF service is complete, so it's time to build the client to consume the service. Add a new Windows Forms Application project to the current solution. Name the project `Client`.

Add a service reference to the ticketing WCF service. In the Add Service Reference dialog, click the Discover button and locate the Ticketing WCF service (see Figure 20-41). Click OK.

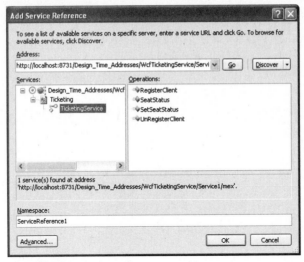

Figure 20-41

Populate `Form1` with the controls shown in Figure 20-42. Set the `Size` property of `Form1` to `477, 387`.

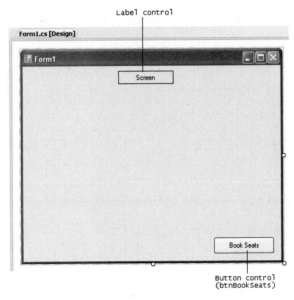

Figure 20-42

In the code-behind of `Form1`, import the following namespace:

```
using System.ServiceModel;
```

Declare the following constants and objects:

```
namespace Client
{
    public partial class Form1 : Form
    {
        int ROWS = 10;
        int COLUMNS = 10;
        const int SEAT_WIDTH = 45;
        const int SEAT_HEIGHT = 25;
        const int START_X = 10;
        const int START_Y = 40;

        static Button[,] seatsArray;

        private ServiceReference1.TicketingServiceClient _client;
        private Guid _guid = Guid.NewGuid();
```

Define the `SeatsOccupied()` static function within the `Form1` class as follows:

```
public partial class Form1 : Form
{
    . . .
    . . .
    . . .
    //---set all occupied seats in red---
    public static void SeatsOccupied(string strSeatsOccupied)
    {
        string[] seats = strSeatsOccupied.Split(',');
        for (int i = 0; i < seats.Length - 1; i++)
        {
            string[] xy = seats[i].Split('-');
            Button btn = seatsArray[int.Parse(xy[0]) - 1,
                int.Parse(xy[1]) - 1];
            btn.BackColor = Color.Red;
        }
    }
}
```

This function accepts a string containing the seats that are occupied. The format of the string is:

```
<column>-<row>,< column >-<row>,...
```

For each seat (represented by the Button control) that is booked, the background color is changed to red.

Define the `SeatStatusCallback` class and implement the `SeatStatus()` method as defined in the `TicketingServiceCallback` interface (defined in the service):

```
namespace Client
{
    public partial class Form1 : Form
    {
        //...
```

```
        }

    public class SeatStatusCallback :
        ServiceReference1.TicketingServiceCallback
    {
        public void SeatStatus(string message)
        {
            Form1.SeatsOccupied(message);
        }
    }
}
```

The `SeatStatus()` method is invoked when the service calls the client's callback. Here, you call the static `SeatsOccupied()` function to update the seats status.

Code the `Form1_Load` event handler as follows:

```
        private void Form1_Load(object sender, EventArgs e)
        {
            InstanceContext context =
                new InstanceContext(new SeatStatusCallback());
            _client = new
                ServiceReference1.TicketingServiceClient(context);
            _client.RegisterClient(_guid);

            //---display the seats---
            seatsArray = new Button[COLUMNS, ROWS];
            for (int r = 0; r < ROWS; r++)
            {
                for (int c = 0; c < ROWS; c++)
                {
                    Button btn = new Button();
                    btn.Location = new Point(
                        START_X + (SEAT_WIDTH * c),
                        START_Y + (SEAT_HEIGHT * r));

                    btn.Size = new Size(SEAT_WIDTH, SEAT_HEIGHT);
                    btn.Text = (c + 1).ToString() + "-" + (r +
                        1).ToString();
                    btn.BackColor = Color.White;
                    seatsArray[c, r] = btn;
                    btn.Click += new EventHandler(btn_Click);
                    this.Controls.Add(btn);
                }
            }
        }
```

These statements basically create an instance of the `InstanceContext` class by passing it an instance of the `SeatStatusCallback` class. Then an instance of the WCF client is created using the constructor that requires an `InstanceContext` object. In addition, the form is dynamically populated with Button controls representing the seats in a cinema. Each Button control's `Click` event is wired to the `btn_Click` event handler.

Define the `btn_Click` event handler as follows:

```
void btn_Click(object sender, EventArgs e)
{
    if (((Button)sender).BackColor == Color.White)
    {
        ((Button)sender).BackColor = Color.Yellow;
    }
    else if (((Button)sender).BackColor == Color.Yellow)
    {
        ((Button)sender).BackColor = Color.White;
    }
}
```

This event handler toggles the color of the seats as users click on the Button controls. White indicates that the seat is available; yellow indicates that the seat has been selected for booking.

Code the Book Seats button as follows:

```
private void btnBookSeats_Click(object sender, EventArgs e)
{
    string seatsToBook = string.Empty;
    for (int r = 0; r < ROWS; r++)
    {
        for (int c = 0; c < ROWS; c++)
        {
            if (seatsArray[c, r].BackColor == Color.Yellow)
            {
                seatsToBook += seatsArray[c, r].Text + ",";
            }
        }
    }
    //---send to WCF service---
    _client.SetSeatStatus(seatsToBook);
}
```

To specify the seats that are selected for booking, a string is created to containing the seats to be booked in the following format:

```
<column>-<row>,< column >-<row>,...
```

Finally, code the `Form1_FormClosing` event as follows:

```
private void Form1_FormClosing(object sender, FormClosingEventArgs e)
{
    _client.UnRegisterClient(_guid);
}
```

Testing the Application

To test the application, press F5 to debug and launch the service. Once this is done, you can debug the client. Right-click the `Client` project in Solution Explorer, and select Debug ⇨ Start New Instance (see Figure 20-43).

Figure 20-43

Run a few instances of the client and you can start to book cinema tickets. As one client books the seats, the other clients are automatically updated.

Calling WCF Services from an AJAX Page

Visual Studio 2008 includes the new AJAX-enabled WCF Service template that enables you to consume WCF services, using AJAX. To try it out, use Visual Studio 2008 to create a new ASP.NET Web Application project. Name the project AJAXWCF (see Figure 20-44).

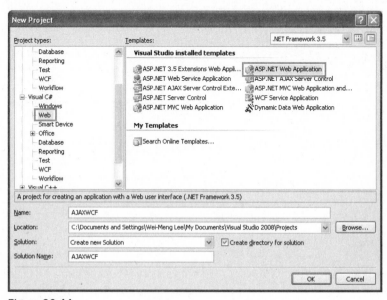

Figure 20-44

Right-click the project name in Solution Explorer, and select Add New Item (see Figure 20-45).

Figure 20-45

Select the AJAX-enabled WCF Service template (see Figure 20-46), name it `Service.svc`, and click Add.

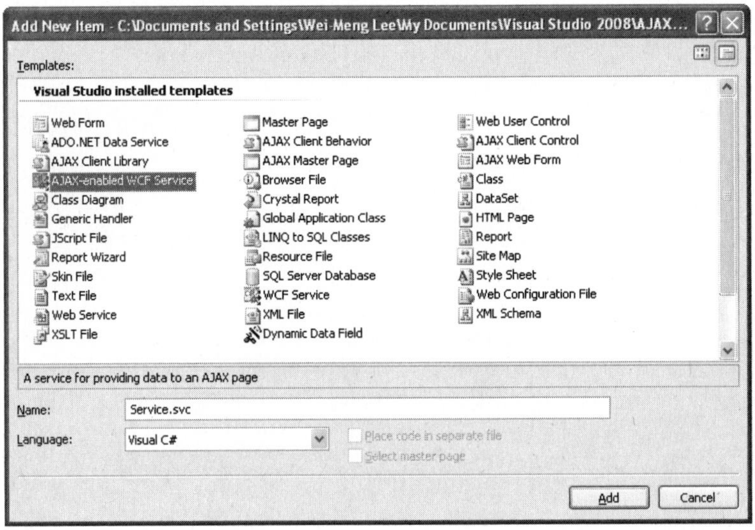

Figure 20-46

Notice that Visual Studio 2008 automatically inserts the `<system.serviceModel>` element into the `Web.config` file:

```
...
    <system.serviceModel>
        <behaviors>
            <endpointBehaviors>
                <behavior name="ServiceAspNetAjaxBehavior">
                    <enableWebScript />
                </behavior>
            </endpointBehaviors>
        </behaviors>
        <serviceHostingEnvironment
            aspNetCompatibilityEnabled="true" />
        <services>
            <service name="Service">
                <endpoint address=""
                    behaviorConfiguration="ServiceAspNetAjaxBehavior"
                    binding="webHttpBinding" contract="Service" />
            </service>
        </services>
    </system.serviceModel>
</configuration>
```

In the `Service.cs` file located in the `App_Code` folder, give the service a namespace of `"WCFService"`, and code the following `GetServerTime()` method:

```
using System;
using System.Linq;
using System.Runtime.Serialization;
using System.ServiceModel;
using System.ServiceModel.Activation;
using System.ServiceModel.Web;
```

```
[ServiceContract(Namespace = "WCFService")]
[AspNetCompatibilityRequirements(RequirementsMode =
AspNetCompatibilityRequirementsMode.Allowed)]
public class Service
{
    // Add [WebGet] attribute to use HTTP GET
    [OperationContract]
    public void DoWork()
    {
        // Add your operation implementation here
        return;
    }
```

```
    [OperationContract]
    public DateTime GetServerTime()
    {
        return DateTime.Now;
    }
}
```

In the Source view of `Default.aspx`, add the following highlighted code:

```
<form id="form1" runat="server">
<div>
    <asp:ScriptManager ID="ScriptManager1" runat="server">
        <Services>
            <asp:ServiceReference Path="~/Service.svc" />
        </Services>
    </asp:ScriptManager>
</div>

<input id="Button1" type="button" value="Get Server Time"
    onclick="return Button1_onclick()" />
<div id="result" />

</form>
```

This adds an instance of the `<ScriptManager>` control to the page and references the WCF service (`Service.svc`). It also adds a Button control to the page.

Insert the following JavaScript code into `Default.aspx`:

```
<body>

<script language="javascript" type="text/javascript">

    function Button1_onclick()
    {
        WCFService.Service.GetServerTime(CallBackFunction);
    }

    function CallBackFunction(result)
    {
        $get("result").innerHTML= result;
    }

</script>

<form id="form1" runat="server">
```

The `Button1_onclick ()` JavaScript function is invoked when the button on the page is clicked. It calls the WCF service and the returning result is retrieved via the `CallBackFunction()` function.

Press F5 to debug the application. You can now click the Get Server Time button to obtain the server time without causing a refresh on the web page (see Figure 20-47).

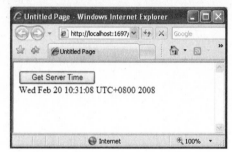

Figure 20-47

Summary

This chapter provided an overview of WCF and explained how it differs from traditional ASMX Web Services. It explored the limitations of Web Services today and examined how WCF aims to provide a better way of writing and hosting your services. The various examples shown throughout this chapter afford concrete illustrations of what WCF offers and hopefully provide enough motivations for you to explore this important technology further.

Part III

Appendixes

C# Keywords

This appendix lists the various keywords in C# that are predefined and have special meanings for the compiler. It is important to familiarize yourself with these keywords because they cannot be used as identifiers in your program. For example, `this` is a keyword in C# that is used to refer to the current instance of a class. Hence, `this` cannot be used as an identifier:

```
string this = "Hello, World"; //---error---
```

To use a keyword as an identifier, you need to prefix the keyword with the @ character. The following statement is valid:

```
string @this = "Hello, World"; //---ok---
```

In C# 3.0, Microsoft introduces the concept of context keywords. Contextual keywords have special meaning in a particular context and can be used as an identifier outside the context. For example, the `set` and `get` contextual keywords are used as accessors in a property definition, together with the `value` keyword, like this:

```
public class Point
{
    Single _x;
    public Single x {
        get {
            return _x;
        }
        set {
            _x = value;
        }
    }
}
```

In this example, the `get`, `set`, and `value` contextual keywords have special meanings in a property definition (x). Using these contextual keywords within the property definition as identifiers is not valid. However, outside the property definition, you can use them as identifiers:

```
static void Main(string[] args)
{
        string get = "some string here...";
        int set = 5;
        double value = 5.6;
}
```

The beauty of contextual keywords is that as the C# language evolves, new keywords can be added to the language without breaking programs written using the earlier version of the language.

C# Reserved Keywords

The following table describes the reserved keywords used in C#.

Keyword	Description
abstract	A modifier that can be used with classes, methods, properties, indexers, and events. Use it to indicate that a class is intended to be used as a base class of other classes, and abstract methods must be implemented by classes that derive from the abstract class.
as	An operator that performs conversion between compatible reference types.
base	Used to access members of a base class from a derived class.
bool	A C# alias of the `System.Boolean` .NET Framework type. Its value can either true, false, or null.
break	Used to transfer control out of a loop or switch statement.
byte	Specifies a data type that can stores unsigned 8-bit integer values from 0 to 255.
case	Used together with the `switch` statement. It specifies the value to be matched so that control can be transferred to the `case` statement.
catch	Used with a `try` block to handle one or more exceptions.
char	Specifies a data type that can store a 16-bit Unicode character from U+0000 to U+ffff.
checked	Used to explicitly enable overflow-checking integer operations.
class	Used to declare classes.
const	Used to specify a field or variable whose value cannot be modified.
continue	Used within a loop such that control is transferred to the next iteration.

Keyword	Description
decimal	Specifies a data type representing a 128-bit data. It can approximately represent a number from ±1.0 × 10–28 to ±7.9 × 1028.
default	Used within a `switch` statement to indicate the default match if none of the other case statements is matched. Can also be used in generics to specify the default value of the type parameter.
delegate	Used to declare a reference type variable that references a method name/ anonymous method.
do	Executes a block of code repeatedly until a specified expression returns false. Used together with the `while` keyword to form a do-while statement.
double	Specifies a data type that represents a 64-bit floating point number. It can approximately represent a number from ±5.0 × 10–324 to ±1.7 × 10308.
else	Used with the `if` keyword to form an if-else statement. `else` defines the block that will be executed if the expression specified in the `if` statement is evaluated to false.
enum	Used to define an enumeration.
event	Used to define an event within a class.
explicit	Defines a cast operation that requires the programmer to explicitly select the cast to be performed.
extern	Declares a method that is implemented externally.
false	Used as either an operator or as a literal. One of the possible values in a bool variable.
finally	Used in a `try-catch` block to contain code that cleans up the code even if an exception occurs. Statements contained within a finally block are always executed.
fixed	Prevents the garbage collector from relocating a movable variable.
float	Specifies a data type that represents a 32-bit floating point number. It can approximately represent a number from ±1.5 × 10–45 to ±3.4 × 1038.
for	Encloses a block of statements that will be executed repeatedly until a specified expression returns false.
foreach	Used to iterate through a collection of items.
goto	Used to transfer control of a program to a labeled statement.
if	Determines if a statement (or block of statements) is to be executed based on the result of a Boolean expression.
implicit	Used to declare an implicit cast operation.

(continued)

Keyword	Description
in	Used in a `foreach` statement to specify the collection you want to iterate through.
int	Specifies a data type that represents a signed 32-bit integer number. It can represent a number from −2,147,483,648 to 2,147,483,647.
interface	Used to define an interface, which is a definition that contains the signatures of methods, delegates, and events. An interface does not contain any implementation.
internal	An access modifier to indicate a member that can only be accessed within files in the same assembly.
is	Used to check if an object is compatible with a given type.
lock	Marks a statement block as a critical section so that other threads cannot execute the block while the statements within the block are being executed.
long	Specifies a data type that represents a signed 64-bit integer number. It can represent a number from −9,223,372,036,854,775,808 to 9,223,372,036,854,775,807.
namespace	Used to organize your code so that it belongs to a globally unique type.
new	Used to create objects and invoke a class's constructor. Also can be used to explicitly hide a base class's member in a derived class. When used in a generic declaration, it restricts types that might be used as arguments for a type declaration.
null	Represents a null reference that does not refer to any object.
object	A C# alias of the `System.Object` .NET Framework type.
operator	Used to overload a built-in operator or provide a conversion operator.
out	Indicates arguments that are to be passed by reference. It is similar to `ref`, except that `ref` requires the variable to be initialized before it is passed.
override	Extends or modifies the abstract or virtual implementation of an inherited method, property, indexer, or event.
params	Specifies a parameter array where the number of arguments is variable.
private	An access modifier used to indicate a member that can only be accessed within the body of the class or struct in which it's declared.
protected	An access modifier used to indicate a member that can only be accessed within its class and derived classes.
public	An access modifier used to indicate a member that can be accessed by all code.

Keyword	Description
readonly	A modifier that indicates fields that can only be initialized at declaration or in a constructor.
ref	Indicates arguments that are to be passed by reference.
return	Terminates execution of a method and returns control to the calling method.
sbyte	Specifies a data type that represents a signed 8-bit integer number. It can represent a number from –128 to 127.
sealed	Specifies a class that does not allow other classes to derive from it.
short	Specifies a data type that represents a signed 16-bit integer number. It can represent a number from –32,768 to 32767.
sizeof	Used to obtain the size in bytes for a value type.
stackalloc	Used in an unsafe code context to allocate a block of memory on the stack.
static	A modifier to indicate that a member belongs to the type itself, and not to a specific object.
string	Specifies a data type that represents a sequence of zero or more Unicode characters. Also an alias for the System.String .NET Framework type.
struct	Denotes a value type that encapsulates a group of related variables.
switch	A control statement that handles multiple selections by matching the value of the switch with a series of case statements.
this	Refers to the current instance of the class. Also used as a modifier of the first parameter of an extension method.
throw	Used to invoke an exception during runtime.
true	Used either as an operator or as a literal. One of the possible values in a bool variable.
try	Indicates a block of code that may cause exceptions. Used with one or more catch blocks to handle the exceptions raised.
typeof	Used to obtain the System.Type object for a type.
uint	Specifies a data type that represents an unsigned 32-bit integer number. It can represent a number from 0 to 4,294,967,295.
ulong	Specifies a data type that represents an unsigned 64-bit integer number. It can represent a number from 0 to 18,446,744,073,709,551,615.
unchecked	Used to suppress overflow-checking for integral-type arithmetic operations and conversions.

(continued)

Keyword	Description
unsafe	Denotes an unsafe context, which is required for any operation involving pointers.
ushort	Specifies a data type that represents an unsigned 16-bit integer number. It can represent a number from 0 to 65,535.
using	A directive for creating a namespace alias or importing namespace references. It is also used for defining a scope at the end of which an object will be disposed.
virtual	An access modifier to indicate a method, property, indexer, or event declaration and allow for it to be overridden in a derived class.
volatile	Indicates that a field might be modified by multiple threads that are executing at the same time.
void	Specifies that a method does not return any value.
while	Executes a statement or a block of statements until a specified expression evaluates to false.

Contextual Keywords

The following table describes the context keywords used in C#.

Keyword	Description
from	Used in a LINQ query. A query expression must begin with a `from` clause.
get	Defines an accessor method in a property or indexer. It retrieves the value of the property or indexer element.
group	Used in a LINQ query and returns a sequence of `IGrouping<(Of <(TKey, TElement>)>)` objects that contain zero or more items that match the key value for the group.
into	Used in a LINQ query and can be used to create a temporary identifier to store the results of a `group`, `join`, or `select` clause into a new identifier.
join	Used in a LINQ query for associating elements from different sources.
let	Used in a LINQ query to store the result of a subexpression to be used in a subsequent clause.
orderby	Used in a LINQ query to sort the result of a query in either ascending or descending order.

Keyword	Description
partial	Denotes that the definition of a class, struct, or interface is split into multiple files. Also denotes that a method's signature is defined in one partial type and its definition is defined in another partial type.
select	Used in a LINQ query to specify the type of values that will be produced when the query is executed.
set	Defines an accessor method in a property or indexer. It assigns a value to the property or indexer element.
value	An implicit parameter in a set accessor. It is also used to add or remove event handlers.
where	Used in a LINQ query to specify which elements from the data source will be returned in the query expression.
yield	Used in an iterator block to provide a value to the enumerator object or to signal the end of iteration.

B

Examining the .Net Class Libraries Using the Object Browser

To be successful in .NET programming requires not only that you know the language you are using (C# in this case) but that you be familiar with the classes in the .NET Framework class library. Navigating the huge number of classes in the class library is a daunting task, and it takes a developer many months to get acquainted with the different classes. This appendix summarizes the features of the various versions of the .NET Framework and explains how to use the Object Browser feature in Visual Studio 2008 to browse the available namespaces and classes in the .NET Framework.

Versions of the .NET Framework

The .NET Framework 3.5 builds upon the previous versions of the .NET Framework, namely, version 2.0, 2.0SP1, 3.0, and 3.0SP1. This is evidenced by the set of assembly references available in the Add Reference dialog (see Figure B-1).

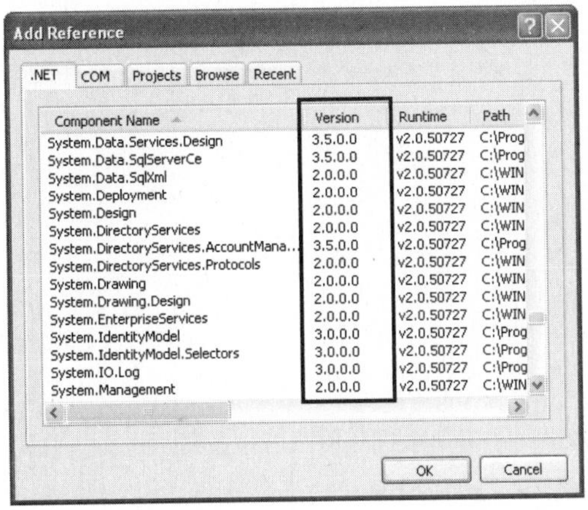

Add Reference
.NET
COM
Projects
Browse
Recent
Component Name
Version
Runtime
Path
System.Data.Services.Design 3.5.0.0 v2.0.50727 C:\Prog
System.Data.SqlServerCe 3.5.0.0 v2.0.50727 C:\Prog
System.Data.SqlXml 2.0.0.0 v2.0.50727 C:\WIN
System.Deployment 2.0.0.0 v2.0.50727 C:\WIN
System.Design 2.0.0.0 v2.0.50727 C:\WIN
System.DirectoryServices 2.0.0.0 v2.0.50727 C:\WIN
System.DirectoryServices.AccountMana... 3.5.0.0 v2.0.50727 C:\Prog
System.DirectoryServices.Protocols 2.0.0.0 v2.0.50727 C:\WIN
System.Drawing 2.0.0.0 v2.0.50727 C:\WIN
System.Drawing.Design 2.0.0.0 v2.0.50727 C:\WIN
System.EnterpriseServices 2.0.0.0 v2.0.50727 C:\WIN
System.IdentityModel 3.0.0.0 v2.0.50727 C:\Prog
System.IdentityModel.Selectors 3.0.0.0 v2.0.50727 C:\Prog
System.IO.Log 3.0.0.0 v2.0.50727 C:\Prog
System.Management 2.0.0.0 v2.0.50727 C:\WIN
OK
Cancel

Figure B-1

The assemblies have different version numbers — some are version 2.0, while some are 3.0 and the rest 3.5. That is to say, when you develop a .NET 3.5 application, your application is actually using a combinations of .NET 2.0, 3.0, and 3.5 class libraries.

The assemblies for the different versions of the .NET Framework are located in the following directories on your development machine:

❑ **Version 2.0** — `C:\WINDOWS\Microsoft.NET\Framework\v2.0.50727`

❑ **Version 3.0** — `C:\Program Files\Reference Assemblies\Microsoft\Framework\v3.0`

❑ **Version 3.5** — `C:\Program Files\Reference Assemblies\Microsoft\Framework\v3.5`

When you install Visual Studio 2008 on a computer without the previous versions of the .NET Framework, all of these assemblies are installed automatically. The following sections discuss the key components contained in each version of the .NET Framework.

.NET Framework 2.0

The .NET Framework 2.0 is a major upgrade of the .NET Framework and is shipped with Visual Studio 2005. The previous versions of the .NET Framework — 1.0 and 1.1 — are completely separate from each other; each has its own set of assemblies and Common Language Runtime (CLR). In fact, a computer can have three different versions of the .NET Framework installed — 1.0, 1.1, and 2.0. Each of these frameworks can exist on its own and does not rely on previous versions.

The main features in .NET Framework 2.0 are:

❑ Common Language Runtime (CLR)

❑ Support for generics

❑ Compilers for the .NET languages — C#, VB, C++, and J#

❑ Base Class Library

❑ ASP.NET

❑ ADO.NET

❑ Windows Forms

❑ Web Services

The .NET Framework 2.0 SP1 updates the CLR and several assemblies.

.NET Framework 3.0

The .NET Framework 3.0 ships with Windows Vista and is built on top of the .NET Framework 2.0. Hence, installing .NET Framework 3.0 also requires .NET Framework 2.0 to be installed. .NET Framework 3.0 ships with three new technologies:

❑ Windows Presentation Foundation (WPF)

❑ Windows Communication Foundation (WCF)

❑ Windows Workflow (WF)

The .NET Framework 3.0 SP1 updates the CLR and several assemblies shipped with the Framework.

.NET Framework 3.5

The .NET Framework 3.5 includes several new technologies and is shipped with Visual Studio 2008. The main features in .NET Framework 3.5 are:

❑ Language Integrated Query (LINQ)

❑ New compilers for C#, VB, and C++

❑ ASP.NET AJAX

❑ New types in the Base Class Library

Using the Object Browser

Because of the sheer size of the .NET Framework class libraries, it is always a daunting task for beginners using this framework to navigate through the large number of classes available. Fortunately, Visual Studio 2008 ships with the Object Browser, a utility that enables you to quickly search through the list of class libraries available in the .NET Framework.

To use the Object Browser (see Figure B-2), launch Visual Studio 2008 and choose View ⇨ Object Browser.

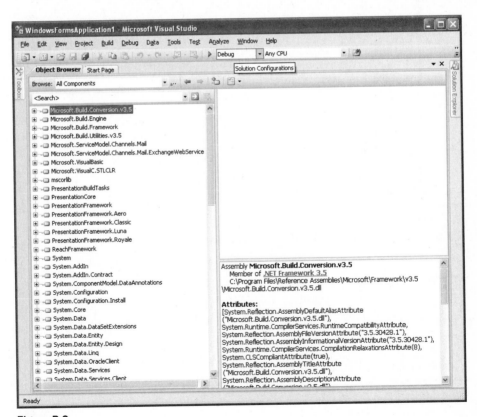

Figure B-2

The left panel lists the assemblies (.dll files) available. You can expand on each assembly to view the namespaces contained within it.

Figure B-3 shows some of the information displayed by the Object Browser.

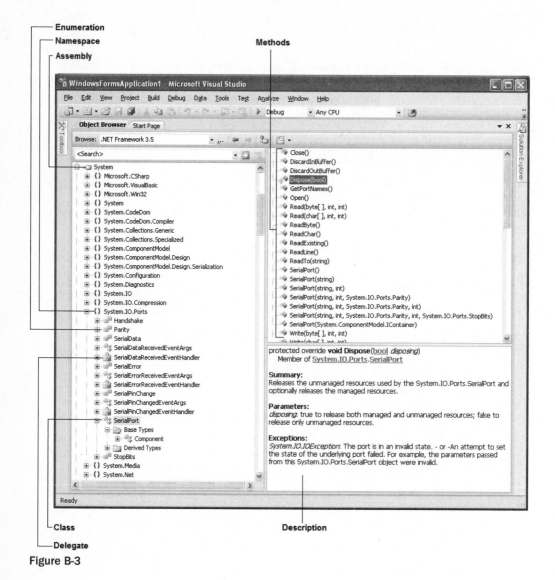

Figure B-3

You can expand a namespace to reveal the classes, delegates, and enumerations contained within it. Select a class and its associated members (methods, properties, events, and so on) are displayed in the top-right panel. Selecting a member of the class provides a detailed description of the member, such as its summary, parameters, and exceptions.

At the top of the Object Browser, you can select the list of components that you want to view (see Figure B-4).

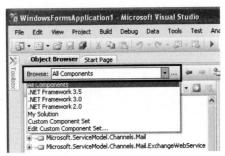

Figure B-4

If the component you want to view is not listed in the Object Browser, select Edit Custom Component Set and choose the component you want to view in the Edit Custom Component Set dialog (see Figure B-5).

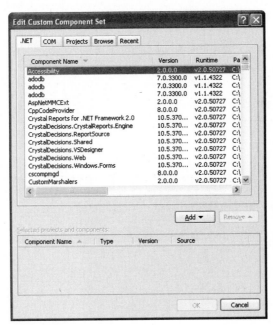

Figure B-5

The most useful feature of the Object Browser is its search capability. Say that you want to perform compression for your application and you are not sure which class to use for this purpose. Simply type a keyword (compression, for example) into the search box (see Figure B-6) and press Enter.

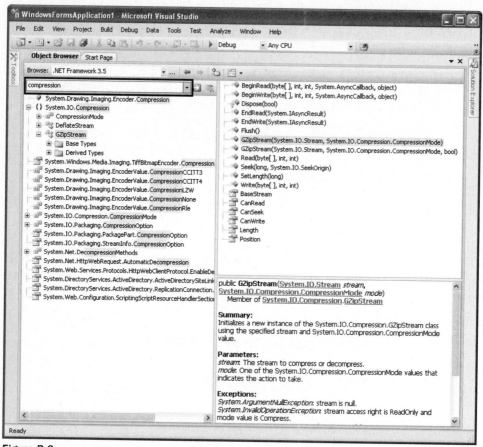

Figure B-6

The Object Browser lists all the namespaces, classes, and so on that are related to the keyword you entered. In this example, you can find the System.IO.Compression namespace that contains the classes you need to use (see Figure B-7) — DeflateStream and GZipStream.

Clicking on a namespace shows you which assembly contains that namespace. System.IO.Compression, for example, is contained within the System.dll assembly.

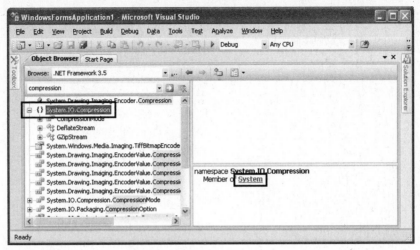

Figure B-7

Clicking an assembly link takes you to the assembly where you can examine all the namespaces contained with it (see Figure B-8). In this example, you can see that the System assembly is a member of the three versions of the .NET Framework — 2.0, 3.0, and 3.5. That's a useful feature because if you use an assembly that belongs only to .NET Framework 3.5, for instance, then you need to ensure that the computer running your application has the latest version of the Framework.

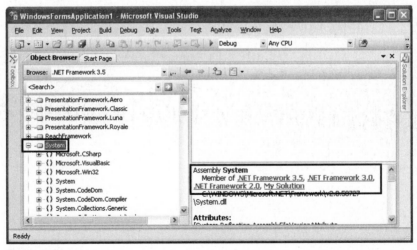

Figure B-8

Once you have selected an assembly, you can also click the Add to Reference button (see Figure B-9) in the Object Browser to add a reference to the assembly.

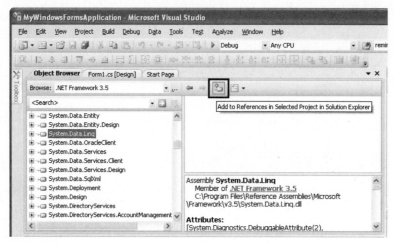

Figure B-9

Generating Documentation for Your C# Applications

Documenting your code is probably the last thing you would do in your typical project cycle. While the importance of writing documentation has been stressed umpteen times, developers usually devote the best part of the project cycle to building new features, and then finally do a mediocre job at the end writing the dreaded documentation. Borrowing the popular "clean as you go" phrase found in a lot of kitchens, the best way to churn out top-quality documentation for your project is to document as you go.

In Visual Studio 2008, you can document your code using the XML code documentation feature. This appendix shows you how to generate MSDN-style documentation for your project using Visual Studio 2008 and a third-party documentation generation tool — Sandcastle.

Inline Documentation using XML

To see how XML documentation works, create a new class library project in Visual Studio 2008 as shown in Figure C-1. Name the project PointClass.

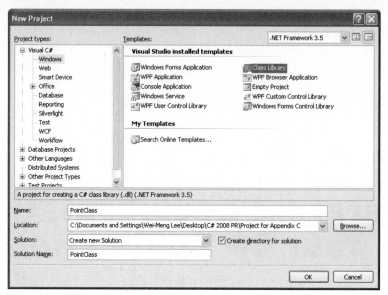

Figure C-1

Populate the default `Class1.cs` with the following class definition:

```csharp
using System;
using System.Collections.Generic;
using System.Linq;
using System.Text;

namespace PointClass
{
    public class Point
    {
        //---static variable---
        private static int count;

        //---properties---
        public int x { get; set; }
        public int y { get; set; }

        //---constructors---
        public Point()
        {
            count++;
        }
        public Point(int x, int y)
        {
            this.x = x;
            this.y = y;
            count++;
        }
```

```
//---overloaded methods---
public double Length()
{
    return Math.Sqrt(
        Math.Pow(this.x, 2) +
        Math.Pow(this.y, 2));
}
public double Length(Point pt)
{
    return Math.Sqrt(
        Math.Pow(this.x - pt.x, 2) +
        Math.Pow(this.y - pt.y, 2));
}
    }
}
```

The definition for the `Point` class contains the following members:

- ❏ A static private member named `count`
- ❏ Two properties — x and y
- ❏ Two overloaded constructors
- ❏ Two overloaded `Length()` methods

To add XML comments to the class, type three slash (/) character in succession: ///. Figure C-2 shows that when you type /// before the `Point` class definition, an XML comments template is automatically inserted for you.

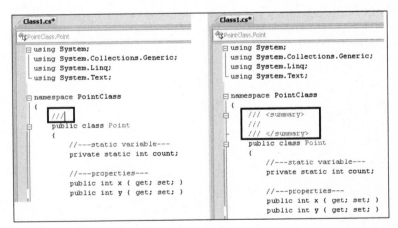

Figure C-2

The `<summary>` tag is inserted by default, but you can insert additional XML comment tags within the XML comments template, as shown in Figure C-3.

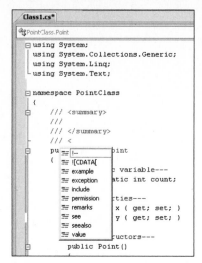

Figure C-3

Following is a list of XML documentation tags. You can find a similar list with a link to each tag's description (its uses) at `http://msdn.microsoft.com/en-us/library/5ast78ax.aspx`.

`<c>`	`<para>`	`<see>`
`<code>`	`<param>`	`<seealso>`
`<example>`	`<paramref>`	`<summary>`
`<exception>`	`<permission>`	`<typeparam>`
`<typeparamrefs>`	`<value>`	`<include>`
`<remarks>`	`<list>`	`<returns>`

Using the `Point` class definition, insert the XML comments highlighted in the following code:

```
using System;
using System.Collections.Generic;
using System.Linq;
using System.Text;

namespace PointClass
{
    /// <summary>
    /// The Point class contains 2 properties, 1 overloaded
    /// constructor, and 1 overloaded method
    /// </summary>
    /// <remarks>
    /// If you need to use the Point class in the System.Drawing
    /// namespace, be sure to reference it using the fully
    /// qualified name, i.e. System.Drawing.Point
    /// </remarks>
```

```
/// <history>
/// [Wei-Meng Lee]   5/12/2008   Created
/// </history>

public class Point
{
    //---static variable---
    private static int count;

    //---properties---
    /// <summary>
    /// Property for x-coordinate
    /// </summary>
    /// <returns>
    /// The x-coordinate
    /// </returns>
    public int x { get; set; }

    /// <summary>
    /// Property for y-coordinate
    /// </summary>
    /// <returns>
    /// The y-coordinate
    /// </returns>
    public int y { get; set; }

    //---constructors---
    /// <summary>
    /// Default constructor
    /// </summary>
    /// <remarks>
    /// Creates a new instance of the Point class
    /// </remarks>
    public Point()
    {
        count++;
    }

    /// <overloads>
    /// Constructor
    /// </overloads>
    /// <summary>
    /// Constructor with two parameters
    /// </summary>
    /// <param name="x">Parameter x is assigned to the x-coordinate</param>
    /// <param name="y">Parameter y is assigned to the y-coordinate</param>
    /// <remarks>
    /// Creates a new instance of the Point class
    /// </remarks>
```

(continued)

(continued)

```csharp
            public Point(int x, int y)
            {
                this.x = x;
                this.y = y;
                count++;
            }

            //---overloaded methods---
            /// <overloads>
            /// Calculates the distance between two points
            /// </overloads>
            /// <summary>
            /// Calculates the distance of a point from the origin
            /// </summary>
            /// <returns>The distance between the current point and the origin
            /// </returns>
            /// <example> This sample shows how to call the <c>length()</c>
            /// method
            /// <code>
            ///     Point ptA = new Point(3, 4);
            ///     double distance = ptA.Length();
            /// </code>
            /// </example>
            public double Length()
            {
                return Math.Sqrt(
                    Math.Pow(this.x, 2) +
                    Math.Pow(this.y, 2));
            }

            /// <summary>
            /// Calculates the distance of a point from another point
            /// </summary>
            /// <param name="pt">A Point object</param>
            /// <returns>The distance between the current point and the
            /// specified point
            /// </returns>
            /// <example> This sample shows how to call the <c>length()</c> method
            /// with a point specified
            /// <code>
            ///     Point ptA = new Point(3, 4);
            ///     Point ptB = new Point(7, 8);
            ///     double distance = ptA.Length(ptB);
            /// </code>
            /// </example>
            public double Length(Point pt)
            {
                return Math.Sqrt(
                    Math.Pow(this.x - pt.x, 2) +
                    Math.Pow(this.y - pt.y, 2));
            }
        }
    }
```

Take a look at the documentation you have done for one of the overloaded `Length()` methods:

```
//---overloaded methods---
/// <overloads>
/// Calculates the distance between two points
/// </overloads>
/// <summary>
/// Calculates the distance of a point from the origin
/// </summary>
/// <returns>The distance between the current point and the origin
/// </returns>
/// <example> This sample shows how to call the <c>length()</c>
/// method
/// <code>
///     Point ptA = new Point(3, 4);
///     double distance = ptA.Length();
/// </code>
/// </example>
```

You will notice that there is a new element — `<overloads>` — that is not in the list specified in the MSDN documentation. The `<overloads>` element is used to give a general description for methods that are overloaded. You will see the effect of this element later when you generate the documentation using the third-party tool. You only need to specify the `<overloads>` element on one (any one will do) of the overloaded methods.

You can also include code samples in your documentation using the `<example>` tag. To format a word (or sentence) as code, use the `<c>` tag. For multiple lines of code, use the `<code>` tag.

Because the XML comments that you add to your code may make reading difficult, you can hide the comments by clicking the minus sign (–) on the left of the code window. To reveal the XML documentation, click the plus sign (+) as shown in Figure C-4.

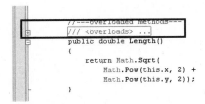

Figure C-4

Once you have inserted the XML comments in your code, right-click the project name in Solution Explorer and select Properties. Select the Build tab and check the XML Documentation File checkbox (see Figure C-5). This indicates to the compiler that after the project is compiled, it should consolidate all the XML comments into an XML documentation file. By default, the XML document will be saved to the bin/Debug folder of your project.

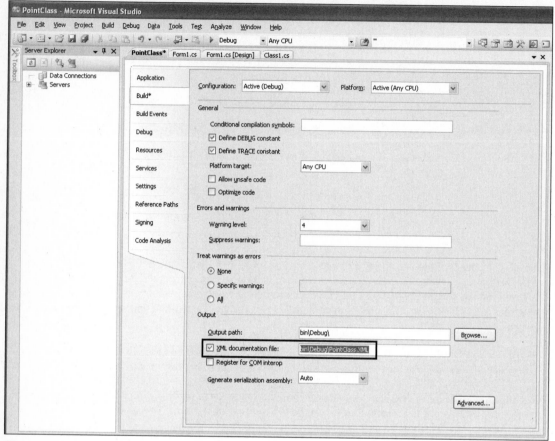

Figure C-5

Build the project by right-clicking the project name in Solution Explorer and then selecting Build. The XML documentation file is now located in the bin/Debug folder of your project, together with the `PointClass.dll` library. Figure C-6 shows what the XML file looks like.

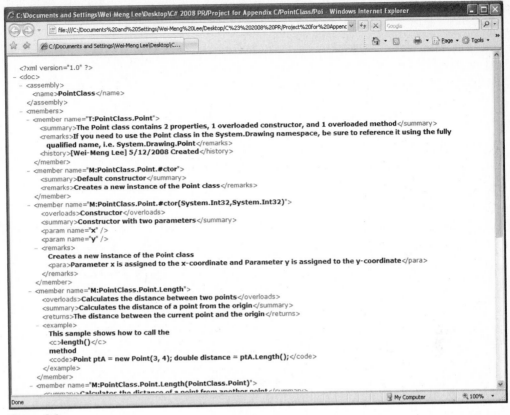

Figure C-6

Generating the Documentation

With the XML documentation file generated, you have two options in terms of using the documentation:

❑ Write your own XSLT transformation style sheets to transform the XML document into a readable format such as HTML, PDF, and so on.

❑ Use a third-party tool to automatically parse the XML documentation into the various documentation formats it supports.

The second option is the easier. For this purpose, you can use the free Sandcastle tool that generates documentation in several different formats, including the MSDN-style HTML Help format (.chm), the Visual Studio .NET Help format (HTML Help 2), and MSDN-Online style Web pages.

Downloading and Installing Sandcastle

To use Sandcastle to generate your documentation, first ensure that you have HTML Help Workshop by checking for the existence of the following folder: `C:\Program Files\HTML Help Workshop`.

If the folder is not there or does not contain `hhc.exe`, you can search for it and download it from Microsoft's web site.

Next, download Sandcastle from `http://codeplex.com/Sandcastle`.

By itself, Sandcastle is a command-line tool and all interaction with it is via the command line. To make your life easier, you can download the Sandcastle Help File Builder, a graphical user interface (GUI) tool that makes Sandcastle easy to use.

Once Sandcastle is downloaded and installed, download the Sandcastle Help File Builder from `http://codeplex.com/SHFB`.

Download the Presentation File Patches from the Sandcastle Styles Project site (`http://codeplex.com/SandcastleStyles`). Extract the Presentation folder and overwrite the Presentation folder in the Sandcastle folder with it (in `C:\Program Files\Sandcastle`; see Figure C-7).

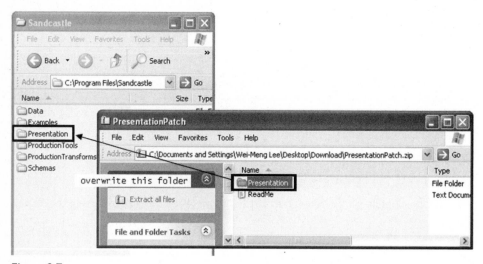

Figure C-7

Due to the continual development of the Sandcastle project, these screen shots may differ from what you actually see on your screen.

Finally, you should run the `BuildReflectionData.bat` batch file (located in `C:\Program Files\EWSoftware\Sandcastle Help File Builder`) to build the reflection data for the version of the .NET runtime you are using.

If the C:\Program Files\Sandcastle\Data folder already contains a folder called Reflection, you need to delete that folder before running this batch file.

Launching Sandcastle

Once Sandcastle and the Sandcastle Help File Builder are downloaded and installed, launch the Sandcastle Help File Builder by selecting Start ⇨ Programs ⇨ Sandcastle Help File Builder ⇨ Sandcastle Help File Builder GUI.

You should see the window shown in Figure C-8 when the Sandcastle Help File Builder is launched.

Figure C-8

You can choose the type of documentation you want to generate from the `HelpFileFormat` drop-down listbox (see Figure C-9).

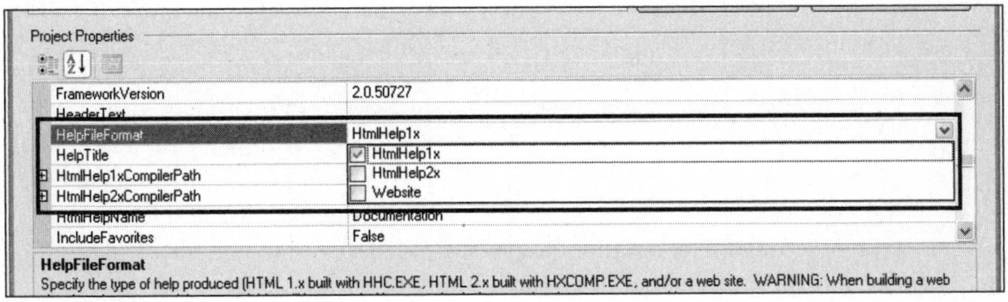

Figure C-9

Click the Add button to add the assembly filename that you want to generate the documentation for (see Figure C-8). Once the assembly is selected (`PointClass.dll` in the bin/Debug folder, in this case), the XML document filename field is automatically selected (the same name as the assembly, but with an `.xml` extension).

You can add multiple projects into the same documentation by adding each assembly into the Sandcastle project.

Finally, set the `ShowMissingNamespaces` property to `false`.

Building and Viewing the Documentation

Once you are ready to build the documentation, click the Build the Help File button in the toolbar (see Figure C-10).

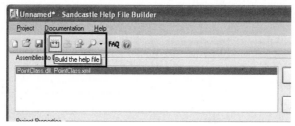

Figure C-10

You will be asked to save the project. Name it `Documentation`. Sandcastle will then generate the documentation. Afterward, you can view it by clicking the View Help File From Last Build button in the toolbar (see Figure C-11).

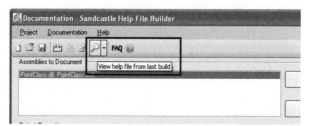

Figure C-11

> **Ensure that your Sandcastle project is saved in a folder whose name does not contain any special characters (such as #, ?, &, and +). If not, you won't be able to view the documentation properly.**

Figure C-12 shows the generated documentation (the tree view on the left is shown with all the nodes expanded to reveal the full documentation).

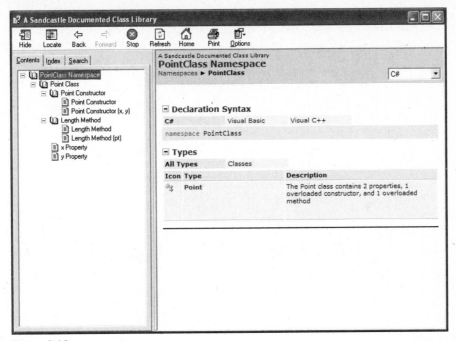

Figure C-12

Let's just take a look at the documentation for the overloaded `Length()` method as illustrated in Figure C-13.

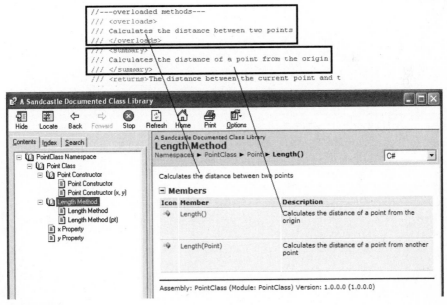

Figure C-13

As you can see, the text in the `<overloads>` element is used to provide a general description for the overloaded method, while the actual description for each overloaded method is detailed in the `<summary>` element.

Click on the first overloaded method of the `Length()` method to see the relationship between the documentation tag and the actual documentation, as shown in Figure C-14.

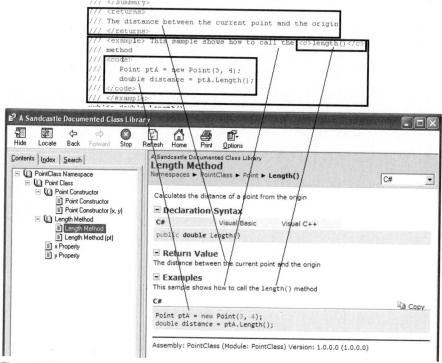

Figure C-14

If you had earlier checked the WebSite item in the `HelpFileFormat` property of the project, the documentation would look like Figure C-15.

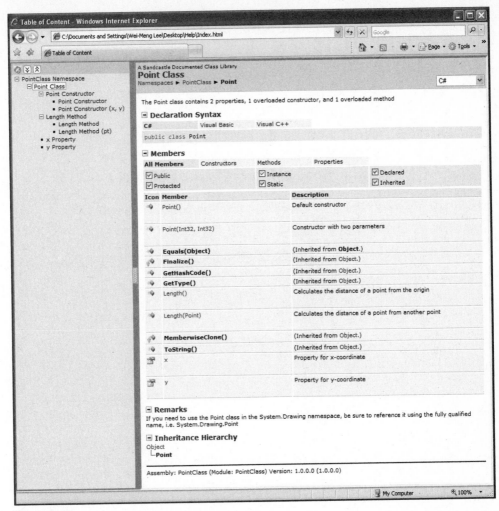

Figure C-15

Distributing the Documentation

You specify the location of the generated documentation by setting the OutputPath property in the properties section in Sandcastle. By default, the documentation is always saved in the Help folder of the project's folder (see Figure C-16).

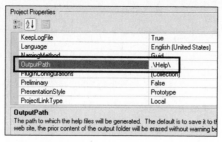

Figure C-16

The Help folder contains a single `.chm` file (Documentation) and a log file (`LastBuild`; assuming you only checked the HelpFile1x item in the `HelpFileFormat` property; see Figure C-17).

Figure C-17

To distribute the documentation with your class, you simply need to provide the file with the `.chm` extension.

If you checked the WebSite item in the `HelpFileFormat` property of the project, the Help folder will contain a list of files and folders. Simply load the `Index.html` file to view the documentation. To distribute your documentation, you need to distribute all the files and folders within the Help folder.

Index

M

S

Get more from Wrox.

978-0-470-18757-9   978-0-470-19137-8   978-0-470-19136-1

wrox™
An Imprint of **WILEY**

Available wherever books are sold or visit wrox.com